# Arm
## with Nagorn

the Bradt Travel Guide

**Deirdre Holding**
**Tom Allen**

edition
5

www.bradtguides.com

Bradt Travel Guides Ltd, UK
The Globe Pequot Press Inc, USA

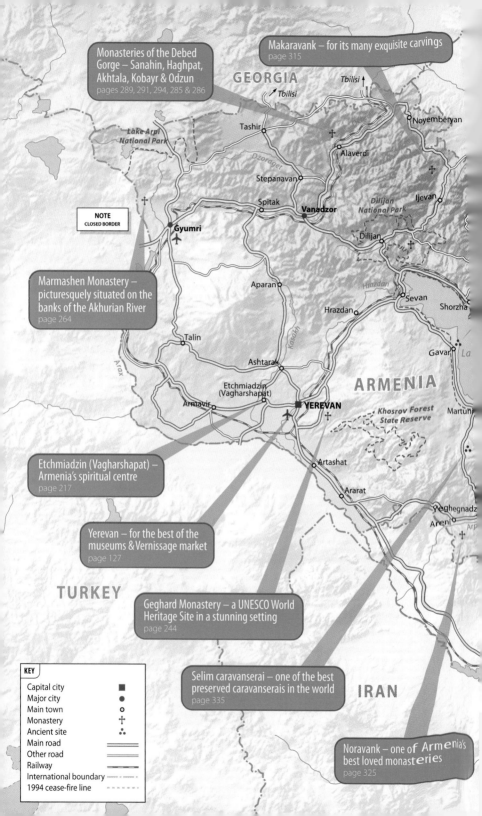

Makaravank – for its many exquisite carvings
page 315

Monasteries of the Debed
Gorge – Sanahin, Haghpat,
Akhtala, Kobayr & Odzun
pages 289, 291, 294, 285 & 286

GEORGIA

Tbilisi ↑

↗ Tbilisi

Noyemberyan

Tashir

Lake Arpi
National Park

Dzoraget

Alaverdi

Stepanavan

Spitak

Dilijan
National Park

Ijevan

NOTE
CLOSED BORDER

Gyumri

Vanadzor

Dilijan

Marmashen Monastery –
picturesquely situated on the
banks of the Akhurian River
page 264

Aparan

Hrazdan

Sevan

Shorzha

Hrazdan

Talin

Kasakh

Gavar

La

Ashtarak

ARMENIA

Arax

Etchmiadzin
(Vagharshapat)

YEREVAN

Khosrov Forest
State Reserve

Martuni

Armavir

Etchmiadzin (Vagharshapat) –
Armenia's spiritual centre
page 217

Artashat

Yerevan – for the best of the
museums & Vernissage market
page 127

Ararat

Yeghegnadz

Areni

Arp

TURKEY

Geghard Monastery – a UNESCO World
Heritage Site in a stunning setting
page 244

KEY

| | |
|---|---|
| Capital city | ■ |
| Major city | ● |
| Main town | ○ |
| Monastery | ✝ |
| Ancient site | ∴ |
| Main road | |
| Other road | |
| Railway | |
| International boundary | |
| 1994 cease-fire line | |

Selim caravanserai – one of the best
preserved caravanserais in the world
page 335

IRAN

Noravank – one of Armenia's
best loved monasteries
page 325

# ARMENIA WITH NAGORNO KARABAGH

**Dilijan National Park** – with more than 200km of waymarked hiking trails & five important monasteries
page 305

**NOTE**
**CLOSED BORDER**

**Field of khachkars, Noratus** – site of Armenia's largest collection of khachkars
page 234

**Tigranakert** – site of an ancient fortified city on a dramatic escarpment together with its museum in a medieval castle
page 388

**AZERBAIJAN**

**Dadivank** – the final resting place of 1st-century apostle & martyr St Thaddeus
page 391

**NOTE**
**CLOSED BORDER**

**NOTE**
**1994 CEASE-FIRE LINE**
**CLOSED BORDER**

ambarak

van
ke Sevan
tional Park

Vardenis

*Tartar*

Martakert

**NAGORNO KARABAGH**
**(Self-declared Republic of Artsakh)**

**NOTE**
**1994 CEASE-FIRE LINE**
**CLOSED BORDER**

Jermuk

*Aghavnoget*

Stepanakert

Shushi

Sisian

Goris

Hadrut

*Vorotan*

**NOTE**
**CLOSED BORDER**

**Tatev Monastery** – one of Armenia's most famous sites, now served by the world's longest cable car
page 350

**NAKHICHEVAN**
**(Azerbaijan)**

Kapan

*Voghji*

Kajaran

*Arox*

*Arevik National Park*

*Shikahogh State Reserve*

**N**

**Bradt**

**Petroglyphs of Ughtasar** – hundreds of ancient carvings are scattered on this extinct volcano
page 345

Meghri

↘ *Tehran*

| 0 | | 50km |
| 0 | | 30 miles |

# Armenia Don't miss...

### Monasteries
The monastery of Hovhannavank, perched right on the edge of the cliff above the deep gorge of the River Kasakh, is just one of Armenia's many fascinating monasteries in beautiful surroundings (JS/AWL) page 189

### People
Good food, such as this tasty hand-made cheese, plays a very important part in the life of the Armenian people (SS) page 96

## Mountains

Armenia's mountains provide many magnificent settings. Mount Khustup in southern Armenia forms a stunning backdrop to the town of Kapan (DH) page 362

## Exquisite stone carvings

Khachkars, carved memorial stones, such as this one at Noravank, are an important, conspicuous and beautiful feature of Armenian decorative art (JS/AWL) page 48

## Apricots

Armenians claim, with some justification, that their apricots are the best in the world (VA/S) page 4

# Armenia in colour

*above* Yerevan's Republic Square is certainly one of the finest central squares created anywhere in the world during the 20th century (E/S) page 152

*left* Yerevan's thriving outdoor café culture comes to life from spring right through to autumn (SS) page 141

*below* Tamanyan Sculpture Park, below Yerevan's Cascade, plays host to a diverse and regularly changing collection of sculptures from around the world (a/S) page 162

above     Yerevan is a city of many statues and sculptures such as this one of *The Men*, depicting characters from a Soviet-era film of the same name popular with Armenians (DH) page 163

right     Men playing backgammon or chess is a common sight in Yerevan and throughout Armenia (MN)

below left     As well as providing impressive views over Yerevan, the Cascade houses the Cafesjian Centre for the Arts, featuring exhibitions, installations and performances all year round (a/S) page 161

below right     The Genocide Memorial is an impressive and poignant reminder of the 1915 Armenian genocide. On 24 April, Genocide Memorial Day, thousands of people come to lay flowers (FJ/S) page 171

*above*    This spectacular view from Selim Caravanserai is just one of the breathtaking panoramas you'll see when hiking across the country on the Transcaucasian Trail (TA) page 114

*left*    Mountain biking remains a little-known activity in Armenia, but the abundance of dirt roads makes it a playground for the intrepid rider (TA) page 114

*below*    Wild camping is universally tolerated in Armenia, and made more practical by the numerous picnic shelters and freshwater springs scattered throughout the country (TA)

## AUTHOR

Born in Liverpool, **Deirdre Holding** moved to Scotland in 1963 and graduated with a degree in medicine from the University of St Andrews. It was at university that she met her husband, Nicholas, and they married in 1970. Among many shared interests was one in the communist world and they made their first visit to the Soviet Union in 1973. The downfall of communism enabled them to travel more freely around the former Soviet bloc, and sparked their interest in Armenia. Deirdre retired early, in 2003, after a career in the  Scottish National Health Service as a consultant eye surgeon. Nicholas wrote the first two editions of the Bradt guide to Armenia. After his death in 2008, Deirdre took over the authorship, having always been closely involved with the guide. She updated the book for the third edition (2011) the fourth edition (2014). She maintains her interest in Armenia and has continued to visit the country. She still lives in Scotland.

## UPDATER

**Tom Allen** was born in the East Midlands in 1983 and studied computer science at the University of Exeter. Graduating in 2005 and desperate to escape the screens, he developed a keen interest in adventure travel, deciding on the bicycle as the best way to travel the world long-term on a shoestring. In early 2008, having pedalled from England, he first arrived in Armenia, where he met his future wife Tenny. After travelling across 32 countries by bicycle he returned to Yerevan, where he and Tenny married in 2009. Their unlikely  love story became the subject of an award-winning documentary film, *Janapar*. In the years since, Tom has learned the Armenian language and explored every corner of the country. The dramatic landscapes and heart-warming hospitality of the Caucasus inspired him to create a long-distance walking route across the region, and in 2016 he launched an expedition to design and map the Armenian section of what would become the Transcaucasian Trail. Tom's experiences place him well to uncover and communicate aspects of the country that would otherwise be missed, while his global perspective on travel ensures that such advice remains as objective as possible.

## PUBLISHER'S FOREWORD  *Adrian Phillips*

When we published the first edition of this groundbreaking guide I noted that Armenia seemed to have everything: a fascinating history, vibrant culture and rewarding natural history. And in Nicholas Holding we had an author who could do justice to this marvellous yet little-known country. Sadly, Nicholas passed away after the second edition was published. Since then, Deirdre Holding – who travelled with Nicholas, her husband, during his journeys around the country – has picked up the reins and ensured that each subsequent edition is scrupulously updated, and Tom Allen, who lives in Armenia, has continued the excellent work for this edition. Armenia remains well off the beaten track, and adventurous travellers have the benefit of Tom's latest discoveries in this fascinating land.

Fifth edition published January 2019
First published 2003
Bradt Travel Guides Ltd, IDC House, The Vale, Chalfont St Peter, Bucks SL9 9RZ, England
www.bradtguides.com
Print edition published in the USA by The Globe Pequot Press Inc, PO Box 480, Guilford, Connecticut 06437-0480

Text copyright © 2019 Deirdre Holding
Maps copyright © 2019 Bradt Travel Guides Ltd; includes maps data © OpenStreetMap contributors (under Open Database License)
Nagorno Karabagh chapter and additional text updated by Mark Johns
Photographs copyright © 2019 Individual photographers (see below)
Project Manager: Claire Strange
Cover research: Pepi Bluck, Perfect Picture

ISBN: 978 1 78477 079 2

**British Library Cataloguing in Publication Data**

A catalogue record for this book is available from the British Library

**Photographs** Alamy Stock Photos: eFesenko (eF/A), Rastislav Kolesar (RK/A); Ivan Vdovin (IV/A); Tom Allen (TA); AWL images: Jane Sweeney (JS/AWL); Adrian Chan (AC); Deirdre Holding (DH); Dreamstime.com: Graphics.vp (G/D), Salajean (S/D); Michael Nyholm (MN); Maria Oleynik (MO); Shutterstock.com: VahanAbrahamyan (VA/S), alionabirukova (a/S), bayazed (b/S) Emena (E/S), Fat Jackey (FJ/S), Lev Levin (LL/S), Maros Markovic (MM/S), Anton Martinov (AM/S), VahanN (V/S); ruzanna (r/S), HroSev (HS/S), Piotr Sitnik (PS/S), Vitaly Titov (VT/S), Marc Venema (MV/S); SuperStock (SS).

*Front cover* Noravank (eF/A)
*Back cover* Freshly baked *gata* at Geghard (SS); Vorotan Canyon (TA)
*Title page* Long view to Ararat (SS); apricots (HS/S); khachkar (AM/S)

**Maps** David McCutcheon FBCart.S (base mapping, modified by Bradt Travel Guides, provided by ITMB Publishing Ltd (www.itmb.com) 2019); colour map base by Nick Rowland FRGS

Typeset by Ian Spick, Bradt Travel Guides and www.dataworks.co.in
Production managed by Jellyfish Print Solutions; printed in the UK
Digital conversion by www.dataworks.co.uk

My husband and I first went to Armenia in 2001, on holiday. We were enthralled by the country: its landscapes, the wild flowers, the many medieval monasteries and churches, its unique alphabet, the welcome given to us, its complex history at so many crossroads – geological, historical, political and religious. But there were frustrations. There was virtually no information in Armenia itself. Even road signs were in short supply. Yes, there was internet information but how many printouts can be packed before a suitcase is overweight? Many times we bewailed the absence of a practical and informative guidebook, such as the Bradt guides we had used elsewhere.

So when, after our return, Nick was asked to write the first Bradt guide to Armenia he accepted willingly. We enjoyed getting to know the country better and feeling that we were making some contribution. It was also hard work! It wasn't just the journeys on dreadfully pot-holed roads but also the research involved. I remember Nick once spent the whole day researching an apparently authoritative statement that a certain cave held a colony of fruit bats. Fruit bats? In Armenia? It turned out that the species of bat referred to wasn't fruit-eating at all and it was in fact quite another species which actually inhabited the cave!

Armenia has been one of the things which has helped me to cope with the enormous gap left in my life by Nick's death. I continue to find the country endlessly fascinating and have come to realise how much more there is to be known than we ever grasped during our early visits. I hope this edition reflects at least some of this increased appreciation of what Armenia was and is, and what it has to offer the visitor.

From the start our hope was that the Bradt guide to Armenia would inform and make a visit there even more enjoyable than it is bound to be. That continues to be my hope for this edition.

At Bradt Travel Guides we're aware that guidebooks start to go out of date on the day they're published – and that you, our readers, are out there in the field doing research of your own. You'll find out before us when a fine new family-run hotel opens or a favourite restaurant changes hands and goes downhill. So why not write and tell us about your experiences? Contact us on ☏ 01753 893444 or e info@bradtguides.com. We will forward emails to the author, who may post updates on the Bradt website at w bradtupdates.com/armenia. Alternatively, you can add a review of the book to w bradtguides.com or Amazon.

## NICHOLAS HOLDING

Author of the first two editions of the Bradt guide to Armenia, Nicholas Holding was born in Wigan (then in Lancashire, but now part of Greater Manchester). He moved to Scotland in 1965 and graduated from the University of St Andrews with a degree in electrical engineering. Nicholas and Deirdre met at university and they married in 1970. After a career in the Scottish electricity supply industry, Nicholas took early retirement in 2000. This enabled him to devote more time to his many interests among which were music (especially opera and in particular Russian opera), literature of the 18th and 19th centuries, wine and food (he became an excellent cook after retirement). He was by nature a forward planner. That, combined with a facility with timetables, made him an efficient organiser of trips to many parts of the world. His ease with timetables stemmed from a childhood interest in trains. A continuing fascination with natural history also started early in life; as a child he spent many hours familiarising himself with the contents of his local ponds. During the last 15 years of his life he developed a particular interest in moths and became County Moth Recorder for two counties in Scotland. Nicholas had an extraordinarily good memory. During his life he amassed a vast fund of knowledge on many subjects, including what he liked to call 'useless information', enabling him to hold forth on any number of disparate subjects.

When asked to write the guidebook to Armenia he applied his characteristic thoroughness to the task, seeking out information and occasionally revealing in his writing his dry sense of humour and his delight in the obscure and esoteric. Nicholas wrote the first two editions of the guidebook to Armenia, the first published in 2003, the second in 2006. He became ill not long after the second edition was published and, although he always hoped to write the third edition, his death prevented that. He died in 2008. Nicholas's original work forms much of the backbone on which this guide is built; those who knew Nick can still glimpse his personality in that part of the text which is his.

## DEDICATION

In memory of Nick.

# Acknowledgements

**DEIRDRE HOLDING** My greatest debt is to my late husband, Nicholas, whose original work for the first and second editions still comprises a significant part of this present edition, the fifth. Without his foundation I could not have contemplated writing this guidebook.

I thank Tom Allen for updating this latest edition, bringing his wide knowledge of adventure travel and, notably, of hiking to the task, thus adding an important dimension to the guidebook.

I remain grateful to Saro Boick for driving me cheerfully and safely the length and breadth of Armenia, on roads both good and bad, and who also assisted greatly as interpreter; to the staff at Armenia Travel + M in Yerevan, particularly Kristina Gharibyan and Nina Dadayan, for their willing efficiency when making arrangements; to Hasmik Shahverdyan for giving me so much of her time and company in Yerevan and for finding the answers to innumerable questions; to Carl Meadows of Regent Holidays for his help; to Andrew Selkirk, Editor-in-Chief of *Current Archaeology*, who allowed some reciprocal cribbing from his writing on archaeology in Armenia; to Tina Walkling, also for archaeological insights particularly in relation to petroglyphs; to David Sayers (author of the Bradt guide to the Azores) for continued use of his guidance on botanical matters; to Anahit Shahverdyan, our original adviser, interpreter and guide to all things Armenian, whose past contribution to the language section was invaluable.

I would also like to thank the very many people in Armenia, and in Nagorno Karabagh, who gave freely of their time, knowledge and practical help, so contributing much to this guidebook.

In their dealings with me the staff at Bradt have encouraged and helped, shown patience and understanding, all laced with cheerfulness and humour.

**TOM ALLEN** First and foremost I thank my wife Tenny for originally convincing me to stay in Armenia, as well as for her patience during the challenges of updating this latest edition. Special thanks to Raffi Kojian for making available his endless knowledge of Armenia's historical sites and research sources. Thanks to Sevada Petrossian for his expert guidance on Yerevan's architectural history; to Alessandro Mambelli for his feedback on my drafts as a fellow western European in Armenia; to the staff and members of Impact Hub Yerevan for responding to my many requests for contacts in the provinces (and providing an excellent working space to get the writing done); to the Transcaucasian Trail and Trails For Change NGO teams for their many tip-offs on little-known sites of interest; and to the many Peace Corps volunteers who happily hosted and guided me in communities across the country. I would like to echo Deirdre in thanking the many Armenians from all sectors of society who so willingly gave of their time and knowledge to make this new edition what it is, and to the amenable and encouraging yet thorough and professional staff at Bradt. Finally, I would like to raise a toast to all those in Armenia I have the pleasure to know who are putting so much energy and faith into changing Armenia for the better in myriad ways. *Genats!*

# Contents

# Introduction

This is a guidebook to the present-day Republic of Armenia together with the territory of Nagorno Karabagh. In the English-speaking world, an individual's knowledge of this fascinating country generally falls into one of two categories. Most people know nothing about it at all, not even where it is. The others, a small minority, not only speak the Armenian language, although neither they nor their parents were born in Armenia, but also have some knowledge of Armenian culture and Armenia's often tragic history. This is because Armenia has one of the most successful and supportive diasporas in the world, upon which present-day Armenia is still very dependent. So far as Nagorno Karabagh is concerned, the contrast is even more stark with the diaspora being wholly familiar with its recent past while few others would claim even to have heard of it, apart from those who are well informed politically and might recall its name as the scene of some half-remembered conflict around the time that the Soviet Union disintegrated.

This book is aimed primarily at the general visitor who is interested in exploring the country and understanding something of its long and complex history. Nevertheless, even fairly knowledgeable members of the diaspora should also find it useful as they, like virtually all other visitors to Armenia, often confine themselves to only half a dozen or so of the more popular places. It appears that few visitors know anything about the many other sights in Armenia which warrant a visit, let alone this mountainous nation's huge potential for off-the-beaten-track exploration. As a consequence, only a handful of visitors to Armenia spend more than a week in the country. Many visits last a mere four or five days; still more are brief sideshows to wider tours of the Caucasus. This book seeks to rectify that regrettable situation and demonstrate that Armenia has huge potential for a broad range of visitors. Not just for general sightseeing, although its spectacular gorges and medieval buildings certainly provide plenty of excellent opportunities for that, but also for activities such as hiking, cycling, wine tourism, birdwatching, architectural and archaeological tours, historical visits, botanical trips, horseriding, caving and even skiing. Although many visitors will probably continue to combine a visit to Armenia with one to neighbouring Georgia, there is quite enough in Armenia alone to occupy several holidays without ever going to the same place twice.

Armenia is actually a very easy country to visit. Its people are overwhelmingly friendly, helpful and welcoming. Most nationalities no longer need a visa to enter the country or can easily obtain one on arrival. There is relatively little crime and the risk of theft or being short-changed is much lower than in most Western countries.

Is Armenia in Europe? It certainly feels far more like a southern European country than an Asian one and it is a member of the Council of Europe and the Organization for Security and Co-operation in Europe. In addition, the Armenian people have been Christian for 1,700 years and from 1828 to 1991 they were ruled by another country whose culture, the Bolshevik Revolution notwithstanding, was fundamentally Christian. On a more practical level, Armenia has an international telephone dialling code (374) in the European sequence, the British post office charges the European rate for letters sent to Armenia from Britain, and Armenia competes annually in the Eurovision Song Contest. Having said all of that, visitors familiar with the cultural traditions of the Middle East – the cuisine, the traditional music and dancing, the hospitality, even certain aspects of language – will find much that feels familiar in Armenia.

The main drawback has long been the language barrier, although this is now far less of a concern in Yerevan and in other places used to dealing with tourists. Outside the centre of Yerevan and the more popular destinations in the regions, few people speak English or any other western European language. The main second language is still Russian (though English is now taught in schools), so visitors travelling on their own may well find it convenient to consider employing an English-speaking guide or driver or else arrange accommodation in advance. Either can be done through one of the Yerevan travel agents or an overseas agent who specialises in the country.

The infrastructure continues to improve with good hotel accommodation now available in most places. However, there are still parts of the country where homestays remain the best option, providing an insight into Armenian family life. Roads are also improving. Most main routes now have a good asphalt surface although secondary roads can still be poor. While all villages can be reached by minibus there are many places of interest which are not served by public transport. For these, one of Armenia's cheap taxis is a viable alternative. If hiring a car, it is generally cheaper to hire one with a driver than to drive oneself, although the car may then be older. Depending on the expected destinations a 4x4 vehicle can be requested, essential for getting to some places and quite helpful for many others. Good road maps are available but the lack of detailed maps for walking, such as the British Ordnance Survey maps, means that Armenia's vast potential for hiking remains relatively difficult to access for the independent visitor, though this is also changing fast with huge improvements in open-source digital mapping data such as OpenStreetMap.

As well as the improvement in hotels and roads most towns, especially the capital, have seen much new building and a significant improvement in the reliability of the water supply. On the other hand, many villages remain largely unaltered. Huge advances have been made on the technological side with Armenia leap-frogging from an antiquated and cumbersome Soviet-era telephone system to one of the most advanced mobile phone and internet systems. Armenia continues to change rapidly and it is likely that some comments made in this book will quickly be superseded.

The amount of information available to tourists has increased enormously. At many historic sites welcome information boards, in several languages, have sprung up and there has been a huge improvement in museum displays and labelling. A significant amount of restoration of historic sites has been, and is being, carried out, some of it good, some of it questionable.

Political and economic problems remain for Armenia. Perhaps the most obvious to visitors is the unresolved question of the status of Nagorno Karabagh, resulting in the continued closure by Azerbaijan and Turkey of their respective borders with Armenia. The refusal of Turkey to recognise as genocide the 1915 massacre of Armenians in the Ottoman Empire continues to influence Armenia's relations with Turkey. However, the Velvet Revolution of spring 2018 was underpinned by a commitment by its leadership to eradicate corruption and tackle many of these fundamental political and economic issues. The mood at this point in Armenia's journey is one of hope, yet also the knowledge that much hard work still lies ahead.

Armenia will never become a mainstream tourist destination like Mallorca or Florida, but few visitors to Armenia leave disappointed, apart from wishing that they had had more time in the country. The authors very much hope that this guide will encourage others to explore not only the popular sites but also more of the off-the-beaten-track places. They will be rewarded by seeing enthralling sights in a country in transition. After centuries of foreign domination Armenia is now once again an independent nation preserving for future generations its unique heritage. Many of the best things in Armenia have not changed: the hospitality of the people, the wonderful quality of seasonal fruit and vegetables, its magnificent landscapes and the abundant ancient sites, both prehistoric and medieval. It remains a country well worth visiting.

**AN IMPORTANT WORD OF WARNING** Do not try to take a copy of this book into Azerbaijan. It will be confiscated at the border.

**NOTE ON TRANSLITERATION** There is no standard transliteration from the Armenian alphabet into English. For example, the principal city of northwest Armenia can appear in English as Gyumri, Gyumry, Giumri, G'umri or even Kyumri, while the province of which it is the capital is Shirak in English, Schirak in German or Chirak in French. Some transliteration schemes even resort to letters borrowed from Czech and Slovak such as č, š and ž, which few English-speakers know how to pronounce anyway.

For place names in this guide the authors have usually followed those found in official government listings of place name transliterations, occasionally those that will be found on local signage and maps, or otherwise those used by Brady Kiesling and Raffi Kojian in *Rediscovering Armenia* (page 408). Occasionally this does result in combinations of consonants appearing such as those in Smbataberd, Aghjkaghala and Ptghni, but these are actually quite close to the Armenian pronunciation. Some places are known to local residents by names other than their official ones and this has been noted in the text.

So far as surnames are concerned (many of which are used as street names), native Armenians tend to prefer the transliteration '-yan', while the diaspora and particularly those of Western Armenian lineage tend to prefer '-ian'. Names in this book tend to follow the former convention, again with due consideration for how such words will be found transliterated in-country on maps and signs, with some exceptions where a particular form has become historically established (eg: Orbelian). In this guide the transliteration Karabagh has usually been preferred to Karabakh, except where an organisation itself uses the latter form.

**AUTHORS' FAVOURITES** Finding genuinely characterful accommodation or that unmissable off-the-beaten-track café can be difficult, so the authors have chosen a few of their favourite places throughout the country to point you in the right direction. These 'authors' favourites' are marked with a ✳.

## MAPS
**Keys and symbols:** Maps include alphabetical keys covering the locations of those places to stay, eat or drink that are featured in the book. Note that regional maps will not show all hotels and restaurants in the area: some establishments may be located in towns shown on the map.

**Grids and grid references:** Some maps use grid lines to allow easy location of sites. Map grid references are listed in square brackets after the name of the place or sight of interest in the text, with page number followed by grid number, eg: [130 C3].

**LISTINGS Accommodation** is marked with a price code and listed alphabetically in descending price code order (**$$$$$–$**); the few hotels where a standard double including breakfast is over AMD100,000 are highlighted. Unless otherwise stated, all accommodation listings include breakfast and Wi-Fi as standard. As **cafés and restaurants** vary very little in price across the country, they are not marked with price codes, although the very expensive and very cheap are noted within their individual entries. The exception to this is in Yerevan, where the range of pricing is considerably wider; as such, listings are marked with price codes and presented in descending order of price (**$$$$$–$**). If no days are specified in the opening times, assume that the venue is open seven days a week. For a breakdown of price ranges, see the inside front cover and pages 93 and 142.

**HISTORIC SITES** Prices and opening hours/days are included where they apply. Otherwise assume the site is free and always open.

# Part One

## GENERAL INFORMATION

**Location** A landlocked country in the southern Caucasus between the Black Sea and the Caspian Sea bordered by Georgia, Azerbaijan, Iran and Turkey. The border with the self-declared Republic of Artsakh (Nagorno Karabagh) is not recognised internationally. Yerevan, the capital, is on the same latitude as Naples, Madrid and New York. It is on the same longitude as Volgograd, Russia, Baghdad, Iraq and Sana'a, Yemen. It would be 5 hours' flying time from London if such a flight existed.

**Area** 29,800km$^2$ – similar to Belgium and the US state of Maryland. Note, however, that following the 1994 ceasefire the territory administered is 31,200km$^2$.

**Status** Unitary parliamentary republic with universal adult suffrage.

**Population** 3.02 million resident in the country at the date of census (October 2011), with an official 2016 estimate of 2.92 million. 98.1% are ethnic Armenians, 1.2% Yezidis, 0.4% Russians, 0.3% other. The balance comprises a wide range of nationalities.

**Major cities** Yerevan (the capital, population 1.1 million); Gyumri (122,000); Vanadzor (86,200). Note that the Yerevan population figure covers only those living within the city. Urban sprawl into the surrounding provinces results in a much larger figure for the Yerevan conurbation.

**Administrative divisions** The country is divided into the capital (Yerevan) and ten provinces (*marzes*): Shirak, Lori, Tavush, Aragatsotn, Gegharkunik, Kotayk, Armavir, Ararat, Vayots Dzor and Syunik.

**Language** Armenian, an Indo-European language. Russian is also widely understood but western European languages are not, although English is becoming better known, mainly in the capital.

**Alphabet** The unique Armenian alphabet, currently with 39 letters, was devised around AD405.

**Religion** Very predominantly Armenian Apostolic. There are a few Roman Catholics, mostly in Shirak province, and there are several sects seeking converts. The Yezidi religion is related to Zoroastrianism and the Kurds are Muslim.

**Currency** Dram (AMD), divided theoretically into 100 luma.

**Exchange rate** £1 = AMD625, US$1 = AMD488, €1 = AMD551 (November 2018).

**International telephone code** +374.

**Time** GMT + 4 hours.

**Electricity** 220V AC; European two-pin plug.

**Weights and measures** Metric system.

**National flag** Three horizontal stripes: red, blue, orange.

**National anthem** 'Land of Our Fathers, Free, Independent' (*Mer Hayreniq, azat, ankakh*); words adapted from a poem by Mikayel Nalbandyan (1829–66); music by Barsegh Kanachyan (1885–1967).

**Symbols of Armenia** The classical symbol is the *khachkar* ('cross stone'). The grape and pomegranate are also used as symbols as is the eagle which appears on the country's coat of arms.

**Public holidays** Page 104.

# 1

# Background Information

## GEOGRAPHY AND CLIMATE

**GEOLOGICAL FEATURES** Visitors to Armenia can hardly fail to be aware of two key geological features of the country: the **Lesser Caucasus** mountain range that dominates much of the country, with the **dormant volcano of Mount Aragats** being the highest peak at 4,090m; and the frequency of **earthquakes**. The two are both accounted for by the theory of plate tectonics, which posits that the outermost shell of the earth, the lithosphere, is formed of a dozen or so large, rigid slabs of rock, together with many smaller ones. These slabs, called tectonic plates, are around 75km thick and comprise a thin outer crust plus the solid part of the mantle. The plates float on the liquid part of the mantle, which is several hundred kilometres thick, and the slow movement of the plates is due to convection currents caused by heat escaping from the earth's core. As the enormous plates move, they grind against each other and stress builds up until there is a sudden movement of one plate against another, resulting in an earthquake. Armenia is on the line where the Arabian plate, moving at about 2.5cm per annum, is colliding with the larger Eurasian plate to its north, and it is consequently very prone to earthquakes, some of them catastrophic – the Spitak earthquake of 1988, for example, levelled the town and took an estimated 25,000–50,000 lives.

About 25 million years ago the Caucasus Mountains were formed as a consequence of this collision. Quite young as mountain ranges go, they are largely composed of volcanic rocks such as basalt, andesite and tuff, all three of which have been used as building materials in Armenia. **Basalt and andesite** are liquid magma which has escaped to the surface during the collision of the plates and then solidified. **Tuff**, by contrast, is formed when small rock fragments which have spewed from a volcano become fused together. Tuff has long been the building material of choice in Armenia, and its distinctive pink-grey hue is now highly characteristic of the country's architecture. Today the biggest working tuff quarry is close to the town of Artik in Shirak province.

Another consequence of the volcanic past is that the semiprecious stone obsidian can be found here. **Obsidian**, which occurs in a range of colours and is used to make jewellery, is a glassy rock formed through the very rapid solidification of lava. In Armenia it occurs most commonly in the Hrazdan region. Apart from these volcanic rocks, Armenia also has substantial deposits of the sedimentary rock **limestone** and in some of these are extensive though little-known cave systems. The most important mineral deposits are of copper (7.4 million tonnes, of which 4.5 million tonnes are at Kajaran), molybdenum (711,000 tonnes, of which 600,000 tonnes are at Kajaran) and gold (268 tonnes, of which 97 tonnes are at Sotk), explaining Armenia's reliance on mining as a major industry from Soviet times until the present day.

**GEOGRAPHICAL FEATURES** Armenia is a very high country, comprising the far northeastern reaches of Eastern Anatolia (often referred to in a historical context as the Armenian Plateau or Western Armenia; page 20), together with the mountains separating it from the lowlands of Georgia and Azerbaijan. The lowest points are in the Debed Valley at the Georgian border in the northeast and the Arax Valley at the Iranian border in the southeast, respectively lying at 380m and 430m above sea level, while the average elevation is 1,370m. Some 90% of the land is over 1,000m, and about half exceeds 2,000m in elevation. The Lesser Caucasus Mountains dominate the northeastern, central and southern regions, with the northwest giving way to high, hilly steppes fissured by deep gorges, and the western region spreading out across the Ararat plain. The volcanic soil in the valleys makes for fertile land, but irrigation is essential because of the low rainfall. Even so, Armenia is a net importer of food. The growing of food crops is unfeasible in much of the mountains, although many of the alpine meadows are used for the production of hay, and fruit orchards and vineyards thrive on the lower, gentler slopes. As befits the Armenians' history as a herding people, the mountains support a large population of cattle, as well as occasional sheep and goats, and livestock and their herders can be encountered even in seemingly remote and inaccessible places during the summer months. About 16% of the land is arable, while 42% is pasture and about 9% is forest. **Fruit growing** is important. Fruits as diverse as pomegranates, grapes, strawberries, peaches, persimmons, quinces and apples are grown. Two fruits native to Armenia and which were consequently first eaten here remain important although they have now spread to the rest of the world. One is the **apricot** – its scientific name reflects this – *Prunus armeniaca* – and Armenians claim with some justification that their apricots are the best in the world. Apricot stones 6,000 years old have been found at archaeological sites and today there are about 50 varieties in the country. The other is the **sweet cherry** or mazzard, *Prunus avium*, from which all the world's 900 varieties of sweet cherry have been cultivated. It spread to the West very early and was known in Greece by 300BC. Walnuts, almonds and hazelnuts grow wild in Armenia and they too are now extensively cultivated. Also of great importance is the fact that wheat was possibly first cultivated, perhaps about 10,000 years ago, in an area that would later become part of ancient Armenia. Two native species of wheat, *Triticum urartu* and *T. araraticum*, still grow in protected fields in the Arax Valley. The importance of both culinary and medicinal herbs, collected wild from the hillsides and forests, can be seen in any Armenian market.

A major feature of the country is **Lake Sevan**, one of the world's largest high-altitude lakes at 1,900m above sea level. There is commercial exploitation of fish stocks although the introduction of alien species has led to the virtual extinction of the endemic trout.

Armenia has a number of **significant rivers** which all flow east into the Caspian Sea. **Hydro-electric schemes** on these rivers are important as the only indigenous energy resource within the country which has been developed apart from a small wind farm on the top of the Pushkin Pass in Lori province. Hydro-electric schemes provide around one-third of electricity requirements and – for better or worse – small hydro-electric schemes are under construction throughout the country. Another third of electricity is generated using **nuclear power** and the balance is **thermal generation** mostly using imported gas. Electricity is exported to Georgia and there are seasonal exchanges with Iran. Gas is mostly imported from Russia by pipeline through Georgia although the Armenian and Iranian gas networks are also linked. Armenia itself has no known reserves of coal, oil or gas but geological and seismic surveys for oil and gas have started.

**CLIMATE** Armenia generally has a highland continental climate with hot, dry summers (June to September) and cold winters (December, January and February being the coldest months). However, the weather does vary regionally, even to the level of neighbouring valleys, owing to the formidable topography, differences in elevation, and other factors affecting local microclimates. Variation in elevation and terrain thus often has more influence on the weather than simple north–south distances. Gyumri, for example, is famously cold compared with lowland Yerevan, even although the distance between them is only 122km. Armenia's very highest mountains see at least partial snow cover all year round (see also page 127 for Yerevan's weather). Dilijan and its surrounds are sometimes referred to as 'semi-rainforest' due to the high level of rainfall. April and May are the wettest months: although this usually means thundery showers, the rain can be continuous for long spells. Spring can be very short, the weather changing from wintery to summery in just a few days. During the hottest months of June, July and August low humidity does mitigate the high temperatures, though Yerevan can be stifling nonetheless, prompting many Yerevantsis to head for the mountains and lakes. Autumn is relatively long and often very pleasant.

**ARMENIA'S BORDERS** Prior to the 1988–94 war with Azerbaijan, the landlocked Soviet Socialist Republic of Armenia was bordered to the north by Georgia, to the east by Azerbaijan, to the south by Iran and to the west by Turkey and by the exclave of Azerbaijan known as Nakhichevan. The borders totalled 1,254km: 164km with Georgia; 566km with Azerbaijan; 35km with Iran; 268km with Turkey; and 221km with Nakhichevan. The area of the country was 29,800km², slightly smaller than Belgium or slightly larger than the American state of Maryland. At this time, the borders with Georgia and Azerbaijan, also under Soviet rule, were administrative rather than physical, with no barriers to movement for Soviet citizens.

The ceasefire in 1994 (page 26) left a considerably altered picture of the newly independent nations of the South Caucasus and their borders. First, five small Azeri-populated enclaves within Armenia, which had been *de jure* parts of Azerbaijan under the Soviet administration, as well as one small Armenian enclave within Azerbaijan's borders, had been annexed by their surrounding powers. Secondly, Nagorno Karabagh, which had been an autonomous region within Azerbaijan with a significant ethnic Armenian population, had unilaterally declared itself independent from Azerbaijan and aligned itself with its ethnic neighbour, Armenia. Thirdly, Armenia, which had supplied military support to Nagorno Karabagh during the war, was left in control of a considerable area of the territory of Azerbaijan proper that surrounded the original Soviet region of Nagorno Karabagh – the so-called 'buffer zone'. Much of this strategically occupied land gradually fell under the administration of the new self-declared Nagorno-Karabakh Republic, since 2017 the self-declared Republic of Artsakh, with maps (especially Armenian-made) beginning to depict it as a single territory comprising all the land that remained under Armenian control, irrespective of its disputed status. Relatively few people remained in these occupied regions of Azerbaijan proper, since the Azeri population fled and Armenian refugees did not choose these territories in which to settle, leaving behind a high proportion of ruined and uninhabited settlements. However, since the ceasefire an estimated 14,000 ethnic Armenians have been resettled in these areas. Despite what is now more than 25 years of de facto self-governance, the international community still recognises the pre-1991 boundaries of Armenia and Azerbaijan, prolonging the ongoing armed conflict over the territory which continues to this day.

1

The borders with **Azerbaijan** and its exclave **Nakhichevan** have consequently been closed and militarised since the early days of the Karabagh war, and the border with **Turkey** was closed unilaterally by the Turkish government in 1993 in solidarity with the Turkic Azeris; despite a brief period in which normalisation of diplomatic relations looked hopeful, the border remained firmly closed at the time of research. The 'border' with **Nagorno Karabagh**, on the other hand, is open to locals and foreigners and is in fact the only way of entering the region, with access from Azerbaijan cut off by the line of contact. Although the northern border with **Georgia** is open to foreigners at three major border crossings, the exact position of the border in some places, especially in Lori province, is disputed. This has led to the closure of several minor border crossings previously used by local people, with the border itself militarised and patrolled. In the south, Armenia's border with **Iran** is demarcated by the River Arax, with a single official crossing point at Agarak bearing all of the traffic between Yerevan, Tabriz and Tehran.

## NATURAL HISTORY AND CONSERVATION

The number of species of animals and plants in Armenia is unusually high, with WWF International labelling the Caucasus one of 35 global biodiversity hot spots. Despite covering just 6.7% of the so-called Caucasus Ecoregion, it is home to 60% of the flora and fauna diversity, according to the UN Economic Commission for Europe. This is largely accounted for by the great altitudinal variation and the diversity of vegetation zones. Armenia is normally described as having **six distinct zones**: semi-deserts, dry steppes, mountain steppes, forest, subalpine and alpine. **Semi-deserts** account for about 10% of the country and occur in the Ararat Valley and adjacent mountain slopes up to elevations of 1,200–1,300m, as well as in the Arpa Valley around Vayk, and in the Meghri region. The land has generally been cultivated for millennia except for a few patches where sand has accumulated and a semi-desert landscape has resulted. Cultivation has required extensive irrigation and these irrigated areas now account for most of the fruit, vegetable and wine production. **Dry steppes** are found at higher elevations than semi-deserts (above 1,500m) in the Ararat Valley and some other areas, but are also found at lower elevations (above 800m) in the northeast in areas which were originally forested. Irrigation of dry steppes has allowed some cultivation of crops and fruit. Treeless **mountain steppes** are the dominant landscape for most of the country, particularly at elevations above 1,500m. In the northeast of the country and also in the south, ridges among these highland meadow steppes often contain patches of forest. Elsewhere, **forests** are usually found on the subalpine slopes of mountain valleys, though in some regions the forests were severely damaged by the cutting of trees for fuel during the energy crises of the early 1990s. The most extensive forested areas are now in the northeast and the far south. **Subalpine meadows** occur at higher elevations than steppes and forests, including highland mountain ranges. **Alpine meadows** occur higher still and are important pasture lands during the relatively short summers at these elevations. So-called **azonal landscapes** (meaning that the soil type is determined by factors other than the local climate and vegetation) cover the remaining 10% of the territory of the country and include wetlands, as well as saline and alkaline areas in the Ararat Valley where the underground waters are close to the earth's surface, resulting in water vaporisation and salt precipitation.

**MAMMALS** Armenia's mammal list was recently increased from 76 to 83 when seven additional species of bat were identified. However, one of the mammals on the list, striped hyena (*Hyaena hyaena*), is probably extinct in the country and the status of Caucasian birch mouse (*Sicista caucasica*) is unknown. Another six are officially classified as endangered: the distinctive Armenian subspecies of mouflon (*Ovis orientalis gmelini*), Persian ibex or wild goat (*Capra aegagrus aegagrus*; often referred to as the Bezoar goat or Bezoar ibex), marbled polecat (*Vormela peregusna*), otter (*Lutra lutra*), Pallas's cat (or manul; *Felis manul*) and Syrian brown bear (*Ursus arctos syriacus*). Despite bears being classified as endangered, their droppings can often be encountered while walking in the mountains, particularly in the Vayots Dzor region, sometimes surprisingly close to habitation. Other interesting mammals include the critically endangered Persian leopard or Caucasian leopard (*Panthera pardus tulliana*), the ongoing subject of a WWF protection programme in Armenia; lynx (*Felis lynx*); wild cat (*Felis silvestris*); wolf (*Canis lupus*); porcupine (*Hystrix indica*); roe deer (*Capreolus capreolus*); wild boar (*Sus scrofa*); and golden jackal (*Canis aureus*). However, none of these large mammals – except perhaps the Bezoar goat – could be described as common sights, and the visitor is perhaps more likely to come across smaller and more abundant species such as red fox (*Vulpes vulpes*), brown hare (*Lepus capensis*), European souslik (*Citellus citellus*) and Vinogradov's jird (*Meriones vinogradovi*), the jird being one of five species of gerbil found in Armenia.

**BIRDS** The standard guide, *A Field Guide to the Birds of Armenia* (page 407), lists 346 species of bird as having been recorded in Armenia up to 1997. However, as there are only a few observers many vagrants and casuals must go unrecorded. Armenia is at the boundary of two faunal zones and the north sees northern species at the southern limit of their range while the south sees southern species and those from the eastern Mediterranean at their northern limit. Raptors (birds of prey) are very common and easy to spot. Five species of eagle breed in Armenia: lesser spotted, golden, booted, steppe, and short-toed snake-eagle. This is in addition to osprey, four vultures, two harriers and a good selection of buzzards and falcons. Other large and conspicuous birds include white and black storks, the former mainly in the Ararat Valley, in whose villages their nests can often be spotted perched on top of electricity poles. The Dalmatian pelican breeds in the country and great white pelicans are year-round visitors. Specialities of the Caucasus include Caucasian grouse and Caspian snowcock, both of which are endangered and difficult to see without a knowledgeable local guide in their subalpine and alpine meadows. Smaller birds of note include both eastern and western rock nuthatches, white-tailed lapwing, Persian wheatear, Armenian gull, white-throated robin and Finsch's wheatear. Raptor migration in autumn is very rewarding as Armenia is on a major flightway between the Black and Caspian seas, with the most numerous species being steppe buzzard, steppe and lesser spotted eagles, and Montagu's and pallid harriers, honey buzzard, Levant sparrow-hawk, lesser kestrel and black kite. September sees migrating demoiselle cranes at Lake Sevan with daily totals of up to 4,500 being recorded.

Visitors interested in Armenia's birds are strongly recommended to join the **Ornithological Society of the Middle East, the Caucasus and Central Asia** (c/o The Lodge, Sandy, Bedfordshire, SG19 2DL, UK; e secretary@osme.org; w osme.org) who can assist with birdwatching trips to the country as well as funding small projects such as the survey of Armash fishponds.

**AMPHIBIANS AND REPTILES** Armenia's dry climate is reflected in the paucity of **amphibian species** and lack of specialities. All eight species in the country have a wide distribution even though only one is also native to the UK. Widespread

European species are marsh frog (*Rana ridibunda*), green toad (*Bufo viridis*), eastern spadefoot toad (*Pelobates syriacus*), European tree frog (*Hyla arborea*) and smooth newt (*Triturus vulgaris*). The others, not included in most field guides, are banded frog (*Rana camerani*), lemon-yellow tree frog (*Hyla savignyi*) and banded newt (*Triturus vittatus*).

By contrast, Armenia is very rich in **reptile species** with a total of 50, although some are now threatened by denudation of the habitat as a result of overgrazing. The Mediterranean tortoise (*Testudo graeca*) may occasionally be encountered as one crosses a track. Ponds may contain one of two species of terrapin, European pond terrapin (*Emys orbicularis*) and stripe-necked terrapin (*Mauremys caspica*).

The **geckos** which can frequently be seen on the outside walls of buildings in the countryside are Caspian rock geckos (*Tenuidactylus caspius*). The Caucasian agama (*Laudakia caucasia*) is a lizard with a decidedly prehistoric dragon-like appearance. Like all agamas, it has a plump short body with a long thin tail, a triangular head and long legs. Agamas are capable of some colour change to match their background. Two **legless lizards** which might be mistaken for snakes (though being lizards rather than snakes they have eyelids and they can shed their tails to escape a predator, a practice known as autotomy) are the slow worm (*Anguis fragilis*) and the European glass lizard (*Ophisaurus apodus*). **Skinks** are lizards which, while not usually completely legless, generally in Europe only have vestigial legs of little or no apparent value for locomotion. The Armenian fauna includes several skinks: two-streaked lidless skink (*Ablepharus bivittatus*); Chernov's lidless skink (*Ablepharus chernovi*); golden grass skink (*Mabuya aurata*); and the Berber skink (*Eumeces schneideri*). The other lizard species are typical lizards belonging to the large family Lacertidae. Ones of particular interest are those with a limited range outside Armenia such as stepperunner (*Eremias arguta*), Balkan green lizard (*Lacerta trilineata*) and Caucasian green lizard (*Lacerta strigata*). Even more unusual is the Armenian lizard (*Lacerta armeniaca*) in which a proportion of the females practise parthenogenesis – in other words without fertilisation by a male they lay eggs which hatch and produce a daughter that is an exact genetic copy of the mother.

**Snakes** are very well represented with 23 species, and they are more commonly seen than in many countries. Interesting snakes include the sand boa (*Eryx jaculus*), one of Europe's few snakes which kill their prey by constriction, mostly small lizards and rodents in this case. Largely nocturnal, it rests by day in rodent burrows or under large stones. Unusually, the snake is viviparous, the female giving birth to about 20 live young which feed on small lizards. The Montpellier snake (*Malpolon monspessulanus*) belongs to the family Colubridae, snakes whose fangs are at the back of the mouth. Such snakes find it difficult to inject their venom into large objects. Unusually for a snake this diurnal species possesses good vision and, when hunting, it sometimes rises up and looks around rather resembling a cobra. The Montpellier snake reaches 2m in length. A much smaller colubrid is the Asia Minor dwarf snake (*Eirenis modestus*) which grows to only 15cm and feeds on insects. Dahl's whip snake (*Coluber najadum*) is another diurnal snake. Very slender, it is extremely fast moving but rarely exceeds 1m in length. Another whip snake is the secretive and weakly venomed mountain racer (*C. ravergieri*). Caucasian rat snake (*Elaphe hohenackeri*) is one of Europe's smaller snakes, growing up to about only 80cm. Very unusually for a snake, it is often found in the vicinity of human habitations where it frequents piles of stones and holes in old stone walls.

Vipers are among the snakes which, unlike the colubrids, have fangs at the front of their mouth. They are consequently much more dangerous because they do not need to get their mouth round the victim in order to inject poison. There are several interesting species in Armenia which have a very limited distribution. Armenian viper (*Vipera raddei*) is now seriously threatened in the country through pasturing and overgrazing, while Darevsky's viper (*V. darevskii*), described as recently as 1986, also has a very limited range and is similarly threatened. Bites from these species can be fatal, as can those from Armenia's more widely distributed vipers. Perhaps the most dangerous of all is the blunt-nosed viper (*V. lebetina*), at 2.5m one of the largest of its genus. An able climber of trees, the danger from this snake lies mainly in the extreme speed of its attack and the method of biting: rather than bite and withdraw, it keeps its teeth lodged in its target and works its jaws to pump more venom in. It is not a snake to be approached lightly, although it generally makes a loud hissing before attacking, thus giving some warning. Hikers in particular should see page 76 for what to do in the event of a snakebite, as well as how to reduce the risk of conflict with snakes in the first place.

**FISH**  Of the 31 species of fish found in Armenia, six have been introduced. Common whitefish (*Coregonus lavaretus*) was introduced into Lake Sevan from Lake Ladoga in Russia with a view to increasing commercial fish production, and this was followed by goldfish (*Carassius auratus*) from eastern Asia. Fish farms are responsible for introducing silver carp (*Hypophthalmichthys molitrix*) from China, and Pacific salmon (*Salmo gairdneri*). Presumably Pacific salmon was preferred to the native Caspian salmon (*S. caspius*) because of the ease of obtaining stock. Grass carp (*Ctenopharyngodon idella*) came from China with the hope of improving water quality in irrigation systems and marshy lakes as it is herbivorous and so helps to control aquatic vegetation. By contrast, mosquito fish (*Gambusia affinis*) was brought from the southeast part of the USA because, as its name implies, it eats mosquito larvae and hence assists in the control of mosquito-borne diseases.

Apart from these exotics there has been some stocking of waters with common carp (*Cyprinus carpio*) which has been introduced to lakes in Lori province as well as Dilijan and Ijevan reservoirs. On the other hand, overfishing of rivers – all too often using electricity, which affects small fish as well as mature specimens – has led to a decline in the abundance of brown trout (*Salmo trutta morpha fario*) and European catfish or wels (*Silurus glanis*). However, chub (*Leusciscus cephalus*) remains common in lakes. Drastic reduction in the water level of Lake Sevan, together with the introduction of competing species such as common whitefish and narrow-clawed crayfish (*Astacus leptodactylus*), has led to the virtual extinction in Armenia of the endemic Sevan trout (*Salmo ischchan*; page 229). Paradoxically, its successful translocation into Lake Issyk-kul in Kyrgyzstan, although having negative consequences for the indigenous Issyk-kul fish fauna, has probably saved this fish from extinction. Stocks in Lake Sevan of Sevan khramulya (*Varicorhinus capoeta*) have also seriously declined but it survives in some of the lake's tributaries.

**OTHER FAUNA**  About 17,000 species of **invertebrate** have been identified in Armenia but this must only represent a small fraction of the total. Two groups may be of particular interest to visitors but for very different reasons. Armenia has three species of **scorpion**, which occur on rocky or stony ground such as that which surrounds many monasteries – an additional reason to stay alert and wear robust footwear when scrambling around such sites. Far more conspicuous is the abundance of **butterflies**. About 570 species of *lepidoptera* (moths and butterflies) have been identified in Armenia, but that is probably a small percentage of the

1

total since it compares with a figure of 2,600 for the UK which, although larger, has a much less suitable climate. A well-illustrated guide to the butterflies of the whole of the former Soviet Union including Armenia (*Guide to the Butterflies of Russia and Adjacent Territories*) is available – it was published in Sofia, Bulgaria, and is obtainable from specialist booksellers worldwide – but unfortunately its two enormous heavy volumes make it difficult even to take to Armenia, let alone carry around. More portable is *A Field Guide to the Butterflies of Turkey*, published in 2007. Obviously it does not cover Armenia specifically, but there is enough overlap to make it more useful than no guide at all. For details of these books see page 408. The American University of Armenia, which published *A Field Guide to the Birds of Armenia*, promised a field guide to the butterflies of Armenia. The original planned publication date was 2012 but at the time of research it had not yet appeared, though an interactive illustrated 'story map' of butterfly species and locations can be found on the website of the university's Acopian Center for the Environment at w ace.aua.am. A 2016 checklist of the dragonflies and damselflies (Odonata) of Armenia can be found at w sites.google.com/site/armenodonata.

**FLORA** Identified so far in Armenia have been 388 species of algae, 4,166 fungi, 2,600 lichens and 430 mosses in addition to the very large total of more than 3,200 species of vascular plants, including some endemic plants found only in Armenia. Vascular plant diversity is highly concentrated in Khosrov Forest State Reserve (page 207), which plays host to 1,849 species – more than half of the total – despite occupying just 1% of the country's territory. Since Armenia's flora is very large it is perhaps surprising that gymnosperms (basically conifers) should be poorly represented by a mere nine species: five junipers, one pine, one yew and two shrubby members of the family Ephedraceae whose American relatives include Nevada joint fir and desert tea.

One third of the forests are oak and they are widely distributed across the country. Of the four species found in Armenia, two are typical of these forests, Caucasian oak (*Quercus macranthera*) and Georgian oak (*Q. iberica*). Caucasian oak is the more frost-tolerant species and is found throughout the country at elevations as high as 2,600m. By contrast, Georgian oak is typically restricted to elevations between 500 and 1,400m, and is mostly found in the north and the extreme south. Other species found in oak forests are ash (*Fraxinus excelsior*), hornbeam (*Carpinus betulus*), Georgian maple (*Acer ibericum*), cork elm (*Ulmus suberosus*) and field maple (*Acer campestre*). A third oak species – Arax oak (*Q. araxina*) – is now declining, probably because of agricultural development.

Another third of the forest are the rain-loving beech forests of northeastern Armenia. They are dominated by Oriental beech (*Fagus orientalis*), which prefers north-facing slopes at an elevation of 1,000–2,000m and can reach over 30m in height; several notable specimens can be seen on walks through the southern portion of Dilijan National Park (page 300). Other species in beech forests include small-leaved lime (*Tilia cordata*), Litvinov beech (*Betula litwinow*) and spindle-tree (*Euonymus europaeus*). Hornbeam forests occur at elevations of 800–1,800m. Other trees found in these forests include the various oaks, field maple, ash, Caucasian pear (*Pyrus caucasicum*) and Oriental apple (*Malus orientalis*). Scrub forests are found in both the north and south of the country occurring at elevations of 900–1,000m in the north, but at much higher elevations in the south (1,800–2,000m). These forests support around 80 species of xeric trees and shrubs, all of which are drought tolerant and light-loving. As well as thorn forest dominated by juniper, broadleaved forests also occur, characterised by species such as Georgian maple, various cherries, pistachio (*Pistacia mutica*), almond (*Prunus dulcis*), buckthorn (*Rhamnus catharticus*) and wild jasmine (*Jasminum fruticans*). There are groves of virgin yew (*Taxus baccata*) in Dilijan National Park and a relict plane (*Platanus orientalis*) grove by the Tsav River in Shikahogh State Reserve (page 366).

A number of Armenia's plants will be familiar to visitors because they have become popular cultivated plants of temperate gardens such as the florist's scabious, the flamboyant oriental poppy, the ubiquitous catmint, burning bush and grape hyacinth. Different types of vegetation can be seen within relatively limited areas, often accessed easily from the principal roads. Abundant and unusual wild flowers are to be found in the mountain habitats typical of Armenia, particularly in late spring and early summer (May–June). It is in central Armenia, for example, that the almost impossible to cultivate, but striking and often bizarre Oncocyclus iris, can be found. Altogether, the extensive alpine meadows, the river gorges and the broadleaved deciduous forests make for a superb area to explore in search of interesting and attractive plants – and one of the great joys of travelling in Armenia is that botanical excursions and visits to ancient churches and monasteries so often naturally coincide.

**CONSERVATION AND ENVIRONMENTAL ISSUES** Conservation has not been a priority in Armenia until recently – unsurprising, perhaps, for a country still coping with the aftermath of a severe earthquake in 1988, the war over Nagorno Karabagh and the associated closure of borders by Azerbaijan and Turkey, and the loss of most of its industrial base following the collapse of the Soviet Union. The crisis resulted in a severe overexploitation of natural resources, with logging and hunting for the basic provisions of food and fuel partly to blame for the diminished state of some of Armenia's forests and its noticeably shy and retiring large mammals. According to the World Bank, Armenia's forests shrank from 20% to 7% of total land area in the 20 years following independence (the figure is now put at 9%), and it is probably fair to say that awareness of such environmental issues is not generally high, although it is increasing. Even where awareness exists, the priority for those who are poor is, understandably, simply to survive, though the organised illegal logging trade is also to blame. There are many active environmental NGOs and international foundations which support conservation activities, and large investments are being made to support environmental education programmes and action for particular species, but it is still early days in terms of positive results on the ground, in spite of considerable relevant expertise in Armenia. The reasons for this are complex but include the vestiges of post-Soviet bureaucracy, corruption and political manoeuvring, and when efforts have been made a focus on brute prevention rather than the creation of alternative choices. Having said all that, conservation priorities are gradually gaining traction, most visibly – for visitors at least – Armenia's potential for ecotourism being harnessed by development organisations and local entrepreneurs alike.

The main environmental issues facing Armenia include pollution and nature conservation, with **mining-associated problems** a particular concern. The Armenian government has in the past made mining a key part of its economic development strategy but there is widespread anxiety, both within Armenia and internationally, on environmental and social grounds. The story of the Teghut mine in the north of Lori province exemplifies many of the concerns. In the early 2000s, a licence to extract copper and molybdenum in one of Armenia's best-preserved forest areas was granted to Vallex Group, prompting years of grass-roots activism by Armenian campaigners. When the open-pit mine opened for business in 2014, its construction involved felling 364ha of virgin forest which was home to six species of flora and 29 species of fauna listed as endangered in Armenia's Red Book. In January 2012 the Parliamentary Assembly of the Council of Europe (PACE) issued a written declaration, signed by 44 parliamentarians representing 27 countries, which referred to the Teghut mining project as a manmade ecological disaster, asserting that the Armenian government had violated its international obligations and Armenian legislation. By 2018, the Danish funders had withdrawn investment on environmental grounds, the mine's operations were suspended, and most of the much-vaunted 1,300 local jobs had been wiped out. Sadly, this was not a particularly unusual story. Protests resurfaced as work began on a new gold mine at Amulsar in southern Armenia (operated by Jersey-registered company Lydian International), set to commence operations by the end of 2018. In response, the new post-revolution Minister of Ecology initiated a nationwide audit of all mining operations, beginning with Amulsar.

**Desertification**, often triggered by deforestation, is another significant problem. Loss of tree cover predisposes the terrain to landslides and leads to fragile topsoil being washed away. The Armenian National Plan to Combat Desertification estimates that 26.8% of the total territory of Armenia faces the threat of extremely severe desertification and only 13.5% is not exposed to any threat of desertification. The loss of forests makes Armenia more susceptible to the consequences of climate change. In 2009 the United Nations Development Programme (UNDP) published a study which looked at the likely effects on Armenia of climate change (*Socio-Economic Impact of Climate Change in Armenia* by Stanton, Ackerman and Resende, Stockholm Environment Institute). The study predicted a rise in temperature; reductions in precipitation, river and lake levels; and an increased risk of heatwaves, droughts, landslides and floods. They suggested that Armenia's future economic development depends on investment to adapt to climate change.

The **Ministry of Nature Protection** is the government agency responsible for protecting the environment, though it also sells mining and logging concessions. In the past, powerful businesses and individuals have seemingly been able to operate in protected areas, and parts of protected areas have allegedly been downgraded in status or fully removed from the area's boundaries to 'allow' such activity, though examples of such questionable practices are thankfully on the decline. There are currently 35 official **protected areas** in Armenia, of which the most significant are Shikahogh State Reserve (page 366), Khosrov Forest State Reserve (page 207), Dilijan National Park (page 300) and Lake Sevan National Park (page 229). Until now, Shikahogh has been the best protected, partly because of its isolated location in the far south of the country but also because of its International Union for Conservation of Nature (IUCN) category Ia status, which forbids any land use other than scientific study and specific, highly regulated forms of tourism. While the will to fulfil their remits effectively is far less lacklustre than in the past, the ministry and the individual protected area authorities generally suffer from a lack of the resources, strategy and expertise needed to effectively enforce the regulations, though progress is slowly being made.

**Non-profit organisations** have stepped in to fill some of the gaps; for example, the **Armenia Tree Project** (w armeniatree.org) aims to repair the damage done to forests and has so far co-ordinated the planting and restoration of more than 5 million trees, work largely carried out by volunteers. The **American University of Armenia** has a research centre, the Acopian Center for the Environment (ACE) (w ace.aua.am), which in 2016 initiated an annual ecotourism conference to draw attention to environmental issues in Armenia and the potential for tourism-based solutions to some of these issues. There is a growing awareness of environmental issues, particularly among the younger generation, and increasingly effective attempts at **civic activism**. In 2011, Trchkan Waterfall (page 269) was the focus of a successful campaign by activists to save it after work had started to dam the river above the waterfall for a hydro-electric scheme. Permission for the scheme had been granted even though the waterfall was deemed a protected area, and plans and licences were never made public as required by Armenian law. The activists made use of the internet to draw attention to their cause, organising a 10,000-signature petition and publicising demonstrations in Yerevan and at the waterfall. Similar direct actions and social media exposés prevented the eviction of several families from their traditional homes on the edge of Khosrov Forest State Reserve, and in 2017 suspended the heavy-handed construction of a tourist resort at Gosh Lake in Dilijan National Park.

**Waste management** is a significant issue which has only recently begun to be tackled. The problem in part is due to the invasion of plastic packaging; most such rubbish goes to landfills, but in rural areas there is no governmental waste-disposal management and people have to dispose of this unnecessary waste as best they can, which often means either setting fire to it in a metal dumpster, or throwing bags of rubbish over the edge of the roadside verge outside the village. The first waste-processing scheme was established in 2011 with sorting plants in Gyumri, Vanadzor and Yerevan, and local projects are beginning to spring up, but there are still no national recycling initiatives in Armenia. Despite a series of awareness campaigns, visitors will still observe a general lack of concern for the environment such as litter, vehicles with high exhaust emissions (although Armenia also leads the world in the use of compressed natural gas to run cars) and the loss of some of Yerevan's green space to illegal constructions.

Other issues transcend national boundaries, and these mainly relate to rivers and water catchment areas, and to the protection of critically endangered species whose territories comprise that of several countries. Indeed, conservation is one of the few spheres in which otherwise conflicted nations have found common ground for co-operation.

# HISTORY

Visitors to Armenia are confronted by the country's history everywhere they look, and not just in the prehistoric sites and splendid medieval monasteries that have long underwritten the country's traditional tourism offer. Other aspects of Armenia's history are reflected in the legacy of Soviet-era apartment blocks identical to those in Kaliningrad or Omsk, and in the huge investment in modern Armenia funded by the country's large, important and wealthy diaspora. Further observations soon strike the visitor: that the oldest surviving building in the country, at Garni, looks Graeco-Roman rather than Armenian and quite different from any other; that there are no Roman remains outside of the museums; that the old churches and monasteries were built within certain very restricted time periods interspersed with long periods from which nothing seems to have survived; that different foreign influences seem to have been significant at different epochs; and that the country's post-Soviet spate of church and monastery restoration shows no signs of stopping. Visitors will also see everywhere signs written in a distinctive and unique alphabet and language, the use of which is a large factor in determining what it means to be Armenian.

Beginning to make sense of all this jumble of impressions necessitates gaining some understanding of Armenia's long and varied history. During this history there were periods of independence as an Armenian nation, though often with the nation divided into separate kingdoms because of internal struggles for supremacy by individual families. These periods were separated by much longer spells of foreign rule, by a whole host of different peoples at different times. The 20th-century regaining of independence after centuries of foreign rule, briefly at first from 1918 to 1920 but then lastingly since 1991, owes little to the nations, notably Britain, which repeatedly let down the Armenian people between 1878 and 1923. However, perhaps the West can take some of the responsibility for the Soviet Union's bankruptcy and collapse.

**THE LEGENDARY ORIGINS OF THE ARMENIAN PEOPLE**  Although most foreigners call the country Armenia or some variation thereof (a notable exception being Georgians, who call it Somkheti), Armenians themselves call it **Hayastan**: literally the 'Land of Hayk'. Genesis 8:4 states that Noah's Ark grounded on 'the mountains of Ararat', an ambiguous phrase that has prompted a long history of (so far unsuccessful) Ark-hunting expeditions. Genesis 10 records that Togarmah was a son of Gomer who was a son of Japheth who had accompanied his father Noah on the Ark. According to Armenian legend, the Armenian people are the descendants of Hayk who was the son of Togarmah and therefore the great-great-grandson of

## ARCHAEOLOGY IN ARMENIA

Armenia has an amazing wealth of archaeological sites. Some of the most important include the Early Bronze Age trans-Caucasian Kura-Araxes-culture site of **Shengavit** (3500–2000BC); the Middle Bronze Age (2500–1000BC) site of **Metsamor** (a copper-mining and major bronze-production site; also a site with ritual rock carvings and where the cemetery revealed rich burials containing looted Babylonian jewellery); the Late Bronze Age (1500–900BC) site of **Lchashen** (where the wheeled wagons in the State History Museum were discovered) and the 9th- to 7th-century BC Iron Age Urartian cities of **Erebuni** and **Teishebaini** (Karmir Blur). These are simply a few, albeit an important few, of the many sites throughout the country. Other places are detailed in this guidebook.

Much excavation was carried out in the Soviet period with results published in Russian-language academic journals, and the amount of information available to non-professional but interested visitors was until recently very limited. This is changing, with excellent displays in Yerevan's History Museum of Armenia (page 176) and the museums at Erebuni (page 172), Metsamor (page 223) and Shengavit (page 174). Archaeologists from the West, in collaboration with local experts, continue to uncover and investigate new sites in the post-Soviet era; one notable foreign expert is Professor Adam T Smith of Cornell University, co-founder and co-director of the joint Armenian–American project ArAGATS (w aragats.arts.cornell.edu).

Visiting some of the ancient sites can leave the visitor feeling less than impressed because after excavation the area often has to be reburied to preserve it. Much imagination is required to clothe the low walls or mounds with their original splendour. Good places to start are the History Museum of Armenia in Yerevan, where many of the rich finds from excavations are on display, and Erebuni, where walls were reconstructed in Soviet days to a height of about one metre. While this has drawbacks, it does allow an impression of what the citadel looked like.

Noah. Their name for their country records this, and Hayk remains a common Armenian name today.

According to the legend, of the three sons of Noah, Japheth and Ham settled with their families in the Ararat region while Shem subsequently moved away to the northwest. Ham's and Japheth's sons gradually spread out to the various regions of the Armenian Plateau. When Japheth's great-grandson Hayk was 130 years old, he travelled south to the city of Shinar (probably what we know as Babylon in present-day Iraq) and worked on the building of the Tower of Babel (Genesis 11). After the Tower eventually collapsed, Hayk, a handsome man and a strong warrior (despite his age) with curly hair and good eyesight, was able to defy even Nimrod (or Bel as he is known in the legend), the tyrannical ruler of Assyria. Nimrod had ordered that he should be worshipped by his people but Hayk refused and moved back north with his family (including his 300 sons) to the lands around Ararat. Nimrod resented Hayk's departure, and ordered him back, even seeking to lure him by reminding him that Armenia had a less favourable climate than Assyria. When Hayk refused, Nimrod marched north with his army (which outnumbered Hayk's) and battle was joined on the shores of Lake Van. Nimrod, according to the legend, wore iron armour but Hayk drew his bow, and shot him with a three-feathered arrow which pierced the armour killing the king. Seeing this happen, the Assyrian army turned and fled. Hayk returned to Ararat and died at the age of 400. The discovery of boundary stones and of Babylonian writings dating from Nimrod's reign confirm the battle and the manner of Nimrod's death as described in the legend.

The name **Armenia**, by which almost everybody else knows the country, was first used by Greek historians about 3,000 years ago, although in legend the name commemorates the great leader of the country, Aram, who was sixth in line of descent from Hayk.

**ANCIENT HISTORY** Crudely worked stone tools found in caves and river gorges and on mountain slopes, including Mount Aragats, have been dated to around 600,000 to 800,000 years ago and more sophisticated ones such as knives to the period between 40,000 and 100,000 years ago. The transition from hunting and gathering to a more settled way of life sustained by agriculture and pastoralism had begun in Armenia in the Arax Valley by about 6000BC. However, the first people to leave significant traces on the Armenian landscape did so in the form of **petroglyphs**, or images carved on rock, which can be found in various regions of Armenia. Those in the Geghama Mountains west of Lake Sevan have been studied in some detail, as have those at Ughtasar (page 345), but the carvings in other regions are similar. They are believed to date mainly from the 5th to 2nd millennium BC. They depict both wild animals such as mountain goats, deer, wild boar, wolves, foxes, snakes, storks and waterbirds as well as domestic animals such as yoked oxen and dogs. Images of hunters using bows are fairly common, some hunters accompanied by their dogs. Humans are depicted, usually in a highly schematic style.

There are also carvings of celestial bodies: the sun, moon and stars. Some of the later carvings show carts and chariots drawn by oxen or bulls with stellar symbols on their fronts and these may be connected with a cult of the sun.

Little is known about those who created the rock art but during the Early Bronze Age, when some of the earlier carvings were created, a series of villages and fortified settlements developed in the Arax Valley based on agriculture and herding but also practising **metalworking**. Local high-quality supplies of ore led to the forging of copper and bronze and later the smelting of iron by around 1000BC. Artefacts found in these settlements include red-black burnished pottery with geometric patterns. Burial goods from the Middle and Late Bronze Ages also suggest a religious belief centred on the sun. Armenia has two monuments from this period which some believe to be astral observatories. At Metsamor (Armavir province) there is a series of stone platforms dated to 2800BC oriented towards Sirius, the brightest star visible, and there are also numerous carvings said to show the position of stars in the night sky together with a compass pointing east. At Karahunj (near Sisian in Syunik province) there is an elaborate arrangement of stones in which holes are bored. Some authorities suggest they had an astronomical purpose, possibly enabling the tracking of solar and lunar phases, while other authorities dispute such astronomical theories for both sites. It has even been suggested that it was in Armenia at this period that the signs of the zodiac were named: certainly the animal signs are all of creatures which would have been familiar in Armenia.

**URARTU** These early peoples spoke a variety of languages but, probably around 1165BC, another people migrated into Armenia and they spoke the language from which present-day Armenian is descended. Their close affinity to the Phrygians (who lived in the north of present-day Turkey) is attested by classical writers such as Herodotus and Eudoxus and this suggests that they came into Armenia from the west.

During the 9th century BC the empire of Urartu developed eventually to incorporate much of Anatolia and most of present-day Armenia. Co-operation under central leadership may have been the result of increasing Assyrian aggression. By the reign of the Urartian king Sarduri I (reigned c840–c825BC) the capital had been established at Tushpa, present-day Van in Turkey. Expansion was achieved through a series of military campaigns with Argishti I (reigned c784–c763BC) extending Urartian territory as far as present-day Gyumri and his successors taking the land west and south of Lake Sevan. Urartian expansion provoked Assyrian concern and in 735BC the Assyrian king Tiglath Pileser III invaded as far as Van. It was not, however, until 715BC that Urartu began to suffer a series of catastrophic defeats, not just against the Assyrians but also against other neighbours, and in 714BC King Rusa I committed suicide on hearing news of the sack of the temple at Musasir. The 7th century BC was to become a period of irreversible decline with Urartu finally disappearing around 590BC: it did, however, outlive Assyria which had fallen to Babylon in 612BC and its name survives to this day in the form of Mount Ararat.

This first state on Armenian territory, Urartu's regional importance briefly rivalled that of its powerful neighbours. An inscription reveals that it had 79 gods of whom 16 were female. Clearly the most important was Tushpa, god of war: he had over three times the volume of sacrifices offered to his nearest rival. Seventeen bulls and 34 sheep were specified, presumably on some regular basis. The accumulation of animal remains in temples must have been a problem: a room at one site yielded to archaeologists 4,000 headless sheep and calves sacrificed over a 35-year period. Armenia's metalworking skills were important in sustaining Urartu and irrigation works supplied water to vineyards, orchards and crops. The empire was more or less self-sufficient in most goods with the exception of tin (needed to make bronze) which was probably imported from Afghanistan. However, fragments of Chinese silk have been found, providing evidence of foreign trade.

Urartu's cities, linked by a network of good roads, were well developed with high walls, moats, and towers at their entrance gates. One Assyrian opponent claimed that the walls reached to 240 cubits – around 120m – but this looks suspiciously like exaggeration to prove his own valour. Van probably had a population of around 50,000 while Armavir had around 30,000. Numerous forts were built throughout the country for defence and as bases for future attacks. They were built in defensible sites and surrounded by walls up to 20m in height and 2–3m in thickness. They were constructed of massive stone blocks up to a height of 2m; above this level construction was in mud brick.

**FOREIGN RULE AFTER URARTU** The Medes dealt the final blow to Urartu in 590BC. What happened to the Armenians subsequently is not clear but during the 6th century BC the Persian Achaemenids under Darius extended their empire to include the country. Political autonomy vanished, a situation that prevailed until the Persians were defeated by Alexander the Great in 331BC. However, the Persians did not seek to impose their culture or religion on their subject peoples though there was in practice probably some influence on Armenian religion – it is thought that the Persians followed an early form of Zoroastrianism which involved belief in a supreme creator God opposed by an uncreated evil spirit. The Armenians did not follow Zoroastrianism absolutely: whereas this disapproved of animal sacrifice the Armenians continued to practise it, notably by sacrificing horses to the sun god. The defeat of the Persians in 331BC did not lead to Greek rule over Armenia, which in fact achieved a greater degree of independence. Alexander's policy in the captured Persian Empire was to continue the existing administrative system under Iranian satraps. For Armenia he appointed Mithrenes who was probably the son of the deposed Persian king Orontes. Mithrenes took the title of King of Armenia. The Greek Empire did not long outlive Alexander's death in 323BC as there was a period of rivalry and war between his erstwhile successors. By 301BC, Seleucus had become satrap of Armenia but his dynasty was to control Armenia only nominally and sporadically with real power in the hands of the Orontid kings, the successors of Mithrenes. The impact of Greek civilisation was, however, increasingly felt and there was a partial revival of urban life which had largely disappeared under the Persians. In around 200BC the satrap Antiochus III was probably involved in the removal of the last Orontid king, Orontes IV, but ten years later he provoked the wrath of Rome through his invasion of Greece. Defeated at the Battle of Magnesia, his own generals then switched sides to Rome and for this they were rewarded by Rome in 189BC with the title of kings of independent Armenia.

**EMPIRE** The settlement with Rome compromised the territorial integrity of Orontid Armenia but also marked the start of a period of territorial expansion which saw the reacquisition, for the first time since defeat by the Medes in 590BC, of much of present-day Armenia. In particular the area south of Lake Sevan as far as the present-day Iranian border was taken back from the Medes. The acquisition of empire reached its apogee under Tigranes the Great who came to power in c95BC, but Tigranes's success clearly created a hindrance to further Roman expansion in the east. Tigranes's father-in-law was Mithridates VI, King of Pontus, and Tigranes unwillingly got dragged into the (third) war between Rome and Pontus when he refused to surrender his father-in-law to the brusque and offensive Roman envoy. Tigranes's new capital Tigranocerta (ie: Tigranakert, one of four cities in historic Armenia bearing the same name), which he had modestly named after himself, consequently fell to a Roman siege in 69BC and, although Tigranes subsequently made good some of the losses, his son deserted him for Rome and formed an alliance with Pompey. Tigranes was forced to make peace and Pompey rearranged the political geography. Armenia suffered considerable territorial losses and Antiochus I, a distant descendant of Darius the Great, became king. For the next 80 years Armenia, although independent, had kings appointed by Rome and it became increasingly dependent on Rome for keeping them in power. In due course Roman authority weakened and by the 50s AD Rome was unable to prevent the Parthians imposing their choice of king, Trdat (Tiridates) I, on Armenia. After a period of instability reflected in further fighting it was agreed by Parthians and Romans in AD63 that Trdat would be king of Armenia but crowned by the Roman emperor Nero.

There then began a fairly stable period for the Armenian kingdom with the kings holding the throne with Roman approval. This was punctuated by the Roman emperor Trajan's policy of expansion which saw Armenia conquered in AD114, only for the Romans to suffer defeat and withdraw after a rebellion in AD116. In AD253, Armenia was captured by the Persian Sassanids and it remained under Persian rule until a Roman victory over Persia in AD298. There were Christians elsewhere in the region from around AD100 and by AD300 there were Christians in Armenia, albeit in small numbers and with few in the elite. Zoroastrianism remained the main religion and animal sacrifice continued to be practised.

**CONVERSION TO CHRISTIANITY** The adoption of Christianity as the state religion of Armenia, the first country in which this happened, is perhaps the single most important event in Armenian history. Although traditionally said to have happened in AD301 there is debate over the precise date, but it had certainly happened by 314. King Trdat III held power, like his predecessors, with the support of Rome against the continuing threat from Persia. The precise date of Armenia's conversion is interesting as it reflects differently on Trdat's motives depending on when it was: 301 was before the persecution of the Christians by the Roman emperor Diocletian in 303 and it was also before the Roman edict of toleration of Christianity in 311 and the conversion of the Emperor Constantine in 312. A later date for Armenia's conversion suggests a much closer alignment with imperial thinking, as adopting Christianity in 314 would have been more than likely to please an emperor who had himself just become a Christian. There is an account of Armenia's conversion which claims to have been written by a contemporary but in reality it was written c460, a century and a half after the events. In this account, well known and much quoted in Armenia, Trdat had St Gregory the Illuminator, who was in his service, tortured to persuade him to give up Christianity. Gregory refused and Trdat additionally realised that Gregory's father had murdered his, Trdat's, father. As a consequence Trdat then had Gregory imprisoned in a snake-infested pit for 12 years at a place now occupied by the monastery of Khor Virap, and he also persecuted other Christians including the nuns Hripsime (whom Trdat tried to rape) and Gayane who were refugees fleeing from Rome. Divine punishment was sent: Trdat is said to have behaved like a wild boar (though in what respect he imitated these animals is not clear), while torments fell on his household and demons possessed the people of the city. Eventually Trdat's sister had a vision after which Gregory was released, the martyrs were buried and the afflicted were cured. Trdat himself proclaimed Christianity the state religion, and Gregory became Bishop of Caesarea.

Conversion required much change in social customs and this change did not happen quickly. In particular Zoroastrianism permitted polygamy and it promoted consanguineous marriages between the closest of relatives as being particularly virtuous. A Church council in 444 needed to condemn the apparently continuing practice of consanguineous marriage, while as late as 768 another needed to emphasise that a *third* marriage is detestable adultery and an inexpiable sin.

**PARTITIONED ARMENIA** By c387 Rome and Persia had decided to abolish Armenia as an independent state and to divide the country between them, a move which was finally accomplished with the removal of the last Armenian king in 428. The intervening 40 years were ones of weakness, decline and foreign domination though with a strengthening Christian presence. Present-day Armenia lies in the part which came under Persian rule after 428. A major hindrance to the acceptance of Christianity was removed through the creation in c405 of the Armenian alphabet by Mesrop Mashtots. This permitted the Scriptures to be made available in Armenian for the first time and for other religious works to be published. Although this important education programme was centred in Persian-controlled Armenia, permission was obtained from the Roman Empire (whose capital had by this time been moved to Constantinople) to set up schools there as well. However, the Persian monarchy's increasing dependence on the Zoroastrian religious establishment led to pressure on Armenian Christians under Persian rule to convert to Zoroastrianism. The first crisis occurred in 450 when taxes were imposed on the Church and the nobility was ordered to convert. The Armenians, in alliance with some Huns, inflicted heavy casualties on a much larger Persian force at the Battle of Avarayr in 451. Although the Armenians were ultimately defeated and their leader Vardan Mamikonian killed, Armenians see it as a moral victory because continuing resistance subsequently resulted in the taxes being removed and freedom of religion granted, although the patriarch and some clergy were executed and many nobles were imprisoned. Persia continued to discriminate in favour of Zoroastrians in making important appointments, a situation which prevailed until the death of the Persian king in 484.

Roman expansion finally restarted in the 6th century but it was to make little headway despite several campaigns against Persia until 591, after which the frontier was redrawn to place some of the western parts of present-day Armenia under Roman rule: the new border ran just west of Garni. However, neither Rome nor Persia was prepared for a new wave of invaders – Arabs who, from the 630s, invaded, fighting in the name of Islam. The Persians were soon defeated and the Romans lost major provinces. By 661, Armenia was under Arab rule though there were promises of religious freedom. Armenian revolts in the early 8th century gave rise to some temporary Arab repression but it was only from the rule of Caliph Umar I (717–20) onwards that Armenian Christianity was seriously threatened. Orders were given that Christian images should be torn down, financial levies were increased and pressure was applied to convert to Islam. This stimulated the creation of a cycle of rebellion, harsher treatment, another rebellion, even harsher treatment, until by c800 annual taxation on Armenia amounted to 13 million dirhams, 20,000 pounds of fish, 20 carpets, 200 mules, 30 falcons and 580 pieces of cloth. Under these conditions many Armenians chose to leave the country for Roman areas.

**RESTORATION OF MONARCHY** Conditions eased in the 9th century to the extent that the caliph agreed in 884 to the restoration of the Armenian monarchy for the first time in 456 years and Ashot I was crowned King of Armenia, the first ruler of the Bagratid dynasty. For the next 40 years, however, Armenia went through a period of continued unrest as different leaders struggled with each other for power and territory. In addition, a prolonged rebellion against the caliph led by his governor in Azerbaijan, who was responsible for collecting Armenian taxes, led to both caliph and governor presenting their own separate tax bills. Armenia was not a united nation but this time was one of a great flourishing of Armenian scholarship, literature and church building. This was particularly the case during the reign of King Abbas (928–52) who succeeded in establishing a degree of security, but during the 960s and 970s after his death, the renewed struggle for succession led to increasing fragmentation of the country and by the end of the 10th century there were five separate Armenian kingdoms – three Bagratid (based at Kars, Ani and Lori); one Artsruni based in Vaspurakan east of Lake Van, and one Syunian in the south of present-day Armenia. Armenia's political fragmentation, however, inevitably left it unable to cope with renewed expansion by the Roman Empire's successors in Byzantium during the 11th century, though Byzantine rule was to be benign in comparison with the new invaders from the south, the Seljuk Turks, who ravaged cities and brought political and economic disruption even to the Byzantium-controlled areas after 1045. The victory of the Seljuk Turks over the Romans in 1071 led to the latter's demise as a significant power and to the establishment of Seljuk rule over Armenia. The immediate consequence of the Seljuk conquest was another period of migration: this time to areas such as Georgia, Ukraine and Syria. A new separate Armenian kingdom arose in Cilicia (on the Aegean coast of Turkey) which was to last until it was overrun in 1375 by the Mamluks, the Turkish military dynasty which then ruled Egypt. Although important in Armenian history, Cilicia lies wholly outside present-day Armenia and is therefore not relevant to this guidebook.

Seljuk power in turn waned and in a series of campaigns culminating in 1204, a Georgian army which included many Armenians defeated the sultan's forces. Georgian influence increased, reflected in the style of a number of Armenia's finest churches in present-day Lori province, only for Armenia to be conquered yet again, this time by the Mongols in a series of campaigns culminating in 1244. High taxation created the usual resentment and rebellion. In 1304 matters worsened for Armenians when Islam became the official religion of the Mongol Empire and religious persecution became a matter of policy. In turn Mongol power declined and between 1357 and 1403, following a series of invasions by the Mamluks, tens of thousands of Armenians were transported as slaves. By 1400, most of Armenia had passed to a Turkmen dynasty called the Black Sheep which ruled for about 50 years before a second Turkmen dynasty, called the White Sheep, became dominant.

**RUSSIA VERSUS TURKEY** The end of the Byzantine Empire came in 1453 when the Ottomans took Constantinople (Istanbul). Further Ottoman aggression saw Armenia itself conquered and taken from the White Sheep, who were now ruling it, by the 1530s. Yet again Armenia became a battleground as hostility grew between the Ottomans and Persia, until in 1639 the two powers agreed that Western Armenia would be controlled by Turkey and eastern Armenia by Persia. A further wave of emigration from the Persian territories began around 1700 because of taxation and persecution; this time many went to India. A local rebellion in southern Armenia led by David Bek, together with invasion in 1722 by Russian forces under Peter the Great, saw Persian rule largely end and in 1724 most Persian territory was divided between the Ottomans and Russia although Persia retained Nagorno Karabagh. David Bek died in 1728 and in 1730 his successor Mkhitar Sparapet was betrayed by Armenian villagers as a result of Turkish threats. That same year David Bek's territory, centred at Tatev, fell to Turkey. Russian expansionism in the area restarted under Catherine the Great. In the conquered lands, largely Muslim, Russian policy was to encourage Christians to settle and Muslims to leave. Starting in 1796 the Russians began a further series of campaigns conquering the west Caucasian khanates. These khanates were effectively autonomous Turkish principalities (although nominally vassals of the Persians under the 1724 treaty) and they occupied an area roughly equivalent to present-day Armenia and Azerbaijan.

At that time Armenians, having been subject to so many varieties of foreign rule, and often persecution, for so long, were scattered throughout the Caucasus and eastern Anatolia rather than concentrated in the Armenian heartland. However, in 1826 Russia began a forced exchange of population which resulted ultimately in the creation of an Armenian-dominated state in the khanate of Yerevan. Russia gained dominance in the South Caucasus by defeating Persia in the war of 1826–28 and the Ottomans in the war of 1828–29, and these victories further encouraged Armenians to migrate into Russian-controlled areas of Armenia while they simultaneously continued to encourage Turks to leave. Conditions in Ottoman-controlled regions were certainly difficult for Christians. Muslim courts did not even allow testimony from them until 1854 and even after that it was usually discounted. Christians paid higher taxes than Muslims, and they were not allowed to bear arms to defend themselves whereas Muslims were. The conditions within Ottoman-controlled Armenia became known in the West through exiles, travellers' publications and official reports, and started to cause wide concern.

**BRITAIN AND ARMENIA**  Britain and Turkey were on the opposite side to Russia in the Crimean War. The treaty which ended the war in 1856 required Russia to evacuate some Armenian areas which it had occupied during the war. Although this was put into effect, British officers on the spot, especially in the 1870s, were still stressing the risk to the trade routes across the Ottoman Empire which they believed were threatened by Russia's renewed interest in southerly expansion. In 1877, the British ambassador in Constantinople went so far as to write (considerably exaggerating) that in the event of a Russian conquest of Armenia: 'The consequence would be the greatest blow ever struck at the British Empire.' Britain therefore supported Turkey against Russia though there was a simultaneous British realisation that Turkey's chance of retaining Armenia would be greater if it treated the native Armenian population better. The British government's concern, however, was with who controlled Armenia and hence the trade routes. It was not with the Armenian people except insofar as their support for Russia would weaken Turkey's hold on the region.

Russia again defeated the Ottomans in 1877–78, thereby gaining control of eastern Anatolia. The three treaties of 1878 are crucial to understanding subsequent British concern over Armenia. The first was signed between Russia and Turkey in March. In it Turkey ceded large areas to Russia and this, of course, increased British concern about the threat to trade routes. In the second, signed in June, Britain promised to defend Turkey against further Russian aggression in exchange for two commitments by Turkey: one was to hand Cyprus over to Britain; and the other was to agree with British reforms which would improve the lot of Christians in the Ottoman territories – principally Armenia. The third treaty, signed in July, restored to Turkey large areas which had been ceded in March. In it Turkey also promised to introduce reforms to improve the lot of the Armenians. Crucially those reforms no longer had to be agreed with Britain, and Russia was to evacuate the specified areas even before the reforms had been introduced. What had been in June 1878 Britain's responsibility to enforce became in July nobody's. Moreover, in July the sultan lost any real threat of action being taken if he did not comply, as the power best able to make him do so, Russia, was the last which Britain wished to see involved. It was this crucial abandonment of British influence on the plight of the Armenians, together with the increasingly harsh and cruel treatment of the Christian Armenians by the Muslim Turks and Kurds, which led the devoutly Christian and humane Gladstone to make the Armenians' plight the subject of the last major speech of his career in

1896. His speech to an audience of 6,000 in his home city of Liverpool led to the resignation of the leader of his party, Lord Rosebery, a fortnight later. There is no doubt that the removal of pressure on the sultan by Britain between June and July 1878 led to the disastrous consequences culminating in the genocide of 1915.

The Muslim Ottoman government saw Christian Armenians as likely supporters of the Christian Russian conquerors: other Christian parts of the Ottoman Empire such as Greece and Bulgaria had already experienced revolution with foreign support. The Armenians meanwhile saw the Ottomans as oppressors of their increasingly nationalistic feelings just as the Greeks and Bulgarians already had. Consequently, the migration of both Christian Armenians and Muslim Turks increased after the Russian victory in 1878. Demonstrations by Armenians for greater autonomy and against the imposition of tribute demanded by local Kurds were violently suppressed (over a thousand demonstrators were massacred on one occasion) and a refusal to pay the tribute demanded by the Kurds in addition to government taxes led to weeks of slaughter. Western ambassadors protested about the excessive violence used against the demonstrators but took no other action, not even when 300,000 Armenians died in the pogroms of 1894–96. Conditions grew even worse when the Young Turk movement, which had previously promulgated a programme of reform and courted the Armenian population, changed tack and adopted in 1909 a policy of 'Turkification' of all Ottoman subjects. This was strengthened by a growing pro-Islam movement. Twenty thousand were massacred among the Armenian community in Cilicia that year, ostensibly to prevent an Armenian uprising.

Meanwhile in the Russian-controlled areas, the climate of liberalism was in recession. The Russian government was no more enthusiastic about Armenian nationalism than the Ottoman, and a policy of 'Russification', similar to that adopted at the time in other parts of the Russian Empire such as Finland, came into being. Armenian schools, societies and libraries were closed. References in print to the Armenian nation or people were banned and Armenian Church property was taken over by the Tsar. Not surprisingly, many Armenians emigrated, principally to the USA.

**WORLD WAR I AND GENOCIDE** The Ottoman Empire entered World War I on the German side, but it was already in a state of rapid decline: between 1908 and 1912 it had lost 33% of its territory and the Armenians were the only significant Christian people to remain under Ottoman rule. In 1915, Russia, which had joined the Allied side, inflicted a disastrous defeat on the Ottomans. The Ottomans saw Russians and diaspora Armenians fighting against them and this inflamed their existing suspicions concerning the loyalty of their Armenian subjects: their knowledge of how they had treated the Armenians would in any case hardly have reassured them concerning their likely loyalty. The 60,000 Armenians serving in the Ottoman forces were quickly demobilised and organised into labour groups in February 1915, only to be massacred by April. It was also ordered that Armenians living in regions near the war front should be moved to the Syrian Desert and the Mesopotamian Valley with the clear expectation that, even if they survived the forced marches under difficult conditions, they would not survive the inhospitable terrain and hostile tribesmen of these regions for long. In reality, not only those Armenians in the frontier regions but also those living nowhere near the frontier regions were deported and then either massacred or left to starve in the desert. Large-scale massacres of Armenians developed, including the Armenian intelligentsia in Constantinople and other cities who were arrested and then murdered on 24 April (a date now commemorated by Armenian communities worldwide as the Armenian Genocide Remembrance Day). There is some dispute as to the authenticity of evidence which suggests that it was the central Ottoman government which ordered the massacres, though they were evidently carefully planned as they were carried out simultaneously in all regions of the Ottoman Empire, but there is no doubt at all that around 1½ million Armenians died in the first genocide of the 20th century. It was recognised as such by the European Parliament in 1987. It is recognised by 29 countries, including Germany, Switzerland, Italy, France, the Vatican, Sweden, Belgium, Argentina, Chile and Canada (but not the UK, although Scotland, Wales and Northern Ireland do) and by 48 US states. However, no Turkish government has ever accepted that these very well-attested events constituted a genocide; the point around which the highly strained Armenian–Turkish relations revolve to this day.

The message of the genocide was not lost on Adolf Hitler, a keen student of history, who, on the eve of his invasion of Poland in 1939, rallied his generals with the oft-misquoted words: 'Who still talks nowadays of the extermination of the Armenians?'

**THE FIRST ARMENIAN REPUBLIC** Following the Russian Revolution in November 1917, Russian forces began withdrawing from the areas of Ottoman Armenia which they had occupied: Lenin was well aware that disillusion with the war was rampant in the Russian army and that withdrawal was necessary to ensure the soldiers' loyalty. Consequently in Anatolia, Armenians were fighting the Ottomans virtually alone. There was a short respite from fighting following the formation in Moscow of the Transcaucasian Federation on 24 April 1918, uniting Armenia, Georgia and Azerbaijan, but ethnic and religious differences led to its demise after scarcely a month in existence. Turkey then started a new offensive attacking Armenia from the west while Russian Menshevik and Turkish forces based in Azerbaijan attacked from the north and east. The Turks advancing from the west were initially successful, retaking the territory west of the Arax River and capturing Alexandropol (Gyumri) on 15 May. They invaded the Arax Valley, occupying the village and railway station of Sardarapat on 21 May from which they launched an offensive towards Yerevan the following day. It was to be a decisive defeat for Turkey. For three days the Turks attacked the Armenian forces under Daniel Bek-Pirumian but were repelled and on 24 May the Armenians went over to the offensive and routed the Turks. The victory at Sardarapat followed by others at Bash-Aparan and Karakilisa (Vanadzor) between 24 and 28 May led to a declaration of independence on 28 May 1918 when the first Republic of Armenia was established under the Dashnak Party. The territories of Nakhichevan and Nagorno Karabagh were incorporated into the Armenian Republic but were excluded from Armenia only a week later when Armenia and Turkey signed a peace treaty at Batum on 4 June. However, Turkey's involvement in World War I ended with its capitulation on 30 October and the question of Nakhichevan and Nagorno Karabagh was automatically reopened.

The Armenians hoped that the victorious Allies would keep their promises and enlarge the borders of the new Armenian state after the armistice in November. Eventually the Treaty of Sèvres in August 1920 granted Armenia borders which were adjudicated by President Woodrow Wilson of the USA in November of that year. Meanwhile, Turkey had invaded Armenia in September and seized part of the country. In parallel to these events the Bolsheviks had invaded Armenia in April 1920 and the combined pressure of Turks and Bolsheviks caused the collapse of the Armenian government, notwithstanding the deliberations about its borders taking place far away in France. In reality, acceptance of Bolshevik rule was for the Armenians the only real defence against the Turks. Armenia was formally incorporated into the Transcaucasian Soviet Federated Socialist Republic on 29 November 1920.

The Bolsheviks made large territorial concessions to Turkey, notably by handing over areas which had been under Russian rule even prior to 1914, including the historic Bagratid capital of Ani and the city of Kars. Soviet historians have claimed that the Bolsheviks wanted a quick agreement with Turkey because they believed that a Turkish delegation was in London where David Lloyd George, much more in favour of newly secularised Turkey under Atatürk than Bolshevik Russia under Lenin, was offering Turkey rule over the Caucasus as a protectorate. This protectorate, the Bolsheviks believed, would include Armenia but, much more important from both Russian and Western perspectives, the Baku oilfields in Azerbaijan. It is, however, more likely that Lenin's real motive was to encourage Atatürk whom he (mistakenly) believed would be an ardent supporter of the communist cause. He probably also believed that Turkey was militarily too strong for Russia to be able to win a campaign in Armenia and these two factors led to Russia's concurrence with Turkey's proposals for the border. Had any Armenians been involved in the Moscow discussions between Russia and Turkey it is inconceivable that Ani would have been relinquished. The Treaty of Sèvres was formally replaced in 1923 by the Treaty of Lausanne, effectively abandoning any pretence of Western support for an independent Armenia and reconfirming the message of 1878 that the Western powers, whatever their feelings about the sufferings of the Armenian people, would relegate action to the 'too difficult' pile.

**SOVIET ARMENIA** From 1921 Lenin made overtures to the new Turkish government, led by Atatürk, which was under attack by Greek forces, Turkey having reneged on its promise to return historic Greek lands in Asia Minor in return for Greek support during the war. By 1921, Greek troops were approaching Ankara. Soviet Russia initially helped Turkey, Lenin still believing that Atatürk was intent on building a socialist state on the Soviet model. Lenin also agreed with Turkey that Nagorno Karabagh, Nakhichevan and Zangezur would be incorporated into Azerbaijan. However, Lenin eventually came to realise that Atatürk had no intention of building a socialist state and withdrew support. Meanwhile, led by Garegin Nzhdeh, an Armenian who had fought successful guerrilla campaigns against the Turks during Bulgaria's struggle for independence, Armenian forces fought a successful campaign in Zangezur (now Syunik in southern Armenia) against the Red Army and the Turks simultaneously. Stalemate developed and Nzhdeh forced Lenin to compromise and accept his terms that Zangezur would be incorporated into the Republic of Armenia rather than into Azerbaijan. He can thus be seen as the person who saved the south of Armenia for the country. Subsequently he went into exile and, after Hitler's coming to power, pursued fruitless negotiations with Nazi Germany in an attempt to regain for Armenia the lands occupied by Turkey. He died in a Soviet prison in 1955 but his remains were secretly returned to Armenia in 1983. In 1987 he was buried at the beautiful (but little-visited) Spitakavor Monastery in Vayots Dzor province. In 2005 he was buried for a third time on the slopes of Mount Khustup in Syunik province.

Between 1921 and 1924 Armenia witnessed a resurgence of intellectual and cultural life and Armenian intellectuals, believing that they at last had a homeland, came from abroad, notably the architect Alexander Tamanyan who had drawn up ambitious plans for the creation of a fine capital for the First Republic and who returned to complete his plans. These resulted in the creation of the buildings around Yerevan's Republic Square, among the finest of all Soviet architectural ensembles. He also planned green belts, gardens and residential areas for a city capable of housing a then unimaginable population of 150,000. Yerevan State University was also constructed and professors were recruited from the West. This was also the era of Lenin's New Economic Policy, forced on him by the failure of communist orthodoxy to deliver material benefit, and limited private enterprise was consequently tolerated.

In 1923, Stalin, who was then Commissar for Nationalities, adopted a divide and rule policy which led to Nagorno Karabagh (whose population was largely Armenian, according to most sources, although this is disputed by Azerbaijan) and Nakhichevan (which had a substantial Armenian minority) being placed in Azerbaijan. Additionally the new Soviet republics were created in such a way that they did not have continuous boundaries: for example, isolated villages deep inside Armenia were designated part of Azerbaijan. This was a deliberate, conscious attempt by Stalin to encourage ethnic tensions between Armenians and Azeris so as to discourage them from uniting together against Soviet rule. A second (Soviet) Transcaucasian Federation was abolished in 1936 and Armenia became a Soviet republic in its own right though still with the artificial 1923 boundaries.

Economic growth was impressive but the abolition of the New Economic Policy caused considerable resentment, especially among farmers. Although Armenia did not suffer deliberate mass starvation during the forced collectivisation of agriculture in the same way as Ukraine did in 1932–33, it did suffer along with other parts of the Soviet Union during Stalin's purges between 1934 and 1939. At least 100,000 Armenians were victims. Persecution of Christians also reached a height in the mid to late 1930s and all churches except Etchmiadzin were closed by 1935. The head of the Church was murdered in 1938 and the entire Armenian political leadership along with most intellectuals was condemned to death for the crime of bourgeois nationalism (ie: being perceived by Stalin as a threat to himself).

Stalin's pact with Hitler in August 1939 did not save the Soviet Union from attack for long and Germany invaded on 22 June 1941. German troops never reached Armenia: they approached no closer than the North Caucasus where the oilfields around Grozny were a principal objective as Hitler simultaneously wanted to secure their output for Germany and to deprive the Soviet Union. About 630,000 Armenians out of a then population of two million fought during World War II (or the Great Patriotic War as it is called throughout the former Soviet Union), of whom about half died.

Armenia experienced rapid growth after 1945 with Yerevan's population increasing from 50,000 to 1.3 million. Huge chemical plants were established in Yerevan, Leninakan (now Gyumri) and Kirovakan (now Vanadzor) and Armenia became one of the most highly educated and most industrialised of the Soviet republics. By contrast, a new wave of repression began in 1947 with the deportees being exiled to the infamous gulag camps of Siberia. After Stalin's death, probably by poisoning at the instigation of the secret police chief Lavrentii Beria, conditions relaxed and during the Brezhnev era (1964–82) dissenters were merely certified insane and kept among the genuinely mentally ill in mental hospitals.

The coming to power of Gorbachev in 1985 saw an upsurge in Armenian nationalism, especially over the question of the enclave of Nagorno Karabagh. Gorbachev refused to allow its transfer from Azerbaijan to Armenia. There were demonstrations in both republics and, especially following Soviet government inaction after the killing in February 1988 of 30 (some estimates claim up to 120) Armenians by their Azeri neighbours at Sumgait, an industrial city north of Baku, many Armenians fled from Azerbaijan to Armenia while at the same time many Azeris fled in the opposite direction. This unprecedented killing shocked the Soviet Union; the perpetrators were tried and sentenced in Moscow. Thereafter ethnic tensions continued to rise and during the fighting over Nagorno Karabagh there were civilian deaths on both sides. Perhaps the incident which gained most international notice and condemnation was the deaths of 161–613 (numbers are disputed) Azeri civilians, fired on by Armenian forces in February 1992, as they tried to leave Khojaly, near Aghdam, as it was about to be occupied by Armenian forces. (Khojaly was used as a military base by the Azeris to shell Stepanakert.) In July 1988, Nagorno Karabagh declared its secession from Azerbaijan and in December the intellectual pressure group known as the Karabagh Committee, which had meanwhile broadened its objectives to include democratic change within Armenia itself, was arrested and held in Moscow without trial for six months. In early 1989, Moscow imposed direct rule on Nagorno Karabagh and rebellion broke out. In November that year Armenia declared that Nagorno Karabagh was a part of Armenia (a claim it no longer makes), as a result of which Azerbaijan closed its borders with Armenia and imposed an economic blockade. The problems this caused were greatly exacerbated because of the closure, as a precautionary measure, of Metsamor nuclear power station following the Spitak earthquake in December 1988.

**THE THIRD REPUBLIC** In July 1990, elections were won by the Armenian National Movement which had developed from the Karabagh Committee. Its leader, Levon Ter-Petrosyan, became president of the Armenian Supreme Soviet which declared independence from the Soviet Union in August. (This was quite legal as, under the Soviet constitution, all republics were nominally free to secede.) The new government took a moderate line over the Nagorno Karabagh dispute and tried to distance itself from the fighting. The collapse of the Soviet Union in August 1991, following the failed putsch against Gorbachev, was followed by a referendum on 21 September in which the population of Armenia overwhelmingly voted in favour of independence. Meanwhile Azerbaijan likewise declared itself independent. However, after Armenia signed a mutual assistance treaty with Russia and certain other members of the Confederation of Independent States (CIS) in May 1992, Russia started supplying arms to Armenia which was able to drive Azerbaijan out of most of Nagorno Karabagh, the area between Armenia and Nagorno Karabagh, as well as border areas with Iran. After the death of around 25,000 combatants a ceasefire was declared in 1994. The closure of the Azerbaijan border in 1989, followed by the Turkish border in 1993 after the capture of Shusha (Shushi), together with frequent sabotage of the gas pipelines in southern Georgia (used to supply gas to Armenia), resulted in Armenia becoming heavily dependent on Iran for supplies.

One possible political solution to the dispute revolved around the idea of Armenia giving up the southernmost part of its territory bordering Iran (ie: Syunik province), previously a notable mixed-ethnicity region of Armenia, in exchange for Nagorno Karabagh. However, the Armenian government's understandable wish to retain a direct link with Iran – not to mention fierce resistance from Armenian nationalist groups against any notion of territorial concessions – made a short-term settlement of the dispute seem unlikely. Meanwhile, Azerbaijan continued to flex its military muscle while apparently hoping that Russia would lose interest in the area and cease supporting Armenia, and international commentators continued to highlight the potential for escalations resulting in a proxy war between Russia-supported Armenia and Turkey- (and therefore NATO-) supported Azerbaijan.

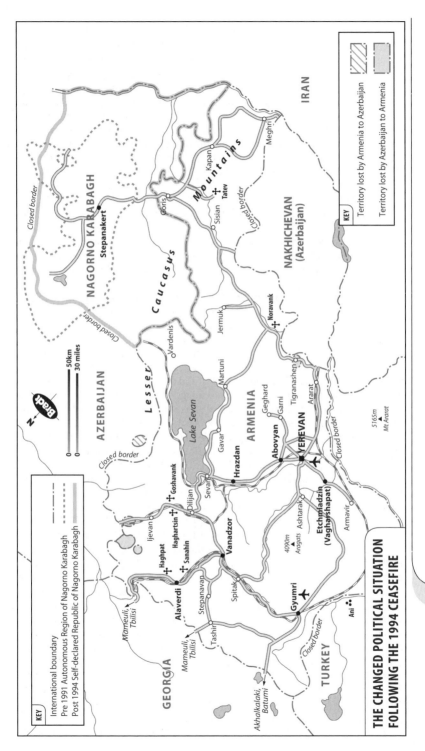

THE CHANGED POLITICAL SITUATION
FOLLOWING THE 1994 CEASEFIRE

**KEY**

Territory lost by Armenia to Azerbaijan

Territory lost by Azerbaijan to Armenia

**KEY**

International boundary

Pre 1991 Autonomous Region of Nagorno Karabagh

Post 1994 Self-declared Republic of Nagorno Karabagh

Armenia adopted a new presidential constitution in 1995 and in September 1996 Levon Ter-Petrosyan was re-elected president. Ter-Petrosyan appointed Robert Kocharyan, a former leader of Nagorno Karabagh, as prime minister and he was elected president in turn when Ter-Petrosyan resigned in 1998. Parliamentary elections in May 1999 brought the opposition Unity Alliance to power with Vazgen Sargsyan of the nationalist Republican Party (HHK) as prime minister and Karen Demirchyan (loser of the presidential election) as speaker, but on 27 October 1999 both of them, along with six others, were assassinated when gunmen stormed into parliament. The trial of the killers in late 2001 did not clarify the motives behind the attack. On 22 March 2000, Arkady Gukasyan, the president of the self-declared Republic of Nagorno Karabagh, narrowly escaped an assassination attempt for which the former defence minister Samvel Babayan was jailed for 14 years. (Released after four years on grounds of ill health, he was in 2017 sentenced to a further six years on charges of illegal arms acquisition and money laundering.)

A bitter struggle for power within the Armenian government led to some senior ministers being ousted and by mid 2001 the People's Party of Armenia (HZhK, led by Stepan Demirchyan, son of the assassinated speaker) was becoming unhappy with its role as junior partner in the ruling coalition. Some of its members joined communists and the Hanrapetutyan (Republican) party of former prime minister Aram Sargsyan (the assassinated prime minister's brother) in blocking an important bill on civil service reform. In August 2001, Kocharyan proposed controversial changes to the constitution while the opposition predictably called on him to resign. In September 2001, HZhK left the coalition and joined the opposition in calling for Kocharyan's impeachment on charges of violating the constitution, condoning terrorism, and causing a political and economic crisis. A further scandal blew up that month when an Armenian resident of Georgia, a member of the pro-Kocharyan Dashnak Party, was beaten to death in the gentlemen's toilet of Yerevan's Poplavok jazz club by members of Kocharyan's bodyguard. The President had just left the club and the bodyguard apparently objected to a remark they had heard the man making. The following month around 25,000 joined anti-Kocharyan demonstrations and 400,000 signed a petition demanding his resignation. A conspicuous feature of the subsequent trial of one of the bodyguards on the fairly minor charge of involuntary manslaughter was the unwillingness of any of the several dozen people who had witnessed the events to come forward and testify, apparently because of fear of what might happen to them at the hands of the police.

In the first round of the presidential election held on 19 February 2003, there were nine candidates, all male, including the incumbent Robert Kocharyan. The official result was that Kocharyan had received 49.48%, but since a candidate must achieve 51% of the vote for an outright victory a second round of voting was required. The entire campaign had been conducted with a great deal of mud-slinging, little discussion of important issues such as education, taxation and welfare, and little in the way of specific proposals for constitutional or legislative change. The reports of international observers from the Organization for Security and Co-operation in Europe (OSCE) differ markedly from those of the CIS observers. Among the shortcomings, the OSCE observers noted that there had been pre-election intimidation, manipulations including schemes to impersonate voters, and the heavy use of public resources in support of the incumbent. The international observers on polling day noted that there were unauthorised people in 23% of polling stations who often acted in an intimidatory manner, as well as cases of ballot-box stuffing and individuals voting more than once, among other irregularities, while the count itself showed a striking disparity both in voter turnout and outcome from the otherwise consistent pattern of results.

The second round with two candidates was held on 5 March and resulted in a win for Kocharyan with 67.44%. The OSCE observers were even more condemnatory of the process. Indeed, this time some polling stations recorded more votes than there were registered voters. Publicly funded television and radio made no attempt to fulfil their legal obligation to report even-handedly and the state-funded newspaper *Hayastani Hanrapetutyan* also gave overwhelming support to the incumbent. The extent of all this election fraud led the observers to conclude that the election 'fell short of international standards for democratic elections'. All this was in complete contrast to the CIS observers who considered the elections to be 'democratic and legitimate' with 'no mass violations of the Electoral Code'. As one local newspaper commented it was rather a 'dialogue of civilisations' with the (mostly Western) European observers having different expectations from those from former Soviet republics.

The parliamentary election held on 25 May 2003 resulted in a similar clash of views although, as on previous occasions, there was less actual malpractice than in the presidential election. Turnout in the poll was 52% with six of the 21 parties and blocs breaking the 5% threshold required to gain seats in the new parliament. The largest share of the 131 seats, 33, went to the pro-government Republican Party (HHK). The Justice bloc, led by Stepan Demirchyan, who had been runner-up in the presidential election in March, took 14 seats. The Communist Party gained a mere 1.6% of the votes and failed to secure a single seat.

The May 2007 parliamentary elections were more decisive: the Republican Party led by Serzh Sargsyan swept to power with 64 seats, placing Sargsyan in the role of prime minister. With the decision in February 2008 of the Rule of Law Party to join the governing coalition, 113 seats in the National Assembly, out of a total of 131, were held by pro-government parties. The only opposition faction in parliament, the Heritage Party, held seven seats while the remaining 11 seats were held by independents who were mostly aligned with pro-government parties. Presidential elections followed in February 2008. Backed by Kocharyan, who was ineligible to run for office for a third time, Serzh Sargsyan was declared the winner with 52.9% of votes in the first round. The election was proclaimed 'largely democratic' by international observers but the result was contested by second-place candidate and former president Levon Ter-Petrosyan, who led ten days of street protests by thousands of opposition supporters claiming that voting was rigged. Clashes between demonstrators and security personnel left ten dead and hundreds injured. Dozens of opposition supporters, and some innocent bystanders, were imprisoned, and Ter-Petrosyan placed under de facto house arrest. A 20-day state of emergency was declared. International groups criticised the detentions as being politically motivated, and the election was later found to have been marred by similar problems as previous elections such as ballot stuffing, intimidation and vote buying. Sargsyan eventually took office as president in April 2008, backed by a strong parliamentary majority consisting of his own Republican Party and its allies.

**THE PRESENT** Transparency International is a non-governmental organisation that publishes an annual Corruption Perceptions Index (CPI), a comparative listing of corruption worldwide, defining corruption as the abuse of entrusted power for private gain which eventually hurts everyone who depends on the integrity of people in a position of authority. Armenia's relative position declined steadily, from 88th place in 2005 to 129th in 2011. For the first time in 2012 it showed an improvement, to 105th place, but then slid backwards, holding 107th place as of 2017. The atmosphere within Armenia during this time was one in which a generally high level of institutional corruption is suspected – if not experienced – by more or less all Armenians. The political events that have paralleled this might be characterised as the Soviet-era old guard of former communists turned 'crony capitalists' growing ever more disconnected from mainstream sentiment, with the corresponding growth of an empowered youth culture unwilling to tolerate ongoing corruption and authoritarianism. A single event brought these trends together to produce a bloodless revolution, which took even its own leaders by surprise and has been (quite correctly) described as the biggest political upheaval in Armenia since the 1991 independence.

In October 2009, after what has been termed 'football diplomacy' (their presidents meeting during football matches between the two countries), Armenia and Turkey signed an accord agreeing to establish diplomatic ties and to reopen the border between the two countries, but the agreement was never ratified by either parliament. The main Armenian objection was the continuing refusal of Turkey to recognise as genocide the massacres of 1915. Difficulties for Turkey included an undertaking to its ally Azerbaijan that it would not open the border with Armenia until the Nagorno Karabagh dispute was resolved. While it was generally accepted that the accord would benefit both countries, the obstacles proved too great and the border remained closed.

Meanwhile the Republican Party (HHK) and its allies, who together held a strong parliamentary majority with Sargsyan as both party leader and president, was coming to be considered unshakeable. In Armenia's 2012 parliamentary elections the party increased its majority with 69 seats (an increase of five seats). Second place went to the Prosperous Armenia Party (BHK), led by prominent business magnate Gagik Tsarukyan, with 37 seats (an increase of 12 seats), while the Armenian National Congress (HAK), an opposition coalition, came third with just seven seats. Three other parties accounted for the remaining 16 seats. The elections were given a mixed assessment by observers, saying that while the election campaign was open and respected fundamental freedoms, and the media offered broad and balanced coverage, there were still significant irregularities in polling stations on voting day. The presidential election was held the following year as usual in 2013, again a foregone conclusion in the eyes of most. Only two of the six candidates received any substantial proportion of the votes: Serzh Sargsyan was re-elected with 59% of the vote, and the American-born Raffi Hovhannisian of the Heritage Party came second with 36.75%. None of the other major non-government parties fielded candidates. The opinions of Western observers were much the same as they had been for the parliamentary elections in 2012 with the additional concern of 'implausibly high' voter turnout recorded for some precincts. In a now-predictable pattern, Hovhannisian and several other opposition figures refused to recognise the legitimacy of the election, and post-election protests followed. No violence was reported during these demonstrations, the shootings of 2008 no doubt still prominent in the memories of many protesters. Armenia's Constitutional Court upheld Sargsyan's election and he was inaugurated for a second term as president in April 2013.

In July of the same year, a government decision to increase public transport prices by between 33% and 100% was met with outrage by locals who saw no corresponding investment in the services, nor any increase in wages. Protests began, involving a notable proportion of young people from the growing middle class. Passengers refused to pay the newly inflated fares which they saw as merely increasing profits for politically connected individuals who owned the operating licences. Widespread media coverage followed and the fare increases were swiftly reversed. The next major demonstrations were to come in June 2015 when a sudden 17% increase in electricity prices was announced. For a second time, the apolitical nature of the issue allowed for much broader participation than the post-election demonstrations of previous years. Major avenues in Yerevan were blocked by 'sit-in' protests and the police use of water cannons to disperse participants only catalysed the spread of demonstrations to other cities in Armenia. Eventually the price increase was reversed, and the electricity grid brought under national ownership. It was noted in the media coverage of what became known as 'Electric Yerevan' that while many of the young, middle-class protesters could in fact have afforded the increase, the outcry stemmed from a perception of corruption and mismanagement of public utilities and an opportunity to express a general mistrust of the government.

In 2013, Sargsyan had set up a commission to draft constitutional amendments that would result in a change to a parliamentary republic whose prime minister would have full executive powers (including command of the armed forces), with the presidency becoming a ceremonial role elected by the National Assembly (ie: parliament). The commission was headed by the chairman of the Constitutional Court and had eight other members, almost all of whom were government officials or others loyal to Sargsyan. In October 2015 the proposed amendments were put to parliamentary vote, passing with 104 votes for to 10 against, resulting in the amendments being forwarded to a public referendum. It had previously been pointed out that, if approved, Sargsyan – who according to the constitution would be unable to run for a third term as president – could in theory be elected by the majority-holding Republican Party (of which he was the leader) to the role of prime minister after the constitutional transition was complete, thereby consolidating his power and that of his party which had controlled the government for 15 years with little serious opposition. Sargsyan had responded by publicly stating that he would not aspire to any government office after his second and last term as president. The opinion of the Venice Commission, which advises the Council of Europe on constitutional law, was that the amendments would provide 'a very good basis for the constitutional reform'. The referendum was held on 6 December 2015. Despite opposition from former president Robert Kocharyan, who had supported Sargsyan's candidacy as his successor, the vote passed with 66.2% in favour and 33.8% against, the turnout of 50.6% just over the threshold required for the result to be valid.

Immediate accusations of widespread vote rigging followed the result, with opposition campaign leaders accusing the organisers of ballot stuffing, intimidation and bribery. International observers also reported serious irregularities. In particular, the Parliamentary Assembly of the Council of Europe (PACE) noted the lack of public debate in the run-up to the vote and concluded that the low turnout reflected 'the fact that the referendum was driven by political interests instead of the needs of the Armenian public'. The European Platform for Democratic Elections (EPDE), a consortium of civil society organisations supporting or conducting citizens' election observations, reported that 'the (ruling) Republican Party of Armenia exerted serious pressure on both observers and journalists'. However, with the changes not due to be implemented until the 2017–18 election cycle, the outrage soon subsided. The first parliamentary election to be held under the new constitution came 18 months later in April 2017. The number of seats available via election had been reduced by the constitutional reforms from 131 to 101, with four additional seats reserved for the representatives of ethnic minorities, making a total of 105. In spite of several opinion polls showing more or less equal rankings for the entrenched Republican Party (HHK) and the increasingly popular Prosperous Armenia Party (BHK), the results of the actual vote were once again dominated by the Republican Party, who won 58 seats with 49.2% of votes. Prosperous Armenia came in second with 31 seats and 27.4% of votes, while the newly formed Way Out Alliance liberal coalition – one of whose leaders was a long-time opposition activist and newspaper editor called Nikol Pashinyan – won nine seats and 7.8% of the vote.

Despite a new computerised system provided by the UNDP with funding from the EU and several Western governments for the purpose of authenticating voters, international observers yet again reported widespread irregularities. The Organization for Security and Co-operation in Europe (OSCE) reported that while the elections were generally well administered, they were 'tainted by credible information about vote buying, and pressure on civil servants and employees of private companies'. Transparency International reported 45 cases of actual or promised bribes in the days leading up to the election. However, with no newly elected head of state to demonise and no fomenting opposition figure, there were no significant protests following the results. January 2018 saw President Sargsyan recommending the candidacy of Armen Sarkissian for the upcoming presidential election, which under the new rules would be voted on by the National Assembly as opposed to the general electorate. Sarkissian, formerly a professor of physics at Yerevan State University and then a research fellow and professor at Cambridge, had had a distinguished international political career as the founder in 1991 of Armenia's London embassy – the first such mission in the West for the newly independent republic – before representing Armenia as Head of Mission to the European Union and serving a further ten years as Armenia's ambassador to the UK. No other candidates stood for election and he was elected on 2 March 2018 with 90 votes out of a possible 105. His inauguration the following month, together with the expiry of Sargsyan's second term, would complete the implementation of the constitutional amendments of 2015. The existing government would be required to resign, and the role of prime minister be opened for nominations to be voted on by the National Assembly, after which a new government would be formed.

Less than a week after Sarkissian's election, Vahram Baghdasaryan, leader of the parliamentary faction of the Republican Party (HHK), joined several other MPs in publicly stating his support for Serzh Sargsyan's candidacy for prime minister, saying that he considered the outgoing president the person 'most capable of carrying this heavy burden', a reference to Armenia's still-unresolved territorial conflict over Nagorno Karabagh in which Sargsyan had played a key military role. Sargsyan himself had refused to rule out this possibility, contrary to his earlier pledges, prompting Nikol Pashinyan, now a backbench opposition MP, to warn that such a cynical move could 'drastically escalate the political situation in Armenia'. After the new president's inauguration on 9 April, the Republican Party held a meeting outside Yerevan in which it unanimously voted to nominate Sargsyan for prime minister. The party's coalition partner the Armenian Revolutionary Federation (ARF) stated its support for the decision, as did many of the Prosperous Armenia Party's MPs. Meanwhile, Pashinyan had travelled to Gyumri to begin a small-scale march called 'My Step', in which he and his supporters intended to walk some 200km to Yerevan, arriving in time to protest the official parliamentary vote on the new prime minister. The march itself drew almost no press coverage, but when Pashinyan and his team arrived in Yerevan they fused almost immediately with a parallel protest movement, dubbed 'Reject Serzh', which had galvanised the same young demographic who had participated in previous apolitical protests. The movement's rallying cry became 'take a step, reject Serzhik', with the charismatic and outspoken Pashinyan its leader by default.

On 17 April 2018 the National Assembly voted 76 to 17, with no abstentions, to give Sargsyan the most powerful official role in the country just eight days after his presidency had ended. The response by protesters was immediate. Acts of peaceful civil disobedience resulted in multiple street closures. Initially heavy-handed responses by the police subsided as it became clear that the peaceful protests, rather than being deterred, were in fact growing in response. Unlike the angry clashes of 2008, the atmosphere on the streets was jubilant as more and more people joined the daily marches, whose times and locations were announced on Facebook by Pashinyan and his campaign team. By 21 April, the initially sceptical had been convinced to join as well, with an estimated 50,000 protesters taking to the streets of Yerevan, a stage built in Republic Square to host nightly rallies, and the fervour spreading with thousands turning out in Gyumri, Vanadzor and other major cities. On 22 April, Sargsyan announced he would meet Pashinyan the following morning for a public discussion. The meeting was scheduled for 10.00 in a conference room of the Armenia Marriott Hotel (page 138) and would be broadcast live in Republic Square outside, across the country on public television, and worldwide via the internet to an increasingly transfixed diaspora. After Sargsyan's opening statement, Pashinyan followed by saying that he had come only to discuss the terms of Sargsyan's resignation. Sargsyan responded with a reference to the events of 1 March 2008, in which eight protesters were shot dead by government forces, and promptly walked out of the meeting, which had lasted less than 3 minutes. Shortly after leaving the building, Pashinyan was detained by riot police along with several key opposition allies, and numerous protesters were arrested throughout the day. This veiled threat of violence, rather than quelling protesters, incited a major escalation; crowds that evening in Yerevan alone swelled to an estimated 115,000. By mid-afternoon the following day, however, Pashinyan and his allies had been released, and just over an hour later, Sargsyan announced his resignation. The number of people (one of the authors of this guidebook included) on the streets of Yerevan that evening has been estimated at 200,000.

On 8 May 2018, after an initial attempt by the Republican Party to block his candidacy, Nikol Pashinyan was elected prime minister of Armenia with a 59–42 margin. All the votes against him came from the Republican Party. Though early in the movement Pashinyan did injure his hand on a barbed wire blockade, the revolution was later described as 'bloodless' and acquired its common name 'Velvet Revolution' after the major victories had been won. Several foreign powers, including the EU and the USA, praised both the campaigners and the state security forces for avoiding escalations to violence. While international commentators were quick to draw comparisons with neighbouring Georgia's similarly peaceful Rose Revolution of 2003, those more connected to the national sentiment of Armenia spoke instead of a movement that had roots not in broader geopolitics but in Armenia's own nation-building challenges, beginning with the dismantling of a corrupt and self-serving establishment. Key tenets of the campaign had been a commitment to law and democracy, the breaking of monopolies and the culture of nepotism, and the conducting of genuinely free and fair elections. Within a few weeks of Pashinyan forming his government, Armenia's National Security Service had begun to investigate a growing list of large-scale corruption scandals, many of which were reported by the previously self-censoring public media. Several high-ranking public officials had been questioned on suspicion of, and in some cases charged with, a veritable catalogue of offences, from money laundering, embezzlement and illegal enrichment to the theft of military hardware and abuses of official power – including immediate family members of Serzh Sargsyan himself. At the time of research the purge was in full swing, showed little sign of abating, and had climbed to the very highest levels of the previous establishment.

## ECONOMY

Between 1960 and 1988 Soviet Armenia achieved growth of 30% in GNP (during the same period, growth of GNP in the USA was 135%) but the following years were catastrophic for the economy. First, the devastating earthquake in northwest Armenia in December 1988 resulted in 25,000 deaths, 20,000 injured and 500,000 made homeless, and caused huge damage to infrastructure. This was to be followed by the break-up of the Soviet Union and war with Azerbaijan. Having had little self-sufficiency under Soviet rule, between 1989 and 1994 GNP fell from US$4,500m to US$652m. By 1994, however, the Armenian government had launched an ambitious economic programme sponsored by the International Monetary Fund (IMF) which resulted in positive growth rates of about 6% or more, until the global financial crisis led to a decline in 2008 and a severe fall in 2009 (to –19.7%). Since then the rate has gradually recovered, reaching 3.8% in 2012 and rising to 7.5% in 2017.

Armenia has been regarded since 2018 as an upper-middle-income country by the World Bank (though this does not reflect the distribution of income). Economic growth is driven mainly by the mining sector, which the pre-revolution Armenian government had prioritised. Also important are remittances from migrant workers which have grown from 4.9% of GDP in 1995 to 13.3% in 2017 (the 20th highest in the world). The financial crisis affected both rural and urban poverty; the poverty rate (at national poverty lines) increased from 26.4% in 2007 to 35.8% in 2010. Even this figure is better than a 1998 estimate of 60–70% of the population living below the poverty line. The support of the diaspora has been and continues to be of considerable importance to the Armenian economy, and poverty rates have again been dropping since the 2010 high, reaching 29.4% in 2016.

Armenia had made a full switch to a market economy by 2009 and in 2018 was rated the 44th most economically free nation in the world by the Heritage Foundation. Consumer price inflation too has been brought under control, falling from a horrific 3,373% in 1994 to as low as –1.3% in 2016, with an average downward trend since 2008 of 9%. The country receives support from international organisations such as the IMF, the World Bank and the European Bank for Reconstruction and Development. Armenia was one of the first to benefit from a special fast-track facility set up by the World Bank to help the poorest countries cope with the impact of the global financial crisis. As of June 2018, the World Bank was supporting 17 projects in Armenia, which include improving rural roads to link villages with highways; reforming the energy sector; assisting rural economic development; modernising several governmental administrative departments; and improving agriculture through irrigation.

Prior to the Soviet collapse in 1991, Armenia had developed a large industrial sector, supplying machine tools, textiles and other manufactured goods to the other Soviet republics in exchange for raw materials and energy. By 1994, most of this had closed. Given the state of the plants, the privatisation of industry has inevitably been slow. There has been a reversion to small-scale **agriculture** away from the large agro-industrial complexes of the Soviet era, but the sector has considerable need for investment and updated technology. Armenia remains a net food importer. This, combined with the lack of energy resources, ensures that Armenia runs a current account deficit. Agriculture employs around 36% of the working population while 17% work in industry and 47% in services – this last figure has increased considerably as the economy has restructured. The unemployment rate in December 2017 was estimated at 18% by the Statistical Committee of the Republic of Armenia. Another source cites 7% of the working population as unemployed although both of these figures are somewhat misleading as many subsistence farmers, tradesmen and owners of small businesses receive no salary as such.

The main **exports** are cut diamonds (which are imported uncut – Armenia has no sources of diamonds of its own), brandy and, increasingly, minerals: copper, molybdenum, ferro-alloys and gold. By value the main export trading partners as of 2016 were Russia at 21%, Bulgaria 8.7%, Georgia 8.1%, Canada 7.9%, Germany 7.9%, Iraq 7.8%, China 5.7%, Iran 4.2% and Switzerland 4.2%. The principal **imports** are natural gas, petroleum, uncut diamonds, cars, foodstuffs and pharmaceuticals. The main import trading partners at the same juncture were Russia at 30.7%, China 11%, Iran 5.1%, Turkey 5% and Germany 5%.

In September 2013 President Sargsyan announced that Armenia would join the **Russia-led Customs Union** and would participate in the formation of the Eurasian Economic Union. The Customs Union of Belarus, Kazakhstan and Russia came into being in January 2010 as a first step towards forming, in 2015, an integrated economic union of former Soviet states, the Eurasian Union, which Russian leaders see as a counterbalance to the European Union. Although it was known that meetings had also been taking place with Russia, Sargsyan's controversial announcement surprised European diplomats because for four years Armenia had been engaged in negotiations with the EU and the following month was expected to initial (along with Georgia, Moldova and Ukraine, which also failed to sign at the last moment) an Association Agreement with the EU, strengthening trade relations while committing Armenia to democratic changes. Russia supplied natural gas to Armenia and was also Armenia's main safeguard in relation to Azerbaijan with a military base at Gyumri; officials in Brussels had no doubt that this leverage was significant in Armenia's decision. After EU diplomats stated that such a move would not be compatible with a free trade agreement with another jurisdiction, a revised Comprehensive and Enhanced Partnership Agreement was signed by Armenia and the EU member states in November 2017 which did not contain a free trade component. However, both Sargsyan and the head of the EU's Armenia delegation stated that dialogues regarding visa-free travel for Armenian citizens to the Schengen Area (enjoyed since 2017 by Georgian citizens) would begin in 2018.

## PEOPLE

The long periods of foreign rule, often accompanied by religious persecution, led to the Armenian people becoming widely scattered and not comprising a majority in any territory. What distinguished them as Armenians was their Church and their language. The **Christian faith** is inseparable for many from the Armenian national identity, their Church binding them together as a people as it has for over 1,700 years while simultaneously uniting them internationally with Christians elsewhere. During the 19th century this changed as a result of the Russian conquest of eastern Armenia. There was a deliberate Russian policy of encouraging Christian immigration and Muslim emigration. Although the Tsarist regime was initially tolerant of Christians who were not Orthodox believers, this changed as a consequence of increasing Armenian nationalism as well as more general concern about national feelings and socialism in the Russian Empire. By the end of the century a policy of deliberate Russification of subject people was being applied. The movement of population resulted, at the start of the Bolshevik regime, in the new Armenian Soviet Socialist Republic having an Armenian majority but with a significant Azeri minority. Similarly, Azerbaijan had many Armenians within its boundaries, a number increased through the boundaries being deliberately gerrymandered. There was little Russian immigration to Armenia in either Tsarist or Soviet periods but the large population movements during the conflict with Azerbaijan between 1988 and 1994 resulted in massive emigration of Azeris and immigration of ethnic Armenians from Azerbaijan.

The population at the 1979 census was 3.8 million of whom 91% were ethnic Armenians. The census in February 1989 gave a population of 3.3 million but is regarded as unreliable since it took place only two months after the devastating earthquake in northwest Armenia which made obtaining data within the region almost impossible. The most recent census in October 2011 gave a figure of 3.02 million, although the real figure, once those temporarily present are deducted and those absent are added, is estimated to be about 2.9 million. According to the census, 98.1% of the population is ethnically Armenian, 1.2% Yezidi and 0.4% Russian, with small numbers of Assyrians, Kurds, Ukrainians, Greeks, Georgians and Iranians.

During the preceding ten years 173,000 people left Armenia and, at the time of the census, 12.6% of citizens were out of Armenia, a figure which includes those who have sought work abroad. The birth rate showed a steady fall from 1991 (from a previously steady rate around 25 per 1,000) to a low of 9.9 per 1,000 in 2001. Since then there has been a gradual rise to 14 per 1,000 at the 2011 census. The fertility rate of women fell to less than half its 1990 rate but has shown a small rise in recent years; however, not to a level which allows the population to reproduce itself. The current total fertility rate is 1.38 (2012 estimate). Experts say that Armenia is facing a serious demographic problem because of the low birth rate and outward migration. In the Soviet Union abortion was the primary method of birth control. Although the abortion ratio (the number of abortions per 1,000 live births) has fallen since independence it remains high at 274, compared with 222 for the EU. Abortion is legal up to 12 weeks' gestation. The number of abortions is probably higher than official statistics suggest as many women choose to end pregnancies using over-the-counter abortifacients. The average number of abortions per woman is eight and some women may have as many as 20. Both surgical and medical abortion are far cheaper methods of birth control than the contraceptive pill, which costs about US$15–20 per month, a price beyond reach of many women. In 2010 only 27% of married women used modern methods of contraception.

A skew in the birth ratio of boys to girls has appeared in recent years, the second worst ratio in the world after China. (The average ratio at birth is boys:girls 106:100. In Armenia it is 112:100.) For economic reasons selective abortion of female foetuses is being practised. Because girls traditionally move to the husband's parental home on marriage, boys are viewed as a greater security for parents' old age. This loss of potential future mothers also has implications for Armenia's demography. As part of a goal to increase Armenia's population to 4 million by 2040, the government announced that from January 2014 parents would receive a lump sum of a million drams for a third and each subsequent child (and a one-off sum of AMD50,000 for a first and second child), though similar pro-natalist policies in other countries have not been shown to be effective. Most regions have recorded a drop in population, the highest drop being in Lori province. Only Kotayk and Armavir provinces recorded an increase. In a reversal of global trends, Armenia's proportional rural population is increasing: as of 2018 some 36.9% of the population lives in villages compared with 32.3% in 1989. Of the 63.1% urban population, 56% is in Yerevan.

One rural feature – not only in Armenia but the whole Caucasus region – is that of villages being predominantly of one ethnicity. This is most evident in the Russian villages east of Vanadzor and in northern Lori. Other villages still have significant Greek-, Yezidi- or Assyrian-speaking populations. It also explains many clusters of ruined villages which are completely abandoned: they were probably inhabited by ethnic Azeris before the war of 1988–94.

**LIFE IN ARMENIA** Life for the majority of people in post-Soviet Armenia is still far from easy. Outside the cities, visitors will note that a great proportion of the population has either reverted to subsistence agriculture if they live in villages or else has sought to become a small-scale vendor of some kind of goods or other if they live in towns. For parents, it is their hope that education will help their children to escape the widespread poverty, and so students from even the most remote reaches of the country can be found mingling in the corridors of Yerevan's many universities. The population has shrunk by about 20% since the 1980s as a result of economic emigration and a low birth rate.

Yet it cannot really be said that Armenians look either despairing or unhappy. They cope with the hardships and family members help each other out. Apparently high poverty and unemployment can also belie the fact that many Armenians working abroad send money back to their families in the homeland. Personal remittances in 2013 comprised nearly 20% of Armenia's GDP, with around half of that estimated to have come from Armenian emigrants in Russia alone. These windfalls sometimes have the odd effect of combining with a culture of flaunting one's wealth to produce typical images of expensive SUVs with private licence plates parked outside decrepit houses with no heating or running water.

The majority of those old enough to remember the Soviet era look back on it as a golden age, though many are too young to remember Stalin's terror, let alone have suffered the purges themselves. The failure of the Soviet Union to deal with the disputes that escalated into the Karabagh war is also often conveniently overlooked. Younger people see things differently, and to an observer their priorities appear much the same as their contemporaries in the West: selfies, Facebook and a preoccupation with defining themselves in opposition to their parents' generation, manifesting most notably in the significant youth component of the 2018 Velvet Revolution. However, they will also be seen lighting candles and crossing themselves in churches, and on Armenian Genocide Remembrance Day it is striking to see all generations represented together for the commemoration in Yerevan.

One of the big changes in the quality of life has been the improvement in the **water supply**. Years ago it was a significant problem: leaking mains meant that the water supply in most towns and cities had to be restricted to a few hours a day to prevent large quantities running away to waste. Sometimes it could even be cut off for days and in both urban and rural areas water had to be stored in quantity for use when needed. Today, considerable progress has been made in the reliability and quality of water and its infrastructure. Now in the towns, at least, there is usually running water 24 hours a day. The situation in villages has also improved greatly, thanks in part to the infrastructure left by the Soviets, although in remoter areas water may still have to be obtained from the village spring or a well in the garden. Improvement in waste-water management and sewerage has also begun, but much remains to be done. The European Bank for Reconstruction and Development and the European

Union have given grants to help upgrade water and sewerage systems, most notably in Yerevan and the Lake Sevan areas. Irrigation networks are also being upgraded.

Virtually every family except for those living in flats grows as much **food** as it can with all the family members, children included, working hard planting and harvesting fruit and vegetables by hand, with pigs, chickens and geese a common sight in and around peoples' backyards. In late summer, women can be found winnowing grain, preserving fruit for the winter by drying it in the sun, and making compotes, jams, pickles and, of course, homemade vodkas to last through the winter. Throughout the year they also join their neighbours in the baking of *lavash*, Armenia's classic flatbread (see box, page 99). Keeping the home clean is difficult for women; not all have domestic appliances. The level of dirt is increased by the wood-burning stoves which are very common and the seas of mud which almost engulf villages, particularly in late winter at the time of snow-melt and which are aggravated by the ubiquity of dirt roads and domestic animals.

Many families keep their own **livestock**, and even in towns cattle and sheep can often be seen being chaperoned around the streets. Rather than left out to pasture, animals are generally taken back to the house at night because of the constant risk of wolf attacks. In some areas free-range pigs wander through the villages and surrounding forests foraging for food. The constant demands of this way of life have resulted in rural Armenians becoming very hard working, with such modern aids as machinery, fertilisers, weedkillers and pesticides remaining unaffordable for many. Together with a lack of suitable agricultural land, such inefficiency has long made Armenia a net importer of food, though the tide has slowly been turning, and in 2016 Armenia for the first time recorded a net export of food products. For well-educated professionals, life is not necessarily much easier: salaries are low, particularly in the public sector; there is serious underfunding of education and health; career prospects are limited; and entrepreneurship has long been hampered by bureaucratic and corrupt state institutions, not to mention the dominance of business opportunities by oligarch 'brotherhoods', though 2018 seems to have marked a turning point in this regard. Though largely concentrated in Yerevan, a growing middle class and a boom in the retail and leisure industries has been visibly under way for some time, prompting repeat visitors to the city to comment on the rapid rate of superficial changes year on year. Such changes can also be seen in other major urban centres of Armenia and seem likely to trickle out to the provinces in the years to come.

Despite many years of difficulties, Armenians are generous to a fault. Desperately poor people welcome you into their homes and lay out vast spreads of refreshments, often unintentionally embarrassing Western visitors who feel awkward about accepting from those who obviously have so much less (an embarrassment soon cured with a shot or two of homemade *oghi*). Especially in rural areas, people remain fascinated by the few non-diaspora foreigners who do appear, and are genuinely touched that people from so far away could even have *heard* of Armenia, let alone be interested enough to visit. Having said that, pride in the country's history and language is intense, with Armenians well aware of the artistic and spiritual achievements of their great monasteries and of the contributions made by many distinguished Armenians in history.

## LANGUAGE

**Armenian** is an Indo-European language which split off at an early stage on its own branch, thus few similarities can be found with any other language. It has its own unique alphabet created in AD405, originally with 36 letters, with three more being added later. It is a so-called synthetic language – the construction of one word with declensions and various endings gives as much information as a whole phrase in English. There are two forms of Armenian: Eastern Armenian (as spoken in Armenia and certain diaspora communities including those in Iran, Georgia and Russia) and Western Armenian (as formerly spoken in Anatolia and still spoken by the members of the diaspora whose ancestors came from this region). Although different, the two are mutually intelligible if the speakers intend to make it so. For further information see page 396.

The second language is **Russian**, which is spoken virtually everywhere. **English** is becoming more common but can only be relied upon in places popular with tourists. Outside Yerevan, apart from the larger hotels, it is common to find that no English is spoken. Other European languages are even less well known although of course interpreters can be employed. Independent travellers can hire an English-speaking guide and an increasing number of drivers of hired cars also speak some English. Learning the Armenian alphabet and a few common words certainly enhances a visit to Armenia, and, as everywhere, Armenians are delighted if a foreigner makes even a small effort to speak their language.

## RELIGION

Ethnic Armenians are overwhelmingly members of the Armenian Apostolic Church, whose head, the Katholikos, has his seat at Etchmiadzin. The Katholikos is elected, following the death of his predecessor, by an electoral college of around 400 delegates comprising members of the senior clergy and representatives of all branches of the Armenian Church worldwide. The present Katholikos, Karekin II, was elected in 1999. The Church is called Apostolic because Christianity is believed to have been brought to Armenia by Jesus's disciples Bartholomew and Thaddeus (or Lebbaeus as he is called in St Matthew's gospel). It is also sometimes called the Gregorian Church because it was founded in Armenia by St Gregory the Illuminator. Most visitors to Armenia will visit several of the churches. The layout and form of worship are quite different from that in the West. They are more similar

### CHURCH NAMES

The great majority of Armenian churches are dedicated to a small number of people or events. Although this guidebook uses English names throughout, visitors will often see an English transliteration of the Armenian name used on the spot. Apart from a few dedicated to Armenian saints, the common ones are:

| | |
|---|---|
| Surb Amenaprkich | Holy Redeemer |
| Surb Astvatsatsin | Holy Mother of God |
| Surb Astvatsnkal | Holy Wisdom of God |
| Surb Arakelots | Holy Apostles |
| Surb Grigor Lusavorich | St Gregory the Illuminator |
| Surb Hakob | St Jacob |
| Surb Hovhannes | St John (usually the Evangelist) |
| Surb Haratyun | Holy Resurrection |
| Surb Karapet | Holy Herald (ie: St John the Baptist) |
| Surb Nshan | Holy Sign (of the cross) |

to the Orthodox Church but there are even here some major differences in that Armenian churches do not have an iconostasis with its royal doors and, doctrinally, the Armenian Church has not adopted the views of the Council of Chalcedon (AD451) concerning the duality of Christ's nature. The Armenian Church did not participate in the Council of Chalcedon, which met on 8 October. It was not convened until after the Battle of Avarayr (page 19) on 26 May, a battle which left Armenia in confusion with her patriarch and bishops either in prison or exile. The Armenian Church maintains as lawful the decrees of the first three ecumenical councils, Nicaea (AD325), Constantinople (AD381) and Ephesus (AD431). These three councils were equally recognised by both the Western and Eastern Churches; their decisions could thus be seen as emanating from the Universal Church. The split between eastern and western Christianity came later. The seemingly interminable controversies over the nature of Christ (still unresolved 16 centuries later!) concerned the closeness of the two natures of Christ (the divine and the human), with the theological debates taking place amid political and hierarchical dissensions. In simplistic terms the council of Ephesus affirmed a close union of the two natures; the council of Chalcedon inclined to a distinctness and separateness of the two natures.

At one end of the church will be a raised altar dais called a *bema*. In active churches a curtain can be drawn across it during parts of the service (see below) and during Lent. A legacy of the Soviet period was a shortage of priests, but numbers are increasing as are seminaries to train priests. (Training for the priesthood lasts seven years.) New churches are being built and old ones renovated, although in some places there is still a shortage of money to pay priests and undertake repairs. Accordingly, many churches do not have regular worship and an individual priest might have to look after several churches.

When visiting any Armenian church it is normal to buy candles on entry and then to light them (matches are provided), placing them upright in the trays of sand and water. The only exception to this rule is the new cathedral in Yerevan where candles are forbidden (there is a special chapel for them to the southeast of the cathedral). Women do not need to wear headscarves unless taking communion. It is correct to leave a church walking backwards so as not to turn one's back on God, though visitors will be forgiven for forgetting this custom.

In an echo of pre-Christian pagan tradition, it is still common for an animal (and more particularly, the salt with which the animal will be seasoned), always male and usually a ram or a cock, to be presented by a family for **sacrifice** (*matagh*) in thanksgiving for some event, such as recovery from a serious illness, or as a particular request to God. Sacrifice is usually carried out by the priest outside the church after the Sunday service. First, the priest blesses the animal and salt at a special stone called the *orhnakar* (blessing stone) and then he sacrifices the animal at the *mataghatun* (sacrifice house). It is partly a form of charity, since some of the meat from the slaughtered animal will be given to the poor, although the donor's family and friends will eat the rest, always boiled and never roasted or barbecued. The animals destined for slaughter are beautifully groomed before being offered to God in this way. Families will sometimes slaughter a cock themselves, and evidence of such sacrifice is not uncommon at small shrines and churches. Another frequent sight outside churches or at other holy sites is a tree or shrub to which numerous scraps of cloth are tied. Each scrap is attached by a person making a private prayer.

**WORSHIP** Worship usually lasts for about 2½ hours, the service having been extended by additional prayers at various times over the centuries. Despite its length there were traditionally no seats but pews are now becoming more common. Worship is quite different from that in Western churches. Visitors need not attend the whole service (which usually starts at 10.30) and can come just for part except that at some churches (notably Sevan) the building is so crowded that it is difficult either to enter or to leave. (Geghard is a good option on a Sunday morning for those staying in Yerevan with access to transport.) Even for those with no knowledge of the Armenian language the beauty of the singing is deeply impressive.

The devout fast on Sunday mornings before going to church. For the celebrant priest the liturgy begins in the vestry. He acknowledges his sinfulness and how privileged he is to be able to lead the people in worship. The deacon then hands him in turn the various items of the vestments and he puts each of them on with a brief prayer. The priest and deacon now enter the nave but do not go immediately up to the bema. At first they remain among the congregation where the priest symbolically washes his hands and then asks the congregation to pray for his forgiveness. Once they are up on the bema, the curtain is drawn across it to avoid distracting the congregation with the preparations. After the elements have been prepared the curtain opens and the deacons lead the priest in a procession round the altar and down into the nave, walking round the whole church offering incense and inviting the faithful to kiss the cross which the priest carries.

After two hymns the deacon symbolically holds the Gospel book over the priest's head and there is a further procession around the altar accompanied by another hymn. This is followed by readings from the Bible and more prayers. The main part of the service, the liturgy of the Eucharist, starts with the priest removing his crown and slippers in obedience to God's command to Moses at the burning bush. The deacon processes around the altar holding the veiled chalice above his head. At the end of the procession the deacon hands the elements to the celebrant. The so-called kiss of peace which follows is a ritualised greeting everyone makes to their neighbours. A long sequence of prayers and hymns concludes with the curtain being again closed, this time for the priest to receive communion while hidden from view – it is traditional in all Eastern Churches for the celebrant to receive communion out of sight of the congregation. Communion is now distributed: as communicants stand before the priest they make the sign of the cross and say, 'I have sinned against God.' Thereupon the priest places a small part of the bread which has been dipped into the wine directly into the mouth of the communicant who again makes the sign of the cross. This is followed by more prayers and hymns during part of which the curtain is closed while the priest and deacons reorganise the altar. The priest then raises his right hand to bless the congregation in Armenian style – with the thumb and ring finger forming a circle to represent the world and the other fingers pointing upward to represent the persons of the Trinity. The service ends with the congregation kissing the Gospel book.

In Armenia the **sign of the cross** is made in the same way as in the Roman Catholic Church (left breast before right) and not in the same way as practised in the Orthodox Church (right breast before left). The sign is made with the thumb, index and middle fingers held together, representing the Trinity, and the other two fingers touching the palm of the hand, and it ends with the palm in the centre of the chest while saying 'Amen'.

**MARRIAGE IN ARMENIA** Traditional marriage in Armenia differs somewhat from that in many other European countries and in North America. Tourists are almost bound to see weddings unless visiting during either Lent, when weddings cannot be held in church, or during May, Armenians having adopted the old Russian custom of considering that weddings in May will lead to an unhappy marriage. Weddings are particularly common on Saturdays.

The first point to note is that fewer young people than formerly are getting married, but not because they are simply living together as in many Western countries. In general Armenian couples do not do this. Young Armenian couples marry and then expect to have their first child a year or so after the wedding and the wife will stay at home to look after it. A young Armenian man will often not make a proposal of marriage unless he feels confident that he will be able to support his wife and child. In the uncertain economic climate (after decades of Soviet predictability) many young men felt unsure that they would be able to support a family and hence stayed single. Armenia's marriage rate fell by 50% after the Soviet collapse. However, since 2007 there has been a gradual increase in the marriage rate. The problem of housing also arises. Economic uncertainty means that young people are reluctant to borrow money to buy a house or flat and the alternative of living with the husband's parents may or may not be feasible.

A second point to note is that Armenians tend to have quite small families. A couple will generally only have further children if they believe that they can support them. This is similar to the view of many Western couples but economic uncertainty, or at least the perception of it, is greater in Armenia than in the West and this impacts on family size.

As traditionally happened in the West, if a man wishes to marry a woman he will go to her father to ask for her hand in marriage. A difference in Armenia is that he will usually be accompanied by his parents and possibly by other very close relatives such as his brother or sister. Unlike the West, wedding ceremonies are not planned long in advance: rarely more than a month ahead and sometimes only a few days, although this is changing as churches and reception venues become busier; it can now be as long as two or three months. On the wedding day the bride will be helped to get ready by her maid of honour (the equivalent of chief bridesmaid): this is always one of her unmarried sisters if she has any and only a close friend if she has no unmarried sister. It is never a married woman: the concept of a matron of honour doesn't exist in Armenia. The bridegroom's family provides and pays for the bride's dress, the bridegroom and the brother of the cross (the equivalent of best man) bringing it to her family's house on the day of the wedding. The bridegroom will normally also be accompanied by members of his family and friends (though not by his mother) and they, together with the bride's relatives and friends, eat and drink at the house while the bride is putting on her dress and being helped to get ready. Traditionally the bride would have worn a gown of red silk with a headpiece, often made of cardboard, shaped into wings and decorated with feathers. Nowadays she usually wears a long white dress similar in style to those worn throughout the West. The bridegroom often wears a suit, though in a rather more interesting colour than one bought for sober office wear. Relatives and friends, including the maid of honour, tend to dress much as in the West although pale suits for all the prominent younger men are common.

Eventually the bride and bridegroom set off for the church together (no bridegroom waiting for the bride at the altar!) accompanied by their relatives and friends. Traditionally the bride's mother stays at home and does not attend her daughter's wedding: for her to do so is considered to bring bad luck upon the couple. However, this tradition is changing and nowadays the bride's mother often does attend the wedding. The bridegroom's mother has always attended. The couple may have either a church service, a civil ceremony or both. If they opt to have a church service but no civil ceremony their marriage is valid in the eyes of

God although it is not recognised in Armenian law and the couple are, in theory at least, both free to remarry. Nevertheless, many couples do in fact have only a church service: the subsequent rate of separation is in practice low. The wedding party enters the church with a large decorated basket containing wedding favours to be distributed to the guests: in the past these might have been small ceramic containers with almonds in them, but many modern brides choose something much less traditional and there is a demand for such exotica as glass containers decorated with sea shells. During the service the officiating priest puts a ring on the finger of the bridegroom and then of the bride before joining their hands. The bridegroom then makes his vows followed in turn by the bride.

After the ceremony, all present, though still without the bride's mother (if she has stayed at home), traditionally go to the bridegroom's family house for the reception although nowadays a room in a hotel or restaurant is sometimes hired for the occasion. En route there is likely to be a motorcade with blaring horns, and in Yerevan driving three times round Republic Square is an essential and audible part of the proceedings. On arrival at the reception the groomsmen and bridesmaids, holding their flowers aloft, form arches through which the young couple walk and two white doves are traditionally released to symbolise their love and happiness. There is more eating and drinking, this time at the expense of the bridegroom's family (although this too is changing with costs being shared), accompanied by dancing in an amalgam of traditional Armenian and more modern styles. The food will almost certainly be the menu invariably eaten on all Armenian celebratory occasions: *khorovats* – barbecued meat, most commonly pork but sometimes lamb or chicken, accompanied by salads and vegetables together with *lavash*, Armenia's flatbread. There will be the inevitable toasts. Friends, neighbours, and indeed

## ST SARGIS

St Sargis, often called **St Sargis the Warrior**, is remembered for his martyrdom in AD362. Why then is he also known as the Armenian patron saint of love and youth? A Persian legend about St Sargis may explain why.

There was a poor bard, named Gharib, who loved Shah-Sanam, the daughter of a wealthy man. Shah-Sanam returned Gharib's love but her father would not let them marry because he wanted to marry his daughter to a rich man. Bard Gharib decided to go to foreign countries to seek his fortune. Before leaving he asked Shah-Sanam to promise to wait for him for seven years, saying that if he were even one day late she would be free to marry as her father wished.

The seven years were difficult for Gharib. He worked hard day and night to amass a fortune, all the time thinking of his beloved and looking forward to the day when they could meet again. Eventually when the seven years were almost up he had enough money and he started back on the perilous journey but he encountered so many hardships and delays that he feared he would not arrive in time. He prayed and begged St Sargis to help him. St Sargis, seated on his white horse, immediately appeared and, lifting Gharib on to the horse beside him, brought him in a trice to Shah-Sanam's house. Seeing the bard's strength of character and the young couple's love for each other, Shah-Sanam's father gave their union his blessing.

St Sargis is often portrayed on his white horse, a small figure seated beside him. He is buried at Ushi Monastery (page 191).

almost anyone passing, drop in to wish the newlyweds well. The party goes on until everyone has had enough.

That isn't quite the end of marriage customs. Trndaz (Purification) day, 13 February, commemorates the purification of Mary 40 days after the birth of Jesus, as laid down in the rules given in Leviticus, chapter 12. After a church service during the evening, the priest blesses a fire. Candles lit in this fire are then taken to the homes of couples who have been married in the previous year and also to the homes of young women who have become engaged. A fire is kindled at the house using the candles lit from the fire at the church which the priest blessed. Then the couples jump over it to get rid of the small devils hanging from the edge of their clothes. The ceremony is the pretext for a large family celebration.

In some years Trndaz coincides with St Sargis's Day whose date is variable (between 11 January and 15 February) and fixed by the Church calendar. As with so many Armenian customs the actual details vary from family to family but traditionally young people fast on the eve of St Sargis's Day. They then eat unleavened salt bread which has been baked either by their grandmother or by a happily married middle-aged woman, and retire to bed without either drinking or speaking. Their inevitable thirst will supposedly make them dream of the person whom they will marry. If a footprint appears in the bowl of flour left outside the house overnight then the young man of the house will marry in the coming year. On St Sargis's Day itself there is a service of blessing for young people at the church.

## EDUCATION

The Soviet education system was successful in producing a well-educated population, and a literacy rate of 100% was reported as early as 1960. In the Soviet period, Armenian education followed the standard Soviet programme with control from Moscow of curricula and teaching methods. After independence Armenia made changes. Curricula were altered to emphasise Armenian history and culture while Armenian became the dominant language of instruction. Russian is still widely taught now as a second language but the former compulsory clutter – subjects such as History of the Communist Party of the Soviet Union, Dialectical Materialism, Historical Materialism, Foundations of Marxist–Leninist Aesthetics, and Foundations of Scientific Communism – was rapidly jettisoned.

Children formerly started compulsory education at the age of seven, but after independence the starting age was changed to six, giving 12 years of compulsory education. There is also day care for two- to three-year-olds and kindergarten for three- to six-year-olds. The school year normally begins on 1 September ('Welcome Back to School' day) – as in most parts of the former Soviet Union children in all classes can be seen making their way to school immaculately dressed and clutching bunches of flowers for their class teacher. University courses last five years or more, four years for a basic Bachelor's degree and typically another two years for a Master's.

Education has suffered from lack of funding since independence and the low salaries paid to teachers have discouraged young people from entering the profession. As well as school-leaving exams there are additional university entrance exams. A particular difficulty is the gap which has developed between what children have learned during their 12 years at school and what they are required to know to pass the universities' entrance exams. It was hoped that the extension of schooling to 12 years would remove the gap in knowledge but that has not yet happened. The only way to bridge this gap is to pay for extra tuition and so important is their children's education to parents that almost all are willing to pay for it. So highly is education regarded that Yerevan's 12 state universities have, despite the falling population, been augmented by 25 private ones since independence. Armenians who do not seek a university education are very much in a minority despite recent figures showing that only 20% of university graduates find jobs after graduation. The ministry is keen to reduce the number of graduates and to increase the extent of vocational training as there are significant shortages of trained specialists such as hairdressers and construction workers. The most highly regarded degrees and diplomas are those from the state institutions, and especially those of students who scored so well in the entrance examination that they gained a free place. A more recent trend has been the opening of (often diaspora-funded) extracurricular educational establishments which offer diverse learning opportunities, usually free of charge, to Armenian students; notably the Tumo Center for Creative Technologies (**w** tumo.org) with locations in Yerevan, Dilijan, Gyumri, Koghb and Stepanakert, with several more planned.

## CULTURE

### ARCHITECTURE
**Church building**  For some members of the diaspora, to experience Armenia's culture and language on its home territory will be their overriding memory of a visit to Armenia, but for the majority of visitors it is the historic buildings in their dramatic natural settings which will make the greatest impression, above all the monasteries but also to a lesser degree the secular medieval buildings such as fortresses and caravanserais. Only a very few buildings survive from the pre-Christian era: little more than the foundations can be observed of the cities of the Kingdom of Urartu such as Erebuni. By far the best-known pre-Christian building is the sole surviving example of Graeco-Roman architecture in Armenia, built at Garni sometime in the first two centuries AD at a time when the country was an ally of Rome. The Greek style was widely employed in contemporary Roman buildings throughout the empire and the survival of no other buildings in Armenia from this era is largely the consequence of Christians destroying pagan temples after the conversion of the country. Almost certainly others would have been constructed. However, the influence of the Greek style, and before that of the elongated halls of Urartian buildings, can be seen in the early hall or basilica churches.

The early churches were often built on the site of pagan shrines employing the same foundations, and hence they had the same dimensions as the temple which they replaced; moreover, the Christian altar was usually placed directly over the previous pagan one as at Etchmiadzin. From the earliest times the churches were built in stone, most commonly the volcanic tuff which is easily carved and tends gradually to harden when exposed to the atmosphere. The need to build in stone was dictated by the unavailability of suitable timber, even for roofing, and the weight of the heavy vaulted stone roof in turn dictated the need for thick walls to support it, with few windows. Where tuff was unavailable, most commonly in border areas, other volcanic rocks such as basalt or andesite were used.

From fairly early days almost all churches, apart from the earliest basilicas, were built with a cupola supported by a cylindrical structure called a tambour. Tambours are usually circular in cross section when viewed from the interior of the church but are often polygonal on the outside. The preference for churches to have a cupola supported by a tambour is one of Armenian architecture's most abiding features and makes its churches very distinctive. Such domed churches first appeared in the 4th century, the simplest being essentially a dome on a cube with one to four

## ARMENIAN SUNDIALS

Sundials can be seen on the walls of many Armenian monasteries and churches. The details of some are easily seen, such as that on the eastern façade of the small St Stephen's Church at Haghartsin Monastery. By contrast, the elaborately carved sundial at Harichavank is positioned so high up on the eastern wall of the Mother of God Church that binoculars are almost needed to appreciate the detail. Sundials were sometimes placed high up on a wall to avoid them being shaded from the sun by surrounding trees but, if this was originally the case at Harichavank, it is certainly not a problem now. The sundials themselves are not dated and it is not always possible to ascertain if they are contemporaneous with the building they adorn or if they were added later.

Armenian sundials are of the vertical type, with a horizontal gnomon at right angles to the wall. They are semicircular and usually divided into 12 (occasionally 11) equal petal-like divisions, each division representing an hour. Such dials show unequal hours, daylight being divided into 12 periods regardless of the length of daylight so an 'hour' in winter will occupy less time than an 'hour' in summer. The hours are counted from one at sunrise on the horizontal line at the left, to 12 at sunset on the horizontal line at the right. Visitors may be more familiar with sundials showing equal hours, with their divisions of variable width and gnomons at an angle to the vertical, the angle determined by the sundial's latitude.

The divisions of some Armenian sundials carry letters of the Armenian alphabet. Armenian letters were (and sometimes still are) used to represent numbers. The first nine letters of the Armenian alphabet represent the units one to nine, the next nine letters represent the tens (ten, 20 ... 90), the next nine letters the hundreds (100, 200 ... 900), etc. The first ten divisions on a sundial bear the first ten letters of the alphabet, 11 and 12 usually being represented by a repeat of the first two letters. Very occasionally, as seen on a more recently carved sundial at Zvartnots, 11 is shown, correctly, as a combination of the tenth letter (representing ten) and the first letter (representing one). Similarly 12 is shown as the tenth letter plus the second letter of the alphabet.

apses. These central dome churches had exclusively local roots: centrally focused sanctuaries are known from Urartian temples. The dome may have developed from domestic dwellings which used the *hazarashen* method of construction in which stones are progressively added across angles to make an aperture of decreasing size. (This construction is most easily appreciated in some *gavits* (page 49) which have a central opening or *yerdik*.) The domed style rapidly developed after the conversion to Christianity and continued until the Arab invasion and conquest in the mid 7th century. Thereafter no churches were built for over 200 years until the establishment of the Bagratid dynasty in the late 9th century. Under this re-established regime new churches began to be built, initially copying the old style but gradually starting to develop this style to provide greater height and space. Once again church building ceased after foreign invasion, this time by the Seljuk Turks after the middle of the 11th century. Domes were also incorporated into the basilica-style churches, the dome supported by either free-standing pillars or wall piers. Most domed basilicas date from the 9th to 14th centuries.

The establishment of Georgian independence together with the Armenian Zakarid dynasty in the late 12th century led to a renewal of church building and, in particular, to the development of the large monastic complexes with their multiple churches and ancillary buildings which are probably nowadays the most visited tourist sites in the country. Again, the traditional style was used but the quest for greater space was now satisfied by building several churches on the same site rather than by increasing the size of each structure. Inevitably, construction ceased at the end of the 13th century after the Mongol invasions and the Armenian kingdom of Cilicia also ceased to exist in 1375 following the Mamluk invasions. No more churches were built until the 17th century when construction, still in the traditional style, restarted at a time when Armenia was ruled by the Safavid kings of Persia. Church building increased in the 19th century as Armenian national consciousness grew, only to come to a complete stop with the genocide of 1915 in Western Armenia and the Bolshevik Revolution in the east. Independence has led to a resurgence in church building, largely with funds provided by the diaspora, with the traditional style and hallmark tuff generally retained. This can sometimes make it difficult for the visitor to know what is new and what is renovated old, except in a few cases when the insensitive nature of the reconstruction has made it obvious.

**Church construction**  Two overriding practical constraints influenced early church architects: the need to use stone for roofs because of the lack of suitable timber, and the need to withstand fairly frequent earthquakes. The necessary strength was provided by the use of an early type of concrete in a method probably copied from Roman architects. The earliest churches were built of massive stone blocks, with mortar separating them, forming the outer and inner surfaces of the walls; between them was a thin layer of concrete. This concrete was compounded of broken tuff and other stones, lime mortar and eggs. During the 5th and 6th centuries the technique evolved, the slabs of the stone shell becoming thinner and the cement core thicker. The method of construction was then to erect finely cut slabs of tuff or other stone a few rows at a time and without mortar to form the surfaces of the outer and inner walls after which concrete was poured into the cavity between them. This concrete adhered to the facing slabs and formed a solid strong core and it is this core, rather than the thin slabs of tuff, which forms the building's major support. The slabs were varied in size and height to break up the vertical and horizontal rows and thus provide protection against parts of the concrete core falling out during earthquakes. Great thought was given to enhancing the artistic appearance of churches, and different churches had the tuff slabs erected in different ways. In some churches the slabs were carved and either different colours of slab might be employed to provide a contrast or else a uniform colour might be used, sometimes with mortar applied between the slabs to give a completely uniform appearance. As the technique evolved the largest stone blocks gradually came to be reserved for the lowest courses of stonework as well as for corners, and smaller ones were used elsewhere. Although windows were, from structural considerations, never a significant feature of Armenian church architecture, their size and number did tend to increase over time.

**Styles of church**  All the earliest known churches were of basilica construction (ie: rectangular with an apse at the east end) with either a single aisle or three aisles. They sat on a stepped base, or stylobate. The more spacious three-aisle basilicas were built in cities or important religious centres and had pylons, or pillars, dividing the space and supporting the roof. The three vaults of the aisles were covered by a single gable roof with pediments on the short façades. Sometimes the middle aisle, which was wider than the side aisles, was also higher and had a separate roof.

*Khachkars*, carved memorial stones, are an important, conspicuous and beautiful feature of Armenian decorative art. The word khachkar literally means 'cross stone'. In quiet streets in central Yerevan it is possible to see even today the stone carvers at work, using traditional methods to create these endlessly varied monuments in a revival of this ancient tradition. The earliest khachkars date from the 9th and 10th centuries, a period when Armenia had gained effective independence from the Arab caliphate and separate Armenian kings each ruled their individual states. This flowering of Armenian craftsmanship under independence was paralleled in architecture: some of Armenia's finest monasteries date from this period.

The earliest datable khachkar was erected at Garni (page 241) by Queen Katranide, wife of King Ashot Bagratuni I, in 879 in mediation for her person. Securing the salvation of the soul was the most common reason for erecting khachkars but some were put up to commemorate military victories or the completion of churches, bridges, fountains and other constructions. Even unrequited love might be commemorated in this way. The dominant feature of the design is generally a cross, occasionally a crucifix, resting on a rosette or sun disc design, often with a stylised tree of life encompassing the lower vertical of the cross. The four limbs of the cross usually terminate in two triple-loops, perhaps a reference to the Trinity. The remainder is covered with complex patterns of leaves, bunches of grapes or abstract geometrical patterns. Occasionally the whole was surmounted by a cornice showing biblical characters or saints and there is sometimes an inscription recording when, by whom and for what reason the khachkar was erected. The absolute peak of khachkar design was probably between the 12th and 14th centuries. Amazingly elaborate and delicate patterns were created using the same elements of design. Depiction of the Crucifixion and Resurrection became more common and at this time some khachkars came to be erected as a spiritual protection against natural disasters. The supreme masterpieces include that at Geghard (page 244) created by Timot and Mkhitar in 1213, the Holy Redeemer khachkar at Haghpat Monastery (page 293) which was created by Vahram in 1273, and that at Goshavank (page 309) created by Poghos in 1291. Some good examples have been transported to the History Museum of Armenia in Yerevan and the cathedral at Etchmiadzin. There can, however, be no substitute for seeing them where they were originally erected.

The Mongol invasion at the end of the 14th century led to a decline of the tradition and, although there was a revival in the 16th and 17th centuries, the artistic heights of the 14th were never regained.

Some khachkars, often recording donations, are embedded in the walls of monasteries but most are free-standing. Armenia has over 40,000 surviving khachkars. An amazing sight is the so-called field of khachkars at Noratus (page 234), the largest of several groupings in Armenia. This is an old graveyard with 900 khachkars marking graves and the endless variations of design make a visit there particularly rewarding. Examples at Noratus span the whole period from the 10th to the 17th century. Where khachkars are still in their original location, they face west and are best photographed in the afternoon. Since 2010, khachkars, their symbolism and craftsmanship are inscribed in the UNESCO list of Intangible Cultural Heritage.

Some basilica churches had outside galleries, around the north, south and west walls, used when the congregation was too large for the main building, for liturgy on weekdays and for the repentant. St Gregory the Illuminator spoke of the need for repentance beyond the church walls. Galleries arose in the 4th century, were widespread in the 5th and 6th centuries and fell out of use by the 7th century. A variation was a covered porch at the west end. In the late 4th century, rooms each side of the altar apse, or corner rooms at both east and west ends, became a feature of Armenian churches and have remained so.

The incorporation of a cupola as a central feature caused changes to church layout and the basilica style gave way to a more centrally planned church built around the cupola, sometimes with four apses or else with four arms of equal length, or sometimes with three apses and one extended arm. This resulted in what was essentially a cross-shaped church, but the addition of corner rooms between the arms of the cross resulted in many church buildings being more or less rectangular in plan when seen from the outside but with the church itself cross-shaped in plan when on the inside. Churches with a cupola and four arms are often referred to as cross-dome churches although cross-cupola would perhaps be less misleading as most English-speakers think of domes as being hemispherical. The ultimate exemplar of this centrally planned style, the church of St Hripsime at Etchmiadzin (page 220), is still further developed. Four semicircular apses are separated from each other by four circular niches, each of which leads to a square corner room, all this being incorporated within the basic rectangular shape. Another variant of the centrally planned church was to make the entire building circular; most are not strictly circular but polygonal. The best known, the ruined 7th-century cathedral at Zvartnots (page 215), has 32 sides.

The basic style of Armenian church architecture has remained to this day the centrally planned church, built around its cupola and with two or more corner rooms. However, two later developments were the additions of a narthex, or **gavit** as it is known in Armenia, and the building of a belltower. Both gavit and belltower came into being during the great upsurge in monastery building from the 10th century onwards. A gavit is a square room usually attached to the west end of the church and serving as a vestibule, a room for meetings and a burial place for notables. Apart from the relatively few free-standing ones, gavits could also house the overflow when the congregation was too large for the main church. They were sometimes very large with massive walls and, like the other parts of the church, were frequently elaborately carved. Belltowers appeared at monastery complexes from the 13th century onwards and were often detached from the church building itself. The walls of later churches, both the exterior and the interior ones, sometimes incorporate khachkars. There are also occasionally carvings of the donors, often holding a model of the church.

Inside Armenian churches there may or may not be carving but the most conspicuous feature is the altar dais or bema at the eastern end with steps leading up to it. The entire dais forms the altar and in an active church it can be shut off by a curtain, though the curtain is never closed except during parts of services and during Lent. Unlike the Orthodox Church there is never an iconostasis. A few churches have a decorated wooden or stone altar screen, as at Sevanavank or Mughni, but this never obscures the holy table.

In the Middle Ages churches were sometimes fortified. An extra, high wall was added to the outside of the church. Most of these walls were demolished in the 19th century but remnants can still occasionally be seen at, for example, the church of St John at Byurakan, Tsiranavor Church at Parpi and Tsiranavor at Ashtarak.

## VISHAPS – DRAGON STONES

*Vishaps* are menhirs or large carved stones from the first two millennia BC, usually associated with water and thought to have religious significance. Vishap is Armenian for 'dragon' and such stones have a dragon or serpent head carved near the top. These tall stones tend to be somewhat cylindrical or cigar-shaped and are often grey in colour. There are also fish-like vishaps which are usually recumbent. Vishaps are sometimes so weathered, or altered, that the carving can be difficult to make out. A good example stands outside the ethnographical museum at Sardarapat (page 224). They were sometimes re-used. One at Garni has an 8th-century-BC cuneiform inscription. Much later, crosses were added to some, as if to Christianise them. They were probably the forerunners of **stelae**, tetragonal columns on a cube-shaped base erected on a stepped stylobate, which functioned as memorials or gravestones. Stelae often have carvings depicting religious subjects such as the Madonna and Child, angels, saints or biblical scenes eg: Old Testament stories of Abraham and Isaac, the three youths in the burning, fiery furnace and Daniel in the lions' den. There is a good array of stelae in Talin, near the small Mother of God Church. Vishaps may also have been the forerunners of the unusual funerary monuments at Aghdzk and Odzun. The latter is particularly interesting, not only for the wealth of carving on each side of the two obelisks but also etymologically. The name of Odzun probably derives from *odz*, the Armenian for 'snake', and legends relating to Ardvi, not far from Odzun, involve two snakes or dragons (see box, page 288). In Armenian mythology vishaps are dragons which live in the mountains, especially on Mount Ararat.

Some small churches or shrines seem to emerge from the hillside, the eastern end of the roof almost level with the higher ground. This is thought to indicate that the site may originally have been a pagan spring shrine. Flowing water can still occasionally be seen, as in the first cave church at Geghard and in the mausoleum at Kobayr.

A word which visitors might hear when any small church is being referred to is *zham*, as opposed to *vank* for a monastery and *yekeghetsi* for a church. *Zham* is the Armenian word for 'hour' or 'time'. Using it to mean a church dates from when the church was the (only) means of telling the time, either by bell or sundial. *Zham* is also often used to refer to simple hall-like village churches without a dome and often with wooden rather than stone pillars supporting the roof. Such a small church may also be referred to as a *matoor* (chapel). They are rarely thought worthy of being pointed out to tourists but they are widespread and often have interesting older khachkars incorporated into their walls.

While the vegetation on some church roofs is the result of centuries of disrepair, on some small basilica churches it is a traditional, deliberate technique to protect the roof. The roof of stone tiles is covered with a layer of turf which gives a grass-covered roof and, in spring, an attractive church-top meadow. Such turf or sod roofs have historically been used in Iceland, the Faroe Islands and northern Scotland to increase both insulation and watertightness. Modern variations are becoming an increasingly popular eco-friendly option. Most turf roofs are flat or with only a gentle incline but in Scotland, in 2006–12, trials found that turf was just as effective on the steeply pitched roof of a 15th-century tower-house.

**Secular medieval architecture** Two types of secular medieval building will attract the attention of visitors: fortresses and caravanserais. Unlike the churches, neither is distinctively Armenian. Armenia's **fortresses** were sited and built according to the general thinking in castle design of the day and followed the same principles as applied throughout Europe. **Caravanserais** were built along the main trade routes to provide secure lodging for merchants and their pack animals. They are generally rectangular and sometimes surprisingly large, reflecting just how important this trade was. Only a single, fairly small, door was provided so that the caravanserai would be easily defensible against robbers. Inside there were rows of stalls with feeding troughs for animals and booths for the merchants. Armenia's best-preserved example by far is Selim Caravanserai (page 335) in northern Vayots Dzor. Ordinary domestic architecture has not survived, apart from the low stone walls and foundations seen clustered around buildings such as castles and monasteries. Excavations have unearthed important palaces at Dvin, Aruch and Zvartnots. Their architecture parallels that of the churches, with large halls divided into aisles by columns, and galleries along outside walls.

## THE ARTS
**Illuminated manuscripts** If khachkars are the symbol of Armenia, the painting of illuminated manuscripts is undoubtedly Armenia's other great contribution to the art world. The beauty and skill represented in the many surviving examples are rarely equalled and seldom surpassed in other cultures. Extensive sets of pictures were used to illustrate manuscripts of the books of the Bible and obviously books such as Genesis or Exodus, where there is plenty of physical action, lent themselves particularly to this art form, with some manuscripts having up to 750 illustrations. The most elaborate manuscripts tended to be those of the four Gospels which were frequently bound with sumptuous covers of ivory or metalwork. A characteristic feature of these copies of the Gospels is the set of canon tables which were designed to show which passages of the individual Gospels were in agreement with any of the other three. They were arranged with columns of figures under decorative arches, often highly elaborated and usually accompanied by scenes or symbols of the evangelists. Before the Gospel itself there is a picture of the evangelist, again within an architectural structure and also with writing desk, lectern and writing implements.

The purpose of these books was to aid worship. They were made to be displayed on the altar as well as to be used by the priest reading to the congregation. A very few examples survive which predate the Arab conquest in 640. The subsequent repression of Christianity by the Muslims led to the suspension of artistic activity until after the end of Arab occupation in the 9th century. From then the art flourished. The importance of manuscripts to the Armenian Church is comparable to that afforded to icons by the Orthodox Church. The large number that has survived testifies to how valuable they were considered to be and how closely they were guarded in times of war. Manuscripts, particularly those believed to be endowed with miraculous powers, were given special names such as Saviour of All or Resurrector of the Dead. The manuscripts were also thought of as pledges for the salvation of the donors, as treasures in heaven, and they are therefore rarely anonymous productions. The names of the sponsor and the creators are carefully recorded so that they might be recalled by those who used the manuscripts. Given the importance of manuscripts and their beauty, it is unfortunate that the only place in Armenia where manuscripts can readily be seen is the Matenadaran (Manuscript Library) in Yerevan (page 179) where a handful are on display in the five exhibition rooms. In 1997 the Matenadaran

Ancient Manuscript Collection was added to UNESCO's Memory of the World Register in recognition of its world significance.

**Music** Both traditional folk music and classical music have fallen on hard times since 1991 with the reductions in state funding. **Folk music** can now most often be heard on national holidays but a more convenient option is to go to one of the traditional Yerevan restaurants where a folk ensemble plays each evening. The *oud* is a 12-stringed (two strings for each note) ancestor of the lute and guitar with a distinctive bent neck. The *tarr* is another lute-like instrument but smaller than the *oud*. The *kemenche* is a three-stringed violin played with the instrument held vertically resting on the lap. The *duduk* makes the sound most often associated with Armenian music. It is a low-pitched woodwind instrument, with a large double reed, made from apricot wood. The *shvi* (whistle) by contrast is a high-pitched woodwind instrument without a reed and with eight holes, seven for playing plus a thumb hole. The *dhol* is a cylindrical drum with one membrane being thicker to give a low pitch and the other thinner to give a higher pitch. Other distinctive instruments which may be encountered include the *zurna*, a higher-pitched wind instrument than the *duduk* but also with a double reed and made from apricot wood; the *kanun*, a box zither, trapezoid in shape, which is played resting on the player's knee or on a table, the strings being plucked by plectra attached to the fingers; and the *dumbeg* which is an hourglass-shaped drum with a membrane made of lamb skin at only one end, the other end being open.

It was the Russian conquest in the 19th century which brought Western **classical music** to Armenia, and the fusion of the folk-inspired Russian nationalistic composers such as Rimsky-Korsakov and Borodin with the existing Armenian traditional music was to result in a distinctively Armenian style. Full of bright colours and rhythms it is vigorous rather than cerebral, music of the heart rather than the head. The best-known Armenian composer outside the country is undoubtedly **Aram Khachaturyan** (1903–78), though broadcasters frequently and incorrectly refer to him as Russian. In particular his violin and piano concerti are regularly encountered in concert and the ballets *Spartacus* and *Gayaneh* have often been staged outside Armenia. Most people would probably recognise the Sabre Dance from *Gayaneh*. Armenian **opera** has made little impact abroad but in recent years there have been American stagings of *Arshak II* by **Tigran Chukhajyan**, first heard (incomplete) in Italian at Constantinople in 1868, and *Anoush* by **Armen Tigranyan** which was first performed at Alexandropol (present-day Gyumri) in 1912. To make these acceptable to Stalinist censors both had to have their plots changed during Soviet times: the alterations required to *Arshak II* in 1945 at the end of the Great Patriotic War included changing the character of Arshak from that of a tyrannical leader to that of a virtuous and unselfish one, and changing the composer's tragic ending into a hymn of rejoicing. Presumably this was in the hope that the audience would identify Stalin with the now virtuous, unselfish and victorious Arshak. *Arshak II* is considerably influenced by Verdi but *Anoush* aims at a fusion of classical Western music with distinctive Armenian melody and harmony. In Yerevan the **Armenian Philharmonic Orchestra** gives regular concerts and opera and ballet are staged in the Spendiaryan Opera and Ballet Theatre except during the summer break.

Another distinctive Armenian form is that of **liturgical music**. It is sung without instrumental accompaniment and is based on a so-called Phrygian dominant scale rather than the major and minor scales familiar in Western music. The number of surviving compositions is considerable: more than a thousand from the Middle

Ages survive on parchment and the range is diverse, sometimes quick and sprightly, sometimes solemn, sometimes dramatic. Only later did composers start to write polyphonically. The best-known more recent composer is **Komitas** (1869–1935), who wrote many wonderful chants as well as other compositions in traditional Armenian style. To listen to this beautiful music in one of Armenia's churches on a Sunday morning is an experience which every visitor should seek out.

**Dance** Dance in Armenia can broadly be divided into traditional dance and classical ballet, the latter considerably influenced by the Russian school. The **traditional dances** which are encountered in Armenia today are those of Eastern Armenia and as such differ in some respects from the dances of Armenian groups abroad which usually represent the Western Armenian tradition. The energetic men's dance *Jo Jon* (also called *Zhora Bar*) comes from Spitak province. *Mom Bar*, meaning 'Candle Dance', was originally from the Lake Sevan region and is now traditionally the last dance at wedding parties. The candles are blown out at the end of the dance signalling that it is time for guests to leave. Women's solo dances called *Naz Bar*, meaning 'Grace Dance', are improvisatory with intricate hand gestures used to tell stories of love, betrayal, conflict and triumph. In Yerevan in particular, choreographic schools and song and dance ensembles preserve the tradition in a form suitable for stage presentation, although funding is more difficult than in the Soviet era.

The musical accompaniment can be played on traditional instruments or sung (or both). **Costumes** for women are invariably sumptuous, whether based on medieval court dress or on simpler peasant dress. Brightly coloured shimmering dresses are decorated with gold embroidery and pearls. A light lace veil surmounts the embroidered hat. For men costume is simpler: full trousers and embroidered tunics or else the *cherkessa*, traditional Caucasian dress similar to Cossack style, with red, white or black silk trousers, leather boots, woollen or fur hat, and a dagger in the belt. Men's dances are martial and vigorous; women's are graceful with elaborate gestures.

Funding is also more difficult for **classical ballet**, performed at the Spendiaryan Opera and Ballet Theatre. The standard of dance remains high but numbers of Armenian dancers are making successful careers in western Europe and North America and the pool of talent remaining in Yerevan has diminished.

**Drama** In ancient times **Greek drama** was popular in Armenia and several amphitheatres were built during the Hellenistic age including one at Tigranakert, the new capital built by Tigran II. When the Romans sacked the city in 69BC the actors were killed during the celebration games which followed. After the conversion of Armenia to Christianity in the 4th century, drama was suppressed by the Church and there is no record of any Armenian theatre until the 18th century when plays were put on by the Armenian community in Venice. The first recorded performance of a play in Armenia proper since the 4th century is often said to have been of **Alexander Griboyedov**'s *Woe from Wit* in 1827 at the palace of the Yerevan Fortress (now one of two major brandy factories), with members of the Imperial Russian Army as the cast. That seems highly unlikely as this scathing satire on corruption, ignorance and bribery in Tsarist society was banned during the author's lifetime and not staged until 1831.

The **first regular theatre** in Yerevan opened in 1865 and in that year **Gabriel Sundukyan** (1825–1912) published *Khatabala*, which may be said to represent the foundation of a realistic Armenian drama. Theatres were established in several

Armenian communities both in Armenia and among the diaspora in cities such as Tehran and Tbilisi, but those in Ottoman-controlled areas were repressed after anti-Armenian action started in earnest in 1894. During the Soviet period drama blossomed with a healthy diet of Armenian and Russian works as well as Armenian translations of foreign classics, particularly Shakespeare, who translates very well into Armenian. Since 1991, as with all the arts, the curtailment of government subsidies has led to considerable retrenchment although several theatres survive at Yerevan and Gyumri.

**Literature** Written Armenian literature could clearly not develop until the creation of the alphabet by Mesrop Mashtots in the early 5th century and any early pagan oral tradition would almost certainly have been suppressed after the conversion to Christianity. Apart from the Bible, other theological works were soon translated from both Greek and Syriac after the creation of the alphabet. Some of Mesrop Mashtots's pupils also wrote original works: **Eznik** (known in Armenia as Yeznik Koghbatsi) wrote a treatise on the origins of evil and the subject of free will called *Refutation of the Sects* while **Koryun** wrote a biography of Mashtots in about AD443. The *Epic Histories* were written in the 470s by an anonymous cleric and give an account of Armenian history between about 330 and 387, bringing together traditional stories about kings from Khosrov III to Arsaces II, as well as about patriarchs. The author sought to draw parallels between historic and contemporary events and, when he wrote about a dying ruler urging his son to die bravely for their Christian country since by doing so he would be dying in the service of God and the Church, it was undoubtedly meant to apply to his readers.

This tradition of martial resistance and martyrdom was continued in the *History* written by **Lazarus of Parp** (or Ghazar Parpetsi as he is known in Armenia), abbot of the monastery of Vagharshapat (modern Etchmiadzin), which continues the story after 387, when the *Epic Histories* break off, as far as 485. In describing the events of 451, the author shows the Armenians finding the Persians unprepared at Avarayr and then holding off since they wanted martyrdom more than victory. He wrote that the face of one martyr was illuminated before his death as a sign of his imminent transformation into an angel. Widows of martyrs and women whose husbands were imprisoned by the enemy were considered to be living martyrs.

From the late 5th century onwards, **translations from the Greek** were made of secular works including the writings of philosophers such as Aristotle and Plato and of the medical writers Hippocrates and Galen. Meanwhile the writers of histories continued to stress martyrdom. In the *History* by **Yeghishe**, probably written in the late 6th century, the account of the revolt in 451 goes even further than had Lazarus of Parp in emphasising martyrdom and justifying armed resistance as well as giving the clergy a leading role. The Armenians are depicted as treating Persian promises of religious freedom as deceitful.

The period after the Arab conquest was a low point for Armenia generally and it was the 10th century before a literary revival took place. Competition between monasteries for endowments led to an interesting forgery. The *History of Taron* (Taron is the area north of Lake Van) was written sometime between 966 and 988 but claims to have been started in the 4th century by Zenob of Glak, the first Bishop of Taron, and then continued by Hovhan Mamikonian, the 35th Bishop of Taron, in the 7th century. The book states that Glak was St Gregory the Illuminator's first foundation, earlier even than Etchmiadzin, while the truth was that Glak was a new foundation in the 10th century. The supposed history includes a completely bogus story of Glak's possession of miracle-working relics of John the Baptist which had produced divine intervention in war. The purpose of all this monastic skulduggery was twofold. First, it was an attempt to show that Glak, being Armenia's oldest monastery, was worthiest of endowment, more so even than Etchmiadzin and Dvin. Secondly, and even more explicitly, in the book some ascetics pray that anyone who makes generous gifts to the monastery from their 'sinful' wealth should be delivered from tribulation; they are answered by a voice from heaven which assents. Rather more prosaic is the description of the cutting off of enemy noses: 24,000 on one occasion.

The 10th century produced several rather more **reliable histories** while the *Book of Lamentations* by **Gregory of Narek** (c950–1010), a long poem comprising prayers about the wretchedness of the soul, the sinfulness of mankind and the certainty of salvation, remains a classic of Armenian literature. It is the earliest written work still to be widely read and was completed in 1002. Its author is usually considered to be Armenia's greatest poet and it has been translated into 30 languages. Armenia's national epic, *David of Sassoun*, also dates from the 10th century although it was not committed to print until 1873. It recounts the story of David's family over four generations with Sassoun, its setting, symbolising Armenia. David in particular incarnated a symbol of the Armenians who fought foreign oppression in the 7th and 8th centuries.

**Nerses Shnorhali** (Nerses the Gracious) (1100–73) was a great **lyrical poet**, musician, theologian and philosopher who became Katholikos Nerses IV in 1166. His greatest poem *Lament on the Fall of Edessa* (present-day Urfa in Turkey) records the capture of that city in 1144 by the Turks who slaughtered most of its inhabitants together with the archbishop. Nerses is also the author of several hymns still used in the Armenian communion service. By the late 13th century, poems on love and other secular themes began to appear and grow as an important force in Armenian literature. The greatest of these poets, **Constantine of Yerznka** (modern-day Erzincan in Turkey), wrote poetry of springtime, love, beauty and light, allegorically exalting the Christian mysteries. Constantine broadened the scope of Armenian poetry, moving away from religious terminology towards the imagery of the natural world. This was taken even further until in the 15th and 16th centuries pure love poetry came to Armenia. Its first great exponent was **Nahapet Kuchak** (meaning 'little patriarch' in a mixture of Armenian and Persian), who is thought to have lived near Lake Van in the 16th century but may have lived earlier and elsewhere. His poems have deep, often erotic, emotional passion, stunning imagery and wit, and are as vividly alive today as when they were written. **Sayat Nova** (c1712–95), born in Tiflis (Tbilisi), was perhaps the culmination of this tradition. Poet and composer in Georgian, Persian and Azeri Turkish as well as Armenian (the name means 'king of songs' in Persian), he considered himself a builder of bridges between the various ethnic cultures of Georgia, writing of courtly love and the beauty of his unattainable beloved.

The development of the **novel** throughout the Western world in the late 18th century inevitably impacted upon Armenia. The first great Armenian novelist was **Khachatur Abovyan** (1805–48). He was the first author to abandon the classical Armenian language and use modern spoken Armenian for his works. His most famous novel is *Armenia's Wounds*, set during the Russian conquest of Armenia from Persia in 1826–28 and dealing with the Armenian people's suffering under foreign domination. Abovyan was also a noted translator of Homer and Schiller. Further impetus to the quest for Armenian identity was given in the novels of the other great 19th-century Armenian novelist, **Raffi** (pen name of Hakop Melik-Hakopian) (1835–88). The grandeur of Armenia's historic past was recalled in novels such as *The Madman* (1881), *Samvel* (1886) and *The Spark* (1887).

The writings of **Hovhannes Tumanyan** (1869–1923) encompass **fables and epic poetry**. An admirer of Shakespeare and translator of Byron, Goethe and Pushkin, it is regrettable that his work is not better known outside Armenia. He wrote patriotic verse with titles such as *In the Armenian Mountains*, *Armenian Grief* and *With My Fatherland*, but also legends such as *A Drop of Honey* in which the eponymous drop is the cause of a war. The work, based on a medieval legend, concludes with the few terrified survivors asking themselves what caused the worldwide conflagration. Tumanyan moralised without preaching, notably in works such as *My Friend Nesso*, a story about how the most handsome boy in the village turns into an evil, dishonest man and ends up dragging out a deprived life at the bottom of society. Similarly, *The Capture of Fort Temuk* traces the criminal path which leads from simple ambition to treason. Most Armenians consider that Tumanyan's masterpiece is *Anoush*, a tragic story of village life in which Anoush's brother kills her lover for breaking a village taboo. The work is much more than a simple story, the author expressing his philosophy of life, his ideas about the existence of man and the world of human passions. His ardently expressed love for Armenia led to his being tried in 1908 for anti-Tsarist activities and he was later very active in seeking to help victims of the genocide.

Tumanyan appears on the AMD5,000 banknote while the figure on the AMD1,000 note is the poet **Yeghishe Charents** (1897–1937). Born in Van, then under Turkish rule, Charents was involved in anti-Turkish activity as part of the Armenian self-defence corps as early as 1912. His early work reflects this in pieces such as *Three Songs to a Pale Girl* (1914) and *Blue-Eyed Homeland* (1915). In 1915, he moved to Moscow to continue his education at the university thereby witnessing the Bolshevik Revolution and becoming greatly influenced by its ideology. In 1918, he joined the Red Army. Returning to Yerevan an enthusiastic supporter of communism in 1919, at this stage of his life his writings covered topics such as civil war in Russia and Armenia, world communism, famine, poverty, World War I and the Bolshevik Revolution. From the mid 1920s there is a gradual change in his work as he became disillusioned with communist rule and increasingly

## AVETIK ISAHAKYAN

The poet, writer and public activist Avetik Isahakyan (1875–1957), whose image appears on the AMD10,000 note, was an establishment figure in Soviet days. Born in Alexandropol (Gyumri) he studied philosophy and anthropology in Leipzig. On his return in 1895 he joined the committee of the Armenian Revolutionary Federation which supported armed groups and sent financial aid to Western Armenia. After twice being arrested and imprisoned by the Tsarist authorities he left the Caucasus. Fearing that pan-Turkism was aimed at the extinction of the Armenians and believing that Germany, Turkey's ally, could prevent it he went to Berlin and participated in the German-Armenian movement. The massacres of the genocide confirmed his fears. In his social and political articles he wrote about the Armenian cause, putting forward genocide accusations. At the same time his poetry was coloured by images of the massacres. Between 1930 and 1936 he again lived abroad, acting as a friend of the Soviet Union. On his return to Armenia he continued to be involved with social matters and was elected to the Academy of Sciences and was president of the Writers' Union of the Armenian SSR. He was twice awarded the Order of Lenin. His poems are filled with sorrow and lament for humanity and are permeated with love for his homeland and the Armenian struggle for freedom. He is buried in Yerevan's Komitas Pantheon.

nationalistic. His satirical novel *Land of Nairi* (1925) starts to reflect this but his last published collection of poems, *Book of the Road*, published in 1933, was to make him notorious. One poem called 'The Message', ostensibly in fulsome praise of the genius of Stalin, contains a second message hidden in the second letter of each line: *Oh! Armenian people, your salvation lies only in your collective power.* Inevitably deemed nationalistic by the Soviet authorities he was arrested shortly afterwards by the NKVD (forerunner of the KGB). He died in prison, an early victim among the tens of millions killed at Stalin's behest, although it was claimed by the Soviet authorities that he had committed suicide while on hunger strike. All his works were banned until his rehabilitation in 1954, the year after Stalin's death.

Later Armenian writers could inevitably have no personal experience of a pre-Soviet world or even of the genocide. **Hovhannes Shiraz,** born Hovhannes Karapetyan (1915–84), however, came much closer than most since his mother was widowed by the genocide shortly before his birth. Growing up in considerable poverty, he attracted attention when his first work *Beginning of Spring* was published in 1935. He acquired the name Hovhannes Shiraz, by which he is better known, because one writer commented that his 'poems have the fragrance of roses, fresh and covered with dew, like the roses of Shiraz' (Shiraz is a city in Iran). His work includes parables and translations as well as a great deal of poetry, and is immortalised for Armenians by such lines as: 'Let all nations reach the moon, but Armenians reach Ararat.' A critic of Armenia's corrupt Soviet government, his protests included publicly urinating one evening on the statue of Lenin in Yerevan.

**Gevorg Emin** was born in 1919, slightly later than Shiraz. Qualifying as a hydraulic engineer in 1940, his knowledge of the technological world of dams, pipelines and power stations is reflected in the concrete images and complex relationships between people and technology which he employs metaphorically. Subtle and witty, his work was translated into Russian by Boris Pasternak. A more establishment figure than Shiraz, his book *Land, Love, Era* was awarded the Soviet State Prize for Literature in 1976.

**Paruyr Sevak** (1924–71) was another staunch critic of the corrupt Soviet government to the extent that most Armenians believed that his death was murder at the hands of the KGB rather than the result of a road accident – and certainly the spot where the alleged accident took place is a straight unobstructed section of road with little traffic. The tenor of his writings is conveyed in titles such as *The Unsilenceable Belfry* (1959) and *Let There be Light* (1971). He is considered one of the greatest Armenian poets of the 20th century.

Not all Armenian writers spoke Armenian as their native language. The novelist **Gosdan Zarian** (1885–1969) was the son of a staunchly Armenian father who was a general in the Tsarist army and he was brought up speaking Russian and French but not Armenian. His youth was spent in various Western countries where he frequently ate with Lenin in Geneva and knew Picasso in Paris. He started to learn Armenian only in 1910, studying with the Mkhitarists on the island of San Lazarro in Venice. He moved to Constantinople in 1913 and two years later was one of the few Armenian intellectuals who managed to escape the genocide, in his case by fleeing via Bulgaria to Rome. He returned to Istanbul in 1920 and in 1922 moved to Yerevan. Thoroughly disappointed with the Soviet regime, he left in 1925 and spent a nomadic existence including spells in the USA and Lebanon before returning to Armenia in 1961. His poem *The Bride of Tetrachoma*, first published in Boston in 1930, was republished in Yerevan in 1965 while a bowdlerised edition of his novel *The Ship on the Mountain*, first published in Boston in 1943, appeared in Yerevan in 1963.

1

Probably the best-known Armenian writer outside Armenia is **William Saroyan** (1908–81). Born to Armenian parents at Fresno, California, he sprang to fame in 1934 with his first book *The Daring Young Man on the Flying Trapeze*. His first successful Broadway play *My Heart's in the Highlands* was first performed in 1939. He was awarded both the New York Drama Critics' Circle Award and the Pulitzer Prize for *The Time of Your Life* (1939), but he refused to accept the latter since he believed that 'Commerce should not patronise art.' A prolific writer, Saroyan acknowledged Armenian culture as an important source of his literary inspiration and his work gave international recognition to Armenia. A year after his death, half of his cremated remains were interred in the Komitas Pantheon in Yerevan, while the other half remained in Fresno.

**Painting** Russian expansionism into Armenia and subsequent greater contact with western European painting greatly influenced the development of Armenian realistic painting in the 19th century. The first notable painter to break away from the medieval manuscript tradition was **Hakob Hovnatanyan** (1806–81), whose family had been painters for nearly 200 years. (His grandfather's grandfather had contributed to the decoration of Etchmiadzin Cathedral in the late 17th century.) He painted portraits of his contemporaries in an original manner which fused elements of the painting of illuminated manuscripts with European traditions of portraiture: everything in these portraits is expressed through the face, above all the eyes, and the hands of the conventionally posed sitter.

By contrast **Hovhannes Aivazovsky** (1817–1900), often referred to as Ivan Aivazovsky – its Russian equivalent – shows little Armenian influence. He was born to an Armenian father at Feodosia in the Crimea and painted wonderful seascapes, calm seas with beautiful lighting effects, violent storms sometimes with men struggling to survive (over half his seascapes) or surprisingly vivid pictures of the historic sea battles of the Russian navy. Though with few equals to his ability to capture the many moods and colours of the sea, his non-marine pictures are decidedly more pedestrian. His achievements were probably more recognised internationally than is the case with any other 19th-century Armenian painter and he was even awarded the Légion d'Honneur in 1857.

Another recipient of the Légion d'Honneur was **Zakar Zakarian** (1849–1923), who left his home in Constantinople to train as a doctor in Paris but later turned to painting. His still lifes with their careful composition and interplay of light and dark frequently incorporate a glass of water, interpreted by his contemporaries as expressing his feeling from his Paris home of the tragic events in his homeland. **Gevorg Bashinjaghian** (1857–1920) developed the painting of landscapes with his calm, serene views, mostly of Armenia although he also travelled. **Vardges Sureniants** (1860–1921) was a much more versatile artist. Like Bashinjaghian a painter of landscapes, he also painted many Armenian subjects and his 1895 painting *Desecrated Shrine* was a response to the massacres of the Armenians by the Turks. He additionally painted historical subjects; he was a gifted book illustrator and in 1899 was chosen to illustrate Pushkin's *Fountain of Bakhchisarai* as part of the centenary celebrations; and as a stage designer he was chosen by Konstantin Stanislavsky in 1904 to design his Moscow production of Maurice Maeterlinck's symbolist drama *Les Aveugles* (*The Blind*).

The landscapes of **Yeghishe Tatevosyan** (1870–1936) reflect the strong influence of French painters as well as of his teachers in Moscow, and the French influence is even stronger in the works of **Edgar Shahin** (often gallicised as Chahine) (1874–1947) who studied in Paris. **Vano Khojabekian** (1875–1922) was a complete contrast: a primitivist who on his arrival in Yerevan in 1919 created some moving scenes of the plight of the refugees who had escaped the Turkish massacres. **Hovsep Pushman** (1877–1966) was another painter of still lifes, mostly incorporating oriental statuettes with titles such as *The Golden Decline of Life* and *The Murmur of Leaves*.

Probably the most brilliant and certainly the most influential Armenian artist of the early 20th century was **Martiros Saryan** (1880–1972), whose works mirror the creative intellectual ferment in the artistic world of the day and show an amazing feel for colour and form. He was born near Rostov-on-Don in Russia and studied in Moscow. His first visit to Armenia in 1901 resulted in the cycle *Stories and Dreams* which shows much symbolist influence. From 1909 he turned towards a more representational style using large areas of single colour with great

## CHESS

For a small country of only three million inhabitants, Armenia has a remarkably high standing in the world of chess, being ranked tenth in the world by the World Chess Federation (FIDE) (March 2018). As well as the Armenians claiming Garry Kasparov, the man considered by many to be the greatest chess player of all time, as one of their own due to his maternal lineage, Armenia also has one of the highest concentrations of chess grandmasters. As of March 2018, FIDE listed 31 active (male) Armenian grandmasters, two women grandmasters, 21 international (male) masters and six women international masters. Armenia's number one player, Levon Aronian, was ranked as world no. 2, having won the World Cup in 2005 and 2017. Four Armenians are in FIDE's top 100 players. At the international Chess Olympiads Armenia's men's team won the gold medal in 2006 and 2008 and the bronze in 1992, 2002 and 2004. Armenia was the World Team champion in 2011. The country has hosted many international competitions including the 32nd Chess Olympiad in 1996 and the Fifth World Team Championship in 2001.

Chess has a long history in Armenia, being known since the 9th century and mentioned in manuscripts from the 12th and 13th centuries. It was popularised during the Soviet era and competitions started in 1927 with the founding of the Armenian Chess Federation. Its popularity increased with the successes of Tigran Petrosyan who was World Champion from 1963 to 1969 and a member of the Soviet team which won the Chess Olympiad nine times between 1958 and 1974.

The Chess House in Yerevan (50a Khanjyan St; ☎010 554923) was opened in 1970 and since 1984 has been officially named after Tigran Petrosyan whose statue stands beside the building. It is home to the Armenian Chess Federation (w chessfed.am) whose current president is Serzh Sargsyan, former president of the Republic of Armenia. The Federation's website has details of competitions and live coverage of games. The Chess Academy of Armenia (w chessacademy.am) was founded in 2002 under the auspices of the Armenian Chess Federation. Supported by the government, it organises chess tournaments and is the leading centre for chess training. In 2011 Armenia became the first country to make chess a mandatory part of the school curriculum for all seven- to nine-year-olds, allocating funds to the Chess Academy to draw up courses, create textbooks and train instructors. Funds were also allocated to equip chess classrooms in every school.

attention to shapes and contrasts and the qualities of light. Another artist working through the revolutionary period was **Hakop Kojoyan** (1883–1959). He produced haunting landscapes as well as works which take a stylised medieval approach and book illustrations for authors such as Gorki. His *Execution of Communists at Tatev*, however, seems likely to have been painted for political reasons.

The Soviet period saw those Armenian painters who remained in the country and were approved by the regime supported, while others were harassed regardless of their talent. **Gyorgy Yakulov** (1884–1928) worked as a stage designer in Tiflis and Yerevan before being invited to Paris by Diaghilev where his work had immense success. He travelled in both China and Italy and his paintings reflect an attempt to combine traditional orientalism with the Italian High Renaissance. **Sedrak Arakelyan** (1884–1942) was a follower of Saryan whose own lyrical landscapes successfully capture ephemeral moments in the Armenian countryside. Another follower, **Harutyun Kalents** (1908–67), was one of the children who escaped the genocide of 1915. His parents both died and he was brought up in an orphanage in Beirut. Not surprisingly his work reflects the tragic circumstances of his childhood. **Minas Avetisyan** (1928–75) is regarded particularly highly in Armenia. His work came to prominence in 1962 at the *Exhibition of Five* in Yerevan. Again a follower of Saryan, much of his work was destroyed either in a fire at his studio in 1972 (widely believed in Armenia to have been deliberately started by the Soviet security forces) or in the 1988 earthquake which destroyed his frescoes at Leninakan (present-day Gyumri) and the museum dedicated to his work at Jajur, his native village. He himself was tragically killed when he was knocked down by a car which had mounted the pavement. According to some sources this was the work of the KGB. A complete contrast to these followers of Saryan is **Alexander Bazhbeuk-Melikyan** (1891–1966), who can be regarded more as a follower of Degas. He painted women; in warm clear colours, whether exercising on a swing or combing their hair, they are elegant and at ease.

**Yervand Kochar** (1899–1979) was a sculptor and designer as much as a painter, and his best-known work in Armenia is perhaps the striking statue of David of Sassoun on horseback which stands outside Yerevan's main railway station, while the works most noticed by visitors may be the statue of Vardan Mamikonian, also on horseback, which stands on Yerevan's green belt at the southern end of Buzand Street; his *Melancholy* on Buzand Street itself, outside the Armenian Centre for Contemporary Experimental Art, opposite Vernissage; and the eagle which stands at the gates of Zvartnots Cathedral. The three-dimensional quality of his paintings tends to express his interest in sculpture and he created some amazing three-dimensional paintings, examples of which are in the Yervand Kochar Museum, Yerevan, and the Pompidou Centre, Paris. An immensely gifted artist, he lived and worked in Paris from 1923 until 1936 but then, although highly successful there, he returned to Soviet Armenia. After his return he was accused of the Soviet crime of formalism and suffered periods of imprisonment. While in Paris in 1930 he married Melineh Ohanian, his second wife. (His first wife, Vardeni – whom Kochar married in Paris in 1925 – and their daughter both died of TB in 1928.) Although Melineh was of Armenian descent, she had been born in France and the Soviet government would not allow her to enter the Soviet Union. Neither was Kochar ever allowed to leave, not even during the period of the Khrushchev thaw. In 1966 an exhibition was held in Paris of the works Kochar had produced in France. Melineh and a group of prominent Parisians petitioned the Soviet authorities to allow Kochar to travel to attend the exhibition but neither he nor the pieces of his post-Paris period were allowed to leave. Melineh committed suicide in 1969. Kochar married his third wife, Manik Mkrtchyan, in 1945.

Petros Konturajian (1905–56) was another child who was orphaned by the genocide of 1915. He went to Paris and became a successful painter of the city under the influence of Cézanne and the Cubists. In 1947, he returned to Armenia but he failed to come to terms with Soviet conditions and committed suicide. **Hakop Hakopian** (1928–75) also moved to live in Armenia at a similar age to Konturajian but was able to adapt, perhaps because life under Brezhnev was less intolerable than under Stalin. His still lifes and landscapes have a dramatic quality expressing deep anxiety. **Girair Orakian** (1901–63) is another painter who was driven from his home city of Constantinople. He spent most of the rest of his life in Rome. His paintings expressing the struggles between life and death for the poor can again be understood against his childhood background.

If Ivan Aivazovsky is Armenia's best-known 19th-century painter outside the country, the best-known 20th-century one is probably **Garnik Zulumian**, also known as Jean Carzou (1907–2000). He worked as a stage designer as well as a painter and engraver and his paintings do often reflect a decorative and theatrical quality. Claiming that Picasso was no painter at all, he alleged the only truly great painters were Claude Lorrain, Watteau and Dalí. Carzou's response to the Armenian earthquake of 1988 was the painting *Armenia: Earthquake. Hope*, in which a naked woman is shown standing over ruins against a background of Armenian buildings and mountains.

Foremost among artists born after the establishment of Soviet power is **Sergei Parajanov** (1924–90). Although better known as a film director (page 181), he also created a wide range of extraordinary works of art including collages and mosaics which were frequently made using everyday materials – perhaps he developed this technique during his involuntary periods in Siberian labour camps. Many of his works display strong egocentricity. Of the more contemporary artists, the one whose work visitors are most likely to notice is **Ara Shiraz** (1941–2014), as his 9m-high sculpture of Andranik Ozanian riding two horses is at the foot of the slope leading up to Yerevan Cathedral.

# 2

# Practical Information

## WHEN TO VISIT

The best time for general sightseeing and touring tends to be in **May** and **June**, or else **late September** and **October**. The former sees the wild flowers at their very best, the landscapes greener and the lower regions (including Yerevan) not yet stiflingly hot, though it can be stormy. The latter is drier and the heat of summer has subsided, but of course there are few flowers and much of the country is parched and brown. As compensation, the brilliant autumn colours of Armenia's forested regions are truly striking. Visibility is also better during these periods of late spring and late summer/autumn, with a higher chance of a good view of Mount Ararat. Having said all of that, midsummer visitors will enjoy reliably fine and sunny weather, and respite from the worst of the heat can be found in the plentiful mountainous regions and the temperate forests of the northeast and south – indeed, the highest reaches frequently remain snowbound until July. Seasonal fruit and vegetables are abundant in the summer and always available on roadsides. Winter is the low season as far as tourism is concerned, due to dependably cold weather and snow; however, much of the national road network is kept clear for travel, and some may of course see the snowy mountains as an opportunity. Relatively cheap skiing opportunities pull in many Russian visitors, and the timing of Persian New Year in late March ensures that the streets of Yerevan are packed with Iranians long before the first Western tour groups arrive. At any time of year, visitors to Armenia should take into account the regional variations in climate due to the country's diverse range of landscapes and elevations.

## HIGHLIGHTS

Armenia's **religious heritage sites** are uniquely popular attractions that form many visitors' strongest impressions of the country. Any risk of overload is compensated for by the fact that they are often situated in **stunning natural landscapes** that offer good hiking opportunities. Though there are literally hundreds of such sites, **Noravank** with its splendid gorge and wonderful carvings is at the top of most 'must-see' lists, with at least a half-day's worth of walking in the vicinity. **Khor Virap**, about as close as you can get to Mount Ararat without leaving Armenia, is a worthwhile stop on the same route from Yerevan, especially if visibility is good. Other comparable sites are the monasteries of **Haghpat**, **Goshavank**, **Haghartsin** and **Amberd** (together with its adjacent fortress), **Selim Caravanserai**, the field of khachkars at **Noratus**, and the prehistoric stones at **Karahunj**. The rock-carved monastery of **Geghard** is another must-see, easily reached from Yerevan and often combined with a visit to **Garni Temple**. **Tatev Monastery**, with its dramatic clifftop setting, can now be reached by the world's longest cable car, as well as by road.

Less visited but among the more unique sites include the wonderful **carvings** at **Makaravank**, the reconstructed fortress of **Smbataberd** on its ridge (together with the nearby **Tsakhatskar Monastery**), **Spitakavor Monastery** (another good walk), **Akhtala Monastery** (with its wonderful frescoes), **Kobayr Monastery** (a short uphill walk again with some excellent nearby hiking), the petroglyphs at **Ughtasar** (requiring a 4x4 or a very long hike), and the monastery of **Harichavank** (together with the other small churches of the area). Some of Yerevan's museums and art galleries are also must-sees, especially the **History Museum** and the **National Gallery** (in the same building), the **Matenadaran** for a glimpse of Armenia's wonderful illuminated manuscripts, and the equally illuminating **Armenian Genocide Museum-Institute and Tsitsernakaberd Memorial Complex**, which is less harrowing and more educational than it might sound.

Beyond the cultural and historical sites, outdoor enthusiasts may explore Armenia's rich **natural heritage** via more than 200km of waymarked trails in **Dilijan National Park**; the gorges of **Vayots Dzor**; the **Debed Canyon** in Lori province; and, in Syunik province, around **Mount Khustup** and **Tatev**. For the truly adventurous, the volcanic **Geghama Mountains** represent some of the most unique landscapes anywhere in the Caucasus.

## SUGGESTED ITINERARIES

A minimum of two or three days should be devoted to **Yerevan**, though if you plan to visit any museums do check the opening hours when researching your trip: Mondays are usually non-working days. Try to be in Yerevan at the weekend when the **Vernissage arts and crafts market** is in full swing (page 156). An extra two or three days in the city would allow for some worthwhile day trips to nearby sites. In planning a trip round the rest of the country, there are three major factors to consider: whether to use public transport and taxis or to hire a car (and, if so, whether to hire a 4x4); whether or not one wishes to do any hiking; and whether some of the chosen places to visit will be inaccessible because of snow.

The following suggested two-week itinerary is focused on heritage sites, covers a great deal of the country, and could be tailored to suit individual requirements:

**DAYS 1–3** Yerevan (or split time in Yerevan between start and end of tour).

**DAY 4** Travel to Gyumri (page 258) visiting Talin (page 201), Mastara (page 202) and Harichavank (page 268) en route. Visit Marmashen (page 264) from Gyumri. Overnight in Gyumri.

**DAY 5** Travel via Spitak (page 276) to Stepanavan (page 279). Visit Lori Berd (page 280). Then travel via Kurtan (visit Hnevank, page 283) to the Dzoraget/Alaverdi area for overnight (page 273).

**DAY 6** Visit the monasteries of the Debed Gorge: Akhtala (page 294), Haghpat and Sanahin, with an excellent walk between the two (page 289) and Kobayr (page 285). Overnight in the Dzoraget/Alaverdi area (page 273).

**DAY 7** Travel via Noyemberyan (page 317) and Ijevan (page 311) to Dilijan (page 300) visiting Makaravank (page 315) en route and also Haghartsin (page 306). Visit Goshavank (page 309). Alternatively, travel via Vanadzor (page 275) visiting Goshavank and Haghartsin. Overnight in Dilijan.

**DAY 8** Visit Sevanavank (page 232), the field of khachkars at Noratus (page 234) and Selim Caravanserai (page 335) before descending into Vayots Dzor (page 319). Overnight in Vayots Dzor.

☞ **Note** that some of the places mentioned are not served by public transport or only by infrequent public transport. If using a mixture of public transport and taxis more time would be required.

**DAY 9** Hike to Tsakhatskar and Smbataberd (page 332). Overnight in Vayots Dzor.

**DAY 10** Hike to Spitakavor (page 330). Overnight in Vayots Dzor.

**DAYS 9 AND 10 – ALTERNATIVE** If not wishing to hike, visit Yeghegis (page 334), Tanahat Monastery (page 331) and Jermuk (page 337).

**DAY 11** Visit Tatev (page 350). Then return to Goris (page 354) or Sisian (page 347) for overnight.

**DAY 12** Visit Karahunj (page 346). Then travel via Gndevank (page 337) to Vayots Dzor for overnight.

**DAY 13** Travel via Noravank (page 325) and Khor Virap (page 244) to Yerevan for overnight.

**DAY 14** Visit Garni Temple (page 242) and Geghard (page 244). Visit Etchmiadzin (page 217). Overnight in Yerevan.

**NAGORNO KARABAGH** If you want to visit the self-declared Republic of Artsakh (ie: Nagorno Karabagh) then on the 11th day, after visiting Tatev, continue to Stepanakert (page 382). Registering with the Nagorno Karabagh Foreign Ministry, either in Yerevan or Stepanakert (page 375), is essential before visiting other parts of the territory. Gandzasar and Dadivank (pages 390 and 391) can be combined in a single day and the opportunity should be taken to visit Shushi (page 385). If there is time, head to Old Khndzoresk (page 357), which is not far off the Goris to Stepanakert road.

**THE EXTREME SOUTH** Anyone wishing to travel to the extreme south of the country could do so on the 12th day after visiting Karahunj. Travel via Goris (page 354), stay overnight in Kapan (page 358) and visit Meghri (page 363) for the day, or stay overnight in Meghri, ideally travelling there on the older road via Kajaran and back on the newer one through Shikahogh State Reserve (page 366).

## TOURIST INFORMATION

Tourist information offices exist in Yerevan and in several major towns and tourist destinations. The country's official tourism web portal (w armenia.travel) was relaunched in early 2018. While still in beta version at the time of research it does offer a comprehensive brochure-style overview of the country, the main attractions and a calendar of major festivals and events. The best **internet source** of background information on Armenian historical sites (including those in Nagorno Karabagh and elsewhere outside Armenia), including many lesser-known sites not covered in this guide, remains Armeniapedia (**w** armeniapedia.org). The Armenian Monuments Awareness Project (AMAP) (**w** armenianmonuments.org) is usually behind the information boards at many heritage sites, and the website has some useful information. For road navigation, both Google Maps and OpenStreetMap coverage of Armenia have improved dramatically in the last few years and smartphone apps give accurate directions in 99% of cases. For more useful websites, see page 410.

The most useful printed **maps** of the country published in Armenia are by Collage Ltd (4 Saryan St, Yerevan; ◣010 520217; **e** collageltd@gmail.com; **w** collage.am). The pocket atlas *The Roads of Armenia*, costing AMD2,500, covers the country together with Nagorno Karabagh at a scale of 1:300,000. It has small street plans of Yerevan, Gyumri and Vanadzor. Roads, rivers, railways, mountain summits and historical sites are shown, and names are given in both Armenian and English. Collage Ltd also publishes *Armenia & Mountainous Karabakh*, at a scale of 1:400,000, costing AMD2,500. Place names are in both English and Armenian (there is also a version in English and Russian). Both the above maps show distances between towns and road numbers. Collage Ltd also publishes a map of *Yerevan* (AMD2,500) with greater Yerevan at a scale of 1:17,000 and the city centre at 1:7,000; and a *Yerevan Guide Map* (AMD1,500) to a slightly smaller scale (greater Yerevan 1:20,000, city centre 1:8,000). There are occasional minor inaccuracies on the Collage maps; these are noted where relevant to descriptions in this guidebook.

Outside Armenia, several folded sheet maps of the country are available from online retailers and from specialist high-street outlets such as Stanfords (7 Mercer Walk, London WC2H 9FA, UK & 29 Corn St, Bristol BS1 1HT, UK; ◣+44 (0)20 7836 1321, +44 (0)117 929 9966; **e** sales@stanfords.co.uk; **w** stanfords.co.uk), produced by international mapping agencies including Reise Know-How at 1:250,000 and ITMB at 1:430,000 (together with Georgia), and Gizi Map at 1:1,000,000 (as part of the Caucasus region).

# TOUR OPERATORS

## INTERNATIONAL OPERATORS

The following tour operators can make arrangements to travel to Armenia or else operate group tours themselves.

## UK

**Birdquest** Two Jays, Kemple End, Clitheroe, Lancs BB7 9QY; ◣01254 826317; **e** birders@birdquest. co.uk; **w** birdquest-tours.com. Specialists for serious, in-depth birdwatching. Sometimes includes Armenia in regional tours.

**Birdwatching Breaks** Cygnus Hse, Gordons Mill, Balblair, Ross-shire IV7 8LQ; ◣01381 610495; **e** enquiries@birdwatchingbreaks.com; **w** birdwatchingbreaks.com. A serious birdwatching company with some trips to Armenia.

**Explore Worldwide** Nelson Hse, 55 Victoria Rd, Farnborough, Hants GU14 7PA; ◣01252 884737; **e** sales@explore.co.uk; **w** explore.co.uk. Offers an 'On Foot In Armenia' trip & a 'Land of

the Golden Fleece' trip (the fleece was kept at Colchis, near present-day Batumi on the Black Sea coast of Georgia). The 16-day trip spends 5 nights in Armenia & a 4-day Azerbaijan extension is available.

**Go Barefoot Travel** Handel Hse, 95 High St, Middlesex HA8 7DB; ◣020 3290 9591; **e** info@ gobarefoot.travel; **w** gobarefoot.travel. Focusing on sustainable/responsible tourism & offering a 9-day tour of Armenia inc some walking, with flexible dates.

**Kudu Travel** 14–16 Norland Rd, Holland Park, London W11 4TR; ◣020 8150 3367; **e** kuduinfo@ kudutravel.com; **w** kudutravel.com. Offers a 13-day tour which includes some walking.

**Martin Randall Travel** Voysey Hse, Barley Mow Passage, London W4 4GF; ◣020 8742 3355; **e** info@martinrandall.co.uk; **w** martinrandall. com. Specialises in highbrow cultural holidays. Offers an 8-day historical group tour, with lecturer.

**Naturetrek** Mingledown Barn, Wolf's Lane, Hants GU34 3HJ; ☎ 01962 733051; e info@naturetrek.co.uk; w naturetrek.co.uk. Offers 8- to 9-day tours in spring, concentrating on birds, butterflies & flowers. Aims to donate 10% of the proceeds to be invested in the conservation of British & European butterflies.

**Regent Holidays** 6th Floor, Colston Tower, Colston St, Bristol BS1 4XE; ☎ 020 7666 1244; e regent@regent-holidays.co.uk; w regent-holidays.co.uk. Can organise any itinerary in Armenia & Nagorno Karabagh (combined with Georgia & Azerbaijan if required) for individuals or groups. It also offers group tours to Armenia & Georgia & short city-break tours to Yerevan. The authors have had personal experience of this firm's efficiency, flexibility & helpfulness over many years.

**Secret Compass** 14 Whitehouse St, Bristol BS3 4AY; ☎ 020 7096 8428; e info@secretcompass.com; w secretcompass.com. Expedition & adventure travel company offering a unique 8-day group trek in southern Armenia. Can also arrange bespoke expeditions.

**Silk Road Tours** 8 Oak Cottages, Green Lane, London W7 2PE; ☎ 020 728 2478; e info@silkroadtours.co.uk; w silkroadtours.co.uk. Offers a 9-day tour to Armenia, 14-day tour to Armenia & Georgia, & a 14-day tour to Armenia, Georgia & Azerbaijan.

**Travel Local** w travellocal.com. A UK-based website where you can book direct with selected local travel companies, allowing you to communicate with an expert ground operator without having to go through a 3rd-party travel operator or agent. Your booking with the local company has full financial protection, but note that travel to the destination is not included. Member of ABTA, ASTA.

**Undiscovered Destinations** PO Box 746, North Tyneside NE29 1EG; ☎ 0191 296 2674; e travel@undiscovered-destinations.com; w undiscovered-destinations.com. Offers 15-day group tours to Armenia & Georgia, as well as tailor-made tours.

**Wild Frontiers** Unit 6, Hurlingham Business Park, 55 Sulivan Rd, London SW6 3DU; ☎ 020 7736 3968; e info@wildfrontierstravel.com; w wildfrontierstravel.com. Can tailor any itinerary for individuals but also offers a 9-day tour to Armenia inc 2 nights in Nagorno Karabagh, a 9-day horseriding trek in Armenia & a 15-day Caucasus itinerary.

## USA

**Levon Travel** 408 East Broadway, Glendale, CA 91205; ☎ +1 818 552 7700, +1 800 445 3866; w levontravel.com. Yerevan office: 10 Sayat Nova Av; ☎ 010 525210, 525284; e sales@levontravel.am; w levontravel.am.

**Sidon Travel** 428 S Central Av, Glendale, CA 91204; ☎ +1 818 553 0777, +1 800 826 7960; e info@sidontravel.com; w sidontravel.com. Yerevan office: 9 Nalbandyan St; ☎ 010 522967; e yerevan@sidontravel.com.

**Sima Tours** 2064 Sproul Rd, Broomall, PA 19008; ☎ +1 610 359 7521; m +1 610 304 5948; e info@simatours.com; w simatours.com. Yerevan office: 50 Teryan St; ☎ 010 589954, 548715.

## Austria

**Biblische Reisen** Stifsplatz 8, 3400 Klosterneuburg; ☎ +43 2243 353 770; e info@biblische-reisen.at; w biblische-reisen.at. Runs group tours concentrating on churches & monasteries.

## Georgia

**GeorgiCa Travel** Erekle II St, Tbilisi; ☎ +995 32 225 21 99; e georgica@caucasus.net; w georgicatravel.ge; see ad, page 124. Arranges Caucasus combination tours to Armenia, Georgia & Azerbaijan.

## Germany

**Biblische Reisen** Silberburgstrasse 121, D-70176, Stuttgart; ☎ +49 7116 19250; e info@biblische-reisen.de, info@biblical-tours.com; w biblische-reisen.de, biblical-tours.com. Runs group tours concentrating on churches & monasteries.

**Ventus Reisen** Krefelder Strasse 8, D-10155 Berlin; ☎ +49 3039 100 332/3; e office@ventus.com; w ventus.com. Group tours & individual arrangements.

## Israel

**Breeza Tours** 27 Lishanski St, Rishon Letzion; ☎ +972 3 9625020; e info@breeza.co.il; w breeza.co.il. Group & individual tours.

**Eco-Field Trips** 11 Nes Ziona St, Tel Aviv; ☎ +972 3 5100454; e mail@eco.co.il; w eco.co.il. Group & individual arrangements.

**Wild Trails** 68 Odem St, Arad; ☎ +972 58 4960748; e info@wild-trails.com; w wild-trails.com. Adventure-tour specialist with a particular focus on Nagorno Karabagh.

## Italy

**Metamondo**  Via Ca' Rosso 21a, 30174 Mestre
(VE); +39 41 8899 211; e info@metamondo.it;
w www.metamondo.it. Group tours.

## Netherlands

**Koning Aap Reizen**  Entrada 223, 1096 EG
Amsterdam; +371 20 788 7700; e info@
koningaap.nl; w koningaap.nl. Offers 8-day tour
to Armenia & 23-day tour to Armenia (10 days) &
Georgia.

## Russia

**Caucasus Explorer**  933–69, Zelenograd,
Moscow; +7 499 653 90 19; e info@caucasus-
explorer.com; w caucasus-explorer.com. Extremely
knowledgeable specialist operator serving not just
Russian but international clients, offering tailor-
made mountain hiking, photography & wine-
themed tours to many unvisited parts of Armenia
& Nagorno Karabagh, as well as other parts of the
North & South Caucasus.

**LOCAL OPERATORS**  All the operators listed
here are based in Yerevan, unless noted otherwise.
Visitors who do not speak Armenian are strongly
recommended to deal with operators who have
experience in making ground arrangements for
travel agents from the West, since they will have
staff who speak reasonable English, while operators
dealing mainly with the large Armenian-speaking
diaspora market may not. Tour operators can arrange
all types of accommodation, inc rural homestays that
may not appear on maps or in regular tourist guides,
as well as guides & interpreters, car hire with or
without a driver, & special-interest & general tours.
They can also help with theatre tickets & virtually
anything else a visitor may want. Armenians are very
flexible & most things are possible. The following
list is representative – there are more than 200 local
operators in Armenia, a full list of which can be
found at w spyur.am/en/yellow_pages/yp/1667.
The Union of Incoming Tour Operators of Armenia
(w touroperator.am) is a non-profit association
whose listed members must meet strict criteria for
quality, ethics & transparency.

**AM Travel**  21/3 Pushkin St & 15 Khorenatsi
St; 010 526226, 526121; m 099 526220, 094
526225; e info@amtravel.am; w amtravel.am.
Offering a variety of themed tours inc food & wine,

arts, music, etc, as well as traditional cultural-
historical tours.
**Armenia Travel**  4 Vardanants St; 010 563667,
545330; e incoming@armeniatravel.am;
w armeniatravel.am; see ad in 2nd colour
section. Can organise almost anything for groups
& individuals. The authors have had personal
experience of this company's efficiency & flexibility
over many years.
**Envoy Tours**  54 Pushkin St; 010 530369;
w envoytours.com. Attached to the long-running
hostel of the same name. Daily tours of Yerevan,
daily day trips near the city, & other short (2- to
5-day) cultural tours.
**Geographic Travel Club**  26 Ghazar Parpetsi St;
010 527162/26; e incoming1@geotravel.am;
w geotravel.am. Offers cultural, pilgrimage, wine
& brandy tours & more. Also organises heli-skiing
on Mt Aragats.
**Hyur Service**  50 & 96 Nalbandyan St; 010
546040, 546080; e contact@hyurservice.com;
w hyurservice.com. Long-established agency
offering a wide range of services, such as apts,
tours & group transport.
**One Way Tour**  16 Ghazar Parpetsi St; 011
362131; m 091/094 362131; e info@onewaytour.
com; w onewaytour.com. Wide variety of day trips
as well as longer cultural/adventure itineraries.
Also covers Nagorno Karabagh & Georgia.
**Saberatours-Sevan**  32–38 Hanrapetutyan St
(at Europe Hotel); 010 525555; e incoming@
saberatours.am; w saberatours.am. Offers tours, car
hire, apts, etc in Armenia but is also a specialist in
travel to & from Iran, being the sales agent for Iran
Aseman Airlines, 1 of the Iranian companies that flies
between Tehran & Yerevan. It can also arrange land
transportation to & from Iran, & Iranian visas.

## Special interest operators

**Arevi Tour**  093 306556; e info@arevi.am;
w arevi.am; f AreviTrekHigher. Offering package
& bespoke tours & support services inc hiking,
trekking, mountaineering, backcountry skiing &
4x4 tours in remote mountain regions, as well as a
hotel in Yeghegis village (page 323).
**Armenia Holidays**  7 Abovyan St; 010 582292,
543311); e info@tourism.am; w tourism.am.
Offers a wide range of tours inc camping, hiking/
trekking, cycling & 4x4 tours.
**Armenian Astronomical Society**  Byurakan
Astrophysical Observatory, Byurakan; 010

525505; e aregmick@aras.am; w aras.am/
SciTourism/eng/. Offers various scientific tour
opportunities, inc astronomy at the Byurakan
Observatory (page 196).
**Armenian Travel Bureau** 24b Baghramyan
Av; 010 563321; m 093 885642, 077 563321;
e info@atb.am; w atb.am. Offers a wide range of
tours inc biking, birding, botanical, wine, winter, spa,
archaeological, faith-based & more. Sister office in
Moscow, Russia (Office 115, Pavilion 'Armenia', VVC,
119/68 Prospekt Mira Av; +7 495 772 9871).
**Avarayr** 1 Buzand St; 010 563681/524042;
e avarayr@arminco.com; w avarayr.am. A long-
established company offering camping, hiking/
trekking tours as well as cultural visits.
**Bezoar Travel** 10 Hrachaya Kochar St; m 096/041
553488; e bezoartravel@gmail.com; w bezoartravel.
com. Offering a variety of bespoke services with a
focus on guided hiking & trekking. Can also arrange
multi-country itineraries. Has Persian- & Arabic-
speaking guides as well as English-speakers.
**Discover Armenia (DA) Tours** 51/18
Artashisyan St; m 091/098/041 407211; e info@
da-tours.com; w da-tours.com. Experienced in
arranging adventurous itineraries inc hiking &
trekking, 4x4, skiing, caving & more. Also provides
fixing services for film & TV productions.
**Dream Riders** 42 Bagratunyats St; m 077
093030; e contact@dreamriders.am;
w dreamriders.am. Motorcycle tour & rental
specialist, offering 5 itineraries from 4 to 16 days
as well as bespoke services, with a fleet of 650cc
Japanese dual-sport bikes.
**Ecotour** Apt 40, 40 Charents St; m 094 136661;
e info@ecotour.am; w ecotour.am. Specialising
mainly in wildlife & botanical tours, being
associated with the Young Biologists Association of
Armenia, with highly knowledgeable local guides.
Also offers a range of other themed tours.
**Exotic Armenia Tours** 1/2 Tsitsernakaberd
Hwy; 060 448712; m 044 200290; e info@
exoticarmeniatours.com; w exoticarmeniatours.
com. Offers hiking & winter tours as well as apt
rental & multi-country tours.
**Exploring Armenia** m 099 613778;
w exploringarmenia.tours; explorarme.

Small operator with a professional archaeological
background, specialising in archaeological tours
combined with hiking & trekking.
**Gardman Tour** Apt 2, 47/1 Khanjyan St;
010 545353; e info@gardmantour.com;
w gardmantour.com. Adventure tours in Armenia
& Georgia inc mountain biking, hiking/trekking,
4x4, winter tours.
**Get Treated** 2/2 Melik Adamyan St; 095
010563; e info@gettreated.co; w gettreated.co.
Medical tourism specialist offering dental work,
laser eye surgery & more. Agents in the UK ( 0800
088 5110) & USA ( +1 855 818 0070).
**Grand Tour Armenia** 5 Nalbandyan St; m 077
131504, 099 131504; e grandtourarmenia@gmail.
com; jeeptourarmenia. Jeep tours – 1-day,
7-day & tailor-made – to off-the-beaten-track
Armenia & Nagorno Karabagh.
**Seven Springs Tour** 45/15 Komitas St,
Yerevan; 010 232440; m 094 912008;
e info@7springstour.am, incoming@7springstour.
am; w 7springstour.am. Offers hiking,
birdwatching & botanical tours.
**Sky Club** 16/1 Kalents St; m 098 055119;
e skyclubarmenia@gmail.com; w paraplan.am.
Paragliding specialist & pioneer, offering tandem
flights & lessons at several locations in Armenia,
with a sister hostel business in Yerevan (Glide
Hostel; page 140).
**Transcaucasian Trail Armenia** 2/2
Melik Adamyan St; m 096 553488, 094
121592; e armenia@transcaucasiantrail.org;
w transcaucasiantrail.org. Offers regular group
fundraising treks on sections of the long-distance
trail (page 114). All proceeds are invested in the
long-term sustainability of the project. Can also
organise bespoke guided treks.
**Up The Rocks** 8/38 Margaryan St; m 093
337937/318006; e info@uptherocks.com;
w uptherocks.com. Offers specialist guiding
services for rock climbing, alpine climbing &
backcountry skiing.
**Wild Armenia** 60 Griboyedov St; m 094 820661;
e info@wildarmenia.com; w wildarmenia.com.
Offering a spread of adventure tours inc treks to
remote mountain ranges.

## RED TAPE

Citizens of all EU member states and Schengen Area member states are entitled to
enter Armenia for up to 180 days per year without a visa, as are passport holders of

the following countries: Argentina, Australia, Azerbaijan, Belarus, Brazil, Georgia, Iran, Japan, Kazakhstan, Kyrgyzstan, Macao, Moldova, Montenegro, New Zealand, Qatar, Russian Federation, Serbia, Switzerland, Tajikistan, Ukraine, UAE, UK, Uruguay, USA and Uzbekistan. Visitors must of course have a valid passport, with at least six months' validity recommended by most foreign travel advice bureaus. Rules change; see the website of the Ministry of Foreign Affairs (w mfa.am/en/visa/) for the most up-to-date information.

Holders of passports from all other countries require a **visa**. The easiest way for visitors from eligible countries to obtain one is **on arrival**; again, consult the website above for the most up-to-date list. At Zvartnots International Airport, where most visitors arrive, it is straightforward and quick. Single-entry tourist visas are available for 21 or 120 days. The fee must be paid in Armenian drams (AMD3,000 for a 21-day visa, AMD15,000 for a 120-day visa). It is easy to change money in the airport, but a considerable commission is charged, so change the minimum required and get a better deal later at one of the many bureaux de change in the city centre. ATMs are also available for withdrawing local currency. When coming down the escalator in arrivals, note that the visa desks and exchange kiosks are directly ahead. Bear in mind that if you have disembarked with a plane full of Armenians you may well be the only one who needs to apply for a visa. Overland travellers can obtain visas at Ayrum railway station and the Bavra, Bagratashen and Gogavan road crossings with Georgia, and at the Agarak land border with Iran. The procedure here may be slower, especially for those last off the bus or train. Border crossing points can only issue single-entry visas (3-day transit, 21-day or 120-day tourist visas).

The second method, which is compulsory for certain nationalities, is to apply for a conventional visa through an **Armenian embassy** abroad (page 70). The application form for a conventional visa can be downloaded from the Ministry of Foreign Affairs website (w mfa.am) and applications should be made to the appropriate embassy. The fees for a conventional visa are the same as for those obtained on arrival (see above). Visas for children under 18 are issued free of charge. Multiple-entry visas are only available through an embassy.

A third way of obtaining a tourist visa is to obtain an **electronic visa** over the internet. Simply go to the web page of the Ministry of Foreign Affairs (w evisa.mfa.am), complete the application page and pay the fee by credit card. The visa is normally issued within two working days and confirmation that it has been issued is sent electronically. It can then be collected on arrival. A valid e-visa allows entry through Zvartnots and Shirak International airports and the land border crossing points at Bagratashen, Bavra, Gogavan and Agarak. E-visas currently cost US$15 for a 21-day visa and US$60 for 120 days (so more expensive than obtaining either a visa on arrival or a conventional visa through an embassy).

For any type of visa other than a tourist visa, an invitation is required. In the case of **business trips** it must be certified by the Consular Department of the Ministry of Foreign Affairs or for private trips by the Passport and Visa Department of the Ministry of Internal Affairs. Multiple-entry visitor visas are available and transit visas may be required for stops in Armenia en route to other countries for nationalities not exempt from visa requirements. (For more details see the website of the appropriate Armenian embassy; page 70).

**Tourist visas can be extended** at the Passport and Visa Department of the Republic of Armenia in Yerevan (17/10 4th District, Davtashen; 010 530182; w police.am/en) for AMD500 per extra day. Locals (including taxi drivers) will know this by its old Soviet acronym of OVIR. Overstaying your visa carries a potential fine and you may be prohibited from returning to Armenia for a year or more.

**ARMENIAN EMBASSIES ABROAD**   See the website of the Ministry of Foreign Affairs of the Republic of Armenia (**w** mfa.am) for up-to-date official listings. For a list of foreign diplomatic missions in Armenia, see page 151.

## GETTING THERE AND AWAY

**BY AIR**   Yerevan has two airports: **Zvartnots International** (three-letter airport code EVN), 10km west of the city, and **Erebuni** (now used only by the military), closer to the centre on the south side. Direct air routes to and from Yerevan tend to reflect the locations of major Armenian diaspora communities within flying distance, particularly in Russia, Europe and the Middle East, though other routes have begun to spring up as tourist numbers increase. Zvartnots is fully up to international standards with signage in English as well as Armenian. Trolleys are available for AMD500 each or AMD2,500 for a trolley and a porter who will carry up to three items of baggage. Additional items of baggage are extra. **Note** that on leaving the airport the tag on your luggage may be checked against that on your ticket or boarding pass, so do not discard it. There is a duty-free area in arrivals after passport control, a small tourist information desk (not always staffed in the middle of the night) and a concierge for the official airport taxi service just before the arrivals exit.

The departure hall has a well-stocked **duty-free** area where there are typical Armenian specialities such as crafts, dried-fruit sweetmeats, coffee and herbal teas as well as the usual alcohol (including local wine and brandy which cost less here than in central Yerevan), perfume, clothes, luggage, etc, and a small range of books, mostly in Armenian. There is a small business lounge on the first floor, accessible via a lift that can be found within the duty-free area.

**Airlines flying to Yerevan**   Armenia's national carrier, Armavia, filed for bankruptcy and stopped operating in April 2013. In October 2014 its successor, Air Armenia, followed suit. Third time lucky: **Armenia Aircompany** (**w** armeniafly. com) is now the only Armenian airline operating international commercial passenger flights, serving destinations in Russia, the Middle East and Europe at the time of research.

Many foreign airlines operate routes to Yerevan. However, there were no direct flights from London at the time of research, nor indeed from most western European capitals besides those with significant Armenian communities (such as Paris and Vienna). Air travel from Europe to Armenia therefore tends to involve at least one change of plane and relatively high fares for the distance involved, due in part to the high landing fees.

Please note: as airlines change schedules frequently, these listings are intended only as an indication of the situation as of June 2018. A **full timetable** for Zvartnots Airport is available at **w** zvartnots.aero.

✈ **Aegean Airlines**   **w** aegeanair.com. Flies 3 times a week from Athens, with good connecting flights throughout Europe.

✈ **Aeroflot**   12 Amiryan St, Yerevan; **\** 010 532131; **w** aeroflot.ru. Flies 4 times daily from Moscow to Yerevan with good connecting flights throughout Europe & long-haul connections to the USA & elsewhere.

✈ **Air France**   9 Alek Manukyan St, Yerevan; **\** 010 512277; **w** airfrance.com. Offers 2 flights a week from Paris.

✈ **AtlasGlobal**   110 Nalbandyan St, Yerevan; **\** 011 345345; **w** atlasglb.com. Flies 4 times a week from Istanbul Apr–Oct, once a week Nov–Mar.

✈ **Austrian Airways**   9 Alek Manukyan St, AUA Business Centre, Yerevan; **\** 010 512201/2/3;

Zvartnots Airport office ✆060 373029; **w** austrian. com. Operates 4 flights a week from Vienna.

✈ **Brussels Airlines** **w** brusselsairlines.com. Commenced twice-weekly flights during the summer season in 2018.

✈ **Czech Airlines** 2 Baghramyan Av, Yerevan; ✆010 564099; **w** csa.cz. Resumed seasonal twice-weekly flights between Prague & Yerevan in 2018 after a 4-year hiatus.

✈ **flydubai** 7 Movses Khorenatsi St, Yerevan; ✆010 536774; **w** flydubai.com. Operates multiple daily flights from Dubai with connections throughout the Middle East, as well as Africa, South & Central Asia, & Europe.

✈ **Germania Airlines** Sidon Travel, 9 Nalbandyan St, Yerevan; ✆060 535251; **m** +374 77 522967; **w** sidontravel.am. Regular flights between Berlin & Yerevan commenced Jun 2018. This local travel agency is the authorised representative in Armenia.

✈ **LOT Polish Airlines** 7 Argishti St, Yerevan; ✆010 510284; **w** lot.com. Flies twice a week from Warsaw.

✈ **Mahan Air** Elite Voyage, 50 Nalbandyan St, Yerevan; ✆010 564045; **f**. Daily flights from Tehran. Tickets available in person from this agency on presentation of valid travel documents.

✈ **Qatar Airways** 3rd Floor, Yerevan Plaza Business Centre, 9 Grigor Lusavorich St; ✆060 380080; **w** qatarairways.com. Daily flights from Doha, with good long-haul connections worldwide.

✈ **Red Wings** **w** flyredwings.com. Fast-growing Russian carrier that launched direct flights from Moscow DME to Yerevan in spring 2018.

✈ **S7 Airlines** 34 Tumanyan St, Yerevan; ✆010 544110; **w** s7.ru. Twice-daily flights from Moscow with good connections to the UK via British Airways codeshares.

✈ **Ukraine International Airlines** 15 Mashtots Av, Yerevan; ✆010 531800; Zvartnots Airport office ✆060 373002; **w** flyuia.com. Flies 5 times a week from Kiev with good connections throughout Europe, with a new weekly service from Odessa starting Jul 2018.

In addition to the list above, a number of Russian and CIS airlines serve Yerevan on fairly limited and often seasonal schedules, which may be useful for long-term travellers on multi-country itineraries involving Central Asia and Russia. Direct flights to Yerevan operate from Aktau, Ashgabat, Astana, Krasnodar, Minsk, Novosibirsk, Odessa, Rostov-on-Don, Samara, Sochi, St Petersburg, Surgut, Voronezh and Yekaterinburg. Buying tickets can be an adventure, as many of the airlines have no offices in either Yerevan or at the airport. While tickets can be booked through a local travel agent, it is not possible to easily contact many of these airlines direct without knowledge of Russian, and the flights may not be included in online searches due to varying levels of non-compliance with IATA regulations. A similar situation awaits those who wish to fly to or from one of the many Middle Eastern destinations served by smaller airlines, including direct routes from Baghdad, Beirut, Damascus, Sharjah, Sharm-el-Sheikh, and Tel Aviv. Often the best source of information on the schedules of these airlines is the online departure board at **w** zvartnots.aero.

As an indication of cost of air travel from the **UK** as of August 2018 a return fare of £300 or less (economy fare, including taxes) from one of the London airports can usually be found if booked early enough. This figure can rise to £500–600 for travel in high season at short notice, or drop below £200 in the low season and if you are lucky with the timing of your booking. From UK airports outside London, a low-cost flight to one of the European hubs listed above followed by a direct flight to Yerevan can be a good option. In general, Aegean, Aeroflot, AtlasGlobal and Ukraine International tend to have the most reasonable prices, but cheaper fares can prompt low-budget travellers to fly to Georgia instead (particularly Kutaisi) and travel to Armenia by land.

Most **passengers transiting Russia** (who are not citizens of Armenia) no longer require transit visas as was the case in the past. Note, however, that passengers must have a connecting through ticket and must not leave the airside part of the airport. While Russian transit visas are not needed for foreigners spending less than 24 hours at the airport, they are required for a longer period. They can be obtained from the consular office at the airport (06.00–01.00 daily) although anyone who needs a Russian transit visa is strongly advised to obtain one before travelling.

**Airport transfer** The **city centre** can be reached via city bus number 201 (every 30mins 07.00–22.00, then once per hour 22.30–07.00; AMD300), with stops at Yerevan Central Bus Station, Republic Square and Mesrop Mashtots Avenue, terminating at Yeritasardakan metro station on Abovyan Street. The journey takes 20–30 minutes and the same price, schedule and stops apply to the return journey. **Airport Service** (↘010 595900, 060 430000; m 098 828200; e airportservice16@ gmail.com; w zvartnots.aero/en/taxi-service) is the official taxi service of Zvartnots Airport, which has a desk in the arrivals hall beyond customs. The English-speaking assistants will helpfully arrange your journey for you and take card payment if necessary. The journey takes about 20–30 minutes depending on your destination; expect to pay around AMD5,000–6,000 to the centre. You can save significantly by using a taxi-hailing smartphone app (page 87) or haggling with the unofficial taxi drivers who occupy the arrivals hall 24 hours a day – fares as low as AMD2,000 are not unheard of.

**Other international airports** Shirak International Airport (three-letter airport code LWN) at Gyumri has flights to and from a small number of Russian destinations (page 71).

**BY RAIL** Overnight trains between **Tbilisi** and Yerevan run year-round and are operated by South Caucasus Railways (↘184 from any Armenian number; w ukzhd.am). In the summer holiday season (15 Jun–1 Oct) the service is extended to the Georgian seaside town of Batumi and runs every day, taking at least 16 hours, though the travel time tends to decrease year on year as the service is upgraded. The train departs Yerevan at 15.25 and costs AMD11,000–27,000 to Batumi, depending on class (see below). In winter the service between Yerevan and Tbilisi runs on alternate days. From Yerevan it departs 21.30, arrives 07.50, is supposed to take 10½ hours, and costs AMD8,000–18,000. All tickets are offered at concessionary rates for children and teenagers. Because the alternate days are continuous, departure dates will not be consistently odd nor even, making it necessary to check either at the station, by telephone (↘184) or on the clunky website (w https://ticket.ukzhd. am//Pages/shedule.aspx). The return train from Tbilisi leaves at 20.20 and arrives in Yerevan at 07.00, but check times as well as days if intending to travel. En route the train calls at several stations, including Ayrum, Sanahin, Vanadzor, Gyumri and Armavir, but mostly at inconvenient hours of the night. When it comes to onward travel plans, it is worth mentioning that the service is not noted for its punctual arrival times.

The sleeper trains have three ticketing classes: *platzkartny* (third-class reserved seats in open carriages which convert into berths, often the most social option for the solo budget traveller); *coupé* (second-class closed compartments with sleeping berths for four); or *luxe* (first-class compartments for two). Third-class ticket holders will be asked to pay extra for bedding. Toilets on the train are not noted for their cleanliness, and food is not available, so bring some with you. The ride is highly scenic but the best bits are hidden in the dark except, to some extent, in midsummer. Border crossings also fall in the early hours of the morning, passport checks disturbing any chance of an uninterrupted night's sleep. Tickets, one-way, are bought at the stations and can be purchased up to about ten days in advance – highly advised during the school holiday season, when the trains quickly fill up with families of Armenian holidaymakers heading for the Black Sea coast.

**BY BUS** It is easy to travel by bus from either Georgia or Iran. There are also services from Turkey and Russia which in both cases travel via Georgia. Citizens of most Western countries, including most of those exempt from the Armenian visa requirement, should not need transit visas for Georgia. Nor, in theory, should a Georgian transit visa be required for holders of Armenian visas spending less than 72 hours in Georgia. If you do need a Georgian transit visa they can now be obtained at the border. Tickets should be bought in advance if at all possible. The baggage allowance on buses is 20kg with excess being charged at AMD250 per kilo. Most buses to destinations outside Armenia leave from Yerevan Central Bus Station (6 Admiral Isakov Av, just past the brandy factory on the road to Zvartnots Airport; \010 565370). This is also where agencies selling tickets to international destinations can be found.

**From Georgia** direct buses leave Tbilisi at 08.00 and 10.00 daily, taking 7 hours for the journey to Yerevan at a cost of about GEL44 (Georgian lari) (US$25). Drop-offs at destinations on the route can be negotiated and should cost less. The return service also operates at 08.00 and 10.00; the cost is about AMD10,000. *Marshrutkas* (minibuses) also travel between Tbilisi and Yerevan, approximately hourly 10.00–16.00, leaving when full. In both countries, bus tickets are purchased at the stations (Ortachala bus station and at the main train station in Tbilisi; Central Bus Station in Yerevan), and can be bought a few days in advance, though you can usually just turn up and get a seat. Minibus 'tickets' usually take the form of a direct cash payment to the driver; it is usually possible to pay in GEL or AMD regardless of direction. **Note** that times and routes can change so check locally if intending to use these services. At the time of research, the reconstruction of the Debed Gorge road has diverted many bus routes to Tbilisi via Dilijan and Noyemberyan, as opposed to the regular Vanadzor/Alaverdi route; it seemed likely that the work would be completed by the end of 2018.

**From Iran** the overnight bus leaves from Azadi bus terminal (ie: the western bus terminal) in Tehran daily at 13.00 and is scheduled to arrive in Yerevan 20–24 hours later, though the exact arrival time depends on how long is spent at the laborious border crossing. The fare is the equivalent of about US$50 in Iranian rials, which includes drinks, refreshments and a generously sized and comfortable reclining seat. Tickets can be purchased from Iran Payam No office at the bus terminal itself (\+98 21 44 669001/4), the office in the Armenian district of east Tehran (Narmak St, 85 Square, No. 44, Tehran; \+98 21 77 253878), or online (Iranian bank cards only) at w safar724.com. The southbound service leaves Yerevan at 10.00 daily; tickets cost AMD17,000 from Tatev Travel Agency (19 Nalbandyan St, Yerevan; \010 524401; w tatev.com). Both directions include a stop on the outskirts of Tabriz to drop off and pick up passengers, and two stops for meals at roadside restaurants. As Armenia's popularity grows among Iranian tourists, multiple daily departures are being added, particularly around Persian New Year and other Iranian public holidays.

Coming **from Turkey**, buses operate between Yerevan and Istanbul via Georgia, leaving Istanbul's Emniyet Garajı bus terminal on Thursdays between 09.00 and 10.00. From Yerevan, buses depart on Saturdays at 07.00 and Sundays at 10.00. The service is aimed primarily at Armenians living in Istanbul and is scheduled to take

36 hours, including two international border crossings. While the fare is cheap at the equivalent of US$50, it is a long and hellish ride, likely only of interest to those with vast amounts of luggage or who have a serious aversion to flying. The advice is to check details before travelling and to book a ticket three to seven days in advance at the bus station agency Rob Tours (\010 519006; m 096 519006, 093 471032). Most nationalities can buy a Turkish visa on arrival at the border crossing, but do check before travel.

## HEALTH  *with Dr Felicity Nicholson*

All travellers to Armenia should ensure that they are up to date with **immunisation** against tetanus, polio and diphtheria (now given in the UK as an all-in-one vaccine, Revaxis, which lasts for ten years), and hepatitis A. Hepatitis A vaccine (eg: Havrix Monodose or Avaxim) comprises two injections given about a year apart. The course costs about £120 (but may be available on the NHS), it protects for 25 years and can be given even close to the time of departure. Travellers to more remote areas or those visiting friends and relatives may be advised to be vaccinated against typhoid fever. In addition, some visitors, depending on what they are likely to be doing, may be advised to have protection against hepatitis B (see below) and rabies (see opposite). Visitors should ensure that they take any essential medications with them as drugs can be difficult to access. Medications may have totally different names even when transliterated.

Consider also taking antibiotics with you (available only on prescription in the UK). **Tuberculosis** is very common in Armenia, with an average annual incidence of greater than or equal to 40 cases per 100,000 people. The disease is spread through close respiratory contact and occasionally through infected milk or milk products. The vaccine is usually only recommended for those aged 16 or younger who will be spending three months or more living and working with the local population. For those aged 17–35, a case-by-case assessment needs to be done. The vaccine is less effective the older you are, so it would only be used for those over the age of 35 if they had never been vaccinated and were going to Armenia as health-care workers.

**TRAVEL CLINICS AND HEALTH INFORMATION** A full list of current travel clinic websites worldwide is available on **w** istm.org. For other journey preparation information, consult **w** travelhealthpro.org.uk (UK) or **w** wwwnc.cdc.gov/travel (US). Information about various medications may be found on **w** netdoctor.co.uk/travel. All advice found online should be used in conjunction with expert advice received prior to or during travel.

**MALARIA** In 2011, the World Health Organization (WHO) granted Armenia malaria-free status. Previously it occurred in the Ararat Valley, roughly between Khor Virap and Yeraskh, with the Armash fishponds (an area popular with birdwatchers) being especially implicated. Anyone planning to spend significant time at the Armash fishponds is advised to check the current status of malaria in Armenia.

**HEPATITIS B** Vaccination against hepatitis B can take six months to become effective and as the disease is most likely to be picked up through inadequately sterilised needles or syringes the best way of avoiding it may be to take an emergency medical kit which contains these items. Do note, however, that a shorter course is available if there is no time for the full course. Three injections are needed for the best protection and can be given over a three-week period if there is time for those aged 16 or over. The shortest course for those under 16 is two months. **Hepatitis A** vaccine can be given in combination with hepatitis B, as Twinrix, although two doses are needed at least seven days apart to be effective for the hepatitis A component and three doses are needed for the hepatitis B. Hepatitis B vaccine is always recommended when working in medical settings and also with children. Children aged 1–15 can be vaccinated with Ambirix, which consists of two doses a year apart so one dose is sufficient before travel. When the course is completed there is long-term protection against both diseases.

**RABIES** Vaccination is essential for anyone likely to be in close contact with animals or for those who are going to be more than 24 hours from medical help. Pre-exposure vaccination comprises three doses over a minimum of 21 days, and all three doses are required to change the treatment needed should you be exposed. If you have had all three pre-exposure doses, then you still need two more doses of vaccine if you are bitten or otherwise exposed, the first ideally on the day of exposure (or as soon afterwards as possible) and the second post-exposure dose three days later. If you have not had the pre-exposure doses you will need rabies immunoglobulin (RIG), which is expensive (around US$800 a dose) and is often unavailable. Post-exposure prophylaxis should be given as soon as possible although it is never too late to seek help as the incubation period for rabies can be very long.

Rabies is spread through an infected bite, scratch or lick even on intact skin from any warm-blooded animal. Dogs are the most likely source in Armenia. If you think you have been exposed then wash the wound immediately and thoroughly with soap and running water for about 10 minutes. Then douse the wound with iodine or a strong alcoholic solution (vodka may be the most immediately available) and go straight to medical help.

**Note** that it is important to seek medical help even if you have had the full three-dose course of pre-exposure immunisation, as explained above. Inform the medical staff of exactly what immunisation you have, or have not had – this can save a lot of worry, and unnecessary expense. Medications, including vaccines, have to be paid for in Armenia.

**TRAVELLERS' DIARRHOEA** Like anywhere else, travellers' diarrhoea can occur in Armenia and visitors should take the usual sensible precautions such as handwashing before eating. Tap water is generally safe to drink thanks to recently upgraded mains water infrastructure, though individual sensitivity obviously varies. The water from Armenia's many natural freshwater springs (page 104) is safe. Free public drinking water fountains, known as *pulpulak*s, are common in all urban areas; note that they are fed by the same sources as the taps. Bottled water is easily available. Where the water quality is dubious, brush your teeth with bottled or boiled water. Food such as fruit and cheese bought at markets for picnics should be well washed in the spring water which flows at most picnic sites. Food you have washed and peeled yourself, and piping hot foods, should be safe. Raw foods, cold cooked foods, salads which have been prepared by others and ice cream are potentially risky, and foods kept lukewarm in hotel buffets may be dangerous, but do keep a sense of proportion.

**SUN** Remember that Armenia is a sunny country and that the lower temperatures at the higher altitudes can mask the strength of the sun. Particularly for outdoor pursuits, sunscreen (SPF 30+), a wide-brimmed hat and appropriate sunglasses should not be forgotten.

**SNAKEBITE** Armenia is home to several venomous snake species, at least three of which are considered deadly. Snakes rarely attack unless provoked, usually preferring to get out of the way of humans as soon as they detect any vibration. Wear stout shoes and long trousers in areas where there may be snakes. Avoid long grass and areas of loose rock, or else stamp your feet or hit the ground with a stick or walking pole to alert any nearby snakes of your approach. Most snakes are harmless and even venomous species will dispense venom only in about half of their bites, so even if you are bitten you are unlikely to have received venom. Many so-called first-aid techniques such as cutting into the wound or applying a tourniquet are dangerous and do not work. The only effective treatment is antivenom. If you are bitten by a snake which you think may be venomous:

- Keep calm. It is likely that no venom has been dispensed.
- Prevent movement of the bitten limb by applying a splint.
- Keep the bitten limb below heart height to slow the spread of any venom.
- If you have a crêpe bandage wrap it round the whole limb (eg: toes to thigh) as tightly as you would for a sprained ankle.
- Evacuate to a medical facility which has antivenom. If within an hour's drive of Yerevan go to the Republican Hospital, Department of Toxicology, 6 Margaryan Street (reception: 010 340020; toxicology dept 010 343166) or, for children, to the Muratsan Hospital Complex, 144 Muratsan Street (010 450230). All main hospitals in the regions should have antivenom.
- NEVER cut or suck the wound.
- NEVER give aspirin. Paracetamol is safe.
- DO NOT apply ice packs.
- DO NOT apply anything to the wound.

Treatment with antivenom requires identification of the snake. Ideally the snake should be killed, if that can be done safely, and taken to show the doctor. Beware! A dead or even a decapitated snake can still exhibit a bite reflex and can leak venom through its fangs. It is wise to handle it with a stick and transport it in a leak-proof container. For a well-referenced depository of information about snakes in Armenia, see w herp-am.narod.ru/Armposn.htm.

**HIV/AIDS**  As of 2016 the CIA World Factbook estimates the prevalence rate at about 0.2% of the adult population. This compares with the prevalence rate in the UK of around 0.2% and in the USA of 0.6%. If you must indulge, use condoms or femidoms, which help to reduce the risk of transmission.

**HEALTH IN ARMENIA**  Life expectancy remains among the highest in the CIS at 71.6 years for men and 77.7 for women (according to the World Health Organization). The health-care system in Armenia has been undergoing significant reforms and improvement although there remains much to be done. The focus has been on strengthening primary health care: rebuilding or modernising local outpatient units and providing them with new equipment; merging outdated, dilapidated and inefficient hospitals; retraining doctors and nurses and aiming to provide specialist services in the regions, not just in Yerevan. The World Bank (through the Health System Modernisation Project) is assisting the Armenian government in its aim to modernise the health system and improve the key health indicators of the population.

A **reciprocal health agreement** for British citizens, which meant that health treatment (excluding drugs but including dental) was free on producing a UK passport, lapsed in 2016. Most UK-based insurers define Europe as including Armenia in their travel policies. Many US health insurance policies do not include Armenia so special cover needs to be purchased. In spite of improvements, the UK Foreign Office and the US State Department still advise that medical facilities are generally poor, especially outside Yerevan. It is prudent for all visitors to ensure that their insurance will cover repatriation, or at least evacuation, in the event of serious illness or accident.

Visitors at the time of research still had to cope with a fair amount of **passive smoking**. Cigarettes are produced locally and consumed in large quantities; around 58% of men over 20 smoke, one of the highest rates in Europe. Public awareness of the risks of smoking has been growing thanks to health warnings on cigarette packets and the fact that advertising is banned except at point of sale. Recent years have seen some cafés and restaurants adopting a no-smoking policy; see the excellent online map Smoke Free Yerevan (w smokefreemap.arthurdolmajian.

> **TICK REMOVAL**
>
> Ticks should ideally be removed complete, and as soon as possible, to reduce the chance of infection. You can use special tick tweezers, which can be bought in good travel shops, or failing this with your finger nails, grasping the tick as close to your body as possible, and pulling it away steadily and firmly at right angles to your skin without jerking or twisting. Irritants (eg: Olbas oil) or lit cigarettes are to be discouraged since they can cause the ticks to regurgitate and therefore increase the risk of disease. Once the tick is removed, if possible douse the wound with alcohol (any spirit will do), soap and water, or iodine. If you are travelling with small children, remember to check their heads, and particularly behind the ears, for ticks. Spreading redness around the bite and/ or fever and/or aching joints after a tick bite imply that you have an infection that requires antibiotic treatment. In this case seek medical advice.

com). A broad spread of **prohibitions** on smoking in public places (including cafés, bars and restaurants) were due to come into force by the end of 2018; listings in this edition of this guidebook no longer highlight non-smoking establishments on the assumption that such information will be redundant by the time of publication, but delays in legislation are of course possible.

## SAFETY

Most visits to Armenia are trouble free. Crime levels are low, but visitors should of course take sensible precautions. Generally, the risk of being a victim of crime is statistically much less likely than in most western European and American cities, and this notion is supported by countless anecdotal accounts of safe and trouble-free visits. Far greater risks are either tripping up on pavements in need of repair after dark or else falling into holes dug during the pavement's reconstruction. Watch out, too, for missing manhole covers. These risks have reduced, at least in the centre of Yerevan, but can still be a problem elsewhere.

The military situation does mean that all areas along the 1994 ceasefire line with Azerbaijan should be avoided because of the presence of snipers on both sides, exchanges of fire between which still happen on a regular basis, affecting civilians living in the vicinity. The road from Ijevan to Noyemberyan, for example, is specifically warned against by British government-issued travel advice, but it is not the only afflicted area. There remains a serious problem in areas of Nagorno Karabagh from **mines** and unexploded ordinance (page 370), as well as in adjoining areas of Armenia that experienced fighting. To the best of the authors' knowledge, all places mentioned in this guide are safe to visit and sights where the unresolved conflict means that safety is problematic have been excluded or specifically highlighted as such. However, visitors to Nagorno Karabagh who do encounter difficulties should note that consular services are unavailable there. Those wishing to procure more detailed information on the threat of landmines should refer to the websites of the HALO Trust (w halotrust.org) for Nagorno Karabagh or the Armenian Centre for Humanitarian Demining and Expertise (w chde.am) for Armenia itself, including the borders between Armenia and Nagorno Karabagh.

Visitors must not attempt to cross the borders with Georgia or Iran apart from at the recognised border crossings. Visitors are unlikely to be in great physical danger (unless attempting to swim the River Arax) but are at risk of being detained and questioned by the authorities, sometimes simply for taking photos within the vicinity.

Armenia's death rate in road-traffic accidents has historically been proportionately much higher than that in much of the West, despite considerably lower traffic levels. The Armenian figure is likely to grow even further as the improved roads tempt drivers to higher speeds and increasing traffic levels mean that it is even more dangerous than it was previously to drive round blind bends on the wrong side of the road. In fact the old pot-holed tracks, where speeds inevitably stay low as drivers seek to avoid the deepest ruts, have undoubtedly helped to keep the accident rate down. The legislation dating from Soviet days making the wearing of seat belts compulsory is now actively enforced by the traffic police, as are speed limits (page 89). Soviet-era vehicles with few or no safety features are gradually being ushered out by modern imports with airbags, seat belts and other such novelties.

Pedestrians should be extremely careful at pedestrian crossings. Often drivers do not give pedestrians priority at such crossings, even though there is a hefty fine if caught disobeying. Be especially aware of traffic turning right at crossroads and of drivers running red lights.

Telephone numbers for the **emergency services** are: **Ambulance** 103; **Fire** 101; **Police** 102. Dialling 911 will also work for general emergencies.

**WOMEN TRAVELLERS** There are no general safety problems for women as the strongly traditional family values ensure that they will not receive unwelcome attention; certainly, in cities and at the popular tourist sights. However, solo female travellers in remote, rural areas where foreigners are rarely encountered should take precautionary steps to avoid normal friendly behaviour being misinterpreted, as cultural misunderstandings have been known to happen.

## NOTES FOR TRAVELLERS WITH A DISABILITY    *Mark Davidson*

As Armenia is a former republic of the Soviet Union, attitudes towards travellers with disabilities are still very much entrenched in the communist era. However, like other countries in the region, it is slowly changing to reflect outside influences as it tries to increase its tourist trade for those with disabilities.

**PLANNING AND BOOKING** There are few specialist travel agencies running trips to Armenia. Companies such as Visit Armenia (w visitarm.com) may be able to offer trips to the area.

**GETTING THERE** The main airport in Armenia, Zvartnots International Airport, has facilities for those in wheelchairs including disabled toilets and other amenities. However, Shirak International Airport may lack the same facilities.

**ACCOMMODATION** A number of hotels in Armenia have wheelchair access, such as the Grand Hotel Yerevan (14 Abovyan St, Yerevan; 010 591600; w grandhotelyerevan.com; page 138) or Best Western Congress Hotel (1 Italy St, Yerevan; 010 591199; w congresshotelyerevan.com; page 138).

**VISITING PLACES** Armenia has a number of historical sites and many will be difficult for wheelchair users to gain access to. Garni Temple, for example, has a number of steps and may cause problems for those who struggle on their own unless they are accompanied by an assistant.

Unfortunately, public transport does not have full access which may cause problems if you are unable to board buses unaided.

**TRAVEL INSURANCE** Many UK-based insurers consider Armenia part of Europe for the purposes of their policies; check the small print or call to confirm. A number of operators offer policies for people with pre-existing medical conditions, including Orbis ( 0845 338 1638; w orbisinsurance.co.uk). If you intend to do any amount of mountain hiking, ensure that your policy includes cover for trekking at appropriate altitudes.

Medical facilities within Armenia are improving but still limited. The main hospitals in Yerevan are somewhat basic but are able to cater for those travellers who are in wheelchairs or have impediments. Hospitals in other parts of the country lack the facilities of those in the capital, though modernisation is taking place. In remote areas the nearest military hospital is often the best bet.

**OTHER TRAVELLERS** Armenia has very few facilities for visitors with **mobility issues,** although ramps for wheelchair access have appeared in one or two hotels, and pedestrian infrastructure upgrades now tend to consider wheelchair users. Subway steps feature death-defyingly steep wheelchair ramps from Soviet times: it may not be wise to attempt these alone.

**Travelling with children** is not a problem from the social aspect. They are welcome anywhere. Family life is important to Armenians – they would find the concept of a child not being allowed into a restaurant, for example, very strange. Nappies and baby food are available in Yerevan and other major towns, often from pharmacies. Most restaurants and hotels will respond to parents' requests about food preparation. In Yerevan, the Grand Candy café (54 Mesrop Mashtots Av; ✆010 565686; w grandcandy.am) is specifically geared towards children and some other cafés have play areas. There are funfairs near the cathedral and in Victory Park and amusements for smaller children in Children's Park on Beirut Street. Some swimming pools have facilities for children, for example Waterworld, and good weather brings out street amusements in a number of towns. See below for advice on taking children to historical sites.

**Homosexuality** was decriminalised in 2003 but is still an unacceptable lifestyle in Armenian society. The website of the NGO Pink Armenia (w pinkarmenia.org) provides a contemporary perspective on the ongoing social challenges facing the LGBT community. The British government advises homosexual travellers to exercise discretion in Armenia. It is common in Armenian culture to see two female friends holding hands in the street and not uncommon to see two men hug and kiss each other in greeting; these signs of affection are not an indication of sexual orientation.

**OTHER DANGERS AND ANNOYANCES** The **traffic police** who used to spend much of their time stopping motorists for 'routine checks' (and who were reputed to seek bribes) are now more usefully employed enforcing the seat belt laws, speed limits and, more recently, the law forbidding littering by motorists. They do still sometimes stop cars for routine document checks (page 90), particularly those with foreign number plates. Foreign drivers who believe they are being incorrectly accused of a traffic violation should ask to see the respective law in writing and to see video footage from the camera installed in every traffic police car.

As mentioned elsewhere in this guide, there is a general danger from earthquakes, poisonous snakes, deep holes concealed by long grass at several sites, and various other hazards ranging from the potential for dehydration when it's hot to the possibility of frostbite when it's cold. The vast majority of visitors suffer none of these, although it is rather difficult always to take precautions against **earthquakes**. It's worth noting that old Soviet-era apartment buildings are among the more vulnerable. If visiting such flats, be aware that the staircases are often in poor condition with limited illumination. (The US Federal Emergency Management Agency gives advice on what to do during an earthquake at w ready.gov/earthquakes.)

It is necessary to **supervise children** very closely at many historic sites. Do not expect Western health and safety standards, with warning signs and guard rails, to have reached all parts of Armenia. Apart from the deep holes concealed by long grass, and the snakes, which find convenient lairs in the piles of fallen stones, much of the masonry of less-frequented buildings is precarious and Armenian castle builders were adept at siting their fortresses on the top of precipices. Even at touristy places such as Noravank the cantilevered steps which give access to the second floor of the mausoleum require considerable care. To reach a few of the less popular sites requires a tough hike and appropriate footwear – it may not be a long walk to Baghaberd, for example, but it is extremely steep and made difficult by unstable scree and a lack of clear waymarking.

Hikers in general and visitors to some of the more remote sites should beware of **giant hogweed** (*Heracleum mantegazzianum*, or *borshevik* in Russian and *bldrghan* in Armenian). This is a tall plant of the family Apiaceae, endemic to the Caucasus, whose white flowers are held in flat-topped umbels, recognisable to many as a giant version of common cow parsley or angelica. The plant needs a constant supply of water and sunlight, and thus can often give away the location of a spring or stream in the mountains or a forest clearing. While on a hot summer's day this creates the temptation to beat a path to the water source, the juice of the stem in combination with ultraviolet rays (ie: sunlight) causes **phytophotodermatitis**, manifesting as severe blisters followed by long-lasting scars. If your skin comes into contact with this liquid you should wash it off with fresh water immediately. The hollow stems sometimes tempt children to use them as peashooters with the result that their lips and hands are burned and require treatment. (Curiously enough, this noxious weed is also pickled and eaten.)

## WHAT TO TAKE

Apart from obvious items such as **walking boots**, **sunglasses**, a **mobile phone** and a compass if you're going hiking, or **binoculars** if you're birdwatching, there are a few other items which are best brought into the country. Any **medications** that you may need should be brought as these may be difficult to obtain, particularly away from Yerevan. Consider bringing a small **torch** or head torch and carry it around, as it is needed when visiting the subterranean rooms at a few sites and may also be useful on the stairs of Soviet-era flats, in poorly lit subways and in bedrooms where the light switch is sometimes a long way from the bed. **Memory cards** are easily obtainable and printing of digital images readily available. **Digital camera batteries** are hard to find – a good place to look for them is at Zigzag photographic chain (page 151). **Clothing** is largely dependent on the time of year, the altitude of the places visited and activities planned, but do note that Armenians recognise foreign tourists by their casual clothes, with shorts, flip-flops and sun hats a dead giveaway. Armenians regularly dress much more smartly and stylishly than most Westerners, particularly women. If there is any likelihood of being invited for dinner into somebody's home, or going to an orchestral concert or the opera, it is worth taking something smarter. Note that Armenian women generally do not have piercings other than their ear lobes, men do not wear earrings, and tattoos are very uncommon. The temperature can change rapidly during late April/early May, going from chilly conditions to warm summer in a couple of days, with thunderstorms frequent. Likewise, in October you may be walking around Yerevan one day in short sleeves and sandals and the next day be wishing for gloves. At these times of year it is advised to take layers of clothing and a jacket for cool mornings and evenings, as well as waterproofs appropriate to your activities.

Armenia's **electricity** supply is at a voltage of 220V and a frequency of 50Hz. It uses standard continental European plugs with two round pins. This means that British and Irish appliances need only a simple cheap **adaptor** to match their plugs with Armenian sockets. Such adaptors are easily bought at home but cannot easily be found in Armenia except on arrival at the airport so they should be taken. However, in North America electricity is supplied at 110V and 60Hz. This means that American appliances require not only an adaptor (to cope with the different

Binoculars are a fabulous tool for getting close to nature – seeing animals well without disturbing them. But with hundreds of models available, and prices ranging from £20 to £2,000, selecting the right pair can feel daunting – whether it is an inaugural purchase or an upgrade. This guide aims to help.

**BUYING BINOCULARS: THE BASICS** To start, three guiding principles. First, what's right for me may not be for you. Binoculars are a personal thing, so never buy without testing. Second, prepare for trade-offs between weight, performance, practicality and price. Third, buy the best you can afford. You get what you pay for. My Swarovski 'bins', bought in 2004, remain as brilliant as on day one.

Binoculars are described in off-putting jargon. So let's explain the basics. Binocular names include two numbers, respectively the magnification factor and objective lens diameter (in mm). An 8x56 binocular magnifies objects by eight times through a 56mm-wide lens. Larger numbers usually mean heavier and more cumbersome binoculars, which are less convenient for travelling. I advise sticking to the ranges 7–10 (magnification) and 30–56 (lens). Avoid apparent marvels such as 20x50 'ex-army' binoculars, which are rubbish and heavy!

The ratio between the two numbers influences how much light the binocular lets in – and thus how bright the image is in dingy conditions. The larger the ratio, generally, the better such low-light performance. I favour a ratio of 1:4 (eg: 8x32) or 1:5 (eg: 8x42); but up to 1:7 (eg: 8x56) may enhance use in shady forests or at twilight.

Numbers aside, binoculars are either 'roof-prisms' (H-shaped, slimline) or 'porro-prisms' (M-shaped, chunky). For tight budgets, porro-prisms arguably offer better value. Although pricier, roof-prisms tend to be better quality, easier to handle and more compact for travelling. All things being equal, they get my vote.

shape of the pins of the plug) but also a **transformer** to cope with the different voltage. These should be bought before leaving home, though they can be found at bigger markets such as Petak. In addition American devices where the mains frequency is important (such as electric clocks) will not work correctly in Armenia. Also in the case of computers and hi-fi equipment it is necessary to check whether or not particular components will function correctly on frequencies of both 50Hz and 60Hz.

Very few Armenian sinks have **plugs**, even in Western-style, modern hotels. If you want to be able to fill a sink with water, take a one-size-fits-all plug with you.

Visitors considering any amount of **hiking**, **cycling** or **camping** (or other specialist outdoor pursuits) are advised to bring all necessary equipment; while not impossible to find in Armenia, such equipment is still relatively rare, often poorly maintained or of poor quality, and expensive.

## MONEY AND BUDGETING

**MONEY** Armenia is still very much a **cash-based society**, particularly outside Yerevan. Some hotels and shops accept credit cards, but many do not, cash or bank transfer being the only accepted form of payment in many smaller regional hotels and restaurants. The same is true of taxis, though some of the available apps do offer a card payment feature. When card payments are accepted they tend to be

**TESTING BINOCULARS: WHAT TO LOOK FOR** Pick them up. Is the weight evenly distributed? Can you hold them steady? Spectacle-wearers need eyecups that roll or slide so that the binocular offers 14–17mm of 'eye relief'. Now look through the optics. You want a wide field of view – but no need to go overboard. Ensure the image is sharp, ideally right to the edge of vision. How close can you focus? If you anticipate watching insects, choose a pair that focuses on your feet. Check that colours look natural – with no blue or yellow cast. Finally, examine a backlit object: if it is fringed yellow or purple, choose another pair.

**WHAT MAKES BINOCULARS REALLY GOOD?** Consider each candidate binocular's finer characteristics, which sort wheat from chaff across years of service. 'Fully multi-coated' lenses and prisms are recommended; they maximise light transmission, contrast and clarity. Look for an image so sharp it sears your eyes. Extra-low dispersion (ED) or high-density (HD) lenses correct colour fringing. Depth-of-field is important: you want to minimise time spent refocusing from a close animal to a distant one. Durability is key: seek high-strength but ideally lightweight housing. Weatherproofing is vital to keep out dust and water. Finally, if things go wrong, you want the manufacturer to stand by its product, offering a lifetime warranty. There's a reason why my Swarovskis go on … and on …

*James Lowen (w jameslowen.com) is a wildlife expert, award-winning writer and author of four Bradt wildlife titles.*

restricted to cards issued on the Visa or MasterCard (as well as the native ArCa) networks; American Express is rarely accepted. Bus and train tickets tend to be cash only and cannot be bought online. Even if relying on ATMs and card payments in towns and cities, remember that in more remote places you will need to take all of your cash with you. (The low crime rate means that carrying more cash than you would normally do at home is safer than might be imagined.)

Armenia has **ATMs** in all major towns operated by various banks, either hole-in-the-wall types or standalone units in supermarkets, most of which accept international cards – look for the logos by the machine advising what cards will work there. Maximum daily withdrawal limits vary; the bank VTB (in Russian script *ВТБ*) seems to have the highest at the time of research (your domestic bank will also impose a limit). Small-denomination notes are available and tend to be preferred for small purchases: consider withdrawing AMD99,000, for example, instead of AMD100,000.

With the increased prevalence of ATMs it is no longer essential to bring all your funds in cash, but this is still an option. It is very easy to **exchange** US dollars, euros, roubles or pounds sterling at one of the innumerable exchange offices, banks or supermarket kiosks in the country. It is usually possible to exchange other currencies in the centre of Yerevan. There is less concern now about accepting notes in less than pristine condition, but it can still prove difficult to get rid of ones which are torn or marked.

After the collapse of the Soviet financial markets, the Armenian dram (officially abbreviated to AMD) replaced the rouble as the national currency on 29 November 1993. Each dram is made up of 100 luma, though the subunit is mainly nominal. The initial exchange rate was US$1 = AMD14, but by the end of 1994 this had inflated to US$1 = AMD400. It has fluctuated in the years since but generally held steady: at the end of June 2018 the 30-day average rate was US$1 = AMD483, £1 = AMD642 and €1 = AMD564. There were originally five denominations of banknotes: AMD10, 25, 50, 100 and 200. Inflation subsequently forced the addition of AMD500, 1,000 and 5,000 notes. In 1997, these were superseded by a second series of banknote depicting famous Armenian males. These notes depict: AMD500 – Alexander Tamanyan (1878–1936; page 162; note rarely seen); AMD1,000 – the poet Yeghishe Charents (1897–1937; page 56); AMD5,000 – the writer and poet Hovhannes Tumanyan (1869–1923; page 55); AMD10,000 – the poet Avetik Isahakyan (1875–1957; see box, page 56); and AMD20,000 – the painter Martiros Saryan (1880–1972; page 59). An AMD50,000 note was introduced in 2001, dedicated to the 1,700th anniversary of the adoption of Christianity, which depicts Etchmiadzin; and an AMD100,000 note in 2009, depicting King Abgar V of Edessa, a vassal of Tigran the Great, though sightings of these higher denominations are rare. In 2017 a commemorative new AMD500 note depicting Noah's Ark, Etchmiadzin Cathedral and Mount Ararat was issued. Notes up to and including AMD500 have now been replaced by coins, though the AMD500 note is technically still legal tender. In 2018 a third series of banknotes was due to be issued, commemorating the 25th anniversary of the national currency and adding a new AMD2,000 note but omitting the AMD100,000 note. At the time of research the new designs were yet to be unveiled.

Although all purchases in Armenia should be paid for in drams, there are a few places where dollars are welcome. Vernissage market in Yerevan is one: most of the stallholders even quote prices in dollars (though they will of course accept drams).

**BUDGETING** Apart from Western-style hotels, which charge Western prices, most things of interest to visitors are cheap. It is difficult to spend much more than AMD5,000–6,000 on a full meal at a regular Armenian restaurant, and a street snack will cost AMD100–1,000. In a café an Armenian coffee will cost AMD150–300, a cappuccino AMD1,000–1,500, while a half-litre of local beer in a bar or café costs AMD600–800. When thirsty in the countryside, you can make free use of one of the excellent freshwater springs, but you can buy a litre bottle of water for under AMD250. A 90g block of local-brand chocolate to keep you going will set you back about AMD400–450 while a Mars bar is AMD250–300. A loaf of local bread or a sheet of *lavash* for your picnic will cost AMD80–150. Fruit and salad ingredients bought in markets or at roadside stalls are cheap when in season, eg: tomatoes might cost AMD200/kg. Postcards home cost between AMD300 and AMD500 with an additional AMD240 for postage; and the T-shirt to prove that you've been to Armenia is priced between AMD3,000 and AMD6,000.

Public transport fares are low and the longest minibus journey from Yerevan (to Meghri) costs AMD5,000. The longest train journeys, such as from Yerevan to Gyumri on the regular daily service, cost AMD1,000. Car hire with driver is often cheaper than without for anything but the smallest and cheapest of hire cars, but don't necessarily expect a new vehicle. Typical rates are AMD25,500–27,300 per day for a private car or AMD32,760–59,000 for a 4x4 including fuel; prices will depend on the cost of fuel. The driver's expenses such as meals and accommodation must also be met if he is away from home.

A standard antibiotic such as ciprofloxacin might cost AMD1,000 for 10 tablets; paracetamol or ibuprofen AMD200 for 10 tablets.

**Tipping** in restaurants is discretionary, but the etiquette is much the same as in Europe at approximately 10% of the bill. Taxi drivers do not expect to be tipped but it might be prudent if a lot of waiting or luggage loading and unloading has been involved. If you have engaged the services of a guide, interpreter or driver and are pleased with their performance you may wish to show appreciation with a tip – again 10% is standard.

## GETTING AROUND

Note that all public transport fares quoted are for a single journey unless stated otherwise. Return tickets are not sold.

**BY RAIL** There is only a handful of domestic train services, but some of them may be of use to visitors, as well as providing a break from the (often hair-raising) taxi and marshrutka journeys. Travelling by train is also relatively cheap. Tickets are bought at stations. A timetable, in Russian, is available on request at Yerevan's main railway station (see below), and electronic departure boards list the day's services. Timetable and ticket price information is available at w ukzhd.am, but this may differ from the real situation as timetables change from year to year (and according to season). Do check times before travelling, either by visiting the station in person or by calling ✆ 184 from any Armenian mobile or landline phone (English is spoken). Trains are, on the whole, efficient, although relatively slow. It is possible to book tickets and seats up to 40 days in advance, although (with the exception of the summer service to Batumi) trains are rarely so busy that seats can't be found.

To reach Yerevan's **main railway station**, take the metro to Sasuntsi Davit station which adjoins the railway station. The station is open 24 hours; the international ticket office is open 09.00–18.00, the local ticket office 07.30–19.30. Daily trains leave for **Gyumri** (AMD1,000) at 7.55, 14.25 and 18.25; journey time 3 hours, 10 minutes. Return departure times are 8.25, 11.45 and 1815. There are frequent stops en route at many towns in Armavir and Shirak provinces; see the published schedules for detailed information. A weekend express service (Fri–Sun only; AMD2,500) commenced operations in March 2018, with departures from Yerevan at 10.00, returning from Gyumri at 17.10. Another useful route is from **Yerevan to Hrazdan** (AMD300), extended in summer (approx 15 Jun–30 Sep) to **Sevan** (AMD600) and **Shorzha** (Sat–Sun only; AMD1,000). Trains run daily except on Wednesdays. They do not, however, leave from the main railway station but from **Kanaker** station in Yerevan's northeast suburb of the same name. The station is hidden down a narrow winding lane which heads eastwards off the northern section of Zakaria Kanakertsi Street. A small sign, in Armenian and Russian and attached to a gas pipe, points the way. (The train actually starts at **Almast** station in Yerevan's Zeytoun district. You can embark here, but the station consists simply of a platform whereas Kanaker station is staffed – not that it matters, as tickets are purchased on board.) Winter trains leave Kanaker at 08.30 and 19.25 (10mins earlier from Almast) and arrive in Hrazdan 1½ hours later. They leave Hrazdan for Kanaker at 07.15 and 18.40. The summer extension arrives in Sevan town

2

at 10.50, and terminates in Shorzha at 12.10. The return train leaves Shorzha at 16.30 and stops at Sevan town at 18.00. Dates of the extension to Sevan/Shorzha are decided on an annual basis and times can change, so check beforehand.

Virtually the whole of Armenia's operational rail network is electrified at 3,000V DC. The track has the standard Soviet gauge of 1.524m rather than 1.435m which is the norm in western Europe and North America. Apart from the passenger services round Yerevan, which are operated by multiple units, other trains are hauled by twin-unit locos of class VL10: VL stands for Vladimir Lenin. They were built at Tbilisi, Georgia, and Novocherkassk, Russia, between 1967 and 1977. The many railway tracks, crossings and bridges elsewhere in Armenia, such as in the Aghstev Valley between Dilijan and Ijevan, raise obvious questions about the infrequency of passenger services today. As well as various goods trains still operating, it's worth remembering that in Soviet times the international rail network would carry passengers as far afield as Iran, Russia, Azerbaijan and Turkey. The abandoned rail infrastructure is, unfortunately, all that's left, though talk of recommissioning various sections of these lines still bubbles away.

**BY BUS** All towns and cities are linked by **minibus** (marshrutka or *mashrutni*) services, and a few larger **buses** ply some of the same routes, costing a little less and taking a little longer. They are cheap: the maximum minibus fare to Stepanakert or Meghri, both of which are several hundred kilometres away, is just AMD5,000. Minibuses are driven more recklessly than buses and are consequently considerably quicker, if somewhat more challenging to the sensitive passenger! Yerevan is the central hub for almost all routes: when travelling between the north and south of the country by bus, it is invariably necessary to travel via the capital.

While it is possible to go almost anywhere you might want to go either by minibus or with a combination of minibuses and taxis, the problem for the visitor tends to be finding out where the bus leaves from and at what time, as this is very much dependent on the whim and demand of the almost exclusively local Armenian clientele. Outside of Yerevan, timetables are not formalised or available online. Public transport sites and apps such as **w** rome2rio.com are unlikely to have any reliable information on such services. Although many routes leave from the Central Bus Station, many leave from other places, resulting in there being about half a dozen additional bus stations in Yerevan (see box, opposite). Their locations usually correspond to the direction in which it is easiest to exit Yerevan towards their destination. The locals will generally ask someone who knows or who knows someone else who knows; Armenia is small enough for the grapevine approach to work very effectively. Visitors may be best off following their example and asking at their hotel, hostel or homestay, whose staff will probably be able to find what you need to know with a few phone calls. If you have arranged accommodation ahead in another part of Armenia, the staff there will probably be able to tell you how best to get there from your current location.

At the time of writing, Yerevan Central Bus Station can be reached by minibus routes 11, 13, 23, 24, 33, 59, 68 and 75, and bus routes 2, 5, 23, 31, 47, 56, 67 and 68; however, do check (say 'Kilikia?' inquisitively to the driver) when boarding as routes change frequently. The station is a large A-frame building which functions from 07.00 to 17.00, with left-luggage lockers available the same hours. There are a couple of decent cafés nearby and various street food options in the vicinity. Almost all international bus services depart from and arrive here.

The details on the opposite page of the stations from which buses/minibuses of possible interest to tourists depart are an indicative guide only; changes are frequent. Note also that buses are gradually being replaced by minibuses on many routes.

## BUS AND MINIBUS DEPARTURES FROM YEREVAN

This information is current at the time of research (June 2018). Note that you are advised to check bus times before travelling; phone numbers are provided where available. Places of departure are subject to change; happily, the trend seems to be to consolidate departures from fewer locations.

**Central Bus Station (aka: Kilikia)**  6 Admiral Isakov Av; ✆ 010 565370. Reachable by many bus/minibus routes from the city centre. Departures to: Alaverdi, Aparan, Armavir, Artik, Ashtarak, Etchmiadzin (Vagharshapat), Jermuk, Maralik, Spitak, Stepanakert (Nagorno Karabagh), Stepanavan, Tashir, Vanadzor.

**Gai Bus Station**  Gai Av, Nor Nork, 1st district, just down the side street by the Mercedes-Benz showroom. Reachable via several bus/minibus routes. Departures to: Garni, Goght.

**Intertown Bus Station**  Sevan St, adjacent to (west of) the main railway station. Best reached by metro (Sasuntsi Davit station). Departures to: Abovyan, Agarak, Artashat, Ararat, Dvin, Goris, Gyumri, Kapan, Meghri, Norashen, Sisian, Urtsadzor, Vayk, Vedi, Yeghegnadzor.

**Northern Bus Station**  1 Tbilisyan Hwy; ✆ 010 621670. Reachable via bus route 259. Has a timetable posted on the door. Departures to: Berd, Chambarak, Dilijan, Gavar, Ijevan, Martuni, Noyemberyan, Sevan, Vanadzor, Vardenis.

**Raykom Bus Station**  24 Azatutyan Av at the junction of Nersisyan St. Reachable via several city bus routes. Departures to: Arzakan, Hrazdan, Tsaghkadzor.

Large towns often have minibus services to local villages; ask locally at the bus stations. Information is provided in the regional chapters of this guidebook where available. Minibuses other than those provided by organised tours do not serve tourist sites per se: a taxi is often the only practical way to reach such sites. For particularly large groups it is worth noting that private bus and minibus hire is possible, best organised by a local travel agent (page 67).

**BY TAXI**  Taxis in Armenia are so plentiful and cheap that they are often treated as if they were another form of public transport, even for intercity and international journeys: taking a taxi from Yerevan to Tbilisi can prove surprisingly cost-effective if shared with other passengers. Bus stations and other transport hubs always have plenty of waiting taxis but be wary of being ripped off; they can also be flagged down in the street (look for a green light in the windscreen), and if you see a taxi stationary at the side of the road then it is probably available. You are also well advised to avoid taxis without meters wherever possible and to insist that a meter be switched on if the driver does not immediately do so. On the whole, taxi firms and drivers do not speak English, so if phoning for a taxi it is best to ask your hotel or host to do it for you. A more convenient arrangement for non-Armenian-speaking visitors – at least in and around Yerevan – is to download and use a regional **smartphone taxi app**, such as ggTaxi, UTaxi or Yandex, which will summon a driver to your precise location and comes with the added bonus of displaying the price of the journey on screen.

On top of a minimum charge of AMD500–700, prices are in the order of AMD100–120/km for a regular car to AMD200–250/km for a larger and/or more luxurious vehicle. If you are hiring a private taxi for a long journey, be sure to agree the price before setting out. Most journeys within central Yerevan cost less than AMD1,000 and should rarely exceed AMD500–700 within the very centre. Telephone numbers of some reliable Yerevan taxi firms are given on page 133.

**BY AIR** While no **domestic passenger airlines** yet operate in Armenia at the time of research, there are Soviet-era aerodromes on the outskirts of most of the main regional cities (some still used by the military), and interest has been shown by the government and the private sector in reviving domestic commercial aviation on this basis. The Prime Minister's 2017 end-of-year report mentioned that the General Department of Civil Aviation was assessing the potential for developing the sector, and US$2 million was meanwhile invested in the **reopening of Kapan airport** in the far south of Syunik province. The first scheduled passenger flights were set to commence in June 2018, with the price of a one-way ticket announced at AMD20,000, but the resignation of the provincial governor (who was personally involved in its funding) in the aftermath of the Velvet Revolution appears to have stalled the project. Such a service, if it does one day come to fruition, would cut the journey time from Yerevan to Kapan from 5–6 hours by (bad, mountainous) road to about 40 minutes by air on a 19-seater Czech-made L-410 Turbolet. Flights would operate according to Visual Flight Rules (VFR), ie: during daytime only and subject to visibility. While the intended market is clearly businesspeople involved in south Syunik's mining operations, it has been commented that the service could also serve to boost tourism to the city and surrounding region, which currently sees a tiny fraction of visitors to Armenia, in part due to the region's perceived remoteness and the inconvenience of travel. It remains to be seen whether this will prove to be the case, or whether other provincial airports will follow suit, but the basic infrastructure is – theoretically – already in place.

Armenia's first **charter helicopter** flights were announced in 2018 by the private firm Armenian Helicopters (**m** 044 888333; **e** info@armheli.com; **w** armheli.com).

**DRIVING** The **road network** in Armenia is based on infrastructure developed under Soviet rule, and as such the driving rules and road layouts will be familiar to those who have driven in other former Soviet and Eastern bloc countries. As a rule of thumb, routes between towns and cities tend to be paved to varying levels of quality, whereas local access roads to and between villages set off from these routes tend to be of dirt. Much improvement in the state of the roads has taken place since the struggles of the 1990s, but many roads remain poorly maintained and pot-holes continue to be a problem (see box, page 89). Drivers will also encounter assorted livestock, either going out to pasture in the morning, returning in the evening or simply grazing on the roadside. The latter are not usually much of a problem being either tethered or looked after by a nearby herder.

Vehicles drive on the right and drivers must give way to the right, even on roundabouts, unless the road you are on is signed as the through road by the main-artery yellow-square sign. It is only permitted to turn left across the carriageways in places marked with a dashed white line. Crossing a solid white line in the middle of the road – even to overtake a slow-moving vehicle – is an easy way of violating the rules, and you may be fined if caught doing this. Dual carriageways may have either a solid white line or an actual central reservation; in any case they will have a central slip lane or a section of dashed white line for left turns. In the absence of either, the procedure is to carry on past the turn-off you want, do a U-turn at the next signed U-turn location, drive back to the junction you wanted and turn right. The same procedure is followed when turning on to a dual carriageway when there is not a tunnel, overpass or crossroads: turn right and continue straight until you can make a U-turn on to the desired carriageway at an official location. Be aware that vehicles may be slow or stationary in the outside lane while performing these manoeuvres themselves, so what you may think of as the 'fast lane' is not necessarily so where these left-turn or U-turn

The publisher has requested that roads on the maps be marked according to whether they are **tarmac** or **dirt** roads. This distinction undoubtedly has some value but it can also be misleading: tarmac roads are not always good roads, likewise a dirt road is not necessarily synonymous with a bad road. There are four main categories of road surface in Armenia: good tarmac (often extremely good); bad tarmac (occasionally appallingly bad); dirt (which can sometimes be good but which is much more likely to be difficult); and narrow jeep tracks which should only be tackled with a serious 4x4, in good weather and with a driver who is used to such terrain. The tarmac/dirt distinction is useful in wet conditions. Some dirt roads become seas of mud after rain. This applies especially to roads within villages, where the daily passage of animals from their accommodation within the village to the fields and back ensures that village streets end up like farmyards.

Armenia's roads have improved enormously in the past 20 years. Most major routes now have good tarmac, and the international-standard highway known as the North–South Road is under construction. There can be problems with pot-holes, especially after the severe winters which are the norm in Armenia. Perhaps even more difficult than the pot-holes themselves are the stretches of road where pot-hole repair is under way and rectangles of road surface have been removed but not yet made good.

Some tarmac roads have had no maintenance for many years and are in a bad condition, sometimes so bad that local drivers have created multiple alternatives by going off-road. These 'off-road' dirt tracks may be noticeably better than the road itself. Occasionally one comes across a bad stretch on a road which is otherwise good. The transition can be disconcertingly abrupt.

As soon as one turns off a main road one is likely to encounter a dirt road; but not always as there is a programme of upgrading rural roads. Regard such surfaced side roads as a bonus! There is a handful of really good dirt roads but these are exceptions.

Throughout the book we have tried to indicate where road conditions are other than standard. Of course a road surface can change quickly, for the better with upgrading or for the worse with adverse weather conditions.

locations exist. If you need to stop, do so on the hard shoulder, which on busier roads are usually generously wide (and often inhabited by locals selling their produce).

Name signs for entering/leaving a village or town relate to the administrative area of the settlement – it may be some way to the first building. Conversely, if the village is located off the main road, the exit sign may be just a few metres after the entry sign.

**Speed limits** are 60km/h within settlements (as demarcated by the name signs), 90km/h on rural roads (except parts of the new North–South Road where it is 100km/h) and 40km/h in tunnels (for which headlights are compulsory). Speed cameras have been installed in many places, both in Yerevan and on rural roads. The traffic police are proactive in stopping drivers who break speed limits; police are obliged to show a driver photographic or video evidence, which should include the number plate, place and time of the alleged speeding offence. The amount of any fine relates to how much over the speed limit the car was travelling, starting at AMD10,000. **Seat-belt compliance** is also being enforced, with fines for any driver or front-seat passenger not wearing one. Rear seat belts are not compulsory, though obviously recommended. For infringements the driver is issued with a note of the fine which must be paid at a bank or at an automated payment terminal within 30 days.

In **winter**, the main through routes are generally kept clear of snow, though it may be a day or two after heavy snowfall before the snowploughs finish clearing all the roads. Winter tyres are not compulsory but are strongly recommended. Access is still possible to most permanently inhabited villages, but this is inadvisable in anything other than a 4x4 and with experience of driving in such conditions. Snow chains are not readily available and those seen on 4x4s in rural areas are probably homemade. You may be lucky enough to find them in a specialist vehicle outfitting shop such as Avtoapakineri Ashkhar (9 Artsakh Av, Yerevan; \010 431101), which also sells a range of **4x4 accessories**.

Drivers must carry their licence and proof of vehicle insurance in their name at all times. You can drive in Armenia on an **International Driving Permit** (IDP 1949), which is only valid when presented together with your domestic licence. Drivers of **foreign-registered motor vehicles** must carry valid temporary importation documents for the vehicle, which are issued at land borders upon entry; a modest 'ecological tax' is levied with the exact fee depending on the emissions class of your vehicle. The duration of your permit can be up to 30 days. Compulsory third-party insurance must also be purchased from one of the many kiosks if you haven't made other arrangements. Overstaying with a vehicle can incur a fine, so if you plan to keep your foreign-registered motor vehicle in Armenia for longer than your original permit allows, you must apply for an extension at the vehicle customs processing facility in the southern suburb of Noragavit (127/21 Arshakunyats Av; \060 547304; w customs. am). The correct entrance to the enormous warehouse is at the building's northern corner. Ignore the queues on the ground floor and proceed up the stairs inside the entryway to the first floor to begin the process, which should take less than an hour. Extensions of up to one year can be obtained free of charge; bring photocopies and originals of the documents issued at the border, your passport's photo page and your car's registration documents, and be aware that your vehicle may be requested for inspection in person. The alternative is simply to leave and re-enter Armenia at one of the road border crossing points. The driver named on the original permit must be in possession of the vehicle when it departs, ie: another driver cannot take the vehicle out of Armenia on your behalf.

**Unleaded petrol** (*benzin*) is available from roadside filling stations in three categories: regular (92 octane), premium (95 octane) and super (98 octane). Regular diesel is also widely available (but rarely the cleaner-burning Euro diesel). At the time of update, regular cost AMD450 per litre, premium AMD470 and super AMD490. Diesel cost AMD470 per litre. Many vehicles in Armenia are dual-fuel, petrol and gas (CNG, compressed natural gas), gas being significantly cheaper at AMD180 per cubic metre. Gas filling stations are usually separate from petrol and diesel stations. When filling up with gas, all occupants must leave the vehicle: a waiting area of variable comfort is usually provided, and refreshments if you're lucky. Petrol, diesel and gas are readily available in towns and on main routes leading out of towns, but stations are less frequent when off the main roads. As everywhere, it is sensible to fill up before embarking on a long journey. Consider carrying additional fuel if heading off-road for extended periods. In a pinch, most Armenian men will be familiar with the process of syphoning fuel from a tank through a hose and will probably be able to rustle up the equipment to do it.

Roadside garages (ie: mechanics' workshops) are ubiquitous throughout the country, perhaps due to the swarms of ageing Soviet automobiles still plying the roads that break down on a daily basis. This means that in case of **breakdown** you'll never be far from a tyre change or similar basic operation. For a more serious issue, especially with a modern vehicle, you are better off visiting the official dealership or service centre, which will almost certainly be in Yerevan, where most major automobile brands are represented. A flatbed truck (*evacuator*) to transport a broken-down vehicle can be found easily enough; most towns will have a few parked up on the main streets waiting for business, especially near popular filling stations, and the phone number of the driver will usually be shown on the side. The ggTaxi app also allows evacuators to be ordered.

Those looking for **basic parts** (tyres, batteries, bulbs, etc) and repair shops should look on Hrachaya Kochar Street and Nar-Dos Street in Yerevan, which are the main districts for auto repairs.

**Parking**  With the increase in traffic, on-street parking in central Yerevan can be a problem. It is free except in private areas (where a fee of AMD100–200 will be collected, usually by an elderly man, on leaving) and in the red-line areas. These on-road red lines, together with yellow noticeboards (Armenian and English) detailing fees and how to pay, cover all administrative areas of the city. The first 5 minutes are free; thereafter it is AMD100 per hour; 500 per day; 1,000 per week; 2,000 per month; and 12,000 per year. Hourly and daily payments can be made via SMS, the fee being taken from a prepaid mobile phone account. Other rates can be paid by bank transfer at any bank branch or online. The system is policed by both fixed and mobile surveillance cameras and there is a fine of AMD5,000 for non-payment.

**Pedestrians**  Especially in Yerevan, it can feel as if drivers are completely oblivious to pedestrians. Great care should be taken when crossing roads, even at signalled pedestrian crossings. Vehicles approach at high speed with apparently no intention of stopping. Drivers turning right are allowed to proceed at pedestrian crossings if there is no-one crossing but should otherwise give priority to pedestrians. Failure to do so carries a fine, if caught, of AMD30,000 but the risk of being caught must be slight, given the number of drivers who flout this law. Pedestrians can be fined AMD3,000 for jaywalking; use subways or pedestrian crossings wherever possible.

**Car hire**  Cars can be hired with or without a driver. Many local tour operators (page 67) can arrange private car hire, tailoring car and driver to particular requirements. For all car hire, a valid driving licence and passport must be presented, a refundable deposit is required, and payment is by credit card. Other terms and conditions, including minimum age, vary between firms.

Several **international car-hire companies** are established in the country and have offices and/or pick-up locations in Yerevan and Zvartnots International Airport. Rates range from AMD22,000–100,000 per day; 4x4 options are available and if you are planning any serious off-road driving it is advisable to hire a truly capable vehicle (as opposed to a 4x4-style SUV designed for road use). **Local** competition is provided by an increasing number of companies in Yerevan (page 92), some of whom offer that rarest of opportunities: to hire and drive a Lada Niva. All firms must ensure that their cars comply with regulatory standards including MOT.

*International companies*

🚗 **Enterprise**  5/1 Northern Av (within Ibis Hotel), Zvartnots International Airport; 📞060 376060; m 099 376060; w enterprise.com

🚗 **Europcar**  8/1 Abovyan St; 📞010 544905; m 099 586822, 096 400044; e info@europcar.am; w europcar.am

🚗 **Hertz**  7 Abovyan St; 📞010 584818; m 091 480485; e info@hertz.am; w hertz.am

**Sixt** 10/1 Northern Av (within North Avenue Hotel), Zvartnots International Airport; ☎010 505055, 060 373366; m 096 660361, 091 373366; e info@sixt.am; w sixt.am. Head office at Fora LLC, 42 Acharyan St (Avan district).

*Local firms*

**ArTourRent** 10/6 Pushkin St; ☎010 566359; m 094 383890; e info@artourrent.am; w artourrent.am

**Autorent** 13/2 Zakyan St; ☎010 547766; m 091 347766; e info@autorent.am; w autorent.am

**Caravan** 50a Mashtots Av (next to Nairi cinema, entrance from Isahakyan St); ☎010 529292; m 098 559292; e info@caravan.am; w caravan.am. Car hire with or without driver.

**Hyur Service** 96 Nalbandyan St; ☎010 546040; 19 Sayat Nova Av (within Ani Hotel); ☎010 541903; m 093 504040; e contact@hyurservice.com; w hyurservice.com

**Tourorent** 4 Tigran Mets; ☎010 541025; m 093 462212; e tourorent@gmail.com; w tourorent.am

**HITCHHIKING** Light traffic and poor transport links make hitchhiking sometimes more of a necessity than a preference if you don't have your own means of transport. Western fears surrounding the practice would be seen as paranoia in the far more trusting culture of Armenia. This means that hitchhiking, as well as being generally safe, is also extremely easy – it is not unlikely that the first car you flag down will stop to pick you up. In fact, there are few reasons one could not rely on it as a means of transportation around the country (much of the research for the fifth edition of this guidebook was undertaken by hitchhiking). Beware, however, of dead-end roads to sites of interest that may see precious little traffic on the return journey, particularly later in the day. The usual global precautions apply: solo female travellers may be more comfortable hitchhiking with a partner; keep your valuables on your person; and trust your intuition. In Armenia specifically, be aware that drink-driving is an issue, so don't be afraid to stop and get out if you suspect a driver is over the limit. Be aware also that your generous car-owning companion may sometimes turn out to be a taxi driver at the end of the journey; establish before anything else that you are expecting a free *avtostop*, not a paid taxi ride. It is not customary to offer payment for the journey, though it would be polite to offer a contribution on a longer trip if the driver stops to refuel.

## ACCOMMODATION

Yerevan has a vast range of hotels within the central area. Some visitors might prefer, particularly in midsummer, to stay outside the central district, where a few good options also exist. Expect to pay Western prices at the upmarket international hotels. There are also some less expensive hotels, mostly built in the Soviet era for tourist groups and since renovated. Small mid-range hotels are plentiful. Budget travellers have a number of hostels to choose from. An alternative is a homestay (bed and breakfast). For those staying longer than a few days, renting an apartment is an economical option. More information about Yerevan accommodation is given on page 137.

Outside Yerevan accommodation is improving and good hotels are available in most of the places tourists are likely to want to stay. Some of these hotels are newbuilds while others are **renovated Soviet-era hotels**. The latter vary from barely acceptable to excellent. There are still some Soviet-era hotels that were used to house refugees in the early 1990s, have never recovered, and are not recommendable unless you are on the lowest of budgets and there are no other options. Soviet-era hotels tend to be renovated and reopened floor by floor as resources become available. A chain of upmarket **Tufenkian hotels** (w tufenkianheritage.com) has been developed in restored buildings. Though they are no longer the only upscale hotels rural Armenia has to offer, they aim to showcase Armenian history and culture with furnishings handmade by Armenian artisans from local materials in a modern yet distinctively Armenian style. There are four Tufenkian hotels – on Lake Sevan, in the Debed Canyon, in Dilijan and in Yerevan.

Some hotels have **self-catering facilities**. These may be in the form of **cottages** or *dachas* – separate small buildings which can accommodate between four and eight persons, although the number is flexible as extra beds can often be erected. Such cottages in Soviet times tended to be in hotels with large grounds and were originally for families spending the whole of their holiday in one place. However, the concept of cottages has been happily adapted to new establishments and it is quite common for a hotel to comprise several small buildings rather than one large building. This preference for individual units can also be found in restaurants where instead of one large dining room there are multiple private rooms each with a single table.

Another feature of the Soviet era was the **residences** run by various bodies to provide accommodation for their members while on holiday. They are therefore usually in pleasant surroundings. Some of these have been sold off, while in other cases they remain in the hands of the original owner. It is possible to stay at most of them and they are generally inexpensive. The standard varies enormously. The privatised ones are usually well managed, some having been upgraded, some still needing a lot of new investment. Soviet-era residences were usually large establishments offering a variety of activities as well as accommodation. Now renovated, such establishments often call themselves 'hotel resorts'. This usually means that the hotel offers a number of facilities (such as sauna and swimming pool) as well as activities (various sports, horseriding, etc) all within the hotel complex.

Yet another feature of the Soviet era was the **spa hotel** or **sanatorium** which provided various therapeutic treatments for guests. More and more of these are being upgraded, most noticeably in the town of Jermuk. They combine their medical and hotel functions and are often relatively inexpensive for the facilities offered. It is perfectly possible to stay there without being a patient but prices usually include treatment (and full board) whether you take it or not.

**Motel**-type accommodation, often associated with roadside eating places on the main routes, is increasing. Such accommodation is generally aimed at locals on long journeys or professional drivers. **Hostel** accommodation in Armenia is still very limited. There are several backpacker hostels in Yerevan (page 139) but very few elsewhere. When hostels are advertised in provincial towns they rarely resemble the communal dormitory-style establishments to which Western backpackers and

## ACCOMMODATION AT A GLANCE

Where cards are accepted it is noted under individual reviews (with the exception of Yerevan where most hotels do accept cards); otherwise, it is better to assume establishments are cash only. Within price code categories hotels are listed in alphabetical order. Prices are for a standard double/twin room in high season. Breakfast and tax are included unless otherwise stated.

2

**HOTEL PRICE CODES**

| | |
|---|---|
| $$$$$ | AMD60,000+ |
| $$$$ | AMD45,000–60,000 |
| $$$ | AMD30,000–45,000 |
| $$ | AMD15,000–30,000 |
| $ | <AMD15,000 |

budget travellers are accustomed. Instead they are more like basic guesthouses and often found in converted homes.

Travellers to the provinces looking for a more cultural experience are strongly recommended to stay at **homestays** (Armenia's term for bed and breakfast establishments, operated within family homes), which are available seasonally throughout the country and provide a real insight into Armenian family life – particularly as convivial and generally excellent meals can be organised. Giving your business to homestay owners is also a powerful means of spreading earning opportunities around the country and directly to those providing the service, as opposed to big businesses and middlemen – particularly important in a country such as Armenia where rural life is hard and income prospects limited. The one real snag is, of course, the language barrier: Russian, not English, is the second language for most rural Armenians. Many visitors enjoy homestays in spite of this, as Armenian hospitality is invariably warm, good-humoured and attentive.

Homestays can be arranged through a Yerevan travel agent (page 67) or one of the few regional information centres; don't expect to find more than a handful of those available on online maps and booking websites, and then only in the towns, rather than the villages. Particularly where options are few, proprietors in a given region will often know each other; your host may be able to arrange accommodation with a partner homestay further down the road. (It is also not unknown for tourists simply to ask around when they arrive in a village – indeed in many villages it may be the only choice. Of course there is an element of pot luck in this method, but it is impossible to imagine a foreigner being left stranded without a bed. Ad hoc accommodation will always be offered eventually, and offering a fair contribution towards the cost of your stay is encouraged.)

Expect to pay about AMD10,000–12,000 for a twin or double room including breakfast. Solo travellers can expect to pay AMD5,000–6,000 for single occupancy of the same room. Dinner is normally AMD3,000–5,000 per person, including drinks. You will need to give the host enough time to prepare an evening meal (eg: requesting it at breakfast time or the previous day) but you'll get a feast. A lighter meal of salads, cheese, etc can usually be provided at much shorter notice. If you want to drink beer or wine, it's usually best to buy it in advance yourself, as you'll probably otherwise be presented with a choice of homemade spirits or sweet red wine, which are an acquired taste to most Western palates. Even if you cannot manage to stay, do try to fit in one or two home-cooked meals. As with homestay accommodation, such meals can be organised through a Yerevan travel agent. While the water situation (page 37) has improved greatly in most parts of Armenia, some rural places still face difficulties and water may only be available for limited periods each day. Occasionally you may have to fill the WC cistern by ladling water stored in the bath. Hot water may not be continuously available or may be restricted to a single heat-on-demand electric shower. Bedrooms will be typically be private rooms with two to three single beds each (double beds are uncommon). There will usually be one bathroom for everyone, shared between you and the household.

**Rented accommodation** can be arranged through Yerevan travel agents or some online booking sites and is a good option for those wishing to stay for more than a day or two. The price varies according to the standard and size of apartment; expect to pay AMD14,000–27,000 per day for a one-bedroom apartment. Many Soviet-era flats have an unpromising approach, with dark, dilapidated stairways and lifts that do not always function, but the flats themselves are usually renovated to modern standards and are spacious and comfortable. A spate of construction means that rented accommodation in newly built Western-style apartment blocks is now more common than in years gone by, though they aren't necessarily any more comfortable or well located than a renovated Soviet-era flat. Hyur Service (page 67) can arrange rented accommodation; also try Airbnb (**w** airbnb.com) or **w** booking.com, or **w** list.am for longer-term rentals if you don't mind negotiating with the landlord yourself.

It is generally acceptable (and indeed practical in remote mountainous areas) to **camp** anywhere, except on what is obviously private property. Pasture lands tend to be unenclosed and access is therefore rarely an issue. It is prohibited in the State Reserves but is tolerated in National Parks. Campers should be aware of the responsibility they have to conserve the environment, and practise Leave No Trace principles. There are very few permanent campsites with facilities as found in the West; those that do exist are mentioned in our regional accommodation listings. In their absence, it is sometimes convenient to make use of *besedka*s (a Russian word meaning 'pavilion'; the proper Armenian word *taghavar* is never used). These are simple open-sided picnic shelters often found near popular sites of natural beauty in the countryside and are usually close to a spring. They often have primitive barbecue facilities. Some tour operators (page 67) include overnight camping during their treks; these are usually in established locations used by local guides and outdoor groups in order to reach specific sites or on established trekking routes. Again, the best-known locations are mentioned in the relevant chapters of this guide.

The **accommodation price codes** (see box, page 93) used in this guide are based on the price of a double room in peak season, usually late May/June to the end of October, although for accommodation in winter-sports areas winter is the peak season (and here, at weekends, it can be very busy). Even in the peak summer season it should not be difficult for individual visitors to find accommodation

## FINDING AN ADDRESS

Addresses in Armenia can be confusing, at least to visitors from the UK. It is the whole building, sometimes covering a large area, which is numbered rather than individual premises or entrances. Thus, several shops may all have the same address because they are in the same building and two addresses, eg: numbers 2 and 6 on the same street which look as if they will be fairly close together, can be a surprising distance apart. If a building occupies a corner site with wings on two (or more) streets the whole building has a number relating to one of the streets on which it stands. Premises in that building, even if their entrance is from another street, will still give the first street as their address. It is quite common therefore to have to go round the corner to get in. For example, the Jazzve café with an address of 8 Moskovyan Street in Yerevan is actually on parallel Isahakyan Street, as the building stretches round three sides of a square. If an address number has a suffix, such as 4a or 4/1, it is possible that it is round the back of the building. Most large blocks have courtyards round the back and many premises are entered via these courtyards, particularly residential apartments in buildings where shops occupy the ground floor. The address may even be in a separate building within a courtyard or in a row of buildings behind the row which fronts on to the street.

However, the familiar pattern of even and odd numbers on opposite sides of the street is used, as is numbering buildings from the town centre outwards.

Practical Information    ACCOMMODATION

2

although the choice is obviously greater if you book in advance. Groups do need to book in peak season. Prices usually include **breakfast**; where this is not the case the cost is stated in individual accommodation entries. Breakfast rarely costs more than AMD2,000. A few hotels do not include **tax** in their price; again, this is noted in our reviews. As explained on page 82, Armenia is a cash-based society and, although cards are becoming more widely accepted, most accommodation (apart from big hotels in Yerevan and some other towns) has to be paid for in cash. Where an establishment outside of Yerevan accepts **cards**, this is noted under individual reviews in this guide. Although the position may change, it should be assumed that cards are not accepted in locations beyond Yerevan unless it is positively stated that they are. Some hotels offer lower prices outside their peak season. One person occupying a double room will usually pay less than two people occupying the same room – the iniquitous single-occupancy surcharge has not reached Armenia. Often there will be a range of prices for double/twin rooms in hotels. The price depends on the size of room and whether there is a separate sitting room.

## EATING AND DRINKING

Traditional Armenian cuisine has much in common with Turkish, Persian or Arab cooking, all of whose empires at one time made subjects of the Armenians. It has much less in common with the cooking of Russia, which also ruled Armenia but whose cuisine reached the country relatively recently and is unknown in diaspora communities elsewhere in the world. Russia's culinary legacy can be seen on the shelves of any mainstream supermarket and on most restaurant menus, as well as in some forms of street food. (Note that most Armenian foodstuffs bought in supermarkets tend to carry the date of manufacture, not to be confused with a best-before date which may also be included. Packaged perishable goods such as dairy products carry use-by dates.)

In comparison with the diversity, freshness and seasonality of dishes experienced in an Armenian household, the menus of mainstream restaurants and hotels tend to be repetitive and predictable. Most restaurant menus, especially away from Yerevan, feature little more exciting than *lavash*, cheese and a few Russian-style salads followed by barbecued meat and vegetables. Therefore, the only way most visitors can begin to appreciate the range of Armenian home cookery is to include in their itineraries homestays (page 94) with dinner included, or else to book a meal in a private house through a travel agent. Having said that, it is also true that the quality, variety and number of restaurants, especially in Yerevan, has improved out of all recognition since Soviet days when surly staff informed customers that everything they asked for was unavailable and meals took hours as the staff vanished for a rest. Nowadays, the problem for unaccustomed foreigners is quite the reverse: main courses may arrive before the starter is eaten! This is not poor service; it is due to the normal Armenian custom of serving everything together at once. Avoid this if you wish by ordering one course at a time, or by specifying the timings, about which some restaurant staff will now ask you in advance. Otherwise, embrace local tradition, order a spread of dishes and have these placed in the middle of the table so everyone can sample a little of each.

The quality of ingredients is extremely high because Armenia produces a wide range of excellent fruit and vegetables as well as meat (pork, chicken and lamb), much of which comes from smallholdings and can be considered as natural as anything in the West with an 'organic' certificate on it. Red meat in particular is as free-range as it gets, with industrial livestock farming more or less unheard of

– the herds that block provincial roads on a daily basis are a testament to this. Beef tends to disappoint, not just because it is cooked to oblivion but because it is predominantly from Caucasian brown cattle, a breed developed between 1930 and 1960 by crossing Swiss brown bulls with cows of the local lesser Caucasus breed. The resulting meat does not compare to Aberdeen Angus, Beef Shorthorn or Hereford; nor has classic French butchery made it this far east. The practice of eating beef and lamb fresh rather than hanging it after slaughter also tends to make it tougher and less flavoursome than in the West. For these reasons, many will order meat dishes made using minced beef and lamb rather than whole cuts.

The quality of Armenia's **fruit and vegetables** is notable, partly because Armenians grow what the climate favours, partly because the produce has not travelled from another continent, and partly because flavour is considered more important than size or appearance. Apricots, native to Armenia, are probably the most famous produce, but throughout the growing season you'll find market sellers and the ubiquitous roadside vendors piling their stalls with peaches, nectarines, multicoloured cherries, apples, pears, quinces, grapes, figs, pomegranates, plums, melons, watermelons, tomatoes, squashes, aubergines (eggplants), peppers, asparagus, cucumbers, courgettes (zucchini), sweetcorn, onions, potatoes, carrots, peas, beans, cabbages, okra, a whole range of mushrooms and herbs, almonds, walnuts and hazelnuts – and that's just the cultivated examples. The world of wild herbs and vegetables, gathered by villagers and appearing alongside the more recognisable fare, is more fascinating still.

A staple ingredient of traditional Armenian cookery is **bulghur**. Traditionally it is made by boiling whole grains of wheat in large cauldrons until they begin to soften, upon which they are removed and dried in the sun. The grains are cracked open and the kernels divided into categories depending on size. This process ensures that they will keep for years without deteriorating. Fine bulghur is preferred for *keufteh* (page 101) while coarse bulghur is preferred for pilaffs and soups.

A warning to **vegetarians**: although it is extremely easy to have a meat-free diet in Armenia, some Armenian dishes may not be what they seem from the menu. For example, 'mushroom soup' or salad may contain as much chicken as mushroom and, because the ingredients may be chopped fine and mixed up together, it will be impossible to avoid the meat. **Vegans** will be troubled to find egg making its way into all sorts of unlikely things. Always ask before ordering.

**BREAKFAST** Most Armenians make do with a cup of coffee (*soorj*) or tea (*tay*) together with bread (*hats*) and butter (*karag*), jam (use the English word), honey (*mergh*) and cheese (*baneer*). Another preserve which may appear at breakfast is *muraba*, composed of various whole fruits in a thick syrup, although it can also be offered as a sweetmeat with tea or coffee, the syrup used to sweeten the beverage. Occasionally a version of a **tomato omelette** (*lolikov dzvadzegh* or simply *omlet*) will be offered, in which onions are first gently fried, then chopped tomatoes added and finally whipped eggs poured on (sometimes with a little cream and curry powder added) for the final cooking. Yoghurt (*matsoon*) and sour cream (*smetan* or *t'tvaser*) is also likely to be on the table. In smaller establishments you will be asked the evening before what you will want and when. In homestays the uneaten food from the night before (of which there will be a great deal, since Armenian hosts would never allow a dish to be emptied) will also be laid out. It is not unknown for the evening's undrunken brandy also to be proffered at breakfast. The main **Yerevan hotels** offer something considerably more than this (though minus the brandy) with a whole buffet breakfast available and a variety of omelettes, but this is pandering to

2

Western hotel eating habits rather than being authentically Armenian. Nor can one or two Soviet-style guesthouses which offer semolina and boiled beef be regarded as remotely Armenian. To cater for foreign tastes, various Yerevan cafés now serve up Continental-style breakfasts, including faithful reproductions of French croissants and pastries, and perhaps not quite so faithful Full English breakfasts. Breakfast is often served relatively late by Western standards, rarely before 08.00 and frequently not until 09.00.

On a special breakfasting occasion, visitors may encounter **khash**, which can perhaps be translated as 'cow heel soup'. Most Western visitors have trouble stomaching it, but a *khash* party is a staple Armenian ritual. *Khash*, which traditionally is never eaten by one person dining alone, is sometimes served in restaurants but usually it is a ritual for a group of friends who will have fasted the previous evening (though it is also known as a hangover cure). The cow heels (and sometimes other parts of the animal, such as the head or stomach) are boiled all night with neither salt nor herbs. By morning a thick, gelatinous broth has been produced and the meat has flaked off the bones. Just before serving at breakfast time, crushed garlic and salt are added. The broth is then eaten by crumbling dry *lavash* into it. The soaked *lavash* is traditionally transferred to the mouth using hands alone, though nowadays a spoon is normally used. It is always accompanied by greens, radishes, yellow chilli peppers and mineral water, and sometimes by red chillies and pickles as well. It is also accompanied by vodka (perhaps a better explanation for its hangover-curing effects), ideally mulberry vodka (*t'ti oghi*), of which considerable quantities are drunk in a series of toasts, the first of which is '*Bari luys*' ('Good morning') and the last of which is to the maker of the *khash*.

**LUNCH** Many restaurants start serving meals by noon and service is continuous until late evening. Armenians argue that one should eat when one is hungry rather than be guided by the clock. Traditionally, though, lunch is a fairly light meal with the main meal being taken after work. For visitors, lunch is often an excuse to buy some fresh produce at the market. The basis for *hats paneer*, meaning 'bread and cheese' and local slang for more or less any lunchtime picnic, is **lavash**, Armenia's classic flatbread (see box, opposite) which is traditionally unleavened. It is baked rapidly in an oven set into the ground called a *tonir* and comes in the form of large, thin sheets which cool just as rapidly as they cook but are irresistible when still hot. Usually eaten fresh on the day of baking, lavash can be readily stored by allowing it to dry, then sprinkling a little water on it before eating. In villages where there is no market people still bake it in their own houses, often several women saving on fuel and having a social morning by baking bread together, each making enough to last the family for a few days or longer.

Tomatoes, cucumbers and mixed herbs, together with cheese and/or sour cream, make an excellent filling. Other possibilities obtainable at any market are the spiced dried meats such as *basturma*, which is dried, salted and flattened beef surrounded by a dried mixture of paprika, garlic and cumin, or *sujukh*, which is spiced and salted minced beef (sometimes mixed with pork or lamb) formed into a sausage and then dried. In the Sevan area, smoked fish can be bought to make another variant.

An alternative lunch would be to call at one of the roadside **barbecue** stalls which are common on the main roads in summer. They offer the ubiquitous Armenian menu of *khorovats*: seasoned meat (usually pork but sometimes chicken, lamb or beef) threaded on to flat metal skewers and barbecued over wood coals, scattered with chopped onion and herbs and wrapped in *lavash*, often served with salads and

The *tonir*, or oven, in which **lavash** is baked is a large cylindrical clay structure sunk into the ground. A fire is lit in the bottom of the tonir and baking begins when the walls of the oven are hot enough, as lavash is cooked on the actual wall of the oven.

Traditionally lavash dough consists simply of flour, salt and water. When several women from the same family or same village join together to make a large batch an efficient mini production line ensues, with one woman rolling out pieces of dough on a floured baking board, a second skilfully stretching the dough into very thin sheets by throwing it to and fro in the air and then laying it on a special padded implement, a *batat*, which has a handle on the non-padded side. It is said that the dough should be stretched to about 30x60cm and should be no more than 1½mm thick. The dough is then swiftly and firmly applied by means of the *batat* to the wall of the tonir to cook. This takes only a few seconds. It is then removed from the tonir with a long metal hook, often by a third member of the group, and added to the pile of cooked lavash, which in public bakeries usually diminishes at a similar rate. The skill lies in judging the correct moment to remove the lavash from the tonir and the oldest member of the group is often granted this important task. The surface of the blisters which form when the dough comes in contact with the heat should be nicely browned.

vegetables. Watching and smelling the food cooking and then eating it either in the open air or under an awning is one of the pleasures of travelling in Armenia. Prices are usually a little lower than you would pay for a similar meal in a restaurant. In towns it might be possible to find a café selling the traditional regional fast food *lahmajo*. This tasty speciality comprises a thin dough base covered, in similar style to a pizza, with tomato, herbs, spices and very small pieces of meat. It's normally rolled up or folded and eaten like a sandwich. Other commonly found street snacks include Middle Eastern-style **shawarma** (aka: doner kebab), **jhingalov hats** (flatbreads stuffed with minced wild herbs; page 379), Georgian-influenced **khachapuri** and – if you're desperate or on a budget – the cheap Russian **piroshki** (doughy, deep-fried pasties filled with potato or minced meat).

**DINNER** The main meal is eaten in the evening. **Bread** will certainly be provided, usually *lavash*, but some restaurants, particularly in Yerevan, will also include a selection of regular leavened breads in the same basket. The meal usually begins with a selection of **salads** which can incorporate both raw and cooked vegetables, peas, beans, herbs, fruits, nuts, bulghur, eggs and meat. In season romaine lettuce is used but in winter cabbage is substituted. Often the salads will double up as an accompaniment to the main course. Popular salads include cucumber and tomato salad (*varoong yev lolikov aghtsan*), also known as summer salad (*amarayin aghtsan*), green bean salad (*kanach lobov aghtsan*), kidney bean salad (*karmir lobov aghtsan*), aubergine salad (*s'mbookov aghtsan*), potato salad with sour cream (*t'tvaserov kartofili aghtsan*) and wild sorrel salad (*avelukov aghtsan*) made with distinctive braids of the dried plants, reconstituted and boiled. (While *aghtsan* is the correct Armenian word, the English 'salad' is also widely understood.) Middle Eastern mezes (such as hummus) and Russian salads (made with root vegetables and too much mayonnaise) are not uncommon.

Practical Information   EATING AND DRINKING

2

The second course would traditionally have been **soup**, although this is not now often served in summer, and restaurants frequently have none available. Some of the soups are actually so substantial as to be main courses, while others are cold concoctions for summer. Armenian soups are excellent so take any opportunity to try one – if you can manage yet more food. One summer soup is *jajik*, chilled yoghurt and cucumber soup, which can either accompany the main course or precede it. Other cold soups made with apricots, cornelian cherries *Cornus mas*, currants, mulberries or sweetbriar *Rosa rubiginosa* can be served as either a first course or a dessert. More substantial traditional soups for winter include *tarkhana abour* made with yoghurt, mint and onion, *shoushin bozbash* (lamb soup with apple and quince) and *ms'sov tsiranabour* (lamb soup with apricots), as well as borrowed dishes such as Georgian *kharcho* and Russian *borscht*. More homely soups, often offered in homestays, are *spas* (yoghurt and shelled wheat), *aveluk* (wild sorrel) or *yeghinj* (nettle). You may also come across *harissa* (not to be confused with the spicy sauce of North African cuisine), a thick Middle Eastern soup of wheat and chicken which is filling if rather unexciting.

The main course is usually based on meat or fish. **Fish** is obviously less common than in countries which are not landlocked but common whitefish (*sig*) from Lake Sevan is sometimes available and also trout (*ishkhan*) from Armenia's rivers. Trout and sturgeon are available from the Armash fishponds and other fishfarms.

Restaurants rarely offer slow-cooked dishes, although they certainly form a big part of traditional Armenian cookery. **Chicken** (*hav*) is far more likely to be roasted, perhaps with a stuffing (*plavov ltsvats hav*) based on rice or bulghur and with some vegetables or dried fruit, or else it might be barbecued (*khorovats*) or fried (*tapakats*). **Game** is very rarely offered, probably because so little of it survives, but if you do come across it, it will usually be rabbit, hare or venison. **Lamb** (*gar*), **mutton** (*vochkhar*) and **beef** (*tavar*) are all popular and a huge variety of meat stews are cooked in domestic homes with ingredients from quinces (*ms'sov serkevil*) and apricots (*ms'sov tsiran*) to artichokes (*ms'sov gangar*) and leeks (*ms'sov bras*). These fascinating, delicious and often celebratory dishes are usually served with a rice pilaff (*brndzov plav*) or bulghur pilaff (*dzavari plav*), but the chance of finding one on a restaurant menu is practically zero. You will, however, find lots of **barbecues** (*khorovats*) using lamb, pork (*khoz*), beef, chicken or, occasionally, veal (*hort*), of which **pork** and chicken are usually the safest options. You may also have to choose between cuts of red meat, usually fillet (*filé*), chops on the bone (*chalaghach*) or ribs (*mat*). The meat will come sprinkled with chopped onion and herbs, often with barbecued vegetables on the side, of very high quality but not necessarily prepared or cooked with the flair and imagination shown in an Armenian household. A popular way of cooking green vegetables, such as asparagus and beans, is to fry them and then add whipped eggs. The result is rather like scrambled eggs with vegetables and could form a meal in itself although it is usually served as a side dish.

Other iconic Armenian dishes include the very popular ***dolma*** (a Turkish word meaning 'stuffed'), of which there is a whole range. They comprise leaves, vegetables and very occasionally fruits which have been wrapped around or stuffed with a seasoned minced meat and rice mixture, arranged in a large covered pan, and simmered slowly in a flavoured sauce on the stovetop. Vine leaves or cabbage leaves are most commonly used depending on the season (hence 'summer dolma' and 'winter dolma'), but the range of vegetables and fruits used in Armenian homes is staggering: aubergines, peppers, courgettes, tomatoes, apples and quinces. For the stuffing, special dishes could involve some combination of minced beef or lamb, rice, bulghur, dried fruits, chopped vegetables, yoghurt and a mixture of herbs and spices. Needless to say, a visit to an Armenian home is necessary to encounter this kind of range, but some restaurants do include the more common dolma on the menu. During religious fasting seasons such as Lent, the meat is usually substituted by lentils or other pulses.

*Keufteh* is another classic of Armenian cookery. It is bulghur which has been mixed with finely chopped vegetables and herbs and often with lamb as well. Again there are innumerable variations depending on the cook and the availability of seasonal ingredients. It can be cooked or uncooked, hot or cold, and some have two separate mixtures, one for the core and one for an outer shell. In the popular *sini keufteh* the inner stuffing is made from butter, onions, minced lamb, pine nuts and spices while the outer shell comprises bulghur, more lamb, onion and other spices. It is prepared in a baking dish before being cut into squares and then baked. It can be eaten hot or cold with vegetables or salad.

**DESSERT AND PASTRIES** Dessert as often as not consists of **fresh fruit**, sometimes accompanied by cheese (*paneer*). In summer **ice cream** (*baghbaghak*) is served but is generally mass-produced. **Pastries** are more often eaten with a cup of afternoon tea or coffee or in the late evening. Armenia's best pastries are those which exploit its fruit and nuts. *Baklava* is widely available and exists in many forms. Layers of buttered filo pastry stuffed with some combination of nuts (often walnuts), apples, cheese and cream are formed into rolls or diamonds and then baked. Afterwards it is covered either with honey or with a sugar and water syrup that has been flavoured with lemon. Another popular pastry is *gata*, a dense, bun-like cake baked with a mixture of butter, flour, sugar and (sometimes) ground almonds inside. Freshly baked, the large flat rounds (looking more like bread than

### EATING OUT IN ARMENIA

It is relatively cheap to eat out in Armenia, except for the more upmarket places in Yerevan which charge Western prices. Main courses usually cost somewhere between AMD2,500 and AMD4,000 and it is easy to have a full meal (which in Armenia usually comprises salads/sides and a main course) for AMD5,000–6,000 per person. A bottle of wine will add somewhere between AMD2,500 and AMD5,000, half a litre of beer AMD600–800 and two coffees AMD500–1,000. There is not usually a significant price differential between restaurants and cafés. Restaurants which fall outside this price range are noted under their individual entries, or in the case of Yerevan ordered by descending order of price category. A light course, such as an omelette, may well cost under AMD1,000 and a savoury street snack can be had for as little as AMD100. Most restaurants open at noon and cafés about 10.00. Most will stay open until midnight or until the last customer has gone. For picnics or for those self-catering, markets provide a wide range of food at budget prices. Supermarkets have a bigger range but are often more expensive. Another option is to patronise the roadside stalls which sell seasonal fruit and vegetables (page 97).

Outside Yerevan, some local cafés and restaurants do not have a printed menu. You are simply asked what you would like – somewhat disconcerting when you have no idea what is available! The standard fare of salads, cheese, bread, barbecued meat (*khorovats*) and vegetables is usually available. Other staples such as an omelette and fried potatoes can probably be provided but it is worth asking what they suggest. In cold weather, soup may be on offer.

cake) are often sold at tourist sites such as Geghard. Packs of bite-sized *gata* are also available from supermarkets and bakeries, though they look quite different. Also excellent are the **dried fruits** such as apricots, peaches or plums which are commonly sold stuffed with nuts and lovingly arranged in decorative, almost floral patterns as gifts. Another interesting and enjoyable novelty is **fruit or sour *lavash***, thin sheets of dried fruit purée. Plum was the classic fruit to use but nowadays a wide range of fruits is employed.

**DRINKS** Armenia is justly renowned for its **brandy**, its **coffee** and its **spring water**. Other drinks, such as some of the **herbal teas** – particularly the thyme (*oorts*) tea – are well worth trying, and the modernisation of the wine industry has led to a noticeable up-tick in the quality of local **wines**. Armenian alcohol consumption is at the bottom end of the European range, though the latest World Health Organization statistics claim that 85% of what is consumed is in the form of spirits. Although beer can be drunk freely, social etiquette has established formal rules for the drinking of wine and spirits in group situations. They may only be drunk when eating, and each table has its *tamada* (toastmaster) who is responsible for making toasts: no-one drinks without a toast. Toasts can be extremely long, with persons around the table requesting the *tamada* to be allowed to toast. The theory is that the *tamada* is able to regulate the alcohol intake of those present and stop people getting drunk. Unfortunately it doesn't always work because the *tamada* himself sometimes (!) ends up inebriated, forcing everyone else to keep going. This ritual can be challenging to visitors, who feel pressured to down a shot of brandy or vodka out of politeness when they don't really want to, yet are forbidden to enjoy a sip of wine with the food because the toast never comes to an end! Women will be let off more lightly, but it is considered highly unorthodox for men not to drink on demand: it is perhaps better to excuse oneself after the first shot. Armenians themselves often prefer to drink brandy or vodka with meals rather than drink wine, quite contrary to Western habits. Indeed, drinking even Armenian wine is largely the prerogative of foreigners, at least beyond the classic wine-producing regions.

Armenia's drinks industry today should be understood in the context of two heavy blows in the late 1980s. First, Soviet president Gorbachev launched a strong anti-alcohol campaign and then, during the blockade years in the early 1990s, goods could not get to the main market in the rest of the CIS. As markets could not import Armenian products other, often inferior, suppliers were only too happy to step into the void. As a result of both these factors production and sales fell considerably, bottoming out in 1996. Today, conditions are much improved. The wine industry in particular has developed at breakneck speed in recent years, being seen as an important part of both Armenian culture and the country's economic prospects – and the beer industry seems to be heading in a similar direction.

Armenian **brandy** (*konyak*) sprang to prominence at the Yalta conference in 1945 when Stalin plied Winston Churchill, the British prime minister, with it and Churchill declared that it was better than any French brandy. Many would still agree, and much in the way of embellishment has since been added to the story, including the spurious claim that Churchill henceforth requested a bottle in every hotel room he stayed in. Although called cognac in Armenia and the rest of the former Soviet Union, this is forbidden under Western trade rules which specify that cognac must be produced in the Cognac region of France, and in any case Armenian brandy is usually seen being thrown back after a toast rather than sipped gently from a crystal snifter. It comes in a variety of qualities. At the bottom of the range is three star, so called because it has been kept (in oak casks) for three years after fermentation. Up to six years the number of stars indicates age, but for six years and beyond special names are given. The Ararat factory in Yerevan, founded in 1887 and well worth the guided tour if time allows, offers Ani (six years old), Select (seven years old), Akhtamar (ten years old), Celebratory (15 years old), Vaspurakan (18 years old) and Nairi (20 years old). Prices range from AMD4,690 for a 500ml bottle of three star to AMD8,410 for Ani, AMD12,300 for Akhtamar and AMD34,700 for Nairi. Prices in the duty-free at Zvartnots International Airport are lower, but note the caution about airline regulations on liquids on page 107. About 70% of production is exported to Russia. Other quality producers are Noy and MAP who also export a large proportion of their production. There are around a dozen smaller firms producing inferior products.

**Vodka** (*vodka* if store-bought or *oghi* if homemade) is distilled by more than 45 small and medium-sized companies in Armenia, including Avshar, Vedi-Alco, SGS (based in Nagorno Karabagh), Garib and Artashat-Vincon. Production has been increasing steadily since 1996 and in 2000 Armenia began exporting its vodka, mainly to the USA and Cyprus. As well as ordinary vodka, several traditional Armenian varieties are made in people's homes, such as mulberry (*t'ti*) vodka, grape (*khagho*) vodka and apricot (*tsirani*) vodka. Many of the vodkas are pleasant enough, particularly the fruit-flavoured ones, but they do not compare in quality to the brandy. The price of vodka (AMD990–10,000 for 500ml) depends on the quality and what it is made from. Armenian vodka is cheaper than Russian and fruit vodkas more expensive than ordinary vodka. You can buy a 500ml bottle of decent fruit vodka for AMD5,000–7,500.

Armenia grows a range of grape varieties but the climate does not lend itself to the 'cool climate' grape growing that is becoming more popular in the New World, and the **wineries** (more than 15 in Armenia) have in the past had insufficient funds to be able to invest in temperature-controlled fermentation. However, the industry is rapidly modernising and a considerable number of different white and red wines are available, many of the reds being sweet or semi-sweet. The best-known grape variety in Armenia is Areni noir, used for making red wines; try those from Karas, Koor, Takar or Hin Areni. Some enjoyable white Armenian wines include those made by the Ijevan winery (page 313) from the Georgian Rkatsiteli grape, as well as from the same wineries mentioned above. A good champagne-style sparkling white is produced by Keush. Although some very cheap wine is available, the more drinkable bottles cost about AMD1,800 to AMD2,000 and a good red wine about AMD4,000–5,000, slightly more in a restaurant whose mark-ups rarely exceed 25%. The Armenian for wine (*ginee*) can be preceded by the appropriate adjectives: red (*karmir*); white (*spitak*); dry (*chor*); or sweet (*kaghtsr*). Wine degustations can be enjoyed at several wineries in Vayots Dzor (page 324) and elsewhere; Yerevan has several specialist wine merchants, such as In Vino (page 147).

Although imported **beer** (*garejoor*, but mostly people use the name of the brand they want rather than the generic word for beer) is available, usually from Heineken or Russia's Baltika brewery, three indigenous brands are ubiquitous throughout the country: Kilikia (brewed in Yerevan), Kotayk (brewed in Abovyan) and Gyumri (indeed brewed in Gyumri). All can be characterised as pale European-style lagers. Smaller breweries include Dilijan, Alaverdi and Sevan. Lovers of ales and craft beers will find slim pickings beyond Yerevan, though specialist beer-houses do now exist (page 146). The regular brands cost around AMD390–450 for a 500ml bottle bought from a supermarket or convenience store, rising to AMD600–800 in a bar or café in central Yerevan. Draught (*ltsnovi*) beer from the same breweries is also available in some bars and restaurants.

*Haykakan soorj*, **Armenian coffee** (also called *sev soorj*, black coffee, or Eastern coffee), is excellent and the perfect end to a meal, ideally accompanied by a glass of brandy. It is brewed in a *jazzve* – a small long-handled copper pot – using very finely ground beans, traditionally heated on a bed of hot sand and served in small cups in a similar way to Turkish coffee. It is usually served slightly sweetened (called *normal* with the stress on the second syllable) and even visitors who drink coffee without sugar at home may prefer it this way. If coffee is desired without any sugar then ask for *soorj arants shakari* or simply *dar* (meaning bitter). In a café, Armenian coffee costs around AMD150–300. Instant coffee is also available and tastes just like it does everywhere else. Tea (*tay*) in Armenia can be either a standard brand of tea bag dunked in a cup or a more refined herbal infusion in a pot. Some wonderful teas, especially thyme tea (*oortsov tay*), may be encountered made from a whole gamut of different herbs and flowers collected from Armenia's hillsides during the summer and then dried.

**Water** (*joor*) is another joy in Armenia. The water from Armenia's mountain springs is delicious and always safe to drink. Many of these springs are located by the sides of roads or tracks or at monastic sites and, quite often, picnic tables are provided. It may seem bizarre to recommend spring water, but all visitors should make an effort to try it. **Bottled mineral water** (*hankayeen joor*) is also available. The 'mineral' epithet should be taken literally: not just carbonated tap water, this often tastes strongly of the dissolved mineral compounds. Jermuk is the most common source but Dilijan, Bjni, Byurakan, Byuregh and Noy can also be found alongside other soft drinks in the refrigerators of every store and restaurant. Carbonated and still are both widely sold. If you ask for bottled water it will be assumed that you want sparkling; if you want still water ask for it without gas (*arants gaz*).

Another drink often consumed with meals and street food is **tan**, a refreshing and slightly salty yoghurt drink, similar to its Turkish and Iranian counterparts *ayran* and *doogh*. Homemade versions tend to be more palatable than the sour store-bought varieties.

**Pasteurised fruit juices** are generally available in small 250ml or larger 1-litre cartons or bottles, as is the usual international range of bottled soft drinks together with some local competitors. A particular joy which might be encountered during a homestay is sweetened fruit juice (*kompot*) made from the family's own fruit trees. Cornelian cherry (*Cornus mas*) juice is especially recommended. Occasionally one of the more traditional restaurants will have a novel juice on offer: sea buckthorn juice is one possibility. Despite its name, sea buckthorn (*Hippophae rhamnoides*), a small tree of the oleaster family, grows in Armenia. Travellers on the dual carriageway between Yerevan and Lake Sevan will often see locals selling the sour berries and their bright orange juice on the roadside. Groceries stock a wide variety of good locally produced fruit juices; if sugar has been added it will usually say so on the packaging.

## PUBLIC HOLIDAYS AND FESTIVALS

### PUBLIC HOLIDAYS

| | |
|---|---|
| New Year's Day | 1 January |
| Christmas Day | 6 January |
| Army Day | 28 January |
| International Women's Day | 8 March |
| Good Friday | March/April |
| Easter Monday | March/April |
| Day of Motherhood and Beauty | 7 April |

| Genocide Memorial Day | 24 April |
| Victory and Peace Day | 9 May |
| First Republic Day | 28 May |
| Constitution Day | 5 July |
| Independence Day | 21 September |
| Earthquake Memorial Day | 7 December |
| New Year's Eve | 31 December |

Genocide Memorial Day and Earthquake Memorial Day are called 'commemoration days' rather than public holidays. On Genocide Memorial Day everything is shut as on a public holiday. Earthquake Memorial Day is now a working day, although with civic commemoration ceremonies.

**FESTIVALS**  Festivals in Armenia tend to be national events, focusing on religious events and dates, or local affairs devoted to seasonal produce and rural traditions, with events dedicated to fruit, vegetables, wine, vodka and baking; even *khorovats* (barbecued meat) has its own festival, as if an excuse was needed. No one reliable source of online information in English exists at the time of writing, but the website of Repat Armenia (**w** repatarmenia.org) is a good place to begin, as is the official tourism portal (**w** armenia.travel). In addition, almost all smaller and regional festivals can be found as public Facebook events. Additional information is included in regional chapters of the guide where appropriate.

The following should not be considered a comprehensive list, but it does cover the most established and long-running events in the Armenian festival calendar.

**New Year and Christmas**  In Armenia, as with all Eastern churches, Christmas (which falls on 6 January) is celebrated after New Year. Though you'll see more than a few acknowledgements of the Western Christmas dates and traditions, it is the two weeks from 31 December that are the main period of continuous family and church-centred celebration. In the weeks before New Year the shops are busy with people shopping – principally for food although also for presents. Food, especially family meals, forms the important focus of the festivities. For three days before New Year's Eve so much food is prepared that you would think there was going to be a two-month siege! Everyone wants to make sure that there are generous helpings for all the extended family members who will visit. Everyone visits everyone else. Even if your aunt has visited you one day, you will still go and see her the next. On New Year's Eve a large piece of meat is cooked, often roast leg of pork, as well as numerous accompanying dishes and desserts, in preparation for visitors who start to arrive after the midnight bells. A small gift is always taken for whoever you are visiting, often a box of chocolates or a bottle of wine or vodka. Presents are given on New Year's Eve rather than at Christmas and it is Kaghand Papi, Grandfather Kaghand (see box, page 106), who brings them for small children. Both the birth of Jesus and his baptism are remembered on 6 January. At the church service water is blessed, consecrated oil (chrism or, in Armenian, *meron*) is poured into the water and a cross is dipped into the water to symbolise Christ's baptism. This water is then distributed to the faithful who will either drink it or wash their hands and faces in it.

Christmas is a religious festival. The family goes to church on either Christmas Eve or Christmas Day, the main family meal taking place on the other day. Again, large amounts of food are prepared for the many visitors who will come. A pilaff and baked fish are always included.

In Russia, and some other Slavic cultures, the traditional character of Ded Moroz (the literal meaning of the Russian being 'Grandfather Frost' but often translated as 'Father Frost') played a similar role to that of Santa Claus or Saint Nicholas in the West. Ded Moroz has his roots in pagan beliefs and was originally a wicked sorcerer who stole children, but under the influence of Christian Orthodox tradition he became a kind person who gave gifts to children at New Year. In the officially atheist Soviet Union the celebration of Christmas was discouraged and New Year celebrations, which included the arrival of Ded Moroz with gifts, were promoted. He, or a local counterpart, was introduced into other parts of the Soviet Union and into eastern European counties in the Soviet bloc, despite his being alien to them. Since the collapse of the Soviet Union countries such as Slovenia, Bulgaria, Poland and Romania have reverted to their traditional characters associated with Christmas.

In Armenia it was Dzmer Papi (literally 'Grandfather Winter' but usually more euphoniously translated as 'Father Frost') who was introduced during the Soviet period. There seems not to have been a pre-Soviet equivalent. Since independence, Dzmer Papi has been replaced by Kaghand Papi (Grandfather New Year) – possibly based on a figure from ancient mythology.

**Easter** A night-time Easter Eve church service is attended followed by a family meal on Easter Sunday (*zatik*). As with Christmas, fish forms the centrepiece of the meal and there will also be green vegetables cooked with whipped eggs and a sweet pilaff. There are egg fights for the children, with hard-boiled eggs which they have painted or dyed the previous day. The pointed ends of the eggs are engaged first then, when they have all cracked, the blunt ends are tested. The winner is the one whose egg lasts the longest without breaking. The eggs are then made into an Easter sandwich with *lavash*, greens (usually tarragon) and cheese.

**Vardavar** The Vardavar Festival, held on a Sunday in summer, is a date for which visitors should be well prepared. The precise date is fixed according to the church calendar and varies from year to year. Being 14 weeks after Easter, it usually falls in July. Vardavar nowadays commemorates the Transfiguration, the incident described in St Matthew's Gospel, chapter 17, when Christ took three disciples up Mount Sinai where his appearance was transfigured as he talked with Moses and Elijah. Its origins, however, are pre-Christian: Vardavar was formerly associated with Aphrodite (Anahit) and rose petals were scattered on the worshippers (*vard* is the Armenian word for 'rose'). Nowadays in place of rose petals the festival involves children (and childish adults) collecting water, stalking passers-by, and then thoroughly drenching them. It is worth mentioning that nobody can opt out of participation: anyone who leaves the safety of their home is fair game. The more water-affluent children will have managed to stockpile many buckets' worth: do not wear smart clothes or indeed any clothes which might be damaged by water, nor expect your ownership of a very expensive smartphone to make the slightest difference. It is also unwise, despite the temperatures in summer, to drive around with car windows open without being confident that no children are lurking out of sight behind a tree or wall – unless you have by this point accepted your fate and decided to go with the flow. Adults can and do retaliate against the water throwers, for example by using their own stockpiled supplies to effect revenge on the miscreants below by aiming at them from the safety of the balconies of their apartments, or by investing in an arsenal of expensive, high-powered water pistols and going mobile in cars and SUVs. Even the fire brigade have on occasion been known to indulge.

Armenia is not the only country to have such a festival – Thailand and Myanmar (Burma) both have similar festivals to celebrate the Buddhist New Year. In Poland and Hungary water throwing is practised on Easter Monday when the boys throw it on the girls – the more gallant married men spray perfume on their wives but this variant has not yet reached Armenia.

In short, the advice is simply to enter into the spirit of the festival: especially in Yerevan it can actually be refreshing to be soaked in the July heat and you will soon dry off.

**Areni Wine Festival** Held annually on the first Saturday of October, Areni Wine festival has become one of the staple events of Armenia's festival calendar, with tourists and Yerevantsis taking a 1½-hour road trip to the heart of Vayots Dzor's wine region to sample the homemade wines of more than 150 producers, as well as of the growing number of commercial wineries in Armenia and Nagorno Karabagh. Festivities kick off at 13.00 in Areni itself and (predictably) continue until the last drop has been drunk. For this reason you may wish to arrange local accommodation as opposed to driving back the same night.

The festival's popularity has sparked a similar venture in Yerevan itself called **Yerevan Wine Days**, in which the streets are closed for an evening and wine producers set up shop on the roads. The first, highly successful event took place in May 2017; it was reprised in May 2018 and is planned to continue annually.

## SHOPPING

In town centres most shops open at 09.30 or 10.00 and then remain open until 19.00. Shops rarely close for lunch. Some, especially food shops and markets, open daily but many specialist shops such as bookshops remain closed on Sundays. In residential areas small shops and kiosks are open for very long hours – often till after midnight – while roadside stalls on main routes are sometimes open 24 hours.

Also open 24 hours are some branches of the main supermarket chains which have appeared in recent years, most prominently SAS and Yerevan City. These supermarkets, and indeed all shops in Armenia, are well stocked and visitors should be able to buy most of what they need, especially in the towns. (See page 81 for items which should be brought from home.) Apart from at a few designer shops on Northern Avenue in Yerevan, shopping is relatively inexpensive.

The widest range of **souvenirs** is to be found in Yerevan. Obvious items to take home include the increasing number of books of photographs of Armenia (see page 150 for bookshops) and Armenia's highly regarded brandy (easily obtainable in markets, shops and specialist brandy outlets) – but remember airline restrictions on liquids in hand luggage and buy from duty free whatever you want to carry on *after* going through security; anything bought beforehand will be confiscated. Remember too, if your flight is not to your final destination, that liquids bought after security on the initial leg of your flight must be in a sealed, transparent, tamper-proof shopping bag containing the original receipt (the duty-free outlet at Zvartnots will do this for you), or they will almost certainly be confiscated at security during transit checks. Craft items are also obvious souvenirs. There is no doubt that the best place to buy crafts is at Vernissage in Yerevan (page 150), but

2

By law, exporting any work of art which is more than 75 years old from Armenia requires approval from the government's Department of Cultural Heritage Preservation at 51 Komitas Avenue, third and fourth floors. For those without linguistic skills, it is advisable to get the dealer to sort it out. You need to take the item, together with two photographs, to the third floor – the Department of Expertise – and pay a small initial fee. You then go to the fourth floor – the permit department – with the photographs and the papers issued on the third floor. You pay a further sum which depends on the valuation of the expertise department. The sums due are variable but in the past they have been around 3–5% of the valuation. Generally the permit is then issued on the spot. However, if the item is considered to be of national importance museums and art galleries have a month to exercise the option to buy it. If none want it an export permit will be issued. This procedure is not required for items less than 75 years old, but the date, name of the author and his/her signature should be appended.

This may be rigorously enforced in the case of paintings (sometimes even those painted last week by an unknown artist and bought at Vernissage) and handmade carpets, but often less so in the case of other items such as carvings or embroideries. In the past, there were reports of customs officers at the airport citing rules written and unwritten and refusing to allow the export of paintings in particular, despite the purchaser having the correct paperwork. Bribery was reported to work in these cases, though such days have seemingly passed.

they can also be found on souvenir stalls at some of the more popular tourist sites and in other outlets in the capital (page 150). The cathedral shop at Etchmiadzin also has a good range of articles. Typically Armenian are carpets (and, for those who want something cheaper than a full-sized floor covering, bags and waistcoats made from carpet offcuts), wood and stone carvings, embroidered articles (from large tablecloths to handkerchiefs; see box, page 158) and jewellery incorporating Armenia's semiprecious obsidian (page 3). Paintings for sale are displayed at weekends at the Painters' Vernissage in Martiros Saryan Park to the northwest of the opera house in Yerevan, and at the main Vernissage itself.

Large and small towns in the provinces have all the basic facilities such as shops, banks, post offices, etc. Large out-of-town supermarkets are also springing up on major transit routes through the country. Almost every village has a well-stocked shop and many petrol and gas stations have a small shop attached.

## ARTS AND ENTERTAINMENT

As in most countries, but perhaps more so than usual in Armenia, access to the arts and to formal entertainments is concentrated in the capital. All the major **museums and art galleries** are in or near Yerevan (page 176). Other towns do have small museums and art galleries, many of which are worth visiting, but they do not compare to those in Yerevan. Labelling in English has improved enormously but many museums, even important Yerevan museums, make few concessions to non-Armenian-speakers.

Entrance fees are low by Western standards, rarely being more than AMD1,000 and often much less. The entrance fee for children is usually lower than the adult rate. If an English-speaking guide is available, this costs about an extra AMD2,500–5,000. The most commonly encountered foreign-language guided tours are English and Russian. Other languages are much rarer; if available they are noted under individual entries. Most museums are closed on Mondays, a few on other days. Opening hours and days are stated in individual entries.

**Theatres and concert halls** are also concentrated in Yerevan (page 147). Performances are usually in Armenian, apart from opera which may be sung in the original language. Theatre tickets cost AMD1,500–15,000 and are usually bought from the venue although tickets for one venue, especially if it is not in the town centre, may sometimes be sold at another. Box offices display posters showing which tickets they are selling. Tour operators can arrange tickets and it is also possible to buy them online.

In Soviet days most towns had a **cinema** but this is no longer the case; only Yerevan has cinemas, including two refurbished ones and a newly built one (page 147) which show films in English. Tickets cost AMD1,500–5,000 for evening screenings, AMD500 for matinées. The annual **Golden Apricot International Film Festival** (3 Moskovyan St; ✆010 521042; **e** info@gaiff.am; **w** gaiff.am) takes place in Yerevan during July. The first festival in 2004 attracted 148 films by 70 film-makers from 20 countries – it has since grown considerably. The festival takes as its theme 'Crossroads of Cultures and Civilisations' and welcomes films representing various nations, ethnicities and religions, collectively depicting the richness of the human experience. The opening of the festival is marked by a traditional blessing of Armenia's famous apricots. **Sunchild International Environmental Festival** (Apt 15, Khanjyan St 47/1, Yerevan; ✆010 585884; **w** sunchild.fpwc.org), whose date

## A NOTE ABOUT SITE NAMES

English versions of Armenian site names sometimes result in tautology if the Armenian name incorporates the type of place it is. The names of two of Armenia's most visited monasteries, Tatev and Noravank, illustrate the problem. In Armenian the former is called Tatev Vank; two words, the first being the name of the place, the second being the Armenian word for monastery. It is therefore correctly called, in English, Tatev Monastery. The other monastery is, in Armenian, Noravank; one word with two parts, *nor* (new) and *vank* (monastery). Usually it is, correctly, referred to just as Noravank but occasionally the tautological Noravank Monastery appears. While this has the merit of indicating what sort of place is being referred to, it can grate on the ears of purists. (Strictly speaking it should be translated as New Monastery but it never is.)

A similar dilemma arises with names which have the suffix *berd* (fortress), *ler* or *sar* (mountain), *get* (river), *dzor* (gorge) and *lich* (lake).

The following compromise has been adopted for headings **in this guide** in the cause of clarity. Where a name incorporates one of these descriptive suffixes, the heading is given in the form Noravank (monastery). Where the descriptive term is a separate word in Armenian it is translated and given as part of the full name eg: Tatev Monastery.

A related problem is caused by the fact that some places are habitually referred to in a translated form eg: Lake Arpi (not Arpi Lich), while others usually retain their Armenian form eg: Akna Lich (not Lake Akna). In such cases the name most commonly used in English is employed.

and venue change each year, began in 2010 and aims to raise national awareness of environmental issues through the medium of film; in 2018 it was held in July in the village of Vardahovit. Many foreign embassies and cultural centres also organise smaller-scale film festivals showcasing the best of their national film talent in Armenia.

Armenia is a country of **statues**. This is an active art form, perhaps not surprising in a land with such a long history of carving (witness the thousands of khachkars). New statues appear regularly throughout the country. Some are described in this guide but visitors are likely to see many more. Khachkar carving continues to be an active art form; see box, page 48.

More modern forms of entertainment, held at **contemporary music venues**, **casinos** and **nightclubs**, are on offer in Yerevan (page 146), as are some **sports** (page 149). The Armenians are good at entertaining themselves and have certainly taken to the café culture; witness the large number of busy cafés in Yerevan's city centre and spilling out on to the streets. Wine bars, pubs and lounges (page 146) are a relatively recent but rapidly growing phenomenon, at least in Yerevan. Strolling, a pastime which seems to have disappeared from much of Western life, is alive and well in Armenia and visitors may enjoy rediscovering this art, particularly on balmy summer evenings when the pedestrianised parts of downtown Yerevan are thronged with people.

## SPECIAL-INTEREST VISITS

Armenia lends itself to special-interest visits and several operators offer hiking, trekking, camping, motorbiking, mountain-biking, 4x4, winter sports including ski touring, paragliding, hot-air ballooning, archaeological and other special-interest tours and experiences (page 67).

Anyone interested in **birdwatching** should contact the Ornithological Society of the Middle East, Caucasus and Central Asia (w osme.org). There are two specialist birdwatching British companies which sometimes include Armenia in regional tours (page 65).

The diversity of accessible vegetation zones means that **botanical tours** are very rewarding. These can be arranged either via the Botanical Institute in Yerevan (❩010 568690) or a couple of local tour operators (page 68). Tours to **watch mammals** such as Bezoar goats and even bears are also possible.

**Cycling** and particularly **mountain biking** has much greater potential than is currently being realised. Some of the local tour operators listed on pages 67–8 offer mountain-biking tours and it is possible to hire and buy equipment in Yerevan (page 136). The Cycling Armenia website (w cyclingarmenia.com) lists a number of suggested leisure and touring routes, both on- and off-road, as well as practical information. Boo Mountain Bike Park (f boomtbpark) near Vanadzor hopes to build Armenia's first purpose-built mountain-bike trails. See page 114 for detailed comments on cycling in Armenia.

**Horseriding holidays** are also available at a number of locations. There is a Yerevan riding school (page 149), an activity centre near Ijevan, Tavush province (page 313), and a horseback tour operator in Gomk village, Vayots Dzor province (page 323). Hire of horses can be arranged when visiting Khosrov and Shikahogh state reserves (pages 207 and 366).

Most of the country away from the Ararat Valley has huge **hiking and trekking** potential; see opposite page for detailed comments, as well as page 67 for a large number of local tour operators who can arrange hiking and trekking tours.

**Mountaineering** is offered by some specialist local operators. Independent mountaineers should contact the Armenian Mountaineering and Hiking Federation (1 Artsakh Av; w armalp.am) whose office doubles as a well-stocked outdoor equipment shop and rental centre. Armenia has superb **caving** with more than 10,000 caves in most regions of the country, often concentrated along the river gorges. Most of the caves are little known, although there is an active Armenian Speleological Society (✆010 582254, 620248). The Armenian Extreme Club (w armextremeclub.wordpress.com) also has knowledgeable staff. In Vayots Dzor province, the proprietor of the Vayots Dzor Tourism Centre and Hotel at Vayk (page 324) leads caving expeditions; information is also available at the Arpa Protected Landscape Visitor Centre (page 328). Reportedly some of the best caving, though only for the experienced, is in this province. Magil Cave is in the gorge which leads to Noravank and is 1.7km deep. Stone tools and artefacts have been discovered in the cave, as well as more recent ceramic fragments from the 9th century onwards. The cave is home to thousands of insectivorous bats. The passageway is horizontal and varies from just enough for a person to crawl through to a spacious 10–15m in width. Because of damage in recent years this cave is no longer as freely open to visitors as it once was. Other caves are strictly for the expert. At 3.3km, Archeri (Bears) Cave near Yeghegnadzor is Armenia's longest, with some of the most spectacular stalactite and stalagmite formations in Europe. Unlike Magil it is far from horizontal, with a vertical range of 145m. The cave gets its name from the remains of bears found here. Mozrov Cave, about 7.6km west of Arpi, has fine speleothems (mineral deposits of calcium carbonate precipitated from solution); again, access is currently restricted due to vandalism and a guide is required.

**Winter sports** including **downhill skiing** are available at Tsaghkadzor (page 250) and Jermuk (page 337). **Cross-country skiing** can be arranged via Shirak Tours (page 258) and at Ashotsk village north of Gyumri (page 265). **Backcountry skiing** and **ski touring** are offered by an increasing number of specialist local operators (page 67); see also the website of the Armenian Alpine Club (w armenianalpineclub.org).

Byurakan Astrophysical Observatory (page 196) offers events and tours for amateur **astronomers**.

## HIKING AND TREKKING

**HIKING AND TREKKING** Given the dramatic mountain landscapes that dominate much of Armenia, it is perhaps surprising that the potential for independent hiking and trekking has remained so neglected for so long. Among the obstacles for those who attempted to explore the remote corners of the country without a guide were a complete lack of detailed topographical maps, a very limited selection of marked trails (which were often impossible to follow), and no reliable sources of information beyond a few hobbyist websites.

The situation can perhaps be traced to general issues that have faced Armenia in the last couple of decades, the economic collapse following the Soviet dissolution leading to more pressing concerns than keeping footpaths maintained. As the economy began to improve, knowledge of the best hiking opportunities – often historical trails between villages and nearby monasteries and fortresses, or trading routes used to pass otherwise impenetrable terrain by horse or donkey-cart – became a scarce resource, the domain of a handful of local guides who competed for a slice of a tiny market and felt understandably reluctant to share their secrets.

Things stayed this way until very recently, when Armenians realised that putting resources into bringing the trails up to international standards could benefit not just foreign hikers but guides, homestay operators and village shop owners; indeed, a whole set of supporting industries. At the time of research the picture is rapidly changing, with hiking trail development projects on regional, national and international levels, led by a variety of agencies from government bodies to international organisations to local NGOs and individuals. Signage is being standardised nationwide, and most of the short trails already well known to tourists and guides are now clearly waymarked. **Long-distance trails** currently in the process of being built or extended include the 500km **Janapar Trail** (**w** janapartrail.org; page 381), which connects Armenia and Nagorno Karabagh, and the Armenian leg of the **Transcaucasian Trail** (**w** transcaucasiantrail.org; see box, page 114), a more adventurous route which will be 750km long when complete, with plans to continue north into Georgia. Shorter regional hikes are covered throughout this guide.

Walkers and hikers who prefer to ramble unmolested by signposts and trail markers will be pleased to know that one is free to roam practically anywhere in the Armenian backcountry, with the exception of private property (where there may be fierce guard dogs), the state reserves of Khosrov and Shikahogh (where a guide is obligatory; pages 207 and 366), and of course anywhere near the militarised borders. The sprawling network of 4x4 tracks found in the mountains – still regularly used by locals in the summer months for herding, haymaking and firewood collection – is extensive enough to walk from one village to the next on them without ever feeling too isolated; indeed, one could (and people have) crossed the entire country this way. If you're lucky you may stumble upon the occasional ancient footpath in the forest or a rock-hewn staircase winding its way up a sheer cliff to a stunning vantage point – such are the rewards awaiting the pioneering and adventurous.

The best source of **general information** on hiking in Armenia is the aptly named HIKEArmenia foundation, whose website (**w** hikearmenia.org) features interactive maps and practical information for walks and hikes all over the country, as well as an accompanying smartphone app. In July 2018 it also opened a hiking information centre in Yerevan (5 Vardanants St; ✆011 445326; **e** info@hikearmenia.org; **w** hikearmenia.org; ⊕ 10.00–19.00 Mon–Fri), providing support and information for local and international hikers to plan and prepare for their adventures, as well as commonly requested supplies such as gas canisters for many types of camping stove. Those in need of **hiking and camping equipment** have few options, but the shop attached to the Armenian Mountaineering and Hiking Federation office (1 Artsakh St, Yerevan; ✆010 434911; **e** info@camp.am; **w** camp.am) carries a good selection.

**Topographical maps** with a level of detail useful to outdoor enthusiasts remain non-existent, though things are changing. The best such maps in general are still the Cold War-era Soviet military maps, of which scanned sets of the original printed maps for Armenia can be downloaded from **w** maps.vlasenko.net or **w** loadmap.net at 1:100,000 and 1:200,000 scales, or accessed via the Soviet Military Maps app for Android smartphones by German mapping agency Atlogis (**w** atlogis.com). The map sheets are named according to a standardised system; there is a useful online tool at **w** gpsmapsearch.com/osm/nom.htm that will tell you the map code for any location. Scans of the 1:50,000- and 1:25,000-scale maps – the equivalent of the UK Ordnance Survey Landranger and Explorer series – do also exist in digital form but are impossible to find without going to lengths on a par with infiltrating the KGB itself. What sources there are change frequently, coverage is inconsistent, and there is a distinct sense of mystery around them (as one website notes, those that are available are most likely sourced from 'the stocks kept on board freight train wagons sitting in Riga captured by the Latvians during the break-up of the Soviet Union'). Note that the maps have not been updated in nearly half a century; while the accurate and useful contours and topographical features may be more or less the same, roads and tracks may have had their alignments changed or been abandoned, and rural settlements may now be known under different names or no longer exist (and in any case are labelled in Cyrillic script). Map keys are not printed on individual sheets; among the most important elements for hikers are dashed black lines indicating dirt tracks or paths, and the Russian abbreviations *вод* (water, ie: a spring) and *коч* (nomad camp, ie: a summer herding settlement in the Armenian context). For the truly keen, an exhaustive English-language guide to interpreting the notation of these maps (originally produced for the US army in the 1950s) can be downloaded from w lib.berkeley.edu/EART/pdf/soviet.pdf.

In combination with the much-improved OpenStreetMap coverage of Armenia (w openstreetmap.org) and aerial imagery from Google Earth (w google.com/ earth), the Soviet maps are usually sufficient to plan routes between most rural locations where no recognised trails exist. In addition, users of the online popular route-sharing community WikiLoc (w wikiloc.com) have managed to log and share a wide variety of hikes and treks, though be aware that these are not curated and are unlikely to correspond to any visible route markings on the ground, and in some cases can be genuinely misleading as to the existence of a viable route. Do cross-reference any downloaded routes with other sources and be prepared to turn back if necessary. The lack of up-to-date mapping is being more keenly felt as interest gathers in the potential of hiking as a driver for tourism: the first detailed hiking-specific map (covering Dilijan National Park at a scale of 1:25,000) was due for publication by Cartisan (w cartisan.org) in early 2019.

Certain **safety concerns** need to be highlighted, particularly if hiking away from established trails. The first is the currently limited capabilities of the Armenian emergency services in a medical evacuation scenario. No official mountain rescue service exists at present; rescue operations are likely to be carried out by the military and/or members of the small mountaineering community, and there is just one military helicopter available for civilian search and rescue scenarios in the event of an SOS call. Hikers venturing into the backcountry should take sensible precautions, including informing others of their plans in advance, carrying the full range of SIM cards for maximum mobile phone coverage (if not a satellite communicator), and ensuring that their travel insurance covers what is likely to be classified a 'risky activity', including the costs of a medical evacuation and repatriation.

The second is the **dogs**. Shepherds' dogs, which are likely to be found wherever there are animals out to pasture, are there to guard their herds on behalf of their owners (who will always be nearby) and will react defensively if they feel that your presence is a threat. Familiarise yourself with the subject of canine aggression and read up on how to interpret the dogs' behaviour and how to respond appropriately during such a confrontation. Very few such encounters escalate into serious incidents, but those that do are almost invariably a result of the victim being unaware of the correct course of action.

Finally, Armenia plays host to a few potentially hazardous species of wildlife – both flora and fauna – that hikers are among the most likely to come across. Bears, wolves and leopards may sound frightening, but there are no recorded incidences of such animals attacking hikers (indeed, if you spot a Persian leopard in the flesh you will be the first human to have done so for many decades). Of far greater concern are giant hogweed (page 81) and stinging nettles in the category of plants and, in

2

## THE TRANSCAUCASIAN TRAIL IN ARMENIA

Though the idea of a long-distance hiking trail across the Caucasus had existed for some time, it became a reality in 2016 with the founding of the **Transcaucasian Trail Association** and the first trail-building effort in the Upper Svaneti region of Georgia. At the same time an expedition funded by Land Rover and supported by the UK's Royal Geographical Society was launched to explore and map possible routes for a branch of the trail through Armenia and southern Georgia. At the time of research (June 2018), an 85km length of the Armenian section of the trail had been built to connect the sights of Dilijan National Park (page 300), with a second section under construction in southern Vayots Dzor (page 339) and a remote route pioneered through the Geghama Mountains to join the two. Additional provinces are expected to be tackled year by year. The finished southern route is planned to stretch for around 1,500km from Batumi on the Black Sea coast, following the Lesser Caucasus Mountains through southern Georgia and Armenia and finishing in Meghri in the far south. A northern route traversing the Greater Caucasus range will be similar in length and hopes to connect Georgia and Azerbaijan, with significant sections open in the Svaneti region and more being worked on. Though the founders of this extremely ambitious project expect it to be a decade or so before the route is declared complete, significant steps have already been taken, and a British hiker successfully completed the prototype 1,500km Armenia–Georgia route in August 2017. The effort is heavily volunteer-focused and there are several ways by which interested visitors may participate beyond simply hiking the route. For more information, see w transcaucasiantrail.org.

the animal kingdom, several species of venomous snakes which may be disturbed by unwary hikers. All can be avoided by taking sensible precautions (page 76).

**CYCLE TOURING AND MOUNTAIN BIKING** It is not uncommon to see travellers defying the mountainous roads of Armenia on two wheels, and the growth in popularity of **cycle touring** has been noticeable in recent years. As well as cyclists flying in and out of Yerevan to ride in Armenia, neighbouring Georgia provides an easy second country to explore on a single trip. Long-distance riders pedalling east from Europe through Turkey and Iran also sometimes detour via the Caucasus, with Tbilisi and Yerevan both stopovers for overland travellers collecting Iranian visas. There is some spectacular riding to be had in Armenia, as long as you aren't afraid of a few ups and downs: particularly in the southern half of the country it is impossible to avoid long and often steep climbs over some tremendous mountain passes. Nagorno Karabagh is by all accounts even more extreme. High elevations also make for thinner air, and so for that and the above reasons a good level of prior **fitness** is strongly recommended.

When **planning routes**, don't expect to find any dedicated infrastructure or tourist information for cyclists. Finding pleasant routes on quiet roads is easy enough if a few rules of thumb are followed. Avoid the bigger highways whenever possible, as you'll find much more pleasant riding on the provincial roads. Avoid in particular the stretches of the M1 between Gyumri and Yerevan (go via Spitak and Aparan), the awful M4 dual carriageway from Yerevan to Lake Sevan (take the scenic route along the gorge; page 248), and the first part of the new M2 North–South Road heading southeast from Yerevan (take the H8 to Vosketap and then the H10 via Vedi). Often where there is a new main road you will find a more or less parallel alternative from a previous era of road building – try asking locals for the 'old road' (*heen janapar*). When the main road is the only option, there is often a generous hard shoulder to ride on. Destinations (ie: towns with accommodation) tend to be spaced well for the daily distance ranges of most cyclists. Many scenic routes can be found in the gentler terrain of the Shirak and Lori provinces in the north and in Gegharkunik and Kotayk provinces in the centre of Armenia, with the road around Lake Sevan providing a particularly nice loop, especially on the quieter eastern shore. Those heading northeast to Tavush or south to Vayots Dzor and Syunik will find tougher riding and fewer options – there is only one continuous paved route between Yeghegnadzor and Meghri on the M2 (with the exception of the highly recommended new M17 route south of Kapan through Shikahogh Reserve), and with several passes over 2,000m it is only really suitable for the fittest and/or most masochistic riders, or those heading for Iran who have little choice in the matter.

In terms of **safety**, local drivers are used to unpredictable sights on the roads and will generally show you courtesy as they pass, but it is always a good idea to wear high-visibility clothing. Badly lit tunnels may be encountered, and roads through forested regions will be more shaded in the summer, so bring lights – especially rear lights – for visibility. Every cyclist knows that dogs love to chase people on bicycles, and Armenia is no different in this respect. Dogs in Armenia are disciplined by being shouted at and having rocks thrown at them by their owners; you may wish to mimic the former and perhaps mime the latter, or administer a good spraying from your water bottle.

Bring your own bike and equipment, including tools and spares, as bike shops are few and far between. Most airlines classify bicycles as sporting equipment and will carry them if suitably packaged in a bag or box, with fees varying by airline. Your **choice of bicycle** should take into account the local terrain and road conditions – a racing bike suitable for the UK lowlands may have you cursing up the climbs in Armenia, so ensure your bike has an adequate range of gear ratios to tackle the long, steep hills. Pot-holes, poor road surfaces and the number of dirt roads that may make for interesting detours or alternative routes indicate that a mountain bike (or a road touring bike with tough wheels and mixed-terrain tyres) may be a wise choice. **Bike shops** carrying parts for high-end modern bicycles are non-existent outside Yerevan and thin on the ground even in the city. See page 136 for information on specific retailers, workshops and bike-hire outlets in Yerevan.

Much of the hiking advice on pages 112–13 regarding maps and route-finding applies to off-road **bikepacking** and **mountain biking**: the network of 4x4 tracks linking Armenia's villages and crossing its mountains makes it a playground for the intrepid rider, and all the better if you come equipped to camp. Get off the beaten track and you're likely to see nobody but a few hardy locals on horseback or in rusting Soviet jeeps for days on end. Beware, however, that gradients can be impossibly steep in places if maps and elevation profiles are not thoroughly considered in advance. Expect to still have to get off and push occasionally. The poor condition of many of these tracks calls for a bike with front suspension, with extra care taken on loose, rocky and badly rutted descents. It's best to avoid the spring and early summer if possible, as melting snow together with wetter weather can turn dirt roads into mudbaths – go later in the summer or autumn when the land has dried out.

Taking **bicycles on public transport** can either be very easy or a chore, depending on what mood the driver is in. With no regular intercity bus services, you are restricted to negotiating carriage of your bicycle on overloaded minibuses. If there is no roof rack this may involve partial disassembly of your bike, and you would do well to keep an eye on the manner in which it is loaded on to the vehicle. Expect an extra charge for this, though there is no standard rate. The only exception is the seasonal train to Lake Sevan (page 85), which is a cheap and easy way to get yourself and your bicycle out of Yerevan to somewhere more pleasant and eliminate a vertical kilometre of climbing in the process.

The abundance of roadside stalls and convenience stores on Armenia's roads means that carrying lots of **food** is rarely necessary unless you're going off-road and remote. You'll also find plenty of roadside picnic shelters, particularly in scenic areas such as river gorges and mountain passes. Freshwater **springs** are a common sight on the road in the mountains of Armenia – the water in all such springs is drinkable, not to mention refreshingly cold in the summer, and they're usually accompanied by a lay-by and a picnic shelter. There are no particular restrictions on **camping** in the countryside and you'll find the locals very tolerant of you setting up your tent away from the road: anyone who does find you is more likely to invite you for a shot of vodka than to kick you off their land.

## HISTORIC SITES

In this guide, prices and opening hours are included where they apply. Otherwise assume the site is free and always open.

There may appear to be some confusion between the terms **church** and **monastery** at times. This is because at some sites only the church of a monastery survives but the site is still referred to as a monastery. With more and more churches becoming active places of worship, it is now common for the church itself to be locked at night although the site as a whole may still be accessible. Larger churches, and especially those in well-known historic sites, will be open all day, at least 09.00–18.00 and often longer. Active churches in small villages are now sometimes kept locked unless there is a service taking place, but it is often possible to gain entrance. The caretaker, having seen visitors arriving, may well just appear. If not, it is often possible to contact the keyholder, who usually lives nearby, by asking anyone who happens to be around. The keyholder will also sell candles to visitors: it is customary on entering an Armenian church to light candles (page 40). Most other sites (**fortresses, caravanserais, prehistoric monuments**) are always open, being in any case impossible to close.

## MEDIA AND COMMUNICATIONS

**MEDIA** Armenia has two public **television** networks, Armenia 1 (H1) and Armenia TV, and over 40 private television companies. They are of little interest to those who do not speak Armenian and, indeed, many Armenians themselves prefer to watch Russian television. The independent television station A1+ posts news on its website (w a1plus.am) in both Armenian and English.

The printed **press** is almost entirely in Armenian. Investigative journalists have in the past been periodically assaulted by thugs employed by those who had vested interests to protect. Censorship was prohibited under a 2004 media law but libel and defamation are punishable by prison terms and journalists have been sentenced under these laws. The US-based NGO Freedom House reports that self-censorship is common, particularly in regard to reporting corruption (though the environment has been somewhat different since May 2018; page 33) and the Nagorno Karabagh situation.

**Radio** does not play a large part in the life of Armenians, being mostly listened to in the car. Public Radio of Armenia is the national, state-run station. There are also many private radio stations; we are told that the quality is not good.

The **internet** is now the main source of news for many Armenians. As a result there is much more in the way of English-language reporting and analysis available: try **w** news.am/eng, **w** evnreport.com, **w** azatutyun.am and **w** hetq.am/en.

**TELEPHONE** Enormous strides have been made in modernising the outdated Soviet-era telecommunications network. The network was bought out by VEON, headquartered in Amsterdam and doing much the same across former Soviet Central Asia, and rebranded from ArmenTel to Beeline in 2008. Beeline (**w** beeline. am) holds all landlines and 19% of the cellular network. There are two other phone companies, VivaCell-MTS (**w** mts.am) which holds 57% of the cellular market and Ucom (**w** ucom.am), a relative newcomer, which holds 24% after acquiring the Armenian arm of French telecoms giant Orange in 2015. Mobile phones are ubiquitous and there is good coverage throughout the country; many people own several phones to take advantage of free call time to other users of the same network. SIM cards are free, and all three operators offer a variety of tariffs, languages and ever-changing special offers. The simplest option for most visitors is to pay a one-off sum for a prepaid package comprising data, call time and an SMS allowance which lasts for 30 days and can be renewed if needed. For those going off the beaten track, VivaCell-MTS is said to have the best coverage of remote regions, though getting two or even three SIM cards to cover all bases might be wise.

All three operators have 24-hour desks in the arrivals hall at Zvartnots International Airport where SIM cards can be obtained. Note that an identification document is required by Armenians and foreigners when registering a SIM card, so your passport will be needed. All companies have multiple outlets in Yerevan and throughout the country where prepaid or post-paid cards are available. Top-up cards can also be bought at numerous supermarkets, shops and kiosks. This method is gradually losing favour to automatic payment terminals which are prominently

2

positioned on the pavements of towns and cities. Many ATMs will also process mobile phone payments.

Your own mobile phone will work in Armenia on a roaming basis if you arrange this with your provider before leaving home. The advantage of course is that you can keep your own mobile number and any smartphone apps that depend on it; the disadvantage is that it is usually more expensive than using an Armenian SIM card. To use an Armenian SIM card in your own phone it will first have to be unlocked. This can usually be done (at your own risk) cheaply and quickly at one of a great many mobile phone repair booths in Yerevan, but if staying in the country for more than a few days a cheaper and more convenient option may be to buy a basic mobile phone in Armenia. The mobile companies have some very reasonable packages and repair kiosks usually have a display window full of secondhand handsets.

**Dialling Armenia** from abroad, the country code is 374 followed by the local area code, excluding the initial 0 (much as with UK numbers). In this guide, area codes are included in individual phone numbers, and there is also a list of the main geographic codes in the box on page 117. Codes are always given for mobile numbers. Yerevan has two codes (010/011), and phone numbers for Yerevan have the relevant code included with the individual numbers. For numbers outside Armenia (eg: tour operator listings), the country code is included with the individual number.

**International calls** from Armenia can be made from landlines or mobiles as elsewhere. If using a landline, a cheaper option than direct dialling is to purchase an **international call card** available from shops, kiosks, newspaper stands, etc. Instructions are on the card but essentially you dial the number on the card, followed by the scratch number, then follow the voice instructions.

In Yerevan and a few other places calls can be made from **public card phones** in the streets, these cards being on sale at post offices and kiosks. The preferred instant messaging apps in Armenia at the time of update are WhatsApp, Viber and Facebook Messenger.

**INTERNET** Internet services have also improved greatly in recent years. All types of connection are available, including data packages for mobile phones via the three main companies (page 117). Free **Wi-Fi** is widely available in hotels and cafés, as well as metro stations and airports, and in an increasing number of outdoor public spaces. On the rare occasion when Wi-Fi is unavailable at a given accommodation option, this is stated in the listing. Although not as numerous as they used to be, there are still a handful of **internet cafés**, charging about AMD500 per hour, mostly now full of teenage boys playing extraordinarily violent computer games rather than backpackers emailing Mum. A curious feature of previous Armenian use of the internet was that it could not cope with the Armenian alphabet and, surprisingly, not even the Cyrillic alphabet with any reliability. Therefore Armenians emailing each other tended to transliterate these languages into Roman letters. Having got used to doing this, many Armenians continue to do so, although using the Armenian alphabet is no longer a problem thanks to the Unicode system and a large range of compatible fonts. Problems can arise, however, if you're carrying out internet searches, because of the lack of standardisation of transliteration (page xi).

**POSTAL SERVICES** The national postal service **Haypost** (w haypost.am) is under Dutch management. Post offices throughout the country have been modernised in recent years and new services introduced. Post offices, in Haypost's blue, white and orange colours, are widespread; even quite small villages have one. Recent letters from the UK have arrived three to four weeks after being posted, much better than in the past when they often never arrived at all. Post sent abroad from Armenia is usually quicker and more reliable than vice versa. Items have taken as little as six days from Yerevan to Scotland but two weeks is average. It can be slower from the provinces. There is a standard charge of AMD240 for postcards sent abroad. Letters are charged by weight; for those going abroad the cost is AMD350 for letters up to 20g, AMD870 for 20–100g, etc. In additional to Haypost, most international couriers are represented in Armenia.

For visitors who wish to receive parcels, it may be better to use one of the relatively new international shipping services such as Globbing (43/34 Mashtots Av, Yerevan; \060 616616; w globbing.com). Invented to cater for locals who wanted to order things online in the West and have them arrive reliably, users ship their items to personalised receiving addresses in the UK, USA, Russia, Germany or China, where the company consolidates them, ships them in bulk to Armenia, clears customs (there is a monthly customs allowance per customer of AMD200,000 and up to 30kg), and makes the packages available for collection at one of their depots (currently four in Yerevan and one in Stepanakert). Pricing is calculated by dimensional weight and usually works out much cheaper than sending by regular international post where large packages are concerned.

## BUSINESS

**Corruption** in official bodies was long known to be widespread in Armenia and the resulting dissatisfaction was one of the major contributing factors to 2018's Velvet Revolution, with the country ranking 107 out of 180 in Transparency International's Corruption Perceptions Index 2017. 'Perhaps the most critical challenge the government faces is … breaking up the near monopolies/oligarchies held by a small group of well-connected businessmen on the import and sale of a range of critical products,' wrote the US Department of Commerce at the time. 'These pose significant barriers to entry for both domestic and foreign businesses, and harm competition and consumer welfare.' The true extent of this situation only began to take concrete form in the revolution's aftermath when widespread investigations were launched and the shocking results began to reach the local media (page 33). In such light it is difficult now to imagine a regression to the former state of affairs.

Business practices as such are not widely different from those in the West but it is absolutely vital to be certain of the competence of **interpreters** when translating between Armenian and Western languages: many problems arise because what is apparently the same word or phrase does not mean precisely the same in two different languages. Business hours are 09.00–17.00. At work men and women are on an equal footing although, as explained on page 42, it is customary for a married woman to stay at home to look after the couple's children while they are young. On a semi-social level, most business visitors find themselves being taken out to restaurants by their hosts for lengthy meals and numerous toasts (page 102). They may also be taken to historic sites, particularly at the weekend.

## BUYING PROPERTY

It is easy to purchase property in Armenia, and many Armenians from the diaspora take advantage of the fact. Foreigners can buy an apartment or house outright, although they cannot buy land unless they are either of Armenian descent or else buy it through

2

a company (which can be foreign-owned): they can only lease land, which can be for up to 99 years. Prices are highest in central Yerevan at about US$5,000/m², while one of the newly built apartments on Northern Avenue currently costs US$2,500/m². Prices drop gradually the further from the centre one travels, with suburban prices being about half this. Prices in towns near Yerevan tend also to be relatively high with prices in other towns considerably lower. When looking for anywhere to buy, only ever consider stone-built property or good quality newbuilds: the poor quality of Soviet prefabricated construction was demonstrated vividly in the 1988 earthquake. Property is widely advertised in the local press, including the Armenian-language newspaper *Gind* (published every two weeks and with a corresponding smartphone app of the same name), and the Craigslist-style website w list.am, or you could use a broker to find you something, though they rarely speak English. A broker's fee is typically 3% of the purchase price. Brokers will also handle the paperwork, whether or not you purchase through them, for a fee of around US$250.

Sound advice on buying a property in Armenia can be found at w armeniapedia. org, together with recommended brokers and websites.

## CULTURAL ETIQUETTE

As is made clear throughout this guide, Armenians are extremely hospitable and, especially in rural areas, visitors will often be invited into people's houses for coffee. Accept with good grace, however poor the family; the invitation is sincere and the family will be genuinely pleased to see you. If dining with a family, including at a homestay, expect to be plied with far more food than it is humanly possible to eat. You are by no means expected to finish everything (leftovers are eaten the following day), but it is polite to at least try every dish. See the section on drinks (page 102) for the rules on toasting and the section on breakfast (page 97) if you have the fortune to be invited to a *khash* party.

If invited to someone's home for a meal, a small gift for the host, who will have spent very many hours preparing the meal, is appropriate – a box of chocolates or flowers (but always an odd number of flowers; an even number is for the cemetery).

When visiting churches, it is customary to buy candles (expect to pay AMD60–100 each) and then light them before sticking them in the trays of sand. Matches are provided. There is no particular need to dress more conservatively than elsewhere in Armenia, but women should wear a headscarf if intending to take communion. It is correct to leave a church walking backwards (so as not to turn one's back on God) but foreigners will not be chastised for not doing so.

Armenians do tend to dress more smartly than Westerners and also more formally. In particular going to someone's house for dinner, or to the theatre, is an occasion for formality (suit or dress) rather than for dressing down. Shorts are worn by both sexes in summer in Yerevan but are much less common elsewhere.

It is normal to greet people any time you meet them outside a town. Just say 'Barev dzez' – 'Hello'. Expect people in rural areas to be very curious about where you come from, what you are doing, and what you think about Armenia. It is very hard not to interact with local people, although the language barrier is considerable unless you speak either Armenian or Russian. Very few people speak English and even those who do, including English-language teachers, may not understand what is said to them since they are unaccustomed to hearing English spoken by native speakers of the language.

With very few exceptions, Armenians of all ages love having their photograph taken, although it is of course polite to ask before taking a portrait shot. In general, people will happily pose. You may well be remonstrated with by old ladies if you fail to take their photograph while photographing the monument by which they are sitting, and children will quite often pester you to take their picture.

In the West, although we are not necessarily conscious of it, we often smile at someone we are speaking to, even if we do not know them and are encountering them in a superficial business situation, as in a bank or enquiry office. However, this is not always the case in Armenia and it can be surprisingly disconcerting for a foreigner. It is not that the person is surly or doesn't want to see you, it is just that Armenians tend not to smile unless they know you or there is something to smile at, such as a joke.

Again, in the West, we are accustomed to think that if a door is firmly shut it probably means that the place is either closed or one is not meant to enter. This is not the case in Armenia. If the place looks shut it is worth trying the door: the premises may well be fully open for business. Even in the National Gallery the large forbidding doors to some of the rooms may be firmly shut (sometimes for so prosaic a reason as to keep out the cold) but one is meant to open them to continue the tour of the art gallery.

Some large hotels have an entry hall devoid of furnishing or people. Go up to the next floor and you will find a fully functioning hotel. If a hotel, restaurant or shop looks deserted when you arrive, don't panic, someone will soon appear.

## TRAVELLING POSITIVELY

Tourism is a growing industry with the potential to do much to alleviate Armenia's ongoing economic struggles – 29.4% of the population is still officially below the poverty line according to Armenia's own National Statistical Service, a figure that has held steady for over a decade. You would never guess this from a day in central Yerevan, of course, where the wealth is disproportionately concentrated. As a responsible traveller, therefore, one of the best actions you can take is to plan to spend more of your time (and money) in the provinces, where small tourism businesses still struggle to bring in enough customers to make their endeavours sustainable. Indeed, many of the country's most spectacular cultural and natural sites are sufficiently distant from Yerevan to warrant overnight stays. So consider multi-day excursions rather than day trips, homestay accommodation wherever possible over business hotels, local guides rather than those supplied by Yerevan agencies, and buying your food locally rather than bringing snacks from city supermarkets.

Beyond responsible tourism, the demand for solutions to many of Armenia's wide-ranging problems has resulted in a very active non-profit sector, with NGOs and foundations formed to support work in almost every conceivable niche. Beyond the large, well-known international development agencies such as the EU, USAID and UNDP, many smaller and more enigmatic organisations have been founded and funded by Armenians from the diaspora, for whom the issues they have chosen to tackle are those to which they have a particular personal connection. Those wishing to support efforts in specific sectors would do well to research them thoroughly; the following is a selected list of organisations with which the authors have had personal contact or involvement.

### CHARITIES AND NGOS
**Armenia Tree Project** 57/5 Arshakunyants St, Yerevan; ☎010 447401; w armeniatree.org.

Founded in 1994 with headquarters in Yerevan & Woburn, MA, conducting environmental projects to advance the reforestation of Armenia, combat desertification & assist the population in using trees to improve their living standards. It has co-ordinated the planting & restoration of more than 5 million trees since its inception, with 4 regional tree nurseries, a permanent staff of 80 & hundreds of part-time workers. Volunteering opportunities are available through Birthright Armenia (see opposite) & donations can be made through its website, through which printable donation forms are also available.

**Armenian Monuments Awareness Project (AMAP)** 101 Pavstos Buzand St, Door 1, Apt 6, Yerevan; ☏ 010 532455; e contact@armenianheritage.org; w armenianheritage.org. An NGO which aims to stimulate sustainable economic development arising from tourism at Armenia's historical, cultural & natural monuments. It also aims to assist in monument preservation & is the body behind much of the welcome recent increase in information at historic sites. Contact it by email if you wish to consider a donation.

**HALO Trust** Carronfoot, Thornhill, Dumfries DG3 5BF, UK; ☏ +44 1848 331100; e mail@halotrust.org; w halotrust.org. This non-political, non-religious NGO & the largest humanitarian mine-clearance organisation in the world undertakes mine clearing in Nagorno Karabagh (see box, page 375; also w halotrust.org/minefreenk). Some governments are withdrawing funding from the Nagorno Karabagh sphere of operation, eg: the UK's Department for International Development has excluded Nagorno Karabagh from its mine-action strategy since 2011, despite previously funding mine clearing there. Governmental monies can only be used within the pre-1991 boundaries of Nagorno Karabagh so mine clearance outside these boundaries is entirely dependent on other sources. All donations, whatever the size, are welcome & can be made via the website or sent to the HALO Trust's headquarters. Anyone wishing their money to be used specifically for Nagorno Karabagh should state this or donate through the Karabagh-specific page on the website.

**Hayastan All-Armenian Fund** Hayastan All-Armenian Fund Great Britain, c/o Armenian Vicarage, Iverna Gardens, Kensington, London W8 6TP; w himnadram.org. Founded in 1992 as a means whereby all Armenians worldwide could contribute to the development & stability of newly independent Armenia. Help is given

where it is most needed, whether that be infrastructure, economic development, job creation or humanitarian relief. Projects range in size from a new classroom for a village school to 150km of new road, & they also cover green projects such as the planting of trees to replace those cut down for firewood during the electricity shortages of 1992–95. All contributions to programmes great & small are welcome, & not only from members of the diaspora. Donations can be made via the website or through 1 of the local branches.

**OneArmenia** 5th Floor, 2/2 Melik Adamyan St, Yerevan; e contact@onearmenia.org; w onearmenia.org. An NGO focused on creating sustainable jobs through innovative, crowdfunded projects, with headquarters in Yerevan & Santa Monica, CA. Its cutting-edge projects have spanned sectors from small-scale agriculture to wine tourism to hiking trails to the technology industry. Donations are made on a recurring or per project basis, with 3–4 new campaigns each year.

**Orran** 6 First Yekmalyan St, Yerevan; ☏ 010 535167; e orran@orran.am; w orran.am. A charity established in 2000 with its headquarters in Yerevan. It aims to help the poorest in society, mainly children & the elderly. Visitors are welcome. Donations can be made via its website or by cheque in US dollars to 2217 Observatory Av, Los Angeles, CA 90027, USA.

**Oxfam** Oxfam has worked in Armenia since 1998 to support refugees who fled to Armenia during the Karabagh conflict & the communities in which they settled. It now assists small farmers & women's groups & monitors the impact of government policies on the poor. A visit to Oxfam's projects can be arranged via Margarita Hakobyan at Oxfam's office in Yerevan (Apt 19, 23 Davit Anhaght St; ☏ 010 208808). Donations can be sent to Oxfam Hse (John Smith Drive, Cowley, Oxford OX4 2JY, UK; w oxfam.org.uk). Anyone who wishes their donation to go specifically to Armenia should state this when donating.

**Tekeyan Centre** 50 Khanjyan St, Yerevan; ☏ 010 573057; e info@tekeyancentre.am; w tekeyancentre.am. The stated aim of the organisation, a British-Armenian charity based in London & Yerevan, is to unite all Armenians to develop & spread Armenian culture, science & art all over the world. On a practical level it has provided free textbooks to schools in Armenia & Nagorno Karabagh &, together with the British

Embassy in Yerevan, raised funds to install a heating system in the Lord Byron School (page 264) in Gyumri. Anyone wishing to donate, either specifically for the Lord Byron School or more generally, can contact the British Embassy (enquiries.yerevan@fco.gov.uk) or the Tekeyan Centre itself.

**Trails For Change** 3 Moskovyan St, Yerevan; e info@trailsforchangengo.org; w trailsforchangengo.org. An NGO founded in 2017 to address the lack of hiking infrastructure in Armenia & Nagorno Karabagh, making the region's natural heritage more accessible to visitors & creating income opportunities for isolated villages in the process. The organisation trains & employs young Armenians to build new trails & to maintain existing routes. Donations can be made online.

**Transcaucasian Trail Association** #106-262, 4200 Wisconsin Av NW, Washington, DC 20016, USA; e info@transcaucasiantrail.org; w transcaucasiantrail.org. US-based non-profit organisation co-ordinating efforts to build the first long-distance hiking trail across the Caucasus, inc Armenia. Donations can be made online with monthly/annual membership options; one-off donations of US$500 or more can be requested to fund projects in Armenia specifically.

**World Vision International** Head Office, Opal Drive, Fox Milne, Milton Keynes MK15 0ZR, UK; 919 2nd Av, 2nd Floor, New York, NY 10017, USA; e info@worldvision.org.uk; w wvi.org/armenia. An organisation with Christian underpinnings which includes Armenia in its worldwide aim of working with children, families & their communities to enable them to reach their full potential by tackling the causes of poverty & injustice. Often works by sponsoring individual children. Sponsors receive annual reports about the child/family they sponsor.

## VOLUNTEERING ORGANISATIONS

**ARK Armenia** 4/4 Charents St, Kapan; ℡093 812683, 098 887894, 095 887895; e arkarmenia@gmail.com; w arkarmenia.com. Small environmental NGO based in the southern city of Kapan, offering volunteering opportunities on an ad hoc basis through the Workaway & WWOOF platforms (page 124). Projects include mapping & marking hiking trails, providing language support to tourists in the local area, & running permaculture operations & training sessions.

Popular with backpackers who often stay at the eco-camp in Kapan itself or the summer house in nearby Arachadzor.

**Armenian Volunteer Corps** 37 Hanrapetutyan St, Yerevan; ℡010 540037; e info@avc.am; w armenianvolunteer.org. A major volunteer placement organisation partnering with a wide range of other NGOs to offer placements of 1 month to 1 year, similar to Birthright Armenia (see below) but for participants of all backgrounds. It also offers support with living arrangements & logistics, as well as language classes, excursions & socials.

**Birthright Armenia** 37 Hanrapetutyan St, Yerevan; ℡010 540037; e info@birthrightarmenia.am; w birthrightarmenia.org. Founded in 2003 to offer young people with Armenian heritage the opportunity to experience immersion in their ancestral homeland through volunteering. Those with at least 25% Armenian lineage (ie: 1 grandparent) are eligible to apply. The organisation provides not just placements but also accommodation, excursions & language classes, & reimburses travel expenses for qualifying participants, with alumni 1,500 strong & counting.

**European Voluntary Service (EVS)** w europa.eu/youth/volunteering/evs-organisation_en; f FindYourEVS. The Armenian branch of the EU-funded youth volunteering charity EVS works with NGOs in Armenia to make volunteer placements available to 18–30-year-olds for 2–12-month periods. Most costs are covered; applicants must be legal residents of 1 of the participating countries.

**Transcaucasian Trail Armenia** e armenia@transcaucasiantrail.org; w transcaucasiantrail.org. Local branch of the international project. Volunteering opportunities are offered seasonally & typically take the form of 'trail-building camps' in areas of natural beauty, performing building & maintenance work on sections of the trail, with an emphasis on teamwork, minimal impact & environmental education.

**US Peace Corps** 33 Charents St, Yerevan; ℡010 513500; w peacecorps.gov/armenia. Since 1992 this well-known US government-funded international programme has posted more than 1,000 American volunteers to Armenia. As with other Peace Corps programmes worldwide, participants spend several months or even years often posted to remote parts of the country in a challenging, full-immersion environment.

**Workaway** w workaway.info. An increasingly popular web portal connecting global travellers & organisations/entrepreneurs to make informal volunteering opportunities available, based on the principle of working a certain number of hours or days/week in exchange for bed & board. Hosts are encouraged to ensure their volunteers have ample time off to travel & explore, & that the 'cultural immersion' aspect of their experience is respected & prioritised. Listings in Armenia are somewhat thin on the ground but worth exploring by interested visitors nonetheless.

**WWOOF** w wwoof.net. Similar to Workaway (see left) but with an emphasis on organic farming. There is no official co-ordination in Armenia, though opportunities are independently offered.

# Part Two

## THE GUIDE

ARMENIA PROVINCES

# 3

# Yerevan

Armenia's rapidly modernising capital sits at the foot of the mountains on the edge of the Ararat plain, straddling the gorge of the Hrazdan River which flows southwest from Lake Sevan to join the Arax south of the city. The deep gorge skirts the centre of Yerevan on its western side and consequently many visitors only see it as they cross Victory Bridge into the city from Zvartnots International Airport. Yerevan is the cultural and financial capital of Armenia and has in recent years developed into a pleasant, thriving and visitor-friendly hub of cosmopolitan life. Particularly around Republic Square, the central area also boasts some of the finest Soviet-era buildings in the whole of the former USSR, and among the new high-rise apartment blocks there is a surprising range of older architecture, owing largely to the fusion of Armenian and Russian styles, with a sprinkling of Persian influence too.

Housing a population of just over a million, Yerevan's suburbs sprawl in contrast to the compact city centre. The lower districts towards Ararat are at an elevation of around 900m above sea level and the hillside districts to the north reach 1,200m. Precipitation is light at 277mm per annum with May being the wettest month (43mm) and August the driest (8mm). The average temperature (measured over 24 hours) varies from –3°C (27°F) in January to 26°C (79°F) in July, though these averages mask considerable variation: night-time lows in January are around –15°C (5°F) while daytime highs in July can reach 44°C (111°F). Yerevan is a very sunny place, with an average of 2,579 hours of sunshine annually (there are 8,760 hours in a year) and only 37 days classed as non-sunny. This combination of dry heat and fierce sun in July and August leads many Yerevantsis to escape to cooler climes outside the city. Consequently, it might be best to visit the city from April to June (though late spring can be stormy) or in September and October, rather than at the height of summer.

## HISTORY

Yerevan's fortunes have waxed and waned considerably over time, and though it was never the capital of Armenia prior to 1918, as a recognisable settlement it is actually very old: Armenians celebrated the 2,800th birthday of Yerevan in 2018. The Urartian king Argishti I (ruled c784–c763BC) established a garrison of 6,600 troops at Erebuni in the southeast part of the present city in 782BC, thus making Yerevan older even than Rome which is traditionally claimed to have been founded in 753BC. About a century later, the Urartian king Rusa II (ruled c685–c645BC) chose a different site, Teishebai Uru (City of [the God] Teisheba) overlooking the Hrazdan River which he believed would be less vulnerable to attack by the Scythians. It is now known as Karmir Blur (Red Hill) in the western part of the modern city. Erebuni had grown within a hundred years to be a substantial settlement but the establishment of Teishebai Uru caused its rapid decline.

Proximity to the fertile plain ensured that Yerevan remained a significant settlement as, along with the rest of Armenia, it was caught up over the centuries of turmoil, its size fluctuating considerably as the degree of urbanisation in the country varied. Eventually it was almost totally destroyed by an earthquake in 1679. The collapsed bridge over the Hrazdan was quickly replaced by a new four-arch structure and Yerevan's importance began to rise again as it found itself close to the frontier line where the Persian, Turkish and Russian empires were jostling for supremacy. At the time of the earthquake, Yerevan itself was under Persian rule, with a mixed Christian and Muslim population. In 1684, at the request of the French king Louis XIV, Shah Suleiman II permitted French Jesuits to establish a mission here to try to persuade the Katholikos to accept the supremacy of the Pope and bring the Armenian Church into the Roman Catholic fold. The missionaries achieved little and greatly lamented the loss of the excellent Yerevan wine when Shah Hussein, who had succeeded his father, banned all wine throughout the Persian Empire in 1694. A new main church to replace those destroyed in the earthquake was erected in 1693–94 and a new central mosque in 1765–66.

Russian southward expansion into the Caucasus began under Peter the Great in 1722, ostensibly with the object of protecting Orthodox believers. It was a fairly gradual process. In 1801, Russia formally annexed eastern Georgia as the new Russian province of Tiflis and installed Prince Paul Tsitsianov, Georgian born but Russian educated, as governor. In 1804, Tsitsianov led a 5,000-strong Russian army south and attacked Yerevan on 1 May. Despite besieging the town from 2 July until 3 September he was forced to withdraw but the following year he was asked by two Armenian notables to try again so as to save the Christian population of Yerevan from Muslim oppression. His haughty reply was to the effect that he did not care even if the Christians at Yerevan were 'dying in the hands of unbelievers' because 'unreliable Armenians with Persian souls' deserved in his view to 'die like dogs' since they had done nothing to help him when he was besieging the city. Tsitsianov was killed at Baku in 1806 and in 1808 Russia made a second attempt, this time under Field Marshal Ivan Vasilievich (1741–1820) but had no more success. Eventually General Ivan Paskevich (1782–1856), a veteran of the Battle of Borodino, succeeded and led victorious Russian troops into Yerevan on 2 October 1827. On this occasion the Tsar awarded him the title Count of Yerevan but he subsequently gained the additional title Prince of Warsaw as a further token of the Tsar's appreciation when he was responsible for killing 9,000 Poles during the second Polish uprising against Russian rule in 1831.

The Russian conquerors found a town which in 1828 had 1,736 low mud-brick houses, 851 shops, ten baths, eight mosques, seven churches, seven caravanserais and six public squares all set among gardens surrounded by mud walls. On the one and only visit to Yerevan by a Tsar, Nikolai I in 1837 described the city as a 'clay pot'. Matters changed only slowly in what was still a garrison town; the principal Russian settlement in Armenia was Alexandropol (Gyumri) rather than Yerevan. Occasional traces of 19th-century Yerevan can still be found, although Yerevan's importance was to change out of all recognition with its proclamation as capital of the First Armenian Republic on 28 May 1918. The brilliant Russia-born Armenian architect Alexander Tamanyan (1878–1936) drew up a master plan in 1924–26 for what was now the capital of Soviet Armenia. It envisaged the complete rebuilding of the large central square with imposing new buildings constructed of tuff surrounding it. From this square would lead broad avenues, and encircling the whole central area would be a green ring of parkland. Quite a large part of this did in fact come to pass (see *A Walk Around Yerevan*, page 152).

Tamanyan did not, of course, foresee the 30-fold expansion of the city's population during the Soviet era to an estimated 1.1 million with its dreary urban sprawl of apartment blocks. There was in practice considerable local enthusiasm for expanding the city since any Soviet city with a population exceeding one million was considered to be of 'all Union importance' and entitled to benefits which included a metro system and a crematorium. In the post-independence era the main construction focus has been on modern high-rise apartments bought up by absentee diaspora Armenians and luxury houses for the new elite, together with the hotels, embassies and other such paraphernalia which any capital city attracts. Unfortunately this has been at the expense of many of old Yerevan's historical buildings, whose remnants grow ever more sparse. The construction of the central pedestrian boulevard Northern Avenue between 2002 and 2007, despite being part of Tamanyan's original plan, was the source of much controversy as it involved the demolition of hundreds of occupied Soviet-era apartments and many even older houses, the original inhabitants of which were reportedly offered meagre compensation in comparison with the value of the luxury apartments built in their place.

Much of the basic infrastructure in the city centre, including roads, pavements, public squares and green spaces, has been upgraded and modernised since Soviet times. In parallel, the café and restaurant scene has boomed with the result that some streets seem to consist of little else! Today, downtown Yerevan appears as manicured and bustling a capital city as any other. This is in stark contrast to the outlying suburbs and industrial areas which in most cases still appear as run-down as ever – not to mention the precarious living conditions encountered elsewhere in Armenia.

## GETTING THERE AND AWAY

Most visitors to Armenia begin their stay in Yerevan, the vast majority arriving **by air** at Yerevan's Zvartnots International Airport. For information about airlines, the airport and transport to the city centre, see page 70. Those arriving **by bus** from Iran, Georgia, Turkey or Russia (page 73) or **by train** from Georgia (page 72) also usually arrive in Yerevan. The capital has the best sources of information and hosts much of the cultural life, and is where bookings (for tours and guides, accommodation outside of Yerevan, etc) can most easily be made. Many of the important historical sites can be reached on day trips from the capital and all public transport to the provinces goes to and from Yerevan.

Yerevan is also the place to **hire a car or 4x4**. Especially if you wish to reach off-the-beaten-track places and/or if your itinerary is tightly scheduled, a vehicle will give you a higher degree of independence and control over your travels. See pages 88 and 91 for more information on driving in Armenia and hiring a vehicle. Taxis (page 87) are also cheap and abundant and can provide a viable alternative to a hired vehicle. For example, a taxi for the 120km from Vanadzor to Yerevan costs around AMD12,000. It is also possible to hire taxis and drivers on a daily basis; this is usually best done via a travel agent or through your hotel or hostel.

It is possible to independently reach most places in Armenia from Yerevan by **public transport**, but note that the transport is primarily to serve locals, not tourists, so if a tourist site is not near a town or village it will rarely be served directly. In these cases, local taxis are often the only option – apart from hitchhiking (page 92), walking or cycling, of course. Most public transport is in the form of buses or minibuses (page 86) which are cheap, if cramped and occasionally hair-raising; even the longest journeys (eg: Yerevan to Meghri) cost just AMD5,000. Daytime

3

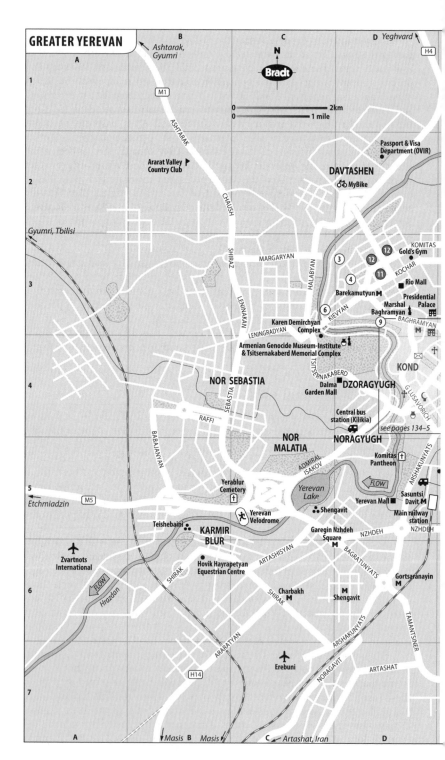

# GREATER YEREVAN

Ashtarak, Gyumri

Yeghvard

Gyumri, Tbilisi

Etchmiadzin

N

Bradt

0 — 2km
0 — 1 mile

Passport & Visa Department (OVIR)

DAVTASHEN

MyBike

Ararat Valley Country Club

KOMITAS

Gold's Gym

KOCHAR

Rio Mall

Barekamutyun

Presidential Palace

Marshal Baghramyan

BAGHRAMYAN

Karen Demirchyan Complex

Armenian Genocide Museum-Institute & Tsitsernakaberd Memorial Complex

KOND

NOR SEBASTIA

Dalma Garden Mall

DZORAGYUGH

Central bus station (Kilikia)

see pages 134–5

NOR MALATIA

NORAGYUGH

Komitas Pantheon

Yeblur Cemetery

Yerevan Lake

FLOW

Sasuntsi Davit

Yerevan Mall

Main railway station

Yerevan Velodrome

Shengavit

Teishebaini

KARMIR BLUR

Garegin Nzhdeh Square

NZHDEH

Gortsaranayin

Zvartnots International

Hovik Hayrapetyan Equestrian Centre

FLOW

Hrazdan

Charbakh

Shengavit

Erebuni

Masis

Masis

Artashat, Iran

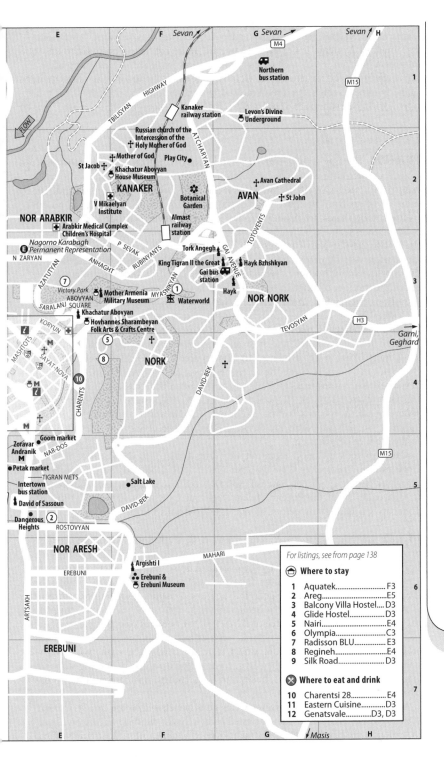

For listings, see from page 138

⊖ **Where to stay**
1   Aquatek..........................F3
2   Areg..............................E5
3   Balcony Villa Hostel....D3
4   Glide Hostel..................D3
5   Nairi.............................E4
6   Olympia.........................C3
7   Radisson BLU.................E3
8   Regineh........................E4
9   Silk Road......................D3

✖ **Where to eat and drink**
10  Charentsi 28..................E4
11  Eastern Cuisine............D3
12  Genatsvale.............D3, D3

trains are even cheaper, the most expensive journey costing only AMD2,500, but much of Armenia is not covered by rail. There are, however, some routes to and from Yerevan which may be useful to visitors (page 85). A final alternative – particularly for visiting sites in the vicinity of Yerevan – is to join one of the many one-day **minibus tours** that are organised by accommodation providers and tour operators in Yerevan (page 67).

## GETTING AROUND

**BY METRO** The metro (w yermetro.am) consists of one line together with a short branch in the southern suburbs. It is safe, efficient and cheap, and if your journey happens to intersect with its route it is usually the fastest way to get around. The main line runs from the north side of the city across the central district and out to the south. Trains are usually formed of two or three coaches and run every 5–10 minutes from 06.30 to 23.00. A flat fare of AMD100 is charged and entry to the platforms is by plastic tokens which can be purchased from the ticket office at any station. As stop names are not displayed on board the trains, it is necessary to listen to the announcements (which are made in English and Armenian) or else count the number of stops in order to alight at the correct station. The entrances to stations are marked on the surface either by the blue Armenian letter Մ, which is a capital M (for Metro), or by the Latin/Cyrillic letter M.

The stations, while not a match for (say) Moscow's more intricate specimens, are individually decorated and host an array of ever-changing exhibitions. The stops most likely to be of interest to visitors are, from north to south: Marshal Baghramyan [134 C1] (near the British embassy and the American University); Yeritasardakan (Youthful) [135 G2] where the green belt crosses Abovyan Street; Hanrapetutyan Hraparak (Republic Square) [135 F5] which is just beyond the square's eastern corner; Zoravar Andranik (Commander Andranik) [135 E7] opposite the new cathedral; and Sasuntsi Davit (David of Sassoun) [130 D5] next to the main railway station.

Other stations include Barekamutyun (Friendship) [130 D3] in the north and Gortsaranayin (Factory) [130 D6], Shengavit [130 D6] and Garegin Nzhdehi Hraparak (Garegin Nzhdeh Square) [130 D6] in the south, with a separate branch to Charbakh (from the Persian *chahar bagh*, meaning 'four gardens') [130 C6]. There are ten stations altogether, along a total route of 13.4km.

**BY BUS** Introduced in 1949, a quaint fleet of **trolleybuses** charge a flat fare of AMD50 and are the cheapest public transport in the city. Their routes are limited, but easily identifiable by the overhead power lines. Modern **buses** cover a more extensive range of routes, for which the flat fare is AMD100 within the city (you pay the driver as you get off). The most conspicuous means of transport is still the **minibus** (*marshrutka* or *marshrutni*), with some 125 routes covering the whole city, also for a flat fee of AMD100, the vehicles operating at frequent intervals until the small hours. Unlike regular buses, minibuses only halt at bus stops on demand: you must flag down from the roadside the one you wish to board, and subsequently ask the driver to drop you off at the upcoming stop (say '*gangaroom gangnek*'). As with buses and trolleybuses, it is conventional to pay when getting off.

Bus, minibus and trolleybus routes can be impenetrable to the non-Armenian-speaking visitor because destinations listed in the vehicles' windows are displayed only in Armenian (and then sometimes by their Soviet-era names). Absurdly, the only official source of route information is an Armenian-language PDF file downloadable from the Ministry of Transport website (**w** mtcit.am). Routes also change frequently with no warning. While this situation remains unresolved, some unofficial **information** can be found in English on WikiRoutes (**w** wikiroutes.info/en/erevan) and in Armenian at **w** marshrut.info. A handful of unofficial smartphone apps have sprung up, too, including **Yerevan Routes**, which at the time of research was the most comprehensive and actively maintained, covering buses, minibuses and trolleybuses, with route maps and lists of destinations for each service in English, Russian and Armenian.

**BY TAXI** Taxis (page 87) are plentiful and cheap, so much so that many visitors treat them as another form of public transport. Fares within central Yerevan are usually under AMD1,000 and often no more than the minimum fare shown on the meter (usually AMD500–700 for the first 4–5km and AMD100/km thereafter; sometimes AMD120/km if travelling far from Yerevan). Always ensure that the driver has switched on the meter before you begin your journey or you may be overcharged. There are a few designated taxi ranks, but taxis can always be found at the train and bus stations, the main markets and near many road intersections. They can also be hailed on the street; unoccupied cars generally display a green light in the windscreen, switching to red when occupied.

On the whole, taxi firms and drivers do not speak English so if phoning for a taxi it is best to ask your hotel or host to do it for you. Much more convenient is to use one of several regional smartphone apps such as **ggTaxi**, **UTaxi** or **Yandex**. These are particularly useful for non-Armenian-speakers as they will hail a taxi to your precise location on a map, displaying the fare on screen to eliminate any potential disagreements.

During rush hours, traffic moves slowly due to congestion. If you have an appointment, allow more time than you think necessary and consider a (much faster) metro journey instead if appropriate to your route. There are dozens, if not hundreds, of taxi firms in Yerevan including the following popular and reliable examples:

🚗**Airport Service** ✆010 595900, 060 430000; 📱 098 828200. Official taxi service of Zvartnots Airport (page 70).
🚗**Aquataxi** ✆010 200090; 📱 043 209005

🚗**Milena** ✆010 731010; 📱 095 731010. 20% discount for Yerevan Card holders.
🚗**Mobitaxi** ✆011 707707
🚗**Taxoline** ✆060 644644

**ON FOOT** The 'little centre' (*pokr kentron*) of Yerevan is compact enough to explore on foot and if you are reasonably fit it is well worth doing so (not least because the alternative is usually sitting in a traffic jam). The area within the green belt can be crossed in about 20 minutes, and almost nowhere of interest within this central zone is more than half an hour's walk from anywhere else. Beyond this zone to the north, the mountains begin, distances increase, and taxis and public transport begin to look more and more appealing. By exploring on foot, however, you will find hidden pockets of the city usually out of bounds to vehicles, such as enclosed communal courtyards within each block that give a good flavour of inner-city neighbourhood life, and the clusters of historical buildings and backstreets, such as Kond district (page 169), that comprise the oldest surviving parts of Yerevan.

**BY BICYCLE** Cycling in Yerevan can be an ordeal, with big, busy boulevards and bullish drivers – a shame, as the city centre's compact and relatively flat layout otherwise lends itself naturally to bicycle use. Dedicated cycling infrastructure extends to a single meandering 'tour' painted in white on a few roads and

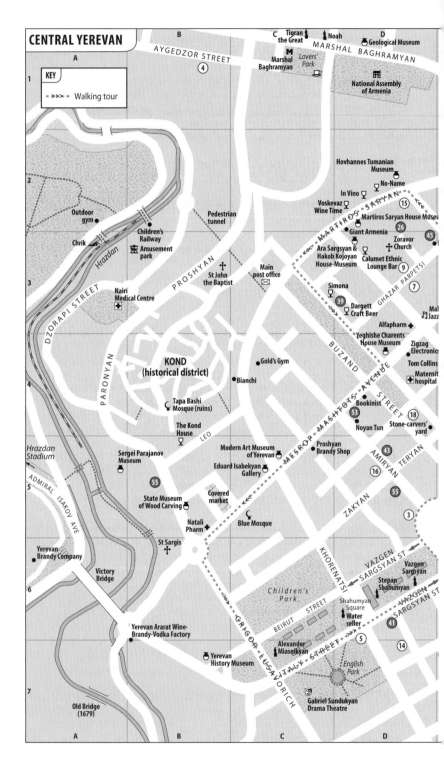

# CENTRAL YEREVAN

**KEY**

▪ ►►► ▪ = Walking tour

AYGEDZOR STREET

Tigran the Great
Noah
Geological Museum

Marshal Baghramyan

MARSHAL BAGHRAMYAN

Lovers' Park

National Assembly of Armenia

Hovhannes Tumanian Museum

No-Name

In Vino

Voskevaz Wine Time

MARTIROS SARYAN

(15)

Martiros Saryan House Museum

Giant Armenia

(26)

(45)

Zoravor Church

Ara Sargsyan & Hakob Kojoyan House-Museum

Calumet Ethnic Lounge Bar (9)

GHAZAR PARPETSI

(7)

Pedestrian tunnel

PROSHYAN

St John the Baptist

Main post office

Simona

(39)

Dargett Craft Beer

Mal Jazz

Outdoor gym

Children's Railway

Amusement park

Chrik

Hrazdan

DZORAPI STREET

Nairi Medical Centre

Alfapharm

Yeghishe Charents House Museum

Zigzag Electronics

BUZAND

Tom Collins

Maternity hospital

KOND (historical district)

Gold's Gym

Bianchi

PARONYAN

MESROP MASHTOTS AVENUE

STREET

Bookinist

(53)

(18)

Tapa Bashi Mosque (ruins)

Noyan Tun

Stone-carvers' yard

The Kond House

LEO

Modern Art Museum of Yerevan

Proshyan Brandy Shop

(43)

AMIRYAN

TERYAN

Hrazdan Stadium

Sergei Parajanov Museum

Eduard Isabekyan Gallery

(16)

(55)

ADMIRAL ISAKOV AVE

(55)

State Museum of Wood Carving

Covered market

ZAKYAN

(3)

Natali Pharm

Blue Mosque

KHORENATSI

VAZGEN SARGSYAN ST

Yerevan Brandy Company

St Sargis

Vazgen Sargsyan

Victory Bridge

Stepan Shahumyan

VAZGEN SARGSYAN ST

Children's Park

BEIRUT STREET

Shahumyan Square

Water seller

(41)

Yerevan Ararat Wine-Brandy-Vodka Factory

GRIGOR LUSAVORICH

Alexander Miasnikyan

ITALY STREET

(5)

(14)

Yerevan History Museum

English Park

Old Bridge (1679)

Gabriel Sundukyan Drama Theatre

A       B       C       D

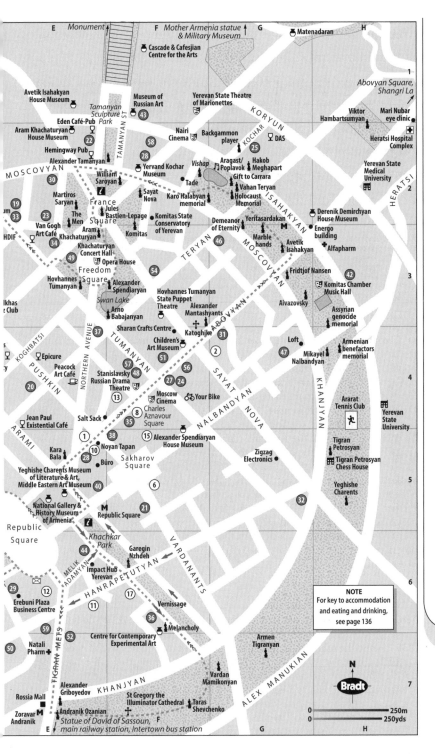

E Monument ↑

F Mother Armenia statue ↑
& Military Museum

G

🎷 Matenadaran

H

Cascade & Cafesjian
Centre for the Arts

1

Abovyan Square,
Shangri La

Avetik Isahakyan
House Museum

Museum of
Russian Art

Yerevan State Theatre
of Marionettes

KORYUN

Viktor
Hambartsumyan

Mari Nubar
eye clinic ●

Tamanyan
Sculpture
Park

43

Eden Café-Pub

Nairi
Cinema

Backgammon
player

KOCHAR

DAS

Heratsi Hospital
Complex

Aram Khachaturyan
House Museum

22

58

25

Hemingway Pub

28

Vishap

Aragast/
Poplavok

Hakob
Meghapart

Yerevan State
Medical
University

Alexander Tamanyan

Yervand Kochar
Museum

Gift to Carrara

MOSCOVYAN

30

William
Saroyan

Tade

Vahan Teryan

HERATSI

Martiros
Saryan

Sayat
Nova

Karo Halabyan
memorial

Holocaust
Memorial

2

19

France
Square

Jules
Bastien-Lepage

Komitas State
Conservatory
of Yerevan

Demeanor
of Eternity

Yeritasardakan

Derenik Demirchyan
House Museum

33

23

The
Men

TERYAN

Marble
hands

Energo
building

Van Gogh
Art Café

Aram
Khachaturyan

Komitas

MOSCOVYAN

Avetik
Isahakyan

Alfapharm

HDIF

34

Khachaturyan
Concert Hall

49

Opera House

Fridtjof Nansen

42

Freedom Square

54

Komitas Chamber
Music Hall

3

Hovhannes
Tumanyan

Alexander
Spendiaryan

Hovhannes Tumanyan
State Puppet
Theatre

Alexander
Mantashyants

Assyrian
genocide
memorial

Swan Lake

Arno
Babajanyan

Aivazovsky

Sharan Crafts Centre

Katoghike

31

Loft

Armenian
benefactors
memorial

37

Children's
Art Museum

2

47

Mikayel
Nalbandyan

Epicure

51

SAYAT

Peacock
Art Café

57

56

KHANJYAN

Stanislavsky
Russian Drama
Theatre

48

27 24

Ararat
Tennis Club

Yerevan
State
University

20

13

Moscow
Cinema

Your Bike

NALBANDYAN

NOVA

Jean Paul
Existential Café

Salt Sack

8

Charles
Aznavour
Square

Tigran
Petrosyan

1

38

35

Tigran Petrosyan
Chess House

Kara
Bala

10

Noyan Tapan

15

Alexander Spendiaryan
House Museum

Zigzag
Electronics ●

Yeghishe
Charents

28

Büro

Sakharov
Square

Yeghishe Charents Museum
of Literature & Art,
Middle Eastern Art Museum

40

6

5

National Gallery &
History Museum
of Armenia

Republic
Square

M

Republic Square

21

32

Khachkar
Park

Garegin
Nzhdeh

VARDANANTS

44

Impact Hub
Yerevan

MELIK
ADAMYAN

HANRAPETUTYAN

17

29

12

Vernissage

6

Erebuni Plaza
Business Centre

11

36

Melancholy

59

52

Centre for Contemporary
Experimental Art

Armen
Tigranyan

N

50

Natali
Pharm

Rossia Mall

Alexander
Griboyedov

KHANJYAN

St Gregory the
Illuminator Cathedral

Vardan
Mamikonyan

Bradt

7

Zoravar
Andranik

Andranik Ozanian

Statue of David of Sassoun,
main railway station, Intertown bus station

Taras
Shevchenko

ALEX MANUKIAN

0       250m
0       250yds

NOTE
For key to accommodation
and eating and drinking,
see page 136

pavements, together with a few parking racks installed by private businesses. That said, leisure cyclists are quite a common sight on the pavements and in traffic-free areas such as Northern Avenue and Freedom Square, owing to the increasing popularity of cycling among the youth. Visitors who do choose to cycle and are not accustomed to heavy traffic and aggressive driving are advised to do as the locals do: stay off the main roads and ride (carefully) on the pavements alongside the pedestrians – there is usually plenty of space. There are a few places to **hire bicycles**: in the centre, try Your Bike [135 F4] (17 Tumanyan St; m 094 403902; f YourbikeArmenia), the Armenia Marriott Hotel on Republic Square [134 D5] (page 138) or Giant Armenia [134 D2] (17/2 Martiros Saryan Street; ✆ 011 265241; f GIANTArmeniaofficial; ⊕ 10.00–22.00 daily). Giant also sells bikes, parts and accessories, as does the Bianchi store [134 C4] (26/3 Martiros Saryan St; ✆ 010 600106; e info@celestebikes.am; w celestebikes.am; ⊕ 11.00–20.00 daily). Slightly further out of town in Davtashen district is Yerevan's biggest and (currently) best bike shop, MyBike [130 D2] (2 Sasna Tsrer St; ✆ 010 707007; w mybike.am; ⊕ 10.00–20.00 daily), which deals in the Trek and Cube bicycle brands (among others), as well as hires and repairs. See page 114 for general comments on cycling in Armenia.

## TOURIST INFORMATION

Yerevan has two official **tourist information kiosks** (⊕ 10.00–22.00 daily). One is located beyond the east end of Republic Square at the southwest corner of the park [135 E5] and the other by the bus stop north of France Square and the opera house [135 E2]. These very welcome installations opened in June 2018 after many years during which Yerevan had no government-run tourist information centre. The staff speak English, Russian and Persian and can assist with organising tours, transport and accommodation, and the kiosks display calendars of cultural events throughout the summer tourist season, which can also be downloaded from w yerevan.am. Free printed city maps are available in several languages. Throughout Yerevan,

English-language signposts are installed at all major intersections to help visitors locate the main streets and sites of interest.

Several unofficial free maps and leaflets are widely distributed; one of the best is **Inside Yerevan** (**w** onearmenia.org/inside-yerevan), a free, crowdsourced map showcasing the less well-known sights of the city centre. Other free maps are produced by the bigger tour operators as a way of promoting their services. Detailed maps and atlases of Yerevan are produced and sold by Collage (4 Martiros Saryan St; **w** collage.am; ⊕ 10.00–18.00 Mon–Sat). Armenian Virtual College (**w** avc-agbu. org) produces a free multimedia ebook about Yerevan, while the website and app Spotted By Locals (**w** spottedbylocals.com) has some interestingly obscure tips. Those with a special interest in Yerevan's cultural-architectural heritage should refer to the **Other Yerevan** project (**w** otheryerevan.am), a website, app and downloadable PDF map pinpointing and providing background information about hundreds of noteworthy buildings and features, as well as suggesting six themed walking routes by which to view them.

Guided **walking tours** of Yerevan are available, including a popular free walk led by local guide Vako Khakhamian (reservations required, starts daily at 17.00 from Republic Square; **m** 093 498985; **f** YerevanFreeWalkingTour). Many hostels and hotels also run their own walking tours or will refer you to partner guides. For a list of local tour operators in Yerevan, see page 67. Note that some agents offer a variety of services which may be of use to visitors, such as Hyur Service, which offers apartment and house accommodation, house cleaning and laundry, and interpretation/translation services.

##  WHERE TO STAY

The development of new **hotels** in Yerevan has been considerable in recent years, with most of the big international chains for both the business and leisure markets now represented, as well as some very good independent boutique hotels. The result is an overall dip in prices relative to the level of service, as the market has diversified in response to increased visitor numbers. The **hostel** scene for backpackers and budget travellers, previously the domain of a single pioneer (Envoy Hostel on Ghazar Parpetsi Street), has also flourished; dorm beds can now be had for genuinely shoestring prices as a result (though beware that the quality of some 'hostels' can vary enormously, sometimes being little more than a recently vacated Soviet-era apartment hurriedly listed on a booking website). Many established hostels offer day trips and other out-of-town excursions; some offer free walking tours of Yerevan and other socially oriented events. Some of the mobile phone numbers listed for hostels can be used with instant messenger services such as WhatsApp/Viber/Telegram to contact the hosts. Another option for the budget traveller is a **homestay** (bed and breakfast), particularly as dinner can be requested and will prove to be a much more authentically Armenian experience than most restaurants will provide. The homestay concept is likely to be more relevant outside of Yerevan, however; indeed, in the more remote areas it may be your only option, and a highly recommended one at that (page 94).

For a general overview of hotel **prices**, see page 92. During the winter most Yerevan hotels charge a lower rate. Some hotels away from the central area provide free transport to and from the centre; this can be quite a pleasant option in the heat and humidity of midsummer, particularly for those who prefer to spend their evenings in quieter neighbourhoods – prices tend to be lower too. Unless otherwise stated, all the places we list accept **credit cards** and include free

Wi-Fi, and are included on one of the two Yerevan city maps in this guide. Unlike elsewhere in Armenia, almost all accommodation staff in Yerevan speak good English, and frequently other European languages too.

## CENTRAL YEREVAN

🏠 **The Alexander** [135 E5] (114 rooms) 3/4 Abovyan St; ☎011 206000; e info@ thealexanderyerevan.com; w starwoodhotels. com. Part of Starwood's 'Luxury Collection' brand of exclusive properties & the chain's first in Armenia, opened in Apr 2018 in a very central location with entrances on Northern Avenue & Abovyan Street. Contemporary designer décor in sgl/dbl/trpl rooms & several opulent suites. Spa, fitness centre & indoor pool combine with a variety of business services, a penthouse restaurant & a cigar lounge. At the time of research the most expensive hotel in Armenia at AMD174,600 for a dbl or AMD524,000 for the Abovyan Suite. **$$$$$**

🏠 **Armenia Marriott Hotel** [134 D5] (256 rooms) 1 Amiryan St; ☎010 599000; e armenia. marriott@marriott.com; w marriottarmenia.com. Absolutely central with an attractive façade on Republic Square. The building dates from 1954 but has been completely modernised & the rooms greatly enlarged. En-suite dbl rooms & a variety of suites; all have separate living & sleeping areas. Choice of 2 restaurants & outdoor café on Republic Square. 24hr bar & fitness centre (free for guests) with small new outdoor swimming pool. Prices exclude 20% tax & b/fast. Variety of b/fast options AMD7,200–12,000 pp. **$$$$$**

🏠 **Best Western Congress Hotel** [134 D6] (126 rooms) 1 Italy St; ☎010 591199; e sales@hotelcongressyerevan.com; w congresshotelyerevan.com. International chain hotel built in 2001, pleasant & brightly decorated. Fitness centre & sauna. Nice outdoor swimming pool & lounge area. Restaurant. Prices exclude 20% tax & b/fast. **$$$$$**

🏠 **Grand Hotel Yerevan** [135 F4] (104 rooms) 14 Abovyan St; ☎010 591600; e welcome@ grandhotelyerevan.com; w grandhotelyerevan. com. Yerevan's oldest hotel was built in 1927, became the Soviet state-run Intourist, was refurbished in 1998 & was rebranded (again) in 2017. Among the most elegant & classical of Yerevan's upscale hotels & well located on the buzzing Charles Aznavour Square. Standard sgl/dbl rooms somewhat small but very well appointed; a variety of bigger deluxe & suite rooms available.

Stunning rooftop swimming pool & bar. Italian restaurant among the best in town. 24hr bar with live music every evening. B/fast AMD7,000pp. **$$$$$**

🏠 **Hyatt Place Yerevan** [135 E6] (95 rooms) 26/1 Vazgen Sargsyan St; ☎011 221234; e yerevan.place@hyatt.com; w yerevan.place. hyatt.com. Upscale international chain hotel opened late 2013 just off Republic Square, behind the main post office & close to the business district. Spacious, modern en-suite dbl/twin rooms with tea- & coffee-making facilities, large LCD TVs, iPhone docking alarm clocks, etc. Fitness centre free for residents. Ground-floor Gallery Café (open to non-residents) ⏰ 06.30–23.30, serving a mix of Armenian platters & European light meals. Buffet b/fast inc hot items cooked to order. **$$$$$**

🏠 **Republica Hotel Yerevan** [134 D5] (255 rooms) 7/1 Amiryan St; ☎011 990000; e info@republicahotel.am; w republicahotel.am. International-standard but locally owned upscale boutique hotel, opened in 2014 just off Republic Square. Very tasteful sgl/dbl/twin/trpl/suite rooms, all en suite & with generously sized beds; deluxe rooms have small balconies. Restaurant serves refined Armenian dishes, with live jazz on Thu evenings & wine tasting on Fri evenings (free for residents). Outdoor Tap Station bar & restaurant serves a better than avg European menu of pizza, burgers, etc as well as draught beers from local brewpub Dargett (which is under the same ownership; page 146). Non-smoking throughout. **$$$$$**

🏠 **Tufenkian Historic Yerevan Hotel** [135 F6] (83 rooms) 48 Hanrapetutyan St; ☎060 501030; e historicyerevan@tufenkian.am; w tufenkianheritage.com; see ad, page 126. One of Tufenkian's four boutique hotels in Armenia, the Yerevan property opened in 2012 next to the Vernissage arts & crafts market, built in a mix of classic European & modern Armenian styles. The lobby houses a ground-floor café-bar & restaurant; a carpet showroom with weaving demonstrations showcases James Tufenkian's entrepreneurial roots. The reasonably priced Kharpert Restaurant serves Western Armenian revival cuisine in a modern style. **$$$$$**

🏠 **Ani Plaza** [135 G4] (262 rooms) 19 Sayat Nova Av; ☎010 589500; e info@anihotel.com; w anihotel.com. Armenia's biggest (& once best) hotel occupies a 14-storey tower block, built in 1970 & renovated from 2002 onwards. A vast range of room sizes available, though the décor in some now looks a little dated. Branch of Hyur Service travel agency in lobby. Restaurant, swimming pool & gym on-site. **$$$$**

🏠 **Bass Boutique Hotel** [134 B1] (41 rooms) 3/1 Aygedzor St; ☎010 261080; e bassboutiquehotel@gmail.com; w bass. am. Located at the northwest edge of the city centre near the American University, 100m from Marshal Baghramyan metro station. Built in 1995, it was the first private hotel to be opened after independence. Pleasant staff & good food. Restaurant, café & wine-tasting cellar on-site. Sauna & jacuzzi. **$$$$**

🏠 **Hotel Aviatrans** [135 E5] (55 rooms) 4 Abovyan St; ☎060 484444; e hotel@aviatrans. am; w hotelaviatrans.am. A comfortable, relatively small, central hotel with very helpful reception staff. Built in 1998, renovated 2008. Restaurant. Currency exchange, Avis car hire & gift shop within hotel. **$$$$**

🏠 **Hotel Europe** [135 E6] (47 rooms) 38 Hanrapetutyan St; ☎010 546060; e info@ europehotel.am; w europehotel.am. Attractive & well-regarded central hotel of French design near Vernissage art & craft market, with sgl/dbl/twin/ suite rooms. Generous European buffet b/fast. French spoken. **$$$$**

🏠 **Ibis Yerevan Center** [135 F4] (255 rooms) 5/1 Northern Av; ☎010 595959; e H7309@accor. com; w accorhotels.com. International chain hotel opened in 2016 midway along Northern Avenue. The 11 floors of twin/dbl en-suite rooms are clean & bright with refrigerators & safes. Casual lobby with 24hr bar & helpful desk staff. Third-floor restaurant & terrace open to public serving light European dishes for lunch & dinner. Underground parking & Enterprise car hire (page 91) on-site. Room pricing is 'dynamic', ie: based on demand, but good value due to the brand's no-frills approach. Free ironing facilities & luggage room. B/fast AMD5,000 or AMD4,000 booked in advance. **$$$**

🏠 **Villa Delenda** [134 D4] (8 rooms) 22 Koghbatsi St; ☎010 253141; m 098 561156; e info@villadelenda.com; w villadelenda.com.

Possibly the most romantic & charming centrally located guesthouse, occupying a converted 19th-century town house originally built by the Mnatsakanian brothers. Interior décor reflects this heritage with amazing attention to detail; each guest room is uniquely furnished & named. Proceeds from this & sister properties in Aygedzor district of Yerevan & Gyumri fund the ongoing work of the charity that owns & operates it. Handmade ceramics boutique in basement. Dinner for groups by arrangement. **$$$**

🏠 **Kantar Hotel & Hostel** [134 D7] (16 rooms, 40 dorm beds, 5 apts) 10 Deghatan St (reception on 7th floor via lift); ☎011 700017/18; e info@kantar.am; w kantar.am. Relaxed & informal but well-appointed hotel/hostel in the south of the city centre offering en-suite twin/dbl rooms & dorm beds. Lower rates for rooms with shared bathrooms. Dorm beds AMD6,000–8,000 depending on season. Well-equipped kitchen for use of guests. Plentiful communal areas create a convivial atmosphere. Also has 5 apts for 2–8 people. **$$–$$$**

🏠 **Center Hostel** [135 F5] (3 rooms, 10 dorm beds) Apt 31, 4 Vardanants St; ☎010 528639; m 093 444333; e info@center-hostel.com; w center-hostel.com. Close to Republic Square on a quiet residential street. Colourful, renovated dbl/twin rooms are among the cheapest in town, as are dorm beds in 6-/4-bed rooms. Lockers, towels, bed-linen inc. Laundry extra. Cards not accepted. **$**

🏠 **Envoy Hostel** [134 D3] (6 rooms, 40 dorm beds) 54 Pushkin St (entry from Ghazar Parpetsi St); ☎010 530369; e info@envoyhostel. com; w envoyhostel.com. Yerevan's original backpackers' hostel is still clean, well organised & central with 24hr reception, spacious toilet/ shower-rooms (separate male/female), common room, kitchen. Dorm beds in 8-/4-bed rooms; private rooms sleep 1–4 with en-suite & shared bathroom options available. The tour operator arm (w envoytours.com) arranges trips in Armenia & Nagorno Karabagh & free daily walking tours of Yerevan. Sister properties in Tbilisi, Georgia & (strangely) Phnom Penh, Cambodia. **$**

🏠 **Hostel Bivouac** [134 D3] (24 dorm beds) 9 Ghazar Parpetsi St; ☎010 536170; w hostelbivouac.com. In the thick of the nightlife but certainly not a 'party hostel', this quiet

**3**

backpacker joint opened in 2017 & is furnished in a modern Western vein with individually curtained bunks for privacy, each with a lockable drawer. Price depends on size of dorm; 6-/8-/10-bed rooms available. Small communal area & kitchen adjoins a leafy backyard terrace. 24hr reception. Unlimited hot drinks inc. Laundry & bath towels extra. **$**

**One Way Hostel** [134 D2] (6 rooms, 40 dorm beds) 41 Tumanyan St; **m** 041 532625; **w** onewayhostel.com. Cosy hostel on the 5th floor of an apt block (no lift); very convenient for the pub & bar district. Set up by a popular tour operator (**w** onewaytour.am) which is consequently eager to promote its day trips to guests. Dorm beds in 8-bed rooms, also sgl/dbl/twin private rooms. B/fast AMD1,000. A second property is now open at 5 Belyakov St; to reach it, go through the archway at the north corner of Sakharov Square [135 F5]. **$**

## OUTSIDE THE CENTRE

**Radisson BLU** [131 E3] (142 rooms) 2/2 Azatutyan Av; **\** 010 219900/219901; **e** info. yerevan@radissonblu.com; **w** radissonblu.com/en/hotel-yerevan. Opened in 2005 & previously the Golden Palace, this remodelled 5-star luxury hotel overlooks the city a 15min walk from the top of the Cascade, next to Victory Park, with dbl/trpl/suite rooms available. Sauna, swimming pool, spa & beauty salon, indoor/outdoor restaurants & several bars all on-site. Popular with business execs & the Middle East's nouveau riche. **$$$$$**

**Aquatek Hotel** [131 F3] (29 rooms) 40/2 Myasnikyan Av; **\** 010 588888; **m** 091 500202; **e** info@aquatek.am; **w** aquatek.am. Part of the Aquatek water park, inc swimming pools, other water amusements, gym & sauna, to which hotel guests have free access (it is also open to the public). Sgl/twin rooms are bright, modern & overlook the swimming pool. All bedrooms are upstairs; no lift. **$$$**

**Nairi Hotel** [131 E4] (120 rooms) 121/7 Armenak Armanakyan St; **\** 010 652121/655151; **e** reservations@hotelnairi.am, marketing@hotelnairi.am; **w** hotelnairi.am. In hilly Nork district (necessitating a bus/taxi from the centre), this 8-floor hotel opened in 2012 & has a restaurant, swimming pool & sauna. **$$$**

**Olympia Hotel** [130 C3] (30 rooms) 64 Barbusse St; **\** 010 271850; **e** info@olympia.am; **w** olympia.am. Near the east end of Kievyan Bridge overlooking the Hrazdan River, with sgl/dbl/twin/suite rooms. Restaurant & café with summer outdoor seating. Outdoor swimming pool. **$$$**

**Regineh Hotel** [131 E4] (57 rooms) 235/1 Armenak Armanakyan St; **\** 010 654020; **e** reservation@hotelregineh.am; **w** hotelregineh.am. Pleasantly airy & bright hotel. A stiff climb up from the city in Nork district but with good views towards Mount Ararat. Dedicated to the memory of the owner's wife. Swimming pool. **$$$**

**Silk Road Hotel** [130 D3] (13 rooms) 53/2 Aygedzor St; **\** 010 265214; **w** silk-road.am. Charming boutique hotel in the low-key residential district of Aygedzor near the edge of the gorge. Lavishly decorated in a historical style showcasing Armenian art & handicrafts with a lovely garden & patio, making up for its slightly out-of-the-way location (20–25mins' walk down to the centre). Also excellent for group meals. Excellent b/fast. Understandably popular. **$$$**

**Areg Hotel** [131 E5] (14 rooms) 80 Burnazian St; **\** 010 456213, 077 567439; **e** info@areghotel.com; **w** areghotel.com. Located near the main railway station & easily accessible by metro. A pleasant small family-run hotel in a quiet suburban street. Can arrange tours & cottages at Lake Sevan. **$$**

**Balcony Villa Hostel** [130 D3] (6 rooms) 3/1 Emin Hovsep St; **\** 010 264449; **e** balcony.hostel@gmail.com. Perched on the edge of Hrazdan Gorge & a 10min walk from Barekamutyun metro, this is a quiet & friendly family-run hostel accommodating up to 20 guests with a lovely garden/terrace. Dorm beds & dbl/twin rooms available. **$**

**Glide Hostel** [130 D3] (12 rooms) 16/1 Kalents St; **\** 010 274027; **m** 094 060586; **e** hostelglide@gmail.com; **w** hostelinyerevan.am. Quiet & cosy family-run hostel a 3min walk from Barekamutyun metro, next to the Kalents museum (**w** galentz.am). Private sgl/dbl/twin/trpl rooms or beds in shared twin/trpl rooms. Unlimited tea/coffee inc; no other meals but kitchen for use of guests. Named 'glide' as one of the family is president of the Armenian Paragliding Sport Federation – paragliding trips are indeed offered (**w** paraplan.am)! **$**

Yerevan's dining scene caters for all tastes and covers a vast range of cuisines considering the country's otherwise conservative attitude towards food. Of special note is the proliferation of **Levantine** restaurants established by Syrian-born Armenians fleeing the civil war, who have brought with them the ever-popular regional cuisine of the eastern Mediterranean. Bars and nightlife venues have also proliferated, again often under the initiative of business-savvy diaspora Armenians, and now a range of options await, from basement bars and themed pubs to trendy wine bars, brewpubs, rooftop cocktail lounges and avant-garde underground music venues. Summer sees the opening of additional outdoor cafés and open-air lounges along Yerevan's green belt and also surrounding the opera house (note that some charge a premium for sitting in so-called VIP areas with comfortable armchairs).

**Restaurants**, cafés and street food outlets can be found throughout the centre but are particularly concentrated between the foot of the Cascade, the opera house and the bottom end of Northern Avenue; along Tumanyan Street and within a block of its intersections with Parpetsi, Teryan and Abovyan streets; along the rest of the length of Abovyan Street; and along Martiros Saryan Street between the Tumanyan and Aram Street junctions, which is now the go-to district for Yerevan's trendy 20-somethings. The strings of restaurants lining the bottom of the Cascade park are all of a good standard (perhaps surprisingly, considering their somewhat touristy location), providing plentiful summer outdoor seating in pleasant surrounds; prices are only a little higher than elsewhere. The best **bars**, pubs, lounges and other nightlife venues are mainly gathered in and around the rectangle formed by the adjoining sections of Tumanyan, Saryan, Aram and Parpetsi streets. **Nightclubs** (at least of the type understood by Western visitors; see page 146) and underground music venues are usually obscurely located in basements or backyards with only the entrance-ways visible; several exist in the region between Poplavok Park on Isahakyan/Moskovyan Street and Koryun Street.

Most restaurants open at noon and cafés around 10.00, but an increasing number of cafés and coffee shops in central Yerevan are open by 09.00 or earlier. Those in business-oriented hotels may open earlier still. Most restaurants will close at around midnight or when the last customer has gone; bars, lounges and music venues later still, particularly at weekends; and a small handful of restaurants remain open 24 hours. Few restaurants have **websites** and those which do exist are often not informative; better to look at online reviews and photos for an idea of what to expect. There are exceptions, and websites which are useful have been listed in our reviews. Try w yerevanresto.am for a locally authored view of the dining scene. The smartphone app Dinebook (w dinebook.am) allows users to make restaurant reservations and is available in Armenian, Russian and English.

Outside the central area of Yerevan there are innumerable small bakeries and **fast-food outlets** where you can get a cheap *khachapuri*, *piroshki* or *shawarma* (page 99). Bars and nightclubs, on the other hand, are almost non-existent outside the centre. The website and app w menu.am allows users to order almost any menu item from any restaurant in Yerevan and have it delivered by bicycle or moped for a small fee, which may be useful for visitors staying far from the centre and wanting a night in.

Note that **restaurants and bars within hotels** are not included in the list on pages 142–6. Hotel restaurants listed on pages 138–40 are open to non-residents. All listings are included on one of two Yerevan city maps on pages 130–1 and 134–5, unless otherwise noted. Additionally, listed establishments are open seven days a week unless otherwise indicated.

Main courses in most of the traditional Armenian-style restaurants usually cost somewhere between AMD2,500 and AMD5,000 and it is easy to get a full meal (a main course with salads or sides and an alcoholic drink) in such places for AMD5,000–8,000 per person. A light meal in a café, such as an omelette, may cost about AMD1,000–1,500, and a savoury street snack can be had for as little as AMD100. Beyond the established favourites there is now considerably more choice than in previous times. Cheap but still good quality canteen-style restaurants can be found, particularly for lunches, and upscale dining options are now more plentiful. For this reason, unlike elsewhere in this guide, Yerevan's cafés and restaurants are listed with the following price codes:

**AVERAGE PRICE OF MAIN COURSE**

| | | |
|---|---|---|
| Expensive | $$$$$ | AMD10,000+ |
| Above average | $$$$ | AMD5,000–10,000 |
| Mid-range | $$$ | AMD3,000–5,000 |
| Cheap and cheerful | $$ | AMD1,200–3,000 |
| Rock-bottom | $ | AMD600–1,200 |

## CENTRAL YEREVAN

✕ **Dolmama** [135 F5] 10 Pushkin St; \010 568931; w dolmama.am; ⏰ 11.00–23.30. Established in 1998 & perhaps Yerevan's most highly respected traditional restaurant – there is a certain prestige to being seen eating here. Very expensive even by Yerevan standards; whether it's worth the money depends on who is paying (!) but the cuisine certainly remains top of the line. **$$$$$**

✕ **Ankyun** [135 F5] 4 Vardanants St; \010 544606; w ankyun.am; ⏰ 11.00–midnight. A delightful family-run Italian-style restaurant. Prices are above avg but well worth it for the quality of the food – the fillet steak is among the best in town. **$$$$**

❋✕ **The Club** [135 E2] 40 Tumanyan St; \010 531361; w theclub.am; ⏰ 10.00–midnight. Extremely good haute cuisine with an Armenian touch in this classy & long-established basement restaurant, which also incorporates a souvenir shop & bookshop, as well as a separate tea & coffee room. Reservations advisable. Occasional live music in evenings is usually of the gentler variety. Informative website includes the menu, with prices, plus details of special events. Excellent steak tartare. Good for a romantic evening meal. **$$$$**

✕ **Aperitivo** [135 E2] 1/3 Tamanyan St; m 055 586584; ⏰ 07.30–02.00. The current pick of the many European-style café-bars with outdoor seating near the bottom of Cascade. Open very early with a range of substantial b/fasts (inc English, vegetarian, avocado on toast, etc) & good Italian-style coffee; alternatively, a good evening spot for wine or sangria. **$$$**

✕ **Asador** [135 G2] 28 Isahakyan St; \044 002200; ⏰ noon–midnight. New in 2018, this classy, modern restaurant serves a refined international menu of classics & fusion dishes with emphasis on top-quality centrepiece ingredients, many of which are flown in. Not cheap but the prices reflect the excellent quality. **$$$**

❋✕ **Dalan Art Gallery & Café** [135 F4] 12 Abovyan St; m 099 580658; ⏰ 08.30–00.30. Walk through the intimate gift shop to reach the large restaurant in its delightful vine-shaded back garden. Serves a very good pan-Armenian menu inc unusual items not found elsewhere; the grilled fish with rice is particularly good. Some indoor seating available upstairs; the space also functions as a gallery & is worth a quick look. Reservations recommended. (*Dalan* means 'archway' in Armenian.) **$$$**

✕ **Gastropolis Food Market** [135 D6] 2 Vazgen Sargsyan St; \011 511511; ⏰ 09.00–midnight. Newly opened in 2018, this self-service food court serves freshly made global cuisine from a variety of themed counters inc Asian, pizza, pasta &

grill, as well as hot drinks, wines & draught beer from Dargett (page 146). W/day lunch customers mainly from corporate offices; quieter for visitors in evenings & at w/ends. **$$$**

**✲ ✗ Lavash** [135 F4] 21 Tumanyan St; 010 608800; **m** 091 608800; **w** lavash.restaurant; 08.00–midnight. Immensely popular new restaurant from the owners of the Tavern Yerevan (see below) chain, serving inventive new recipes & twists on Armenian/Caucasian classics with an emphasis on showcasing local ingredients. Despite fine-dining aspirations it remains modestly priced. Good for light lunches as well as evening dinners. Reservations highly recommended. **$$$**

**✗ Our Village** [135 F3] 32 Tumanyan St; 010 548700; noon–23.00. Tourist-oriented restaurant decorated with old coffee pots, radios, etc. Serves only Armenian produce & drinks. Live folk music in the evenings. Staff wear traditional costume, & menus (singed at edges) have carefully placed holes burned in them. Reservations recommended. Vegetarians might enjoy the mushroom *manti*. **$$$**

**✗ Tavern Yerevan** [134 D5 & 134 B5] 5 Amiryan St 010 545545; **m** 099 545545; 10.00–midnight); 7 Paronyan St 010 530563; **m** 091 530563; 10.00–midnight); **w** pandokyerevan.am/en. A chain of large, lavish restaurants specialising in classic Armenian/Caucasian banquets & all accompanying revelry. Serves dishes such as *khash* & *harissa* in winter, *dolma* in summer. Ever popular with locals celebrating special occasions. **$$$**

**✲ ✗ Wine Republic** [135 F2] 2 Tamanyan St (entrance on Isahakyan St); 055 001100; noon–midnight. With a double-bill menu of European & Asian dishes, this trendy restaurant near Cascade has proved a hit with expats craving spicy pad thai, Japanese *gyoza* or Chinese chow mein. Also serves good quality pasta dishes, burgers, salads, etc; the seafood is also worth a look. Excellent wine selection, as the name implies, but serves draught beer too (if you ask for it). **$$$**

**✲ ✗ 12 Tables** [135 E2] (entrance on Spendiaryan St) 40/63 Tumanyan St; noon–23.00 Mon–Sat. Cosy & welcoming basement dining room & café decorated with mid-20th-century European retro chic. Wallpaper aside, the food is delicious & wholesome & the menu inventive & unique. Vegetarians will be very happy

here, as will their wallets. On-site gift s worth a look. **$$**

**✗ At Gayane's** [134 D2] 35b Tumanya St; 010 530320; 10.00–23.00 Tue–F 09.00–23.00 Sat–Sun. Found by following the alley to the right of Jazzve (page 145) for about 100m into the yard beyond. Dining here feels like attending a giant dinner party: Gayane, the host, serves traditional home-cooked food in this old-fashioned but tasteful ground-floor apt conversion & entertains diners with her piano playing. Quite the experience & rather good value. **$$**

**✗ Black Angus** [135 E5] 2/5 Abovyan St & 39/9 Mashtots Av; **w** blackangus.am; 10.00–02.00. Understandably popular with those craving a Western-style burger after endless *lavash* & *khorovats* in the regions. AMD200 markup for 'Angus beef': if you notice the difference your taste buds are better than ours. A vast range of burgers from AMD1,400 (mini veggie) to AMD3,000 (big Angus classic double cheese). Also serves pizzas & salads. All beer is international. Take-away available. **$$**

**✗ Caucasus Tavern** [135 G5] 82 Hanrapetutyan St; 010 561177; **w** tavern.caucasus.am; 24hrs. Expansive, old-fashioned, tavern-style restaurant with a frankly biblical menu of Armenian, Georgian, Persian & other 'Caucasian' dishes which are all helpfully pictured on the menu for the uninitiated. Live folk music in the evenings. Good for groups; reservations advisable. **$$**

**✗ Derian Restaurant** [135 F6] 1/3 Buzand St; 011 750750; 11.00–midnight. The pick of the Syrian-Armenian restaurants to have sprung up in recent years & very handy from Republic Square or Vernissage (page 156), serving utterly delicious eastern Mediterranean cuisine. If you have the stomach, the *chi kofte* (raw minced beef & bulghur wheat) is quite divine. Those who prefer their meat cooked should try the *shish tawuk* or *khash-khash* kebab. Classics inc hummus, tabbouleh, etc also available. **$$**

**✗ Eat & Fit Healthy Café** [134 D3] 80 Aram St; 011 588080; 08.30–midnight. New in 2017, this pleasant, low-key café serves a range of light meals, wraps & salads, snacks & drinks. Its definition of 'healthy' revolves around raw food & organic ingredients with lots of fresh vegetables, legumes & pulses, nuts & seeds;

yours may of course differ but the results are in any case delicious. Good for b/fasts & lunches. **$$**

✗ **Genatsvale** [135 H3] 12 Isahakyan St; ☎010 277999; w genacvale.am; ⊕ 10.00–midnight. Flagship city-centre branch of the Georgian restaurant chain serving classic Georgian dishes inc *khinkali, khachapuri, kharcho, ostri* & more. Menus are well illustrated. Live traditional Georgian & Armenian music in evenings. Good quality & value. **$$**

✗ **Lagonid** [135 G4] 37 Nalbandyan St; ☎010 580804; ⊕ 10.00–23.00. Yerevan's original Middle Eastern restaurant is a little out of the way but worth it for the falafel & *fatte* & the very low prices. Try also the shredded lamb with pistachio rice; the *crème toum* (garlic cream) served with the grilled meat dishes is another winner. **$$**

✗ **Nima** [135 E7] 6/3 Tigran Mets Av; ☎041 038885; ⊕ 09.00–midnight. Small but bright Iranian-run basement diner serving classic Persian dishes inc *ghormeh sabzi, fesenjan, khoresht-e gheimeh*, etc, as well as kebabs & grills, always with enormous portions of perfectly cooked rice. A great opportunity to try authentic Iranian cuisine if you haven't had the pleasure. **$$**

✗ **Tumanyan Khinkali Factory** [135 F4] 21/1 Tumanyan St; ☎010 582352; ⊕ 09.30–midnight. This basement restaurant is known for being the best in town for its speciality, Georgian *khinkali*, which are large ravioli-like dumplings, boiled or fried & containing minced meat, cheese or mushrooms: 4–6 dumplings pp is about right, usually ordered in bulk for the whole table. Eating them is an art: forget cutlery, pick them up by the 'handle' & slurp away (discarding the handle). All else is merely an accompaniment. **$$**

✗ **Artashi Mot** [135 E2] 31 Moskovyan St; ☎010 501333; ⊕ 09.00–midnight. One of countless cheap *shawarma* & fast-food joints but the quality here is distinguished by the meat being cooked over charcoal instead of gas. Indoor & outdoor seating. Good & cheap *khinkali* also. For vegetarians, a meatless *shawarma* is just AMD400, or try the mushroom *khorovats*. **$**

✗ **Blizzard Lunch** [135 E6] (entrance on Petros Adamyan St) 26/1 Vazgen Sargsyan St; ☎010 555193; ⊕ 11.00–15.00 Mon–Fri. If you're looking for a cheap, wholesome lunch near

Republic Square on a w/day, try this well-hidden self-service lunch canteen beneath the southeast corner of the Erebuni Plaza business centre. It's ostensibly aimed at office workers but technically open to all. A full meal & drink is unlikely to cost more than AMD2,000. **$**

✻✗ **Gaidz Lahmajo** [135 E5] 5 Nalbandyan St; m 077 332118; ⊕ 10.30–20.00 Mon–Sat. Another Syrian-Armenian success story, this family-run underground canteen hidden in plain sight serves several variations on *lahmajo, zaatar* bread & other such specialities. W/day lunchtimes get very busy; other times quiet & incredibly good value. Try the cinnamon & tahini cookies. **$**

✗ **The Italian** [135 E6] 51/53 Hanrapetutyan St; ☎012 255555; ⊕ 07.30–midnight. As the name implies, an Italian restaurant & coffee bar conveniently close to Vernissage & Republic Square which happens to serve the most authentic Neapolitan-style pizza in town. Also good for a morning coffee & pastry. **$**

✗ **Jhingalov Hats** [135 G3] 62 Teryan St; ☎010 582205; ⊕ 10.00–22.00. *Jhingalov hats* (see box, page 379) is a typical herb-stuffed flatbread from Nagorno Karabagh. This place serves nothing else & is good for when you want a quick, tasty & cheap (vegetarian) snack without having to spend time choosing; it is among the best outside Karabagh. One portion costs AMD700 & is ample unless you are very hungry. Goes well with tomato juice. **$**

✗ **Ost Bistro** [134 D4] 20 Mashtots Av; ☎010 539580; ⊕ 10.00–22.30. No-frills fast-food joint whose *pièce de la résistance* is its Adjarian *khachapuri*, a heart-stopping cheese-filled dough boat slathered with eggs & molten butter; the best you'll find outside of Georgia. One of these for b/fast will last you all day. It also bakes a good *lahmajo*. **$**

✗ **Zatar Pizza** [135 E6] 24 Hanrapetutyan St; ☎010 525106; ⊕ 10.00–22.45 Mon–Sat, 10.00–16.00 Sun. *Zaatar* is a classic Levantine spice mix named after the endemic herb of the *thymus* genus. This Syrian-Armenian-run fast-food restaurant specialises in all varieties of the delicious Middle Eastern b/fast 'pizzas' built around the flavouring, though it is actually busiest at lunchtimes. Quick service & very good value if you're lucky enough to get a table; try the 'cheese special'. Take-away also available. **$**

**Artbridge Bookstore Café** [135 F4]
20 Abovyan St; 010 521239; w artbridge.am;
08.30–midnight. This long-running bookshop/
café remains of the few places open early in the
morning; good for b/fast, which is available all day.
Also soups, salads & pastries. Their French toast is
the best in town. $$$

**Mirzoyan Library** [135 E7] 10 Mher
Mkrtchyan St; 010 520828; noon–20.00
Tue–Sun. Originally a photography gallery &
events space but now an increasingly popular café.
Located through an archway in one of Yerevan's last
remaining 19th-century buildings, with delightful
wooden balconies surrounding a quiet courtyard. A
good afternoon getaway from the crowds around
Republic Square, serving a (somewhat pricey)
range of teas, coffees, light snacks & alcoholic
drinks. Regular free exhibitions in the gallery
space. $$$

**✳ Baguette & Co** [135 F4] 28 Tumanyan
St; 011 202299; 08.30–23.00. If you're
desperate for an authentic French croissant or *pain
au chocolat* with your cappuccino, this is the place
to get it. The open-plan bakery puts out delicious
sweet & savoury snacks & sandwiches all day.
Good coffees & a variety of b/fast deals until late
morning. Take-away fresh bread & pastries also
available. $$

**Brioche** [135 E2] 31 Moskovyan St; 011
561111; 08.00–midnight. Another French-
inspired early risers' coffee shop, serving a good
range of cakes & pastries. Outdoor seating area
somewhat noisy beside the Baghramyan–
Moskovyan intersection, but the interior is
pleasant. $$

**Café Central** [135 G4] 30 Abovyan St; 010
583990; w cafecentral.am; 10.00–midnight.
Popular long-running coffee shop – the name
is pronounced the French way – with outdoor
seating. Good salads & cakes/desserts as well as
good value main courses. Also sells coffee beans/
ground coffee. $$

**Crumbs Bread Factory** [135 E3]
37 Mashtots Av; 010 537013; 08.30–
midnight. Bright & modern new café with a good
selection of herbal teas, light meals & snacks, &
freshly baked bread & pastries. Excellent soups. A
good value lunch spot at this end of town. $$

**Dip n Dip** [135 E4] 1 Northern Av; m 041
858016; w dipndip.com; 10.00–01.00 Mon–
Sat, 08.00–midnight Sun. Strictly for those with

no regard for sugar intake, the centrepiece of this
(originally Lebanese) dessert café is its 3 molten
chocolate fountains (dark, milk & white), of which
theatrical use is made for every last menu item bar
the caramel *pain perdu*. There is a 'lucky dip' page at
the end of the menu if you're struggling to decide
how best to give yourself type 2 diabetes. $$

**✳ The Green Bean** [134 D5 & 135 F1] 10
Amiryan St 010 529279, 08.30–23.00);
38 Isahakyan St 055 529277, 08.00–
midnight). A small chain of attractive eco-
friendly cafés established back when non-
smoking venues were still unheard of, sourcing
locally made, preservative-free products.
Excellent coffees, soups & real homemade
lemonade. A 3rd branch is within the American
University. $$

**Jazzve** [134 D3] 35 Tumanyan St; 010
533663; w jazzve.am; 09.00–22.00. Also
at 2 Abovyan St, 18 Abovyan St (inside Moscow
Cinema), 8/1 Isahakyan St, 16 Komitas St & among
the open-air cafés in front of the opera house.
Established in 2003, this reliable chain of coffee
shops is decorated in literary style, with menus in
the form of newspapers. Good coffee, cold drinks,
desserts & a full meals menu, though service can
be somewhat chilly. *Jazzve* is the Armenian/Turkish
word for the long-handled copper pot in which
Armenian coffee (*haykakan soorj*) is made; here it
is still prepared traditionally on a hot bed of sand
rather than over an open flame. $$

**Natura Gold** [135 F4] 11 Abovyan St; 010
569091; 10.00–midnight. Originally a tea
house serving speciality teas & desserts, this tiny
but welcoming gem of a café now serves snacks &
main courses too, with a very pleasant back garden
in summer. Also sells loose leaf tea from around
the world. $$

**Thomas Twining** [135 F4] 22 Abovyan
St; 010 543070; 11.00–midnight. A busy
basement tea shop cheerfully decorated with tea-
making apparatus. Serves a vast range of teas, all
well described on the menu (also sold loose). Also
serves snacks such as crêpes, savoury & sweet, as
well as main courses. $$

**Melody** [135 E3] 34/6 Tumanyan St; 010
569320; approx Apr–Oct; 09.15–01.30 Mon–
Sat, 09.15–midnight Sun. Right on the corner of
Tumanyan & Mashtots, this cheap open-air café
is the most reliable among the many surrounding
the opera house. Somewhat gruff service but

food always good with a very varied menu. Excellent value for money. $–$$

⛻ **Aeon** [135 E4] 3a Teryan St; ☎010 538766; m 095 538766; w aeonyerevan.com; ⊕ noon–midnight. So-called anti-café/time-club charging by the hr rather than by the order; ie tea/coffee/snacks inc. Blurs the line between café & cultural centre with an almost hostel-like vibe. Big selection of books, games, instruments, etc & an ongoing events calendar. Discount packages for those who wish to stay longer & work. Relaxed upstairs lounge with beanbags. A good place to meet people, work, read or simply relax. $

## OUTSIDE THE CENTRE

✖ **Charentsi 28** [131 E4] 28 Charents St; ☎010 572945; w charentsi28.com; ⊕ noon–midnight. Right on the edge of the central area but worth seeking out. In a fully restored old house with an ambience, as they say, of 'casual elegance'. Detailed menu consists of a carefully chosen mix of traditional Armenian & contemporary world food. Good for groups on special occasions. $$–$$$

✖ **Eastern Cuisine** [130 D3] 16/1 Komitas Av; ☎010 271620; ⊕ 24hrs. Located northeast of Barekamutyun metro station & thus useful if on your way to the Republic of Artsakh (Nagorno Karabagh) permanent representation (page 375). Extensive menu of regional cuisine with outdoor seating in pleasant gardens. $$

✖ **Genatsvale** [130 D3] 35/2 Komitas Av ☎010 277999, ⊕ 24hrs); 23 Vahram Papazyan St ☎010 326161, ⊕ 10.00–midnight); w genacvale.am. See page 144. $$

# NIGHTLIFE

A number of (usually small and intimate) bars, pubs and live music venues host a spectrum of contemporary world music, as well as bands and DJs from the local underground scene, and are very welcoming to foreign visitors. Events listings are best found on the websites (or more commonly Facebook pages) of the venues in question. For specialist electronic music genres and DJs, try Resident Advisor (w residentadvisor.net/events/armenia). Do be aware that the term 'nightclub' in a local context usually refers to a striptease club! The Western meaning (ie: a night-time venue for music and dancing) is usually known as a 'disco'; the mainstream venues all offer a similar experience and generally appeal to locals, diaspora Armenians and Russians.

## PUBS, BARS AND LIVE MUSIC

⚲ **Calumet Ethnic Lounge Bar** [134 D3] 54/23 Pushkin St; m 095 359229; ﬁ; ⊕ 17.00–midnight. Cosy Calumet, Yerevan's original hippie basement bar, is still going strong with its east-meets-west décor, regular live music & trendy young crowd of locals, expats & hostel-dwelling backpackers. No less popular after nearly a decade, though closes rather early (unless you're invited to a lock-in).

✳⚲ **Dargett Craft Beer** [134 D3] 72 Aram St; m 096 870870; ﬁ; ⊕ 11.00–midnight Sun–Thu, 11.00–01.00 Fri & Sat. Not Yerevan's first brewpub but the first to make such a splash. More than a dozen 'craft beer' varieties all brewed on-site in this spacious, industrial-style beer house & restaurant. Lots of outdoor seating for warm summer nights. Excellent mixed menu of posh pub food; try the *tarte flambée*. Also serves the only draught cider in the whole of Armenia.

⚲ **DAS** [135 G2] 9 Koryun St; m 095 418008; ﬁ dasaridu; ⊕ 20.00–late Thu–Sun. Bar & left-field music venue hosting a rolling events schedule with resident DJs, bands & regular promoters as well as one-off gigs. Check its Facebook page for what's on.

⚲ **Eden Café-Pub** [135 E2] 1a Tamanyan St; ☎010 544644; ﬁ; ⊕ 10.00–03.00 Mon–Sat, 10.00–midnight Sun. Regular-looking Cascade café by day which morphs into a lively & intimate party venue by night. Good cocktails.

⚲ **Epicure** [135 E4] 40 Pushkin St; m 095 105020; ﬁ EpicureYerevan; ⊕ 10.00–02.00. Cosy, classy & relaxed café-bar with light meals during the day & DJs blending a variety of chilled world music into the night. A notably open & progressive atmosphere, yet not at all touristy.

**Hemingway Pub** [135 E2] 1a Tamanyan St; m 098 349882; 🔲; ⏲ 17.00–04.00. Late-night dive bar (it's in the basement) near Cascade, mostly good for prolonging festivities well after other venues have shut. Loud, cramped & crowded as a consequence but can be good fun.

**\*🍷In Vino** [134 D2] 6 Martiros Saryan St; 📞010 521931; w invino.am; 🔲; ⏲ 11.00–midnight. This wine bar & merchant is the original & best on Martiros Saryan Street; the many copycats attest to its success. The cellar is augmented by classic European cheese & meat platters. Staff highly knowledgeable & happy to make recommendations based on taste. If you're new to the Armenian wine scene but don't have time to visit a winery, this is the place to start.

**🍷Jean Paul Existential Café** [135 E4] 42/1 Aram St; m 041 044201; 🔲 navavarfish; ⏲ 19.00–03.00. Head straight upstairs to this bohemian living room/bar in which you too may drink wine & discuss existential matters until the early hrs.

**🍷The Kond House** [134 B5] 46 Leo St; m 091 013801; 🔲; ⏲ 18.00–02.00. Climb the steps, follow the alley & keep going when you think you're lost. Aiming perhaps to recreate a bohemian Yerevan underworld of old, this sprawling Kond mansion-bar is a curious mix of crumbling concrete, creaky floorboards, Soviet furniture & cosy nooks filled with bearded hipsters discussing serious matters over shots of homemade vodka. (The distillery is in the basement.)

**🍷No-Name** [134 D2] 4 Martiros Saryan St; ⏲ 17.00–midnight. No name had been chosen for this bar at the time of research; hence, locals started calling it the 'no-name bar' and it seems to have stuck. Small, chilled & friendly space set back from Martiros Saryan Street opposite the eponymous museum, serving a good jug of sangria & much else.

**🍷Simona** [134 C3] 80 Aram St; m 095 426619; 🔲; ⏲ 19.00–03.00. Lively (but not too lively) late-evening cocktail bar with a cool young crowd & live DJs spearheading a vinyl revival in Yerevan. Plentiful seating, too, but not so much you can't find the dance floor.

**🍷Tom Collins** [135 E4] 31 Pushkin St; m 055 743252; 🔲; ⏲ 17.00–04.00. One of the longer-running & more traditional pubs & open late; also good value compared with some of the upscale alternatives. All-you-can-eat crayfish on Wed nights for AMD3,500 pp.

**🍷Van Gogh Art Café** [135 E3] 31/3 Tumanyan St; m 095 140694, 091 433705; w vangogh.am; ⏲ noon–03.00. Snacks & salads until 18.00, alcohol & music thereafter in this well-established basement bar with galleries of local art.

**\*🍷Voskevaz Wine Time** [134 D2] 6 Martiros Saryan St; 📞060 706262; 🔲; ⏲ noon–midnight. Gourmet retro-chic wine bar serving delicate & artful gastronomic accompaniments to your balloon-glass of fine wine, with an excellent first-floor aspect over the buzzing street below. One of our top picks on Martiros Saryan's hipster strip.

## ENTERTAINMENT

Posters detailing upcoming cultural events are published on billboards outside theatres and concert halls, as well as in the more popular coffee shops, bars and the like. Printed listings are no longer readily available; at the time of research the most reliable sources were **Facebook's events listings** (w facebook.com), favoured by most local promoters due to the network's enormous popularity in Armenia (events can be discovered simply by searching for 'events in Yerevan' or by visiting the official page of the venues in question). **TomsArkgh** (w tomsarkgh.am), literally 'box office' in Armenian, is an excellent English-language website and smartphone app that also functions as an online ticket sales platform, accepting Visa and MasterCard payments. **Yerevan Events** (w yerevanevents.am) is another actively updated website but only in Armenian at the time of research (though your web browser may auto-translate its contents).

**CINEMA** International films are usually screened in Russian, but several cinemas also show a selection of the most popular **films in English**. KinoPark [130 D5] within **Yerevan Mall** (34/3 Arshakunyants Av; 📞 011 888888; w kinopark.am) generally has several screenings per day, as does the Russian chain Cinema Star (w cinemastar.ru) with locations within **Dalma Garden Mall** [130 D4] (3 Tsitsernakaberd Hwy; ☏060 755555) and **Rio Mall** [130 D3] (8 Vahram Papazyan St; ☏011 281888). Of the older establishments, **Nairi Cinema** [135 F2] (50 Mesrop Mashtots Av; ☏010 542829) and **Moscow Cinema** [135 F4] (18 Abovyan St; ☏010 521210) have occasional English-language programming with tickets available via TomsArkgh (page 147); the latter is the usual venue for the annual **British Film Festival**, organised by the British Council (w britishcouncil.am). The week-long annual Golden Apricot International Film Festival (page 109) takes place in Yerevan during July in several venues. The annual **Sunchild International Environmental Festival** (w sunchild.fpwc.org) includes an environmentally themed documentary film programme.

**CASINOS**  All Yerevan's casinos were closed and moved outside the city limits in the early 2000s. The road to the airport is thickly populated, and there are quite a few on the Sevan highway, including the vast, tourist-oriented **Shangri La** complex (5 Tbilisyan Hwy; ☏060 488000; w shangrila.am).

**CLASSICAL MUSIC**  The **Spendiaryan Opera and Ballet National Academic Theatre** [135 E3] (54 Tumanyan St; ☏010 533391/565803/586311; e info@opera.am; w opera. am), also known simply as 'opera', stages regular opera and ballet except during July and August. Schedules are announced two or three weeks in advance. As well as online (page 147), tickets (AMD1,500–15,000) can be bought in person from the box office (⊕ Mon–Sat 11.00–19.00) just behind the theatre to the northeast. The **Aram Khachaturyan Concert Hall** [135 E3] (46 Mesrop Mashtots Av; ☏010 560645; e philharmonic@apo.am; w apo.am), in the northern half of the same building, is the home of the Armenian Philharmonic Orchestra and hosts concerts throughout the season. The **Komitas Chamber Music Hall** [135 H3] (1 Isahakyan St; ☏010 526718) presents regular concerts by the Armenian Chamber Orchestra.

**THEATRES**  Apart from the Spendiaryan Opera and Ballet National Academic Theatre (see above) there are at least 15 other theatres in Yerevan, listed on the interactive online map of Yerevan (w maps.yerevan.am/en). All, except the **Stanislavsky Russian Drama Theatre** [135 F4] (7 Abovyan St; ☏010 569199), which performs in Russian, perform exclusively in Armenian. There are two puppet theatres which may appeal to non-Armenian-speakers: the **Yerevan State Theatre of Marionettes** [135 F1] (43 Mesrop Mashtots Av; ☏010 562450) and the **Hovhannes Tumanyan State Puppet Theatre** [135 F3] (4 Sayat Nova Av; ☏010 563244).

**JAZZ**  The main jazz club is **Poplavok** [135 G2] (41 Isahakyan St; ☏010 522303, in Aragast restaurant, page 161) where reservations are always required. It has the dubious distinction of being the location of the 2001 murder of a Georgian Armenian by presidential bodyguards in the men's lavatories (page 28). The **Malkhas Jazz Club** [134 D3] (52 Pushkin St; ☏010 531778) is a bar/restaurant serving Armenian and European cuisine which also stages live jazz. It is owned by Levon Malkhasyan who is considered to be the godfather of Armenian jazz. **Cafesjian Centre for the Arts** (page 179) hosts concerts, including jazz and classical. More jazz events at other venues are listed at w tomsarkgh.am/en in the relevant category. The **Yerevan Jazz Festival** seems to be gaining traction, having now run annually since 2016, although the time of year has so far varied from April to October.

**SPORTS AND FITNESS** Sports facilities continue to increase in number and quality. Two branches of the international chain **Gold's Gym** [134 C4 & 130 D3] (27/1 Amiryan St & 40/1 Komitas Av (entrance from Nairi Zaryan St); w goldsgym. am) provide world-class fitness facilities, English-speaking personal trainers and classes, spas and saunas, and in the Komitas branch an Olympic-size swimming pool. Most upscale hotels have fitness centres and some offer memberships to non-residents. There is a free outdoor gym in **Hrazdan Gorge** near the Children's Railway [134 B2] with a nearby plunge pool and outdoor shower. During good weather, billiard and table-tennis tables appear in parks and can be hired by the hour. Tennis courts and equipment can be hired at the **Ararat Tennis Club** [135 H4] (2 Alek Manukyan St; 010 570648; f) in Yerevan's green belt near Yerevan State University; coaching is apparently always available and there is an adjacent clubhouse and café. Tennis, basketball, golf and minigolf are available at **Ararat Valley Country Club** [130 B2] next door to Vahakni Residential Community. At **Play City** [131 F2] (35 Acharyan St; 010 288377; e info@playcity.am; w playcity.am), in Yerevan's northeast suburb of Avan, activities include bowling, karting, paintball, billiards and minigolf. Winter visitors will find Swan Lake [135 F3] (page 163) transformed into an **ice-skating rink**, with another, larger, rink in Yeraz Park at the north end of Azatutyan Avenue where it becomes the Tbilisyan Highway.

In terms of **spectator sports**, the **Karen Demirchyan Sport and Concert Complex** [130 C4] (Tsitsernakaberd Hill, entrance from Kievyan St; 011 755502) hosts a variety of international sports fixtures. The 54,208-seat **Hrazdan Stadium** [134 A5] (4/1 Hrazdan Gorge Rd; 010 585191) is the largest multi-use stadium in Armenia and the home stadium of the national football team. Replacing the Soviet-era velodrome demolished in 2012 is the new **Yerevan Velodrome** [130 C5] (27/8 Admiral Isakov Av; m 099 770857; w velodrome.am), hosting training sessions and competitive events.

**Riding** Riding lessons for all ages and abilities and hire of horses can be arranged at the **Hovik Hayrapetyan Equestrian Centre** [130 B6] (39 Shirak St, Charbakh; 010 465000; m 099 465000; e info@hhec.am; f horseridingschoolyerevan; ⊕ 09.00–19.30 Tue–Fri, 10.00–16.00 Sat–Sun) in the Shengavit district of southwest Yerevan.

**Swimming** Several of the larger city-centre **hotels** (including Ani Plaza, Best Western Congress, Armenia Marriott, Metropol, Regineh and Grand Hotel Yerevan) have swimming pools to which non-residents are admitted for a fee. Gold's Gym on Nairi Zaryan Street (see above) has an Olympic standard (ie: 50 metre) swimming pool and diving boards, available with gym membership. Among the other venues are:

**Aquatek** [131 F3] See page 140 for contact details. ⊕ 09.00–22.30, last entrance 21.00; Jun–Oct Mon–Fri adult/child AMD6,000/3,000, Sat–Sun AMD7,000/3,500; Oct–Mar prices about AMD1,000 lower. Other facilities extra. Non-residents can visit the swimming pools & other water amusements.
**Ararat Valley Country Club** [130 B2] 50 Gevorg Chaush St; 043 177220; w vahakni.com; ⊕ swimming pool: Jun–Sep 10.00–20.00;

adult/child Mon–Fri AMD5,000/3,000, Sat–Sun AMD8,000/4,000. The club has a very pleasant outdoor swimming pool area & bar to which non-members are admitted, as well as facilities for tennis, basketball, football, minigolf & golf (9 holes).
**Erebuni Plaza Business Centre** [135 E6] 26/1 Vazgen Sargsyan St (off Republic Sq); 010 510451; e info@erebuni-plaza.am; ⊕ 08.00–16.00; single visit AMD4,000, 12 visits AMD30,000.

The centre has a gym & small swimming pool which are available to visitors.
**Waterworld** [131 F3] 40 Myasnikyan St; \010 638998; ⊕ Jun–Sep 13.00–20.00. Admission price is by height, adult approx AMD5,000. It is popular with Yerevan residents during the heat of summer so it can be busy. Especially suitable for families with children, as there is much to keep them entertained.

## SHOPPING

Yerevan has every type of retail outlet imaginable, from expensive shops on Northern Avenue selling internationally known designer brands to that part of Vernissage specialising in secondhand nuts and bolts. Several huge American-style shopping malls now exist in suburban areas. Some pedestrian underpasses in the centre have a host of small shops. For cheap clothes try **Rossia Mall** [135 E7] above Zoravar Andranik metro station. For homemade dried fruits, *basturma* and other dried meats, dried mountain herbs, cheese and other **traditional produce** it is worth visiting **Goom Market** [131 E5], the covered market on Khorenatsi Street off Tigran Mets Avenue about 500m south of the cathedral. The covered market on Mesrop Mashtots Avenue now houses a supermarket (page 164) in place of the previous traditional bazaar, although there are still a few market stalls selling fresh fruit and vegetables at the entrance and the building is as impressive as ever. The biggest trading centre for imported goods – particularly household appliances and electronics – is **Petak** ('beehive') **market** on Sevan Street [131 E5].

Craft items and artwork of all types can be bought at the **Vernissage** open-air market [135 F6] (page 156) and it is by far the best place to buy souvenirs; even if you don't intend to buy anything a trip to Yerevan would not be complete without a visit. There are several good art, handicraft and souvenir shops on **Abovyan Street** including Salt Sack [135 F4] (3/1 Abovyan St) and Dalan Art Gallery and Café (page 142). Worth a look elsewhere are Peacock Art Café [135 E4] (10 Northern Av), Sharan Crafts Centre [135 F4] (6 Sayat Nova Av), Tade [135 F2] (8 Moskovyan St; w mstade.com), the ceramics showroom beneath Villa Delenda (page 139) and the entrance hall of 12 Tables (page 143). Armenia's only World Fair Trade Organization-certified handicrafts outlet at the time of research is that of the non-profit Homeland Development Initiative Foundation, or HDIF [134 D3] (13/6 Ghazar Parpetsi St; w hdif.org), which employs a network of artisans in villages throughout Armenia.

One of Yerevan's biggest **bookshops** is Noyan Tapan [135 E5] (8 Abovyan St; w noyantapan.am) which has the range of Collage maps (w collage.am; page 65) and a good selection of books in English. Artbridge Bookstore Café (page 142) specialises in foreign-language publications and has a wide selection of English-language books on Armenia. Bookinist [134 D4] (20 Mesrop Mashtots Av; w books. am) is a large bookshop mostly stocking books in Armenian and Russian but there is an English section. The same is true of the newly opened Zangak (7 Abovyan St; w zangak.am). **Secondhand books** are sometimes found at the west end of the Vernissage (page 156); also there are several Little Free Library (w littlefreelibrary. org) locations in Yerevan.

**Brandy** can be bought from most markets and supermarkets but specialist dealers include the Proshyan Brandy Shop [134 C5] (18 Mesrop Mashtots Av; w proshyan.am), Noyan Tun [134 D4] (12 Amiryan St; w noyantun.am) and both of the big brandy distilleries (page 170). In Vino (page 147) is one of the first and best boutique **wine merchants**, selling a range of Armenian and world wines, with very knowledgeable staff. It also functions as a wine club with special events. If intending to take alcohol home with you, remember airline regulations on liquids (page 107); the duty-free outlet at Zvartnots International Airport sells all popular Armenian wines and spirits (except homemade *oghi*).

If you need a good **photographic** dealer, try the **Zigzag** chain [134 D4 & 135 G5] (24 Mesrop Mashtots Av & 20 Sayat Nova Av). Those looking for quality **hiking and camping equipment**, including canister gas, should visit Dangerous Heights [131 E5] (1 Artsakh Av; \010 434911; m 098 911000; w camp.am) or the HIKEArmenia information centre (page 112); there are also a couple of hunting and fishing outlets within Petak (see opposite) that sell cheap accessories. **Cyclists** are better catered for than in previous times; see page 136 for a list of suggested retailers.

Several **supermarket chains** have arisen in recent years and many branches are open 24 hours. They are well stocked, though not necessarily cheaper than convenience stores (and usually more expensive for fresh produce). They do in addition have 24-hour currency exchange kiosks. Brands include SAS, Yerevan City, Krpak, Nor Zovk and Parma. Many can be connected to oligarch families and some have been the target of public boycotts and criminal investigations in the aftermath of the Velvet Revolution (page 33).

## OTHER PRACTICALITIES

**BANKS AND EXCHANGING MONEY** Banks are generously scattered in all areas of the city, but queues for money exchange can be long at busy times of day. If all you want to do is change some cash it is much quicker to go to one of the currency exchanges in the supermarkets (see above).

**EMBASSIES AND CONSULATES IN YEREVAN** For guidance on how to find a full list of Armenian embassies abroad, see page 70.

**France** 8 Grigor Lusavorich St; \010 591950; e cad.erivan-amba@diplomatie.gouv.fr; w am. ambafrance.org
**Germany** 29 Charents St; \010 523279; e info@eriw.diplo.de; w eriwan.diplo.de
**Malta** 28 Koghbatsi St; m 094 542499
**Nagorno Karabagh (self-declared Republic of Artsakh)** 17a Nairi Zaryan St; \010 249705; e ankr@arminco.com

**UK** 34 Marshal Baghramyan Av; \010 264301; e enquiries.yerevan@fco.gov.uk; w gov. uk/world/armenia. Note that due to ongoing technical issues the embassy was operating from a temporary location in Yerevan at the time of research.
**USA** 1 American Av; \010 464700; e usinfo@ usa.am; w usa.am

**INTERNET** Free **Wi-Fi** is available in practically all hotels, cafés and restaurants, as well as via several citywide hot spots. All of the major mobile phone network operators (page 117) have pay-as-you-go data packages available with their (usually free) local SIM cards. Internet cafés are nowhere near as ubiquitous as they once were and the few that remain tend to specialise in gaming rather than internet access per se. To find one the best plan is to ask around; expect to pay about AMD500 per hour. Many hotels make a computer available to guests; the larger hotels have 'business centres' with several terminals as well as printing and scanning facilities.

**MEDICAL ISSUES** Most hotels can help with finding a **doctor** and embassies may have lists of specialists. **Hospitals** have 24-hour emergency departments; there is a rota for receiving patients. To call an **ambulance** in an emergency, dial \911 or 103; patients needing hospital admission will be taken to the receiving hospital.

Hospitals also have casualty departments where patients can self-refer if needing immediate treatment. Possible hospitals include:

➕ **Arabkir Medical Complex Children's Hospital** [131 E2] 30 Mamikonyants St; ☏010 231352/236883

➕ **Heratsi Hospital Complex** [135 H2] 58 Abovyan St; ☏010 561778/563508

➕ **Nairi Medical Centre** [134 A3] 21 Paronyan St; ☏010 537742. Usually favoured by international visitors, with English-speaking doctors & the ability to deal with travel insurance claims.

➕ **Shengavit Medical Centre** [130 D6] 9 Manandyan St; ☏010 440530; w mcshengavit. am. Recently renovated & re-equipped to international standards.

➕ **V Mikaelyan Institute** [131 E2] 9 Hasratyan St; ☏010 281790/281990

There is also a 24-hour emergency **dental service** but apparently it is staffed by relatively inexperienced, newly qualified dentists so anyone with a problem may prefer to attend one of the many private dental clinics, some of which have 24-hour cover. Again, embassies may hold lists of dentists. **Pharmacies** abound and are indicated by a green cross and the Russian word аптека ('apteka', ie: apothecary). Chains with branches throughout the city include **Natali Pharm** at 3 Mashtots Avenue [134 B5] and 10 Tigran Mets Avenue [135 E7] (full list at w spyur.am/natalipharm), and **Alfapharm** at 23 Mashtots Avenue [134 D3] and 38 Abovyan Street [135 H3] (full list at w spyur.am/alfapharm).

**POST OFFICES** A convenient, central post office is that on Republic Square [135 E6] (page 154; ⊕ 08.00–19.00 Mon–Sat, 10.00–16.00 Sun). It has a philatelic corner for anyone interested in stamp collecting. Yerevan's main post office is at 22 Martiros Saryan Street [134 C3]. Each postal district also has its own branch. See also page 118.

## WHAT TO SEE AND DO

**A WALK AROUND YEREVAN** Central Yerevan is eminently walkable and the following route may be comfortably completed in a day, including stops for refreshments and to take in the various points of interest. If you intend to visit many of the museums or follow the suggested additional routes, however, it may be worth splitting the route over two (or more) days, perhaps walking from Republic Square to the Cascade on the first day, and continuing from the Cascade back to Republic Square on the second.

**Around Republic Square** Visitors to Yerevan are inevitably drawn to the large (3ha) and imposing **Republic Square** [135 E5–E6], which in Soviet times was called Lenin Square and is certainly one of the finest central squares created anywhere in the world during the 20th century. Described by the cultural geographer Diana Ter-Ghazaryan in 2013 as Yerevan's 'most important civic space', in April 2018 it fulfilled this epithet as the location of the most significant public demonstrations of the Velvet Revolution (page 33), with numbers exceeding 100,000 and crowds overflowing into the nearby streets. The building on the northeast side, directly facing the fountains, is the **History Museum of Armenia** [135 E5] (page 176) of 1926, with its white symmetrical colonnades; the **National Gallery of Armenia** (page 178) storeys, in a similar colour, were added from the 1950s onwards. It is sometimes claimed that Yerevan needed a large new art gallery after 1945 because many valuable works of art were brought here for safekeeping during the war years from other Soviet cities and never subsequently returned; the collection is almost certainly the finest in the former USSR apart from those of Moscow and St Petersburg. The water of the **fountains** outside the museum 'dances' in time to classical music on summer evenings; lighting is used to enhance the effect after dark. This unusual spectacle, which draws large crowds every night, was invented by Abraham Abrahamyan, a professor in the electronics department of Yerevan University. Each winter, a giant Christmas tree is erected in the square. To the left of the history museum entrance is the 'seven springs' *pulpulak* (page 75).

Underneath the square is a **large bunker** converted from former residential basements during the Cold War to protect officials from danger in the event of a nuclear attack. Since independence, suggestions have been made that it could be handed over to the museum as an additional display area but lack of funding, together with tensions over Nagorno Karabagh, will probably ensure that it retains its original purpose for the time being.

To the left of the museum across Abovyan Street on the northwest side of Republic Square is a former **government building** designed by Samvel Safaryan (1902–69) and built in the 1950s. It incorporates much Armenian detail and housed the Ministry of Foreign Affairs until 2016. As you continue anticlockwise, across Amiryan Street you will see the curving façade of the **Armenia Marriott Hotel** [134 D5] (page 138), opened in 1958 and now very popular with the diaspora and the diplomatic elite. During refurbishment by the Marriott chain, a secret floor was discovered with a 1.5m-high ceiling: it was used by the KGB to spy on guests.

Still continuing anticlockwise, you will cross a broad street with fountains down the middle. In the centre of the street formerly stood the statue of Lenin designed by Sergei Merkurov (1881–1952), erected in 1940 to mark the 20th anniversary of Soviet power and speedily removed, along with its huge pedestal, after independence. Standing where the statue once stood and looking at the hillside behind the museum it is possible to see the statue of **Mother Armenia** [131 E3] on an even larger plinth, 34m high, constructed in 1950 as the Victory Memorial in memory of the Great Patriotic War. The forged copper statue of Mother Armenia, a heroic figure holding a sword, was designed by the sculptor Ara Harutyunyan and erected in 1967. Very provocatively for this date, the statue with sword takes the shape of the cross. Mother Armenia actually stands in the space occupied from 1950 until 1962 by a 16.5m-tall statue of Stalin; at 21m Mother Armenia is, perhaps symbolically, taller than Stalin used to be. A Soviet writer in 1952, one year before Stalin's death, claimed:

Topping the Memorial Building is a statue of Stalin in a long greatcoat of which one lap is thrown open, showing the figure caught in a forward stride. In this statue wrought in Armenian bronze, the sculptor S Merkurov (NB: The same who was responsible for Lenin), has depicted Stalin in a characteristic pose of dynamic movement, supreme composure and confidence. Stalin stands with one hand in his coat-breast and the other slightly lowered as though his arm, swung in rhythm with his step, has for one brief moment become frozen in space. Stalin's gaze rests upon the splendour of the new Armenian socialist capital, upon its new handsome buildings, its wide green avenues, upon the central square in the opposite end of the town. There, Lenin, in his ordinary workday suit, has swung abruptly around in that characteristic, impetuous, sweeping way of his, so dear and familiar to every Soviet man, woman and child. The statues are very tall and the impression is that the two great leaders exchange glances of deep understanding as they survey the prospering life around them, so much of it the handiwork of their own genius, their self-abnegating labours, their perspicacity, the wisdom that enabled them to see far into the future.

A flower bed has replaced Lenin whose statue, with head detached, lies stored in the courtyard behind the History Museum; some walking tour leaders may be able to get you past the security guards to view it, though photography is forbidden. The sculptor of the vanished Lenin and Stalin as well as of Stepan Shahumyan, Sergei Merkurov (page 262), devoted his whole working life to immortalising communist leaders. Born in Alexandropol (present-day Gyumri), Merkurov studied in Paris where he was much influenced by Rodin before going on to sculpt many of the leading figures of his day as well as to create striking monuments to such figures as Chekhov and Pushkin.

The next building on the square, also built in 1956–58 and with a curving façade, houses a **post office** [135 E6] which is accessible through the left-hand door. Although not the main post office of Yerevan, this one has a pleasing stained-glass window behind the counter depicting a woman in Armenian costume holding a telegraph tape. The building housed the Ministry of Transport and Communications until 2016. Eagle-eyed visitors may spot the Masonic Square and Compasses symbol within the upper façade's detail (though given that Freemasonry was outlawed by the Soviets it is by no means a clear symbol of their involvement).

The final building, on the southeast side of the square, was partly built under Tamanyan's direction in 1926, though only completed in 1941. An irregular pentagonal structure with one curved side, it is possibly Tamanyan's masterpiece. An elegant colonnade above arches forms a gallery along the whole façade and is combined with Armenian detail in the capitals. The archway to the inner courtyard is surmounted by a clocktower which usually flies the red, blue and orange Armenian flag; the building is home to the offices of government ministers.

**To the cathedral** Leave Republic Square along the street that runs between the post office and the government buildings. It is named **Tigran Mets Avenue** in honour of King Tigran II (the Great) who ruled Armenia from c95BC to 55BC. The street bends right after a few metres between buildings which mostly date from the 1920s and 1930s.

As you emerge from Tigran Mets Avenue, to the left on the corner of **Khanjyan Street** you will see a **bronze statue** [135 E7] dating from 1974 of Alexander Griboyedov (1795–1829), the satirical playwright whose best-known play, *Woe from Wit*, was only performed and published posthumously. Its hero is branded a lunatic when he arrives in Moscow full of liberal and progressive ideas – a dangerous practice in either the Tsarist or the communist era. Griboyedov was also a diplomat and instrumental in Russia's peace negotiations with Turkey following the war of 1828–29 when Russia gained control of much of Armenia (page 21).

Just past the statue, the striking building on the right with a two-part curved roof is the former Russia cinema, now **Rossia Mall** [135 E7]. Underneath it is the **metro station** originally called Hoktemberyan ('October' in honour of the October revolution of 1917), but now renamed Zoravar Andranik (Commander Andranik) in honour of **Andranik Ozanian** (1865–1927). Born in Western Armenia, Ozanian became head of the Armenian self-defence troops in the 1890s until in 1905 he moved west to seek assistance for the Armenian cause. He subsequently participated in the liberation of Bulgaria from Ottoman rule in 1912–13 before organising Armenian units to fight alongside the Russian army against Turkey during World War I. Being more in sympathy with socialist ideals than the new Armenian government led by the Dashnak Party he left in 1918 for Bulgaria and then moved to the USA, dying in Fresno, California. His last expressed wish was to be buried in Armenia. Although he was originally interred in Fresno, after a few months his coffin was moved to Europe and he was reinterred among the renowned in the cemetery of Père Lachaise in Paris. He was finally brought to Armenia in 2000 and now rests in the Yerablur Cemetery in Yerevan where the dead from the Karabagh war are buried. His **statue** [135 E7], unveiled in 2003, can be seen at the foot of the slope leading up to the cathedral. It depicts him brandishing a sword while rather uncomfortably riding two horses at once, one of which is crushing a snake beneath its hoof. Continuing straight on for a block brings you to the covered **Goom Market** [131 E5], which spills out on to the surrounding streets. It is a good place to buy dried fruits and other homemade delicacies.

The **cathedral** [135 F7], straight ahead up the slope to the left, is dedicated to St Gregory the Illuminator (as he is always called, although St Gregory the Enlightener would be a better translation since his achievement was converting Armenia into a Christian country). It was consecrated in September 2001 to celebrate what was officially the 1,700th anniversary of Christianity becoming the state religion and to this end symbolically has seating for 1,700 people in the main church, although a further 300 can be accommodated in the smaller chapels dedicated to St Trdat, the king who adopted Christianity as the state religion, and his wife St Ashken. There is also a *gavit* and a belltower. The cathedral may well be the first church in Armenia which visitors see but, even apart from its modernity, it is in several respects atypical. It was one of the first churches in Armenia to introduce seats. Traditionally there were no seats in Armenian churches as the congregation stood throughout the service. Secondly, there are no candles. It is normal on entering an Armenian church to buy candles and then to light them. Here candles are forbidden and may only be lit in a separate building on the southeast side. Thirdly, there is an organ. Fourthly, the church is well lit, having many windows as well as a large metal chandelier. Fifthly, by Armenian standards it is enormous with a total area of 3,500m² and a height of 63m. It has been described as having more the atmosphere of a concert hall than a place of worship but it is conspicuously busy with numerous Armenians of all ages visiting and a constant succession of weddings, particularly at weekends. (See page 41 for information about Armenian wedding customs.) Rather incongruously, near the entrance is a baldachin brought from the church of St Gayane at Etchmiadzin, underneath which is a casket containing some of the relics of St Gregory which were brought here from the church of San Gregorio Armeno, Naples, where they had been kept for more than 500 years. They were a gift from Pope John Paul II on the occasion of the cathedral's dedication. Other relics of the saint have been built into the cathedral's foundations.

Leave the cathedral by the main door through which you entered and walk back down the slope. At the foot of the slope do a U-turn to the right into the part of the **circular green belt** in Tamanyan's 1926 plan which was actually created. This part in summer now holds a children's funfair; beyond it, walk through trees and cafés. The first **statue** encountered is of Taras Shevchenko (1814–61) [135 F7], the Ukrainian poet and artist whose literary works are regarded as the foundation of Ukrainian literature and the modern Ukrainian language. Armenia and Ukraine have educational links. Both, together with Moldova, are Eastern partners in the Athena project, co-ordinated by the European Universities Association, which aims to contribute to the development, reform and modernisation of the higher education systems in the three countries. The co-ordinator for Armenia is Yerevan State University and, for Ukraine, the Taras Shevchenko National University of Kiev. European Union partners include universities in Portugal, Finland and the Netherlands. Continue along the green belt until a radial road crosses it. Here there is another **statue** [135 G7] of a warrior on horseback. It is Vardan Mamikonian, the leader of the Armenian forces killed at the Battle of Avarayr (page 19) in AD451 when his troops were overcome by a much larger Persian force. Made of wrought copper and unveiled in 1975, it is by Yervand Kochar (1899–1979), other examples of whose work include the fine statue of David of Sassoun outside the main railway station and several paintings in the National Gallery of Armenia.

**Around Vernissage** [135 F6] Instead of continuing along the green belt, take the pedestrian subway under Khanjyan Street to reach the eastern end of the celebrated **arts and crafts market** of Vernissage. (*Vernissage* is a French word, literally meaning 'varnishing' or 'glazing' but also used in the sense of 'preview', or 'private viewing', at an art gallery.) Occupying the area between Buzand and Aram streets as far as the Hanrapetutyan Street intersection, Vernissage is unquestionably the most popular place in Armenia for tourists to buy souvenirs and craft items. A huge range of items is sold within the rows of covered stalls, for the most part by the people who made them. Though it operates every day, the stalls swell considerably at the weekend, which is the best time to absorb the buzzing atmosphere. The range covers carpets, embroideries, wood and stone carvings, paintings, metalwork and the like, and the quality ranges from the superb to the tacky. It is generally possible to pay in either drams or US dollars and, while bargaining is acceptable and indeed expected, you may feel that the prices in the first place do not really reflect the work that has gone into some of the items for sale and that asking for a reduction would be unreasonable. As well as craft items there are also the scant remains of the diverse flea market that accompanied the arts and crafts before the market's remodelling in 2016, with hawkers selling everything from Soviet-era radios, cameras and medals to secondhand books and cookware. Particularly adventurous weekend visitors may also enjoy travelling back in time with a lunch stop at the unmarked **Soviet-era canteen** which exists to serve extremely cheap meals to the vendors. The dingy entrance is located midway along Aram Street to the right of the Naregatsi Arts Institute. The matriarch who runs it will calculate your bill – which will struggle to exceed the value of a single AMD1,000 note – on an abacus, and likely force you to drink a shot of vodka with her before you take a seat.

Outside the **Armenian Centre for Contemporary Experimental Art** [135 F6] (1/3 Buzand St; w accea.info; ⏰ 11.00–17.00 Tue–Sat) opposite Vernissage to the south is another **statue** [135 F6] by Yervand Kochar, his bronze *Melancholy*. The gallery itself hosts an ongoing programme of worthwhile exhibitions, as well as occasional performances in its small theatre. West of Hanrapetutyan Street begins the remodelled 'park of khachkars', at whose east end is a 2016 statue of the Armenian military hero **Garegin Nzhdeh** (page 24) by sculptor Gagik Stepanyan. Positioned throughout the park are 13 khachkars, all replicas of specimens found at various locations in historical Armenia beyond the present-day republic, as well as four replica cuneiform inscriptions from the 7th century BC. At the northwest end is **Hanrapetutyan Hraparak** [135 E5] (Republic Square) metro station.

## Abovyan Street from Republic Square to Tumanyan Street

Cross Nalbandyan Street via the pedestrian subway incorporated into the metro station. This underpass is known as Aleppo Market, revived by refugee Syrian Armenians and now a good place to buy imported Syrian olive oil, herbs, spices, condiments and other items. Climb the stairs on to Aram Street and continue straight on along the back of the art gallery. Before turning right into Abovyan Street, look first at the two buildings to the left which are at the bottom end of Abovyan Street adjoining Republic Square. **Abovyan Street** is one of the most popular streets for tourists to walk along, hence the plethora of souvenir shops, cafés and hotels; it also has some of the best Tsarist-era buildings. It is named after Khachatur Abovyan (1805–48), a teacher and writer whose best-known novel, *Armenia's Wounds*, is based around the events of the Russo-Persian war of 1826–28. **Number 2** Abovyan Street, on the left-hand side as one faces Republic Square, is a red and black Neoclassical building constructed in 1880 as a boys' secondary school on a site where it had originally been planned to build Yerevan's cathedral. In Soviet times the building was adapted for chamber music concerts and is now the Arno Babajanyan Concert Hall. **Number 1** on the opposite side is slightly newer having been built between 1900 and 1914 to house a trading business; it is also constructed of red and black tuff but is in the then-fashionable Art Nouveau style.

Before continuing up Abovyan Street it may still be worth continuing about 300m down **Aram Street**, opposite the road you have walked from Vernissage. The object of the detour is a **stone carvers' yard** [134 D4] on the left where khachkars and other items are still created from tuff in the traditional way. To see these carvers at work is to witness the successors to over a thousand years of tradition. A little further along Aram Street on the right is the maternity hospital with four **bronze sculptures** of 1982, *Maternity* by Yuri Minasyan. Return via Aram Street to Abovyan Street and turn left up the hill. On the left is the start of **Northern Avenue** linking Republic Square with Freedom Square, part of Tamanyan's master plan of 1926 on which construction finally started (amid much controversy as it required the demolition of several residential blocks) in 2002. Either walk up Northern Avenue at this stage or walk down later from the theatre. The eight- and nine-storey buildings on Northern Avenue, built in tuff of various colours, combine modernity with a definite Armenian character. International boutiques and cafés occupy the ground-floor shops while the upper stories are a mixture of private apartments, hotel accommodation and commercial spaces.

South of the lower end of Northern Avenue is a **statue** of an old man holding a bunch of roses. Created by the sculptor Levon Tokmajyan and erected in 1991, it originally marked the exact spot where the old man it portrays used to stand in the 1930s. His real name was Karapet, but the locals gave him the name '**Kara Bala**' [135 E5], Turkish for 'black boy', because of his dark complexion (see box, page 159).

Yerevan  WHAT TO SEE AND DO

3

## ARMENIAN EMBROIDERY

Visitors will probably be most aware of embroidery during their visit to Vernissage, Yerevan's arts and crafts market (page 156). Here many colourful hand-embroidered articles are on sale, ranging from small items such as handkerchiefs to larger-scale works such as tablecloths. Much of the embroidery is based on the celebrated Armenian illuminated manuscripts, one of the most popular subjects being letters of the Armenian alphabet in the form of birds. The technique used is known as freestyle embroidery or needle painting and some of the results are exquisite. Other styles of Armenian embroidery, such as Aintab, are types of drawn thread work or cut work, akin to Hardanger embroidery. Yet another variety is an interlaced embroidery technique, also known as Marash or Maltese Cross embroidery.

One theory is that these various types were introduced into Europe from Armenia at the time of the Crusades (1096–1270) as a result of the known commercial, military and social contacts between the Armenian kingdom of Cilicia on the Aegean coast of Turkey and the Crusaders.

A technique which may be less familiar to visitors is Armenian knotted needle lace. Superficially this resembles crochet in appearance but the loops are knotted together rather than looped together, thus making it more robust because even if some threads are damaged the whole will not unravel. The stitches are made with an ordinary sewing needle, not with a crochet hook. Once the basic knotting technique is mastered, the skill lies in regulating the size and shape of the loops and many different patterns are known with evocative names such as Ararat, Yerevan and Arek, the last based on the circular sun design common in other Armenian art forms and often seen on khachkars.

There is a good display of Armenian embroidery in the Hovhannes Sharambeyan Folk Arts and Crafts Centre in Yerevan (page 180) and in the ethnographical museum at Sardarapat (page 223). Etchmiadzin Cathedral Museum (page 219) houses examples of ecclesiastical embroidery.

**Number 8**, on the right-hand side of Abovyan Street, was built in the 1880s, again in Neoclassical style. After 1937 the building housed the Soviet Central Committee and the office of Comsomol, the Soviet youth organisation; there was formerly a red star in the top arch of the masonry. It retains one of its original wooden doors. On the opposite side of the street at **number 1/4** is the dark façade (now incorporated into a later building) of the Gabrielyan mansion, built in 1910 by the architect Meghrabyan and combining Classical and Art Nouveau elements.

Continue uphill across **Pushkin Street**. The **first building** on the right, with salmon-coloured stucco and red trim, dates from the 1870s. A plaque on the wall commemorates the playwright Maxim Gorky's one-night stay in the building in 1928. Opposite it, on the left, is the red tuff **Khanzatyan mansion** and just above that is the **Hovhannisyan mansion**, a large building dating from 1915–16 which incorporated a hospital on the ground floor. Note the windows which incorporate a Star of David in the framework.

Slightly higher up the hill, still on the left, is the **Stanislavsky Russian Drama Theatre** [135 F4] built in 1937 in Constructivist style but considerably altered in 1974 when it gained a façade of yellowish tuff. Its architect Karo Halabyan (1897–1959) worked on several interesting Soviet-era projects including Krasnopresnenskaya metro station in Moscow and the post-war reconstruction of Stalingrad.

Opposite the Stanislavsky theatre is the small square, once called Zodiac Square because its fountain incorporates each sign of the zodiac, since renamed **Charles Aznavour Square** in honour of the composer, singer and actor (1924–2018) who was born in Paris in 1924 to Armenian parents who had fled the Turkish massacres. The square was created in the 1920s by demolishing a 17th-century Persian mosque together with the church of Sts Peter and Paul which also dated to the 17th century. The Grand Hotel Yerevan, designed by Nicoghayos Buniatyan (1884–1943), has its entrance on the square and dates from 1926. At one time Yerevan's most elegant hotel, it once again boasts five-star status. Its red tuff construction with wrought-iron balconies in traditional Armenian style contrasts oddly with the grey stonework of the entrance surmounted by white Ionic columns. Across the square is the **Moscow Cinema** [135 F4] which dates from 1933. Between the hotel and the cinema is the **exhibition hall of the Painters' Union** used for temporary shows. The square is host to statues of creatures made from bits of machinery – a surprisingly lifelike bear and an enormous spider. There is also a giant chess set, popular with children.

### Abovyan Street from Tumanyan Street to the green belt
Continue uphill across **Tumanyan Street**, beyond which Abovyan Street widens considerably and is lined with trees. Most of the buildings here date from the 1940s. On the left is the **Children's Art Museum** [135 F4] which is well worth visiting (page 180). Continue across **Sayat Nova Avenue**.

First on the left is the remaining part of the only one of Yerevan's churches to have at least partially survived the 1679 earthquake. Known as the **Katoghike** [135 F3] (literally 'cathedral', singularly inappropriate for the tiny building still standing), its current form dates from 1936 when the main church, a substantial basilica without a dome rebuilt in 1693–94, was demolished in the name of urban redevelopment. It was known that there had been a church on this site since the 13th century but until the demolition was under way nobody realised that the apse and sanctuary actually comprised this old church. Inscriptions of 1229 and 1282 on the newly revealed southern façade as well as one of 1264 on the wall proved this to be the case. Public and scientific outcry won the newly revealed church a reprieve, and the

---

### KARA BALA

Kara Bala was said to have come from a well-to-do family and was married to a beautiful wife; they had a son. Kara Bala grew roses. He would take his roses to Astafian Street (as Abovyan Street was then known) where he would stand and give them to girls. In particular he was said to be passionately in love with the famous actress Arus Voskanian who used to walk along Abovyan Street to the theatre, and he gave her one red rose every morning. However, she had another admirer, a Turkish man, and this made Kara Bala so jealous that he murdered his rival, for which he was subsequently tried and imprisoned.

On his eventual release he found that his wife and son had left him, that he didn't have a house and a garden any more and that his roses had been uprooted. 'I am not Kara Bala any more, I'm Dardy Bala' ('dard' means sorrow in Armenian), he kept saying, wandering sadly around the town with a bottle of wine. However, he didn't stop giving flowers. Whenever he came across flowers he gave them to women and many in Yerevan still remember him going up to young couples in the 1960s to present the girl with a bunch. Eventually he died and his frozen body was found one morning sitting on a rock.

surrounding buildings were demolished to make way for a plaza and a large new church dedicated to St Anna (this time built next to rather than around the old one). Since independence, Katoghike has resumed a religious function and services are now held here, although it is so tiny that there is hardly room for the officiating priest let alone any congregation. To either side of the *bema* are carvings, some of which appear to have been defaced.

Continue up the hill. Just beyond Katoghike is a **statue** of Alexander Mantashyants (1842–1911) [135 F3], an Armenian industrialist, financier, oil magnate and philanthropist. He was born in Tiflis (Tbilisi) and spent his childhood in Iran, entering his father's cotton business at an early age. In 1869–72 he visited England, staying in Manchester, then a world centre of the cotton and textile industries. Later he bought most of the shares of the Tiflis Central Bank and became the bank's chairman. He invested heavily and successfully in the developing oil industry and funded the Baku–Batumi pipeline, launched in 1907 and, at 835km, the world's then longest pipeline. At his death he was one of the richest individuals in the world. Among other philanthropic activities he helped to found the Armenian Charitable Society in the Caucasus, donated 250,000 roubles to build the residence of the Katholikos in Etchmiadzin, sent young Armenians (including the composer Komitas) to study at European universities and built the Pitoewski (now Rustaveli) Theatre in Tiflis. Perhaps his most famous donation was some 1½ million francs in 1904 to build the Armenian church of St John the Baptist in Paris. On the right, plaques on numbers 28, 30 and 32 commemorate residents of these buildings which were put up in the 1930s to house artists and intellectuals. Slightly higher up, also on the right, is a 1930s Art Deco building sporting the Russian word for bread. Continuing uphill, Abovyan Street meets the circular green belt. Steps lead down to a pedestrian underpass beneath Moskovyan Street which houses the subterranean Metronome Shopping Centre. The continuation of Abovyan Street uphill is dealt with on page 168.

**The green belt** The walk round Yerevan continues by ascending the steps on the left-hand side halfway along the underpass to emerge into the circular green belt with Moskovyan Street on the left and Isahakyan Street on the right. The first **statue** [135 G3] encountered, an old man with a walking stick, dates from 1965 and is of the poet Avetik Isahakyan (1875–1957) whose early work reflected sorrow and anguish for the fate of humankind. He left Armenia in 1911 as a result of Tsarist oppression but returned in 1936. The statue is by Sergei Baghdasaryan. To the right just past the statue, the building which looks like a large upside-down spaceship is **Yeritasardakan** [135 G2] (Youthful) metro station which opened in 1981: the name reflects the number of students in this part of the city owing to the proximity of several universities.

Further along is a large pair of **marble hands** [135 G3], a gift from Yerevan's twin city of Carrara in Tuscany; Yerevan achieved its first twinning in 1965 when it was linked with both Carrara and Kiev. Yerevan's response to the gift was to send in return a model of a spring of water carved in tuff and decorated with Armenian motifs – an exact copy stands a little further on across Teryan Street. Just before crossing Teryan Street the **statue** of a woman, *Demeanor of Eternity* by Msho Charntir [135 G2], was installed to mark both Yerevan's year as World Book Capital in 2012 and the 500th anniversary of Armenian printing. The apparently single figure actually shows two women, one on each side, holding a large book. It is dedicated to the history of the preservation of the *Homilies of Mush*, the largest Armenian manuscript in the world, now preserved in the Matenadaran. The manuscript, written in 1200–02 and historically associated with the Holy Apostles Monastery in Mush (now in eastern Turkey), was saved from destruction during the 1915 genocide (when historic artefacts were also destroyed) by two women. The huge parchment manuscript, weighing 28kg, was too heavy for one woman so they divided it into two parts and each aimed to carry her portion to eastern Armenia. One woman reached Etchmiadzin and handed hers to the church. The other woman died on the way but managed to bury her half in the grounds of the monastery at Erzurum (also now in eastern Turkey). Here it was found by a Russian soldier who took it to Tbilisi and handed it over to the Armenian community, whence it was transferred to Armenia in the 1920s, thus reuniting both parts of this priceless book. Immediately across **Teryan Street** is a **memorial** [135 G2] to the victims of both the Jewish Holocaust and the Armenian genocide. Uniting the two khachkar-like halves of the memorial is a brass representation of the eternal flame. The Armenian inscription reads 'Live but do not forget'; presumably the Hebrew reads likewise.

Continuing along the green belt, the next **statue** [135 G2] is of a pensive-looking individual. This was erected in 2000 of the poet Vahan Teryan (1885–1920) after whom the street was named. A little further, on the right, is the copy of Yerevan's gift to Carrara (see opposite) and to the left a small memorial monument to the architect Karo Halabyan (1897–1959) [135 G2] whose designs include the Sundukyan (page 165) and Stanislavsky (page 158) theatres in Yerevan. Next is a small artificial lake; the **Aragast** restaurant [135 G2] on the north side is itself built in imitation of a boat. Just beyond the lake is a fish-like *vishap* [135 F2]. The remainder of Tamanyan's planned circular green belt back to Republic Square was never built, so at this point the tour reverts to city streets. At the end of the green belt to the right across Isahakyan Street is a **statue** of Hakob Meghapart (15th–16th century) [135 G2], the founder of Armenian printing, who published the first Armenian books in Venice in 1512–13. Just beyond, in the partly pedestrianised Gevorg Kochar Street, is a delightful **statue** of a man in the final stages of a round of backgammon [135 G2].

A visit to the **Matenadaran** [135 G1] (page 179) can conveniently be made from here by turning right up **Mesrop Mashtots Avenue**, formerly Lenin Prospekt (and often still referred to as 'Prospekt' by bus and taxi drivers) but renamed in honour of the inventor of the Armenian alphabet. The museum faces down the street with a **statue** of Mesrop Mashtots outside.

## The Cascade

[135 F1] The walk continues straight on down Mesrop Mashtots Avenue. Turn right on either Isahakyan Street or Moskovyan Street to reach the park at the foot of the Cascade. With abundant cafés lining each side of the park, this may be a good place to break the walk, perhaps after climbing the **Cascade**. This enormous limestone stairway was designed to be a large artificial waterfall tumbling down from the monument commemorating 50 years of Soviet rule but it was left uncompleted at the demise of the Soviet Union. Its privatisation and subsequent funding from the Cafesjian Family Foundation allowed revitalisation of the project and the establishment within the Cascade complex of the **Cafesjian Centre for the Arts**. Renovation started in 2002, with the Centre for the Arts opening at the end of 2009. Work to extend the Cascade up to the plaza at the top, from where there is an excellent view of the city, remains stalled, with the unfinished foundations blighting what could be a magnificent centrepiece for the city. The plaza can, however, be reached by continuing up the backstreets and steps from the top of the Cascade, or by road from the city centre. There is also a series of escalators under the steps, accessible from the western entrances, and this started to operate again in November 2002 after being out of use since 1997, thus saving the residents living at the top of the hill a climb of around 500 steps. It operates from 08.00 until 20.00. The occasion of the escalators' reinstatement also saw the unveiling of a statue of a fat cat. The self-satisfied-looking, well-fed cat, 2.5m high in bronze covered in black, is the work of the Colombian artist, Fernando Botero (b1932), and one of several of his cats located in capital cities. It was a gift from Gerard Cafesjian and was the first exhibit of the arts centre to arrive. It was reported in the local press that while the cat was greeted with smiles by the local residents, accustomed to statuary of Soviet dimensions, the loudest cheers were for the reactivation of the much-missed escalators. Another Botero **statue**, of a fat, naked, stunted gladiator wearing a helmet, has joined the collection of statues in the **Tamanyan Sculpture Park** at the foot of the Cascade after originally being placed at the top when it arrived in 2005. Since then the exhibition has continued to expand, including works by several British artists including Lynn Chadwick (1914–2003) – the one entitled *Stairs* is particularly appropriately located – Barry Flanagan (1941–2009), including an especially attractive *Hare on Bell*, Tom Hill (b1986), Saraj Guha (b1966) and Fiona Campbell. There are also works by US-born sculptors Peter Woytuk (b1958), Christopher Hiltey (b1953) and Robert Indiana (b1928).

On the **plaza** above the Cascade, the approach enlivened by some colourful sculptures, as well as the tall monument (referred to simply as 'Monument') commemorating 50 years of Soviet rule, there is also a low square grey building, a monument to Stalin's victims. Across **Azatutyan Avenue** is the entrance to **Victory (Haghtanak) Park** [131 E3], at the east end of which stands **Mother Armenia** (page 153) with its Military Museum (page 181). In the centre of the park is a statue inscribed 'No to war'. Within the park are various fairground amusements and a boating lake, which in the early morning is a popular place for locals to exercise.

In the gardens below the Cascade is a **statue** [135 F2] of Alexander Tamanyan, much of whose work has already been seen on this walk. In this work by Artashes Ovsepyan, carved from a single block of basalt and mounted on a marble plinth, his hands are resting on a plan of the city; a detail of the plan itself is recreated on the front right corner of the plinth. It has been suggested that this was the first statue of an architect in the entire world. Tamanyan, author of the original plan for the Cascade, stands with his back to it and stands with his back to it, facing one of his finest buildings, opened in 1933, the Yerevan State Opera House.

Between the statue of Tamanyan and his opera house is **France Square**, so named following a visit in 2006 by the President of France. In 2011 a **statue** by Rodin of Jules Bastien-Lepage, a 19th-century naturalist painter, was gifted by France to Armenia and stands in the centre of France Square. Unfortunately, the 1.75m statue is dwarfed by the vast size of the busy junction and the only way to see it without risking one's life is with binoculars or by visiting in the middle of the night when the traffic is less. The diagonal junction centred on the statue divides the park around the square into quadrants. At the northeast corner stands the **statue** of a rather consumptive-looking William Saroyan [135 F2] (page 58). Opposite him, on the other side of Mashtots Avenue, is a bust of Sayat Nova (1712–95), composer and poet in the Armenian, Georgian, Azeri and Persian languages. Also in the eastern quadrant of France Square is a 1986 **statue** of a man leaning back on a tree: he is the composer **Komitas** (1869–1935) [135 F3] whose career is outlined on page 53. Behind him is the **Komitas State Conservatory of Yerevan** [135 F2] with busts outside of Bach, Shostakovich, Khachaturyan and Beethoven. The western quadrant of

France Square has at its centre a **statue** of the painter Martiros Saryan (1880–1972) [135 E2]. Rather appropriately the park is used at weekends for painting sales; indeed, this location was a precursor to the now more popular Vernissage (page 156). A little to the south, the **sculpture** *The Men* [135 E2] depicts well-known characters from a Soviet-era film of the same name directed by Edmond Keosayan and popular with Armenians.

**Around the opera house** The southern quadrant of France Square merges with the opera house and its surrounding recreational area and gardens. Opened in 1933 as the Yerevan State Opera House, it was renamed two years later as the **Spendiaryan Armenian Theatre of Opera and Ballet** [135 F3] after Alexander Spendiaryan (1871–1928), an Armenian composer who trained with Rimsky-Korsakov. (Note that the oval building also houses the **Khachaturyan Concert Hall**; its entrance is on the north side of the building.) Spendiaryan's most famous work is the opera *Almast*, based on the poem *The Capture of Tmkaberd* by the poet Hovhannes Tumanyan (1869–1923) and set in 18th-century Crimea. The noble and beautiful Almast is betrothed to Tatul, ruler of the Armenian fortress of Tmkaberd which is under attack by Nadir, Shah of Iran. Nadir deceives Almast into betraying Tatul after which she is killed by the bored Nadir in the poem, but treated very differently in the opera, which has a denouement more in keeping with Soviet Armenia in the 1920s. In it the Armenian forces rise up, liberate the fortress and collectively sentence Almast to exile. Left uncompleted at Spendiaryan's death, *Almast* received its premiere at Moscow in 1930 and its first Yerevan performance shortly after the new opera house opened in 1933.

At the back of the opera house (ie: on the north side nearer the Cascade) is a **statue** [135 F3] of the Armenian composer who is perhaps the best known outside the country, Aram Khachaturyan (1903–78; page 52). Round the front (ie: the south side) in Freedom Square, as you face the building, the **right-hand statue** [135 F3] is the eponymous Spendiaryan while to the **left** [135 E3] is Tumanyan, a second of whose poems was the source of the most famous Armenian opera, *Anoush*. With music by Armen Tigranyan it is another tragedy typical of the time when it was composed, although it does contain much attractive Armenian dance music; it was first seen at Alexandropol (Gyumri) in 1912.

Southeast of Freedom Square is **Swan Lake** [135 F3], which hosts occasional free outdoor concerts, film showings and major sporting event screenings, and in the winter is converted into an ice-skating rink. A **sculpture** [135 F3] of composer and pianist Arno Babajanyan (1921–83) was erected at the south end in September 2002, but had to be removed before its official unveiling because its expressionistic style met with far from universal approval. Passers-by said that the work of sculptor David Bejanyan was 'an insult' and even the Armenian president at the time, Robert Kocharyan, questioned whether it was appropriate. The main objections were to the exaggerated facial features and the long fingers which, it was claimed, made Babajanyan look almost like a bird. Bejanyan did agree to take the work away to make the hands more realistic and to 'correct' the face, but he said that his new and unrealistic approach had made his sculpture different from other monuments in the city. When the statue was returned after its 'correction', any changes were imperceptible. More recently, Swan Lake gained international media coverage in April 2015 during Kim Kardashian's much-publicised visit to her ancestral homeland, when her husband **Kanye West** staged an impromptu free concert on a stage above Swan Lake. West jumped into the water mid-performance, causing hundreds of fans to follow suit. Police closed down the event and the incident was reported by MTV, *NME*, *TIME* magazine and other international media outlets. (The body of water was thereafter locally dubbed 'Swanye Lake'.)

## Mesrop Mashtots Avenue and Martiros Saryan Street From the opera house
you can walk down Northern Avenue to return to Republic Square, completing the eastern half of the walk around Yerevan, or you can continue by walking down Mesrop Mashtots Avenue and turning right on to Tumanyan Street. At this point a detour can be made to visit **Zoravor Church** [134 D3] which is hidden behind Soviet apartment blocks. Turn left along Ghazar Parpetsi Street, then first right into narrow Parpetsi 9A street. The church is in the yard at the end of this small street, surrounded by trees. It dates from 1693 with renovations in the late 18th century and 1990s. It was built on the site of a 9th- to 13th-century monastery said to house the relics of St Anania (mentioned in chapter 9 of the Acts of the Apostles by the Greek form of his name, Ananias, as the Christian sent to Saul, later St Paul, to cure Saul's blindness after his conversion experience on the road to Damascus). The underground mausoleum of St Anania survives beneath the chapel immediately west of the church. Continue to the end of Tumanyan Street, where the building on the opposite side of the T-junction is the 1953 museum of **Hovhannes Tumanyan** (1869–1923) [134 D2] (page 55). Tumanyan, beloved of Armenians the world over as the author of many favourite childhood bedtime stories, is represented here by over 18,000 items, as well as a reconstruction of his last apartment in Tiflis. Turn left on to **Martiros Saryan Street**; the first point of interest on the left is the Martiros Saryan House Museum [134 D3] (page 181). Saryan (1880–1972), whose impressionistic landscapes are nowadays much reproduced, lived and worked between 1932 and 1972 in the original two-storey mansion (another of Tamanyan's works); the attached three-storey gallery was added in 1967. Beyond here and mainly on the west side of the road are a number of trendy cafés, wine bars and restaurants. Continue to the junction with Aram Street, opposite Yerevan's main post office. From here it is possible to climb the steep cobbled street to the left of the post office to explore the historical **Kond** district [134 B4] (page 169).

Follow Martiros Saryan Street to the junction with Aram Street – the former is some 20m higher in elevation than the latter (one of the technical factors explaining why Tamanyan's 'green belt' did not come to fruition in this part of the city). Follow Aram Street down to the newly renovated park that runs between Aram and Buzand streets. A worthwhile detour from here is immediately to double back and follow the pedestrian tunnel beneath Martiros Saryan Street to the **Children's Railway** (see box, page 173) and amusement park down in the gorge (✆010 527263; ⊕ summer only – from late Apr, depending on the weather – 10.30–23.30 daily; the train leaves when it is full – there is usually not long to wait; child or adult AMD300). Otherwise, rejoin **Mesrop Mashtots Avenue** and turn right, continuing another two city blocks past the junctions with Amiryan and Khorenatsi streets.

Behind elaborate doors on the left lies the **Blue Mosque** [134 C5], built in 1765 and the only one surviving in Yerevan. During Soviet days it was the museum of the city of Yerevan but in 1999 it was renovated in Persian style at the expense of the Iranian government and is now functioning as a mosque once more, though you will not hear a call to prayer. The grounds (⊕ 10.00–13.00 & 15.00–18.00 daily) with shrubs and trees form a peaceful oasis. Just past the mosque on the opposite side is a building which has caused great controversy. It is the 1940s-built **covered market** [134 B5], known locally as *pak shuka*, designed by Grigor Aghababyan (1911–77). It is immediately recognisable by its arching entrance and Armenian decoration on the façade. Until 2012 it was a huge arched market hall bustling with traders selling every kind of foodstuff. Despite being on the Culture Ministry's list of historical buildings which cannot be redesigned without government permission, it was privatised and the interior demolished by one of Armenia's richest oligarchs who had links to the government and owned one of Armenia's largest supermarket chains (a branch of which now occupies much of the building's interior). A few metres further along Mesrop Mashtots, beyond the market and mosque, go straight ahead through the underpass beneath Grigor Lusavorich (Gregory the Illuminator) Street. You quickly reach the Hrazdan Gorge close to **St Sargis Church** [134 B6]. The present church replaces the one destroyed in the 1679 earthquake. It was built during the period 1691–1705 and rebuilt between 1835 and 1842. Further extensive rebuilding including a taller cupola took place from 1971 onwards and was completed in 2000. From the church there are good views over the Hrazdan to Victory Bridge, Ararat, the stadium and the Genocide Memorial.

**Italy Street and Beirut Street**  Return to Grigor Lusavorich Street and turn right in the underpass to emerge on the east side of this street facing south. After one block there is a **park** on the left, formerly called Kirov Park and now **Children's Park** [134 C6]. Keep straight on past the park as far as the next street on the left. To the right across the road is City Hall, a striking new building complete with a clocktower. Finished in 2005, it houses the municipal offices for the city government and the **Yerevan History Museum** [134 B7] (page 179). The carvings on the southern façade represent the 12 capitals of Greater Armenia, from Urartian Van to present-day Yerevan. The carving over the entrance to the museum is a plan of Yerevan, and that over the entrance to the municipal offices is the tree of life over the circular symbol of eternity.

Turn left from Grigor Lusavorich Street into what was in his lifetime called Stalin Street but is now called Beirut Street. Between here and the parallel Italy Street is a 1980 granite **statue** [134 C7] of Alexander Myasnikyan (1886–1925), a professional Bolshevik revolutionary who was appointed Commissar for Armenia in 1921. He was reported to have died in an air crash although rumours arose that he had really been poisoned on the orders of Stalin because of disagreements over Western Armenia. The park between Beirut and Italy streets, formerly lined with rose gardens, was undergoing full reconstruction at the time of research.

Cross over to **Italy Street** to enter **English Park** [134 D7] via one of the two metal gates, formerly named the Park of the 26 Commissars in honour of the 26 Bolsheviks who set up a short-lived government in Baku which was deposed as the Turkish army approached. They fled to Turkmenistan but were captured and executed in September 1918. In the southern corner of the park is the **Gabriel Sundukyan Drama Theatre** [134 C7] whose company was created in 1925. The inaugural performance was of the play *Pepo* by Gabriel Sundukyan (1825–1912), a story about love versus exploitation set in Tiflis and first performed in 1871. There is a statue dating from 1976 of the eponymous Pepo in the park, as well as a bust of Sundukyan which dates from 1972. The present 1,140-seat building was built in 1966 and was reopened after renovation in 2004; a Soviet-era velodrome next to it was demolished in 2012, as was the circus beyond it.

Continue along Beirut Street or Italy Street, depending on which side you care to walk. At the northeast end of the park between the two streets is a bronze **statue** erected in 1970 of a boy holding a large jug of water. It is a reminder of the days when such youths used to sell water along the dusty streets of the old town. Beyond the next big intersection, known as Shahumyan Square, is another **statue** [134 D6], this time of Stepan Shahumyan, again created by the same Sergei Merkurov who was

3

responsible for the now vanished Lenin and Stalin. Stepan Shahumyan (1878–1918) was an Armenian who was instrumental in imposing Bolshevik rule in Azerbaijan and one of the 26 commissars after whom English Park was formerly named. He is further commemorated in having two towns named after him: Stepanavan in Lori province and Stepanakert in Nagorno Karabagh. The granite statue, erected in 1931, is the oldest on this walk. Beyond it, between the walkways in the middle of the street, is a **fountain** with 2,750 jets, one for every year of Yerevan's existence up to the time that the fountain was installed in 1968. Halfway up is a **statue** of Vazgen Sargsyan [135 E6] (page 28) after whom the continuation of Beirut and Italy streets is named. These streets extend as far as Republic Square which is where the walk started. In the warmer months, when the fountain is operating, the surrounding outdoor cafés are pleasant places to rest.

**The eastern part of the green belt** The part of the green belt not already covered in this walk is perhaps not as attractive as the northern section but it nevertheless has some worthwhile sculptures. From the **statue of Vardan Mamikonian** [135 G7] continue along the green belt instead of turning left to Vernissage as described on page 156. The first sculpture encountered is a **basalt statue** [135 G7], by Artashes Hovsepyan, of the composer Armen Tigranyan (page 52), holding a musical score, perhaps that of his best-known opera *Anoush*. The next, after walking past a sports complex and across Sayat Nova Avenue, is a **bronze monument** [135 H5] by Nikoghayos Nikoghosyan to the poet Yeghishe Charents (page 56), the pain depicted in the sculpture echoing his life. On the left is the **Tigran Petrosyan Chess House** [135 H5] with stylised chessmen on its curved façade. Opened in 1970, it is home to the Armenian Chess Federation (see box, page 59). Since 1984 it has been officially named after the former world chess champion Tigran Petrosian (1929–84) whose statue stands beside the building. It is also home to the Henrik Gasparyan Olympic Chess School. Gasparyan (1910–95) won the National Chess Championship ten times, became an international master in 1950 and was an internationally renowned chess composer, especially of endgame studies. In good weather chess is played outside – you may be invited to join in a game!

Shortly after this on the right, across Alek Manukyan Street, is the main campus of **Yerevan State University**. There are a number of **statues** on the square in front of the building. Centrally are Mesrop Mashtots (362–440), creator of the Armenian alphabet, and Sahak Partev (338–439); the latter was Katholikos 387–428. Active in promoting education he, with Mashtots, translated many works including the Bible into Armenian. To the right, as one faces the university, is Anania Shirakatsi (610–85), mathematician, astronomer and geographer. To the left is Movses Khorenatsi (410–80), author of the *History of Armenia*, the earliest historical account of Armenia. It is probably best to stay on the Khanjyan Street side of the green belt and use the underpass to negotiate the road which crosses the green belt before returning to it to find the **bronze statue** [135 H4], also by Nikoghayos Nikoghosyan, of Mikayel Nalbandyan (1829–66) who looks out across the street bearing his name. Nalbandyan – writer, philosopher, journalist and poet (the words of Armenia's national anthem are adapted from one of his poems) – was a revolutionary democrat who travelled widely throughout Europe, visiting Warsaw, Berlin, Paris, London and Constantinople. Returning to Russia he was imprisoned in the Peter and Paul fortress in St Petersburg by the Tsarist government, spending three years in solitary confinement. He was subsequently exiled to a remote area 800km southeast of Moscow and died of TB in prison aged 37. In *A Reference*

*Guide to Modern Armenian Literature*, Kevork Bardakjian (Professor of Armenian Language and Literature, University of Michigan) described Nalbandyan as 'an outspoken publicist whose lively and bold style, at times crude and arrogant, was almost invariably laced with irony'. The sculptor seems to have caught the essence of the man.

Across Nalbandyan Street is a **memorial** entitled *To the Innocent Victims of the Assyrian People in 1915*. Like the Armenians, the Christian Assyrians suffered at the hands of the Ottoman Turks. It is estimated that 250,000–300,000 Assyrians were slaughtered by the Ottoman armies during World War I, about two-thirds of the entire Assyrian population. Some fled to the Caucasus; there are still villages in Armenia with a significant Assyrian population. The next **statue** [135 G3] is by Yuri Petrosyan. Set in bronze it depicts the painter Hovhannes Aivazovsky (page 58), well known for his dramatic seascapes. He stands, palette in hand, among the waves. Perhaps, therefore, it is appropriate that the final **statue** on this part of the green belt should be Fridtjof Nansen (1861–1930) [135 G3], the Norwegian polar explorer and diplomat who visited Soviet Armenia in his role as League of Nations Commissioner for Refugees. He tried to help Armenian refugees from the massacre in the Ottoman Empire, proposing to the League of Nations that 360km$^2$ within Soviet Armenia be irrigated to allow the settlement of 15,000 refugees. Although the plan failed because the money was not forthcoming, Nansen's reputation remains high in Armenia. The statue was erected in 2011 to mark the 150th anniversary of Nansen's birth. A stamp was also issued to mark the anniversary – it was the second time Nansen had been so honoured in Armenia, a previous stamp having been issued in 1996.

**ELSEWHERE IN YEREVAN** Some of the sights covered in this section can be easily reached on foot. Others probably require transport, unless you are a keen walker or cyclist, and these are noted under individual entries.

## Around the railway station

[130 D5] (The easiest way to get here is to catch the metro to Sasuntsi Davit (David of Sassoun) station.) Tamanyan's plan was for a new central railway terminus but this was never realised and the main station is in an industrial area south of the centre. The fine **station building** dates from 1956 and is a striking structure, though since the closure of the borders with Azerbaijan and Turkey and the suspension of rail routes to Russia it now sees much less traffic. The long façade has, uniquely for Armenia, a tall central spire that would not be out of place in St Petersburg. The finial of this spire is, equally unusually, still topped by a purely Soviet symbol being a form of the design of the coat of arms of Soviet Armenia adopted in 1937 and replaced after independence in 1992. The coat of arms was based on a design by the well-known Armenian artist Martiros Saryan and depicts the five-pointed Soviet star above Mount Ararat with a bunch of grapes and ears of wheat below. The coat of arms also bore the well-known slogan 'Proletarians of all lands, unite!' but the railway station does not appear from ground level to enjoy this embellishment.

In front of the station, in the square of the same name, is a very fine equestrian **statue of David of Sassoun** [131 E5] mounted on his horse Dzhalali, by Yervand Kochar (page 60). The epic stories of David of Sassoun date back to the 10th century though they were not written down until 1873. They recount the fortunes of David's family over four generations, Sassoun symbolising Armenia in its struggle against Arab domination. The statue shows David brandishing a sword which is ready to fall on the invaders while water flows from a bowl over the pedestal, symbolising

3

that when the patience of the people is at an end there will be no mercy for the oppressors. David's crest of honour was a sword of lightning, belt of gold, immortal flying horse and sacred cross.

More prosaically, outside the station market (see below) is positioned a **steam engine**. It is $E^u$ class number 705–46, built in 1930 and one of around 11,000 E-class 0-10-0s built between 1912 and 1957 as the standard design for hauling heavy freight trains. This is the largest number of any steam locomotive design ever constructed. In the $E^u$ variant, to which this particular example belongs, the superscript U stands for *usilennyi* – 'strengthened'. Until his recent passing away, the last driver of the train, born in 1927, had a collection of personal memorabilia in the train, including photographs of Stalin, which he was happy to show anyone who was interested. Today, railway enthusiasts may instead visit the small **railway museum** (⏲ 10.00–17.00 Mon–Fri) that has been established in the station building; maybe also worth a quick look while waiting for a train. If it is closed, ask at Enquiries.

To the right of the main railway station is the entrance to *kayarani shuka* (station market). It is essentially a food market with wonderful displays of fruit, herbs, vegetables, breads, cheeses, spices, jams, pickles and, of course, Armenia's delicious dried fruit and nut sweetmeats. (There is also an early morning street market outside the station itself where producers sell fruit and vegetables, usually in bulk, but by the time most tourists are likely to be at the station the traders are already packing up.)

**The north end of Abovyan Street** Abovyan Street has some worthwhile buildings beyond Isahakyan Street where it crosses the green belt. On the left corner of Abovyan and Isahakyan is the **Energo building** [135 G3], which houses Armenia's main electricity utility company. Constructed in 1940 of black tuff, it was designed by Hovhannes Margaryan (1901–63) who was also responsible for the Yerevan Brandy Company building (page 170). As you cross Koryun Street, the building of black tuff on the right corner is the **Yerevan State Medical University** [135 H2] of 1938. Continuing uphill along Abovyan Street, on the left side you will see a small park housing the **original university observatory** designed in 1926 by Tamanyan but superseded by the Byurakan Astrophysical Observatory (page 196) on Mount Aragats. At the entrance to the park is a **statue** of Viktor Hambartsumyan (1908–96) [135 H2], a prominent astrophysicist and one of the founders of the observatory. On the right-hand side of Abovyan Street there is a **Neoclassical building** of 1905 which originally housed the Guyanyan Mirzoyan School for Girls but now houses the university faculty of theology. After an elaborate wrought-iron fence (still incorporating a hammer and sickle design, alternating with the staff of Aesculapius), complete with stone posts and flowerpots that encloses a hospital courtyard, is the **Mari Nubar children's eye clinic** [131 E3] which includes a series of pyramids in the frieze below the cornice. This building stems from an initiative in Egypt taken on Easter Sunday (15 April) 1906. Armenians had been prospering in Egypt, and particularly so since the British occupied the country in 1882. Numbers of Armenians there were also being swelled by refugees from Ottoman oppression as well as from the Armenian–Azeri conflicts. The driving force behind the initiative was Boghos Nubar Pasha (1851–1930), an Armenian whose father, Nubar Pasha, had been prime minister of Egypt on five separate occasions between 1872 and 1895. The initiative saw the founding of the Armenian General Benevolent Union (**w** agbu.org), whose mission was to establish and subsidise schools, libraries, workshops, hospitals and orphanages for the benefit of Armenian communities throughout the Middle East and adjacent regions, and the Yerevan children's eye hospital was built in 1927–29 under the auspices of this organisation. Boghos Nubar Pasha was to be leader of the Armenian delegation at the Paris peace conference of 1919. The newly decorated building is still an eye clinic but no longer just for children.

Abovyan Street opens out into **Khachatur Abovyan Square** [131 E3], in the centre of which is a statue of Abovyan himself sculpted by Suren Stepanyan and unveiled in 1950. This was not the statue of Abovyan originally intended for this site. That one, made of bronze, was sculpted in Paris in 1913 by Andreas Ter-Marukyan, and packed up for shipment but then, owing to some misunderstanding, it was forgotten and lay undisturbed for 20 years. When it was finally delivered in 1935 it was first erected on Abovyan Street near the Moscow Cinema, then moved to the children's park by the Hrazdan River, before finally in 1964 being taken to the Abovyan House Museum where it remains. The building on the right as you enter the square is a children's hospital of 1939. The Hovhannes Sharambeyan Folk Arts and Crafts Centre of 1941 is just beyond that (page 180). The square is locally referred to as *plani glukh* (head of the plan), a reference to its position at the furthest extremity of Yerevan prior to the creation of Tamanyan's master plan for the city.

### Marshal Baghramyan Avenue to the American University (It is convenient to walk up one side and back down the other side of this broad avenue.) Baghramyan Avenue has some striking buildings and provides a contrast to the centre of Yerevan (architecturally, if not in volume of traffic). It is home to a number of foreign embassies as well as to Armenia's National Assembly (ie: parliament) building and former presidential palace. Starting from the northwest corner of **France Square** [135 F2], walk up the south side of the street. Near the bottom on the left is the **Union of Writers building**, built in 1954 and renovated in 2010. Higher up is the imposing **National Assembly building** [134 D1] (designed by Mark Grigorian in 1949–50), set in beautifully kept grounds behind tall fences. Across Demirchyan Street is **Lovers' Park** [134 C1] (⊕ Mar–Nov 07.00–02.00, Dec–Feb 07.00–01.00 daily) which was fully renovated by the Boghossian Foundation and reopened in 2008. It is favoured not only by lovers but also by young mothers with their children and older folk enjoying a rest on one of the benches in the shade (though woe betide anyone who attempts to sit on the grass). There are a couple of cafés, notably Achajour, so it is a good place for a drink before continuing. A little higher up, across the road, are the **British embassy**, steps leading up to the **American University of Armenia** built in 1979 (ironically as the Community Party headquarters), and the **bronze statue** [134 C1], by Norayr Karganyan, of Marshal Baghramyan after whom the avenue is named. Hovhannes Baghramyan was born in Russia to Armenian parents. He fought in World War I; then in the Turkish–Armenian war, taking part in the Armenian victory at Sardarapat in 1918 (page 223); and then in World War II commanding forces which expelled the Nazis from the Baltic states. He is buried at the Kremlin Wall Necropolis in Moscow. Cross the road and turn round at this point to walk back down to the centre of town. Opposite Lovers' Park, the former (until April 2018) **presidential palace** [130 D3] of 1956 is on the left. Just within its grounds (⊕ noon–19.00 Sun) are **two marble statues** by Levon Tokmajyan: Tigran the Great on the left and Noah on the right.

### Kond The district of Kond [134 B4], on the west side of central Yerevan, is one of the few places where it is still possible to see a few of the **old houses** which, until the early 20th century, were typical of the whole of Yerevan. The easiest way to

find the remaining (as of 2018) old houses is to enter Kond up the steep cobbled slope from Saryan Street, just below building 24, or to climb the first narrow alley on the right after turning on to Leo Street. The area of small houses with their flat roofs, narrow alleys and small courtyards was earmarked for reconstruction during Soviet times but little was done. Almost a century later the residents continue to await a decision on the fate of their homes; the risk that it will all be torn down still too high to make the district of interest to investors. Within Kond is **St John the Baptist Church** [134 C3], a medieval church destroyed in the 1679 earthquake and rebuilt in 1706–10 and again in the 1980s. The busy church has an interesting carving (presumably modern) over the north door. In the south of the district is what was once the Safavid-era **Tapa Bashi Mosque of 1687** (Tapabashi was the name of the district under Persian rule, meaning 'top of the hill'). Its walls, arches, columns and roof sections have been integrated into several homes, the remains easily distinguished by their pointed archways and red brickwork. Several other architecturally significant buildings and features can be found – often in people's private backyards – and have been meticulously documented by the Other Yerevan project (w otheryerevan.am; page 137). A few local tour operators offer walking tours specifically focused on Kond.

**By Victory Bridge** [134 A6] The high-level Victory Bridge dates from 1945, its name celebrating victory in World War II. Victory Bridge, 200m long and 34m above the river, supersedes the red tuff bridge constructed following the collapse of its predecessor in the 1679 earthquake and rebuilt in 1830 after the Russian conquest of Yerevan. The four arches of the 1679 bridge, 80m long and 11m above the river, can be seen to the south of Victory Bridge, the central two arches spanning the river itself; the smaller side ones originally crossed irrigation canals. Most visitors see the **Hrazdan Gorge** through which the river flows only as they cross Victory Bridge. In spring, when all is green and the poppies are flowering, driving or walking in the gorge is pleasant, but in the summer it can be hot – perhaps this is why a small (free) open-air bathing pool known as **Chrik** [134 A3] was built some 200m west of the Children's Railway on the south bank of the river by a footbridge, complete with a small changing room. There is an **outdoor gym** [134 A2] by the road over the bridge. Huge entertainment complexes and restaurants have taken over large portions of the gorge but, thankfully, much remains unspoiled and fun to explore.

At each end of Victory Bridge are prominent buildings associated with Yerevan's alcohol business. At the west (airport) end is the **Yerevan Brandy Company distillery and museum** [134 A6] (2 Admiral Isakov Av; \010 510100/540000 (tours); w araratbrandy. com; tours approx AMD4,500–10,000 depending on the types of brandy tasted) which stands on a plateau high above the bridge; the large Ararat sign is a reference to the brand name used for many of their brandies. The distillery was founded in 1887 and is now owned by the French Pernod Ricard company. The building itself was designed by Hovhannes Margaryan and built in 1944–50. Its façade, displaying nine arches, can be best appreciated when approached by the long flight of steps from the valley below. Guided tours of the storage facilities and museum, with sampling of the products, can be arranged but the actual production is not shown.

At the other (city) end of the bridge the large, rather forbidding building constructed of basalt, which faces the bridge, houses the snappily named **Yerevan Ararat Wine-Brandy-Vodka Factory** [134 A7] (w brandy.am), which in spite of its name is responsible for the Noy brand of brandy. Built in 1937, its shape and dimensions are exactly those of the former citadel that occupied the site. Its architect Rafael Israelyan (1908–73) was also responsible for the very fine memorial commemorating the Battle of Sardarapat in Armavir province. It is often stated that the first performance of Griboyedov's *Woe from Wit* was actually given in a room of the fortress by Russian army officers in 1827 but this seems unlikely (page 53).

## Armenian Genocide Museum-Institute and Tsitsernakaberd Memorial Complex [130 D4] A trip to the genocide memorial and museum at Tsitsernakaberd (Swallow Castle) is strongly recommended for any visitor who wishes to understand the backdrop against which the various concepts of modern Armenian nationhood are set, and the sentiments expressed by many Armenians towards present-day Turkey.

In 1965, as Armenians throughout the world commemorated the 50th anniversary of the 1915 genocide, the lack of any tangible symbol in Armenia itself was conspicuous enough to catalyse protests. The Genocide Memorial was created in response and completed in 1967. The architects Kalashyan and Mkrtchyan succeeded in creating a striking and appropriate monument. Although the ideal approach is to mount the flight of steps leading up to it, most visitors are likely to approach instead from the car park, in which case the first thing they will notice is the collection of trees, each of which has been planted by a distinguished visitor, in many cases foreign dignitaries representing countries that have formally recognised the genocide. Separating the museum from the monument is a 100m-long memorial wall of basalt carved with the names of villages and towns where massacres of Armenians by the Ottoman army are known to have taken place. The **memorial** itself has two parts. There is a 44m-tall stele reaching to the sky symbolising the survival and spiritual rebirth of the Armenian people. It is riven, however, by a deep cleft which symbolises the separation of the peoples of Western and Eastern Armenia while at the same time emphasising the unity of all Armenian people. Adjoining the stele is a ring of 12 large inward-leaning basalt slabs whose shape is reminiscent of traditional Armenian khachkars. The 12 slabs represent the 12 lost provinces of Western Armenia; their inward-leaning form suggests figures in mourning, or perhaps refugees huddled around a fire. At the centre of the circle, but 1.5m below, burns the eternal flame. The steps leading down are deliberately steep, thus requiring visitors to bow their heads in reverence as they descend. Each year, on the anniversary of the genocide, the surrounding wall is piled so high with flowers – one per visitor – that the flame itself is lost to sight.

The **museum-institute** (w genocide-museum.am; ⊕ 11.00–17.00 Tue–Sun; free guided tour in Armenian, English, French or Russian) was added in 1995 to commemorate the 80th anniversary of the massacres. A circular subterranean building designed by the same architects as the memorial, the museum is well labelled in Armenian, English, French and Russian. Rather than overtly authoring a narrative of the tragedy, attention is instead drawn to contemporary anecdotal and factual sources, often by non-partisan observers, with the intention that the bigger picture reveals itself indirectly. Much information is given on the number of victims in different parts of Western Armenia and there are many photographs taken by German army photographers who were accompanying their Ottoman allies during World War I. There are also examples of foreign publications about various aspects of the genocide, including reports by British, American and German officials on the maltreatment of the Armenians. One typical exhibit reproduces the letter sent by Leslie A Davis, the American consul at Harput (west of Lake Van) to his boss, the American ambassador at Constantinople on 24 July 1915. It reads:

3

I do not believe that there has ever been a massacre in the history of the world so general and thorough as that which is now being perpetrated in this region, or that a more fiendish, diabolical scheme has ever been conceived in the mind of man.

**Erebuni**  [131 F6] Erebuni, a protected archaeological reserve on a hilltop in the southern part of the city, is the original settlement of Yerevan and gave the modern city its name. At the time of research it could be reached by marshrutkas 11, 14, 45, 50, 55 and 68, or trolleybus number 2, all of which can be caught from outside Zoravar Andranik metro station (page 154). Visitors can see the partially excavated **remains** of the site of the city's citadel, together with interesting objects found here which are now housed in the museum at the bottom of the hill. When visiting the site it is useful to go to the museum first, as the model of Erebuni there gives a good idea of the general layout. A guidebook in Armenian, Russian and English is available which deals also with the sites of Teishebaini (Karmir Blur) and Shengavit (page 174). The informative website (**w** erebuni.am) deals with all three sites.

Erebuni was discovered by chance in 1950 during exploration of Arin Berd Monastery which had later been built on the site. A cuneiform inscription was uncovered which can be dated to 782BC. It states: 'By the greatness of [god] Khaldi, Argishti, son of Menua the powerful king of Biaini and ruler of Tushpa city built this splendid fortress and named it Erebuni, strength to Biaini.' (Biaini was the Urartian name for their country; Urartu is the Assyrian name.) Argishti was the Urartian king Argishti I (ruled c784–c763BC) who established a garrison here of 6,600 troops, the first Urartian settlement on this side of the Arax. Its heyday lasted for only about a century until the Urartian king Rusa II (ruled c685–c645BC) chose

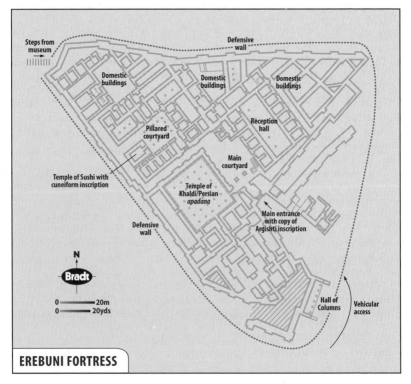

EREBUNI FORTRESS

Children's railways were a Soviet Union phenomenon although a few were built in other cities of the Soviet bloc, such as Budapest. They were not constructed as fairground amusements but to train children aged 9–15 in the operation of real railways. The first opened at Tbilisi, Georgia, in 1935. Yerevan's opened in 1937 and was extensively renovated in the late 1950s. (The second children's railway in Armenia, at Leninakan (Gyumri), never reopened after being damaged in the 1988 earthquake.) It runs during the summer when children are not at school, the first day of operation usually being Genocide Memorial Day (24 April). It is now simply a recreational amusement; children no longer perform all the tasks under adult supervision. Both children and adults can ride on the train. The line is 2.1km in length along the Hrazdan Gorge and starts from a gaily painted station whose architecture was clearly influenced by Yerevan's main railway station. It also incorporates stained-glass windows depicting birds. To reach it from the city, walk west from Mashtots Avenue along the broad street which has defunct fountains down the middle (called Aram Street to the north and Buzand Street to the south). From the far end a long pedestrian tunnel leads to the gorge and the children's railway.

All children's railways have a track gauge of 750mm. The original steam locomotive, coal-burning 0-8-0 number 159-434, is of a design built in the 1930s mainly for forestry work. Although still on view, it is apparently unserviceable. The usual motive power is a diesel hydraulic, currently number TY2 096 dating from 1958. The route is a single track towards Victory Bridge. There are no facilities for the locomotive to run round the train at the far end and the coaches are therefore hauled out but propelled back.

a different site, Teishebai Uru (literally 'City of [the God] Teisheba') overlooking the Hrazdan River, which he believed would be less vulnerable to attack by the Scythians. However, Erebuni remained occupied as is testified by archaeological finds from later periods.

As well as the model of the citadel, the **museum** (38 Erebuni Av; \010 458207; w erebuni.am; ⊕ 10.30–16.30 Tue–Sun; guided tour in Armenian AMD1,000, in English, Russian, French & German AMD2,500; adult/child AMD1,000/300 (museum & site) or AMD500/200 (site only)) gives much interesting information about many aspects of life in Erebuni in well-presented displays. Interesting items include three silver rythons (drinking horns in the form of animals), the helmet of King Sarduri II (ruled c763–c734BC) and a large jug, possibly a funerary urn, with bulls' heads. There is also a good selection of jewellery, ceramics and weapons found on the site. The central courtyard of the museum is a reconstruction of the palace courtyard. Of particular interest is the stone, actually found at Tanahat Monastery, Syunik (not the better-known Tanahat Monastery, Vayots Dzor). It has a cuneiform inscription dedicated to the Urartian king Argishti II (ruled 714–685BC) but the stone was made into a khachkar in the 11th century by which time no-one of course could read the inscription. A tuff **statue** of Argishti I on his chariot, by Levon Tokmajyan, stands on the street outside the museum.

The shape of the hill on which Erebuni is built necessitated a triangular shape for the **citadel**. It had walls around 12m high, the lower 6m being formed of two parallel walls of large stone blocks with rubble filling the space in between the rows and large

Yerevan   WHAT TO SEE AND DO

3

buttresses providing additional strength. Above the stone blocks clay bricks were used which were then covered with plaster. Within the citadel was the royal palace, temples and service premises, everything being connected by stairways because the slope of the hill necessitated the buildings being constructed at different levels. A **good view** of the walls can be had from below and it is worthwhile walking along the path which follows them right round the outside. It can be accessed from near the vehicle entrance to the site or from steps which lead up from the left side of the museum.

Entering the site from the access road and car park the first building on the left is the reconstructed **Hall of Columns** used to greet dignitaries. It has a blue wall with a frieze and the present roof is supported by six wooden columns. Continuing up the main entrance slope and steps, near the top of the steps is a copy of the **Argishti stone** erected here in 782BC (the original, as referred to on page 172, is kept in the museum). Just after going through the entrance-way a narrow alley goes off right to the **necropolis**. To the southwest of the central square was the **temple of Khaldi**, the chief god. It was crowned by a tower with a flat top that was probably used for sending smoke signals which would have been visible from far across the plain. Following the collapse of the Urartian kingdom and the installation of a Persian vice-regent at Erebuni, the temple was converted for use as a 30-column *apadana* (**reception hall**). Part of this has been reconstructed and the design of frescoes can be seen generally with figures of gods between horizontal bands in contrasting colours.

Northwest of the Khaldi temple was a **pillared courtyard**, probably used by the king for important meetings, together with a **small temple** devoted to Sushi, another of Urartu's 79 gods, and used by the royal family. At its entrance is another cuneiform inscription. The palace's **main reception hall** was northeast of the central square. Surrounding the main buildings were living quarters for the garrison and for servants, together with buildings for storing produce such as meat, fruit, wine, sesame seed oil, and milk products in *pithoi* (large urns) sunk into the ground to keep them cool. Different parts of the site are stated to have had different functions but this is not obvious when walking round the ruins.

**Karmir Blur** [130 B5] The site of Teishebai Uru to which the Urartian king Rusa II moved his capital from Erebuni in the 7th century BC is now known as Karmir Blur (Red Hill) or Teishebaini. It is in the southwest suburb of Karmir Blur on the south side of the Hrazdan Gorge and is probably most easily found by taking a taxi. The site of the city, citadel and palace occupied about 0.45km². Today there is not a lot to see apart from the bases of the massive megalithic walls which surrounded the citadel and evidence of some excavated buildings of the town, but the situation, on the edge of the gorge, is impressive. Walking around the hill not only gives an impression of how huge a city Teishebaini must have been but also affords excellent views of the gorge itself. Many of the articles unearthed during excavation are on display at the History Museum of Armenia (page 176). Archaeological evidence indicates that the city was destroyed by fire after a Scythian raid at the beginning of the 6th century BC, possibly at night, the large number of human remains suggesting that the inhabitants had no time to escape. The name derives from the reddish colour of the hill caused by the upper tuff walls of the citadel crumbling in the heat of the fire and turning a more intense shade of red. The ancient site was discovered in 1939, 2½ millennia after it was buried, following the finding of a cuneiform inscription of Rusa II.

**Shengavit** [130 C5] This important Early Bronze Age site, occupied from c3500 to c2000BC, sits on a low mound on the south bank of the Yerevan Lake, an artificial reservoir formed by damming the Hrazdan River in the 1960s. Discovered in 1936 and excavated in 1958–83 it occupies some 10–12ha. In the 1970s the Soviet authorities erected a hospital on about half of the site, in spite of protests from local archaeologists. After independence there was no funding for maintenance of the site and its small museum, and almost half of the site was sold illegally to private individuals. After sustained lobbying by Shengavit's director the illegally privatised land was returned to the Shengavit Historical and Archaeological Culture Preserve in 2012.

The official entrance to the preserve and its museum (⊕ 10.30–16.30 Tue–Sun) is via the grounds of the hospital, entered from Bagratunyats Avenue. Go round to the far side of the hospital where you will find a small chapel. Left of this is the locked door of the site. Ring the doorbell (high up to the left of the door) and a member of staff will come and let you in. Some improvements to the maintenance of the site have been made, thanks to funding from outside donors, and further excavations undertaken. The small museum has been upgraded and is well worth visiting. The exhibits on display are much the same as in the History Museum of Armenia (where many of the finds from Shengavit are housed) but this small museum is less overwhelming and there is the added satisfaction of knowing that the objects were found in the dwellings adjacent to the museum.

There are hopes that funding may one day be forthcoming to preserve the excavations, improve conditions in the museum and make the site attractive to visitors. Excavations show both round and rectangular dwellings and a surrounding cyclopean wall. Finds (some of which are on display in the History Museum of Armenia) include terracotta figurines, pottery, tools, domestic items, evidence of copper smelting and a gold pendant.

**Avan and Kanaker** Now suburbs in the northeast of Yerevan, Avan and Kanaker were originally villages; something of their old character can still be seen in their maze of small streets and low houses. Both contain minor sites for those who have time and want to see off-the-beaten-track Yerevan.

**Avan** Lying to the east of the M4 main road from central Yerevan towards Abovyan and Lake Sevan, Avan can be reached by buses 58 and 59. By car, follow the M4 north out of Yerevan and take the slip road just next to Water World. Bear left at the fork and then turn immediately right on to Khudiakov Street. For **Avan Cathedral** [131 G2] turn left just after a large cemetery. (If lost, ask for Katoghike, or Tsiranavor as it is sometimes called locally.) Built in AD591, the cathedral is in a ruined state that belies its immense architectural importance as the prototype of the much better-known masterpiece, St Hripsime in Etchmiadzin. Avan Cathedral was the first four-apse church in Armenia to have western corner rooms in a centric composition. Uniquely, its corner rooms are circular (St Hripsime's are rectangular). As at St Hripsime they are reached via four three-quarter-circle niches. It is thought that the church had five domes: the main central dome and one over each corner room. A good example of a fish-shaped vishap has been used for the internal lintel of the west entrance. For the **church of St John** [131 G2] turn left at the far end of the cemetery. Dating from the 5th or 6th century and rebuilt in the 13th century, the black and red tuff church has been in ruins since the massive earthquake of 1679. A single nave basilica, it retains its original stepped base and has a Greek cross on the lintel of the entrance. Its most notable feature is the intricately carved *bema* front which has an openwork central boss clutched by the feet of birds (now headless) on each side.

3

The **Botanical Garden** [131 F2] (1 Acharyan St; w botany.sci.am; ① 08.00–23.00 daily; AMD300), founded in 1935 both as a scientific institution and recreational area, has suffered badly from underfunding since the collapse of the Soviet Union. It is a good place for walking and jogging but the educational aspect is limited. The large circular greenhouse is worth seeking out, housing many tropical species with a central upper gantry that can be accessed via a spiral staircase. Behind it is a nursery where ornamental plants are cultivated for public spaces in Yerevan.

North of Avan and technically in Arinj district is one of Yerevan's most idiosyncratic attractions, **Levon's Divine Underground** [131 G1] (9 Fifth St, Arinj; m 077 178850; ■; ① 10.00–20.00 daily). Modern legend has it that in 1985, Levon Arakelyan, having been asked by his wife to dig a hole in their yard to store potatoes, was commanded by God to continue excavating. This he did 18 hours a day for the next 23 years until his death in 2008. Levon's wife subsequently opened the resulting network of subterranean passages and chambers to the public and turned the house into a museum dedicated to his astonishing achievement.

**Kanaker** Situated a little west of Avan, Kanaker can be reached by taking Azatutyan Avenue from the top of the Cascade. Where Azatutyan Avenue branches and becomes the Tbilisyan Highway, fork right on to Zakaria Sarkavag Street and follow the winding road to reach the **Khachatur Abovyan House Museum** [131 F2] (page 182). A little further along the main street, turn left on to Sixth Street. This brings you first to **St Jacob Church** [131 E2] and then to **Mother of God Church** [131 F2]. Both churches were rebuilt after the 1679 earthquake (original dates unknown but probably early) and are very similar in style, being three-aisled barrel-vaulted basilicas with elaborate carving round doors and windows. St Jacob was restored in 1990 after being a barn in Soviet days; Mother of God more recently still. Further along the main street is a **khachkar shrine** of 1265 in a stone frame with pointed roof. Carrying on, you reach the **Russian church of the Intercession of the Holy Mother of God** [131 F2], a striking contrast with its blue roofs, gold domes and bright white interior with iconostasis; the compound opposite is a Russian military base. A few hundred metres beyond and on the right a sign points down a narrow track to **Kanaker railway station** [131 F1] (page 85) from where summertime trains depart for Lake Sevan.

**YEREVAN'S MUSEUMS AND GALLERIES** Like any other capital city, Yerevan has a plethora of museums. There are some which most visitors agree are 'must-sees' and should be fitted in if at all possible. Others are very worthwhile even for those without a special interest in the subject covered. Yet others will probably appeal only to those with a special interest. Some indication of these groups is given in the entries below, although it is inevitably subjective. Non-Armenian-speakers should note that some museums, particularly some of the smaller house museums, have information only in Armenian. For biographical details of persons whose house museums are listed, see individual entries in the index.

## Must-sees

*History Museum of Armenia* [135 E5] (4 Republic Sq; ☏010 520691; e info@ historymuseum.am; w historymuseum.am/en; ① 11.00–18.00 Tue–Sat, 11.00–17.00 Sun, last entry 45mins before closing; pre-booked guided tours in English, Russian, French, German & Italian AMD5,000; adult AMD2,000) The museum displays are on three floors; it is difficult to do justice to it all in one visit. The third floor covers the Palaeolithic to the Iron Age as well as the kingdom of Urartu and some

Gai Avenue (also known as Hayk Avenue) in the northeast of Yerevan is the main road out towards Garni and visitors heading there frequently notice the four **statues** [131 G3] alongside the road. The **first**, on the left, made of copper and dating from 1975, is of a man wearing a lion skin and aiming his bow either at Turkey or at the block of flats opposite. This is Hayk, great-great-grandson of Noah and legendary founder of the Armenian people (the Armenians' name for themselves is *hay*, pronounced to rhyme with 'eye'). The **second** statue, a figure on horseback to the right of the road brandishing a sword and looking back towards Turkey, is another Hayk, Hayk Bzhshkyan (1887–1937). Born in Tabriz (Persia) he was active in revolutionary movements and also in World War I when he commanded Armenian troops. Subsequently he supported the Bolshevik cause and after service in Siberia became commissar of the military forces in Soviet Armenia. His military career continued but he succumbed, along with 40,000 others, to Stalin's purge of the Red Army. The victims were variously accused of being 'spies', 'Fascists' or 'Trotskyite–Bukharinite'. The bronze statue was erected in 1977, a time when the true cause of death was not acknowledged.

The **third** statue, on the left and opposite a market, is a 2003 marble statue of King Tigran II (the Great) who ruled from c95BC to 55BC. It is by Levon Tokmajyan who also sculpted the statue of Tigran the Great in front of the former presidential palace (page 169). The **fourth** statue, also on the left and dating from 1982, is of Tork Angegh (Ugly Tork). He is shown standing on a pile of boulders, carrying an enormous rock on his shoulders, and with a grotesque expressionistic face. In legend he was a very kind giant and a skilled artist. Eventually, despite his ugliness, he was able to marry the woman he loved after defeating her 20 other suitors.

later periods. The second and first floors cover the rest of Armenian history plus extensive displays of ceramics, national costumes, metalwork and carpets. Most sections have at least limited information in English. The official website has a good downloadable map and 'virtual tour' section. You may prefer to save your visit to the museum until the end of your trip, when the most important exhibits can then be put into the context of sites you have visited, or you may prefer to visit the museum first, the better to clothe the sometimes bare sites with the rich finds from them. Ideally of course one needs to do both!

As with many Armenian museums, one is expected to start at the top and work down. Go up to the **third floor**, through the glass doors which lead to the art gallery, and up the stairs on your left to reach the display covering from two million to 1000BC. These rooms contain a fascinating collection of items showing the enormous wealth of historic objects unearthed in Armenia, bringing to life the ancient history of the country, with finds from so many well-visited sites such as Garni, Lake Sevan, Metsamor and Dvin, as well as less-visited sites such as Artashat, Karmir Blur and Shengavit. Notable items include finds from Karmir Blur such as Argishti I's ritual helmet and decorative shield of the 8th century BC, jewellery from various pre-Christian sites, and the Bronze Age chariot burials from Lchashen, Lake Sevan. Also on display is the world's oldest shoe, excavated in the Areni-1 cave in Vayots Dzor (page 325) and radiocarbon dated to about 3500BC.

Yerevan has two cemeteries of interest. The **Komitas Pantheon** [130 D5], on Arshakunyants Avenue in the southern suburbs of Yerevan, is where Armenia's famous deceased are interred. The individuals most familiar to visitors are likely to be the composers Komitas and Aram Khachaturyan together with the writer William Saroyan. Presumably the reason that only the upper half of Saroyan's body is shown in the 1984 sculpture on his tombstone is that only half his ashes are here: the other half are in Fresno, California.

The cemetery of **Yerablur** [130 C5], on Sebastia Avenue, to the right off the road to Zvartnots, houses the dead from the Nagorno Karabagh war together with Andranik Ozanian, fighter against Turkey in the late 19th and early 20th centuries, and Vazgen Sargsyan, the prime minister who was assassinated in parliament in 1999. Visiting this cemetery, particularly on one of the traditional Armenian days for visiting graves, such as Easter Monday, is even more poignant than at most war cemeteries because the war in which they were killed is so recent (1989–94) and many of the figures tending the graves are the mothers or other close relatives of those who died. Most of the graves carry a picture of the deceased.

On the **second floor** the rooms cover Dvin and Ani, as well as Armenian national costume: it is here the downloadable map (page 177) is helpful. The **first floor** has items brought from churches including stonework from Zvartnots Cathedral, a carved wooden door from Tatev, khachkars and an extensive display of carpets and religious artefacts. The museum also hosts an ongoing programme of temporary exhibitions.

In the covered gallery outside the museum is an explanatory exhibition of stelae, an important category of stonework in Armenia, usually overshadowed by the abundance of khachkars.

**National Gallery of Armenia** [135 E5] (1 Aram St but sharing the same entrance from Republic Sq as the History Museum of Armenia; ☏ 010 567472; e galleryarmenia@yahoo.com; w gallery.am; ⊕ 11.00–17.30 Tue-Sat, 11.00–17.00 Sun; last admission 30mins before closing; pre-booked guided tour in English, Russian & French AMD5,000; adult AMD1,500) The ticket office for the gallery is on the first floor. A **helpful floor plan** leaflet in English is available for AMD300, but you will have to ask for it; it is kept under the counter. Labels include English. After buying a ticket one is expected to take the lift to the **seventh floor** to start viewing but it is possible to go directly to other floors. The collection of Armenian works is on the fourth and fifth floors and includes all the major Armenian painters with a good collection of Aivazovsky's seascapes and works by Martiros Saryan.

The rest of the collection largely comprises paintings from the main European schools. Italian artists represented include Bicci di Lorenzo (*The Betrothal of St Catherine*); Benvenuto Garofalo (*Virgin Mary with the Christ Child*); Jacopo Tintoretto (*Apollo and Pan*); Jacopo Bassano (*Adoration of the Shepherds*); Leandro Bassano (*Good Samaritan*); and Francesco Guardi (*Courtyard with Stairs*). Flemish painters include: Hans Jordaens III (*The Jews Crossing the Red Sea*); and David Teniers the Younger (*Kegl Players and The Village Feast*). Dutch painters include Jan van Goyen (*View of Dordrecht*); Pieter Claesz (*Still Life*); and Jan Wijnants (*Landscape with Broken Tree*). French artists include Louis le Nain (*The Nest Robbers*); Jean Baptiste Greuze

(*Head of a Girl*); and Eugène Boudin (*Sea Harbour*). Among the Russian works Ilya Repin's *Portrait of Teviashova* and Isaac Levitan's *Reaped Field* particularly stand out.

**Matenadaran** [135 H1] (53 Mesrop Mashtots Av; ☏ 010 562578; e contact@ matenadaran.am; w matenadaran.am; ⊕ 10.00–17.00 Tue–Sat; guided tour in Armenian AMD2,500; in English, French, German, Spanish, Italian, Portuguese, Arabic or Russian AMD2,500–5,000 depending on group size; adult/child AMD1,000/100) Enter the **ticket office** from the outside to the right of the main entrance steps. It is worth paying for the English-speaking guide. The Matenadaran was purpose built in 1957 to house 14,000 Armenian manuscripts but the original single display room could show fewer than 1% of them. The museum provides virtually the only opportunity in Armenia to see examples of this important art form. In 1997 the Mashtots Matenadaran Collection of Ancient Manuscripts was inscribed on UNESCO's Memory of the World Programme Register in recognition of its world significance. Following the construction in 2009–11 of an adjacent research institute, more space became available in the old building and further expansion means there are now several display rooms. The original room displays the most valuable items. They include copies of histories (such as a *History of Armenia* by 5th-century Movses Khorenatsi), *Geography* by Anania Shirakatsi (6th century), the *Book of Canons* by Hovhannes Odznetsi (one of the oldest works on church law), the *Homilies of Mush* (the largest manuscript in the collection, page 160), the earliest Armenian printed book (printed in Venice in 1512) and translations of many important works into Armenian, the originals of which are, in some cases, lost. Other rooms display manuscripts from each of the three main Armenian manuscript centres (Cilicia, Vaspurakan and Karabagh), items given by Iran, and maps. Armenians are particularly proud of the copy of Ptolemy's 16th-century map which shows Armenia extending from the Black Sea to the Caspian.

**Armenian Genocide Museum-Institute** [130 D4] See page 171.

**Erebuni Historical and Archaeological Museum-Reserve** See page 172.

**Cafesjian Centre for the Arts** [135 F1] (10 Tamanyan St; ☏ 010 567262; e info@ cmf.am; w cmf.am; ⊕ 10.00–20.00 Fri–Sun; adult AMD1,000, 13–17yrs AMD750, children under 12 free; several categories of annual membership available) The Centre, opened in 2009 within the Cascade, aims to bring the best of contemporary art to Armenia. The exhibits are from the personal collection of the founder, Gerard L Cafesjian, and include items from one of the most comprehensive glass collections in the world. The gallery is on six levels of the Cascade with a dedicated lift from each floor. The Cascade escalators between floors function between 08.00 and 20.00 daily. A fascinating and eclectic collection of objects is displayed with excellent information labels in English. A visit here, together with the Tamanyan Sculpture Park in front of the Cascade, is strongly recommended. (For information on the Cascade itself and the sculpture park, see page 161.)

**Yerevan History Museum** [134 B7] (1/1 Argishti St; ☏ 010 568185; e info@yhm. am; w yhm.am; ⊕ 11.00–17.30 Mon–Sat; tour in Armenian AMD2,000, in English, French, German & Russian AMD3,000; adult/child AMD500/250) Located in the new City Hall (page 165); enter by the far left-hand door. This well-laid-out museum on three floors traces the history of Yerevan from ancient times to the early 21st century. Most items are labelled in English. The first floor is ancient and medieval although the model in the centre shows 19th-century Yerevan, with archaeological sites (Shengavit, Erebuni, Avan, Teishebaini) at each corner; the second covers the 19th century while the third focuses on the 20th century.

## Worthwhile

***Aram Khachaturyan House Museum*** [135 E2] (3 Zarobyan St; ☏ 010 589418; e info@akhachaturianmuseum.am; w akhachaturianmuseum.am; ⊕ 11.00–17.00 Mon–Fri, 11.00–16.30 Sat; guide in English, French or Russian AMD2,500; AMD800) Contains personal memorabilia of Armenia's best-known composer as well as props and costumes from his ballet *Spartacus* and photographs of Khachaturyan with many well-known people including many non-musicians such as Che Guevara, Ernest Hemingway, Sophia Loren, U Thant and Charlie Chaplin. There is an astonishingly vivid painting by Edman Aivazyan of Khachaturyan conducting at the EMI studios in London, painted in 1977, a year before Khachaturyan's death. Few paintings have ever captured so well the spirit of music-making and the museum is worth visiting to see this alone. The museum makes no reference to the composer's falling foul of the Soviet authorities in the late 1940s.

***Children's Art Museum*** [135 G4] (13 Abovyan St; ☏ 010 520951; ⊕ 11.00–16.00 Tue–Sat, 11.00–15.00 Sun; guided tours in English, German & Russian AMD2,500; adult/child AMD500/200) This fascinating gallery has two parts. There is a permanent collection of works of art by children from around the world and there are temporary displays of work by Armenian children on various themes such as Europe, the Bible or Armenian folk stories. The standard of the exhibits, which include other art forms such as embroidery, metalwork and carving, is excellent. The children are given instruction in art and craft techniques and then assigned a theme to tackle. It is worth having a guide especially for the themed Armenian section. The gallery, which is on the corner of Abovyan and Sayat Nova streets, has no sign although there are colourful posters in the window. The official entrance is on Abovyan Street, the exit on Sayat Nova. If you want an English guide (recommended as there is no labelling in English), go to the exit first which is where any members of staff who speak English are to be found. Attractive books of the children's work are on sale and may make good souvenirs.

***Eduard Isabekyan Gallery*** [134 C5] (7a Mesrop Mashtots Av; ☏ 010 500567; e isabekyan100@gmail.com; w eduardisabekyan.com; ⊕ 11.00–17.00 Mon–Sat; AMD500) Opened in 2013, this gallery is well worth a visit for art lovers despite its unprepossessing entrance. Edward Isabekyan was born in 1914 in what is now eastern Turkey. He went on to graduate from Yerevan Art School in 1931 and is regarded as the founder of the thematic compositional genre in Armenia. Between 1967 and 1987 he was the director of the National Gallery of Armenia (page 178) and a hall in this gallery is now devoted to him. Much of his work is based on the history of the Armenian nation and the relationship between these people and their landscape. Following his death in 2007, Isabekyan was buried in Komitas Pantheon cemetery (see box, page 178).

***Hovhannes Sharambeyan Folk Arts and Crafts Centre*** [131 E3] (64 Abovyan St; ☏ 010 569380; ⊕ 11.00–17.00 Tue–Sun; English guide AMD2,500; AMD500) A wide range of embroidery, lace, silver jewellery, stone carving, wood carving, carpets, ornamental metalwork and ceramics. There are numbers of salt containers in the shape of women, a traditional Armenian symbol of the woman as being the essence of the home. Other interesting exhibits include shawls from the

Lake Van area (now in Turkey) which are similar in style to those from the Scottish Shetland Isles. The museum is particularly strong on wood carving.

**Modern Art Museum of Yerevan** [134 C5] (7 Mesrop Mashtots Av; ☎ 010 539637/535359; w mamy.am; ⊕ 11.00–18.00 Tue–Sun; AMD500) On the northern corner of Mashtots and Saryan streets but not directly fronting Mashtots. There is a sign pointing to it on the building in front of it. Founded in 1972, it was the only such gallery in the entire USSR. With additional funds provided by the diaspora it has built up a thought-provoking collection of 20th-century Armenian painting and sculpture.

**Martiros Saryan House Museum** [134 D2] (3 Martiros Saryan St; ☎ 010 580568; w sarian.am; ⊕ Oct–May 10.00–18.00 Fri–Wed; Jun–Sep also Thu); AMD1,000) This three-storey house museum of one of Armenia's greatest 20th-century artists holds around 170 of his works and shows their brilliant colours reflecting a sunny climate. There is information in English about the painter's varied life and the paintings are labelled in English.

**Mother Armenia Military Museum** [131 E3] (Victory Pk, 2 Azatutyan Av; ☎ 010 201400; ⊕ 10.00–17.00 Tue–Fri, 10.00–15.00 Sat–Sun) The free museum is located inside the enormous pedestal, which from 1950 to 1962 supported a statue of Stalin but now supports the statue of Mother Armenia. Originally the whole was devoted to World War II but the upper (ground) floor is now devoted to the Nagorno Karabagh conflict (labels in Armenian, Russian and English). The displays of uniforms, portraits of marshals, etc, are not particularly interesting although camouflage netting is successfully used to create atmosphere on the lower floor (labels here only in Armenian). The museum is notable for succeeding, even in a Stalin-era building, in creating the atmosphere of a church as one enters, and this is echoed in the statue of Mother Armenia, a young woman holding a sword horizontally and forming the shape of the cross.

**Sergei Parajanov Museum** [134 A5] (15 Dzoragyugh St; ☎ 010 538473; w parajanovmuseum.am; ⊕ 10.30–17.00 daily; guided tours in English, French & Russian AMD2,500; AMD1,000) This museum is dedicated to the artist and film director known in Armenian as Sargis Yossifovich Parajanyan (1924–90). It is best to get the English-speaking guide to show you round first, and afterwards to wander round on your own. Parajanov made significant contributions to Ukrainian, Armenian and Georgian cinema, seeing fame with the celebrated *The Colour of Pomegranates* (1969) and increased international recognition posthumously. His unique cinematic style was at odds with socialist-realist principles, at the time the only sanctioned art style, leading Soviet authorities repeatedly to persecute and imprison him and to suppress or distort his films. The displays also illuminate something of his controversial lifestyle. All in all, an extraordinary museum.

**Yervand Kochar Museum** [135 F2] (39/12 Mesrop Mashtots Av; ☎ 010 529326; e kochar.museum@gmail.com; w kochar.am; ⊕ 11.00–17.00 Tue–Sat, 11.00–16.00 Sun; guided tour in English AMD3,000; AMD800) This excellent museum gives a very good idea of the range of work of this interesting and talented artist who was persecuted in Stalinist times. As well as paintings from all parts of his career, including the Tiflis, Paris and Yerevan periods, there are also photographs of some of his monumental sculptures.

## And if there's still time

***Alexander Spendiaryan House Museum*** [135 G4] (21 Nalbandyan St; ☎010 521299/580783; w spendiaryanmuseum.am; ⊕ 10.30–16.30 Tue–Sat, 10.30–15.30 Sun; tour in Russian or English AMD1,500; AMD700) In addition to manuscripts and personal effects belonging to the composer, there is a display on his best-known work, the opera *Almast*.

***Ara Sargsyan and Hakob Kojoyan House Museum*** [134 D3] (70 Pushkin St; ☎010 561160; ⊕ 10.00–16.30 Tue–Sun; AMD300) The ground floor, dedicated to Sargsyan (1883–1959), a sculptor who produced works such as *Hiroshima* and *Mother Armenia*, contains a reconstruction of his studio as well as examples of his work. Sargsyan's granddaughter Anna shows visitors round. Upstairs is devoted to Kojoyan (1902–69), with examples of his work and personal effects. He was a talented book illustrator as well as a painter and is credited with the first Soviet Armenian painting *The Execution of the Communists at Tatev* (1930 – now in the National Gallery of Armenia). There is a striking painting of David of Sassoun on his horse in a style reminiscent of Russian fairy tales.

***Avetik Isahakyan House Museum*** [135 E1] (20 Zarobyan St; ☎010 562424, 587380; w isahakyanmuseum.am; ⊕ 10.30–17.00 Tue–Sat, 11.00–16.00 Sun; tours in Russian & English AMD2,500; AMD500) A museum devoted to the poet (1875–1957) who, after his return from study at Leipzig University, was arrested by the Tsarist police and banished because of his involvement in the Armenian freedom movement. Very much an establishment figure in Soviet days, he was awarded two Lenin prizes and became a deputy to the Armenian supreme soviet. The museum contains personal effects and memorabilia.

***Derenik Demirchyan House Museum*** [135 H2] (29 Abovyan St; ☎010 527774; ⊕ 11.00–16.00 Tue–Sun; AMD500) This house museum is dedicated to the writer (1877–1956) who was best known for his play *Nazar the Brave* (1923). Among the personal effects is Demirchyan's Stradivarius violin.

***Geological Museum*** [134 D1] (24 Baghramyan Av; ☎010 582936; ⊕ 11.00–16.00 Mon–Fri) Covers the geology and volcanic past of Armenia with displays on rocks, gems, minerals, etc, together with palaeontology.

***Hovhannes Tumanyan Museum*** [134 D2] (40 Moskovyan St; ☎010 560021; w toumanian.am; ⊕ 11.00–16.30 Mon–Sat, 11.00–15.00 Sun; AMD500) An interesting museum even for those who do not know the works of this notable writer. There are good explanations in English; it is recommended to read the introductory board just inside the front door. As well as documenting his literary output, the museum offers an insight into Tumanyan's intellectual life and humanitarian activities in trying to help the plight of those caught up in the genocide. Upstairs is a recreation of his apartment, including his very large library and his study, where he had a notice saying 'please do not smoke and please do not ask for books'!

***Khachatur Abovyan House Museum*** [131 F2] (4 2nd St, Kanaker; ☎010 284686; w abovyanmuseum.am; ⊕ 10.00–17.00 Mon–Fri, 10.00–15.00 Sat; tour in English AMD2,500; adult/child AMD500/300) This museum, set in pleasant gardens in the northern suburb of Kanaker, is dedicated to the novelist. The initial view is unusual; the small house in which Abovyan was born is covered, umbrella fashion, with the 1978 display hall. The statue of Abovyan originally intended for Abovyan Square (page 169) stands in the garden. The museum is well presented and labelled in Armenian, Russian and English, so having a guide is not essential but it adds to a visit. Exhibits cover various parts of his life such as an ascent of Mount Ararat, the Russo-Persian war of 1826–28, and his sudden disappearance, possibly at the hands of Tsarist agents.

**Middle Eastern Art Museum** [135 E5] (1 Aram St; ☏010 563641; ⏱ 11.00–17.00 Tue–Sat, 11.00–16.00 Sun; AMD300) Sharing an entrance with the Yeghishe Charents Museum of Literature and Art (see below) and based on the collection of the painter Marcos Grigorian. It has an excellent collection of Persian applied arts with pottery, bronzes and ritual figurines dating back five millennia. Included are exhibits from Persia's pre-Islamic Zoroastrian culture.

**Museum of Russian Art** [135 F1] (38 Isahakyan St (entrance from Tamanyan St); ☏010 560872; w musrussart.am; ⏱ 10.30–16.45 Tue–Sat, 11.00–15.30 Sun; guided tour in English, Russian or Persian AMD2,000; adult/child AMD500/300) Mostly late 19th- and early 20th-century works. Founded in 1984 and based on the collections of Professor Aram Abrahamyan. An attractive gallery with marble floors that make it a wonderfully cool oasis in the heat of summer.

**State Museum of Wood Carving** [134 B5] (2–4 Paronyan St; ☏010 532461; w artwood.am; ⏱ noon–18.00 Tue–Sun; AMD400) This small museum covers the history of Armenian wood carving, applied carving and sculpture. The small sign outside is, somewhat ironically, carved in stone.

**Yeghishe Charents House Museum** [134 D4] (17 Mesrop Mashtots Av; ☏010 535594; ⏱ 10.30–16.30 Tue–Sat, 10.30–15.30 Sun; AMD500). A well-presented museum containing the personal effects of the poet and public activist, whose picture will be familiar to visitors as it appears on the AMD1,000 banknote. The separate **Yeghishe Charents Museum of Literature and Art** [135 E5] (1 Aram St; ☏010 581641; w gatmuseum.am; ⏱ 11.00–17.00 Tue–Sat, 11.00–16.00 Sun; AMD800) is a research centre and archive of Armenian literature, theatre, music and cinema from the last 300 years.

**DAY TRIPS FROM YEREVAN** See page 184 for suggested day trips from Yerevan.

## FOLLOW BRADT

For the latest news, special offers and competitions, subscribe to the Bradt newsletter via the website w bradtguides.com and follow Bradt on:

- 🇫 BradtTravelGuides
- 🐦 @BradtGuides
- 📷 @bradtguides
- 𝓟 bradtguides
- ▶ bradtguides

3

# 4

# The Central Provinces

Central Armenia stretches from the irrigated plains in the shadow of Mount Ararat via the country's highest peak to the large high-altitude Lake Sevan and its surrounding mountain ranges. Almost any of the major sites in these five central provinces – Aragatsotn, Ararat, Armavir, Gegharkunik and Kotayk – can be visited on a day trip from Yerevan except for those in the eastern and southern parts of Gegharkunik; exploring the more remote areas will of course require more time. Cultural-historical destinations include the town of **Ashtarak** together with the fortress and monastery at **Amberd** in Aragatsotn; the monastery of **Khor Virap** in Ararat, with its stunning views of Mount Ararat in clear weather; the churches and cathedral of **Etchmiadzin** and the monument and museum at **Sardarapat** in Armavir; **Sevanavank** in Gegharkunik; and the temple at **Garni** and rock-carved monastery at **Geghard** which are near each other in Kotayk. More idiosyncratic highlights include the **hot springs** in Hrazdan Gorge and its side valleys, **Byurakan Astrophysical Observatory,** and the amazing field of khachkars at **Noratus**. Hikers and nature lovers will find fertile ground in **Khosrov Forest State Reserve**, **Ashtarak** and **Garni** gorges, around **Tsaghkadzor** and **Aghveran**, and in high summer in the volcanic **Geghama Mountains**, of which **Azhdahak** is the highest peak at 3,597m. **Mount Aragats**, at 4,090m the highest point in the present-day republic, offers non-technical summit opportunities in good summer conditions. Those visiting in high summer may also enjoy a spot of Armenian beach life, watersports or simply a cooling swim in **Lake Sevan**. Keen skiers and snowboarders can enjoy a good day on the slopes at **Tsaghkadzor ski resort** between December and March. The following pages make numerous further suggestions.

## ARAGATSOTN PROVINCE

The province whose name means 'foot of Aragats' comprises the land around **Mount Aragats**. The province's geography is extremely varied and it is probably best thought of as being three separate zones: the mountain itself, arid steppe to the west, and the land bordering the gorge of the Kasakh River to the east. Each of these zones has its different attractions. Ashtarak (Tower), the provincial capital, is on the Kasakh Gorge in the southeast of the province and only 22km from Yerevan.

**GETTING THERE AND AROUND** There are **minibuses** from Yerevan Central Bus Station (see box, page 87) to many destinations in the province, including Aparan, Ashtarak, Byurakan, Ohanavan and Talin. From Ashtarak, local minibuses go to some villages, although it is probably easier to hire a taxi in Ashtarak, or even in Yerevan given the relatively short distances involved. See page 87 for information

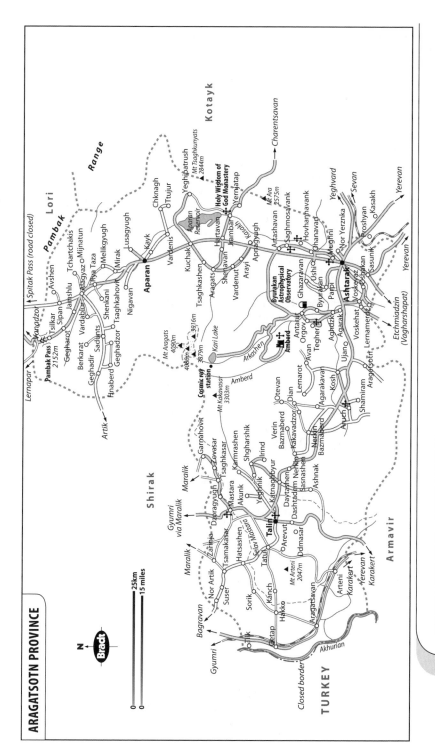

# ARAGATSOTN PROVINCE

185

about **taxis**. The main roads in the province are good; visitors travelling between Yerevan and Ashtarak will find themselves on one of the first completed sections of the new North–South Road. Most places are accessible by **car** and a 4x4 is only necessary if you are intending to explore very remote areas or are driving at higher elevations before the snow has fully melted.

🏠 **WHERE TO STAY** Apart from **homestays**, accommodation in the province is limited, but since almost everywhere can be reached as a day trip from Yerevan this shouldn't prove a problem. Several guesthouses and hotels exist in and around Byurakan and Amberd for those wanting to spend more than a day exploring the various sights on the southern slopes of Mount Aragats. There is a hotel at Kari Lake (see below) which acts as a base camp for Mount Aragats from about mid-June to early September, depending on snow-melt. Ashtarak has several B&Bs as well as a partially functional Soviet-era hotel.

## Ashtarak

🏠 **Ashtarak Hotel** (10 rooms) 16 Sisakyan St; 0232 34393. A candidate for Armenia's best-preserved Soviet hotel, seemingly untouched since the day Gorbachev left yet still open & representing more of a historical experience than a simple overnight stay. At the time of research 10 sgl/twin/quad rooms were operating on 2 storeys of the original building, which is conveniently located in the town centre. Water might work if you're lucky. Staff might be friendly if you're lucky. No b/fast but cutlery & crockery available. Sgl rooms a snip at AMD3,000 pp. **$**

🏠 **Ashtaraki Dzor** (13 rooms) 1 Kasakh Gorge; 0232 36778; m 098 220330; e info@dzor.am; w dzor.am. One of the original post-independence countryside entertainment complexes near Yerevan, still offering lavish Armenian-style feasting facilities by the river north of town as well as a few basic dbl/quad rooms. Restaurant on-site. **$**

## Elsewhere in the province

🏠 **Alagyaz Hotel** (3 rooms) Kari Lake; m 093 396182; ⊕ May–Oct or as season dictates. Simple cottage accommodation & restaurant below the southern peak of Aragats. Priced per cottage; each cottage sleeps 3. Extremely remote location at the last vehicle-accessible point on the road (page 195). B/fast extra. **$$**

🏠 **Byurakan Astrophysical Observatory Guesthouse** [map, page 185] (10 rooms) Byurakan village; 010 525505; m 055 911307, 091 195903, 091 195901; e sona.farmanyan@mail.ru, aregmick@aras.am; w aras.am//SciTourism/eng/index.php. The observatory offers basic accommodation for up to 35 visitors on night-time stargazing tours of the complex, as well as for visiting scientists. Certainly one of the more unique overnight options in Armenia. Price pp depends on room type, size & occupancy. B/fast extra. 7 days' notice preferred. **$–$$**

✗ **WHERE TO EAT AND DRINK** Ashtarak has several good restaurants and cafés (see opposite). There are good **bakeries** at Aparan (page 194) and Mughni (page 189) and **cafés** at Amberd (page 197) and in Byurakan village (page 197). The restaurant at Kari Lake is known mainly for its *khash* (page 195), though other dishes are available. Some filling stations have small shops and cafés attached. Most towns have small shops where you can buy picnic ingredients. See individual destination listings for specific recommendations.

**ASHTARAK** The town of Ashtarak can be considered a satellite of Yerevan, some 20km to its northwest and with a population of around 18,000. It is situated on the **Kasakh River**, whose verdant gorge limits the old town to the east. This river rises in the southeastern corner of Shirak province and then flows south through Aragatsotn to join the Arax south of Yerevan. The town's exposed but desirable location on the well-watered lower flanks of Aragats left it vulnerable to successive waves of invasion and conflict, ceded to Russia by the Persians in 1828 and explaining much of the Tsarist-era construction that remains, as well as scatterings of earlier ruins and quaint tangles of residential backstreets. With numerous irrigation canals and fruit trees lining the streets, Ashtarak has a pleasant and well-kept feel and is compact and interesting enough to warrant a few hours of wandering, with several good restaurants within easy reach. Those wishing to spend time at the numerous surrounding sites of interest may prefer its provincial vibe over the bustle of Yerevan as a base for exploring.

## ✕ Where to eat and drink

✕ **Old Ashtarak** 31 Grigor Ghapantsyan St; m 094 992232; ⨍ HinAshtarak; ⏲ 11.00–23.00 daily. Syrian-Armenian-run restaurant in a classically restored 19th-century house on a quiet backstreet, serving the full spread of Levantine cuisine inc meze dishes, salads, barbecues, bakery items, etc. Excellent quality & amazingly good value. Try the pomegranate molasses-infused *lahmajo*.

✕ **Pascal & Diodato** 12 Abovyan St; m 098 996903; ⏲ 10.00–22.00 daily. One of Ashtarak's better-known restaurants, named after two Armenian coffee merchants who reportedly established Europe's first coffee houses in London & Vienna. Typical Armenian food with shaded outdoor seating in a quiet spot near Karmravor church. Can get busy & certainly on the pricier end of the scale in Ashtarak.

✕ **Tatoents 164** 1 Sajumyan St; m 091 576883; e qotuk@hotmail.com; ⨍; ⏲ open on demand by advance arrangement. Home-cooked meals in a charming historical home of 1837 in which 7 generations of the same family have lived. Excellent food by all accounts & definitely not the usual restaurant fare. Popular with groups; requires reservation at least 24hrs in advance.

🗖 **Ome Anti-café** 25 Grigor Ghapantsyan St; m 041 228225; ⨍; ⏲ 11.00–23.00 daily. Anti-café Ome (rhyming with 'olé') opened May 2018 in the basement of a lovely old house with a big, relaxing garden (formerly Ghapantsyan's house museum). AMD600 for the first hr, AMD200–300 (or less) thereafter depending how long you stay. Drinks, snacks, books & games all available. Popular with young locals.

**What to see and do** Ashtarak is a very walkable town, particularly the older residential districts near the gorge. Historical sites include several fine medieval churches and a **three-arch bridge** of 1664. This has a rather unusual appearance in that the three arches are unequal in size with the southernmost arch almost twice the height of the northernmost. Among Ashtarak's notable figures, the Armenian writer Perch Proshyan (1837–1907) has an attractive **house museum** (10 Perch Proshyan St; ✆0232 33254; ⏲ 11.00–17.00 Tue–Sat, 11.00–16.00 Sun; guided tour in English AMD1,000; AMD300) in a restored 19th-century house in one of the town's older districts, containing memorabilia of his itinerant life in the Caucasus and his work as a novelist, playwright and photographer. Prominently perched atop an outcrop on the east bank of the river between the new and old bridges is the small red tuff **church of St Sargis**, a modern construction on early foundations. Ashtarak's biggest church, **St Marina**, is in the city centre set in well-tended gardens. Built in 1281, it is a cross-dome church with octagonal tambour and an unusually steep-sided cupola. The tambour features attractive decoration in contrasting colours of tuff. Unfortunately the appearance of the whole is somewhat marred by a late 19th-century addition which looks more like a large derelict shed than part of a church.

Ashtarak's other three **churches** are the subject of a local legend which states that three sisters lived here who all loved the same prince, Sargis. The elder two decided to kill themselves to leave the way free for the youngest. One of the elder sisters dressed in an apricot-coloured dress and the other in a red dress and then they both threw themselves into the gorge. The youngest sister learned what had happened, put on a white dress, and threw herself into the gorge after them. The prince became a hermit but three churches appeared at the edge of the gorge: one apricot-coloured, one red and one white. The problem with this legend is that the present colour of these churches doesn't correspond with it, although the names do: Karmravor (Red), the church of the sister wearing the red dress, is apricot coloured (though it does have a red roof); Spitakavor (White), the church of the sister wearing the white dress, is red; while Tsiranavor (Apricot), whose sister wore the apricot-coloured dress, is actually white!

By far the best preserved of the three is the small 7th-century **Karmravor Church** dedicated to the Mother of God. It is one of the few Armenian churches of this period to have survived unaltered, even retaining a roof of tuff tiles and a tiled octagonal cupola. A single aisle cross-dome church, it is one of Armenia's most appealing town churches. An extensive cemetery with khachkars lies to the north and east of the surrounding walls. The other two churches in the legend, 14th-century **Spitakavor** and 5th-century **Tsiranavor**, are both roofless and forsaken but are only a short walk away. Both are perched on the edge of the gorge. **Tsiranavor**, on a three-step base, was a three-aisled basilica. There is evidence of the church having been fortified with remnants of an extra wall on the east, north and west and a rebuilt southern wall with castle-like windows and defensive chutes. **Spitakavor** is a small, almost square church, the apse occupying the full width of the eastern end. From outside the eastern wall there are good views of the gorge, the old bridge and St Sargis Church. The streets south of these two churches lead to a zigzag walkway down to a (newer) **suspended footbridge** above the Kasakh, also with excellent views along the gorge. The large storage jars decorating the gardens passed on the walk are often unearthed in the district, and in early summer you may find yourself feasting on the abundant mulberries and cherries that overhang many of these residential alleyways.

**AROUND ASHTARAK** Several modern Armenian wineries have estates in the countryside near Ashtarak, including **Voskevaz** (✆ 010 202006; e info@voskevaz. am; w voskevaz.am) in the village of the same name and **Van Ardi** (m 094 535050; e info@vanardi.com; w vanardi.com) in nearby Sasunik. Both offer public and private **winery tours and wine tasting sessions**, which may represent a convenient alternative to better-established but more distant wineries in Vayots Dzor.

**Oshakan** Eight kilometres southwest of Ashtarak is the village of Oshakan, whose **5th-century church** was renovated in 1875 with frescoes added in 1960. A tall belfry rises at its east end. It is famous as the burial place of Mesrop Mashtots and the alphabet is spelled out in grass in front. A window has been inserted in the front of the *bema* to allow a view of Mesrop Mashtots's grave. It is possible to descend into the mausoleum via steps to the side of the *bema*. A new **stele** stands at the entrance to the church, commemorating the 1995 visit of Katholikos Karagen I. Carved into the stele is a **sundial** with the traditional Armenian use of letters for numbers. However, whether due to unfamiliarity with the old letter/number system or because of Oshakan's association with the alphabet, the hours are uncharacteristically numbered with a continuous sequence of the first 12 letters of the alphabet (see box, page 46). In the grounds of the church is a collection of 36 **modern khachkars** carved by Ruben Nalbandyan. Each represents a letter of Mashtots's original alphabet, carved with images appropriate to the letter as well as a typical Armenian cross and the circular symbol of eternity. A visit would be enhanced by the company of an Armenian speaker but, armed with a copy of the

Armenian alphabet (page 397), it is possible to appreciate the ideas behind some of them. For example, the Armenian letter 'E' (Է) bears an image of Etchmiadzin, 'M' (Մ) depicts Mesrop Mashtots, and on 'J' (Ջ) water flows from the eternity symbol, *joor* being the Armenian word for 'water'. The first rank of nine can be read as (Ch) rist, (E)tchmiatzin, (S)aint, (M)(A)(SH)(T)(O)(TS).

To the northeast of the church is **Didikond Hill**, visible from the church. A cemetery (medieval to modern gravestones) lies at the base of the hill and on top of the hill are the impressive excavated remains of a 7th–5th-century BC citadel. The remains were discovered when ArmenTel (now Beeline) began to dig pits for the foundation of the mobile phone tower. The huge blocks of dressed stone which form the massive walls of the square fort make one realise why such buildings are termed cyclopean. A road skirts the base of the hill; the dirt track seen where the gas pipe goes up and over leads to the top of the hill. The inside of the small church of St Grigor on top of the hill disappoints; for some reason it is painted a shiny orange colour.

On the northwest edge of the town is the 7th-century **St Sion** (or St Mankanots) church, a small tetraconch (comprising four apses) church, one of only a few such churches in Armenia, the best known being Karmravor Church in Ashtarak. The nearby pillar on a stepped base is traditionally believed to mark the grave of the Byzantine emperor Mauricius (539–602) (or his mother) who was said, by one Armenian historian, to come from the village. In the **gorge** nearby, a **five-arch bridge** dating from 1706 spans the Kasakh.

**Mughni** The village of Mughni, nowadays within the Ashtarak city limits, lies just to the north of the main road at the west end of the high viaduct over the Kasakh Gorge. The 14th-century **monastery of St George** was completely rebuilt between 1661 and 1669 during the period when Eastern Armenia saw a revival of church building thanks to the stable conditions enjoyed under the Safavid kings of Persia. It is one of the finest buildings of this renaissance and it is now surrounded by well-tended gardens. It is notable that the church withstood the earthquake of 1679 which flattened Yerevan and badly damaged the monastery of Hovhannavank to the north. The main cross-dome church has a distinctively striped circular tambour supporting the conical umbrella cupola and different colours of tuff are also used to decorative effect on the gable ends. To the west is an arched gallery surmounted by a belfry whose cupola is supported by 12 columns. Both the west and south doorways are especially notable with elaborately carved tuff of different colours and fine carved wooden doors. Inside the church, fragments of early 19th-century murals survive, notably one showing the baptism of Trdat on the north wall. There is an altar screen, unusual in Armenian churches, also with paintings. The fortress wall of the monastery survives with small towers at the northwest and southwest corners. At the northeast corner the original service buildings have been restored: they originally housed the living quarters of the monks together with the refectory.

**Hovhannavank (monastery)** Situated about 5km north of Mughni, Hovhannavank (Monastery of John) is the southernmost of two sizeable monasteries that are perched on the edge of the gorge, the other being Saghmosavank. They are linked by a signposted 7.5km trail along the gorge (allow 2½–3 hours), but there is little shade in the middle of the day and a spate of new buildings continues to blight the route.

The oldest part of Hovhannavank is a barrel-vaulted **basilica** dating from the 5th century though extensively rebuilt since then. It has a painted wooden altar

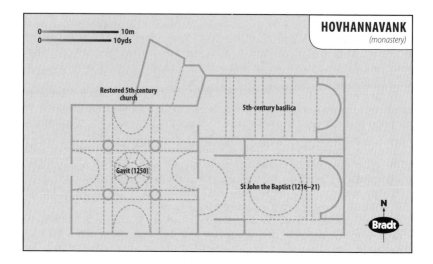

0 ——— 10m
0 ——— 10yds

Restored 5th-century church

5th-century basilica

Gavit (1250)

St John the Baptist (1216–21)

N

Bradt

screen. On the south side of this early basilica stands the **main church**, dedicated to John the Baptist, and erected by Prince Vache Vachutian in 1216–21; the prince was Governor of Ani from c1213 until 1232. The corner rooms of this church are two-storey and those at the west have cantilevered steps. As at some other churches of this period, the front of the altar dais was originally decorated with stars, pentagons and diamonds, and some of this decoration survives. The *gavit* was built in 1250 to serve both the churches and is consequently off-centre. Four pillars divide it into separate sections, each of which is differently decorated; the belfry supported by 12 columns was probably added in 1274.

The cupola of the main church collapsed following an earthquake in 1679 and then again, following another one, in 1919; the latter also damaged the south façade and still more damage resulted from the 1988 earthquake. The 12-sided tambour and umbrella cupola were reconstructed in 1999. Particularly strange is the tympanum of the door from the gavit into the main church. The bas-relief is always said to depict the parable of the wise and foolish virgins with Christ apparently blessing the five wise virgins with His right hand and rebuking the five foolish virgins with His left – except that the virgins appear to have beards. Given the large sickle shape on Christ's left, one wonders if the scene actually depicts the Last Judgement. The church is surrounded by a fortified wall, originally constructed in the 13th century and rebuilt in the 17th. To the north is an extensive graveyard with khachkars.

**Saghmosavank (monastery)** This monastery was, like Hovhannavank, built by Prince Vache Vachutian. Not surprisingly the two monasteries have many similarities, not least in their situation on the rim of the gorge and in the stone used in their construction, although the architectural details are quite different. The oldest part of Saghmosavank (Monastery of Psalms) is the **Zion Church** of 1215 with its round tambour and conical cupola. Inside there are four two-storey corner rooms; those in the west have cantilevered steps going up the west wall of the church, those in the east currently have no permanent means of access but there is a suggestion of cantilevered steps having been present up the north and south walls. The smaller **Mother of God Church** to the south, a plain barrel-vaulted church, was built in 1235 and was followed by the large **gavit** which has an impressive entrance doorway similar to those found at the entrance to mosques. Whether this simply

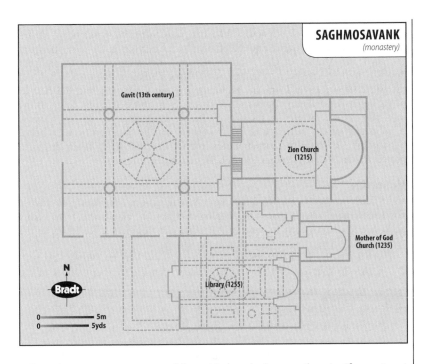

SAGHMOSAVANK
(monastery)

Gavit (13th century)

Zion Church
(1215)

Mother of God
Church (1235)

N

Library (1255)

0 ——— 5m
0 ——— 5yds

reflects the previous experience of the architect or had some other significance is not clear. The layout of the existing buildings required the **library** to be L-shaped when it was added in 1255. It has an apse in its southeast corner with frescoes on the side pillars and carved angels above it. There is a fresco of St Gregory over the door from the library into the Mother of God Church. As at Hovhannavank, a **fortified wall** surrounds the complex and there are splendid views of the Kasakh Gorge.

**Ushi**  To the west of the main road, where Hovhannavank is to the east, lies the village of Ushi with the massive site of **St Sargis Monastery** (5th–17th century). Although in ruins and rarely visited, enough remains to make a visit to these extensive monastery buildings worthwhile. The monastery is 1½km from the main road. Go straight through the village and continue on the dirt road at the end of the tarmac. It brings you to a picnic area below the southeast entrance to the monastery. The large complex (45m by 54m) up on the hillside is surrounded by a defensive wall of 1654 with round towers. The monastery suffered earthquake damage in 1679 and again in 1827. The small **church of St Sargis**, built in the 10th century, was the only structure left standing after the 1827 earthquake. It was restored in 2003–04. The church was built on the site of an earlier 5th-century chapel believed to house the tomb of St Sargis (see box, page 43). Executed by the Sassanid king in AD362 for his Christian beliefs, the saint was originally buried at Namyan, on the southern coast of the Caspian Sea. In the 5th century Mesrop Mashtots had the saint's remains reburied at Ushi.

The **Mother of God Church** (12th–13th century) lies to the south of St Sargis. It was a three-aisle domed basilica (stones from the tambour are laid out outside the monastery complex to the west). The remains of the eastern apse can be seen, with interesting carving on the front of the *bema*. Slightly more intact is the 1246 **gavit** to the south of Mother of God, its western portal and some walls still standing.

Two large windows look out across the Arax plain and in clear weather there are good views of Mount Ararat. Enough of the intricate carving on the portal between the gavit and Mother of God Church remains, indicating what a magnificent doorway it must have been. A gallery and belltower adjoined the western sides of the churches and gavit. Domestic buildings line the south, west and north sides of the defensive wall and others run westwards from above St Sargis. Large as the monastery is, it is dwarfed by the size of a **Bronze Age fortress** on the slopes above. A good idea of the fortress and the monastery can be obtained from an aerial photograph (**w** rogpalmer.cantabphotos.com/081229205050/20) taken during a project to identify archaeological sites in Armenia.

**Mount Ara** Volcanic Mount Ara (2,576m), on the border between Aragatsotn and Kotayk provinces, is a prominent landmark in eastern Aragatsotn. Its ridge is said to resemble the silhouette of a sleeping man, Ara the Handsome, lying on his back; due to its proximity to Yerevan it is a popular destination for hiking in the summer and ski touring/snowshoeing in the winter.

There is a well-visited **cave shrine**, dedicated to Kuys Varvara (Virgin Barbara), also known as Tsaghkavank (Flower Monastery), on the southern slopes of the

## MOUNT ARA – A BOTANICAL FORAY

The extinct volcano of Mount Ara, about an hour's drive north of Yerevan, makes an ideal botanical excursion. The trip takes in semi-desert, mountain steppe, forest, meadows and agricultural ecosystems. There are several trails and tracks for a 4x4; while it is possible to climb to the 2km-diameter crater at the top for the panoramic view; the lower slopes afford much of interest. More than 650 species of vascular plants grow on Ara, almost 20% of the whole Armenian flora.

Timing a visit for flowers is always going to be a compromise. Ara has snow cover from December which may not fully melt until late May. The first flowers to appear in February/March are *Merendera trigyna* and *Crocus adamii*. Irises, tulips and other spring flowers follow. The most luxuriant growth is in May and June including the scented white flowers of *Crambe orientale*, aromatic thyme, crimson poppies and the dark red bugloss *Echium russicum*. You should also see spectacular fields of agricultural weeds, cornflower, poppy, chamomile and blue larkspur. In the moister meadows are lovely violet-purple, almost black *Gladiolus atroviolaceus*, brilliant blue *Anchusa azurea*, white *Anthemis* daisies, the white foam of *Filipendula hexapetala*, various star of Bethlehem (*Ornithogalum*) species and much more.

Ara's northern slopes have remnant forest, remains of much wider cover in the past. Over 40 species of shrubs and trees are present including Caucasian oak (*Quercus macranthera*), birch, maple, aspen, cherry, apple, pear and several species of *Sorbus*. There is also a subalpine crook-stem forest, where trees have been weighed down on their sides by heavy snow and then new growth has grown upwards before the snow melted. On the lower slopes can be found the orchid *Dactylorhiza romana*, an inflated cowslip *Primula megacalyx*, *Veronica gentianoides*, beloved by UK cottage gardeners, and a little later the large-flowered violet-blue *Iris demetri*.

For further information on Mount Ara and details of how to get here, see above and opposite.

Legend relates how Semiramis, Queen of Assyria, was so enamoured by the beauty of Ara, King of Armenia, that she sent envoys to ask him to marry her. He refused: he was already married. Thereupon Semiramis sent her armies to Armenia, with orders to capture Ara alive but he was killed in the battle between the two armies. Grief-stricken, Semiramis, a sorceress, believed she could bring Ara back to life. Failing to do so, she dressed one of her lovers in Ara's clothes to convince the Armenians, who wanted to avenge his death, that Ara was still alive, thus preventing further war. Most versions of the legend agree that Ara was not revived but accounts vary as to how his outline appeared on the mountain. One tale says that when Semiramis buried Ara at the foot of the mountain his spirit rose and formed the mountain's top into his sleeping likeness. Another tale has Ara tied to the mountain and when Semiramis used her magic powers to try to fling him into the void his body landed on top of the mountain, giving it its present contour.

mountain. It is best approached by car from Karbi, where the road crosses the gorge before proceeding straight in the direction of the mountain. Where the asphalt ends, turn right on to a dirt road. From here multiple tracks lead across the initially gently sloping foothills, all heading in the same direction towards an obvious cleft in the mountain. It is possible with a 4x4 to drive all the way to the cave shrine but the steeper later stages are along difficult rocky tracks. A longer route begins from behind the cemetery in Yeghvard (which can be more easily reached from Yerevan by marshrutka) and follows a dirt road – allow a full day if using public transport and approaching on foot via this route.

It is a **pleasant walk** to the shrine from the dirt road (allow about an hour), especially in spring when it is not too hot and flowers cover the hillside. Inside the dripping cave, the focus is the well in the centre of the floor. Its water is said to cure many ailments but only to be effective if you draw the water yourself. Candle stumps and religious art abound, which highlight the site's continued significance to locals (as do the nearby picnic tables and barbecue facilities). From the shrine it is possible to hike up the mountain – aim for the saddle, which is obvious from the foot of the shrine, between two peaks. Numerous possible routes exist, including a loop of the crescent-shaped ridge, though none is marked.

The 17th-century church in **Karbi** does not match its better-known neighbours, Mughni and Hovhannavank, but the three-aisled Mother of God Church has a striking belltower on the west side, its black and red tuff decoration reminiscent of Mughni's.

**APARAN AND AROUND** On a knoll just north of where the H4 road to **Yernjatap** crosses the Kasakh River are the ruins of the **Monastery of the Holy Wisdom of God**, founded in the 5th century and renovated in 1244. It is a peaceful and isolated spot, accessible by a dirt track from where the road begins to descend into the shallow gorge. The black tuff cross-dome church is swathed in wooden scaffolding within and without and a little work has been done on the roof to keep out the elements. The gavit with its massive columns is roofless. Its west portal has elaborate carving, as does the west entrance to the church with its black and red decoration. Some decoration survives on the altar dais and the remains of a red-painted frieze are discernible. Painted decoration can also be seen at the main entrance to the church

The Central Provinces  ARAGATSOTN PROVINCE

4

and on adjacent khachkars. A door in the south wall leads to a small 4th-century barrel-vaulted church.

**Aparan Reservoir** on the Kasakh may be glimpsed to the east from the M3 main road between Hartavan and Kuchak: it supplies Yerevan with drinking water. When the reservoir was created in the 1980s the village of **Zovuni** was submerged, with residents being moved to the suburban village adjoining the north of Yerevan which now bears the same name. Three historic Zovuni monuments were threatened by the rising waters: the important 5th- or 6th-century church of Sts Peter and Paul, the Vardan Mamikonian mausoleum, and a 4th-century chapel or Tukh Manuk shrine (see box, page 212). The latter two were dismantled and reconstructed on higher ground on the east side of the reservoir above the church; the church was left and its ruins can be seen and reached when the water level is low. All three can be reached via dirt roads either from the south or north end of the lake, or a loop can be done via Yeghipatrush. The **mausoleum** of Vardan Mamikonian, hero of the Battle of Avarayr, AD451 (page 19), is reached by going down steps beside the entrance to the adjacent ruined church. Between the mausoleum and Tukh Manuk are some ancient khachkars; a dark pillar-like one may have been a *vishap*. The 4th-century **Tukh Manuk** is built of large blocks. Inside it is typical of such shrines, an array of votive offerings adorning the small apse. A large cemetery occupies the hillside below the shrine.

The **Sts Peter and Paul Church** is most easily reached, if the water level is low enough, by going straight down from the picnic table immediately to the west of the Tukh Manuk, keeping to the right of a small ravine. The church on its stepped pedestal is in a sadly ruined state, making it difficult to appreciate its importance in the development of Armenian church architecture. It was the first to be converted from a three-aisle basilica, with free-standing pillars supporting the roof, to a domed hall church in which the pillars adjoin the walls, thus creating a large unbroken space in front of the altar. The conversion at Zovuni was carried out in the early 6th century. The new pillars, adjacent to the walls but without structural cohesion, supported a dome positioned centrally over the original basilica. An eastern apse was added at the same reconstruction with the result that the dome is asymmetrically positioned in regard to the total length of the interior.

In **Yeghipatrush** is the large 10th-century **Mother of God Church**. Most of the interest lies with the roofless 13th-century **gavit** which is apparently unique in Armenia in having watchtowers at both its northeast and southeast corners. The gavit's west portal has a distinctly oriental appearance, its pointed arch decorated with shell shapes all surrounded by a decorated rectangular frame.

**Aparan** (telephone code: 0252) itself has an undistinguished claim to fame in that it is (unfairly) the butt of many a joke among Armenians about the supposed stupidity of its inhabitants. More positively, the smell of freshly baked bread will likely guide you to the immensely popular **Gntunik Bakery** just south of the main square. The square is named after Tigran Petrosian (1929–84), World Chess Champion 1963–69, and his statue stands here.

Just north of the square, the black tuff **Holy Cross Church** is one of Armenia's oldest, dating from the earliest days of Christianity in Armenia in the 4th century. However, with its brand-new roof and well-tended garden, outfitted with solar-powered street lamps, the overall effect belies its age and significance. It is a three-nave basilica without a cupola, the naves being divided by T-shaped pillars; the roof is barrel-vaulted. At the apse a modern stained-glass window is virtually the church's only decoration. An unusual feature is the row of four large stone blocks, a little like khachkars, which form a sort of half barrier across the chancel in front of the altar dais. The stepped base on which the church stands is larger than the present church and there are the outlines of two other churches to the north.

Aparan has a second functioning church, the restored 4th-century **Teghenyats Church**, set on a rocky knoll within its cemetery. To reach it, take the first right from the main road north of the Holy Cross road. Continue until you see an old wall and follow the wall as it curves to the right. The metal gate in the wall is the entrance to the church grounds.

On the northern edge of town, a striking illuminated **monument** can be seen on a hill to the west. This commemorates three events: the Armenian victory over Turkey in 1918; the genocide of 1915; and the Great Patriotic War (World War II) of 1941–45. The monument is reached through parklike grounds and up a flight of steps. It resembles three apses, each containing a memorial to one of the events.

North of Aparan, the M3 main road passes several villages inhabited by members of the **Yezidi** ethnic minority (page 36). Modern Yezidi cemeteries are distinctive with graves that look almost like small houses; an older cemetery is by the road in the village of **Rya Taza** ('new way' in the Yezidi language) where there are tombstones in the form of horses for the men and much simpler ones, sometimes depicting a cradle, for women. (Constructing tombstones in the form of animals was not associated solely with Yezidis in Armenia as the tombstones of Armenian nobility were sometimes in the form of sheep.)

The main road climbs up through rolling hills and over the **Pambak Pass** (2,152m) into Lori where it reaches the town of Spitak (page 276). The old road between Sipan and Lernatsk via the Spitak Pass has long been closed to vehicles, but it would probably make a nice 16km walk or mountain-bike ride.

**MOUNT ARAGATS** Mount Aragats has four separate peaks, the highest being the northernmost; at 4,090m it is the highest point in the modern-day Republic of Armenia. Aragats's four peaks are situated around the rim of a volcanic crater, broken between the southern and eastern peaks by an outflowing stream. If you are reasonably fit, it is a simple, non-technical hike to the summit of the southern peak, although the thin air at altitude will likely slow your pace. All four peaks can be connected in a single day by an experienced hiker under favourable conditions (perhaps camping by Kari Lake or staying at the base camp hotel for an early start). Whatever your ambitions, it is essential to take the same precautions as when ascending any mountain: do not consider going without walking boots, fully charged mobile phone, compass, waterproofs, warm clothing, water and food. Be aware that the weather can (and does) change rapidly and dramatically. Because clouds often gather round the crater from mid-morning, an early start is recommended to maximise the potential for spectacular views and to minimise the risk of becoming disorientated in cloud.

The easiest approach ascends the southern flank via the H20 road from Agarak, passing Byurakan (page 197) and Amberd (page 197) and continuing as far as the artificial **Kari Lake** at 3,190m, where a restaurant and hotel (page 186) operate during the climbing season (roughly May to October). In early June, look out for *Draba*, *Crocus adami*, *Scilla siberica*, *Pushkinia scilloides* and the delightfully downy *Ajuga orientalis*. July and August see the alpine meadows in full flower. Also by the lake is a **cosmic ray station** (w crd.yerphi.am), inaugurated in 1943 to study astroparticle physics. According to the station's brochure, work currently concentrates on monitoring solar activity as well as on studying the physics of extensive air showers and measuring the incident flux of galactic cosmic rays. Some travellers have reported being able to stay overnight here.

From Kari Lake, it takes about 2 hours to walk to the southern peak (3,879m). Head for the northwest corner of the summit until a rough track is encountered which leads to the top. For those wishing to reach the highest point in Armenia on the northernmost peak (4,090m) note that it takes about 4 hours from the end of the road and should be attempted only by those accustomed to mountain walking. Apart from the break between the southern and eastern summits, the peaks are linked by high saddles and a ridge descends south from the southern peak. Other, longer approach routes are sometimes taken but tend to be the domain of more experienced mountaineers and hikers. In late winter, backcountry ski touring sometimes takes place on the northern slopes.

## The Southern slopes of Mount Aragats

**Byurakan Astrophysical Observatory** East of the H20, just south of Byurakan village is Byurakan Astrophysical Observatory (w bao.am), whose tourism element is looked after by the Armenian Astronomical Society (✆ 010 525505; w aras.am/SciTourism/eng/). The facility was founded in 1946 and is set in very pleasant grounds at an elevation of 1,405m, with a visitor centre, a café and enough curiosities to warrant a couple of hours' visit. The observatory complex includes a quaint house museum dedicated to Viktor Hambartsumyan (page 168), containing many of his personal effects. In-depth guided tours of the whole ensemble, including night-time use of the telescopes for stargazing, can be arranged. There is also a guesthouse on-site (page 186).

The original equipment included a 45cm Cassegrainian telescope (a reflecting telescope in which incident light is reflected from a large concave mirror on to a smaller convex mirror and then back through a hole in the concave mirror to form an image) and a 52cm Schmidt telescope (a reflecting telescope incorporating a camera and consisting of a thin convex glass plate at the centre of curvature of a spherical mirror which thus corrects for spherical aberration, coma and astigmatism). Radio telescopes were added in 1950. In 1960, a larger Schmidt telescope with a 102cm glass plate and 132cm mirror was installed and, in 1965, an important programme began looking for UV-excess galaxies. It continued for 15 years and achieved considerable international renown with 1,500 such galaxies being identified. (In 1968, the observatory was awarded the Order of Lenin.) A larger 2.6m telescope was installed in 1976 and a second survey was started which was also to achieve major international recognition. The object this time was to obtain baseline data for an ongoing survey of 600 quasars, emission-line and UV-excess galaxies, although the detailed work ended up providing information about 3,000 varied objects. Since independence the 2.6m telescope has been refurbished and in 1998 the observatory was named in honour of Viktor Hambartsumyan (1908–96), its founder, whose face used to be familiar to visitors because his picture appeared on the AMD100 banknote until the note was replaced by a coin.

Not to be confused with the observatory – though now under its administration – is the nearby **radio-optical observatory ROT-54**, built between 1975 and 1985 under the leadership of the pioneering Armenian radio-engineer Paris Heruni (1933–2008). The 54m-diameter dish is set into the hillside and can be viewed up close from a perimeter walkway. The building overlooking the dish houses the original control room with all of its equipment still intact. In spite of his amazing engineering accomplishments, Heruni's facility was tragically never brought into commission, being deemed economically unviable by the crumbling Soviet leadership of the time. The site is just northwest of Orgov village, about 7km from Byurakan, and can be reached on a good paved road.

**Byurakan** The village of Byurakan is served by several daily minibuses from Yerevan and has a couple of guesthouses and cafés which are open during the summer tourist season. As well as the well-known observatory (see opposite) it has **two early churches**: the interesting 5th-century church of St John within the village, and the 7th-century Artavazik Church just outside the village in a small ravine.

To reach **St John**, take the right-hand fork from the 'square' in the middle of the village, then first right again, then at the next fork take the upper road to the church. You will come across it quite suddenly, set above the road in beautifully tended grounds with a collection of interesting stones and khachkars. The south façade, which is the first to be seen, immediately suggests several periods of building. The western portion is plain apart from the horseshoe-shaped arch over the door and three high narrow windows, also with curved arches. The eastern portion is plain in its lower half but the upper half has blind arcades and two small round windows, in front of which hang two bells. The blind arcades continue on to the east façade where two of the narrow vertical windows have carved stone grilles (even better seen from inside the church). On the north side the distinction of round porthole-like windows to the east and vertical windows to the west continues. Wrapped around the northeast corner of the church is an extra wall, built externally of large tuff blocks and internally of an early type of concrete (page 47), most easily seen beside the west door. In the Middle Ages churches were sometimes used as fortresses and an extra wall was built round the outside of the church. Remnants of such walls still persist in places; a good example is the Tsiranavor Church in Parpi (page 199). Most such defensive walls have been demolished, as has part of the wall here at Byurakan; old photographs show that the wall once obscured the blind arcades on the south façade. An intricately carved khachkar stands beside the west door. Inside the church there are massive wall piers supporting the arches of the high barrel-vaulted roof. The unusual bema is reached by six steps on each side. Not only is it unusually high but it is also rectangular, a rare shape for a bema in medieval Armenian churches. In spite of the windows being small and high up, this peaceful church feels light and airy.

The second church, **Artavazik**, is much less notable than St John but it has a pretty setting. The tiny ruined cross-dome church is reached by continuing along the right-hand fork from the village square to the far end of the village, then by taking the right fork down into the shallow ravine. The 13th-century belfry over the west door was damaged by lightning.

**Amberd (fortress)** The fortress and church of Amberd are beautifully situated at an altitude of over 2,000m between the gorges of the Amberd and Arkashen rivers and may be inaccessible because of snow as late as May. In late May/June, the fortress and church are surrounded by expanses of bright red oriental poppies, geraniums, various peas including the Persian everlasting pea *Lathyrus rotundifolius*, a relative of the garden-popular perennial pea, and the tall *Nectaroscordum siculum*, an onion relatively rare in the wild but often grown in UK gardens. In nearby grassland grows the striking borage relative *Solenanthus circinatus* with its metre-high stems of bluish-purple flowers. To reach the site, turn west off the H20 road about 14km north of Byurakan. In clear weather spectacular views of the church and fortress can be obtained from the approach road with Mount Ararat in the background, a view all the more impressive because the café does not obtrude when viewing from this direction. The owner of the **café** (⊕ May–end Oct, depending on weather) lives on-site, so opens the café when tourists arrive and closes when they have all gone.

The **church**, a typical cross-dome structure with an umbrella cupola, is older than the present fortress, having been built in 1026 by Prince Vahram Pahlavuni, leader of the Armenian forces who fought against the incorporation of Ani into the Byzantine Empire. The present **fortress** dates from the 12th century although there had been a stronghold here since the 7th century which changed hands several times according to the fortunes of war. The final phase of building took place after the brothers Ivane and Zakare Zakarian captured it from the Seljuk Turks in 1196. Acquired by Prince Vache Vachutian in 1215, it withstood Mongol invaders in 1236 but was finally abandoned in 1408.

The approach to the fortress is from the west, the side least protected by natural defences, and the windowless west wall has defensive towers and steps inside the castle up to what would have been a walkway on top of the wall. The eastern side of the fortress is more domestic in appearance. Inside there is evidence of at least three storeys of small rooms and the many windows of differing styles, looking out towards the church, suggest various phases of rebuilding.

Three small buildings at the foot of the fortress on the east have been restored. That nearest the castle (the **cistern** on the site plan) certainly has evidence of a water-related function. The middle building is a small **chapel** while the easternmost, the 13th-century **bathhouse**, has two rooms each with a dome. Grooves in the wall would have held clay water pipes, similar to those visible at Lori Berd near Stepanavan. A path around the outside of the fortress affords good views of the gorge. It is possible to go inside the castle. Many people scramble up the steep scree-like slope visible from the car park but the easiest (and official) way in is through the door in the east wall; a path goes off between the chapel and cistern. (Note that, inside, some of the walls don't seem too stable.)

**Tegher Monastery**  Another attractive and interesting monastery in this area is Tegher in the village of the same name. It was founded by Prince Vache Vachutian's wife Mamakhatun in 1213. Constructed of basalt and commanding extensive views over the plains below, it can be reached via turn-offs at Antarut or Agarak, depending on whether you are coming from above or below. The oldest part is the **Mother of God Church** with round tambour and conical roof. The front of the altar dais shows seven arches (filled with new paintings depicting scenes from the life of Christ), said to symbolise that this was the seventh church built by the family. To its right is a now blocked-off secret passage down into the river gorge for water and escape. The large **gavit** of 1232 is particularly attractive with decoration around the base of its cupola: the pillars supporting the roof were brought from 10km away. Set into the floor is the grave of the founder and her husband and, more unusually, one grave depicting the deceased as having only one leg and another indicating that the deceased, a stillborn child, had been buried with feet pointing west rather than east. Two small chapels are perched on the west end of the roof of the gavit; entrance to them is only from the roof, presumably by ladder. Perhaps they were used as semi-secret storage areas. A suggestion has been made that the students slept here, the removable ladders being one way of curtailing night-time excursions! In the vicinity are the remains of other buildings including a **bread oven** just below the church. On the adjacent hillock are the ruins of the old Tegher village. Behind the church is a **picnic area** and some visitors **camp** here then walk the 12km over the hills to Amberd.

Continuing south from Tegher the road descends through **Aghdzk** village. On the east side of the village street are the ruins of a 4th-century three-aisle **basilica church**, to the south of which is a **mausoleum**, originally of two storeys but with only the subterranean part now intact. According to the early historians Movses Khorenatsi and Pavstos Buzand, the mausoleum was built in AD364, in the period of the Armenian-Persian war, to house the bones of the kings of the Arshakuni dynasty which had been seized by the Persians but were then recaptured by the Armenian leader Vasak Mamikonian. The carvings in the chamber date from the late 4th or early 5th century and are unique in early Armenian Christian art. On the north wall is Daniel in the lions' den while on the south is a boar hunt. A torch is essential for seeing the carvings.

**THE WESTERN STEPPES OF ARAGATSOTN** The arid steppe which forms the western part of Aragatsotn is a complete contrast to the eastern and central parts of the province and is crossed by the M1 Yerevan to Gyumri road. For convenience the western slopes of Aragats are included here as they too are best accessed from that highway.

**Parpi** Parpi is an attractive village with three interesting churches. The statue in the centre of the village, of a seated man reading a book, is Ghazar Parpetsi, a chronicler and historian born in Parpi around AD442 and best known for his *History of Armenia* written in the 6th century. Nearby is the 5th-century **Tsiranavor Church**. What is particularly interesting about this church is that it is very easy to appreciate the several conversions it has undergone. The 5th-century building was a hall church with relatively wide windows high up. It probably had a wooden roof. In the 7th century the roof was converted into a stone, barrel-vaulted one with the addition of wall piers and arches. Note how the arches supporting the roof have been built in front of older windows in the south and west walls. In the 10th century the church was fortified by building a second wall outside the first; it is this defensive wall which is the first to be seen on arriving. Outside, its construction can best be seen at the ruined east end of the church; inside, it is most obvious blocking the double west window. Entering the church from the west, one first goes through the low doorway in the defensive wall, with its heavy stone door pivoted above and below (a similar door can be seen at Aruch; page 200), and then through the doorway in the earlier wall.

You may have spotted **Targmanchats** (Holy Translator) **Church** up to the right, within a cemetery, on entering the village. Built in the 7th century, rebuilt in the 10th–13th centuries and now fully restored, this small tetraconch church has a wealth of carved detail, most notably on the capitals of the double columns flanking the doorway and the huge lintel with its trinity of large geometric shapes. In the angles between the wings of the church there are half-columns with decorated capitals. Unfortunately the two birds over the east window have lost their heads.

From Targmanchats a third church, **St Gregory**, is visible just across the main road. The restored church may be locked but the grounds are worth exploring. A medieval cemetery spreads over the hill. Around the church, excavations have uncovered what was obviously a large building within which the present church stands and on top of which are more recent graves. Carved stone fragments line the excavation.

**Agarak** West of Ashtarak is Agarak (Farm) where a large site, dating from the 3rd millennium BC, was excavated during the first decade of this century. The site occupies 200ha on an extensive outcrop of tuff. Finds indicate occupation from the Early Bronze to Middle Iron ages, the Urartian period (8th–6th centuries BC), the early Christian era, the medieval period (12th–14th centuries AD) and a final phase from the 17th to 18th century. The foundations and walls of many buildings are visible around the periphery of the site which is signposted on the left just after leaving the village on the M1 heading west. After an information board the track veers right, uphill. Keeping close to the weather-beaten cliff-like rock on your right you reach a 1m³ cavity in the white tuff. At the bottom is a small passageway, 50cm long, which leads into an underground 2m³ chamber. Carved into the walls are large rectangular niches. Apparently a complete skeleton and weapons, thought to be Urartian, were found in this rock-cut sepulchre. A torch is essential if you wish to explore. On the top of the rocky outcrop, removal of the thin layer of topsoil has revealed numerous pits carved into the rock. Some are deep and either rectangular or circular, while others are shallow and have an obvious channel running from them. Some are now filled with water, creating small ponds in which irises and frogs flourish. Yet others look very like the rock-hewn coffins in places such as Lmbatavank. More mundanely, Agarak is also the location of one of Armenia's largest dairies (actually named after Ashtarak), whose products can be found in more or less every grocery and supermarket in the country.

**Kosh** Behind the village cemetery is a hill on which are the remains of a small **13th-century castle** built on an earlier foundation. It is rectangular in shape with round corner towers. In the cemetery itself are the 13th-century **church of St Gregory** complete with two sundials, and the 19th-century **church of St George**. More interesting than either, however, is the nearby 7th-century **church of St Stephen**. The well-preserved church is perched on a ledge so narrow in the side of the gorge that the shape of the roof had to be adjusted to avoid an overhanging rock. One of the church's corners is supported by a pile of rocks, more dramatic before the recent path around the church was laid but still visible. Inside can be discerned the remains of frescoes.

**Aruch** Just south off the M1 main road is the monastery of **Aruchavank** in Aruch village. The large **cathedral church of St Gregory** was built of red and grey tuff in 666 when Aruch was the seat of Grigor Mamikonian, a prince who enjoyed local autonomy during the period of Arab rule. The cupola of the church has collapsed, remaining unrestored when some work was carried out between 1946 and 1948. More recently the windows have been glazed but the cupola is still missing. The church is unusual for one so large in having only a single nave. There are the remains of the frescoes in the apse. A cemetery with recumbent 19th-century gravestones surrounds the church and in the south of the precinct are the remains of Grigor Mamikonian's palace. The main palace building is immediately south of the cathedral. It consists of a three-aisled hall with a row of rooms on its south side. On the north side was another row of rooms and beyond them a gallery. The bases of the columns which supported the roof of the hall are still in place and two carved capitals also survive. To the east of this complex is another separate three-aisled building, possibly a church, possibly a reception hall, the lower parts of its massive pillars still standing. In the Middle Ages the building was fortified, as were some churches, and the remains of the defensive wall built round the outside can be seen. At the east end is a large stone door which pivoted top and bottom, very like that in Parpi's Tsiranavor Church. To the northeast stands a 4th-century, single-nave church.

Away from the centre of the village, Aruch also has a **ruined 13th-century caravanserai**, possibly Armenia's most frequently noticed as it is just a few metres from the M1 Yerevan to Gyumri road on the south side. When built it was on the main route linking the then important Silk Road cities of Tabriz (in present-day

Iran), Dvin and Kars (in present-day Turkey). The caravanserai is commended as a stop for birdwatchers as it is an excellent location for the larks, wheatears and other birds of this arid plain.

For those who enjoy exploring the remains of Bronze Age fortresses, a further detour southeast from Aruch to **Shamiram** may be worthwhile. The remains of the fortress are situated above the merging point of two relatively low but attractive gorges. On the opposite side of the furthermost gorge is a huge tomb field with some very tall standing stones.

**Irind** Between the large cathedrals of Aruch and Talin is the important 7th-century **octagonal church** at Irind, north of the main road. At the time of research, restoration of the main building was nearing completion. Inside there are seven apses of equal size, the eighth being replaced by the rectangular west entrance. The east apse houses the bema and from the two adjacent apses square corner rooms go off eastwards, making the exterior of the church rectangular at the east end as well as at the west. The octagonal tambour rests on the arches over the apses. Each apse has a window and in the tambour there is a window over each apse. Externally there are triangular niches between the apses and the whole rests on a stepped base which follows the church's contours.

**Talin** The next points of interest as you head west are in the small town of Talin just south of the M1 main road, populous enough to have a handful of basic services including a post office, bank, medical centre and pharmacy, as well as a farmers' market. The semi-ruined **cathedral** here is larger and more ornate than that at Aruch. Like Aruchavank it was built in the 7th century, but it has three naves and three polygonal apses and is an altogether more impressive building of red and grey tuff with a 12-sided tambour decorated with arches into which windows are set. There is good 7th-century decoration around some of the windows. The remains of frescoes can be seen. The one in the apse probably depicts the Transfiguration while on the south wall can be seen a portion of the entry into Jerusalem. The cathedral lost its cupola in an earthquake in 1840 and was further damaged by another in 1931, although some restoration was carried out in 1947 and again between 1972 and 1976. The smaller church in the southeast corner of the site is roughly contemporaneous; an inscription records that Nerseh built it 'in the name of the Holy Mother of God for her intercession for me and my wife and Hrapat my son'. Unfortunately it isn't clear which of several Nersehs was involved. Near the small church are a number of stelae with Christian carvings, their shape harking back to pre-Christian vishaps. On the edge of Talin to the south is a very large **ruinous caravanserai**: its sheer size is testament to the importance of the trade routes across Armenia.

**Dashtadem** In Dashtadem, 6km south of Talin, is a large **fortress** whose perimeter walls are entered through an arched gateway over which are interesting carvings of animals. Built according to the best theories of castle building, the gateway requires anyone entering to turn through a right angle thus preventing horsemen charging the entry. Within is a keep of the 9th or 10th century to which half-round towers have been added at some later date and under which large cellars can be explored. An Arabic inscription of the month of Safar 570 (ie: September 1174) on the fortress records that it was then under the control of Sultan Ibn Mahmud, one of the Shaddadid Seljuk princes who ruled in Ani. The keep has been restored, not entirely felicitously, and the small 10th-century chapel against its inner wall has been rebuilt. If the door is not locked it is possible to scramble up on to the walls of the keep from where there are good views but care is needed; there are no safety precautions. There are also good views from the surrounding defensive wall, especially towards the south, across the extensive ruins of an old settlement, to the church of St Christopher. Until recently inhabited by local villagers, the fortress is currently in limbo due to various stalled restoration efforts – no longer a living community, but not an appealing ancient monument either.

Good views of the fortress on its hill can be obtained by continuing south along the M9 main road. About 2km along this road a khachkar marks a track going off left which leads to the restored 7th-century **church of St Christopher**, built of rather forbidding grey stone. Nearby is a rectangular tower with sloping sides; a 13th-century belltower according to the Soviet-era plaque. Around the church is an extensive graveyard in use from the 6th century to the present day.

**Mastara** Mastara is yet another village now bypassed by the main road but the **church** here definitely warrants the short detour necessary to see it. Constructed of red tuff, most of the present structure dates from rebuilding carried out in the 7th century: it has never suffered significant earthquake damage. A surprisingly large construction, it has a massive octagonal tambour supporting a 12-panel cupola. The tambour in turn is supported by eight large arches, or squinches, and eight smaller ones. This unusual design is found in other 7th-century churches which are referred to as being of the Mastara type. Inside the church there is a great feeling of height – it is 21m from floor to cupola. Floor space for worshippers is larger than in plain cross-shaped churches, achieved by rectangular corners protruding between the apses. Thus, internally the church is square with four protruding apses; externally the alternating pentagonal apses and the square corners surround the tambour. The single-storey east corner rooms, built at the same time as the church, are tucked into the angle each side of the east apse. The tambour admits light by a window on each side, those on the cardinal points being wider. The rather incongruous balcony on the west side dates from the building's use as a grain store for the local collective farm from 1935 until 1993. The church is dedicated to St John the Baptist whose relics, brought back from Caesarea by St Gregory the Illuminator, are said to be buried at the site.

**Garnahovit** The road through Mastara continues northeast to another architecturally important church, that of St George, at Garnahovit. The round dome of the huge 7th-century **church of St George**, fully restored, looms over the village. It has the same composition as the much better-known church of St Hripsime at Etchmiadzin (page 220). Rectangular externally, inside there are four apses at the cardinal points and between the apses four three-quarter-circle niches, each of which in turn leads into a square corner room. There is a structurally important difference from St Hripsime. In the latter, the entrances to the round niches are set squarely across the right angles of the basically square floor plan. Here at St George they are positioned asymmetrically: the two eastern ones turned a little to the east, the two western ones to the west. The transition to the octagonal tambour is by arches over the apses and by fan vaults over the round niches. The cardinal sides of the tambour have two large windows, the diagonal sides smaller ones. Externally, niches play an important part in the decoration as well as reducing the bulk of stone. St George has the common triangular niches each side of the apses, here rounded in their upper halves, but there are also niches below the gable on each side and at the corners of the tambour. The twin half-columns with a single capital in the niches of the west façade, typical of the second half of the 7th century, echo the portal frame.

# ARARAT PROVINCE

Ararat province lies to the southeast of Yerevan and has two distinct parts: the irrigated plateau at around 900m elevation which borders the **Arax River** (forming the border with Turkey), and the mountains that limit this plateau to the east which rise to 2,445m at Mount Urts. A fairly large area within these mountains comprises the government-administered **Khosrov Forest State Reserve** (page 207) and the privately run **Caucasus Wildlife Refuge**; to their northeast the land rises to become the Geghama mountain range, which roughly delimits the Gegharkunik provincial border. The fertile plateau enjoys a longer growing season than other parts of Armenia and thus supports a large portion of the country's fruit and vegetable production, from new industrial operations near the highway to quiet terraced orchards in the foothills. To the south, the province is bordered by the Azeri exclave of Nakhichevan; the old road and rail links are of course closed.

**Mount Ararat** is in Turkey, but the name of this province recognises that it is the region of present-day Armenia nearest the biblical mountain: it is only 33km from **Khor Virap Monastery** (page 206) to the 5,165m peak. The whole massif looms high and spectacular above the plateau, and the views are particularly stunning during the early summer (late May and early June) and autumn (late September and October) when visibility is at its best. It is especially beautiful in early morning and late evening.

The provincial capital of **Artashat**, 29km from Yerevan, is on the edge of the plain. Modern Artashat is some 5km northwest of ancient Artashat, established in 185BC by King Artashes I as his capital and retaining that role until the reign of Khosrov III (AD330–38), when the capital was moved to **Dvin** (page 205).

**GETTING THERE AND AROUND** The towns and villages in the province are served by minibuses from Yerevan which depart from the Intertown Bus Station. (See box, page 87 for more information on minibuses.) The few train services are timed mainly for people commuting to Yerevan and are unlikely to be of much use to visitors. Taxis (page 87) are also an option. The main highway from Yerevan to southern Armenia crosses the plateau before following the southern border of the province east and crossing into neighbouring Vayots Dzor province over the Tukh Manuk Pass. This road carries all heavy goods traffic between Yerevan and the Iranian border and is gradually being upgraded to become the North–South Highway. A quieter and more scenic route for visitors with their own transport – especially recommended for cyclists and motorcyclists – follows the H10 via Vedi and Urtsadzor before rejoining the main road before the Tukh Manuk Pass.

**WHERE TO STAY**  *Map, page 204*
Khor Virap and Dvin do not require an overnight stay for visitors starting from Yerevan. Those wishing to visit the southern part of the Khosrov Forest State Reserve or the Caucasus Wildlife Refuge for more than a day have several options, from nearby guesthouses to on-site accommodation and camping. For accommodation near the northern entrance of Khosrov Forest State Reserve, see page 240.

**Sunchild Eco Lodge**  (4 rooms) 7km from Urtsadzor village; m 077 444184; e hello@set.am; w set.am. Upscale non-profit 'green' guesthouse mainly intended for people on Sunchild's tour packages, though anyone can book a room.

Dbl/twin rooms on offer, some en suite. Hiking, mountain biking, horseriding & 4x4 tours available in the privately run Caucasus Wildlife Refuge adjoining (but not to be confused with) Khosrov Forest State Reserve. Kitchen for the use of guests.

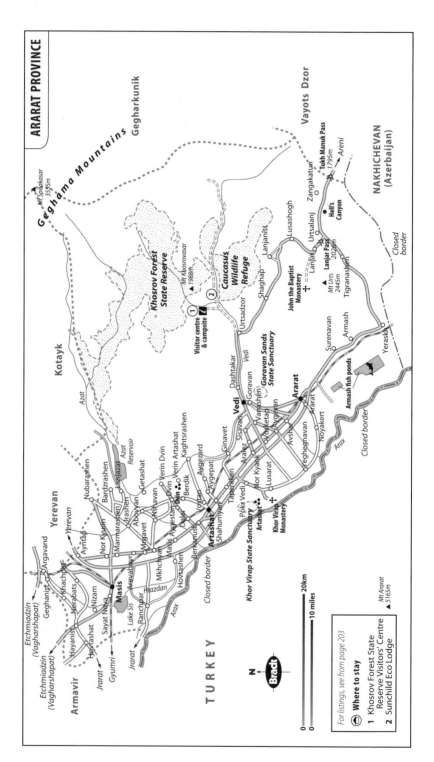

ARARAT PROVINCE

Geghama Mountains

Gegharkunik

▲ Mt Spitakasar
3555m

Khosrov Forest
State Reserve

▲ Mt Khosrovasar
1988m

Caucasus
Wildlife
Refuge

Kotayk

Vayots Dzor

Tukh Manuk Pass
1795m → Areni

Zangakatun

Lusashogh

Lanjanist

Shaghap

Urtsalani
Hell's
Canyon

NAKHICHEVAN
(Azerbaijan)

Lanjar
Lanjar Pass
2025m

† John the Baptist
Monastery

▲ Mt Urts
2445m

Tigranashen

Closed
border

Urtsadzor

① Visitor centre
& campsite ②

Vedi
Dashtakar

Goravan

Goravan Sands
State Sanctuary

Vedi

Surenavan

Armash

Yeraskh

Ararat

Ararat

Armash fish ponds

Closed border

Arax

Noyakert

Yeghegnavan

Avshar

Lusarat

Nor Kyakh

Taperakan

Malez

Sisavan

Vanashen

Noshatap

Aygavan

Ginavet

Aygezard

Azat

Azat
Reservoir

Nubarashen

Bardzrashen

Lanjazat

Getashat

Verin Dvin

Verin Artashat

Kaghtsrashen

Aygepat

Nshavan

Dalar

Dvin

Berdik

Mrganush

Mkhchyan

Hovhari

Hovtashat

Nor Kyurin

Marmarashen

Abovyan

Masis

Aygestan

Dvin

Aygavan

Shahumyan

P'ok Vedi

Artashat

Khor Virap
Monastery

Artashat

Khor Virap State Sanctuary

Berkanush

Arevabuyr

Hrazdan

Ranchpar

Lake Sis

Sayat Nova

Nizam

Khachpar

Geghanist

Norabats

Argavand

Geghanist

Etchmiadzin
(Vagharshapat)

Etchmiadzin
(Vagharshapat)

Jrarat

Gyumri

Jrarat

Hayanist

Armavir

Yerevan

Yerevan

Ayntap

Mygavet

TURKEY

Closed border

N

Bradt

0                    20km

0        10 miles

For listings, see from page 203

Ⓘ Where to stay

1  Khosrov Forest State
   Reserve Visitors' Centre
2  Sunchild Eco Lodge

Mt Ararat
▲ 5165m

204

Dorm-style loft beds also available; bring your own sleeping bag (AMD3,000pp, b/fast extra). HB/FB available. If this is full, try one of the several homestays in Urtsadzor village that partner with Sunchild. $$–$$$

🏠 **Khosrov Forest State Reserve Visitors' Centre** [map, page 208] (6 rooms & campsite) 11km from Urtsadzor village; 📞0234 21352; m 099 006030; e khosrovreserve@gmail.com;

w khosrovreserve.am. Basic self-catering hostel featuring twin rooms with a shared kitchen & bathrooms & dining area. The big advantage is its position near the remote southern entrance of Khosrov Forest State Reserve (page 207). A 4x4 is required, or else walk or cycle the 11km dirt track from the Vedi–Urtsadzor road. Also has a tranquil campsite for several tents (AMD1,000 pp) for which reservations not required. $

✗ **WHERE TO EAT AND DRINK** The highway between Yerevan and Yeraskh has various roadside fast-food joints and groceries, and can be an excellent place to buy fresh **local produce** – the first apricots of the season are often found here. Fresh **fish** from the Armash fishponds becomes available as you approach Yeraskh. The towns of Artashat, Ararat and Vedi have their own shops and basic cafés, but none to warrant a detour. There are a few eating options on the route from Pokr Vedi to Khor Virap. In the smaller villages you may be limited to picnicking. The homestays in Urtsadzor and the Sunchild Eco Lodge (page 203) can provide meals on request.

**DVIN** (🕐 The gate in the fence surrounding the site is usually open. The small museum can be opened whenever the resident caretaker is at home.) The excavated ruins of the former Armenian capital Dvin lie about 10km to the east of the main road, on the southern edge of the village of Hnaberd (rather than the current village of Dvin). Even more so than other ruinous sites in Armenia, it is necessary to apply a large dose of imagination to the series of low walls that is all that is left of a city that once housed tens of thousands of people.

Dvin, whose name comes from the pre-Islamic Middle Iranian language family and means 'hill', was established by the Arsacid king Khosrov III in the 4th century, on the foundations of a 3rd-millennium BC settlement, and served as the capital of early medieval Armenia (page 19) until the Arab conquest in AD640 when it became the seat of the governor. It was badly damaged by earthquakes in 863 and again in 893 but remained a significant town until the 13th century with a population, at its peak, probably of the order of 100,000. The second of these earthquakes destroyed what had been **Armenia's largest church**, dedicated to St Gregory and 58m long by 30m wide. Its excavated foundations can be clearly identified, including the layout from at least two of its three rebuildings. Originally a pagan temple, it was rebuilt as a three-nave basilica with an east apse in the late 4th century. It acquired external arcaded galleries in the 5th century. In the 7th century it was rebuilt as a winged three-nave domed basilica, with apses also on the north and south. This church was slightly shorter, hence the double east apse seen today. Mosaics from its floor are now in the museum. To the east of the church is a glazed display of excavated **ceramic pipes** that once supplied water to the site, similar to those seen in the entrance-way of Tatev Monastery. North of the church are the foundations of the 7th-century **palace of the Katholikos**; a capital from one of its columns is now Dvin's best-known exhibit. East of this palace lay a single-nave **5th-century church**. An **earlier palace** (5th century) lay southwest of the main church.

The small **museum** is surrounded by the caretaker's fruit trees. Its contents include finds from the site including examples of the glassware for which Dvin was renowned, particularly in the 7th century. Outside is a collection of carved stones including two large phalluses. The extent of trade is evident in the finding here of coins minted in

The Central Provinces ARARAT PROVINCE

4

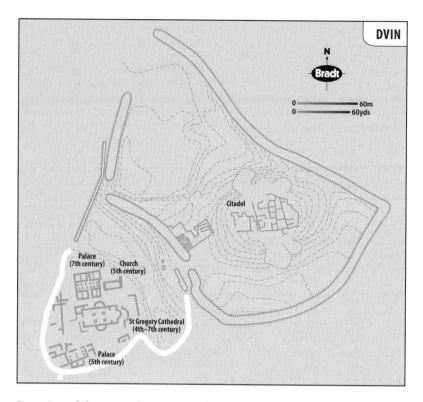

Byzantium while, conversely, coins minted at Dvin have been found in the Baltic states and Scandinavia. Behind the museum a path leads up the hill to the ruins of the **citadel**. While it is difficult to form an idea of Dvin's detailed historic appearance, it is worth making the short walk to the top of the site to gain an idea of the size of the town as well as views over the lower part of the complex and the Arax plain.

**KHOR VIRAP MONASTERY** (⏰ 09.00–18.00 daily) Khor Virap (Deep Dungeon), situated on a small hill in the Ararat plain, can be seen in the distance from the main road which passes 5km to the east: the site is well signposted from the highway. In contrast to Dvin, where few visitors ever go, Khor Virap receives enough people to support several small cafés and snack bars on the approach; there is parking for several coaches, and the site is outfitted with multilingual information boards and vending machines (thankfully the interior of the monastery is now free of tacky souvenirs).

Khor Virap's historical significance is considerable, and there are, in clear weather, superb views of Mount Ararat, whose summit is just 33km away. Architecturally, the monastery is not particularly unusual. It is famous above all as the place where King Trdat III imprisoned St Gregory the Illuminator for 12 years in the late 3rd and early 4th centuries (page 18), and it is still possible to visit the subterranean cell where he was kept. However, although there was a monastery here by the 5th century, the present buildings are much more modern. Construction started in 1669. A large perimeter wall surrounds the **main church** with its 12-sided tambour and cupola. It is dedicated to the Mother of God. Rather plain otherwise, it has an elaborately decorated front to the altar dais. High on the eastern façade is a carving of St Gregory curing the possessed King Trdat.

Access to the cell where Gregory was imprisoned is from the smaller **St Gregory's Church** which is the barrel-vaulted structure at the southwest corner of the walls. To the right of the altar dais is the entrance hole from which a long ladder with 27 steps leads 6.5m down to the surprisingly large underground chamber; the first 2m of descent is very narrow, after which the hole widens. It tends to be stuffy in the chamber because of a lack of air circulation combined with the number of burning candles; those who do venture down should take a torch. (Do not be confused by a second hole to the right of the door of the church. This leads to a separate underground chamber, possibly another prison. The entrance shaft is even narrower than that of St Gregory's cell.)

A path goes from the north side of the monastery to the top of the hill, from where there is a good view of the monastery itself and across the vast irrigated plains on both sides of the border. North of the hill is a small (50ha) wetland area comprising Khor Virap State Sanctuary (administered by Khosrov Forest State Reserve). From this vantage point it is also possible to appreciate something of the scale of **ancient Artashat** which occupied the group of hills surrounding Khor Virap, including the hill on which the monastery was later established. Although it is now possible to see only minor evidence of the city (about which much detail is given on the information boards), it was once a major centre of Hellenistic culture, described by Plutarch as a large and beautiful city, 'Armenia's Carthage', with villas, temples, statuary and an amphitheatre. It was founded as his capital in 185BC by King Artashes I, one of the Armenian kings who ruled with Roman consent after the defeat of Antiochus III at the Battle of Magnesia in 190BC (page 17). Artashat retained its role as capital until the reign of Khosrov III (AD330–38) when it was moved to Dvin (page 205) because the Arax River had changed its course, leaving Artashat without its former defence. The medieval historian, Movses Khorenatsi, described Artashat as being founded at the confluence of the Arax and Metsamor rivers. Such descriptions led to the location of the city being a mystery until the 1920s, the shifting of riverbeds giving a present-day confluence significantly further west than it was when Artashat was built. Excavations were carried out in the 1970s/80s.

On a hillock to the left of Khor Virap as one approaches is a statue of Gevorg Chaush (1870–1907) who led Armenian *fedayi* (armed volunteers) in their struggle against the Turks in Sassoun province, the area in Western Armenia around the source of the Tigris. He was killed in battle.

**KHOSROV FOREST STATE RESERVE** Khosrov is the oldest known nature reserve in the Caucasus, and is sometimes claimed as the oldest in the world, having been founded in the 4th century AD by King Khosrov III after whom the reserve is named (it was in fact founded as a game reserve, though hunting is of course now strictly forbidden). The Soviet Union granted Khosrov reserve status in 1958 and it currently covers 23,214ha of semi-desert, mountain steppe, woodland and subalpine meadow. It is home to a unique range of European and Asian flora and fauna, including endemic, rare and endangered species, such as the Persian leopard, Bezoar ibex and marbled polecat. Lynx, brown bear, wild boar, wolf and Eurasian black vulture also live here. More than half of Armenia's vascular plants (and a third of all those in the entire Caucasus ecoregion) are represented in Khosrov, despite it comprising less than 1% of Armenia's total land area. Unless you are incredibly lucky or specifically here to look for them, you are unlikely to see any of the larger mammals (except perhaps the Bezoar ibex), but the splendid scenery and sites of historic interest will make up for that. A wildfire swept through part

4

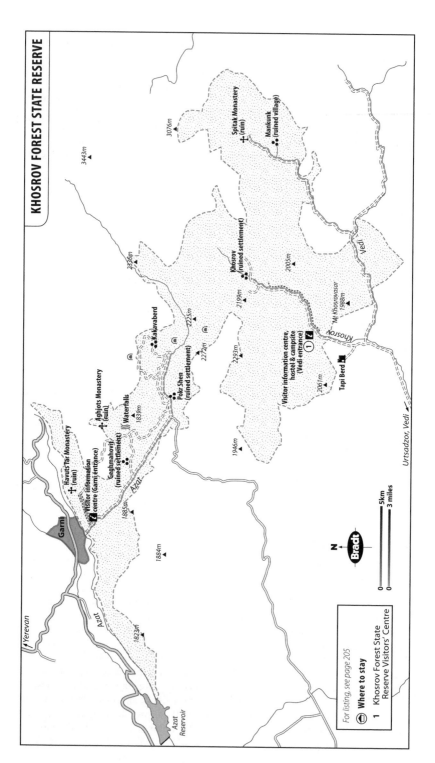

# KHOSROV FOREST STATE RESERVE

*3443m* ▲

*3076m* ▲

**Spitak Monastery**
✝ (ruin)

**Mankunk**
• (ruined village)

*2336m* ▲

**Khosrov**
(ruined settlement)
✝

*2199m* ▲

*2005m* ▲

*2225m* ▲

•• **Kakavaberd**
ⓐ

*2274m* ▲

ⓐ

**Aghjots Monastery**
✝ (ruin)

**Pokr Shen**
(ruined settlement)
••

*2293m* ▲

**Visitor information centre,
hostel & campsite**
(Vedi entrance)
①

*Khosrov*

*Mt Khosrovasar*
*1988m* ▲

*Vedi*

《《 **Waterfalls**

*1839m* ▲

*2061m* ▲

**Tapi Berd** 🏰

**Havuts Tar Monastery**
✝ (ruin)

**Visitor information
centre** (Garni entrance)
ℹ

**Geghmahovit**
(ruined settlement)
••

*Azat*

*1946m* ▲

*Urtsadzor, Vedi*

*1885m* ▲

**Garni**

*1884m* ▲

↑ *Yerevan*

*Azat*

*1823m* ▲

**N**
*Bradt*

0 ————— 5km
0 ————— 3 miles

*Azat
Reservoir*

*For listing, see page 205*

**① Where to stay**

**1** Khosrov Forest State
Reserve Visitors' Centre

of the reserve in the extraordinarily hot summer of 2017, but serious damage was restricted to a region of mature juniper in the Khachadzor district. Conversely, the critically endangered **Persian leopard** (*Panthera pardus tulliana*), also known as the Caucasian leopard, was in early 2018 photographed in the area for the first time in many years by camera traps installed by WWF Armenia (w armenia.panda.org), causing jubilation within the conservation community.

As far as visiting is concerned, Khosrov is best thought of in **two parts**: a northern part entered from Garni (see below) and a southern part entered from a point near Urtsadzor (page 211). Both entrances have official visitor centres to which all visitors must report. Most choose to enter from Garni (which is actually in Kotayk province) as it is closer to Yerevan and can be easily combined with other nearby sites on a day trip; most of the reserve's own historical sites are also best accessed from this entrance. A total of nine official 'ecotourism routes' have been developed, some of which are hiking-only and some of which involve transfers by 4x4. Between them they cover all of the historical sites detailed on pages 210–12, as well as several wonderful natural heritage sites.

All visitors require a **daily permit** to enter the reserve (AMD3,000–4,000 pp depending on which trail you intend to follow), payable upon entry. With the exception of the short Havuts Tar monastery trail from the northern entrance (page 210), it is obligatory to employ one of the reserve's rangers as a guide (AMD10,000/group/day). Any 4x4 transport hired is charged at a rate of AMD500 per km per vehicle; including driver. For the trails beginning at the southern entrance it is possible to arrange in advance for horses to be hired (AMD10,000–15,000 pp). For conservation reasons, overnight stays within the reserve are prohibited, though accommodation (including camping) exists at or near both entrances. These minor inconveniences are more than compensated for by the opportunity to explore in depth one of the most pristine and diverse natural landscapes in the Caucasus and to support the reserve's conservation efforts in doing so.

The administrative **headquarters** of the reserve is in the town of Vedi (79 Kasyan St; ☏0234 21352; m 099 006030; e khosrovreserve@gmail.com; w khosrovreserve. am; ⏰ 09.00–19.00 Mon–Sat). For anyone not organising a guided tour via a local operator in Yerevan, enquiries relating to independent visits should be directed to the very helpful English-speaking staff of the reserve's tourism department, who can make arrangements regarding permits, ranger-guides, 4x4 transport, equipment hire and any other services you may require, as well as overnight stays at the southern entrance's guesthouse and campsite (page 205). There is no requirement to visit the headquarters in person, but it does house a quaint **museum** in which collected specimens of flora and fauna can be viewed. Note that Goravan Sands State Sanctuary, southeast of Vedi, is also administered by the reserve, though of very limited relevance to non-specialist visitors.

**Northern entrance**  Allow two full days to see the main sights in this part of the reserve. All involve walking, some of it strenuous, so good footwear is essential. Trousers and long sleeves give some protection when the walk is through shoulder-high vegetation, some of it thorny. Be sure to take a picnic.

To reach the northern entrance to the reserve **on foot** from Garni take the cobbled track to the left of the temple entrance down into the gorge. Near the end of the short paved section a path goes off to the left. This brings you to a metal gate, entrance to hydro-electric territory. (If you carry straight on down the track which later bears left you end up at the same metal gate by a longer, muddier route.) The guard is usually willing to let people through to walk down; you exit the hydro-electric site near the river. Turn left and continue along the river past the basalt columns to what was a medieval bridge. Having been rebuilt by the American Ambassador's Fund for Cultural Preservation (!) the only suggestion of the old original bridge is the shape of the arch. Cross it and go uphill, following the signs to the **visitor centre**. Allow about 45 minutes from Garni Temple to this point. If **driving**, turn right from the Garni Temple road, then left in front of the information office in the centre of Garni, then second right down to the river. At the river the right-hand turn leads to the basalt columns, the left to the reserve. Go left along the river for about 1km then do a U-turn over the river to wind up the hillside to the visitor centre.

For all sites other than Havuts Tar, a **guide** is required (page 209). The tracks are very rough in places; the reserve staff are expert drivers, very familiar with the terrain. If walking, remember it can be very hot. About 5km from the entrance the tracks to two of the most impressive sites, Aghjots Monastery and Kakavaberd Fortress, diverge at the bridge over a tributary of the Azat. The left track passes the deserted **Baberd** village where there is a 5th-century barrel-vaulted church. After a few more kilometres the reserve vehicle parks beside the Azat River for walks to Aghjots and Kakavaberd.

**Havuts Tar Monastery** The nearest site to the visitor centre (allow at least 4 hours to walk from Garni to Havuts Tar and back), is reached by an easy path which follows the side of the gorge and gives marvellous views both down into the gorge and also of Garni Temple. The monastery is about 3km along this path and, at an altitude of 1,590m, is some 200m higher than Garni Temple. The extensive site comprises two main groups of ruins, eastern and western, with evidence of other structures, or possibly graves, between them. The **western buildings** come into view first but the path approaches the eastern group. Although dating from the 11th–13th centuries the monastery was very badly damaged in the 1679 earthquake and much of what is now seen supposedly dates from its rebuilding in the early 1900s. It must be wondered how much rebuilding actually took place as the appearance of the site is such as to give the impression that Havuts Tar was effectively abandoned in 1679.

The **eastern buildings** were surrounded by a fortified wall which still stands to a considerable height on three sides. The entrance is an arched doorway at the southeast corner. The main church is relatively well preserved and once had a gavit – few traces remain. The western façade and the interior use a mixture of red and black tuff to striking effect and the interior is notable for its carved niches with birds appearing in several. On its north side, work commenced in 1772 on the construction of a new church but it was never finished. Ruins of domestic buildings line the north and south fortified walls.

The west group is dominated by a cross-dome church whose walls are again constructed in a chessboard pattern of red and black tuff. This is probably the **Holy Saviour Church** founded in 1013 by Grigor Pahlavuni (c990–1058), founder also of Kecharis, although some sources state that Holy Saviour is the church in the east group. On the south side of this church is a small vaulted chapel built at a later date.

**Aghjots Monastery** Reach this monastery after a short but steep climb up rocky scree where the scent of thyme, lavender and other aromatic plants fills the air. It is well worth the effort. The monastery, which sometimes seems to merge with the hillside in its overgrown state, comprises the St Stephen Church with its gavit, the church of Sts Peter and Paul (whose carving is the gem of the monastery) with its ruined gavit, together with evidence of other buildings over a wide area. The monastery was sacked by the Persians in 1603 and restored soon afterwards but was then damaged by the 1679 earthquake, despoiled again in the 18th century and finally ruined during Azeri-Armenian clashes in the early 20th century. The **church of St Stephen** was built in the early 13th century and, according to local legend, was founded by St Gregory the Illuminator on the site of the martyrdom of one of St Hripsime's companions, Stepanos by name. The church is a small cross-dome structure missing its tambour and dome. The front of the bema is decorated with carved octagons, all except two containing geometric patterns. Of the other two, one has a pair of birds, the other, wrongly orientated, two heads with tall hats. St Stephen's gavit, added in 1207, is wider than the church and at a lower level. It is ruined but what remains bears a wealth of carving. Ghosting on the west façade of the church shows the position of the gavit arches and how the gavit was added asymmetrically with respect to the church entrance. The **church of Sts Peter and Paul** stands to the north of St Stephen. The strikingly large bas-relief figures of St Peter, on the left, and St Paul, on the right, survive on the church's west façade. Such large figures are very unusual in present-day Armenia although they decorated the 10th-century Holy Cross Church on the island of Aghtamar on Lake Van, once part of Greater Armenia. Present-day examples are on the new church beside Katoghike on Abovyan Street (page 159).

***Kakavaberd (Geghiberd) (fortress)*** This 9th–13th-century fortress (*kakav* is a kind of partridge) must be the most impressive in Armenia. It changed hands many times during its history and is last mentioned in 1224 in historical documents. Three sides of the ridge on which it stands are inaccessibly steep; the walls and towers, 8–10m high, guard the fourth side. From the bridge where the Aghjots and Kakavaberd tracks diverge it is about 8km to Kakavaberd, or 13km from the reserve entrance. From the Azat River it is a strenuous 2-hour climb up to the fortress. The first stretch is uphill through meadows to the base of a high rocky knoll with sheer sides. Skirting the base one enters a ravine which climbs up to the ridge on which Kakavaberd was built. When the fortress first comes into view it looks totally inaccessible but continue up the ravine, sometimes walking along the bed of the stream. Fortunately, the last and steepest climb is through trees which mitigate the heat of the sun. The nearer one gets, the more impressive the high walls with their towers become. Entering the fortress, ingenious use has been made of a sheer rock face. The outer wall has been positioned so that anyone gaining entrance to the fortress had to turn right through a right angle and then go along a narrow passage between wall and rock face, making them very vulnerable to attack from above. Within the fortress not much remains to be seen apart from grassy mounds marking the position of buildings, but the wild flowers are a joy – in early summer there are purple orchids, red poppies, yellow umbellifers, blue harebells, freesias, asphodels, purple vetches, saxifrages, thyme and many more. The panoramic views, especially from the highest point at the far end of the site, are magnificent. Near the entrance a tall ridge of rock forms a natural wall; in it has been carved a tiny chapel, complete with apse, bema and altar.

**Southern entrance** The southern part of the reserve does not boast the same wealth of historic sites as the north but it is better for **wildlife**, having fewer visitors. It contains important bird breeding sites. Most sights (deserted villages, ruined churches, caves) within the southern part of the reserve can be visited in one or two days unless wildlife watching is the main reason for a visit, in which case several days and nights may be necessary. The visitor centre also functions as a self-catering guesthouse and campsite (page 205), though a 4x4 is needed to reach it on the 7km dirt road from Urtsadzor. Three of the nine official ecotourism routes begin from this location, where horses are also available to hire.

**Gevorg Marzpetuni Castle (Tapi Berd)** This is now a small renovated chapel within fortified walls set at the far end of a bowl-like plain surrounded by mountains. It is reached from the dirt road to the Khosrov Forest State Reserve southern entrance, and is visible 1½km before reaching the visitor centre on the left hand side.

**SOUTHERN ARARAT** About 12km east of Yeraskh, the main road crosses the 19km² Azeri exclave of Karki, which has since been renamed **Tigranashen** and partly populated by Armenian refugees from Azerbaijan. Some maps show it as being *de jure* Azeri territory; it has, however, been controlled by Armenia since the Karabagh war.

The remote **monastery of John the Baptist** can be reached on a dirt track from **Lanjar**. The track is poor; the last section needs a 4x4. The monastery is attractively situated among rolling hills. The **Mother of God Church**, built in 1254, has a tall circular tambour and umbrella dome. Over the door is a carving of the Madonna and Child flanked by two angels. Above this is a second carving of Christ with the symbols of the four evangelists at his side and two heads at his feet. Both carvings have a background of deeply incised, ornate, leafy swirls. Inside, the small cross-dome church has an unusual stone altar screen with its own small apse and belfry. The gavit to the west of the church and a mausoleum southwest of the church are both ruined. West of the mausoleum are the two remaining storeys of a three-tier building, the uppermost, a belfry, now lost. It must once have looked similar to the three-storey building at Noravank. The lower storey has no entrance and was probably another mausoleum. The remains of a fortified wall surround the monastery.

Between Urtsalanj and Zangakatun, an unmarked dirt road descends south for 2km to reach so-called **Hell's Canyon**, a favourite **rock-climbing** venue for both trad and sport climbing (visit **w** uptherocks.com for route details). It is also possible, though extremely challenging, to hike right through the canyon, which in some places narrows to just 1.5m in width and requires wading, and in others is overgrown with thorn bushes. Other risks include flash floods and accidentally

---

## TUKH MANUK

Visitors to Armenia will probably best know the words Tukh Manuk as the name of the 1,795m pass between the Ararat and Vayots Dzor provinces. However, they may then become increasingly aware of the term in relation to numerous small chapels or shrines throughout the country, often in remote locations such as hilltops but also common in small villages. Sometimes a corner room of a larger church seems to fulfil the same function. Such shrines are obviously popular, having a multitude of offerings – religious pictures of Jesus Christ or the Virgin Mary, crosses, embroidered items, flowers and other small tokens. It is evident that candles are frequently lit and outside there may be signs of animal sacrifice (page 40).

The shrines are nowadays ostensibly Christian but their roots are thought to originate in pre-Christian times. Literally, *tukh manuk* translates as 'dark youth', a somewhat mysterious figure who seems to hark back perhaps to Zoroastrian Mithra or even further back to a proto Indo-European deity related to Krishna, a manifestation of the Hindu god Vishnu. Interestingly, the name Krishna apparently comes from the Sanskrit for dark or black. No-one quite seems to know who this dark youth is.

top      Built in the 7th century, destroyed by earthquake in the 10th century and lost under layers of debris until the 20th century, Zvartnots Cathedral was a massive round church thought to have been three storeys high (MV/S) page 215

above left      Like its English namesake, Karahunj — known as 'Armenia's Stonehenge' — continues to mystify experts as to its original purpose (SS) page 346

above right      Although there are many groups of khachkars in Armenia, none can rival the 900 at Noratus (MM/S) page 234

below      Garni Temple, as it is called, is Armenia's only Graeco-Roman-style building (MN) page 242

*above*    The cathedral in Yerevan is dedicated to St Gregory the Illuminator (V/S) page 155

*left*    Tatev Monastery, in stunning mountain scenery, is one of Armenia's most popular sites (PS/S) page 351

*below*    Looking up at the dome of Akhtala's Mother of God Church with its superb frescoes (AC) page 296

*above left* Geghard Monastery, partly hewn into the rock and with numerous carvings, is a UNESCO World Heritage Site (r/S) page 244

*above right* The Holy Archangels Church in Etchmiadzin Cathedral precinct is an interesting and unusual modern Armenian church (DH) page 220

*right* The interior of the Sts Peter and Paul Church at Tatev during Lent, with the curtain across the *bema* closed (AC) page 351

*below* The 10th-century monastery of Haghpat is one of several impressive historical sites among the sheer cliffs of the Debed Gorge (SS) page 291

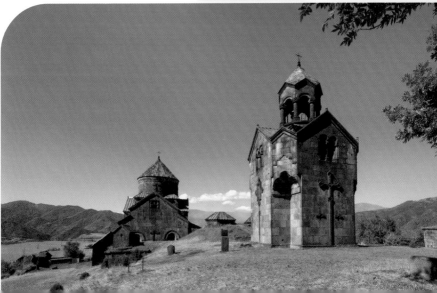

top     Basalt columns in Garni Gorge, known locally as the 'Symphony of Stones' (b/S) page 244

above left     The vividly coloured Caucasian green lizard (*Lacerta strigata*) can be seen in a variety of habitats in Armenia (DH) page 8

above right     The Mediterranean tortoise (*Testudo graeca*) may occasionally be encountered as one crosses a track (DH) page 8

below     The Eurasian hoopoe (*Upupa epops*) is one of 346 bird species recorded in Armenia (LL/S) page 7

*above*    With a surface elevation of 1,900m and a length of 74km, Lake Sevan is one of the world's largest high-altitude lakes (IV/A) page 225

*right*    Parz Lake is one of many starting points in Dilijan National Park for exploring more than 200km of signposted hiking trails (SS) page 310

*below*    The cable-car to Tatev, the world's longest, opened in 2010 and carries passengers high above the valley of the Vorotan River (VT/S) page 351

*top*    Women making *lavash*, Armenia's classic flatbread, in the traditional way (SS) page 99

*above left*    Stone carving remains a flourishing active art form in Armenia (SS)

*above right*    Traditionally women's dances are graceful with elaborate gestures while men's dances are martial and vigorous (SS) page 53

*below*    Bringing the flock down from high summer pastures to winter quarters (MN)

*above left*  Although this famous statue in Stepanakert, Nagorno Karabagh, is officially called *We Are Our Mountains*, it is always affectionately known as *Tatik yev Papik* (Granny and Grandad) (S/D) page 385

*above right*  Ghazanchetsots Cathedral in Shushi, Nagorno Karabagh, is built of strikingly pale stone (G/D) page 387

*right*  The thought-provoking Museum of Missing Soldiers in Stepanakert commemorates soldiers who died during the Nagorno Karabagh war (RK/A) page 384

*below*  Dadivank, one of the largest medieval monastery complexes, is on the northern route between Armenia and Nagorno Karabagh (MO) page 391

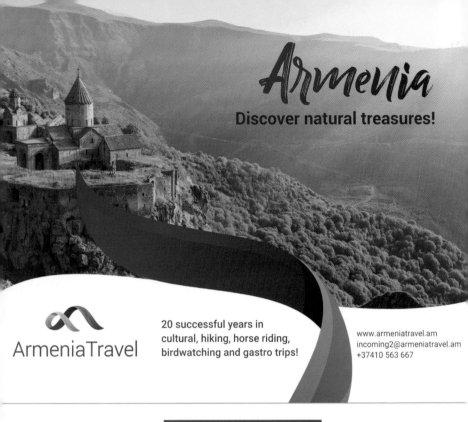

# Armenia

## Discover natural treasures!

ArmeniaTravel

20 successful years in cultural, hiking, horse riding, birdwatching and gastro trips!

www.armeniatravel.am
incoming2@armeniatravel.am
+37410 563 667

crossing into Nakhichevan; it is perhaps best to take a guide if you wish to attempt it! See page 111 for more information on hiking.

In Zangakatun village there is the **house museum of Paruyr Sevak** (page 57) (m 094 034448; ⊕ Mar–Dec 10.00–17.00 Tue–Sun; AMD300) For non-Armenian-speakers who do not know the work of this much-loved Armenian poet there is unfortunately little of interest in the museum. Sevak and his wife are buried in the grounds of what was their home.

## ARMAVIR PROVINCE

The province is named after its capital city, Armavir, which is 46km west of Yerevan along a good dual carriageway. It is unlikely that anyone would choose to stay here as the main concentration of sights is in **Etchmiadzin**, or Vagharshapat as the city is now officially called, only 20km from Yerevan. The churches of Etchmiadzin together with the ruins of Zvartnots Cathedral were added to the UNESCO World Heritage list in 2000. The eastern part of the province merges imperceptibly with Yerevan's western sprawl where it includes Zvartnots International Airport. To the west the province comprises part of the flat and, in summer, hot plain of the broad Arax Valley. The Arax forms the border with Turkey in the south of the province while to the west the border is formed by the Akhurian River. There are several important ancient sites in the province, usually on small hills rising above the flat plain. While there are now little more than low excavated walls to be seen, these sites do hint at the extent and importance of Armenia's distant past. Such sites in Armavir province include **Metsamor**, with its own small museum, Urartian **Argishtikhinili** and Hellenistic **Armavir**. The marshes along the Arax River in the south of the province are the only remaining Armenian breeding ground for the scale insect *Porphyrophora hamelii*, from which was extracted the colourfast, brilliant red dye, *vordan karmir*, used in Armenian illustrated manuscripts and after which the 220ha **sanctuary** encompassing the marshes is named. There is little good hotel accommodation in the province but limited reason to stay here rather than in Yerevan anyway.

**GETTING THERE AND AROUND** Minibuses ply frequently between Yerevan's Central Bus Station (page 87) and the two main towns, Etchmiadzin and Armavir, and from these centres marshrutkas go to local villages. Several other villages are also served directly from Yerevan. The main roads in the province are generally good and the traffic fairly heavy for Armenia. The few **train** services are unlikely to be of use to visitors; there is a daily train from Yerevan to Armavir at 15.50, returning to Yerevan at 16.50 (AMD300). The train to Tbilisi stops at Armavir just before midnight. Slightly more useful are the regular (slow) trains to and from Gyumri which call at Etchmiadzin and Armavir, among other provincial stops – note that the new express train to Gyumri does not stop at either of these stations. See page 85 for more information on trains. As Armavir is flat, with plentiful provincial roads, **cycling** to some of the sites may be an option, perhaps in combination with trains to avoid the hellish industrial outskirts of Yerevan or to shorten the routes to a manageable length.

**✗ WHERE TO EAT AND DRINK** The sights in the province are usually visited as day trips from Yerevan. Etchmiadzin and Armavir have small cafés, and cafés and fast-food kiosks appear along the highway and in the park near Etchmiadzin cathedral precinct in summer. The precinct is also well provided with drinking water fountains. There are two restaurants at Sardarapat (page 223). If you are planning

4

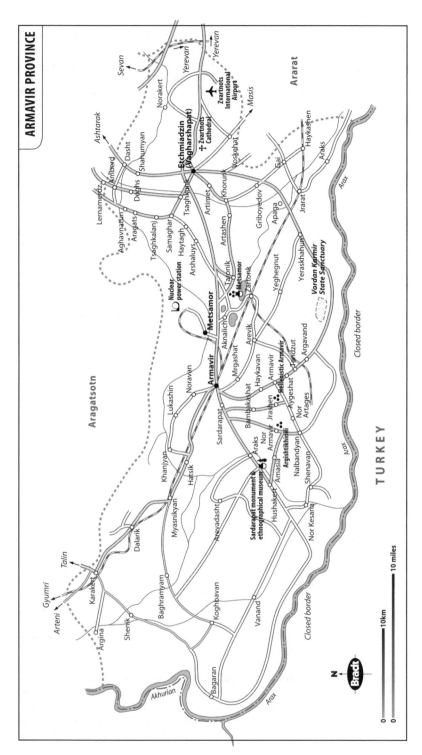

to spend time at Sardarapat or Metsamor in the heat of summer, remember that it can be very hot and there is not much shade at either site. It might be wise to take something to drink with you.

**EASTERN ARMAVIR**  En route to Zvartnots and Etchmiadzin, visitors may notice a red tuff arch at the top of a flight of steps to the north of the main road, but few actually visit it. This is the **Musaler Memorial** commemorating the resistance of Armenians from six villages on the coast of Turkey during the 1915 genocide. Rather than obey Turkish orders to evacuate their homes (and face almost certain death) they built fortifications on the mountain of Musaler and resisted Turkish troops for 53 days; a story depicted in the final scenes of the 2016 Hollywood historical drama film *The Promise*. They were then rescued by French and British naval vessels; some 4,200 people were evacuated to Egypt. After several relocations some settled in Armenia in the present village of Musaler. Inside the red tuff building, with its enigmatic carving and whose shape resembles an eagle, is the **Museum of History of Musaler Battle** (☏ 0237 68373; ⊕ 09.30–17.45 Tue–Sun) which details the events. A second building holds the **Museum of Ethnography of Armenians of Musaler** (with the same opening hours) showing the everyday life of the people of Musaler. An adjacent open space, with rows of low, narrow platforms, is where the traditional *harissa* (a thick porridge-like soup) is prepared. Every year on the third weekend of September descendants of the survivors of Musaler gather to celebrate and partake of the *harissa* which has been simmered and stirred overnight.

**Zvartnots Cathedral**  (⊕ 10.00–17.30 Tue–Sun, last entry 30mins before closing; guided tour in English AMD4,000; car parking AMD100; adult AMD1,300 for foreigners or AMD500 for citizens of Armenia, child AMD100) The ruin of the huge Zvartnots (Celestial Angels) Cathedral, dedicated to St Gregory, lies to the south of the road and the entrance driveway is marked by elaborate gates and an eagle with a ring in its beak gazing back over its shoulder, the work of the famous artist and sculptor Yervand Kochar. The complex comprises the cathedral, the royal palace of Nerses in the southwest, a winery to the south and a modern museum, all set among attractive orchards and rows of newly planted fruit trees (a free and tasty bonus for those whose visits correspond with the June apricot season). Excavations revealed that the cathedral was built on structures which date back to the reign of the Urartian king Rusa II (c685–c645BC). Built between 643 and 652 by Katholikos Nerses III, it is believed to have been a three-storey structure, constructed on a multistep stylobate, but modern artists' impressions of its appearance, such as that on display in the nearby museum, are inevitably conjectural. Intended to surpass even Etchmiadzin Cathedral in its grandeur, it is usually thought of as having been circular but in reality had 32 equal sides. Decorated with frescoes, it was destroyed, probably by an earthquake in 930, to be lost under layers of dirt and debris and even the location was forgotten until its rediscovery in the early 20th century. Some limited reconstruction has been carried out, but protests have caused plans for a more thorough one to be suspended.

The interior of the cathedral consists of four apses; the eastern one housing the bema has a solid wall, while the other three each have six columns forming open semicircles. The massive pillars between the apses supported the upper tiers, tambour and cupola. On the southern side of the bema are the remains of a pulpit and in front is what looks like a baptistery in the floor reached by going down some steps, although it is now labelled as the reliquary of St Gregory the Illuminator, for whom the cathedral is named. Within the outer polygonal wall an ambulatory surrounds the whole inner quatrefoil. At the east end of the quadrilateral structure

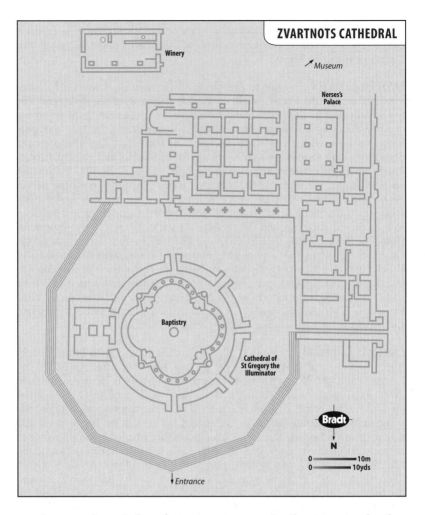

Winery

Museum

Nerses's
Palace

Baptistry

Cathedral of
St Gregory the
Illuminator

**Bradt**

N

0 ━━━━━ 10m
0 ━━━━━ 10yds

Entrance

was the vestry, the equivalent of eastern corner rooms in other Armenian churches. To the east of the cathedral, various stones are laid out according to which storey of the building they are thought to belong. There is some interesting sculptured decoration among the ruins, including one capital on the southeast pillar carved with a fine representation of an eagle. **Nerses's Palace** to the southwest consists of a labyrinth of rooms, well labelled, and a winery with vats sunk into the ground lies to the south.

At the far southwest corner of the site is the **museum** (☏010 545570; ⊕ 10.00–17.00 Tue–Sat, 10.00–15.00 Sun; inc in entrance ticket) which contains a wealth of information in Armenian, Russian and English, with attractive displays of artefacts found during excavation and a wooden maquette depicting how architectural historian Toros Toramanian (1864–1934) believed the cathedral would have looked. Outside the museum is a basalt stele with a cuneiform inscription recording the construction of a canal from the Hrazdan River by King Rusa II. Scattered about the site are metal brackets presumably intended to hold interpretative signboards; at the time of research they appeared to have remained unfinished for several years.

**ETCHMIADZIN** Officially Vagharshapat since 1995, yet still almost universally referred to by its old name, Etchmiadzin is Armenia's fourth most populous city. The central square is Komitas Square, where a statue of Komitas by the same Yervand Kochar responsible for the eagle at Zvartnots was erected in 1969. Attractive parks with fountains and walkways stretch east back towards Yerevan through the city centre. On the south side of the square is one of several entrances to the **cathedral precinct**, beyond which most visitors rarely venture. A few hundred metres west along Khorenatsi can be found the bus station – actually just a section of street – from where minibuses (AMD250) and buses (AMD200) return to Yerevan's Central Bus Station, departing every few minutes throughout the day when full.

**Cathedral precinct** Known in Armenian as the Mayrator ('Mother See', literally 'Mother Seat'), Etchmiadzin became the spiritual centre for Armenia's Christians shortly after the country's conversion in the early 4th century. Today this vast complex houses a religious seminary and all the administrative mechanisms of the Armenian Apostolic Church, as well as being a pilgrimage site for followers of the Church worldwide; its touristic element is in reality a mere sideshow. In recent years there has been, and continues to be, a considerable building programme, with extensive renovation of the main cathedral in progress at the time of research, the roof and belltower clad in scaffolding and much of the interior similarly obscured.

On the basis of archaeological evidence, the first church at Etchmiadzin was of the basilica form but it was rebuilt in the 480s on a cruciform plan with four free-standing piers, four projecting apses which are circular on the interior and polygonal on the outside, and with a cupola. It was this second church, with cupola, which corresponds to Agathangelos's report of Gregory's vision (page 18), a report which fixed in Armenian culture the idea that churches should be cruciform in shape and should have cupolas. Further rebuilding was carried out in the 7th century and Etchmiadzin remained the seat of the Katholikos until 1065 when the then Katholikos Gregory II was forced to flee by the Turkish Seljuk invaders who were ransacking monasteries. He moved to the Armenian principality of Cilicia (roughly the region of present-day Turkey around Adana and Tarsus at the extreme northeast corner of the Mediterranean Sea) and the seat of the Katholikos remained

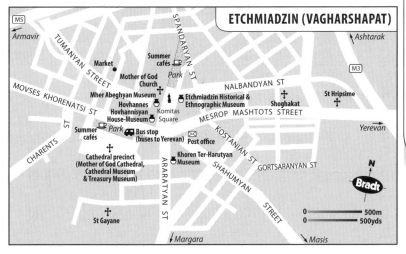

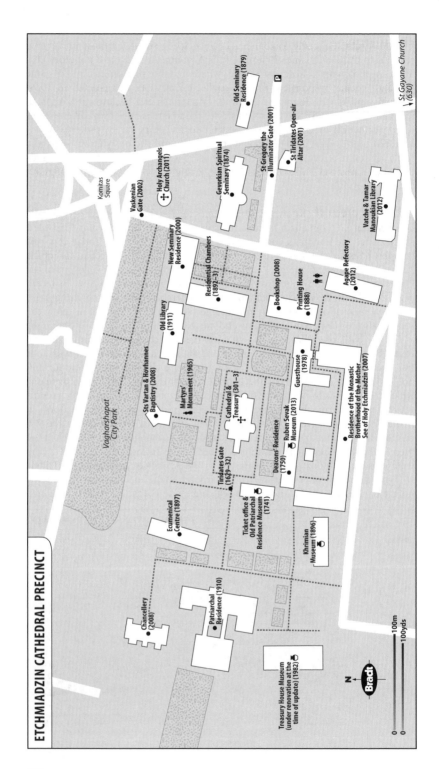

ETCHMIADZIN CATHEDRAL PRECINCT

Komitas Square

Vagharshapat City Park

Old Seminary Residence (1879)

St Gregory the Illuminator Gate (2001)

St Tiridates Open-air Altar (2001)

Gevorkian Spiritual Seminary (1874)

Vatche & Tamar Manoukian Library (2012)

St Gayane Church (630)

Holy Archangels Church (2011)

Vaskenian Gate (2002)

New Seminary Residence (2000)

Residential Chambers (1892–3)

Bookshop (2008)

Printing House (1888)

Agape Refectory (2012)

Old Library (1911)

Sts Vartan & Hovhannes Baptistry (2008)

Martyrs' Monument (1965)

Cathedral & Treasury (301–3)

Guesthouse (1978)

Residence of the Monastic Brotherhood of the Mother See of Holy Etchmiadzin (2007)

Tiridates Gate (1629–32)

Ruben Sevak Museum (2013)

Deacons' Residence

Ecumenical Centre (1897)

Ticket office & Old Patriarchal Residence Museum (1741)

Khrimian Museum (1896)

Chancellery (2008)

Patriarchal Residence (1910)

Treasury House Museum (under renovation at the time of update) (1982)

N

Bradt

100m
100yds
0
0

there even after Cilicia fell to the Egyptian Mamluks in 1375. Ultimately in 1441 a council decided that the seat of the Katholikos should return to Etchmiadzin. There are no records of any immediate reconstruction but the monastery was certainly in a very dilapidated state, with the roof in ruins and some facing stones having fallen, when in 1627 renovation eventually started. A wall was built around the precinct at this time and numerous service buildings were added. However, these were mostly destroyed in 1635–36 during the wars between Persia and Turkey for domination over Armenia and further rebuilding was required. The large three-storey belltower was built over the western doorway in 1654. Three smaller six-column rotundas were added at the beginning of the 18th century; that at the southern apse collapsed in 1921 to be replaced by a new structure.

The **cathedral** (w armenianchurch.org; ⊕ 07.00–21.00; see website for service times) that visitors see now is the site of a pagan temple used as the location for a new Christian church in the 4th century, rebuilt in a quite different style in the 5th century and then very extensively renovated in the 17th. The tambour with its decorative medallions and cupola, the elaborately carved belltower and much of the exterior carving are pure 17th century, as are the surrounding wall and service buildings. The oldest wall of the cathedral is the northern, which is the 5th-century original. The exterior retains two 5th-century figured reliefs with Greek inscriptions, one showing St Thecia and St Paul, the other a cross flanked by two doves. In 1720, frescoes were added inside the cathedral but they were removed in 1891 only to be reinstated in 1956. The interior is still, as in AD480, dominated by the four massive free-standing pillars supporting the tambour. In the very centre is a stepped holy table (the steps representing the hierarchy of angels) bearing many candlesticks and crosses. Surrounded by a framework from which hang lamps and incense burners, it is said to mark the spot where the 'Only Begotten' appeared to St Gregory, telling him to build a church. The frescoes, the use of marble for floor and balustrade, the embroidered curtains, and the candles and crosses on the holy table give a much more decorative feel to the building than exists in any other church in Armenia.

The **Cathedral Museum** (⊕ 10.00–17.00 Tue–Sat, on Sun it opens only after the end of the service – usually around 13.30 but later if there is something special such as an ordination; guided tours only; AMD1,500) is reached through a door to the right of the altar dais. The museum isn't well labelled but English-speaking deacons are available. The **treasury** contains some curious items – including what is claimed to be the lance that pierced the side of Christ, brought to Armenia by the apostle Thaddeus and long kept at Geghard; the hand of St Gregory the Illuminator; wood from Noah's Ark (carbon-dated to 6,000 years old); a drop of St Hripsime's blood, and similar relics – as well as more ordinary ecclesiastical pieces.

Interested visitors can also arrange in advance (through a tour operator in Yerevan; page 67) for admission to the separate **Treasury House Museum** (closed for renovation at the time of update), where a similar collection of historic ecclesiastical items is displayed.

The cathedral is surrounded by pleasant gardens in which original and replica khachkars from different parts of Greater Armenia have been erected; their Soviet-era labels are unfortunately in Russian and Armenian only. The building housing the Treasury House Museum (see above) dates from 1869 and is one of the few Tsarist-era buildings here. The seminary, closed during the Soviet period but reopened in 1997, is another. The carved wooden doors are also Tsarist-era and were made at Tbilisi in 1888. The **Ruben Sevak Museum** was renovated by the French-Armenian philanthropist Hovhannes Chilingaryan, Sevak's nephew. Born Rupen

Chilingiryan in Silivri, modern-day Turkey, Sevak (1886–1915) was an Armenian poet and writer who studied medicine in Switzerland and moved to Constantinople in 1914. The following year, at the onset of the Armenian Genocide, the Ottomans offered Sevak his life if he would accept Islam and marry the daughter of a Turkish official; he chose to be loyal to his family and was executed. Around 200 unique and valuable paintings are displayed in the museum. There is also a collection of the renowned writer's possessions, including charcoal drawings, personal effects and documents, historical items, valuable Armenian works of art and pieces by Western artists. The handwritten letters that Ruben wrote to his wife, Yanni, in French, are deeply touching.

The eastern, **main gateway** into the cathedral precinct commemorates the visit of Pope John Paul II in 2001. Its four tall pillars joined by arches, forming a rectangular space open at the top, suggest the shape of a church without a dome, perhaps representing St Gregory's vision (page 18). On its eastern, outer aspect are the carved figures of St Gregory and King Trdat III facing each other, a central cross between them. On the west face are the figures of the two apostles, Thaddeus and Bartholomew, who are believed to have brought Christianity to Armenia in the 1st century AD.

A **baptismal chapel**, built in 2010 and entered from the north perimeter wall, has provision for infant baptism. A previous provision for adult baptism by immersion (sunk into the floor) no longer exists. Apparently a number of people accidentally fell into it, in spite of it being roped off, and the cathedral authorities thought it safer to remove it. Near the north gate of the precinct is a striking tall round (actually polygonal) building, the **Holy Archangels Church**. Polygonal churches have been a significant feature of Armenian architecture but this is an unusual, modern variant, albeit retaining many traditional features. Very tall for its footprint, with a tambour, topped by an umbrella cupola, almost the same diameter as the lower part of the building, the whole looks like a vertical cylinder. The many windows round the top are separated by crosses which, from a distance, also resemble a ring of people holding hands. The wall of the apse is carved with khachkars and at each side of the bema is a startling representation of a bishop's pastoral staff with serpent finials. The inscription above the entrance reads 'God is love'. On the north side of the exterior is a carving of the 'Descent of the Only Begotten' with a curly-haired Gregory looking on. A sundial adorns the south side. Across lawns and flower beds a long colonnaded white building at present houses a **library** and not much else. It was originally envisaged as a branch of the Matenadaran, allowing extra manuscripts to be displayed, but this has not (yet) come to pass.

The **cathedral shop** (◷ 10.15–19.00 daily), on the left as one approaches the cathedral, has a wide range of books and a selection of tasteful souvenirs.

## St Hripsime

St Hripsime was one of the refugee nuns from Rome in the late 3rd century who were persecuted under the rule of King Trdat III and the king himself tried to rape her. This 7th-century **church** dedicated to her is unquestionably one of Armenia's architectural gems. Built by order of Katholikos Komitas in 618 it now unfortunately finds itself surrounded by undistinguished buildings between the main road in from Yerevan and the bypass. The present church is built over the mausoleum of the saint, which was constructed in 395. The church has proved more resistant to earthquake damage than many more modern buildings and its appearance has remained almost unchanged apart from the addition of a small portico on the west side and a cross on the roof in the 17th century. The belfry was added to the portico in 1790. Standing on a raised paved area above the road and

According to Agathangelos's *History of the Armenians*, written in about 460, St Gregory the Illuminator saw a vision in which the heavens opened and a blaze of light shone upon the earth. Through the light a procession of angels came down to the earth headed by the tall and glorious figure of Christ. Carrying a golden hammer, he descended and struck the ground three times with it. A tall column of fire instantly arose, with a circular base of gold and a capital of cloud and cross of light. Similar visions appeared at three other sites where Hripsime, Gayane and another of their companions were martyred. The columns transformed themselves into churches covered by clouds whose shape was that of a cupola. After the vision faded, Gregory founded the monastery of Etchmiadzin (Descent of the Only Begotten) on the spot where Christ had struck the hammer. In reality the monastery was founded, like many others in Armenia, on the site of a pagan temple whose altar still exists below the present altar.

with the old fortified wall (probably 15th–17th century) on the west side, the pinky-grey tuff church is essentially a cross-dome structure, with a 16-sided tambour. It has four apses and four rectangular corner rooms. Each corner room is, unusually for Armenia, separated from the central part of the church by a circular chamber. The large triangular niches seen on the exterior of each wall helped to reduce the bulk of stone which would otherwise have resulted where the apses and corner rooms join. The northeast corner room is reached by going down steps and further steps lead down to saint's mausoleum. The inside of the dome has decorative stonework and, unusually, a balcony runs round the base of the tambour, giving access to the small towers seen on the outside of the tambour. To the left as one enters the church the large 12th-century khachkar is a rare example of the open-cross type. A **souvenir shop** is to the left of the steps going up to the paved area, and is likely to be open whenever there is the chance of a visitor buying something.

**St Gayane**  St Gayane was the abbess of the fleeing nuns persecuted by Trdat III. Her **church** is slightly later, rather more pleasantly situated, and of quite different style. The present church was built by order of Katholikos Ezr in 630 on the site of Gayane's martyrium. By the early 17th century it was forlorn, the roof having collapsed to leave just the walls and piers standing. Major reconstruction was therefore carried out in 1651–53 and a chapel was constructed under the east apse for the saint's relics. Unlike St Hripsime's church, St Gayane's is of the longitudinal basilica style and with an apse and corner rooms only at the east end. Free-standing pillars support the octagonal tambour. In 1683, a gallery was added at the west end: the three central arches are open while the smaller side ones built to house the remains of dignitaries of the church are blanked off and topped with six-column belfries. This gallery, prominent as one walks from the gate, gives the church a 17th-century appearance even though the main part of the building is older. On Sundays St Gayane's church is a popular place for sacrifices; the *mataghatun* is in the southwest corner of the grounds.

**Shoghakat**  This **church** was built in 1694 by Prince Aghamal Shorotetsi on the site of a chapel dedicated to one of Hripsime's and Gayane's anonymous companions. Coming here after visiting Etchmiadzin's other churches gives a clear picture of both continuity and change in Armenian church architecture. In particular the continued presence of a cupola atop a tambour, octagonal in this case, follows a tradition going back to the 5th century, but a prominent six-column belfry over the porch is evidence of 17th-century ideas. Similarly, the detailed ornamental carving in geometrical patterns could have been created at almost any time in the last 1,500 years. Few tourists ever go to Shoghakat, and certainly it does not compare to the main cathedral or St Hripsime, but it does provide interesting insights and locals claim that it marks the fourth place where St Gregory the Illuminator saw a vision of a column of fire.

**Mother of God Church** If few visitors go to Shoghakat, even fewer come here, yet it has an altar in an Italianate style which is unique in Armenia. The original church of 1767 was wooden and the present stone building dates from the 19th century. The belltower was added in 1982. It was built as the village church for the ordinary people of Etchmiadzin as opposed to the members of the Holy See or of the monasteries and seminaries. Even now it is near a small market and overlooked by blocks of flats. A three-aisle basilica, it has paintings on the square columns depicting Christ, the Holy family and saints. The stepped altar and the painting of the Madonna and Child within its marble frame are covered with a baldachin-like canopy, painted blue and decorated with gold, which is incorporated into the screen across the bema. The screen, including the two doors, one on each side of the altar, has further paintings.

**Elsewhere in Etchmiadzin** If you have spare time in Etchmiadzin there are four other small museums, all near the cathedral precinct. The **Mher Abeghyan Museum** (Komitas Sq, on the left as you face the statue of Komitas; ✆0231 54941) houses paintings by Mher Abeghyan (1909–94) which he donated to his home town of Etchmiadzin. Abeghyan's paintings also hang in other galleries including the National Gallery in Yerevan and the Tretyakov Gallery in Moscow. He was an accepted (and decorated) artist in the Soviet era in spite of painting subjects which were officially forbidden. The Etchmiadzin gallery contains three of his large triptychs including the best known, *Mother Armenia*.

Next door through the archway on the left is the **Hovhannes Hovhannisyan House Museum** (Komitas Sq; ✆0231 53370). Hovhannes Hovhannisyan (1864–1929) was born in the house which is now home to the museum. A poet, linguist, translator and teacher, he was a key figure in the modern Armenian literature movement. He studied in Moscow and travelled extensively in Europe before returning to Etchmiadzin where he lectured on Greek and Russian language and literature. He translated ancient Armenian manuscripts into modern Armenian and also translated works by writers such as Homer, Shakespeare, Goethe, Ibsen, Pushkin and Schiller. He supported the Bolshevik Revolution and the creation of the Soviet Union. He is buried in Yerevan's Komitas Pantheon (see box, page 178). There is no information in English in the museum. For non-Armenian-speakers the main interest is perhaps in the house itself and its furnishings.

On the other side of Komitas Square is the **Etchmiadzin Historical and Ethnographic Museum** (✆0231 53663; ⊕ 10.00–17.00 Tue–Sun). This well-presented museum, with labels in English, has a good section on prehistory including a helpful model of a roundhouse. The ethnographic section has all the usual artefacts as well as some more unusual ones including a contraption for shoeing oxen and cattle, as well as horses, and an anti-wolf dog collar.

The **Khoren Ter-Harutyan Museum** (2 Araratyan St; ✆0231 63877) is across the road from the main entrance to the cathedral precinct. Khoren Ter-Harutyan

(1909–91) was born in Western Armenia (present-day Turkey). He, his mother and his sister were the only members of a large extended family to escape the genocide. They arrived in the USA in 1921. Moving between America, Jamaica and Europe he was a painter, carver and latterly a sculptor. In 1983 he donated the majority of his work to Armenia; sculpture lovers may therefore find a visit to the gallery worthwhile. It is well laid out and labels are in English.

## CENTRAL ARMAVIR

**Metsamor** (Museum, archaeological site and ancient observatory: ☎010 545570 (Monuments Protection Service hotline); m 094 930071; ⊕ site always; museum 10.00–17.00 Tue–Sun; guided tour in English & Russian AMD2,500; AMD1,000) The small red tuff museum of Metsamor (Black Swamp) opened in 1971 and is well worth visiting, showing finds from the excavations at the site with labels in English. A booklet with colour photographs of the museum's most important artefacts is available. Although currently only in Armenian, it makes an attractive memento of a visit; when more money is available it is hoped to produce an English version. Of particular interest is the basement where there is an exact reconstruction of one of the excavated royal tombs. The excavation of royal tombs has shown that the deceased were buried with feet to the east, presumably to face the rising sun, and in the foetal position within a sarcophagus in the early tombs but later lying within a casket. Royalty was buried not only with their jewellery and a supply of food and wine, but also with the domestic animals and decapitated human beings, presumably their slaves, who were slaughtered for the occasion. Also exhibited are some superb examples of gold jewellery, belt decorations in the form of lions, and a weight in the form of a frog made from agate and onyx. This weight, found around the neck of a woman, bears an inscription in Babylonian cuneiform. The ground and upper floors of the museum show examples of ceramics, jewellery, tools and other items including a very large phallus.

The small hill on which the museum stands is the site of an important Bronze Age **citadel**, around 30% of which has been excavated. Although there was occupation here much earlier, the important remains and finds date from around 2000BC. Excavations have revealed an important metalworking industry, a postulated astronomical observatory and considerable evidence of international trade.

The **excavated part of the site** lies just beyond the museum. The walls built in the 2nd millennium BC can be seen; they were strengthened in the Urartian era. Up on the plateau are chambers and pits (those with runnels thought to be related to the metalworking industry) hewn into the rock. However, it is the ancient **observatory** where various markings can be seen on the stones which is likely to be of greatest interest. Archaeologists have suggested that it was used around 2800–2500BC to detect the appearance of Sirius, the brightest star in the sky, which may have been worshipped and which possibly marked the start of the year and indicated the time to start planting crops: at that epoch Sirius was visible in summer rather than in winter as it now is. It should be said that some authorities dispute this astronomical observatory claim. If there is no-one from the museum free to show you the markings, walk along the path beside the megalithic walls in the direction of the power station, heading for a small outcrop of reddish rocks. On the far side of the rocks you will come across steps carved into the rock and it is in their vicinity that the markings are to be found. The easiest ones to see comprise a series of converging lines.

## Sardarapat (Monument and Ethnographical Museum) The Sardarapat
memorial complex is just south of the village of Araks. If using public transport,

the best option might be to travel to Armavir then take a taxi. There are no taxis at Sardarapat so you would have to negotiate a price for waiting – allow several hours. The monument is on a small hill; from the car park at the bottom there is a long flight of steps up to the monument and then a level walk through the gardens to the museum, a total distance of about 1km. For those unable to negotiate the steps or the distance, a road to the museum goes off left just before the car park. There are barriers on the road; if they're closed you may be able to ask for them to be opened.

**✖ Where to eat and drink** There are two restaurants within the Sardarapat complex. **Hazarashen** (📞 0237 69891; m 095 500350; ⊕ 09.30–23.00 daily) serves the standard Armenian fare of salads and *khorovats* at the usual prices, and is built in the form of a traditional Armenian house with a central roof under which large *tonirs* are set into the ground to cook the food about to be eaten. **Vardevar** (⊕ on request for groups & events) is built in a style resembling a gavit with intersecting arches and also has a long room to accommodate traditional Armenian mountain dancing. The inscription at the dining hall entrance has elements of the sentiments inscribed on memorial khachkars and uttered during Armenian toasts:

> Bending down before the names of our great ancestors and inspired by their skilful works we, the grateful descendants, built this dining hall ... when visiting this heroic site it is impossible not to raise a glass to the memory of heroes who sacrificed their lives for the homeland.

**The monument** Sardarapat's striking **red tuff monument**, in the form of two Assyrian bulls facing each other separated by a structure from which bells are hung, can be seen straight ahead from the main road. This 35m-tall structure, contrasting with the massive bulls, is built in a form inspired by the stelae at Odzun, Lori province, and Aghudi, Syunik province.

The monument commemorates the victory by Armenian troops and irregular forces commanded by Daniel Bek-Pirumian over attacking Turkish troops who were coming down the railway from Alexandropol (Gyumri). The Battle of Sardarapat lasted from 22 to 26 May 1918 and was a decisive victory resulting in the declaration of an independent Armenia on 28 May 1918. The monument was unveiled in 1968 to commemorate the 50th anniversary and each year on 28 May celebrations are held here: the bells are tolled and there are performances by folk song and dance groups. Near the monument is a memorial for the dead of the Nagorno Karabagh conflict.

The area surrounding the monument is meticulously well kept, perhaps because it has since 1998 come under the control of the Ministry of Defence: older women sweep the paths with besoms while younger ones weed the rose beds. This commemorative monument is probably unique among those erected anywhere in the former Soviet Union in its appropriateness, stylishness and thankful absence of banal pseudo-heroic bombast. Its designer was the evidently gifted People's Architect of the USSR, Rafael Israelyan (1908–73). At right angles to the approach slope, broad paths through gardens and flanked by eagles lead to a memorial wall covered with symbolic reliefs and penetrated by an arch. From here a path leads to the museum. Outside its entrance stands a convincing example of a vishap and representative examples of other stone monuments.

**The museum** (📞 0237 69996; ⊕ 09.30–17.45 Tue–Sun; parking AMD100; pre-booked guided tours in English, French, German & Russian AMD5,000; adult/

child AMD700/300; admission to the war museum hall costs an extra AMD400 & a guided tour of this room an extra AMD3,000) The **museum** brochure (AMD500) has a good selection of photographs with explanations of the exhibits and also of the memorial. The interesting material is well presented in pleasant surroundings with good labelling in Armenian, Russian and English. Symbolically the museum has only two windows facing outwards: one looking north towards Aragats and the other south towards Ararat. Instead there are large windows on to a central courtyard, and skylights in the tradition of the *yerdik* of medieval Armenian architecture. The displays cover many aspects of life in the Arax Valley, including finds from various archaeological sites; traditional farm and domestic implements; the tools of various occupations such as armourer, blacksmith, hatter and shoemaker; crafts such as carpet-weaving, embroidery and lacemaking; musical instruments; puppets; herbal and mineral medical remedies and much more. A hall of contemporary sculpture has many intriguing pieces. The separate war hall has material about the Battle of Sardarapat.

**Argishtikhinili**  Located just south of Nor Armavir village, this **Urartian site** was founded by Argishti I in 776BC and lasted for about 200 years. It is thought that it was an administrative rather than a military centre but it did have fortified walls as well as palaces, temples and dwellings. It occupied a ridge of low hills, its dimensions approximately 5km x 2km. Excavations were carried out from the 1920s to 1970s and many of the finds are now in the Sardarapat museum. The major digs were covered with earth to conserve them but some foundations and walls are still visible, hinting at what once existed. There is a plaster model of the site, now somewhat weathered, on the western hill.

**Armavir**  The site of the **ancient Hellenistic town** of Armavir is on a hill just southwest of Haykavan. A modern cemetery girdles the base of the hill. The site was occupied from antiquity but was most important as the capital of the Orontids from the 4th to the 2nd century BC. At that time the Arax River ran further north than it does now, its marshes helping to defend the town. When the river changed its course the capital was shifted but the site continued to be inhabited through the medieval period. The climb to the top of the hill, while short, is difficult because of loose scree. On top is evidence of the temple platform and various dwellings.

# GEGHARKUNIK PROVINCE

Gegharkunik comprises the area surrounding **Lake Sevan**, at 1,238.8km² in total area the largest lake in the Caucasus and, with a surface elevation of 1,900m, one of the largest high-altitude lakes in the world. Dimensional measurements vary but according to a European Environment Agency report of 2015 it reaches 74km in length and 32km in width at its most extreme points, with a maximum depth of 79.4m. Historic Armenia was a land of three large lakes, of which Sevan was one; Lake Van is now in Turkey and Lake Urmia (Orumiyeh) is in Iran, hence Sevan's significance in modern-day Armenia. It is a popular summertime destination for families from Yerevan who flock to the northwest shores – and particularly the **peninsula** – at weekends to take advantage of the cool, calm weather and child-friendly beaches. The consequence is that foreign visitors are more likely to have the cultural experience of being invited to a barbecue and *oghi*-drinking session amid roaring jet skis and thumping pop music than a relaxing day on the beach! More

tranquil spots do exist, particularly on the eastern shore, and are noted as such in the following sections.

Gegharkunik also includes most of the beautiful and little-known valley of the Getik River which lies to the northeast of the lake. The Getik rises close to the Azerbaijan border and then flows northwest, separated from the lake by the Aregunyats range of mountains whose highest peak is **Mount Karktasar** (2,743m), flowing into the Aghstev River in Tavush province about 15km east of Dilijan.

The name Gegharkunik recalls early legends. Gegham was the great-great-grandson of Hayk, the legendary founder of Armenia (page 14). Gegham left Armavir and moved north to Lake Sevan where he established the city of Gegh; the name of the province translates as 'Gegham's seat'. The lake he called Geghama Lich (Gegham's Lake), the volcanic mountain range to its west is known as Geghama Lernasheghta ('Gegham's Mountains', or the Geghama Mountains as they are usually referred to in English). The range is actually divided between Kotayk and Gegharkunik provinces; see page 238 for information on the most popular sites of interest and access routes from Kotayk. The whole area around the lake is rich in prehistoric and historic remains. It seems that almost every village has a nearby Bronze or Iron Age fortress, megalithic tomb, medieval settlement or something else of interest.

**GETTING THERE AND AROUND** The northern part of Lake Sevan is quickly reached by the modern M4 highway from **Yerevan** which bypasses all towns en route; the volume of traffic makes it one of the easiest hitchhiking routes in the country. It is still possible to follow the older scenic road along the gorge via Nor Hachn, Argel, Arzakan, Bjni, Hrazdan and Sevan town; for anyone not in a hurry (especially on two wheels) it is strongly recommended to do so. To the north, the M4 main road then connects with **Tavush** province via the Sevan Tunnel; the scenic old road over the Sevan Pass (2,114m) is still serviceable. A mostly good road circumnavigates the lake, though the stretch between Tsapatagh and Vardenis remains in terrible but passable condition for a regular car. From **Vardenis**, the new M11 Vardenis–Martakert Highway, completed in 2017, crosses the **Sotk Pass** (2,367m) into the *de jure* Azeri province of Kelbajar (the Shahumyan province of the self-declared Republic of Artsakh) and on to Martakert in **Karabagh** proper; minibuses from Yerevan to Stepanakert now tend to ply this road instead of the longer route via Goris and it has become the second 'official' point of entry for tourists travelling between Armenia and Karabagh (page 375). In the south of Gegharkunik, a good road connects Martuni and **Vayots Dzor** province via the **Selim Pass** (2,410m), allowing access to several sites of interest on the way, though the pass is closed in the winter due to snow.

Minibuses from Yerevan to Gegharkunik tend to depart from the Northern Bus Station on the highway near Abovyan (see box, page 87) for Sevan, Gavar, Martuni, Vardenis, Chambarak and Shorzha, among other minor destinations. In summer (ie: from mid-June to mid-September, though exact dates can vary annually), the daily train from Yerevan to Hrazdan is extended to Sevan and Tsovagyugh, and on Fridays, Saturdays and Sundays to Shorzha (page 85). If you intend to use this slow but cheap and charming service, do check beforehand (♦184; w ukzhd.am). The train stops in Sevan itself and next to Sevan peninsula, as well as at several other provincial stops en route.

**WHERE TO STAY** There is abundant **lakeside accommodation** at the northwestern end of Lake Sevan, ranging from large Soviet-era guesthouses and new international-standard hotels to small motel-type establishments, cottages and beach huts. It is possible to **camp** overnight at many of the beaches for a small fee. Most of the accommodation is only fully functional in the summer holiday season and caters primarily for Armenian families whose motivations for being there tend to differ from those of foreign visitors, making the area of limited relevance (though it is much less rowdy out of season). The eastern shore is remote from Yerevan and tends to be more relaxing for those wanting a quiet getaway. Accommodation is more sparse but again ranges from basic campsites and cottages to upscale offerings such as the Tufenkian property in Tsapatagh.

Basic hotels and guesthouses operate in the larger **towns** of the province, including Sevan, Gavar, Martuni and Vardenis, which may be of use to those passing through, though the towns themselves have few notable sites of interest. In smaller villages and particularly in the Getik Valley and its side valleys (page 237) there are some pleasant homestay-style **B&Bs** (page 229).

## Around Lake Sevan

**Avan Marak Tsapatagh Hotel** (34 rooms) Tsapatagh; ♦060 501010; m 093 947891; e tsapatagh@tufenkian.am; w tufenkianheritage. com; ☉ 1 Apr–31 Oct, high season Jul & Aug.

Luxurious & tranquil lakeside resort on the far east side of Lake Sevan, 57km from Sevan town and 126km from Yerevan. Its construction reflects the Tufenkian dedication to heritage, incorporating old stone barns. The Zanazan

4

restaurant is in a separate building 250m away; transport is available. Outdoor swimming pool, hot tub & sauna. Wi-Fi. Cards accepted. Prices vary depending on size of room & view of lake. **$$$–$$$$**

🏠 **Best Western Bohemian Resort** (25 rooms, 18 cottages) 102 Yerevanyan Rd, Lake Sevan; ✆ 0261 25885; e info@bohemianresort. am; w bohemianresort.am. One of the few international chain properties on the northwest shore of Lake Sevan, just south of the peninsula & open year round. Restaurants & cafés on-site serve European & Armenian cuisine. Outdoor heated swimming pool (seasonal). Cottages sleep 4; all have 2 storeys with bedrooms upstairs. Buffet b/fast. Reduced low-season rates. High season Jul–Sep. Wi-Fi. Cards accepted. **$$$**

🏠 **Harsnakar Hotel** (34 rooms) Tsamakaberd, Lake Sevan; ✆ 060 748888; e info@ harsnaqarhotel.am; w harsnaqarhotel.am. Another modern mid-range hotel at the northwest end of the lake, perched on a small hill in well-tended gardens. Open all year with very pleasant dbl/twin/suite rooms & a variety of cottages (AMD40,000–100,000), which sleep up to 7. Entrance to the Water World children's aquapark AMD1,500–2,000, depending on height. Private beach. Sports facilities inc swimming pool & sauna, tennis courts, beach volleyball & more. Wi-Fi. Cards accepted, excluding American Express. **$$$**

🏠 **Ashot Yerkat Restaurant/Hotel Complex** (8 rooms) Sevan Peninsula; ✆ 0261 25000; m 091 025000/500043. Near the car park for peninsula monasteries & a little uphill from the busy lakeshore. Mainly a restaurant & still one of the best on the peninsula; it is best to book ahead (2hrs) at busy times. Ideal for coffee & pastries (the baklava is delicious) when visiting Sevanavank. Their barbecued *sig* (see opposite) is also delicious. Twin/dbl/quad rooms in need of renovation but cheap & comfortable enough. **$$**

🏠 **Blue Sevan** (49 rooms) 7km east of Tsovagyugh, Lake Sevan; m 098 288277, 091 288277; e bluesevan@gmail.com; w blue-sevan. com; ⊕ May–Oct. Although the postal address is Chambarak, this hotel is actually on the north shore of Lake Sevan on the M14 lakeside road about 7km from the M4 junction. A well-renovated pleasant hotel set in wooded grounds; like most in the area it is geared towards local families although in a quiet location. Also has cottages,

AMD150,000, which sleep up to 6. Excellent buffet b/fast. Lunch (⊕ 14.00–17.00 daily) can be ordered in advance (AMD4,000 pp). Evening meals not available. Price varies with floor (cheapest on ground floor) & view of lake; discounts for stays of longer than 3 days. **$$**

🏠 **Hotel Lavash** (25 rooms) 29 Vtoraya St, Chkalova; m 093 722727; e info@sevanresort. com; w sevanresort.com. Tranquil spot just south of the Yerevan highway in the direction of Gavar. Part of the Tsovatsots resort complex, built in a tasteful historical style with a restaurant serving an excellent fish barbecue, plus the Bashinjaghyan Tea House & a handicraft shop on-site. Spacious dbl/twin/trpl/quad rooms; those facing the lake have floor-to-ceiling windows & panoramic views. **$$**

🏕 **Wishup Shore** 1km north of Shorzha; m 093 412002; 🅵; ⊕ approx Jun–Sep. Hip beach camp striking a good balance between chilled daytimes & lively evenings, with a bar/restaurant serving all meals. Windsurfing/sailing/canoeing equipment for hire. Popular with trendy Yerevantsis. Daily fee of AMD1,000 to use the beach. Camping AMD2,000 pp; discounts for longer stays & camping equipment for (very cheap) hire. Cottages for 5–6 also available (AMD25–30,000). Bar tabs far too easy to run up. Cards accepted, thankfully. Wi-Fi. **$**

## Martuni

🏠 **Khrchit Restaurant/Hotel** (3 rooms) 24 Kamo St; ✆ 0262 42964; m 099 800600, 091 228881; e qrchit@gmail.com. On the main road just after entering Martuni from the west; a useful landmark is the pair of artificial storks on their nest at the front entrance. En-suite dbl rooms with the advantage of readily available meals. B/fast approx AMD1,000 pp. **$**

## Vardenis

🏠 **Chez Nelly** (1 dbl, 1 twin, 1 sgl) 3 Baghramyan St; m 093 323193, 094 550746; e aslakaren@yahoo.fr; w vardenis.free.fr. Member of the Aregouni association of B&B owners in Vardenis, which has formed a link with people in the town of Romans in France. Children in Vardenis are taught French during the summer months & exchange visits are arranged. With the help of their French partners the Armenian families have been able to upgrade their bathroom & toilet facilities to enable them to take guests. The authors have stayed with 2 of the families in the association. Evening meals can be arranged (AMD4,000 pp). **$$**

🏠 **Naira & Artem Barseghyan's B&B** (5 rooms) 34 Andranik St; ✆ 0269 23147; m 095 473131; e nairabarseghyan@gmail.com; w guesthousevardenis.weebly.com. Founders of the Aregouni association (see opposite). Offering khachkar-carving lessons in a nearby workshop! Fantastic home-cooked food. **$$**

## Elsewhere in the province

🏠 **Hooga Guesthouse** (3 rooms) 8 Sixth St, Kalavan; m 094 486298; e hoogahouse@ gmail.com; w hoogahouse.com. Modern & rather upscale guesthouse-hostel with an international vibe in the remote mountain village of Kalavan.

Somewhat hard to reach, 7.5km by 4x4 from the main road, but worth it if you plan to stay a few nights to explore the natural surroundings & soak up the village vibe. Dorm beds AMD10,000 pp. Very detailed website. **$$**

🏠 **Anna B&B** (3 rooms) 1/2 Paruyr Sevak St, Chambarak; m 098 727382. Useful homestay if passing through Chambarak. Dbl/twin/quad rooms in a rustic family home. B/fast AMD1,500. **$**

🏠 **Mher B&B** (3 rooms) 21/6 Chambarak St, Martuni village (not to be confused with Martuni town, page 236); m 093 065964. One of several good B&Bs in the villages of the Getik Valley, Mher's is particularly memorable for the owner's carpentry as well as his homemade honey wine. Pleasantly situated overlooking the river up a dirt road at the northwest end of the village. **$**

✘ **WHERE TO EAT AND DRINK** Most of the hotels listed on the opposite page have **restaurants** on-site, notably the Tufenkian at Tsapatagh and Ashot Yerkat on the peninsula; any homestay should be able to prepare lunch or dinner with advance notice. All the major towns surrounding Lake Sevan have fast-food outlets and there are innumerable roadside 'bistros' for most of the circumference of the lake (less so between Shorzha and Vardenis). There is an excellent and wildly popular **bakery** on the M4 near Tsovagyugh just north of the M14 junction; try the freshly baked cheese-filled baguette-style *khachapuri* or the dried-fruit-and-nut-filled *gata* if you're lucky enough to get a parking space.

**OTHER PRACTICALITIES** The towns in the province are small but have all basic facilities. Lake Sevan's beaches are very popular with Armenian families and during the school summer holidays from June to September, particularly at weekends, and, especially on the peninsula and its surroundings, it can be very busy.

**Tourist information** is available at Sevan town hall (164 Nairyan St; m 099 199555, 077 023385; e davidtorosyan09@yahoo.com; ⊕ 09.00–18.00 daily) in English, French and Russian. There are no signs either outside or inside the building; keep asking.

**LAKE SEVAN** To those accustomed to the mountain lakes of Switzerland or the lochs of Scotland, Lake Sevan may initially seem bare and windswept. Its real attraction lies in the ever-changing colours of its surface and in the skies above it. It is also, particularly on its southern side, an area with a long history and with a great many interesting places to see. The monastery of Sevanavank was formerly on an island, but falling water levels (see box, page 230) turned it into a peninsula and visitors travel there today by road rather than by boat. Sevan's beaches are the only ones in landlocked Armenia and provide a unique experience for Armenians who cannot afford a beach holiday in upmarket Batumi or elsewhere.

Lake Sevan and much of its shoreline have enjoyed national park status since 1978. The lake itself is fed by 28 rivers, and there is one outflow, the Hrazdan River, which exits the lake at the western end to descend to Yerevan and become a tributary of the Arax. As well as being an important bird habitat, it is home to a variety of endemic and introduced **fish** species. Common whitefish *Coregonus lavaretus*, known as *sig*, were introduced in the 1920s from Lake Ladoga; by

## THE FALL AND RISE OF LAKE SEVAN

In 1910, the Armenian engineer Soukias Manasserian published a book entitled *The Evaporating Billions and the Stagnation of Russian Capital* in which he proposed reducing the depth of the lake from 95m to 45m, using the water for irrigation and hydro-electric generation. (Manasserian also produced a plan to reduce the level of the Aral Sea, a much better-known environmental disaster.) Manasserian's scheme was approved by the Soviet government and was envisaged to result in a reduction in the lake's perimeter from 260km to 80km and its volume of water from 58km³ to 5km³. With a breathtaking lack of realism it was anticipated that this drastic reduction in size would be accompanied by an equally drastic increase in the yield of fish. A typical Stalin-era writer stated that Lake Sevan's 'scraggy, barren shores will be turned into sweet-smelling meadows, groves of nut trees and oak trees … Around it beautiful roads and promenades will be laid … There could be no objection to diminishing the size of the lake.'

Work began in 1933 to implement the scheme. The Hrazdan River outflow was deepened to increase the discharge from the lake, a tunnel was bored, and the lake level started to drop by more than 1m per year. It was not until 1956 that the wisdom of the Sevan venture started to be questioned. Problems were starting to manifest, such as the difficulty of growing the promised trees on the newly exposed shore together with a reduction in fish catch. A 'Sevan Committee' was formed and the Soviet government decreed that the lake level was to be kept as high as possible. The water level stabilised in 1962 at 18m below the original level, but eutrophic algal blooms started to occur in 1964. A 49km tunnel, intended to bring 200 million cubic metres of water each year north from the Arpa River (in Vayots Dzor) into Lake Sevan, was completed in 1981, but the tunnel only succeeded in raising the water level by 1.5m. A second tunnel, 22km long, was initiated to bring water from the Vorotan into the Arpa and thence to the lake, and was completed in 2003.

Matters deteriorated after 1988 as a consequence of the economic blockade of Armenia during the Karabagh War, when the Hrazdan River hydro-electric stations became one of the few domestic sources of electricity. The level of the lake fell 20m below its original level with a surface area of 940km² in comparison with the former 1,360km². The current official policy is to raise the lake level to 1,904m by the year 2031, which will necessitate the demolition of some 1,697 buildings and structures on the drained land. With the lake level already increased to 1,900m at the time of research, newly flooded areas are conspicuous. A 15km section of the main road around the lake has been submerged and rebuilt on higher ground. Some 1,400ha of trees have already been cleared, and it is estimated that a total of 4,000ha will have to be cleared by 2020/21 to mitigate problems caused by submerged vegetation.

contrast the endemic Sevan trout *Salmo ischchan* is now on the verge of extinction, although they survive in Lake Issyk-kul in Kyrgyzstan where the species was introduced. Regulations on fishing do not prevent both species finding their way on to the menus of numerous lakeside restaurants; they can also be bought fresh on the side of the M4 main road, particularly between the Sevan peninsula and the Tsovagyugh junction, as can the introduced crayfish *Pontastacus leptodactylus* (which are literally sold by the bucketload).

The lake is not without its problems. Challenges include outdated waste-water treatment and sewage disposal; recent upgrading work has included a new sewer network in Sevan and waste-water treatment plants for Gavar, Vardenis and Martuni. Another cause for concern is the pollution which could result from a continuing increase in gold mining at Sotk, east of Vardenis. Meanwhile, a lack of robust planning or enforcement of property laws over the years has resulted in plenty of inappropriate construction on the lakeside. Two forces may reverse this trend and help combat some of the ongoing environmental issues. The first is a spread of reformative measures for the territory of Lake Sevan National Park, announced in 2017 by then prime minister Karen Karapetyan (including the establishment of public beaches and the announcement of a pedestrian promenade). The second is the rising level of the lake itself (see box, opposite) which will result in the forced demolition of hundreds of illegal properties. Perhaps this will make way for the continued growth of active watersports such as swimming, sailing and windsurfing, the absence of which had until very recently been somewhat puzzling to foreign visitors given such a prime location.

## ✕ THE WESTERN SIDE OF LAKE SEVAN
## Where to eat and drink

✕ **Bashinjaghyan Tea House** 29 Vtoraya St, Chkalova; m 093 722727; e info@sevanresort. com; w sevanresort.com; ⏰ 09.00–23.00 daily. Adjoining the Hotel Lavash (page 228), this tranquil lakeside eatery is south of the Sevan highway towards Gavar with excellent views over the lake. The fish barbecue & the baklava both come highly recommended.

✕ **Collette Restaurant** On the M4 highway 3.3km north of the peninsula junction; ☏ 0261 60002; ⏰ 24hrs daily. One of several roadside restaurants overlooking the lake north of the peninsula where the road narrows to a sliver. This expansive complex is frequently recommended for its fish dishes, though it represents all the mainstays of Armenian cuisine as well.

☕ **Bohem Studio** 16/13 Sayat Nova St, Sevan; m 055 662119; f; ⏰ 10.30–21.00 daily. Lovely little cosmopolitan community café popular with the younger generation of locals, serving hot/cold drinks & light snacks. Good for a herbal tea & a pancake if you happen to be in Sevan.

☕ **Kellers Beerhouse** 3 Yerevanyan Hwy, Sevan; ☏ 0261 60011; ⏰ 09.00–23.00 Mon–Fri. Easy to spot from the main M4 highway, this is the outlet and beer garden for Sevan's small brewery & may provide very welcome refreshment when passing through. Light, dark & unfiltered draught beers available. Accessed from the westbound lane, so a U-turn may be required.

**Sevan (town)** In spite of an increasing number of new shops and renovated buildings, the town of Sevan itself has a somewhat overlooked feel, perhaps because there is so little of interest to tourists. It is, however, the principal settlement in the northwest region. Most facilities are on or just off the main thoroughfare, **Nairyan Street**. They include the post office and market towards the west end; the town hall (with information office, page 229) and the hospital towards the east end. Sayat Nova Street crosses Nairyan Street about halfway along it. Both the railway station and the bus stand are on Sayat Nova, the railway station to the north, the bus stand to the south. (The bus ticket office is the inconspicuous small triangular building.)

Just outside the town to the west is a **war cemetery** where German prisoners of war lie buried, one of several in Armenia (pages 262 and 277). To get here go west along Nairyan Street to a roundabout, turn right and cross the railway, then take the first left turn. Continue for about 1km looking out for the large plain cross of the war cemetery across fields to the left. Within the cemetery are four groups of three crosses as well as the large cross underneath which is the same inscription as the other German war cemeteries, *Hier ruhen Kriegesgefangene – Opfer des zweites Weltkrieges* ('Here rest prisoners of war – victims of World War II').

**Ddmashen** The village of Ddmashen, 12km west of Sevan, though more easily reached from Hrazdan in Kotayk province, has the 7th-century **church of St Thaddeus**. This domed basilica church is considered to be the fourth most important of this type of construction after Talin, Ptghni and Aruch. It has survived without major alterations, although it received a new 16-sided tambour in 1907 following earthquake damage. The tambour has eight windows; the intermediate façades have niches. There is a single small window in the altar apse and much larger windows in the nave. It is very plain both inside and outside, the only external features being undecorated moulding at the windows. The window arches and the pattern of lighting is typical of early 7th-century churches. To the south of the church is a large cemetery, the grave stones mostly unmarked recumbent slabs.

**Sevanavank (monastery)** This monastery is one of Armenia's most visited tourist sights, set on a hilltop on the small Sevan peninsula (previously an island) and frequented by many tourist buses. It owes its popularity largely to its proximity to the lake and to its accessibility from Yerevan, and is reached via a short footpath from the car park below. The summer train from Yerevan (page 85) makes a stop at the peninsula, from where it is a few minutes' walk to the site. A taxi from the town of Sevan should cost a maximum of AMD1,000, or AMD2,500 return with waiting time. The peninsula gets very busy in high summer, with several private beaches, shops, souvenir stalls, restaurants and accommodation options (pages 227 and 229).

The surviving monastery buildings comprise the Mother of God Church and the smaller Holy Apostles Church, together with a ruined gavit. (**Note:** most sources use the church names followed in this guidebook – the information boards at the monastery name them differently.) An inscription on the **Holy Apostles Church**, the oldest of the churches and the first to be encountered, states that the monastery was founded in 874 by Princess Miriam, wife of Prince Vasak of Syunik, and daughter of the Bagratid King Ashot I. This was a time when Armenia was emerging from subjugation under the Arab caliphate and the church was one of the first to be built in Armenia after more than 200 years of Arab Islamic domination. Not surprisingly the architects resorted to 7th-century practice in developing the design. Despite what the inscription says about Ashot being king, in 874 this was a little premature. By judicious exploitation of others' enforced absence at the caliph's court in Samarra, Ashot was able to amass great power and in 862 the caliph awarded him with the title Prince of Princes. Ashot managed to remain neutral in the wars between the caliph's Arab forces and the Byzantine Emperor Basil I which were being waged when Sevan Monastery was built. The caliph was only to give Ashot the title King in 884, ten years after the date of the inscription; he was later followed in doing so by the Byzantine emperor. Holy Apostles is a typical and plain cross-dome church and, in the absence of corner rooms, its interior shape can be seen from the outside. There is a large doorway between the south and west arms and a small chapel with an apse between the south and east arms. The octagonal tambour has four small windows.

The larger **Mother of God Church** is in similar style and lies to the southeast of the Apostles Church; it too has an octagonal tambour. The small chapels were probably later additions. There are two features of particular interest. One is an extremely elaborate 13th-century basalt khachkar inside the church. At the top right is God the Father with right hand raised in the Armenian style of blessing – tips of thumb and ring finger touching with the other three fingers upright representing the Trinity. He is surrounded by the winged symbols of the four evangelists – eagle, lion, ox and man. At the top left is God surrounded by angels. The central panel shows Jesus on the cross flanked by Mary and St John. To the right of Jesus are panels showing his birth, the ox and ass, and the three kings. To his left are panels showing scales weighing good and evil, three figures and abstract decoration. Below Jesus, God is shown expelling Adam and Eve from Eden. The other notable feature is the wooden altar screen, part carved and part painted. It is most un-Armenian, being a gift in 1824 from the monastery of St Thaddeus, south of Maku in present-day Iran.

Off the Mother of God Church is a ruined gavit in which are displayed pieces of khachkars found hidden in the cupola of the church. Its roof once rested on six wooden columns. The finely carved wooden capitals from the gavit depicting a chalice and the tree of life flanked by two doves are now in the Historical Museum in Yerevan, as are two carved walnut doors also from the gavit, one dating from 1176 and the other from 1486. Northeast and a little uphill from Mother of God Church is the low outline of a third church, **Holy Resurrection**.

The monastery was one of the first seminaries to reopen in Armenia after the Soviet period. In the past being here was not necessarily a matter of choice. The French expert on the Caucasus, Jean-Marie Chopin, who visited the island monastery in 1830, reported that the regime was extremely strict with no meat, no wine, no youths and no women. It therefore served as a reformatory for those monks banished for their misdemeanours from Etchmiadzin. Another visitor reported that as late as 1850 manuscripts here were still being copied by hand. Walking to the end of the peninsula affords good views across the lake as well as some escape from the multitude of visitors thronging the monastery at the height of the season. On the north side of the peninsula is the seminary, and at the tip, protected by a high metal fence, the guesthouse of the president.

**Lchashen and Norashen**  Heading southeast from Sevan along the west side of the lake, the road passes **Lchashen**, site of the discovery of the Bronze Age burial chariots now on display in Yerevan's History Museum of Armenia (page 176). At **Norashen** is one of the world's largest breeding colonies of the Armenian gull (*Larus armenicus*), another being at Lake Arpi in northwest Armenia (page 265). The gulls breed on islands in Lake Sevan and by the late 1990s the reduced water level had turned the islands into peninsulas. This allowed access to predators and domestic cattle, which trampled on the eggs. In addition human activity caused disturbance during the breeding season, all leading to a serious threat to the viability of the colony. In 1999, in a project led by the Acopian Center for the Environment (w ace.aua.am), a channel was dug so that Gull Island was once again an island, allowing the birds to breed more successfully. An area of the lakeside at Norashen has been set aside as a reserve. It is also a good place to see a range of passerines, flowers and butterflies.

**Hayravank (monastery)**  Just south of Berdkunk, the monastery of Hayravank can be seen on a knoll to the left of the road overlooking the lake. The monastery and surrounding rocks are all conspicuously covered with reddish-orange lichen. The monastery consists of a domed four-apse church from the end of the 9th century, a gavit from the 12th and a small 10th-century chapel off the south wall of the church. The topography of the rather cramped site with the ground falling away quite steeply led to the gavit, at a lower level than the church, incorporating the western apse of the church, which now protrudes into the interior of the gavit. The east arch of the gavit spans the church asymmetrically in relation to the west door and crosses the top of the west apse window. The interior of the gavit's short octagonal tambour and dome are decorated with red and grey tuff, thought to be one of the earliest examples of polychrome decorative masonry. Every interior wall of the gavit is covered with carved crosses. The disposition of the buildings means that, of the original church, only the east apse and part of the north apse are visible from the outside. There are many attractive khachkars at the monastery.

**Gavar** Gegharkunik's provincial capital was founded in 1830 as Nor Bayazit (ie: New Bayazit) by Armenian migrants who had left what is now Doğubayazıt in Turkey following the Turkish defeat by Russia. In 1959, it was renamed Kamo, the *nom de guerre* of Simon Ter-Petrosian (1882–1922), one of a number of Bolshevik supporters who raised money for the party by robbing banks, post offices and railway ticket offices (he died in a road accident in Tbilisi). The city changed its name to Gavar, meaning 'county', following the Soviet collapse. The area was historically important: the ridge which runs through Gavar (perhaps best seen from the road to Karmirgyugh), now the modern cemetery, is the site of an early Iron Age fortress thought to be an Urartian royal capital. Tombs from 4000BC and medieval monuments have been found.

Gavar is unlikely to make it on to most visitors' itineraries, particularly as it is bypassed by the main lakeshore road, but it is of course a fully functioning town, with several cafés and restaurants and at least one hotel at the time of research. The central square has the large Mother of God Church (1900), a post office, the Culture Palace where taxis wait and from where minibuses depart, and the tall building of the Soviet-era Khaldi Hotel (4 Kentronakan Sq; m 094 380864) with a bus ticket office (✆0264 26001) at its base. Most of Gavar's industry has drawn to a close but the hosiery factory survives, exporting to the other CIS countries and seeking niche markets elsewhere.

Those who enjoy visiting small village churches will find a number of interest in and around Gavar, and there are other off-the-beaten-track sites such as the medieval settlement of **Kanagegh**. It is also one of several points of access to the Geghama Mountains, and has the singular distinction of hosting an annual **potato festival** in September.

**Noratus (field of khachkars)** Noratus village is home to one of Armenia's most amazing and unique sights: the field of khachkars on the eastern edge of the town. The modern section is quite interesting, but the array of stones from the medieval period onwards is where the range and fascination of the khachkars are overwhelming. Although there are many groups of khachkars in Armenia, nowhere can rival the impression made by the approximately 900 here. It is quite impossible to do justice to the carved stones on a single visit and one can merely wander across the site gazing in amazement: it is quite impossible to take in the riot of carved detail. There are information boards, but visitors may find it useful to carry with them the description of the Noratus cemetery walking tour instituted by AMAP (see **w** armenianmonuments.org/en/monument/Noratus). A small problem is that the numbers on the posts have disappeared: the suspicion is that this is the work of small boys who hope thereby to act as guides! Visitors should note that, like all khachkars which are still in their original positions, these face west and can therefore most easily be photographed in the afternoon.

On the southern edge of the village of Noratus stands the small white 9th- or 10th-century **church of St Gregory** with its relatively high cylindrical tambour. The narrow front of the church combines with the small projecting corner rooms, the high tambour and the conical dome to give the appearance of a space rocket. Behind the east end of the church is a row of ten interesting khachkars. In the centre of the village the larger 9th-century Mother of God Church has been under gradual restoration for several years.

## Dzoragyugh and Nerkin Getashen
Dzoragyugh (Gorge Village) is home to two churches, both of which were founded in the late 9th century shortly after Sevanavank. The larger, ruinous one, Shoghagavank, dedicated to St Peter, is situated on a hill at the western end of the village. The church was built between 877 and 886 and its founder was the same Princess Miriam who founded Sevanavank. The site again has a good array of khachkars, and is where local royalty are thought to be buried, but it is no rival for Noratus. Dzoragyugh's other church was originally built as the Masruts Anapat (Hermitage of Masru). It was subsequently extended and now presents a plain, square appearance. Today it is known as St John the Baptist. It still functions as the village church today and was one of the first to have carpets on the floor and on the altar dais. It is decorated with, among other things, a carpet hanging on the wall depicting the Last Supper (and owing its composition to Leonardo da Vinci) as well as various embroideries. A large wrought-iron chandelier hangs from the ceiling. The lower, older parts of the building are constructed of dark grey, rough-hewn basalt blocks, and contrast rather startlingly with the upper parts and tambour which are formed of red tuff, and some modern repairs effected with dressed grey tuff. Khachkars are lined up beside the west and east walls and also occupy the orchard to the south of the church.

**Nerkin Getashen** (Lower Getashen) was at one time the summer residence and administration centre of the Bagratid dynasty. The large Mother of God Church (part of what was Kotavank) built of dark grey basalt was again founded in the late 9th century, but this time by Miriam's son, Gregory Supan. It is almost square in external appearance thanks to the large corner rooms which conceal the internal cross shape. The dome and parts of the walls collapsed during the 17th century; it still presents an impressive appearance today, as it hopefully also will on completion of ongoing restoration work. Many interestingly carved tombstones and khachkars stand around the church including a row of 17 enormous ones. It is worth exploring the adjacent hill: it is covered with an array of khachkars to rival Noratus and from it one can see the ruins of Kot, the early medieval capital of the region.

## THE SOUTHERN SIDE OF LAKE SEVAN
From Martuni the M10 road over the **Selim Pass** (2,410m) branches off and goes south into Vayots Dzor province, being one of two roads linking northern and southern Armenia which avoids the capital (the other is the new highway through Karabagh; page 377). Its relatively recent paving has reduced sightings of steppe eagles, black vultures and griffon vultures which were characteristic of the rolling uplands on the northern side of the pass. One of Armenia's most interesting sights, the 14th-century **Selim Caravanserai** (page 335), is just over the provincial border in Vayots Dzor. Within Gegharkunik, there is at the southern end of **Gegh'hovit** a ruined 5th-century church dedicated to St George, surrounded by tombstones with much figure carving. There are **petroglyphs** on Sev Sar (Black Mountain) to the east of the road. To the west is **Mount Armaghan** (2,829m), an extinct volcano with a crater lake and a small basalt chapel of 2009 built on older foundations. Accessible via a 7.4km dirt road from the village of

Madina (4x4 required or a 2-hour hike each way), it gives a flavour of the volcanic landscapes found elsewhere in the Geghama range.

**Martuni**  Martuni acquired its present name in 1926: Martuni was the *nom de guerre* of Alexander Myasnikyan, the first prime minister of Armenia in Soviet days. The renaming of towns here manages to create particular confusion as there is another Martuni, also in Gegharkunik province but in the Getik Valley north of the lake. It is always necessary therefore to specify which Martuni one means: the northern one seems usually to be called Martuni Krasnoselsk region even though Krasnoselsk (Russian for 'red village') has officially reverted to its former name of Chambarak. Just to add to the confusion there is a third Martuni in Nagorno Karabagh.

**Vanevank**  In a gorge on the southern side of the village of **Artsvanist** is the secluded and appealing **monastery of Vanevank**. The main church, dedicated to St Gregory and at the left-hand side, was built in 903 by Prince Shapuh Bagratuni together with his sister Miriam, the same Miriam who was also responsible for other churches in the district already mentioned. It was restored at the end of the 10th century by King Gagik I Bagratuni when the surrounding wall was built, parts of which can still be seen, notably on the hillside above and behind the monastery. The rather plain church building is itself basalt but the octagonal tambour is of contrasting red tuff. The right-hand church is barrel-vaulted and without a dome. It has a somewhat elongated appearance and is also built of basalt but has contrasting red tuff at the top of the gable ends. The gavit between the two churches was added at a later date. It has a belltower and in the east part is what appears to be a burial vault.

**Makenis**  With its livestock, dirt roads and dung drying for fuel, Makenis is an evocative village, though the access road is in poor condition. **Makenyats Monastery** is picturesquely situated at the edge of the village overlooking the Karchaghbyur River. According to 13th-century chroniclers, the monastery was founded by Prince Gregory Supan in 851. It is a three-apse cross-dome church built of basalt with a circular tambour and surrounded by a substantial wall. There are large chapels on both sides of the altar dais with carved doorways. Carvings of horses decorate the base of the southern pillar and the inside of the lintel of the main door. At the west gable is a small belfry. The gavit is now ruined but there is a small chapel to the southwest. The river must have changed its course slightly since the monastery was built, as the conspicuous latrine in the perimeter wall is now a few metres from it. There is a good collection of khachkars, some of which have been incorporated into garden walls and one of which has been removed to act as a bridge over a modern irrigation channel. Beyond Makenis is **Akhpradzor**, at an elevation of 2,293m one of the highest permanently inhabited settlements in the country.

**THE EASTERN SIDE OF LAKE SEVAN**  This side of the lake is much less developed than the west side. The road on the eastern side of the lake is mostly in good condition although there are some extremely poor stretches between Tsapatagh and Vardenis. The flat area between Vardenis and the lake used to be the shallow Lake Gilli, a wetland complex of about 1,000ha and an important nesting area for more than a hundred species of migratory waterbirds. In 1960 the Soviet government decided to drain Lake Gilli for agricultural land, mainly wheat and barley cultivation. Although some small areas of wetland remain, many breeding birds were lost. The draining of Lake Gilli and the reduction in the level of Lake Sevan also destroyed important wintering grounds for wading birds, though greater flamingos can still be seen in autumn. The eastern side of the lake has few specific tourist attractions, but there are some pleasant beach resorts (page 227) which tend to be much quieter than those in the northwest. A railway parallels the road, with weekend passenger services to Shorzha in the summer (and regular freight services to and from the gold mine at Sotk). Wild flowers abound in early summer; the embankment can be spectacular with poppies, catmint, vetches and hypericum. On the shore of the lake salvias and iris can be found among the tamarisk trees. At the northern end, look out for the dark purple-pink mounds of *Onobrychis cornuta* and the pinkish-white carpets of rock jasmine (*Androsace* sp) in May/June.

Between the villages of Artanish and Shorzha, the hilly **Artanish peninsula** juts into the lake, on which Mount Artanish rises to 2,460m. A road goes down the flat west side of the peninsula from Shorzha and ends at a few houses and some beaches. A short road leads to Artanish bay on the east side. It is not possible to drive around the peninsula, but you can walk round.

**Vardenis**  Vardenis is the principal town in the eastern part of Gegharkunik and is a convenient stopping place for those travelling to or from Nagorno Karabagh, either by road on the new highway over the Sotk Pass (2,367m) or by foot on the Janapar Trail (page 381). The town has all basic facilities, a couple of B&Bs (page 228) and a handful of eateries. The prominent church dates from the early 20th century.

### ✗ Where to eat and drink

✗ **Hrashk Ojakh Restaurant**  Viktor Hambartsumyan St (1km from the main road on the road to Ayrk); ⏱ 10.00–midnight daily. Serves good fish *khorovats*.

**Ayrk**  A poor road runs southeast to Ayrk which has two small medieval churches. Ayrk itself is pleasantly set in rolling countryside but looks poor and even more run-down than Vardenis with many empty houses, probably deserted by fleeing Azeris and, with little potential employment to attract Armenians fleeing in the opposite direction, they have remained unoccupied. The two churches are about 150m apart. Both have barrel-vaulted roofs and good collections of khachkars. The westernmost church, dedicated to the Mother of God, dates from 1181 and the easternmost, St George's, is slightly later. Between the two are remnants of massive Iron Age fortification walls and in the cliffs below the eastern church are caves, from which we disturbed a little owl (*Athene noctua*).

**Sotk**  The newly upgraded main road between Vardenis and the Sotk Pass (2,367m) across Geghakunik's flat eastern plain bypasses the town of Sotk, or Zod as it was called until 1991 (and often still is). Zod grew from village to town in the 1960s/70s with the industrialisation of the Zod gold mines. The predominantly Azeri inhabitants fled in 1988. If passing, it is worth a short detour to see the **church of St Betghehem**. A long basilica, it has an old feel to it both inside and outside. Dating from the 7th century, there is evidence of several phases of rebuilding, including 13th-century khachkars incorporated into the walls, most notably a complete row in the west wall. The church, today standing in a farmyard, is mostly built of large blocks of stone, and inside four massive free-standing pillars divide the barrel-vaulted church into a wide central aisle and two narrow side aisles.

**THE GETIK VALLEY**  The beautiful but little-visited **Getik Valley** can be reached by heading northeast from Shorzha over the **Chambarak (or Karmir) Pass** (2,176m) towards the town of Chambarak. With the quiet, paved H30 road descending gently among rolling hills before entering the forested valleys of Tavush, it makes for an excellent scenic route from Lake Sevan to the attractions of the Aghstev Valley, particularly for cycle tourists. Several B&Bs (page 229) exist along the route in Chambarak, Martuni and Kalavan.

**Chambarak** itself is something of a backwater and looks as if it has seen better days. The shops, post office, bank, etc are on either September 21st Street (the road on which one enters the town), or Garegin Nzhdeh Street at right angles to it. These are the only tarmac roads in the town, all others being poor dirt roads.

From **Ttujur** village, the H38 unpaved road over the spectacular Ttujur Pass (2,092m) goes off northwards into the eastern part of Tavush province (page 314), eventually reaching Berd. Ttujur means 'sour water', and the village itself does indeed have a mineral water spring, on the south side of the road opposite a small church and grocery store; its iron-rich waters are believed to have medicinal properties.

Further west, the spectacular mountain village of **Kalavan** is reached by turning south and crossing the river at Dprabak to follow a dirt road (4x4 required) for 7km via Barepat. Enterprising local resident Robert Ghusakyan is working hard to realise his vision of Kalavan as a self-sustaining 'eco-village', with environmentally sensitive tourism playing a major part. Notably, Kalavan seems able to reinvent itself in this way in part because its residents are relatively new arrivals: Armenian refugees from Azerbaijan who participated in a 'village swap' with their Azeri counterparts during the early 1990s. In any case, the village represents an ideal hub for several days' worth of hiking in the surrounding forests and mountains – one of the B&Bs (page 229) should be able to organise a guide. Kalavan is also on the newly extended route of the **Janapar Trail** (page 381), which allows backpackers to hike through to Dilijan and eventually Yerevan in one direction, or through to Vardenis and Nagorno Karabagh in the other.

## KOTAYK PROVINCE

The Hrazdan River flows southeast from Lake Sevan to Yerevan, ultimately to join the Arax in the south of the country, and forms the spine of Kotayk province. The main road and rail routes roughly parallel the river and its gorge. The trip from Yerevan to **Garni Temple** and **Geghard Monastery** in the south of the province is probably Armenia's most popular half-day tourist excursion and is well worth making. The provincial capital of Hrazdan is a slowly improving post-industrial town; the mountainous northwest part of the province has long been a popular holiday destination, particularly the town of **Tsaghkadzor**, Armenia's principal ski resort, which also offers pleasant summertime hikes in the surrounding wooded countryside. To the east, split between Kotayk and neighbouring Gegharkunik, are the volcanic domes and cones of the Geghama Mountains. The sights of the Hrazdan Gorge and its side valleys are not as well known as those of the Kasakh in neighbouring Aragatsotn province, but are worth visiting if time permits.

**GETTING THERE AND AROUND**  Most places in Kotayk can be reached by minibus from Yerevan. Services to Hrazdan (AMD1,500) and Tsaghkadzor (AMD2,000) depart from 10.00 onwards from the so-called Raykom Bus Station at the intersection of Azatutyan Avenue and Nersisyan Street, reachable by bus/minibus from Mesrop Mashtots Avenue. There are buses and minibuses to **Garni** and **Goght** villages (from 10.00, departing when full; AMD250) from the bus stand just off Gai Avenue in Nor Nork (turn right at the Mercedes-Benz dealership), which itself is reachable via several bus/minibus routes from the city centre. Note that they do not go as far as Geghard; a taxi from Garni or Goght should cost around AMD2,000–3,000 with waiting time. Trains run from Yerevan's Almast and Kanaker stations to Abovyan and Hrazdan (and beyond in high summer), stopping at several points in Kotayk en route (page 85).

**WHERE TO STAY**  Most sites of interest in the province can be visited as day trips or half-day trips from Yerevan. If you're planning a summer walking or winter skiing holiday in Tsaghkadzor, you will find plentiful hotel and B&B accommodation at

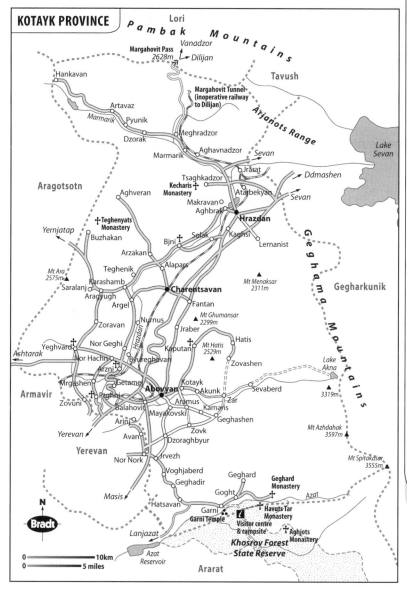

all price points, as well as much in the way of self-catering apartments via Airbnb. It should be noted that as Tsaghkadzor is primarily a holiday destination for locals and Russians, English is still not spoken in many hotels and, in terms of prices, high season tends to be winter rather than summer. If you wish to spend more than a day exploring Khosrov Forest State Reserve (page 207) from its northern entrance (overnight stays within the reserve are forbidden) you can choose from several good options in and around Garni, although it can also be visited by taking several day trips from Yerevan. There is an excellent campsite and B&B in Goght, which makes a good base camp for the area, as well as being immensely popular with overland travellers.

## Tsaghkadzor

🏠 **Tsaghkadzor Marriott Hotel** (97 rooms) 4/1 Tanzaghbyur St; ☎010 294141; w marriott. com. New international-standard 5-star hotel. Contemporary twin/dbl rooms & 3 suites; prices depend on whether room is in the main building or a separate cottage. Pool, sauna & spa on-site. Several restaurants & bars. Free shuttle to ski lift in winter. Cards accepted. Wi-Fi. **$$$$–$$$$$**

🏠 **Bagart Hotel** (6 rooms) 3 Tsaghkunyats Sq St; ☎0223 60295; m 077/091 439695. Small but adequate rooms in the town centre. B/fast extra. Guests can do their own cooking in the kitchen if they wish. Wi-Fi. Cards accepted. Price depends on size of room & whether there is a balcony. **$$**

🏠 **Best Western Alva Hotel** (97 rooms) 40 Tanzaghbyur St; ☎0223 60020/22; m 093 415102; e info@hotelalva.am; w hotelalva.am. Part of the Best Western chain since 2013, this collection of lodges with somewhat basic dbl/twin rooms is extremely convenient for the ski lifts. Cottages sleep 4. Pool & sauna. B/fast AMD4,000 pp. Cards accepted. Wi-Fi. **$$**

🏠 **Jupiter Hotel** (32 rooms) Tsaghkunyats Sq; ☎0223 60616; m 091 460617, 094 460617; e info@jupiter-hotel.info; w jupiter-hotel.info. A variety of twin/dbl rooms; price depends on size, aspect & amenities. Café, bar & restaurant on-site. Sauna. Wi-Fi. Accepts Visa & MasterCard. **$$**

🏠 **Kecharis Hotel** (35 rooms) 20 Orbeli Brothers St; ☎0223 60409/509/609; e info@ kecharis.am; w kecharis.am. A former department store, this well-presented hotel uses its space imaginatively & attractively. Many facilities, inc sauna. Disco w/end evenings in summer. Wi-Fi. Cards accepted. Meals available; order in advance. **$$**

🏠 **Tsaghkadzor General Sport Complex Hotel** (182 rooms) Olimpiakan St; ☎0223 60523/4; e info@sportcomplexhotel.com; w sportcomplexhotel.com. Some 1.5km uphill & south from town centre near the stadium. Originally built to train Soviet athletes for the 1968 Mexico Olympics; sports facilities still used by professional athletes. Sgl/dbl/quad rooms are relatively small but look comfortable. Guests can use the ordinary swimming pool (but not the Olympic pool). Free ski-lift shuttle. Wi-Fi. FB available. Cards accepted. **$$**

🏠 **Writers House Hotel** (79 rooms) 4 Charents St; ☎0223 60445, 010 281081; m 093 013044; e info@writershotel.am; w writershotel.am. In Soviet times this was the House of Creativity of Writers (the statue in front is of writer Yeghishe Charents). Set in attractive grounds & very clean. It is very popular with conferences, & visitors may well find themselves talking to cardiologists or language teachers or some other professional group. Sgl/dbl/twin/trpl/suite rooms have been fully & colourfully renovated. Indoor/outdoor swimming pools. Free ski lift transfer in winter. Wi-Fi. Cards accepted. B/fast AMD1,200 pp; FB AMD4,000 pp. **$$**

## Garni

🏠 **Chez Yvette** (7 rooms) 31 Geghard Hwy; m 055 278076; e chezyvette38@yahoo.fr. Spacious family-run B&B with a large & beautiful back garden & outdoor swimming pool, on the bus route from Yerevan. Dbl/twin rooms across 3 floors, some en suite. Bright & airy top-floor lounge & kitchen for guests. English & French spoken by members of the family. Dinner by arrangement (AMD3,000–5,000 pp). **$$**

🏠 **Narine B&B** (3 rooms) 20 Charents St; m 095 228272. This homestay has long been a popular place to eat & stay. There are views of Garni Temple from the garden & back bedrooms. You don't have to stay here to get a meal but you must give 48hrs' notice to allow the food to be prepared. Groups can also be well fed in the very pleasant garden. **$$**

## Elsewhere in the province

**⌂ Arthurs Aghveran Resort** (60 rooms) Arzakan; \0226 61610; m 091 791227; e info@ arthurs-hotel.am; w arthurs-hotel.am. Upscale holiday resort in the hills at the far end of the Aghveran road, about 12km from Arzakan (northwest of Charentsavan). Suitable for those wanting either a restful retreat or a comfortable base for walking. Swimming pools, indoor sport, gym. Restaurant serves European & Armenian cuisine. Wi-Fi. Cards accepted. Rooms are in several separate buildings & are accessed by steps. **$$$**

**⋏ Camping 3Gs** 4 Third St, Goght; m 094 496094; e info@campingarmenia.com; w campingarmenia.com. Opened in 2015 by a Dutch couple & very highly recommended. Armenia's sole international-standard campsite

is quietly & beautifully situated in Goght village & very convenient for all surrounding sights, as well as hikes in the gorge, the Geghama range & Khosrov Forest State Reserve. Popular with overland travellers who often stay several days & make day trips to Yerevan. Shared kitchens, toilets & showers. Laundry AMD500/ load. Tent pitches AMD3,000 pp/night (own tent) or AMD6,000 pp/night (permanent tent inc bedding). Secure parking for motorbikes, camper-vans & overland vehicles; electric hook-up AMD1,000/day. B/fast not available for campers. Also B&B (w bedandbreakfast3gs.com) with 4 dbl/twin rooms (AMD20,000) & 1 deluxe en suite (AMD25,000), all with b/fast inc. Outdoor swimming pool & sunloungers. Wi-Fi. **$–$$**

**OTHER PRACTICALITIES** Entering Khosrov Forest State Reserve at Garni requires a permit and, for anything beyond the short trail to Havuts Tar monastery, the company of a ranger-guide; both can be arranged at the visitor centre at the entrance to the reserve (page 207). There is free Wi-Fi for the whole of Tsaghkadzor. There is a local **tourist information office** (⊕ 09.00–17.00 daily) within Garni town hall on the main square; English-speaking staff can help with local accommodation, taxis or private cars to Geghard. Next to the office is an **e-bike charging station** installed in 2016 as part of the Green Mobility project (\010 585884; m 098 118881; e greenmobility@sunchild.org; w greenmobility.am) from where **electric-assist bicycles** can be hired.

**GARNI AND GEGHARD** The excursion from Yerevan to Garni Temple and Geghard Monastery is probably Armenia's most popular day trip and well worth making if it is your only opportunity to get a flavour of the country's ancient historical sites. The area also offers relatively easy access to the most popular hikes in the Geghama Mountains, as well as in Garni Gorge and Khosrov Forest State Reserve. Unfortunately the approach to Garni Temple itself has in recent years become laden with the paraphernalia of a mainstream tourist hot spot, attracting a clamour of hostels and B&Bs and everything from wine tasting to *lavash*-baking lessons being touted. Geghard Monastery isn't much better; on a summer Sunday it is entirely possible you will have to queue to get into the main church. Those with any kind of aversion to such environments are strongly suggested to make a very early start and preferably visit on a weekday.

See page 87 for information about public transport from Yerevan to Garni and Goght. If you have private transport, about halfway from Yerevan, near the village of Voghjaberd, it is worth stopping at the **memorial arch** to the writer Yeghishe Charents (page 56) as it offers splendid views across the valley to Mount Ararat. During the descent to Garni the **Azat Reservoir** can be seen to the southwest; a right turn, signposted to Artashat, goes to the reservoir, which is a favoured picnic spot in summer.

**⋈ Where to eat and drink** Garni and Geghard being such popular destinations, restaurant prices tend to be slightly higher than elsewhere in the provinces. Garni has several basic eateries on the road to the temple and there are various roadside options between Yerevan and Geghard Monastery. If on a budget you can make for the usual village groceries, from which a picnic can be put together, as well as plenty of traditional *lavash* bakeries that sell the bread fresh and hot.

✖ **Garni Fish Restaurant** Garni Gorge; m 091 923464, 093 923464; ⊕ 09.00–21.00. Located 2km upstream from the bottom of the descent into the gorge from beside the temple (see below), this restaurant attached to a nearby fish farm is well known for its excellent fish barbecue. Conveniently located on the way to/from the Khosrov Forest State Reserve entrance & visitor centre.

✖ **Garni Toun** 8 Marzpetuni St, Garni; m 096 060470, 091 202757; e info@garnitoun.am; ⊕ 24hrs. Huge restaurant overlooking the gorge & temple, popular with big tour groups, with indoor & covered outdoor seating. Menu is the usual Armenian fare; there is an on-site bakery with working *tonir*. Even has its own small shrine, built on the site of an old sacred place & dedicated to St Thaddeus. Also has 5 somewhat dated dbl/twin hotel rooms (AMD20,000); late-night revelry in high season means a good night's sleep is probably better had elsewhere.

✖ **Goght Restaurant** Beyond Goght village on Geghard Hwy; m 091 115108, 077 115108; ⊕ 10.00–midnight. Our pick of several roadside eateries on the approach to Geghard Monastery,

with a regular Armenian menu & friendly, attentive staff. (Not to be confused with nearby Geghard Restaurant.)

✖ **HyeLandz Eco Village Resort** 2nd St, Geghadir village; m 098 333322; e info@ hyelandz.com; w hyelandz.com; ⊕ 10.00–22.00. Questionable wordplay aside, this pioneering organic farming venture & hotel/restaurant complex has long been a favourite with diaspora Armenians & is conveniently positioned en route to Yerevan. Well signposted from the main road. Friendly & attentive service & tasty home-grown food, if at the upper end of the price spectrum: expect to pay AMD7,000–10,000 pp for a full meal. Do try the homemade wine or walnut liqueur. Larger groups should pre-book.

✖ **Sergei Mot** 2 Alekyan St, Garni; m 091 528087; ⊕ by appointment. Hidden in a quiet, enclosed garden away from the main tourist strip, this family-run kitchen doesn't have set opening times, usually catering for groups by prearrangement, but should be able to cope with walk-ins at lunch or dinnertime during high season. Excellent home-cooked food, by all accounts.

## What to see and do

*Garni Temple* (⊕ 10.00–17.30 Tue–Sat, 10.00–15.30 Sun; guided tours in Armenian AMD1,000, English & Russian AMD2,500; it is possible to arrange evening visits (18.00–23.00) AMD1,200; parking AMD100; adult/child AMD1,000/100) Garni Temple, as it is called, is Armenia's only Graeco-Roman-style building and is one of the few historical monuments in Armenia for which there is an admission charge. Although usually said to be a 1st-century pagan temple, probably devoted to Mithra, more recently some historians have suggested that it is more likely to be the tomb built for a Romanised ruler, probably Sohaemus, in which case the construction would have been around AD175. It is the best-known building on what is an extensive archaeological site, a triangle of readily defensible land jutting out into a bend of the Azat River far below. Archaeologists have discovered the remains of a Neolithic encampment; an inscription in cuneiform from the early 8th century BC on a vishap stone recording the capture of Garni Fortress by the Urartian king Argishti I; a Greek inscription on a huge basalt block recording the construction of a later fortress here by King Trdat I; a 3rd-century royal palace and bathhouse; churches from the 5th and 7th centuries; and the 9th-century palace of the Katholikos. Plainly the site has had a long and important history.

The 'temple' itself was destroyed in the great earthquake of 1679 but well restored between 1969 and 1975. It is easy to see which stones are the surviving originals and which are the modern replacements. The building looks rather like a miniature

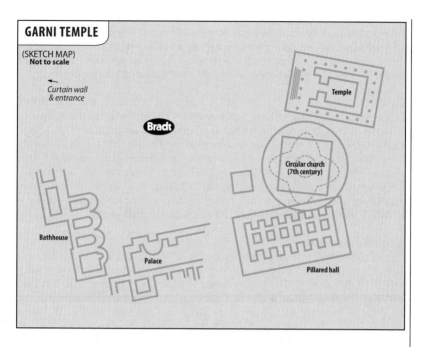

**GARNI TEMPLE**

(SKETCH MAP)
Not to scale

Curtain wall & entrance

Temple

Circular church (7th century)

Bathhouse

Palace

Pillared hall

Parthenon and has 24 columns supporting the roof with Ionic capitals and Attic bases. The frieze depicts a variety of leaves and fruits while the cornice shows the heads of lions exhibiting a variety of expressions. Nine steep steps lead up to the interior in which are a reconstructed and probably inauthentic altar and sacrificial pit. The building differs from most other Graeco-Roman buildings in being constructed of basalt; the use of such a material probably required the employment of Armenian craftsmen skilled in the technique of carving so hard a rock.

Close to the temple are the remains of other buildings. The circular building next to the temple on the west side was a 7th-century church with four apses while northwest of the church was a palace and beyond it a bathhouse. The bathhouse has a mosaic floor which depicts sea gods framed by fish and nereids together with the ambiguous words: 'We worked but did not get anything.' Some further reconstruction was started in the early years of this century and the walls of the church and palace were built up slightly. This does give an idea of the original layout but work on the church in particular was most insensitively carried out using black and bright red stones which looked garish and out of place. There were understandable protests and work was suspended.

**Around Garni** The area has several other sights, notably the churches of Mother of God and St Mashtots and the striking rock formations in Garni Gorge. **Khosrov State Reserve** is also accessed via the gorge (page 207). The **Mother of God Church** in the centre of the town (just to the right and behind the information centre) is a red and grey 12th-century basilica with a small porch incorporating a belfry. Once inside allow a little time for your eyes to adapt to the dim interior, the better to appreciate the red and grey decoration and the unusual, for Armenia, red tuff altar screen in this atmospheric church. The smooth dressed stone of the four square, free-standing pillars contrasts with the rougher stone of the walls and barrel-vaulted roof. The more elaborate **St Mashtots Church** is in the eastern part of the town, set back on the

4

left from the road down to the gorge. It is a small square single-aisle church with a 12-sided tambour with much geometric carving and windows in four of its sides. The pink cupola and roofs contrast attractively with the grey stonework of the walls and tambour. There is more elaborate carving around the door and the windows.

There are two main ways down into the **gorge**: on foot by the path to the left of the temple entrance or by the road which goes down to the river past St Mashtots. In the gorge are the astonishing **rock formations** known locally as the 'symphony of stones' – hexagonal columns of basalt which are similar to those of the Giant's Causeway (County Antrim, Northern Ireland) and Fingal's Cave (Staffa, Scotland), not to mention those in various other locations in Armenia such as along the Arpa and the Vorotan gorges, as well as in the Hrazdan Gorge through Yerevan. The gorge has a flora of drought-tolerant shrubs including *Spirea crenata*, willow-leaved pear (*Pyrus salicifolia*) and the rare yellow *Rosa hemisphaerica*. Herbaceous plants include *Campanula*, *Verbascum* and spiny *Astragalus* (goat's thorn).

**Geghard Monastery** (⊕ during usual church opening hrs 09.00–18.00 daily) One of the great sites of Armenia and on the UNESCO World Heritage list since 2000, Geghard (Spear) Monastery in its gorge setting should ideally be seen when several of the country's less extraordinary churches have been visited. It is then easier to appreciate what makes this one different. Its unusual feature is that it is partly an ordinary surface structure and partly cut into the cliff. The name dates from the 13th century and reflects the bringing here of a spear said to have been the one which pierced the side of Christ at Calvary. (This spear, a shaft with a diamond-shaped head into which a cross has been cut, can now be seen in the treasury at Etchmiadzin. It is inside a gilded silver case made for it in 1687.) Visiting Geghard on a Sunday morning is an enthralling experience with beautiful singing from the choir, and beautifully groomed animals brought for *matagh* (sacrifice) after the service.

The first monastery at this site was called Ayrivank (Cave Monastery). It was founded as early as the 4th century but was burned down and plundered in 923 by Nasr, a subordinate of Yusuf, the caliph's governor of Azerbaijan. Yusuf had just spent five years in prison for rebellion against the caliph. Nasr continued the rebellion, seeking to extend his own power and to enforce conversion of the Christian population to Islam.

Thereafter the monastery declined until the revival of monastery building in the late 12th century. The earliest surviving part, the **Chapel of the Mother of God**, dates from before 1164 and is situated above the road just before the gateway to the main monastery complex. It is partly a surface structure and partly hewn into the rock, rectangular in plan but with a semicircular apse. Adjoining it are other passages and small rooms in the rock.

In total, surrounding the main site are more than 20 other rock-hewn chapels and service premises, many of which have carvings. Also outside the gate are small ledges on to which visitors try to throw stones. If a stone remains on the ledge then the thrower's wish is supposed to come true.

The main buildings of the monastery are surrounded by walls on three sides and a cliff face on the other. Construction was started by the Zakarian family who came into possession of it after they had commanded Armenian forces which joined with the Georgians to defeat the Seljuks. The main cathedral was built in 1215 and is of the cross-dome type, the circular tambour being decorated with graceful arcature and narrow windows and topped by a conical cupola. Between the spans of arcature and on the portals and cornices are depicted a variety of

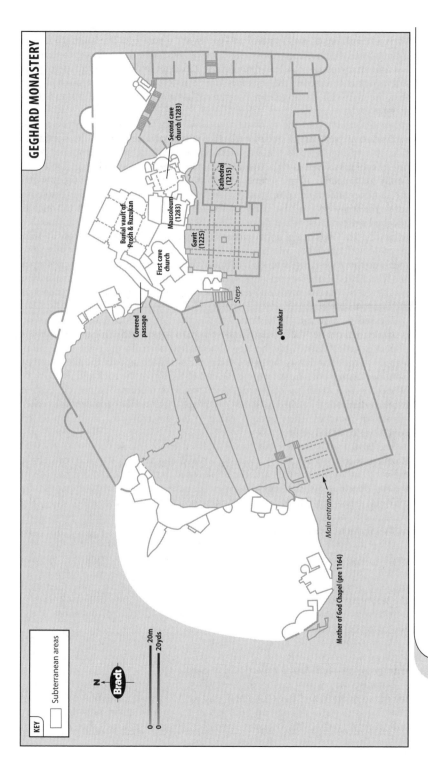

## GEGHARD MONASTERY

**KEY**
Subterranean areas

N

Bradt

0 ____ 20m
0 ____ 20yds

Second cave church (1283)

Cathedral (1215)

Mausoleum (1283)

Burial vault of Prosh & Ruzukan

Gavit (1225)

First cave church

Covered passage

Steps

● Orhnakar

Main entrance

Mother of God Chapel (pre 1164)

birds and animals as well as floral and geometrical patterns. The southern façade is particularly interesting. Above the doorway with two doves facing each other is a lion attacking an ox, the emblem of the Zakarian family. The gavit at the west side which is attached to the rock face was completed by 1225. It is much plainer than the main church though the tympanum has an attractive floral design within an ogee arch.

The Zakarians sold the monastery to the Prosh family who constructed the subterranean part carved out of rock. In the **first cave church**, on the northwest side, is a spring. It bears the architect's name, Galdzag, and incorporates some fine khachkars as well as stalactite decoration around the roof opening. The Prosh family **mausoleum** and the second cave church at the northeast were probably by the same architect and completed by 1283. On the north wall of the mausoleum above the archways is a relief carving of a goat with a ring in its mouth to which is attached a rope whose two ends are round the necks of two lions which are looking outwards. The ends of the lions' tails are dragons looking upwards. Below all this, an eagle with spreading wings grasps a lamb in its talons. Both here and in the rock-cut churches there is much elaborate carving of crosses, geometrical shapes and khachkars. Rather surprisingly, to the right of the entrance to the mausoleum are carved two sirens, mythical creatures with the crowned head of a woman and the body of a bird.

The **second cave church**, dedicated to the Mother of God, leads off from the mausoleum. Some of the khachkars show human figures including one who holds a spear pointing down while he blows an uplifted horn. To the right at the stairs leading to the altar dais is the figure of a goat. At the left side on the altar dais is a stone seat with a lion's head forming the end of the top of the back and to the right of the dais is a khachkar of two doves each side of a cross. The church, despite being underground, retains the same cross shape with tambour and cupola as other Armenian churches. There is an opening to the outside world at the top of the cupola which admits light.

The **gavit** which formed the burial vault of Prince Papak Prosh and his wife Ruzukan was hewn in 1288. It is at a higher level and to reach it, go up the steps at the west end of the complex and then follow the narrow subterranean passage to the right decorated with khachkars carved into the rock. The roof is supported by four pillars and in the floor is a hole looking down into the mausoleum below. The acoustics in this gavit are amazing. Anyone standing here and singing, particularly by the northeast pillar, sounds like an entire choir.

Other features of interest are the small **rock-hewn chapel** adjacent to the steps leading up to the gavit. Over the door is a carving of a figure wearing what appears to be a Mithraic-style hat. The *orhnakar* is in the middle of the paved area within the monastery walls but the *mataghatun* is outside the small eastern gateway. Around the boundary wall are various service buildings; that at the northeast corner is a **bakery** complete with *tonir*. Most date from the 17th century but those at the southwest corner only from 1968 to 1971.

After so much culture it makes a pleasant change, on leaving Geghard, to try the freshly baked *gata*, fruit *lavash* or walnut *sujukh* sold by the many vendors near the entrance. (The plum *lavash* is particularly good.)

Botanists may wish to explore the river valley with its wealth of herbaceous plants, including orchids, and trees. Oriental wild apple *Malus orientalis* and Caucasian pear *Pyrus caucasia* flourish on boulders in the middle of the fast-flowing river and wild grape vine *Vitis sylvestris* scrambles through trees, including *Euonymus*, *Cornus*, *Sorbus* and *Acer ibericum*, on the riverbank.

**MOUNT AZHDAHAK AND THE GEGHAMA MOUNTAINS** To climb **Mount Azdahak** (3,597m) in a day during the seasonal snow-free window from mid-June to late September, most visitors arrange 4x4 transport (at least in the outward direction) from Geghard village to one of several points close to the base of the peak; see page 67 for a list of local specialist tour operators, or ask at one of the local accommodation providers. Reaching the peak entails a relatively simple non-technical hike from the north side, with a little more scree to cross and scrambling required from the south; loose rocks call for sturdy footwear whichever route you use. A snow-fed crater lake below the summit provides a most invigorating swim for the truly daring. Nearby **Lake Akna** is another popular destination; this is best reached by 4x4 from Sevaberd. An unmarked **backcountry hiking route** traversing the entire Geghama mountain range north to south through Kotayk (and other provinces) is being developed as part of the Transcaucasian Trail (see box, page 114); the spectacular route passes through an altogether different landscape from that seen by most visitors, but requires complete self-sufficiency for several days. It should only be attempted by very experienced hikers and only during the summer season from mid-June to late September. Note that the summits frequently attract thundercloud build-up and electrical storms as the day progresses; early starts are advised for this reason.

**NORTH FROM YEREVAN** Yeghvard and Kaputan have churches very similar in style to each other and to the much better-known three-tier Mother of God Church at Noravank. The two churches, both also dedicated to the Mother of God, are small in floor area but disproportionately tall, have two storeys and are topped not by a tambour with cupola but by a belfry supported by columns. The lower storey of each is more or less square; the upper storey is a cross-shaped church. Access to the upper storey was by an external cantilevered staircase of which the top steps were stone while the lower were wooden and have now vanished. The only way now into the upper storey is by ladder. As well as these similarities there are also differences, in part accounted for by the use of contrasting stone (warm pink tuff in the case of Yeghvard but a rather forbidding grey basalt, which is difficult to carve, at Kaputan).

The rather plain church at **Kaputan**, built in 1349, is on a hilltop above the village and the ground around it is strewn with shards of obsidian. The belfry has eight columns; the bell is missing. Among the votive offerings inside the church is a reproduction of Salvador Dalí's *Christ of St John of the Cross*, the original of which hangs in Glasgow's Kelvingrove Art Gallery! After Kaputan the road goes on through the treeless upland to circumnavigate the eroded volcanic cone of **Mount Hatis** (2,529m), with a pleasant hike possible to the summit during the summer months. It is possible to do a loop back to Abovyan although the road surface deteriorates after Zovashen.

**Yeghvard** is most easily reached direct from Yerevan on the H4 road, although it may be convenient to combine it with the churches of the Kasakh Gorge (page 187) and travel to Yeghvard via Ashtarak. The church, which dates from 1301, is set in a well-kept garden in the middle of the village and is highly decorated both externally and inside. The upper church is particularly notable for its very fine carved animals: a lion and a bull on the west façade, an ibex on the north, a leopard killing an ibex on the east, and an eagle with a lamb in its talons on the south. Inside, the apse has radiating black and red tuff and there is geometrical carving around the bema's two doors. The belfry has 16 columns and the bell has been rehung.

Elsewhere in the village are the remains of a (harder to find) basilica church of the 5th or 6th century. Turn left, just after a large shop, near to where you turned right

4

for the two-storey church, and/or ask the way. Yeghvard is also an alternative starting point for the 4x4 drive or walk to Mount Ara and its cave shrine (page 192).

Some 6km north of Yeghvard is the ruined circular **Zoravar Church** at Zoravan. Like all so-called circular churches it is actually polygonal. Just north of the right turn for Zoravan village a track goes off left just beyond a cemetery. Follow the track along the side of the cemetery keeping an irrigation channel to your right. The church can be seen across the hillside. Standing on the lower slopes of Mount Ara looking across the Arax plain to Mount Ararat, the church was built in the second half of the 7th century by Prince Grigor Mamikonian. Some reconstruction was carried out in the 1970s. Standing on a circular base the church has eight apses, the east altar apse being wider than the others. The tambour, cylindrical inside but 12-sided externally, is carried on the apse arches and the pillars between apses. Externally the east apse is pentagonal, the other seven are three-sided. The church was lit by three windows in the east apse, one in each of the other seven apses and four windows in the tambour, at the cardinal points.

Further north **Teghenyats Monastery** is reached from the village of **Buzhakan**, a resort centre in Soviet days and an excellent centre for walking. Parking at the start of the track and walking the last 3km to Teghenyats Monastery makes a very **beautiful walk**. The first section is between fields as far as a half-built guesthouse, construction of which was halted when the Soviet Union collapsed. The track then continues uphill through forest. There is a small river to the right down in the gorge and the track, after winding along the hillside, drops down to ford it. It is difficult to cross when the river is in spate. The track then climbs straight up to the monastery, with springs and places to picnic on the way. The monastery is evocatively situated with the Tsaghkunyats mountain range forming the backdrop. The ruins occupy a large area. The ruinous 10th-century **church** looks as if it had a barrel-vaulted roof and the front of the bema has interesting carvings.

The massive red and black 12th- to 13th-century **gavit**, the best-preserved building, was domed; there is carved decoration on what remains of the base of the tambour. Northwest of the gavit low-walled ruins lead to the remains of the 13th- to 14th-century **dining room**. One enters through the south doorway. Massive pillars on the north side supported what was probably a barrel-vaulted roof. At present the two doorways in the north wall lead only to an earth face. Immediately north of the gavit is a building with free-standing columns which has either been built into the hillside or excavated from it. There is evidence of other buildings to the west, south and northeast of the main complex. The graveyard, with tombstones shaped to look like sheep and horses, covers the hillside to the south of the monastery. Snow can linger up here well into late April; one visit in the spring revealed bear footprints in the snow while further down the valley an array of spring flowers rapidly succeeded the melting snow.

**NORTHEAST FROM YEREVAN** The main road from Yerevan to Sevan bisects the province from south to north, staying above and to the east of the Hrazdan river gorge. Leaving Yerevan it is notable for the number of casinos since they were banished from the city (page 148) and also, in late summer, for the number of sheep herded into pens for sale. To the south of the road, on top of a hill, can be seen what looks like a Russian church. As any local will tell you, it is actually the mansion of Gagik Tsarukyan, one of Armenia's best-known business magnates and founder of the Prosperous Armenia political party.

The first point of interest is the ruinous **church of Ptghni** in the middle of the village to the west of the highway. The church is a large basilica of the 6th century whose cupola and roof have collapsed. The north façade of the church and much of the west end are still standing and were stabilised in 1939–40. Further restoration was undertaken in 1964 which included demolishing a 19th-century church that had been built adjacent. The size of the building is impressive, as is the massiveness of the one surviving arch of the four which once supported the cupola. Over the windows, most notably on the south façade, carvings depict angels, hunting scenes, saints, plants and fruits.

Probably the most noticeable feature of the industrialised town of **Abovyan** (named after the writer Khachatur Abovyan) is the enormous new red tuff **church of St John the Baptist**, dedicated in 2013. Inside there are four full-length murals of four St Johns: on the north wall St John the Evangelist and St John the Baptist, on the south wall St John Chrysostom and St John Mandakouni, Katholikos AD478–90. The church was funded by the same individual whose mansion is visible en route (see opposite). With its lavish furnishing, mass of carvings (some of which are quite interesting) and columned turrets topped with gold crosses, some have seen it as a symbol of the huge gap between rich and poor in Armenia.

**Arzni**, which is signposted off the highway, has a tiny 5th- or 6th-century octagonal church, the **St Kiraki Baptistery**. Octagonal on the outside, four-apsed inside with round windows in the thick walls, it is built on a stepped square base, which is probably older than the church, perhaps pagan. These features make it unique among similar contemporary Armenian buildings. It resembles early Christian baptisteries and may be Armenia's only example of a separate baptistery building. Its red-painted metal roof is anachronistic, as is the house number (No 6) which has been assigned to it! Arzni is a large village and apparently has seven churches. To reach the baptistery continue on the main Arzni road (2nd Street) as it bears left into the village, then take the third turning on the right (5th Street). The baptistery is at the end of the street. Arzni's main claim to fame is that it was developed from 1925 onwards as the Soviet Union's first purpose-built spa. Coming from the highway, where the road into the village bears left, a road goes straight ahead and descends into the Hrazdan Gorge which is lined here with huge guesthouses, mostly derelict and spoiling what must once have been an attractive setting. The sheer number of people who could have been treated here simultaneously with water from the mineral springs is truly amazing. Building works suggest that rehabilitation of the spa may be envisaged.

**Bjni** has a fortress and two interesting churches. The main church is dedicated to the **Mother of God** and dates from 1031. It has a disproportionately large circular tambour and umbrella cupola as well as some fine khachkars from the 13th to 15th centuries. The small belfry was added in 1275 and the fortified wall in the 17th century. Used as a byre in the Stalinist era, it was restored in 1956 with assistance from the Gulbenkian Foundation. Just below the church to the east is the 13th-century **St Gevorg Church** with older khachkars built into the walls. The **fortress**, up on the small plateau within the village, was built in the 9th or 10th century by the Pahlavuni family. Parts of the northern and western walls remain but there are only traces of other buildings in what is a fairly large area. The entrance to the secret passage down to the village can be seen but it is blocked after 40m. The best way up to the fortress is from the east. The **small church** at Bjni on top of a hill beyond the fortress is dedicated to St Sargis and dates from the 7th century. It has an octagonal tambour and retains a roof of tuff tiles.

It is possible to continue from Bjni direct to **Hrazdan** town along the scenic Hrazdan River, rather than returning to the main highway, the road running first along the flat river valley, with rocky cliffs to the right and hills to the left, and then climbing above the river as the gorge narrows. Coming into Hrazdan, the road skirts the western half of the Hrazdan Reservoir. Hrazdan itself has minimal appeal. It was heavily industrialised in the Soviet period and still has a large thermal power station. Within the municipality of Hrazdan, to the west, is the village (sometimes called a suburb) of **Makravan** with the **monastery of Makravank**. The 13th-century church dedicated to the Mother of God has a tall round tambour and a conical cupola. On its south side is the smaller 10th-century Holy Redeemer Church and to the west a ruined 13th-century gavit with many khachkars piled up around the remaining walls. The cemetery has gravestones dating from the 10th to 14th centuries.

**THE HRAZDAN GORGE** The old road along the gorge is slower than the main highway but it gives a very different and certainly more pleasant view of the region. Not only is one much more aware of the gorge itself but also of the surprisingly large villages or small towns, to which one is more or less oblivious when using the main highway.

**Argel** has one of Armenia's largest hydro-electric power plants, the **Argel Gyumush power station**, with a capacity of 224MW. The road across the river actually takes you into the power station grounds then out the other side, an arrangement which is presumably the result of another bridge upstream having been lost. Before reaching the river a narrow alley off left leads to Argel's **St George Church**. Built in 1890, incorporating earlier remains, this restored basilica church is dwarfed by its belltower. A crowded cemetery extends east from the church. Argel is also home to Anna Tatosyan's well-known **lavash bakery**, which draws visitors from Yerevan and elsewhere to watch the bread being traditionally baked, though its primary function remains to feed the village; it is easily located by sense of smell.

**Charentsavan** was founded in 1948 to house workers building the hydro-electric plant and then became heavily industrialised. With the collapse of the Soviet Union there are now vast areas of depressing derelict factories. The well-known Bjni brand of mineral water is, despite its name, bottled in Charentsavan.

As well as a large red and grey three-aisled Mother of God basilica of 1891–97, **Alapars** has two much earlier churches, both on Vardan Mamikonyan Square. The most obvious, because of its incongruous red belltower, is the **Vardan Zoravar Church** built by Prince Grigor in 901, rebuilt in 1901 and recently renovated. Inside it now has a typical village *zham* appearance. Local legend says that one of the stones contains a drop of blood from Vardan Mamikonian, hero of the Battle of Avarayr, AD451 (page 19). Just east is the earlier three-apse cross-dome 7th-century **church of St John**. At first glance it is not obvious that it is a church, the restoration of 1997 having given it a square metal roof in place of what would originally have been a dome. However, it stands on a three-step base, has khachkars embedded in its walls and a new carving of a church over the entrance. On the walls of the south apse are fragments of frescoes. The churches are usually locked but the keyholder, Zina, lives next door at number six; she is willing to open the churches for visitors.

In **Arzakan** several hot springs can be found, which can be rented by the hour from the entrepreneurs who have built informal bathing complexes around them; best to ask locally. A side road goes north through the wooded hills to **Aghveran**, a favourite leisure area for Armenians and a good base for hiking and, in winter, ski touring. The attractive gorge has a range of hotels, holiday homes, former *pansionats* and picnic areas.

## NORTHEAST KOTAYK

**Tsaghkadzor** Tsaghkadzor is Armenia's principal ski resort and the number and range of accommodation options reflects this. It is also an excellent centre for walking and the scope for doing so is extended by using the chair-lift, which operates all year. In summer thousands of anemones (*Pulsatilla armena*) can be seen in grassland a short distance above the chair-lift terminus. A useful brochure containing a map of the town, details of ski facilities and hotels is published by Collage Publishing House in Yerevan.

The **ski resort** (w ropeway.am), used for Olympic training in Soviet days, is located on the eastern slopes of Mount Teghenis and offers a range of pistes for all abilities, as well as some good lift-accessible off-piste skiing just below the summit and above the treeline. The main season is usually from late December to mid-March, depending of course on seasonal variations. The resort is particularly popular with Russians, perhaps due to cheap flights from Moscow and significantly lower prices for accommodation and ski passes than back home; for this reason it can be difficult to find English-speaking staff at the hotels and restaurants. Ski instruction is available, and equipment of variable quality can be hired from a couple of outlets near the chair-lift (AMD5,000/day for skis, boots & poles, AMD7,000/day for snowboard & boots); expert skiers may prefer to bring their own. The **chair-lift** or **ropeway** (⊕ summer 09.30–17.30 daily, shorter hrs in winter; single trip AMD2,000, unlimited day pass AMD12,000, other options available), opened in 1967 and was replaced in 2004 by an Italian company, operating in three sections from the base of the ski slopes to the top at 1,966m. The nursery slope for beginners is at the top of the first lift, where an additional short drag lift operates. Two other chair-lifts operate at different points on the slopes to extend the pisted ski area. Cafés and restaurants operate at all of the main lift termini. There is a **rescue service** (✆ 0223 60030) and any injuries requiring hospital treatment go to the hospital in Hrazdan. In winter a **skating rink** is open in the town's main square.

The **Orbeli Brothers' House Museum** (✆ 0223 60552; w orbelimuseum.am; ⊕ 11.00–18.00 Tue–Sun; adult/child AMD500/200) is, appropriately, on Orbeli Brothers Street opposite Kecharis Hotel. Of the three brothers, Ruben (1880–1943) was a marine archaeologist, Levon (1882–1958) head of the Military Medical Academy and Joseph (1887–1961) an archaeologist who took part in the excavations of Ani as well as being director of the Hermitage Museum in Leningrad. The museum contains personal belongings of the brothers and copies of their publications. An information leaflet in English is available, as is a booklet, produced for the 1,050th anniversary of Ani, detailing Joseph Orbeli's work in Ani with Nicholas Marr, the Georgian-born (of Scottish father and Georgian mother) historian and linguist who undertook annual excavations in Ani between 1904 and 1917. Disappointingly for non-Armenian visitors, there is little accessible detail of the brothers' work in the museum displays.

*Kecharis Monastery* Located at the western end of Tsaghkadzor town centre, the **main church** of Kecharis Monastery is dedicated to St Gregory the Illuminator and was erected in 1003 by Grigor Pahlavuni (990–1059). Given his age, his personal involvement must have been slight. Son of the Lord of Bjni, he was to become a distinguished theologian and writer acquiring the title Grigor Magistros from the Byzantine rulers after their takeover of the kingdom of Ani from Gagik II in 1045. The circular tambour and conical cupola were damaged by an earthquake in 1927 but were restored between 1997 and 2000. To the south of St Gregory's lies the small **Holy Cross Chapel** which dates from 1051. It too has a conical cupola but its circular tambour is decorated with six arcatures. After the construction of these buildings the Seljuk conquest put paid to any further work, the region remaining under their rule until their defeat by the Georgians with Armenian support in 1196.

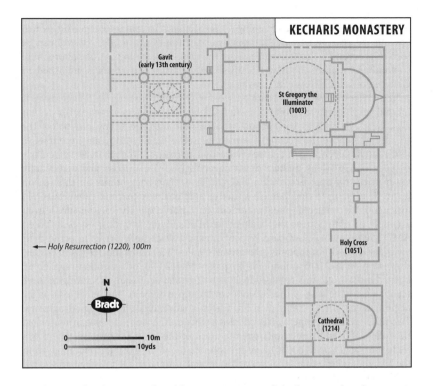

Gavit
(early 13th century)

St Gregory the
Illuminator
(1003)

← Holy Resurrection (1220), 100m

Holy Cross
(1051)

N

Bradt

0 ————————— 10m
0 ————————— 10yds

Cathedral
(1214)

Work immediately restarted and by 1206 St Gregory's had acquired its large **gavit** whose roof is supported by four free-standing columns. The final church, the so-called **cathedral**, lies to the south of Holy Cross and was built immediately after the gavit by Prince Vasak Prosh, being completed in 1214. As in other churches of the period, the corner rooms at the west end have two storeys with the upper storey being accessed by cantilevered stairs. It too has a conical cupola, the circular tambour having 12 arcatures. The Mongol invasions in the late 1230s saw Kecharis badly damaged but it was restored by 1248. Presumably it was at this restoration that the tympanum of the doorway leading from the gavit into St Gregory's acquired its Georgian-style frescoes. The monastery is once more a functioning church with new furnishings and embroidered curtains in all three churches. The embroidered text on the north wall of Holy Cross is the Lord's Prayer. About 100m from the main group of buildings is the small **Chapel of the Holy Resurrection** with its high circular tambour and another conical cupola. It dates from 1220 and was probably used as the family burial vault for the founders of the cathedral.

**Meghradzor and Hankavan** From Hrazdan a road goes northwest along the Marmarik River for 30km to Hankavan. This valley is another favoured holiday area for Armenians but is rarely visited by foreign tourists. It is an attractive road with walking potential and the possibility of bathing in the hot mineral water springs at the end for which Hankavan is known (*hank* means 'mine' in Armenian). The road and railway follow the broad river valley to **Meghradzor** where the (inoperative) railway turns north to enter the Margahovit Tunnel through the Pambak range; a dirt road crosses the ridge to Margahovit from this point (4x4 required) and can be used in summer to access the Pambak ridge and Lori province (page 278).

Meanwhile, the road in the main valley climbs towards a renovated reservoir and beyond that to the village of **Hankavan**, which sports a number of health resorts following in the footsteps of the Soviet-era sanatoria that formerly operated here. Just south of Hankavan, one of the hot springs in the area has been 'privatised' with the construction of three small and two larger hot water pools and changing cubicles. Above the village, an area of some 51.7km$^2$ of the surrounding mountains comprises Hankavan Hydrological Sanctuary.

The Central Provinces    KOTAYK PROVINCE

4

## UPDATES WEBSITE

You can post your comments and recommendations, and read feedback and updates from other readers online at **w** bradtupdates.com/armenia.

# 5

# The Northern Provinces

The three northern provinces of Shirak, Lori and Tavush encompass a great diversity of landscapes. **Shirak** is dominated by rolling hills and treeless steppe, while **Lori** is characterised by its deep gorges and wild-flower meadows and **Tavush** by broadleaved forests and the dramatic cliffs and ridgelines of the Lesser Caucasus Mountains. Visitors who combine a visit to Armenia with one to Georgia are obliged to cross at least one of the three provinces, most commonly Lori, passing through the provincial capital of Vanadzor. The **monasteries** of Sanahin, Haghpat, Haghartsin and Goshavank are all much visited, and others such as Kobayr receive a fair number of visitors, though such gems as Makaravank, Kirants and Hnevank see only a few. Two of Armenia's four **national parks** reside in the northern provinces: Lake Arpi National Park in Shirak province is a significant birdwatching destination, while the valleys and escarpments of Dilijan National Park surround the former spa town of Dilijan with forests that are prime hiking territory.

## SHIRAK PROVINCE

Shirak province is bounded to the west by Turkey and to the north by Georgia. In the south the border with Turkey follows the Akhurian River and bisects the Akhurian Reservoir, whose water is shared between Armenia and Turkey. Mostly a high, treeless plateau possessing a spacious, remote and rugged character, it becomes increasingly hilly nearer the Georgian border and to the east where it borders Lori province. It is known for being one of the colder provinces of Armenia, with particularly drawn-out winters, though the short summers can be pleasantly warm compared with the stifling heat experienced elsewhere in the country. Aside from the provincial capital **Gyumri**, Shirak is off the main tourist routes and fine monasteries such as **Marmashen** and **Harichavank** remain little visited. Those interested in churches should visit **Anipemza** whose roofless basilica church is one of the oldest in Armenia. Though physically inaccessible from the Armenian side, the ancient city of **Ani** is visible across the gorge in present-day Turkey and remains a key historical and cultural heritage site for the Armenians. In the northwest corner of the province is **Lake Arpi National Park**.

**GETTING THERE AND AROUND** The only sizeable city in Shirak is the provincial capital of **Gyumri**. It has good road links to the south (Talin and Yerevan) and east (Spitak and Vanadzor) and there is a border crossing with Georgia, 45km to the north at Bavra, which is open to foreigners.

One of the few functioning **rail routes** in Armenia runs from Yerevan to Gyumri. Trains to and from **Yerevan** run three times daily; an additional weekend express service, which commenced operations in March 2018 (Fri–Sun; AMD2,500), takes

2 hours, with departures from Yerevan at 10.00, returning from Gyumri at 16.45. The regular daily service stops at a long list of intermediary stations, departing Yerevan at 07.55, 14.25 and 18.25, and departing Gyumri at 08.25, 11.45 and 18.15, taking around 3½ hours. It is also possible to catch the Yerevan–**Tbilisi** sleeper train at Gyumri; berths cost AMD8,200 in third class or AMD12,000 in second class, departing Gyumri for Tbilisi at 00.20 every alternate evening all year round. During the summer holidays the service runs daily and extends to Batumi. See page 85 for general comments on train travel.

**Minibuses** depart from and arrive at Gyumri's bus station (*avtokayan*) at the south end of Shahumyan Street. They run between Gyumri and Yerevan's Intertown Bus Station on Sevan Street (half-hourly from 07.00; AMD1,500) with shared taxis plying the same route for a slightly higher fee. Other useful routes include minibuses to Tbilisi (10.30 daily; AMD5,200), minibuses to Vanadzor (hourly from 10.00; AMD800) as well as a bus (16.00 daily; AMD500), minibuses to Tashir via Stepanavan (09.00 daily; AMD2,000/1,500), minibuses to Etchmiadzin (listed as Vagharshapat on the timetable) (10.00 daily; AMD1,500), and a minibus to Armavir (15.00 daily; AMD1,200). For local destinations, a digital timetable in both Armenian and English displays services in Shirak province including Anipemza, Artik, Bavra, Gusanagyugh, Jrapi, Lusaghbyur and Maralik, together with prices. **Taxis** also wait at the bus station: a private taxi to Yerevan should cost about AMD12,000.

Finally, it is possible to **fly** into Gyumri's Shirak International Airport (page 72), which at the time of research was served by flights from Russian destinations with significant Armenian populations.

**WHERE TO STAY** The majority of accommodation in Shirak province is in **Gyumri**, which makes the city a natural staging post for explorations of the surrounding area. Options range from hostels and guesthouses to mid-range B&Bs and hotels and a few upscale places. Being distant from Yerevan, prices are considerably cheaper for equivalent levels of service.

**Homestays** can be found in other areas, including around Lake Arpi, and are best arranged in advance with a local travel agent. In Artik there is a Soviet-era hotel which has a couple of renovated rooms. See page 92 for general comments on accommodation.

## Gyumri
Map, page 259

**Nane Hotel** (16 rooms) 1/5 Garegin Nzhdeh St; 0312 33369; e info@nanehotel.am; w nanehotel.am. This relatively new hotel is aimed at business travellers as well as the leisure market. Facilities are of a high standard. The façade preserves that of a former factory which was destroyed during the earthquake. Pleasant, well-laid-out garden with café. Restaurant & good pizzeria. Cards accepted. A little further from the city centre than the website implies. **$$$**

**Villa Kars** (16 rooms) 182 Rustaveli St; 010 561156; m 098 561156; e info@villakars.com; w villakars.com. Boutique rooms in a characterful restored 19th-century property in Gyumri's historical district. Italian founder Antonio

uses the revenue to support an on-site ceramics training centre & showroom. Uniquely appointed sgl/dbl/trpl/suites for families. Lunch/dinner for groups by advance request. Can organise regional tours & ceramics workshops. Two sister properties in Yerevan (page 139); new restaurant & hostel forthcoming. **$$$**

**Alexandrapol Hotel** (19 rooms) 70 Mayakovski St; 0312 50051; e info@alexandrapolhotel.am; w alexandrapolhotel.am. International-standard hotel located near Gyumri's central square. Opulent (some might say over-the-top) imperial-style façade with matching interior décor & furnishings. Restaurant, bar & room service. Accepts cards. Has a range of suites up to AMD200,000. Perhaps more geared towards Armenia's nouveau riche. **$$**

5

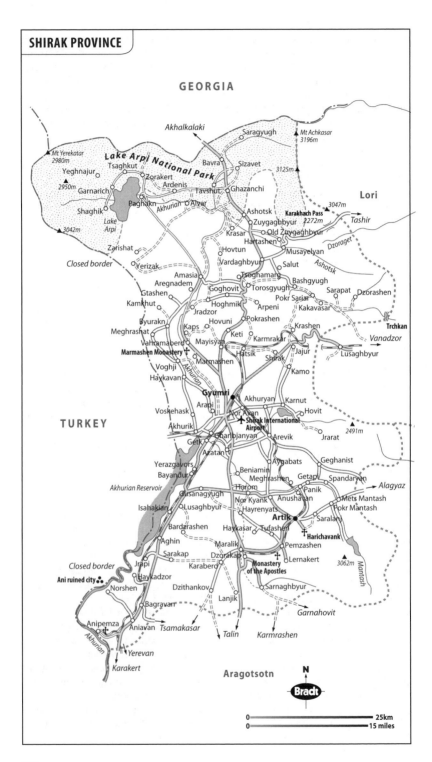

# SHIRAK PROVINCE

**GEORGIA**

Akhalkalaki

Saragyugh

▲ Mt Achkasar
3196m

Mt Yerekatar
2980m

Tsaghkut

Bavra

Sizavet

3125m

**Lake Arpi National Park**

Yeghnajur

Zorakert

Ardenis

Ghazanchi

**Lori**

2950m

Garnarich

Tavshut

Alver

3047m

Paghakn

Akhurian

Ashotsk

**Karakhach Pass**
2272m

*Tashir*

Shaghik

Zuygaghbyur

Lake
Arpi

Krasar

Old Zuygaghbyur

3042m

Hartashen

*Dzoraget*

Zarishat

Hovtun

Musayelyan

*Ashotsk*

*Closed border*

Yerizak

Vardaghbyur

Salut

Amasia

Tsoghamarg

Bashgyugh

Sarapat

Dzorashen

Aregnadem

Goghovit

Torosgyugh

Gtashen

Pokr Sarian

Kamkhut

Hoghmik

Arpeni

Kakavasar

**Trchkan**

Jradzor

Hovuni

Pokrashen

Byurakn

Kaps

Keti

Krashen

*Vanadzor*

Meghrashat

Mayisyan

Karmrakar

Jajur

Lusaghbyur

Vahramaberd

**Marmashen Monastery** ✝

Marmashen

Hatsik

Shirak

Voghji

Akhurian

Kamo

Haykavan

**Gyumri** ●

Akhuryan

Karnut

Arapi

Voskehask

Nor Avan

Hovit

Akhurik

✈ **Shirak International Airport**

Jrarat

2491m

**TURKEY**

Gharibjanyan

Arevik

Getk

Azatan

Aygabats

Geghanist

Yerazgavors

Beniamin

Getap

Spandaryan

Bayandur

Meghrashen

Panik

*Alagyaz*

*Akhurian Reservoir*

Gusanagyugh

Horom

Anushavan

Mets Mantash

Isahakian

Lusaghbyur

Nor Kyank

Pokr Mantash

Hayrenyats

**Artik** ●

Saralanj

Bardzrashen

Haykasar

Tufashen

✝ **Harichavank**

Aghin

Maralik

Pemzashen

Sarakap

Dzorakap

Lernakert

3062m

*Closed border*

Jrapi

Karaberd

**Monastery of the Apostles** ✝

**Ani ruined city** ⁂

Haykadzor

Norshen

Dzithankov

Sarnaghbyur

*Mantash*

Bagravan

Lanjik

*Garnahovit*

Anipemza ✝

Aniavan

*Tsamakasar*

*Talin*

*Karmrashen*

Akhurian

*Yerevan*

*Karakert*

**Aragotsotn**

**N**

**Bradt**

0 ———————— 25km
0 ———————— 15 miles

🏠 **Araks Hotel** (23 rooms) 25 Gorki St; ☎0312 51199; e info@arakshotel.am; w arakshotel. am. This handsome black stone building with an impressive marble entrance hall is a former police HQ. It has been fully restored & has well-appointed rooms. Indoor pool & sauna extra. Lunch/dinner must be ordered in advance. Accepts cards. **$$**

🏠 **Berlin Art Hotel** (15 rooms) 25 Haghtanak Av; ☎0312 57659; e info@berlinarthotel.am; w berlinarthotel.am. Small, attractive 1-storey hotel with clean, modern en-suite dbl/twin rooms, helpful staff & galleries of work by local artists & sculptors. Built by the German Red Cross after the earthquake as a hospital & converted into a hotel in 1996. A clinic still operates on-site & is funded by the hotel proceeds. Lunch/dinner by arrangement. No bar but drinks from reception. Tours of the region, homestays, etc can be organised by the Shirak Tours division. Cards accepted. Discounts for members of humanitarian organisations & long-term guests. **$$**

🏠 **Hotel Plaza Viktoria** (24 rooms) 244/1 Abovyan St; ☎0312 90002; m 043 290003; w hotelplazaviktoria.am. Centrally located, mid-range hotel on northwest corner of Vardanants Square. Opened in 2017 targeting foreign visitors. Very spacious & tastefully furnished en-suite sgl/dbl/trpl/family rooms all with lounge areas. Restaurant (100 seats) open to non-residents. Adjoining café with outdoor seating. **$$**

🏠 **Artush & Raisa B&B** (6 rooms) 1/2 Ayvazovsky St; ☎0312 30815; m 093 350314; e artushdavtyan@yahoo.com; w gyumribnb.com. Long-established budget option in Gyumri with 6 twin/dbl en-suite rooms. Shared kitchen & BBQ, communal garden & games/music room. A 30min walk from Gyumri's main squares, and reachable by minibus or taxi. English spoken. B/fast AMD2,000. Home-cooked lunch/dinner by arrangement. **$**

🏠 **Hostel #1** (22 beds in 3 dorms) 1 Rizhkov St; m 094 115599, 099 090100; 📘 hostel1gyumri. New in 2018, this is a very central & convenient low-budget backpacker hostel from the owners of the Ponchik-Monchik cafés (page 260). Coffee shop on ground floor, hostel & reception on 1st floor with a pleasant terrace. Large mixed main dorm sleeps 16 & is divided into 2 areas; 2nd female-only dorm sleeps 6. Prices from AMD3,000 to AMD5,000 pp depending on demand. Basic kitchen

& dining room; clean toilets & showers. B/fast AMD1,000–1,500. **$**

🏠 **Kama Hotel** (23 rooms) 3/2 Garegin Nzhdeh St; ☎0312 30777; e kamahotel@mail.ru. More hostel than hotel. Near the Russian consulate, with Nane Hotel around the back of the building. No English spoken. Prices range from AMD2,500 pp for 1 bed in a trpl with separate shared toilets, to AMD12,000 for a cleaner dbl with shower. **$**

## Elsewhere in the province

🏠 **Ardenis Ray** (2 rooms) Ardenis village; m 093 824005 (Shakro). Shakro was the manager of the Lake Arpi National Park HQ & is a font of knowledge & an expert taxidermist. He & his wife offer B&B in 2 twin rooms. Facilities are basic but the beds are cosy in what can be a chilly part of Armenia for much of the year & the food is wonderful, the majority being their own produce. Meals available with advance notice (AMD3,000–5,000 for an extravagant lunch, AMD2,500 for a simple dinner). B/fast AMD2,500. **$**

🏠 **Lake Arpi National Park HQ Guesthouse** (1 room) Paghakn village; ☎0245 60909/08. Guesthouse near the park HQ, beside Lake Arpi. One very basic self-catering dbl available with kitchen. Can be arranged through the park HQ or visitor centre, or via Shakro (see above). If no member of staff is around when you arrive, the security guard for the reservoir's dam will call someone for you. **$**

🏠 **Mets Sepasar Tourism Centre** (3 rooms) Mets Sepasar village; m 094 833190. Community-run guesthouse with self-catering facilities, living room, shared bathroom & beds for 7 in twin/trpl rooms. B/fast AMD1,000–2,000. FB available (AMD4,000 pp). A variety of tourism services offered inc biking, horseriding & fishing. **$**

🏠 **Ojakh Hotel** (10 rooms) 3 Yekatughainner St, Artik; ☎0244 51818; m 093 424944. A Soviet-era 7-storey hotel of which 2 floors are in use. B/fast & other meals not inc but available from the restaurant next door. Unrenovated rooms (no hot water, no shower) are decrepit but extremely cheap at AMD3,000 for a dbl & AMD6,000 for a quad. The 2 renovated dbl rooms (inc hot water, en-suite shower-room) look satisfactory at AMD15,000. **$**

**OTHER PRACTICALITIES** Gyumri has all major facilities such as banks, post offices, shops, market, internet cafés, etc. Most are on the main Vardanants Square or

Kaghaghutyan and Ankakhutyan squares. A **visitor information centre** opened in 2017 on Vardanants Square's western edge on Abovyan Street. The helpful staff speak English, Russian, German and Arabic and provide a full spread of information on the city's facilities and local tour operators, as well as free photocopied maps. Gyumri's official tourism portal (**w** visitgyumri.com) is the online counterpart to the bureau, while Travel Gyumri (**w** travelgyumri.com) has some useful information on Shirak province as a whole and can arrange tours. Berlin Art Hotel (page 257) can help to organise rural homestays via their Shirak Tours arm (**w** shiraktours.am), which also arranges tours of the region, including ski touring in winter. A detailed map of Gyumri (both Armenian and English script) is published by Collage (page 65) and can be purchased from the shop adjoining the visitor information centre. The two other towns of note, Artik and Maralik, also have basic facilities.

**GYUMRI**  Gyumri is the principal city of northwest Armenia, the administrative centre of Shirak, and the second largest in the country by population. Characterised by the striking use of black and orange stone in many of its structures, the original settlement has a long heritage dating back to the 8th century BC. In more recent times it was caught up in the long struggles for supremacy between the Persian and Ottoman empires, the oldest surviving buildings dating from the period after Russia gained control of the region following the Russo-Turkish war of 1828–29. A fortress was built to defend the new border and in 1837, when Tsar Nicholas I visited Gyumri, the town was renamed Alexandropol after Nicholas's wife, Tsaritsa Alexandra Fedorovna. That name lasted until 1924 when the city was again renamed, this time in honour of the recently deceased Lenin. Thus, Gyumri was known as Leninakan at the time of the natural disaster that would define its history from 1988 onwards. There is a certain irony in that Lenin's entire system of government was to collapse so soon after a city which had been named in his honour.

At 11.41 on Wednesday 7 December 1988 – when most adults were at work and most children at school – the city was hit by a devastating **earthquake**. The epicentre, which measured 6.9 on the Richter scale, was 30km east of Gyumri in Lori province near the small town of Spitak (population then about 25,000) where every last building was destroyed. The earthquake claimed 60–80% of Gyumri's buildings, depending on which source you refer to, but the scale of the catastrophe was near total: at least 25,000 people were killed and 500,000 made homeless in Gyumri and the surrounding region. Immediately after the earthquake, the Soviet prime minister Nikolai Rizhkov promised the inhabitants that the city would be rebuilt within two years. That timetable was unachievable in the last days of the Soviet Union and, after the Armenian vote for independence in 1991, work on the partly completed buildings ceased. The situation in post-independence Armenia (page 26) took a huge toll on the rebuilding efforts. By 2001 around 40% of the population was still living in shipping containers into which windows had been cut. The rate of improvement increased during the 2000s, and the rebuilding of much of the town centre is now complete. The survival of the older buildings suggests that construction under Tsarist rule was to a higher standard than in the Soviet era. Indeed, the districts north and west of the main Vardanants Square have undergone additional renovation with the intention of showcasing this historical architectural style.

It may not be obvious at first glance, but there still remains much to be done. Behind the new and restored buildings there are still many historic buildings awaiting attention. According to some Armenian news reports, as recently as 2014

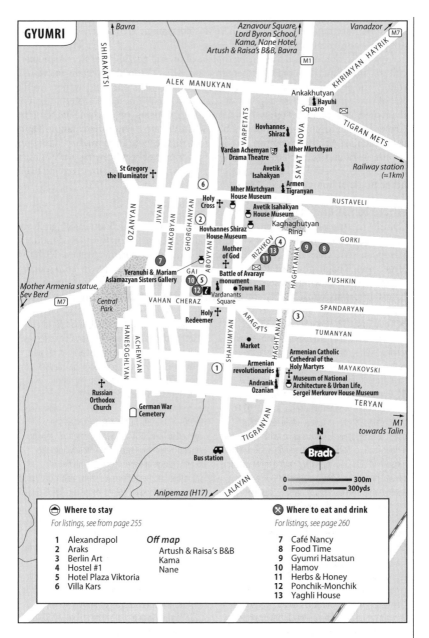

**GYUMRI**

Bavra

Aznavour Square,
Lord Byron School,
Kama, Nane Hotel,
Artush & Raisa's B&B, Bavra

Vanadzor M7

M1

SHIRAKATSI

ALEK MANUKYAN

KHRIMYAN HAYRIK

Ankakhutyan
Hayuhi
Square

TIGRAN METS

VARPETATS

Hovhannes
Shiraz

SAYAT NOVA

Mher Mkrtchyan

Vardan Achemyan
Drama Theatre

Avetik
Isahakyan

Armen
Tigranyan

Railway station
(≈1km)

St Gregory
the Illuminator

(6)

Mher Mkrtchyan
House Museum

RUSTAVELI

OZANYAN

JIVAN

HAKOBYAN

GHORGHANYAN

Holy
Cross

(2)

ABOVYAN

Avetik Isahakyan
House Museum

Hovhannes Shiraz
House Museum

RIZHKOV

Kaghaghutyan
Ring

(4)

(13)

(11)

HAGHTANAK

GORKI

(9)

(8)

Mother
of God

(7)

Yeranuhi & Mariam
Aslamazyan Sisters Gallery

GAI

(10) (5)

Battle of Avarayr
monument

PUSHKIN

Mother Armenia statue,
Sev Berd

M7

Central
Park

VAHAN CHERAZ

(12)

i

Vardanants
Square

Town Hall

SPANDARYAN

HANESOGHLYAN

ACHEMYAN

Holy
Redeemer

SHAHUMYAN

ARAGATS

Market

HAGHTANAK

(3)

TUMANYAN

(1)

Armenian
revolutionaries

Andranik
Ozanian

Armenian Catholic
Cathedral of the
Holy Martyrs

MAYAKOVSKI

Museum of National
Architecture & Urban Life,
Sergei Merkurov House Museum

TERYAN

Russian
Orthodox
Church

German War
Cemetery

TIGRANYAN

M1
towards Talin

N

**Bradt**

Bus station

Anipemza (H17)

LALAYAN

0 ———— 300m
0 ———— 300yds

**Where to stay**

For listings, see from page 255

1  Alexandrapol
2  Araks
3  Berlin Art
4  Hostel #1
5  Hotel Plaza Viktoria
6  Villa Kars

*Off map*

Artush & Raisa's B&B
Kama
Nane

**Where to eat and drink**

For listings, see page 260

7   Café Nancy
8   Food Time
9   Gyumri Hatsatun
10  Hamov
11  Herbs & Honey
12  Ponchik-Monchik
13  Yaghli House

some 4,000–5,000 Gyumri residents still lived in temporary accommodation. On the whole, however, Gyumri is now a bustling and vibrant city like any other. As well as representing an important part of the story of post-independence Armenia, the city is increasingly worth visiting on its own merits, as the welcoming Gyumretsis redefine their city and move forward from the tragedy. There are now adults who have no personal memories of the earthquake itself. That said, there are few who will not remember life during the difficult aftermath. One can only wonder at the psychological trauma: it is said that there was not a single Gyumri resident who did not lose a family member in 1988.

Gyumri is famous for being the birthplace of several **notable figures** in Armenian culture, including the Soviet Armenian actor Mher 'Frunzik' Mkrtchyan, whose statue can be seen in Yerevan's Saryan Park; the lyrical poet and writer Avetik Isahakyan, whose likeness appears on the AMD10,000 note; the internationally renowned jazz pianist Tigran Hamasyan, who appears regularly in concert in Armenia and around the world; and the World/Olympic wrestling champion and gold medallist Artur Aleksanyan. In contrast with the wine and brandy production of other regions, Gyumri has a relatively long heritage of **beer** brewing, with its own namesake beer brand and a factory open for tours, as well as a claim to having been home to the oldest brewery in Armenia.

## ✗ Where to eat and drink  *Map, page 259*

Gyumri has the pick of the province's eateries, many of which are making efforts to represent some of the region's traditional specialities. A new wave of modern European-style cafés has sprung up, mainly around Vardanants Square, Rizhkov Street and Khaghaghutyan Ring, and also in Central Park (page 262) during summer. The following is a selection. There are restaurants in most of the upmarket hotels. Prices are considerably cheaper than in equivalent places in Yerevan.

**✗ Food Time**  58/2 Gorki St; `0312 39999; ⊕ 10.00–23.00 daily. Spacious fast-food cafeteria serving a variety of homemade-style dishes as well as the usual grills, soups & salads. No alcohol. No English menu, but everything is laid out to view.

**✗ Gyumri Hatsatun**  1 Khaghaghutyan Ring; `0312 50808; w gyumrihatsatun.am; ⊕ 09.00–01.00 daily. Caucasian tavern-style restaurant popular with locals & visitors alike, with outdoor & indoor seating. Serves several regional specialities inc *sach* (AMD4,350–6,900), a spiced meat dish for several people, and *khurjin* (AMD2,000), a meat & vegetable dish encased in *lavash*, plus hints of the region's shared culinary heritage (*pide*, *imam bayildi*, *Tartar borek*), as well as the usual salads, barbecues, etc. Extraordinarily good value.

**✗ Hamov**  14 Gayi St; ⬛ hamovlunchgyumri; ⊕ 11.30–16.00 daily. Welcoming & wallet-friendly lunch joint opened in Feb 2018 on the ground floor of a vaulted 19th-century stone building, just off Vardanants Square. Serves a varying range of home-cooked dishes in a canteen style, as well as teas & coffees. Central & very good value. Locally made souvenirs available. Do check out the vintage barbershop opposite.

**☕ Café Nancy**  Gayi & Hakobyan St junction; m 041 262629; ⊕ 10.00–22.00 daily. Quaint, tucked-away little café in a retro European style, opened in 2016 & inspired by the owners' visits to the French town after which it is named. Attracts

mostly a local/foreign tourist clientele. Good selection of b/fast options & good value coffee, as well as light meals along the usual lines of soups, salads, pastas & pizzas. Eclectic global playlist makes a change from Armenian pop music.

**☕ Herbs & Honey**  5 Rizhkov St; w herbsandhoney.am; ⊕ 08.30–23.00 Mon–Sat, 09.00–22.00 Sun. Bright & spacious tea shop opened in Mar 2018 by a Swiss-Armenian, serving natural mountain herbal teas & honey from the nearby village of Ashotsk, along with 'detox' smoothies, homemade fruit syrups, plenty of organic & vegetarian food inc crêpes, soups & cakes, & Swiss-style hot chocolate! Outdoor seating in summer.

**☕ Ponchik-Monchik**  7 Sayat Nova Av `0312 56004; ⊕ 10.00–22.00) & on Vardanants Sq opposite the town hall (⊕ 09.00–23.00). Colourful family-oriented cafés for cheap, filling snacks. *Ponchiks* are light flat doughnuts which come with a sweet vanilla or chocolate custard filling. *Piroshkis* are the meat- or potato-filled savoury versions.

**☕ Yaghli House**  6 Rizhkov St; `0312 52463; ⊕ 10.00–23.00 daily. One of several new cafés on the pedestrian strip. This one serves drinks, light meals, waffles & pastries inc the eponymous local delicacy *yaghli* (from Turkish *yağli* meaning 'fatty'), a sweet puff pastry pouch which goes well with coffee. Menu inc soups, salads & pizza/pasta dishes. Pleasant street seating in summer. Cocktail menu for evening visitors.

**What to see and do** Most sights are within walking distance of central Vardanants Square. A few are a longer walk or a short drive from the centre.

*Central Gyumri* There are more surviving Tsarist-era buildings here than in any other Armenian city and the older central streets offer an insight into 19th-century Russian provincial architecture. These buildings are concentrated in areas to the west and north of the main square, where extensive renovation is taking place to restore much of the district's historical charm. Several historical-style guesthouses, cafés and artisan businesses are springing up here and it is well worth exploring.

On the expansive **main square** (Vardanants Square), two 19th-century churches face each other, **Mother of God** on the north side and **Holy Redeemer** on the south. Both were damaged by the earthquake, the latter suffering considerably when its large central cupola collapsed. Mother of God is functioning again and is busy with many people coming and going. While the church is definitely Armenian the blue altar screen with its painted pictures lends something of an Orthodox feel. Holy Redeemer is still under restoration. The new red and grey stone is being carefully matched to the colours of the old but some is being left plain to distinguish it from the older decorated stonework. The inscription on the monument to the south of Holy Redeemer Church reads 'To the innocent victims, to the merciful hearts', namely the victims of the earthquake and those who came to help. By contrast, Gyumri's largest 19th-century church, **Holy Cross**, which is situated to the north of the centre on Abovyan Street, escaped lightly. For many years following the earthquake it housed families who had lost their homes but it too is now a functioning church again. **St Gregory the Illuminator**, just a few streets northwest, was badly damaged in the earthquake but is also fully rebuilt and operational. Its eastern façade can be seen on Jivan Street although it is entered from Rustaveli Street round the corner and through what is now the entrance to houses. The small **Russian Orthodox Church** (commonly called Piplan Zham, or 'Shimmering Chapel'), in typical Orthodox style with a silver-coloured onion dome, appears to have suffered little damage but is now closed. None of these churches need detain the visitor long but they do combine with the older residential streets to provide one of the few extant pictures of the Tsarist era in Armenia.

The new pale tuff building occupying the whole of the east side of the main square is the **town hall**. Facing it, on the west side of the square, is a monument to those who fought Persian troops in AD451 at the Battle of Avarayr (page 19). Their leader, Vardan Mamikonian, is mounted and below him are four figures representing all ranks of society. Although the Armenians were defeated, subsequent events allowed the battle to be seen as a moral victory and one which preserved the Armenian language, hence the names of the first four letters of the Armenian alphabet carved on the tablet. From the northeast corner of the main square the popular pedestrianised Rizhkov Street (named after the person in charge of organising aid after the earthquake), with its many small shops and a number of open-air cafés, leads to Khaghaghutyan Ring, a major traffic island that also sports several cafés and restaurants. From the southeast corner of the main square the colourful market stretches south towards the bus station. Near the end of the market, at the bottom of Haghtanak Street, is a **statue** of 'Zoravar' Andranik Ozanian (page 154). Behind him, in the parklike central reservation of the dual carriageway, are busts of Armenian revolutionaries. They include Gevorg V (1847–1930), Katholikos during the Armenian genocide and early Soviet period; Garegin Nzhdeh (1886–1955), statesman and Armenian commander; and Nikol Duman (1867–1914), freedom fighter in Baku and Yerevan. Nearby, next door to the Museum of National Architecture and Urban Life (see below), stands the new **Armenian Catholic Cathedral of the Holy Martyrs**, consecrated in 2015 and visited by Pope Francis on his June 2016 visit to Armenia, where he delivered a public mass to some 50,000 attendees.

West from Vardanants Square is **Central Park**. It is a favourite place for Gyumri residents to stroll, its trees giving welcome respite from the summer heat. It has a number of statues including busts of Isahakyan and Shiraz and a statue of Alexander Pushkin, the Russian poet, who visited Gyumri in 1829 on his way to Erzurum (see box, page 279). Near the southern entrance to the park the building with a somewhat dilapidated exterior was once a theatre which, in 1912, staged the première of the opera *Anoush* by Armen Tigranyan (page 52), another native of Gyumri. In the upper, western reaches of the park is a columned Neoclassical rotunda which gives good views over the town to Mother Armenia and Sev Berd (see opposite).

Tucked into an inconspicuous corner of Gyumri just south of the central area is a **German war cemetery** where prisoners of war from World War II lie buried. To reach it go to the southern end of Achemyan Street, which ends as a cul-de-sac with two large metal doors. Go through the left-hand door. You will see the large dark cross up to your right. The cemetery is very like the other German war cemeteries in Armenia (pages 231 and 277). Not far away, next to the small Russian Orthodox Church, is the more formal memorial to the dead of the 19th-century Russo-Turkish war.

The three sons of Gyumri whose house museums are detailed opposite are also commemorated by statues outside the **Vardan Achemyan Drama Theatre** (Sayat Nova Street north of Khaghaghutyan Ring). From north to south the statues represent Shiraz, Mkrtchyan and Isahakyan.

## Museums
**Museum of National Architecture and Urban Life** (47 Haghtanak St; ✆0312 53600; ⏰ 11.00–17.00 Tue–Sat, 11.00–16.00 Sun; tours in English, French & Russian AMD2,000; AMD1,000) This museum is located in a restored 1872 townhouse, the façade of which comprises black and orange-red tuff blocks together with a wrought-iron balcony. Inside are paintings by local artists and rooms furnished as they would have been in Tsarist days. It is particularly conspicuous that virtually all items in the rooms for the wealthier inhabitants came from western Europe and little from Russia, eastern Europe or Asia. This presumably reflects the aspirations of prosperous Armenians (not to mention Russians) under Tsarist rule.

The adjacent gallery, the **Sergei Merkurov House Museum** (same ticket office & details as Museum of National Architecture and Urban Life), was the home of Sergei Merkurov, a prominent Soviet sculptor-monumentalist and native of Gyumri. He was considered to be the greatest Soviet master of post-mortem masks, making death masks of Lenin, Tolstoy and Gorky among many others. The statue of Lenin which stood in Yerevan's Republic Square during Soviet times was his work (page 153). The gallery houses his work.

**Yeranuhi and Mariam Aslamazyan Sisters Gallery** (242 Abovyan St; ✆0312 48205; ⏰ 10.00–17.00 Tue–Sat, 11.00–16.00 Sun; pre-booked tours in English, French & Russian AMD2,000; AMD300) This gallery, which features the paintings and ceramics of Mariam (1907–2006) and Yeranuhi (1910–98) Aslamazyan, born near Gyumri, is well worth a visit. The two-storey gallery is in a black tuff building of 1880 and is reached by going through the archway to an attractive garden overlooked by balconies with carved wooden railings: the entrance is on your immediate right. Yeranuhi's work is displayed on the first floor, Mariam's on the second. Many of the works on display are in strikingly bright colours. Unusually for Soviet times the two sisters were allowed to travel abroad and some of the paintings reflect this. Mariam is the better known of the two sisters. She died in Moscow, but is buried in Yerevan's Komitas Pantheon cemetery.

**Hovhannes Shiraz Memorial House Museum** (101 Varpetats St; ↘ 0312 55142; w shiraz.am; ⊕ 10.00–17.00 Tue–Sat, 10.00–16.00 Sun; tours in English, French & Russian AMD2,000; AMD300) The museum contains items from and about this writer (page 57) of popular patriotic and love poems. A pleasant museum with friendly staff, it is perhaps of less interest to non-Armenians who do not know his work. However, it is worth visiting for the sake of the building itself, an attractive 19th-century, single-storey, black and red tuff house. One notable piece is a gift from Parajanov (page 61). The red cloth, not quite filling the frame, symbolises that Armenia is now just a portion of what it once was but it still has its religion, symbolised by the cross of gold braid, and its language, a quill through the cross.

**Avetik Isahakyan House Museum** (91 Varpetats St; ↘ 0312 57291; ⊕ 10.00–17.00 Tue–Sat, 11.00–14.00 Sun; tours in English, German & Russian AMD2,000; AMD300) The single-storey black tuff house, where Isahakyan (see box, page 56) – the writer whose picture will be familiar from AMD10,000 notes – was born, was built by his grandfather in 1829. The reconstruction of the living areas, with all artefacts belonging to the house, gives an interesting insight into the life of an affluent citizen in 19th-century Gyumri.

**Mher Mkrtchyan Museum** (30 Shota Rustaveli St; ↘ 0312 55174; m 094 987317; ⊕ 10.00–17.00 Tue–Sat, 11.00–15.00 Sun; pre-booked tours in English & Russian AMD2,000; AMD300) Mher 'Frunzik' Mkrtchyan (1930–93) was an actor well known within Armenia for his comic roles, although his personal life contained much tragedy. The museum contains his personal belongings and also props from some of his best-known films.

*Outside the centre* The enormous statue of **Mother Armenia** stands on a hill on the western edge of the town. It was erected in 1975 as a memorial to The Great Patriotic War (World War II) 1941–45 and is reached by climbing a long flight of steps. The climb is rewarded by panoramic views over Gyumri and the surrounding countryside. From here one can walk across to the adjacent hill on which stands **Sev Berd** (meaning 'Black Fortress'), a Russian defensive fortress built in the 1830s after Russia gained control of the region. The circular fortress is usually locked but the keyholder is often here allowing access. Inside is a central well, sunk to a depth of 28m. Living quarters line the walls and from the ramparts there are good views. Russia still maintains a garrison in Gyumri, guarding the border with Turkey. The troops occupy Karmir Berd (meaning 'Red Fortress'), closed to visitors, on the hill to the north of Sev Berd.

Gyumri **railway station** on the eastern edge of the town is a vast edifice which looks typically Soviet from the outside (apart from its roof) but whose entrance hall is reminiscent of the gavit of a church with its central dome, from which hangs an enormous chandelier, and a mosaic of the Armenian symbol of eternity on the floor under the dome. One of the frescoes beside the stairs to the upper floor could, similarly, be given a religious meaning – interesting for a 1977 building. See page 254 for details of train services to and from Gyumri.

The main route north from Gyumri town centre includes the large **Ankakhutyan Square**, its central statue *Hayuhi* representing Armenian independence and freedom,

5

and **Aznavour Square** with its rather ordinary statue of Charles Aznavour, the French singer of Armenian parents who, since the 1988 earthquake, has provided much humanitarian aid to Gyumri. Not far away on Tetcher Street (named after Margaret Thatcher, UK prime minister 1979–90) is the **Lord Byron School** which specialises in teaching English. It was built after the 1988 earthquake with funds provided by the British government and donations from the British public and was opened by Margaret Thatcher in 1990. It is named after Lord Byron (1788–1824), considered one of founders of Armenology (the study of Armenian history, language and culture), in recognition of his knowledge of and work on the Armenian language. A bust of Lord Byron stands in the school grounds.

Some 7km southeast of the city is **Shirak International Airport** (page 72), opened in 1961. The wrought-iron sign indicating the principal road to the airport is easy to miss; coming from Gyumri the dual carriageway to the airport goes off left just after some rails cross the road. A little further south (1.5km) is a more obvious sign but following this second sign will take you via a much poorer road. Local legend has it that the airport was designed to look like an airport in provincial Turkey so that, in the event of a hijacking, a plane could be diverted here and the hijackers then deceived into thinking that they had made it to the West. Though the exterior's distinctly Soviet appearance casts some doubt on this tale, it is said that the normal airport signs could be rapidly changed to ones in Turkish, there were stocks of Turkish uniforms for the staff, and suitable photographs of such people as the Turkish president.

## NORTHERN SHIRAK
**Marmashen Monastery**  (Main church ⊕ 09.00–20.00 in good weather, but if the door is locked when you arrive it is likely that the caretaker will soon appear, having seen visitors arriving) The monastery of Marmashen is beautifully situated in the valley of the Akhurian River, unlike most Armenian monasteries which tend to be sited in elevated positions. It is not on a main tourist route, so sees relatively few foreign visitors. In Vahramaberd turn sharp left on to a dirt road between fields. The road descends into the valley. The monastery can be seen below the road, picturesquely situated by the river and a small reservoir, and surrounded by fruit trees.

Three churches survive, the foundations of a fourth have been uncovered and the remains of many more buildings can be seen, as can parts of the surrounding wall, particularly on the northwest side. The main church, **St Stephen**, was built between 986 and 1029 in red tuff and is in the style of those at Ani, the former capital. It is particularly elegant with decorative arcatures on each façade and columns supporting the corners of the umbrella cupola. Inside, the front of the altar has been restored using the original carved stones where possible but supplemented as necessary with other stones found on the site. Much restoration has been expertly carried out, funded by an Italian-Armenian couple who went to the length of having experiments carried out in Italy to find an ideal mortar to repair the stonework. The church had a 13th-century gavit on the west, its position clearly visible on the church's west façade. The 10th-century church, **St Peter**, to the north of the main church is now roofless. The church on the south side, **Mother of God**, is rather like a smaller version of the main one. The foundations of the **fourth church**, circular and much earlier, lie further west. It was a four-apse church with a small room off each apse. There is a good array of khachkars, those marking the graves of men in front of the main church, those of women to the sides and back. On the small hill to the north of the churches is an extensive cemetery and a ruined chapel.

**Lake Arpi National Park**   This national park in the far northwest of Armenia is on the high Javakheti-Shirak Plateau, a volcanic plateau shared by Armenia, Turkey and Georgia, which includes mountain steppe, subalpine grassland, wetlands and lakes. The territory of the park directly adjoins Javakheti National Park on the Georgian side of the border in a deliberate effort to foster transboundary co-operation between the conservation agencies of the Caucasus (a third contiguous protected area in Turkey was discussed but never implemented). Lake Arpi, the source of the Akhurian River (also referred to locally by its Turkish name, Arpaçay), increased in size in 1950 from 4.5km$^2$ to 22km$^2$ when the river was dammed. The relatively new national park itself was established between 2007 and 2015 and is a Ramsar Convention (The Convention on Wetlands of International Importance) site. The park is a habitat for 670 species of vascular plants, including some Caucasian and Armenian endemics, and for 255 species of vertebrate animals of which more than ten are included in the IUCN Red List of Threatened Species. It is an important staging and breeding ground for migrating birds; over 140 species have been observed around the lake, of which 80–85 were nesting when observed. The park is home to the largest colony of the Armenian gull in the world, is the only Armenian nesting site of the Dalmatian pelican and is the only world habitat of Darevsky's viper. The area has a harsh climate with deep snow cover for up to six months; by the end of October the ground is usually frozen. The milder months are May, June and July, corresponding to the breeding season for birds. Most of the villages around the lake used to be inhabited by Azeris as evidenced by the lakeside Azeri cemeteries.

The lake can be visited as a day trip from Gyumri, but for any serious exploration of the area an overnight stay is necessary. The **visitor centre** in the village of Ghazanchi on the M1 main road has free maps of the park and can arrange local accommodation. Tours and accommodation can also be arranged through the tourist information centre in Gyumri (page 258), and several local tour operators (page 67) offer tours to the lake, including the Gyumri-based Shirak Tours (w shiraktours.am). The park comprises two main territories either side of the M1 main road, of which the lake itself in the western portion will be of most interest to wildlife enthusiasts. The eastern portion rises to meet the ridge of the Javakheti Mountains. A selection of themed walking and mountain-biking trails have been developed, including a route around Lake Arpi itself which is suitable for 4x4s. Nature enthusiasts might also consider crossing into Georgia at Bavra (page 69) and visiting the adjoining Javakheti National Park.

**Ashotsk**   The small village of Ashotsk is notable for being a long-time base for **cross-country skiing** in Armenia. Indeed, the Mikayelyan family – three generations of former and current Olympic champions and team members – live in the village and are in the process of establishing a cross-country ski centre (8 First Street; m 055 352111, 093 352111, 077 352111) with help from the EU. Planned to open in the winter of 2018–19, the centre will comprise basic B&B accommodation, equipment hire and guiding/training services from family members.

**SOUTHWEST SHIRAK**   Heading southwest from Gyumri and parallel to the Turkish border, the H17 road crosses the inoperative railway line between Armenia and Turkey at a level crossing. This railway was originally completed in 1899 as an extension of the Transcaucasian Railway from Poti to Baku, providing a connection between Kars (in present-day Turkey), Alexandropol (now Gyumri) and Tiflis (Tbilisi) at a time when all three cities were in the Russian Empire. The last train to run was in 1993 with the closure of the Turkish–Armenian border during the war.

**Gusanagyugh** has an 11th-century, three-aisled basilica church which, unlike an increasing number of churches, has seen no renovation and so still gives an idea of the state many churches were in following the break-up of the Soviet Union. Nearby are two surviving fragments of wall from a medieval castle. Near the dam of the Akhurian Reservoir – built in the 1970s and one of the largest in the Caucasus – are the ruins of the 10th- or 11th-century **Jrapi caravanserai** which can be seen on the east side of the H17 road, together with a small 7th-century church and the ruins of another, rebuilt as a castle in the 11th century.

**Anipemza** straddles the border with Aragatsotn province. Yereruyk Church, though roofless, is one of the most architecturally important in Armenia and often features in collections of photographs of the country. Its significance rests with its early date (5th–6th century) and the idea it gives of early Armenian church architecture which was modelled on the style of churches in the eastern provinces of the Roman Empire. The basilica-style building is erected on a large plinth approached by steps. The porches are framed by elaborately carved pediments of Graeco-Roman style, contrasting with the different style of the carved window arches and the plain pilasters. There were galleries on three sides, north, south and west, constructed between the eastern and western corner rooms which project beyond the nave. Unusually, the eastern corner rooms are elongated along a north–south axis. The whole site covers an enormous area. To the north are natural caves and pits carved into the rock, some of which may have been for storage: others are coffin-like. Even the name 'Anipemza' has particular significance for Armenians since it reminds them of their inaccessible ruined city Ani; the 'pemza' part of the name refers to pumice which is quarried locally.

The Turkish border, defined by the Akhurian River, is only a few hundred metres from the church and, on a clear day, both Mount Aragats, the highest peak in present-day Armenia, and Mount Ararat, the highest peak in historic Armenia, can be seen. Until some years ago it was possible to obtain permission to go to a specially constructed viewpoint (at Norshen) over the ruined city of **Ani** which is immediately over the border in Turkey. Because access to this viewpoint is now so difficult, AMAP (page 65) has established another at **Haykadzor**. The observation point is 3km from the main road. It is further from Ani and the view is not as good but it has the merit of being free and easily accessible. Take binoculars and hope for a calm, clear day. Note that the several signposts in the region for this viewpoint may mislead the visitor into thinking Ani can be reached from the Armenian side of the border – this is not the case; you must instead make a 300km detour via Georgia and Turkey!

## ANI

That present-day Armenia is cut off from Ani, the 10th–11th-century capital of the Bagratid Kingdom of Armenia, is a consequence of the Soviet–Turkish treaty of 1921 which ceded to Turkey areas – including Kars and Ani – that had been under Russian control since 1877 and had even been awarded to Armenia under the Treaty of Sèvres in 1920. The possible return of Ani to Armenia in exchange for two Kurdish villages further north was raised in intergovernmental talks in 1968 but nothing resulted. In 2016, after a long and troublesome period of neglect, action on the part of the international community finally resulted in Ani's inclusion on UNESCO's World Heritage list. The Turkish government has since stated it a priority site for restoration and conservation.

**SOUTHEAST SHIRAK**  At **Horom** are the remains of one of the largest Bronze Age/ Urartian citadels in Armenia which cover two hills east of the village, opposite the reservoir. Climb up from the road beside the reservoir's dam. From the top the vast extent of the settlement becomes apparent with long stretches of the lower courses of cyclopean walls and evidence of other structures. As always with such sites imagination is needed to reconstruct it in the mind's eye, but it is a good walk and the views from the top are splendid.

Around 25km south of Gyumri the main road bypasses **Maralik**. Turn left on the H21 towards Artik just before the road crosses the railway. On the right, opposite the road junction, there is a gigantic example of Soviet central planning: an enormous cotton-spinning factory, now operating at a fraction of its original capacity. It was typical of Soviet economic policy to site a large cotton-spinning factory far from the sources of cotton (in Uzbekistan and Tajikistan), far from the markets for cloth (mostly in the western USSR), requiring a dedicated railway line to be built to transport materials in and out, and not even near significant sources of power.

Several interesting monasteries lie close to this road. The first, which can be seen across the fields to the right after rounding a hill, is the **Monastery of the Apostles**. A dirt track goes off right across the railway then runs parallel to the railway. Beside a rubbish dump, a grassy track goes off right and curves back to the church. The dome of the 11th-century red tuff church has long since collapsed and there was considerable further earthquake damage in 2009, but it is still possible to get an idea of how the building must have looked. Notwithstanding its damaged state, the building is still used; there are the remains of burnt candles and the cloths and handkerchiefs which believers leave when a special wish is expressed. **Pemzashen** has a complex of three medieval churches at a lower ground level than the present village. The now domeless 6th-century **St Gevorg Church** has three apses within its rectangular walls and an octagonal tambour. The tambour is notable with its four windows alternating with niches and shell-like fan vaults allowing the transition from octagonal tambour to dome. The tympanum over the entrance shows the Virgin Mary holding Jesus with, on the right, an angel and another figure. There was a similar composition on the left, now defaced. The church has two-storey eastern corner rooms but, unusually, these appear to be accessed from outside rather than from inside the church. The small **chapel** to the south, reconsecrated in 2010 to act as the village church, is also 6th century. To the north of St Gevorg are the foundations of a 5th-century basilica. Continuing on towards Lernakert you pass the ruins of a **9th-century cross-dome church**, Holy Apostles, shortly after leaving Pemzashen. There is weathered cable-carving at the portal. The church stands above a small gorge in which is a 17th-century Mother of God Church. As you wind uphill to **Lernakert**, you pass a new church (2005). To reach the 4th-century **church of St John the Baptist**, continue through the village to the end of the tarmac then turn left up a cobbled road. This large barrel-vaulted basilica, restored to a functioning church after its days as a barn in the Soviet era, has a new roof courtesy of the Women's Association of Lebanon. The trim village is said to be one of the oldest in Armenia. It has a khachkar-carver's workshop, on the right as you descend from the church.

The main entry to **Artik** is from the north, crossing the railway line by an improbably large flyover. The centre of Artik is just beyond the flyover but to reach **Lmbatavank (monastery)**, part way up a hill to the southwest of the town, turn immediately right at the end of the flyover. This small 7th-century monastery, whose single-aisle church is dedicated to St Stephen, is built of red tuff and, with its

5

high dome, is very well preserved being particularly notable for its frescoes. There are good views to the north from the hillside location. Scattered around the church are old hollowed-out coffins, also made of tuff. Lmbatavank is a good place to see *sousliks*, a burrow-dwelling member of the squirrel family. If you stay quietly in the car park below the monastery, you may be rewarded by glimpses of them emerging from their burrows in the earthen slope.

**Artik** There are a few older buildings here, but most of the town obviously dates from the post-1945 Soviet period. It was developed as a centre of tuff mining (hence the name of the nearby village, Tufashen) and the recent upsurge in construction work means that unemployment has fallen slightly from its very high level after the collapse of the Soviet Union. The town centre, just beyond the flyover, is recovering from its depressed post-Soviet state with new shops, banks, etc. The town has two old churches adjacent to each other. Both churches were under restoration but work stopped with the collapse of the Soviet Union. The 7th-century **church of St George** is a massive four-apse cross-dome church whose dome has collapsed. Unfortunately it is locked, presumably for safety, but a good idea can be obtained from the outside and from glimpses through the large windows. The exteriors of the south and west apses are pentagonal and are decorated with double-column blind arcades. The arches of the arcades and those over the windows have floral or basket-weave carving. The north apse is round and plain. The curvature of the main east apse is almost obscured from outside by the eastern corner rooms but can still be appreciated at the three large windows. **St Marine** (or Mother of God) to the northwest is even more ruinous. It is a 5th-century cross-shaped church on a three-step pedestal. Although the west door is blocked it is possible to enter by the north doorway, under a huge lintel. The east apse is wide and shallow and is flanked by a narrow apsidiole on each side. The external apsidioles on the west walls of the north and south wings, together with remnants of barrel vaulting, suggest there may have been a gallery round the west end of the church.

**Harichavank (monastery)** (⊕ Harichavank is a working monastery; the compound gates may be shut at night but the monastery & the churches will be open all day) The monastery is at the far end of the main street of the village of **Harich** on the edge of a plateau where two small ravines meet. The monastery was founded by the 7th century and expanded during the 13th. Most of the ancillary buildings were added after 1850 when the Katholikos moved his summer residence here. The original 7th-century church, St Gregory's, has a round dome. From the southwest corner room a secret passage leads down into the gorge and a secret room is concealed above the roof of the same room. Its belltower, resting on large columns, is a 19th-century addition as are the small chapels which adjoin it. The much larger Mother of God Church of 1201 has an unusual 16-sided umbrella dome and much elaborate decoration around the tambour. Inside, cantilevered steps lead to the upper storeys of the western corner rooms which are unusual in having arcaded windows looking on to the nave. In between the two churches is a very large gavit whose porch is particularly finely decorated with small twisted columns and inlaid carved red and black stones which show a striking oriental influence. On the east façade of the Mother of God Church is a relief showing the founders of the church and also one of a lion. An unusual feature is the small chapel perched on top of a high pillar of rock in the gorge; it owes its present inaccessible location to an earthquake. It is possible to walk down into the gorge; a path goes off from the northwest corner of the entrance courtyard. It is quite an easy scramble up to the plateau opposite the monastery. From both gorge

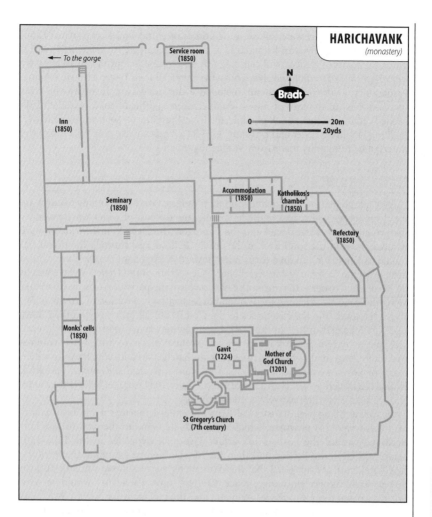

**HARICHAVANK**
(monastery)

← To the gorge

Service room (1850)

N

Bradt

0 ———— 20m
0 ———— 20yds

Inn (1850)

Seminary (1850)

Accommodation (1850)

Katholikos's chamber (1850)

Refectory (1850)

Monks' cells (1850)

Gavit (1224)

Mother of God Church (1201)

St Gregory's Church (7th century)

and plateau the views of the monastery and its defensive walls are refreshingly different from what one would normally see within the monastery complex.

**EASTERN SHIRAK** Jajur is home to the **Minas Avetisyan House Museum** (m 091 498895; ⏲ 10.00–17.30 Tue–Sun; AMD200). This is by no means a typical house museum, rather an excellent small art gallery showing work by this popular dissident painter and his friends. Avetisyan (1928–75) (page 60) was born in Jajur; it was while he was visiting his family here that his Yerevan studio was destroyed by fire in 1972. Rebuilt after the 1988 earthquake, the Jajur gallery opened in 2004. The paintings are colourful, attractive – even joyful – many depicting everyday village life. A visit is well worth the short detour. The gallery, with its cupola-like roof, is at the east end of the village and is signposted off the main road.

The excavated foundations of the **monastery of Chichkhanavank** at **Shirakamut** are actually in neighbouring Lori province but are conveniently visited from Gyumri. They are the starting point for one of the routes to **Trchkan Waterfall** (1,786m above sea level, height 23m) on the Trchkan River, which flows into the Pambak River near Shirakamut. The waterfall is on the border of Shirak and Lori provinces and, although not large by world standards, is one of the largest in Armenia. In 2011, it was the focus of a successful campaign by environmental groups to save it after work had started to dam the river above the waterfall for a hydro-electric scheme. Preparatory work for the scheme included a dirt road (which forded the river several times) to the foot of the waterfall. This very difficult road (4x4 definitely needed) makes it just about possible to drive the 8km or so from Shirakamut. Walking would be easier and certainly less scary. You can also reach the top of the waterfall by rough dirt roads from Vardaghbyur.

# LORI PROVINCE

Largely a high plateau with gentle mountain ranges, Lori's outstanding features are the deep gorges which fissure the landscape, the deepest of which are formed by the principal rivers the **Debed** and the **Dzoraget**. The Debed's main tributary, the Pambak, rises in the southwest of the province, flows east through the provincial capital of Vanadzor and then turns north towards Georgia to join the Kura, whose delta is on the Caspian Sea in Azerbaijan. The section of the Debed Valley close to the Georgian border is the one of the two lowest-lying parts of Armenia (the other being the Arax Valley along the Iranian border) with an elevation of around 425m above sea level. The Dzoraget rises to the west in Shirak province and then flows east past Stepanavan to join the Debed halfway between Vanadzor and Alaverdi. The spectacular gorges of these rivers are excellent places to find eagles, vultures and interesting smaller birds such as rock nuthatches. In addition, they are where many of Lori's most appealing hiking trails and historical sites are to be found. Unlike the Debed, which is on a major transit route, the Dzoraget Valley offers quiet and scenic roads with relatively gentle gradients.

As well as being part of historical Armenia under its former name Tashir, parts of present-day Lori province (which also lends its name to the city-fortress **Lori Berd**) fell within the borders of various Georgian dynasties in the 12th–16th centuries before the Persian and then the Russian empires annexed the territory. It was not until World War I that the Armenians' successful repulsion of Turkish forces at Karakilisa (meaning 'Black Church', now Vanadzor) would lead to Lori's incorporation into Soviet Armenia and thus its inclusion within Armenia's present-day borders. Remnants of Lori's meandering history can still be seen today in historical sites such as Kobayr Monastery (page 285), where Georgian as well as Armenian inscriptions can be seen. The ongoing border dispute with Georgia (involving competing claims to at least two important religious monuments) might also be perceived as a reminder of the region's multi-cultural past.

**GETTING THERE AND AROUND** Vanadzor is the main transport hub. The railway and bus stations adjoin each other at the end of the short dual carriageway which runs from the main square. The bus station has timetables up beside the ticket windows. **Buses** or **minibuses** serve local destinations, including Alaverdi (several times daily from 11.00; AMD800), Bagratashen (border crossing, also continuing to Marneuli in Georgia; several times daily from 08.00; AMD1,000), Stepanavan (4 times daily from 09.50; AMD800) and Tashir (daily at 14.45; AMD800). Major towns served in the neighbouring provinces include Gyumri (via Spitak; 4 times daily from 09.30; AMD800) and Ijevan (via Dilijan; 4 times daily from 08.30; AMD1,000). Most smaller local destinations have one daily service, timed to benefit locals with departures tending to be either in the morning between 08.30

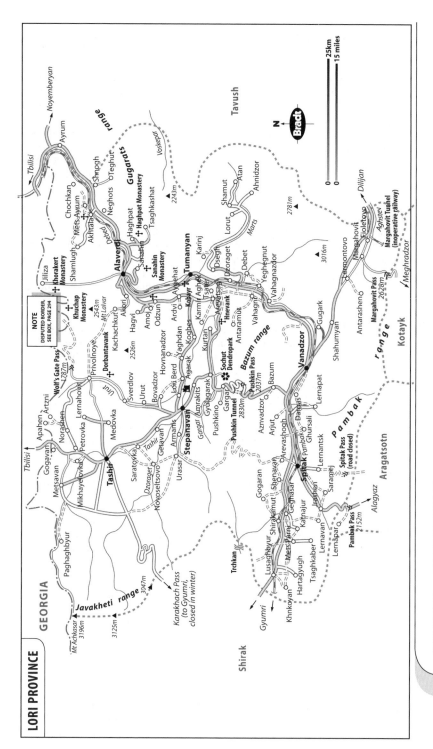

# LORI PROVINCE

**GEORGIA**

*Tbilisi* ↗ *Noyemberyan*

↗ Ayrum

Gugarats range

Tavush

**N** Bradt

25km
15 miles
0
0

Chochkan
Mets Ayrum
Teghut
Shnogh
Neghots
Voskepar
2243m
Shamut
Atan
Ahnidzor
2781m
3016m

*Tbilisi*

Jiliza
**Thorakert Monastery**
Haghpat ✝ **Haghpat Monastery**
Tsaghkashat
Shamlugh
Akhtala ✝
*Debed*
**Alaverdi** ●
Akori
Sanahin ✝ **Sanahin Monastery**
**Tumanyan** ✝
Karinj
Lorut
Dsegh
Marts
Shamut

**NOTE**
**DISPUTED BORDER,**
**SEE BOX, PAGE 294**

**Khuchap Monastery** ✝
2543m
Mt Lalvar
*Dorbantavank* ✝
2526m ▲
Kachachkut
Hagvi
Amoj
Odzun
Ardvi
Aghehat
Koghes
Kobayr ✝
Karmi Aghek
Sat
Dsoraget
Debet
Yeghegnut
Vahagnadzor
Margahovit
Fioletovo ↗ *Dilijan*
Aghstev
Margahovit Tunnel
(inoperative railway)
*Meghradzor* ↙

**Wolf's Gate Pass**
1787m
Privolnoye
Kachachkut
Yaghdan
Hovnanadzor
Kurtan
Agarak
**Hnevank** ✝
Antaramut
Vahagni
Gugark
Dermontovo
Margahovit Pass
2628m

Urut
Sverdlov
Bovadzor
Lori Berd
Gyulagarak
**Sochut Dendropark** ✿
**Bazum Pass**
2037m
Bazum
Shahumyan
Antarashen
*Uruf*
Apahen
Artzni
Lernahovit
Amrakits
Gargar
Pushkino
**Pushkin Tunnel**
2830m
Aznvadzor
Arjut
Batoas
Lernapat
*range*
Kotayk

Gogavan
Norashen
Petrovka
Medovka
Tashir
Getavan
Armanis
**Stepanavan** ●
Gargar
Arevashogh
**Vanadzor** ●
Ghursali
Lernapat
**Pambak**
**Pambak range**

Metsavan
Mikhayelovka
Saratovka
Novoseltsovo
Urasar
Tashir
*Dzoraget*
**Tashir** ◆
Pambak
**Spitak** ✝
Lernantsk
Saramej
**Spitak Pass**
(road closed)
**Aragatsotn**

Paghaghbyur
Gogaran
Lusaghbyur
Shirakamut
Shenavan
Geghasar
Lernavan
Saramej

*Tbilisi* ↙

'Mt Achkasar
3196m
3125m
**Javakheti range**
*Karakhach Pass*
*(to Gyumri,*
*closed in winter)*
3047m
**Trchkan**
Mets Parni
Kahnajur
Jrashen
Lernapat
**Pambak Pass**
2152m
*Alagyaz* ↙

**Shirak**

Gyumri
Khnkoyan
Hartagyugh
Tsaghkaber

and 11.00 or in the afternoon between 15.00 and 16.30. Minibuses depart hourly for **Yerevan** from 08.00, the 120km journey taking 1½ hours (AMD1,200), and to Tbilisi at 08.30 (AMD3,000). Times can change so it is wise to check in advance. The Yerevan–Tbilisi **train** (page 85) passes through in the early hours of the morning and is significantly more expensive, inconvenient and slow than the bus (in both directions). Possibly of more interest is the extended service to **Batumi**, which runs daily during the summer holiday season.

**Taxis** wait at the bus station and can be a convenient way to travel both to local sights and intercity. They should charge AMD100–120/km but for long trips agree a price before leaving. A taxi from Vanadzor to Yerevan costs AMD12,000 and a round trip to the historical sites at Sanahin, Haghpat, Akhtala and Odzun costs much the same. A shared taxi to Yerevan costs AMD2,000.

While the most-used **border crossings** to Georgia are Bavra in Shirak province and Bagratashen in Tavush province, there is also a road crossing at Gogavan in Lori which is open to foreigners. Several other border crossings may appear to exist on maps but are closed on the ground and guarded by the Armenian military who will detain anyone found in these areas without permission. The previously awful main road through the Debed Valley between Vanadzor and Alaverdi was undergoing extensive rebuilding at the time of research, scheduled to conclude in late 2018.

 **WHERE TO STAY** Lori is a relatively cheap area of Armenia and very acceptable accommodation can be had on a low budget. Because of the terrain there is no one place from which it is easy to visit all there is to see. Stepanavan is the best place to stay if wishing to visit Lori Berd or any of the remoter areas north of Stepanavan. For the sights and hikes of the Debed Gorge, several accommodation options exist in Dsegh, Alaverdi, Haghpat and Odzun; the Tufenkian hotel at Dzoraget is a notable upscale option in a very convenient location. Homestays and B&Bs exist in most towns and many villages. Allow at least a full day to visit all the monasteries in the Debed Gorge; longer if incorporating any of the excellent hikes between the sites. Vanadzor is a useful overnight stop when moving from one area to another and offers a glimpse of modern-day urban life outside of Yerevan. See page 92 for general comments on accommodation. Where listings are plotted on a map, it is indicated below.

## Stepanavan

**SH Resort** (8 rooms) 145 Baghramyan St; `0256 22007`; e h_israyelyan@yahoo.com; ⏰ 1 May–30 Nov & 10 days at Christmas. Some way from the centre but a pleasant & modern hotel, aimed primarily at local families on holiday, with large garden & outdoor eating area. Dbl/trpl en-suite rooms on 3rd floor; no lift. Function suite for up to 400 on 2nd floor, so could be noisy during a wedding party. Luxe rooms for a small supplement. Cards accepted. FB AMD9,000 pp. **$–$$**

**Lori Hotel** (12 rooms) 11 Nzhdeh St; `0256 22323`; e info@lorihotel.am; w lorihotel.am. One of several comparable small hotels in the very centre of town. Also has a café (⏰ 09.00–21.00 daily). Dinner AMD2,500 pp. **$**

**Ruzanna's B&B** (1 room) 9 Million St; m 093 230320/226936; e tag_sahakyan@yahoo.com; w stepanavan.net. Located behind the town hall northwest of the Shahumyan museum, this basic family homestay has 1 small dbl room & is currently the cheapest spot in Stepanavan. Outdoor bathroom is the only downside. If fully booked, ask the family about its second B&B in the north of the town across the bridge. Dinner AMD3,000 pp. **$**

## Vanadzor
Map, page 275

**Hotel Argishti** (22 rooms) 1 Batumi St; `0322 42556/7`; m 095 442556; e argishti@freenet.am. A mid-range hotel in the centre of town. Good-sized sgl/dbl/twin/trpl rooms are all en suite, with luxe rooms available. Restaurant serves dinner for approx AMD5,000–6,000. Sauna. Discount for groups. Due for refurbishment in late 2018. **$$**

🏠 **MagHay Guesthouse** (12 rooms) 21 Azatamartikner St; m 091 380305. Opened in 2007 & has since grown year on year. Proprietress Marineh speaks some English. Her quiet guesthouse has rustic & comfortable sgl/dbl rooms in 3 buildings set around a pleasant garden. Some rooms en suite. Lovely dining room & kitchen in a detached conservatory. Prices depend on room size & occupancy. Excellent b/fast; other meals by arrangement (AMD4,000–5,000 pp). Laundry AMD2,000/load. **$$**

🏠 **Hotel Gugark** (20 rooms) 20 Tigran Mets Av; ✆0322 41519. Very central with a new & lavish-looking frontage & lobby right on the city square, but still undergoing renovation inside & only using the 4th floor of the building. One wing is a cheap, no-frills option based on the original Soviet-era edifice; the other upscale & glamorous. Sgl/dbl/twin/family rooms available. No restaurant yet but one is planned. B/fast therefore not available but plenty of nearby places to eat. If & when finished this looks set to be Vanadzor's premier downtown hotel. **$–$$**

🏠 **Downtown Hostel** (3 rooms) 9 Garegin Nzhdeh St; m 077 020299. Entrance from backstreet; rooms on 2nd floor. Clean & modest little hostel with 1 twin & 2 quad rooms of which 1 is en suite. Shared kitchen, lounge & bathroom. Prices per room, not per bed. Guests are free to use the 3rd-floor yoga studio & participate in sessions run by a local group. **$**

🏠 **Green House** (16 rooms) 8d Banaki St; ✆0322 40015; m 091 310070; e greenhousehotel@yahoo.com. Banaki St is parallel to & 4 streets south of main Tigran Mets Av, between Myasnikyan & Nzhdeh streets. A comfortable hotel but the soundproofing is poor. All rooms on ground floor. No evening meals. **$**

🏠 **Hotel Kirovakan** (20 rooms) 1 Mashtots; ✆0322 47010; m 099 417010, 098 417010; e info@kirovakan-hotel.com; w hotelkirovakan. com. This Soviet hotel of 1980 has had several floors renovated to a good standard but still has a somewhat dated atmosphere. Situated at the east end of the town centre with good views of the town from its elevated & highly visible position.

Helpful reception. Accepts cards. Restaurant. B/fast AMD3,000 pp, other meals AMD4,000 pp. **$**

🏠 **Hotel Laguna** (6 rooms) 68a Zoravar Andranik St; ✆0322 50009; m 055 877222, 093 877222, 099 877222; e admin@laguna.am; w laguna.am. Some 2km from town centre on the road towards Dilijan. Behind Soviet-era flats, signposted. No dining room: meals taken either in rooms, in sitting areas on landings or in summer house in the garden. B/fast AMD1,500 pp. Evening meal AMD3,000. Accepts cards. **$**

## Debed Gorge

🏠 **Tufenkian Avan Dzoraget Hotel** (54 rooms) North end of Dzoraget village; ✆060 501010; e dzoraget@tufenkian.am; w tufenkianheritage.com; see ad, page 126. On the river about halfway between Vanadzor & Alaverdi. Airy & atmospheric spa-like interior with simple but attractive décor in dbl/trpl rooms across 2 buildings, with several larger suites up to AMD100,000. Restaurant (page 283) open to non-residents & serves delicious Armenian & Georgian dishes (the *su borek* is excellent). Swimming pool & sauna inc. Extra services available, eg: massage, billiards, guided tours. Stiff supplement for a river view; the mountain view is often quieter. Generous buffet b/fast. Cards accepted. **$$$–$$$$**

🏠 **Hotel Gayane** (6 rooms, 4 cottages) Haghpat village; ✆0253 60618; m 098 994755. This popular hotel is expanding rapidly with en-suite twin/dbl/trpl rooms & cottages for larger groups. Swimming pool. Sheltered BBQ area with an open fire for cooler evenings. English spoken & staff can arrange local tours. Meals extra. **$$**

🏠 **Hotel Odzun** (10 rooms, 2 cottages) 85 1st St, Odzun village; m 091 717404, 095 717404. A Soviet holiday hotel of 1971 which is being renovated to a high standard. On the hillside above Odzun 2.2km from the church (not 1.2km as it says on a sign beside the church). Turn right at the sign then left in 800m on to a tarmac road & keep going uphill. Ignore the first set of rusty gates & continue to the new gates. Set in extensive gardens with its own orchard, swimming pool & BBQ. Accommodation will increase as renovation progresses. Unrenovated rooms cheaper. Cottages sleep 4. Would be a good centre for hiking. Restaurant & café. FB AMD4,000 pp. **$$**

🏠 **Hotel Qefilyan** (16 rooms) Haghpat village; m 055 210210; e info@qefohotel.com.

A comfortable, modern hotel in a superb location overlooking the Debed Gorge. Restaurant. **$$**

🏠 **Agha-Bek B&B** (3 rooms) Dsegh village; m 094 660037 (Marineh Aghbekyan). This B&B is one of several in Dsegh village. Marineh is the church's keyholder & the house is next door to the church. Bedrooms are spacious. Can sleep up to 14. B/fast AMD2,000 pp. **$**

🏠 **Artemi Hostel** (3 rooms) 2 Tumanyan St, Tumanyan village; m 093 625101, 094 433725. Conveniently located midway along the Debed Gorge, Anush's clean & comfortable homestay is a real gem in the region, particularly if you sample her fantastic dinners (AMD2,000–3,000 pp). All ingredients are freshly grown or made by the family, inc the *oghi*. Extra beds can be set up for larger groups. **$**

🏠 **Parisis B&B** (7 rooms) 2 Jrazavan St, Alaverdi; m 091 257323. This budget hostel/B&B in Alaverdi comprises several apts in a Soviet-era tower block with sgl/dbl rooms & (cheaper) dorm beds. The host Taron speaks excellent English & French & is highly knowledgeable about the local area. Small kitchens in each apt for use of guests. B/fast served in the family's own flat on the ground floor. Other meals on request. **$**

## Elsewhere in the province

🏠 **Hekiat Resort** (3 rooms, 4 cottages) 2km from Gyulagarak en route to Sochut Dendropark; m 094 083000. The unsigned collection of buildings by the road just before entering the woods – the name means 'fairy tale'. Dbl/twin rooms available. Well-presented cottages sleep up to 8 (AMD35,000–45,000/cottage). Russian *banyo* (sauna) on-site. Restaurant open to the public & very convenient for visitors to the arboretum. B/fast AMD2,000 pp. FB AMD5,000 pp. **$$**

🏠 **LerMont Guesthouse** (7 rooms) Lermontovo village; m 098 901910; 📘. Conveniently situated by the main road between Vanadzor & Dilijan, this very tasteful mid-range hotel on the edge of the forest has en-suite trpl/family rooms & would make a good base for hiking

in the upper Aghstev Valley. Owner Nork teaches English at the private school in Dilijan. Lunch/dinner by request. **$$**

🏠 **Sochut Resort** (46 rooms) 3km from Gyulagarak next to Sochut Dendropark; m 095 411195; e info@sochut.am; w sochut.am; ⊕ Apr–Oct. Previously a Soviet sanatorium, built in 1955 & transformed into a modern hotel in 2009. Very much aimed at local holidaymaking families with a children's playground on-site, set in spacious, well-tended gardens with ample parking. May suit those with a special interest in the Dendropark (page 279). Restaurant & café. Cards accepted. Price depends on room size & quality. Prices quoted are for FB; discount if you take b/fast only. **$$**

🏠 **Spitak YMCA** (4 rooms) 4a Aygestan St, Spitak; ☎0255 62901; e spitak@ymca.am; w spitak.ymca.am. Built in 2010 as a community centre, with a wide range of facilities for children & adults. In the absence of other accommodation in Spitak it has dbl/trpl/family rooms which visitors can use. Excellent reports from those who have stayed here – 'rooms very clean & comfy with good shower facilities'. Lunch AMD4,000 pp. Dinner only possible for groups of 10 or more. **$$**

🏠 **Carahunge Village Home** (2 rooms) Amrakits village, opposite the Russian church (page 279); m 099 324300; 📘. New in 2018, this 'ecolodge' is set in the peaceful village of Amrakits near the Dzoraget Gorge, having the same clean & colourful vibe as Carahunge's two café-restaurants in Stepanavan & Dilijan. Spacious garden & BBQ area; kitchen for use of guests. B/fast not inc; other meals can be delivered from the Stepanavan café. Additional guest rooms under construction. **$**

🏠 **Geologist's Guesthouse** (8 beds in 2 apts) Gargar village; m 091 402097. Well situated for hiking in the Bazum mountain range & surrounding hills. English-speaking owner & guide Armen has a wealth of knowledge on the local area & its hiking & mountain-biking opportunities. Each of the 2 renovated apts in this village house has 4 beds, lounge area & small kitchen. Lunch/dinner on request. **$**

✗ **WHERE TO EAT AND DRINK** Vanadzor is best catered for in terms of standalone restaurants, though fast-food and basic eateries can be found in all the main towns. Summer cafés spring up seasonally in the parks of the larger settlements. Some of the larger hotels listed on pages 272–3 have restaurants, noted under individual entries. There are various roadside eateries in the Debed Gorge. Off the beaten track it may be necessary to picnic or to dine at homestays.

**OTHER PRACTICALITIES** Vanadzor has all facilities, with Stepanavan, Spitak, Tashir and Alaverdi being reasonably provided. Stepanavan's tourist information centre was no longer functioning at the time of research. **Dsegh** village has a NGO-sponsored **visitor centre**, opened in 2015 (page 284), which will be of particular interest to birdwatchers. The 'Tumanyan Land' **tourist information centre** in **Alaverdi** (**w** toumanian-lori.com) also opened in 2015, sponsored by the local copper mine; the helpful English- and French-speaking staff can assist with all the attractions of the Debed Gorge. Also based in the town is the **Alaverdi Guides** organisation (**m** 094 157137 (Lena); **e** alaverdiguides@gmail.com; **w** alaverdiguides.com), whose English-speaking guides can assist with explorations of the local area. The Vanadzor-based tour operator **Visit Lori** (**e** visitlori1@gmail.com; **w** lori-travel.com) is pioneering white-water rafting and other ecotourism ventures in the province.

**VANADZOR** Vanadzor, the provincial capital, is situated on the Debed River at 1,350m above sea level between the Pambak mountain range to the south and the Bazum range to the north. Prior to 1935, Vanadzor was called Karakilisa (Turkish for 'black church'), after which it was renamed Kirovakan after Sergei Kirov (1886–1934), the head of the Communist Party in Leningrad, whom Stalin arranged to have assassinated because his popularity in the party made him a potential rival. In 1993, the city acquired its present name from the local Vanadzor River. The third-largest city in Armenia by population, it was damaged by the 1988 earthquake but not to anything like the same extent as Gyumri and Spitak, and its central square with buildings of pink tuff and its main shopping street survived more or less intact. Though it was an important industrial centre in Soviet times, most of the former chemical plants making products as diverse as glue and nail polish remover are now closed and the previously acrid atmosphere is now clean and pleasant. Banks, currency exchanges, tour operators, shops and most other facilities can be found on **Tigran Mets Avenue** between the M8 main road and Hayk Square. This stretch of road, along with the side streets on both sides, is also where most of Vanadzor's

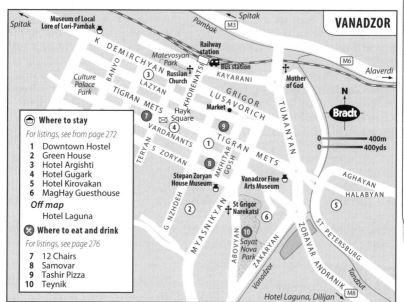

VANADZOR

**Where to stay**
For listings, see from page 272
1  Downtown Hostel
2  Green House
3  Hotel Argishti
4  Hotel Gugark
5  Hotel Kirovakan
6  MagHay Guesthouse
*Off map*
   Hotel Laguna

**Where to eat and drink**
For listings, see page 276
7  12 Chairs
8  Samovar
9  Tashir Pizza
10 Teynik

central eateries can be found. Parallel **Grigor Lusavorich Street** is the market district, including the largest indoor food market in the province. From Hayk Square, around which several governmental offices are situated, Khorenatsi Street leads down to the bus and train stations. The **train station** is almost worth visiting for its own sake to see the enormous and perfectly preserved map of the former USSR's vast railway network on the eastern interior wall of the main hall.

## ✗ Where to eat and drink  *Map, page 275*

✗ **Tashir Pizza** 65 Tigran Mets Av, Vanadzor; ☏0322 44411/01; ⏱ 10.00–midnight. A branch of the national chain, popular with the local youth & serving more than just pizza. Cheap & cheerful.

**12 Chairs** 16/23 Tigran Mets Av, Vanadzor; ☏055 787934; ⏱ 11.00–22.00 daily. New in 2017, this trendy café mostly serves the local market but is one of the more appealing coffee stops on a wander through central Vanadzor.

**Samovar** 84 Vardanants St, Vanadzor; ⏱ 10.00–22.00 daily. This clean & colourful cafeteria & bakery, newly opened in 2018, serves delicious cinnamon-infused tea from large Russian samovars. The sweet & savoury pastries are all freshly baked, inventive & good value. Try its novel twists on the classic Adjarian *khachapuri*. Certainly the pick of the city centre cafés at the time of research.

**Teynik** 1K Abovyan St, Vanadzor; ☏0322 23636; m 055 888636; ☐ AnticafeTeynik; ⏱ 11.00–22.00 daily. Opened in 2017, this is a so-called 'anti-café' in the sense that you pay for the time you spend here rather than for what you order (1st hr AMD500, AMD300/hr thereafter with tea, coffee & snacks inc). Popular with the progressive youth of Vanadzor as well as foreign backpackers. Rolling events calendar on the Facebook page. Musicians encouraged to play the supplied instruments.

**What to see and do** A worthwhile place to start is the **Vanadzor Fine Arts Museum** (52 Tigran Mets Av; ☏ 0322 43938; e info@vanart.org; w vanart.org; ⏱ 10.00–17.00 Tue–Sat, 10.00–16.00 Sun; for guided tour in English, AMD2,000, contact 1 day in advance; AMD500). Founded as a branch of the National Gallery of Armenia in 1974, it has a separate hall dedicated to artists from Lori who often depict local subjects, including landscapes and some fine portraits. The labels include English. Start on the third floor of this spacious and light gallery and work downwards: floors three and two house the paintings; sculptures occupy the ground floor. The **Stepan Zoryan House Museum** (24 Stepan Zoryan St;☏0322 43093; m 093 800138; ⏱ 10.00–18.00 Tue–Sat; tours in English AMD2,000; AMD500) is bright and well presented with enough English to make it accessible. The writer Stepan Zoryan (1889–1967) is best known for his novels and short stories based on Armenian village life. The small **Museum of Local Lore of Lori-Pambak** (23/1 Karen Demirchyan St;☏0322 40555; e museumlori@mail.ru; ⏱ 10.00–18.00 Tue–Sat; guided tour in English AMD500; AMD1,000) houses displays of local artefacts including a good collection of decorative metalwork.

There are three **churches** in the town centre: a small Russian one near the train station; a large new one, St Grigor Narekatsi, at the junction of Myasnikyan and Stepan Zoryan streets; and a third, Mother of God, built in 1831 on the site of an earlier church, where the road to Alaverdi crosses the river. Three city **parks** provide shade for a stroll: Sayat Nova Park near the new church; Matevosyan Park, beside the Russian church, with its children's funfair rides and cinema club; and the Culture Palace Park at the far end of Tigran Mets Avenue.

## WESTERN LORI

**Spitak** West from Vanadzor, the main road and rail lines to Gyumri follow the Debed to pass by the town of Spitak, in the district where cabbages and carrots are grown. Spitak was close to the epicentre of the 1988 earthquake and was completely destroyed by it. Much rebuilding, including a new church, has been funded by the international community but some former factories still lie ruined and derelict. Much of the population lives in areas of housing built with international aid after the earthquake, such areas still known by the name of the country which provided funds and materials. Inevitably the housing was built away from the ruins of Spitak and these areas remain more like villages some distance from the town.

In the rebuilt town centre facilities are concentrated around the large **main square**, actually more like a truncated triangle with a large carved wall at its apex. The new church, **Holy Resurrection**, is a typical cross-dome church with a belltower. A rather nice touch is the carpet-like throws over the pews harking back to traditional Armenian furnishings. Although the town feels as if it is coming to life again, the earthquake cannot be forgotten. Apart from any personal memories of the inhabitants, the old Soviet memorial (see below) is visible from almost everywhere and there are other memorials on Alek Manukyan Street.

On a hill overlooking the town is the official **memorial to the victims of the earthquake**. Visiting it is thought-provoking. First, it is reached by a long flight of concrete steps, most of which have disintegrated and all of which are overgrown by a colourful range of weeds. At the top of the steps one reaches the rather grandiose memorial, now equally neglected with much of its marble cladding having fallen off, giving the appearance that total collapse may not be long delayed. Is there, in the memorial's neglect, implied criticism of the shoddy Soviet building standards which contributed so much to increasing the death toll? Local residents tend to visit individual graves rather than the memorial itself. There is no inscription in any language. Maybe the wild flowers gradually taking over the monument are a more fitting memorial.

Opposite the hill with the memorial is the town **graveyard**. Many of the victims are buried here. Some graves show not only a picture of the deceased but also a clock face with the hands pointing to 11.41, the time the earthquake struck. Those of younger people often show a flower with a broken stalk symbolising a life broken while in full bloom. The graveyard is less neglected than the monument but is clearly little frequented. Perhaps many of the deceased have no surviving relatives. Certainly some of the graves show three generations of victims from the baby a few weeks old to the grandparents. Still remaining in the graveyard is the one-of-a-kind **metallic church** which served in the immediate aftermath of the earthquake and which was erected within 40 days of the disaster.

There is another graveyard in Spitak round the other side of the hill. It is a **war cemetery** where German prisoners of war lie buried. It's a tranquil place – a flowery meadow with rows of metal crosses. Although the identity of each person is known, this is not marked on the grave with the sole exception of one grave where a relative has provided a stone tombstone. There is also a large cross bearing the words *Hier ruhen Kriegesgefangene – Opfer des zweites Weltkrieges* ('Here rest prisoners of war – victims of World War II'). The prisoners worked on the construction of a nearby sugar factory but that was destroyed in the earthquake. The German government pays a local man to look after the graves and to preserve the meadow by cutting the vegetation annually. To reach the war cemetery take the road which runs between the town graveyard and the earthquake memorial, signposted to Gyumri off the main road south to Yerevan. Stay close to the base of the graveyard then continue beyond it, keeping watch for the large black cross up on the hill to the left, behind some small houses. This is the largest of the German war cemeteries in Armenia. Others are at Sevan (page 231), Gyumri (page 262), Artashat and Abovyan.

For the **monastery of Chichkhanavank** and **Trchkan Waterfall**, see page 269.

**SOUTHEASTERN LORI** The road to Dilijan in Tavush province passes above the three Russian villages of **Lermontovo**, **Margahovit** and **Fioletovo** in the valley south of the road. An older, parallel road also links the three settlements, providing an interesting alternative route. The villages are inhabited to varying degrees by Molokans, or as they call themselves, Spiritual Christians (see box, below). Lermontovo, with its typical two-storey blue and white houses with balconies, is the most traditional of the three villages. Fioletovo appears to have a majority of Molokans, although with a significant Armenian presence, while Margahovit looks more Armenian and has an Armenian church. The roads down into the villages are poor, as are the roads within the villages. Other, far less visible Molokan communities can be found in specific parts of Yerevan, Dilijan and Vanadzor, but this valley appears to contain the main concentration. A 27km dirt road provides summer access from Margahovit to Meghradzor in Kotayk province via the Margahovit Pass (2,633m), suitable only for 4x4s or otherwise a very challenging mountain-bike ride. A better walking route runs in parallel and slightly to the east, part of the newly extended **Janapar Trail** (page 381). It is also possible to traverse the ridge east on foot right through to the Sevan Pass (page 298); on a clear day the panoramic views from the ridge are truly spectacular.

**NORTHERN LORI** In addition to those covered here, the region north of Vanadzor and around Stepanavan is also home to a number of little-visited sites and cultural curiosities which are well documented in the 16-page downloadable guide *Mysteries and Sacred Sites of Stepanavan District* by Taguhi Sahakyan, whose family run a local B&B (page 272) and a very informative website (w stepanavan.net).

## THE MOLOKANS OF ARMENIA

Colloquially pronounced 'malakan', this Christian sect emerged in the 16th–17th century in Russia, refusing to obey the Russian Orthodox Church and rejecting the veneration of icons or the cross. True Christians, they believe, must worship only God and recognise the Bible as the Word of God. At the beginning of the 19th century the Russian government started to relocate those, including the Molokans, who did not accept Orthodoxy, exiling them to distant parts of the empire such as the Caucasus. The name 'Molokans' (milk-drinkers, *moloko* being Russian for 'milk') is most usually said to originate from their refusal to obey the dictates of the Orthodox Church which prohibited milk as well as meat during religious fasts. Another theory is that it derives from the name of the Molochnaya River (which translates as Milky River) in south Ukraine beside which the sect settled in 1820. They themselves prefer to think of their name as referring to 'spiritual milk'.

The Molokans maintain their traditional way of life and tend to marry within their own community. After marriage the men grow beards and the women cover their heads. Religious meetings are in houses rather than churches and men and women sit separately. Their economy is based on agriculture (their cabbages, carrots and homemade pickles are well known) although many do seek work in towns, the men particularly in the building trade where they are renowned for their fastidious work, and so speak some Armenian. Children receive their education in Russian. They are pacifists and are well known for being conscientious objectors in times of war. They prefer not to be photographed.

The M3 main road to Stepanavan avoids the Pushkin Pass (2,037m; see box, below) by a 2km-long tunnel, though the original road is still open, providing access to Armenia's only wind farm, its four turbines built in 2005 by the Iranian government.

There is a dramatic change of scenery as you emerge from the tunnel: gone are the bare stony hillsides and in their place are lush wooded ones. Much of this forest comprises the 26km² **Gyulagarak Sanctuary**, first established in 1958. The first village reached is **Gargar**, whose black-and-white church is visible on the left when passing through; with a good guesthouse (page 274) it would make a convenient base for hiking in the nearby mountains and forests. In Gyulagarak is the junction for **Sochut Dendropark** (☉ 10.00–19.00 daily), sometimes referred to as Stepanavan Dendropark; an arboretum covering 35ha which was founded by the Polish engineer-forester Edmund Leonowicz in 1931 for the cultivation and acclimatisation of trees. The ruinous 6th–7th-century single-nave **Tormakadur church** is passed on the right en route on the site of a former village of the same name. The **arboretum** itself contains over 500 introduced species and is maintained for the benefit of tourists, botanists and school groups – even today the Polish government continues to provide funding. Its numerous footpaths make it one of the more pleasant places in Armenia for a stroll (and an example of how the country's other arboretums and botanical gardens might feel if better supported). There is accommodation nearby (page 274) for those with a special interest, as well as vendors by the entrance selling various pine-based products, including a syrup made from the young cones.

After Gyulagarak, the road to Stepanavan passes through **Amrakits** with its fairy-tale but sadly ruined Russian Orthodox church of St Nicholas the Wonderworker, said to have been built in 1846 by Ukrainian Cossacks. Beyond Amrakits the road approaches the gorge of the Dzoraget River. It is worth stopping and walking the few metres to the edge of the gorge; from here there is a good view to the site of Lori Berd, the main historical site in the vicinity (page 280).

**Stepanavan** Stepanavan is known among Armenians as a summer retreat from the stifling heat of Yerevan, surrounded by gently sloping hillsides replete with wild-flower meadows and forests which (for knowledgeable locals) are prime

---

### THE PUSHKIN PASS

Now bypassed by a tunnel, the Pushkin Pass gets its name from Alexander Pushkin who, on a visit to the Caucasus, met there in 1829 a cart carrying the body of Alexander Griboyedov (1795–1829) who had been killed in Persia, an incident described in Pushkin's *Journey to Erzurum*. Griboyedov, whom Pushkin knew well, was a satirical playwright whose best-known play, *Woe from Wit* (1824), was only performed and published posthumously. Griboyedov was also a diplomat and instrumental in Russia's peace negotiations with Turkey following the war of 1828–29 when Russia gained control of much of Armenia, after which he was appointed Russia's ambassador to the previously defeated Persia. Griboyedov was negotiating in Tehran when an angry anti-Russian mob stormed the embassy and massacred the staff. His mangled body, barely recognisable, was being returned on the cart which Pushkin encountered; a scene depicted on the roadside memorial moved from the pass itself to a new location just downhill from the north end of the tunnel. Pushkin's legacy also survives in the tiny nearby village of Pushkino.

mushroom-picking territory. Formerly Jalaloghlu, Stepanavan was renamed in honour of Stepan Shahumyan (1878–1918), an Armenian who was instrumental in imposing Bolshevik rule in Baku, Azerbaijan. Faced with an uprising he fled but was captured and executed by local anti-Bolsheviks, with some British involvement. His statue can be found at the north end of the town centre, in the middle of a large roundabout at the south end of the bridge across the Dzoraget Gorge. The town is mostly composed of two-storey stone buildings and has a spacious, open feel.

To the west of the main roundabout is the bus station from where **minibuses** to nearby villages as well as Gyumri (daily at 14.00; AMD1,500), Vanadzor (4 daily; AMD500) and Yerevan (5 daily from 08.00; AMD1,500) depart. Buses to Tbilisi via the Gogavan border crossing also run in high season.

## ✗ Where to eat and drink

✗ **Carahunge Café & More**  64 Million St; ☏0256 24300; m 099 324300; w carahunge-cafe. com; ⊕ 11.00–23.00 daily. Delicious Western Armenian (ie: Levantine) cuisine inc *zaatar*, *kofte*, *manti*, hummus, etc, as well as pizzas & grills in this popular restaurant-café which opened late 2015 in Stepanavan town centre. A second branch opened in late 2017 in Dilijan (page 301), with a guesthouse in nearby Amrakits village opened in 2018 (page 274).

**What to see and do**  A well-maintained park, with walkways, gardens and fountains, runs south alongside Garegin Nzhdeh Street to an imposing orange tuff building housing the **Stepan Shahumyan House Museum** (⊕ 09.00–17.00 daily; tours in Armenian and English AMD800; AMD400). The large museum building houses quite literally the original Shahumyan homestead, as well as numerous artefacts from Lori Berd (see below); exhibits are labelled only in Armenian. The house itself is of some interest, as is the model of the secret passage to the underground printing press where Shahumyan printed communist leaflets. The area surrounding the museum and central park is home to much of the town's commerce, along with a handful of small hotels and a couple of cafés and restaurants (see above and page 272). Heading south on Garegin Nzhdeh Street eventually takes you to a coniferous forest limiting the southern edge of the town, where can be found a number of family-oriented holiday resorts, popular in summer with domestic tourists. The aromatic air among the pines, particularly during pollination season, is believed to have curative properties for those with respiratory problems.

The **Communist Caves** (signposted on the left on the M3 main road east), where Shahumyan and fellow revolutionaries met, can be clambered down to by the sure-footed. There is not much to see, but the views of the Dzoraget Gorge are good. **St Sargis Church** is signposted left down one of the small side streets also on the main road south shortly after leaving the town centre. Renovated in 2009, it dates from the 13th century. A khachkar, now on the east façade, gives the foundation date in Armenian letters (page 397) as 666. Adding the 551 years needed for calendrical adjustment, this equates to AD1217.

**Lori Berd (fortress)**  Just outside Stepanavan on the north side of the Dzoraget River, Lori Berd is one of Armenia's most impressive medieval fortress sites. To reach it by road, cross the long bridge over the gorge of the Dzoraget River at the north end of the town. At the far end, turn right and continue for about 2km, turn right where signposted on to an unpaved road through the village of Lori Berd, then continue for another 2km. A taxi from Stepanavan costs AMD2,000 for a return trip plus waiting time. It is also possible to **hike** along the bottom of the gorge; allow 1½–2 hours to cover the 6km. From the south end of the bridge, by the bus station, follow the path northwest and down a disused switchback road to the bottom of the gorge. Cross the rickety bridge and turn immediately right. The 4x4 track follows the river to a small weir, then narrows and bears north around the base of the cliffs before climbing from the historical bridge over the Urut via a steep path to the fortress itself.

The triangular site is spectacularly situated between two river gorges: that of the Dzoraget and that of the Urut. The only side of the site not protected by these gorges, which are too steep-sided easily to scale, is the northern one and this was protected by a high stone wall with towers, at the foot of which there was a moat. As well as the area within the fortifications, the town spread outside them and outlying districts also developed across the two gorges. Bridges were constructed to provide access from these outlying districts: that over the Urut survives and can be seen from the eastern part of the site. It can be reached either by a rocky path which descends from the top of the plateau just before the gate or by a steep path which winds down from just inside the gate and which is very slippery in wet weather.

The fortress was built by David I Anhoghin (David the Landless) (ruled 989–1048), member of a junior branch of Ani's Bagratid dynasty, to be the new capital of the Tashir-Dzoraget kingdom: there were five Armenian kingdoms at the time. Though suffering heavy casualties, the Seljuk Emir Kizil managed to capture Lori Berd in 1105 and it subsequently came under Georgian rule following the Seljuk defeat by Davit IV Aghmashenebeli (David the Builder) (ruled 1089–1125). Davit's great-granddaughter Queen Tamar transferred Lori to the ownership of the Armenian Prince Sargis Zakarian for his assistance in inflicting further defeats on the Seljuks between 1195 and 1204. The town subsequently flourished under his rule and that of his son, but in 1228 Shah Jala-Edin of Khoremsk captured the outlying districts and in 1238 the fortress itself fell to the Mongol Khan Jagat, allegedly because the captains charged with organising the defence spent too much time drinking and too little praying, or so their brother-in-law wrote. The town was ransacked and for over 200 years it passed through various hands only to fall to invaders again in 1430. Decline, however, continued and the last inhabitants left as recently as 1931, largely because of problems with the water supply.

The first building encountered is a **bathhouse** with two baths and evidence of pipes running in the walls. In the centre of the fortress can be seen a roofed **rectangular building** which, at first glance, looks like a church. However, it seems to have had a succession of uses, the exterior walls showing several phases of building. Inside, the six square-domed bays (with pillars supporting the arches dividing the bays) and the niche in the south wall facing Mecca suggest that the building dates from sometime during the Muslim occupation which lasted until the 18th century. The building incorporates medieval tombstones and the doorway is flanked by two khachkars; there may have been an earlier church on the site and it is currently in use as a Christian chapel. Built on to the north side is what looks like a dwelling house with fireplace and chimney. Nowadays the building is home to a family of redstarts in the breeding season. In buildings on the side of the Dzoraget Gorge there is more evidence of pipes suggesting a **washroom** or latrine.

## Northwest from Stepanavan

To head north from Stepanavan turn left after crossing the viaduct. For some length the road keeps east of the river at a distance of a few hundred metres. It is well worth stopping and walking across to look down into the immensely impressive gorge. The road passes through a series of Russian villages built by refugees who fled here to avoid religious persecution during the time of Catherine the Great. The houses typically have two storeys with living accommodation for the family being on the upper storey with its balcony, and the lower storey being used for storage. About 15km from Stepanavan the road reaches the small town now called **Tashir**. Founded in 1844, it was originally named Vorontsovka after Prince Mikhail Vorontsov (1785–1856), viceroy to Tsar Nicholas I, who had been brought up in Britain where his father was Russian ambassador. Vorontsov's role in the Caucasus was considerable. Appointed Governor General of New Russia with 'unlimited powers' during the reign of Tsar Alexander I, he was so successful in integrating southern Ukraine into Russia that he was promoted to viceroy in 1845 and his mandate was extended to the newly acquired territories in the Caucasus. In 1935, Vorontsovka was renamed Kalinino after Mikhail Kalinin (1875–1946), the communist functionary who became titular head of the Soviet state. Tashir has the typical two-storey Russian houses, many still with their red roof tiles. It also has all facilities including a supermarket with an in-store bakery in the form of a large *tonir* where *puri*, a Georgian bread, is baked in the same way as *lavash* (see box, page 99). Eaten freshly from the *tonir* it is quite delicious.

The main road continues north for 14km to the border crossing with Georgia at Gogavan, open to foreigners at the time of writing, though it has periodically been closed to visitors so do check before travelling; one of the most reliable sources of up-to-date information on the subject is w caravanistan.com/border-crossings/armenia. At the far end of Tashir, a road branches left from the main road and heads northwest across marshy ground to the village of **Metsavan**. In the village go straight ahead at the roundabout in the main square, on the road to the right of the village hall, straight ahead at the next fork then turn left. This brings you to the newly renovated **church of St George**. On the hillside at the far end of Metsavan (take the road to the left of the first church) is the small 10th-century **monastery of St John**. The church and graveyard are surrounded by a wall made of gravestones. On the west façade of the church is an alcove, a much-used shrine, with what appears to be the upper part of a free-armed cross, unusual for Armenia.

From Tashir it is possible to travel a dirt road to **Privolnoye**, a village with a Russian church and Russian-style houses. The road is good as far as the crossroads for Medovka and Lernhovit. It then becomes a dirt road drivable in good weather (4x4 advised). It is an attractive route, climbing up through rolling grassy hills then down the other side to Privolnoye, the silver onion dome of the Russian Orthodox church of St Michael visible among the red roofs of the village. If you want to see inside the church ask for Vera (the 'e' is pronounced like the 'e' in vent and the 'r' is rolled), the keyholder, and she will be delighted to show you round and may even take you up the belltower. The church was built in 1895 and the roof was renovated in 1991. Only the west end of the nave is in use, forming a tiny Orthodox church complete with iconostasis and royal doors. Restoration of the remainder of the interior has been started but, like so many projects in Armenia, has run out of money.

North of Privolnoye, the H34 provincial road approaches the Georgian border and Khuchap Monastery via the Wolf's Gate Pass; due to ongoing territorial disputes it is controlled by the Armenian military and the region is only passable by special arrangement, if at all (see box, page 294). Heading east, adventurous mountain bikers and hikers may continue on a dirt track over the considerable flanks of Mount Lalvar to reach Alaverdi, a journey of perhaps 20km.

South again towards Stepanavan is the village of **Sverdlov**, named after Yakov Sverdlov (1885–1919), a Bolshevik who was instrumental in overthrowing the elected Russian constitutional assembly in January 1918. The 7th- to 12th-century St George Church with its red tile roof is visible on entering the village; keep going uphill. The church is a barrel-vaulted basilica; the arches supporting the roof spring from four pairs of piers in the side walls. The belltower on the south wall of the church is roofed with stone tiles. Gravestones cover the hillock on which the church stands. Some 3km north of Sverdlov, the **monastery of Dorbantavank** can be seen across fields to the right. Dating from the 6th century, it is a single-nave structure with barrel vaulting and rather tall for its size. Although attractively situated it was insensitively restored during the Soviet era.

## From Stepanavan to the Debed Gorge

Rather than travelling via Vanadzor it is possible to travel to the Debed Gorge by two alternative routes. The first heads east from Gyulagarak and passes the **monastery of Hnevank**. The asphalt road deteriorates badly beyond **Kurtan** but is manageable by car to a point 300m from the monastery and beyond to Dzoragyugh village. For the descent into the Debed Gorge, a 4x4 is necessary to negotiate the abandoned Soviet-built switchback road. Booted eagles and golden eagles can be seen along the gorge, and in early summer this spectacularly beautiful valley is enhanced further by the brilliance of the wild flowers. The monastery itself was founded in the 7th century but rebuilt with a much higher tambour in 1144. The gavit dates from the late 12th century and leads to both the small cross-dome main church on the east and a chapel to the west. Restoration may have diminished some of the charm of the previously undisturbed ruins, but it does enable the visitor to make more sense of the layout. A barrel-vaulted building lies to the west and what was thought to be the refectory a short distance to the east. To the south of the gavit are the low remains of other monastic buildings, all but hidden when the vegetation grows waist-high.

The second route is paved throughout and suitable for all vehicles. From the north end of the bridge over the Dzoraget in Stepanavan, turn right to head east through Lori Berd village and onwards via **Yaghdan**, a village established by Greeks who arrived in the 18th century to work in mining and the only village in Armenia that is still considered 'Greek', with a reported 60–70 inhabitants who identify as such. At the east end of the village, just south of the road, a 13th-century bridge spans the Yaghdandur tributary. The road bears north to pass Aygehat and Ardvi (page 287) before descending from Odzun to the bottom of the gorge south of Alaverdi. This gentle and largely traffic-free route would make for excellent cycle touring.

## THE DEBED GORGE

The M6 main road north from Vanadzor, as well as the railway to Tbilisi, follows the scenic gorge of the Debed River. The gorge is noteworthy for having five of Armenia's finest churches/monasteries and for being a habitat for several iconic bird species; it also has the only stretch of river in Armenia on which **white-water rafting** is officially sanctioned, although still at a very early stage of development at the time of research.

## ✖ Where to eat and drink

✖ **Avan Dzoraget Restaurant** North end of Dzoraget village; m 093 947889; w tufenkianheritage.com; ⊕ 09.00–23.00. Part of the Tufenkian hotel of the same name; page 273.

✖ **Flora** On the M6 main road through Alaverdi; ☎ 0374 22474; m 091 210624. One of the region's more pleasant roadside restaurants on the east side of the river on the way past Alaverdi. The fare is the ubiquitous *khorovats*, but restaurateur Armen has won awards for his barbecuing skills & judges an annual BBQ competition at Akhtala.

✖ **Nurik** 1 Raffi St, Akhtala village; m 094 417912/580787; ■ nurikcenter; ⊕ 09.00–22.00 daily. Attractive & tasteful new NGO-run café & community centre, located at the entrance to Akhtala Monastery & employing local women in serving the site's many visitors. A good selection of hot & cold drinks, soups, salads & the usual *khorovats*. Traditional *lavash* bakery & souvenir shop on-site selling local handicrafts & honey. (*Nurik* means 'little pomegranate'.)

## What to see and do

**Dsegh** Just south of Dzoraget village, a side road crosses the river to follow the valley of a tributary for a few kilometres before turning abruptly left to wind up the side of the valley to the plateau, from where expansive views across wild-flower meadows on both sides of the gorge can be seen. The road reaches the village of Dsegh which has a **visitor centre** (⊕ on demand; m 093 045514 (Eduard)) providing information about the area's bird species and habitats, as well as maps and literature describing five hiking trails of varying lengths beginning from the village. Several B&Bs (page 274) allow hikers to overnight here. In summer, the longest of the trails leading east to the ridge above the villages of Lorut and Atan can be extended to reach Yenokavan and Ijevan in Tavush province, or connect through to the Dilijan National Park trail network near Hovk (page 311), though at least one night's camping would be necessary to complete this excellent trek through the remote mountains.

The main attraction of Dsegh itself is the **Hovhannes Tumanyan house museum** (⊕ 10.00–18.00 Tue–Sun; adult/child AMD500/300), devoted to the poet (1869–1923) (page 55) after whom the village was named until 1969. Although tourists who do not speak Armenian are unlikely to have encountered his works, the museum gives an interesting insight into living conditions in Tsarist days, notably the two older rooms with their rock floors and chest-like bed. The monument outside the museum was erected after the collapse of the Soviet Union when Vano Siradeghyan, Minister of Internal Affairs, decided that the poet's heart should be buried here rather than kept in a jar in the anatomical museum of the medical university in Yerevan. Opposite the museum is the **church of St Gregory the Illuminator** (⊕ 09.00–18.00), built in the 7th century, rebuilt in the 12th–13th centuries by the Mamikonians, restored in 1900 and again in 1969, when it became a museum.

Just below the village of Dsegh is the ruin of a small 12th-century cross-dome church known as Karasun Mankats, or the **40 Children Church**. The story goes that, sometime in the 17th century, 40 children hid in the church from the invading Turks and were never found. The church is notable for an amazing variety of khachkars ranging from simple crosses to those with elaborate decoration. Interestingly a significant proportion of the khachkars show two equally sized crosses side by side. The views from the church over the gorge below are superb. Golden eagles and lammergeiers, Europe's largest vultures, are quite common here and alpine swifts nest in crevices in the valley side.

The church can be reached either by a short steep descent (20mins) from Dsegh or a longer hike (about 1½hrs), with some steep stretches, up from the main road in the Debed Gorge near the Tufenkian Hotel. To get here from Dsegh, take the path to your right as you face the church of St Gregory the Illuminator then turn left beyond the house bearing the sign for 40 Children Church. This path takes you to the edge of the plateau. Walk along the edge to the obvious large khachkar from where a rocky path descends. From here you can see the church. At a suitable point leave the path and scramble down the boulder-strewn slope to the church. Returning to Dsegh the landmark to aim for is the last wooden electricity pole in the gorge (the next one is up on the plateau). This will bring you back to the path to the village.

To get here from the Debed Gorge, start from the bridge across the river to the Tufenkian Hotel and walk northwards along the main road for no more than 500m.

The start of the path up to Dsegh is not very obvious; it goes off to the right just north of a café with a khachkar-like statue. The railway can be seen above the road crossing a small stream. Cross the railway line (beware of trains: this line is used) and the path becomes easier to see going up on the left of the stream. Continue up until you reach a small meadow a little below the plateau on which Dsegh stands. The church is across the meadow to your left. To continue up to Dsegh, see opposite.

Dsegh is also the starting point for visiting the ruined 13th-century **Bardzrakashi St Gregory Monastery** down on the side of the gorge. The monastery is signposted from the village and also at the edge of the plateau where the path into the gorge starts. It is about 2km from the village to the start of the path then a 20-minute walk down to the monastery. The path (slippery after rain) descends through the forest past collections of khachkars and a spring with a drinking trough before reaching the monastery in its peaceful setting.

The main buildings are the 13th-century Mother of God Church with a gavit on its south side and a second smaller church on its north side. All is in a tumbled down and overgrown state, but it is still possible to get an idea of what it must have looked like and there are some wonderful carved details both inside and out, such as the fish high on the eastern façade of the main church. The east façade of the gavit bears the Mamikonian family crest, a two-headed eagle with a lamb in its talons. The gavit is reached first and is entered from the south. The dome and roof, long since fallen, were supported by four free-standing columns and there is an eastern apse which has parted company from the rest of the wall. The Mother of God Church is entered on its south side from the gavit. It too is filled with fallen masonry but arches remain springing from a pillar with a decorated capital. The wide eastern apse has niches with scalloped carving. The second smaller church is difficult to enter, the doorway between the two churches being blocked by yet more fallen masonry. Back on the plateau, about 500m north of the start of the path to Bardzrakashi St Gregory Monastery is the **Sirun Khach** (Beautiful Cross), a large, intricately carved, 13th-century khachkar on a three-step pedestal.

**Kobayr Monastery** The monastery is accessed from close to the town of **Tumanyan**, named after the poet and overlooked by a Soviet-era knitwear factory, which remains in surprisingly good condition and would perhaps make for a good hotel conversion. The distinctive curved arches and imposing columns of many of Tumanyan's buildings and its unusually resplendent town square were the work of a German architect who spent several years as a prisoner of war in the town and decided to put his skills to use. Just south is what looks like a huge abandoned brick factory; it is in fact still operational with a couple of employees stockpiling bricks for the day, long-awaited, when an order finally comes in.

The usual trail head for Kobayr is about 2km further north: look out for a small railway station up above the road on the left. It is a steep 15-minute waymarked hike to Kobayr, one of Armenia's most impressive ruined monasteries. A longer but easier route suitable for 4x4s begins opposite the bridge from the main road to Tumanyan village and is also signposted; park below the monastery and climb the steep and often slippery rock staircase to the western corner of the complex. The fortified monastery complex covered a large area; restoration continues interminably and at a snail's pace, presumably in part because of the difficulty of hoisting materials to the precipitous site. According to an inscription, the **main church** was built in 1171 by Mariam, daughter of Kyurik II. At this time the Turkish Seljuks ruled Armenia but delegated control to local princes. Following Georgian victories over the Seljuk Turks in 1195 and 1202 the monastery came under

Georgian rule, passing into the control of the Zakaryan family who adhered to the Georgian Orthodox Church rather than the Armenian Church. (The Georgian Church differed in having accepted the views of the Council of Chalcedon, which took place in 451, over the duality of Christ's nature.) This explains the existence of Georgian features, notably the Georgian-style frescoes and carved inscriptions. Much of the south side of the complex has descended into the gorge below but the roofless apse and parts of the other walls survive, with Georgian-style frescoes in the apse and chapel, which were restored in 1971. In the apse the frescoes comprise three rows: in the top row the Virgin Mary and archangels; in the middle row Jesus and the Last Supper; in the bottom row figures of saints. The frescoes in the **chapel** on the north side of the church are in a similar style with vivid portrayals of Jesus and the disciples. Immediately southeast of the main church are two small chapels, one of which has a viewing balcony. The belltower/mausoleum, north of the main church, in the centre of the monastery was built in 1279. The mausoleum houses the tombs of Shanshe Mkhargrdzeli and his wife Vaneni and has a spring flowing through it, a feature which may indicate that this has been a religious site since pagan times. The reconstructed belltower surmounting the mausoleum has eight pillars supporting the dome. The **13th-century refectory** is between the main church and the mausoleum slightly up the hill. Surrounding the whole complex was a fortified wall and the well-preserved gateway lies to the north of the main group of buildings together with a further small church dated 1223.

**Odzun and Ardvi**  By **road** from Kobayr to Ozdun, continue north along the main road until the left turn for Odzun in about 7km. It is highly recommended, however, to continue on foot along the waymarked **hiking trail** from just below the monastery itself to Odzun. The 9km medium-difficulty walk will take around 3–4 hours and mostly follows an ancient footpath beneath the dramatic cliffs at the top edge of the gorge, with stunning views of the canyon itself; it's certainly among the most spectacular walks in Armenia. It is also possible to break off from the marked trail midway and climb an ancient stone staircase to the clifftop village of **Aygehat**. The regular route passes the ruined **Horomayr Church** which is right on the edge of the gorge. It was built in the 7th century and rebuilt in the 13th using a darker stone. The darker stone, having scarcely weathered, almost has the appearance of concrete and contrasts considerably with the warm honey-coloured older stone, which has weathered badly. A small central gavit, paved with gravestones, leads into the dark-stone barrel-vaulted church on the south and pale tuff chapel on the north. The tiny **Holy Cross Chapel** can be seen below and in spring the plateau is covered by an amazing carpet of flowers. (The church can also be reached by a shorter route from the top of the gorge.)

**Odzun** itself is on the plateau and the road winds up the valley side to reach it. Several accommodation options exist here. Its **church** is constructed of pink felsite (⊕ usually in the tourist season 10.00–19.00 daily; if it's shut, the caretaker can often be found & the priest lives nearby). It is a large building, dating from the 6th century, reconstructed in the 8th, and one of Armenia's finest basilicas with a cupola. It stands on the site of an early 4th-century church (303–13) which was destroyed by an earthquake in the 5th century. Remnants of the 4th-century church were found under the apse of the present church. Tradition holds that the apostle Thomas ordained priests at Odzun on his way to India and that before he left he buried Christ's swaddling clothes where the present altar stands. A 6th-century inscription above the southern door of the church records this tradition. The two small belltowers at the east end were a much later addition in the late 19th century. The church had an exterior gallery on its north, west and south sides, those on the north and south were arcaded while that on the west had a blind wall with an arched entrance in the middle. The arcades on the north no longer exist but restoration, ongoing at the time of writing, may change this. The gallery ends on the southeast in a small chapel and on the northeast in an open apse. (See page 49 for the historical uses of galleries.) Inside the church there are three naves, the two side naves very narrow. The roof is barrel-vaulted and the rib-vaulted octagonal tambour is supported by four free-standing columns. There are two additional supporting columns at the west end of the church. Carved stones from the 4th-century church were built into the wall of the church, most notably a carving of the Virgin Mary and Christ Child above the font in the north wall. The 2009 fresco in the apse depicts the Virgin and Child in the same postures. The most notable feature of the exterior carving is on the east façade above the central window where Christ can be seen holding open the Gospel of St John with angels below. At each side of the central window on the south side is an angel with traces of another figure, probably Christ. Above the central window on the north side is a weathered full-length figure, possibly another image of the Virgin and Child. The west portal is surrounded by curving foliage and above the tympanum of the west entrance is an enigmatic fragment of a larger carving.

In the surrounding graveyard the clergy were buried near the church and were depicted on the gravestones holding staffs. Beside the church is a most unusual **funerary monument**, one of only two in this style in Armenia – the other is at Aghitu in Syunik province (page 349). It comprises a stepped platform supporting two slender obelisk-shaped carved stelae set between double arches. The carvings on the stelae are divided into panels depicting, on the east and west sides, biblical scenes together with the coming of Christianity to Armenia, and on the north and south sides, geometrical motifs and floral shapes. It has been suggested that the monument might commemorate Hovhannes Odznetsi (see below) who was Katholikos from 717 until 728 and undertook rebuilding work at Odzun, but its style suggests an earlier date and erection in the 6th century seems more likely.

Southwest from Odzun is **Ardvi** (not signposted from the main road: the turn-off is 3km after the leaving Odzun sign). The 10th-century **Holy Resurrection Church** is on the left as you enter the village, a small rectangular structure on a knoll. The roof of the barrel-vaulted nave has collapsed but that of the apse still stands. Two of the gravestones here depict a figure with a smaller figure within it, indicating the grave of a woman who had been pregnant when she died. Beyond the village, 5km after leaving the main road, is the small **monastery of St John** on a hillside. The 17th-century double church and its separate belltower have very low doors, only a little over 1m high. The belltower incorporates an unusual khachkar of a person wearing a hat and high-heeled shoes and carrying two unknown objects.

The small adjoining churches are both barrel-vaulted with thick walls and are entered from the south. In the second church is the tomb of **Hovhannes Odznetsi**. Odznetsi was born in Odzun and was Katholikos from 717 until his death in 728. He is revered in Armenia for his opposition to the influence of the Chalcedonic Byzantine Church and for his negotiations with the Arab rulers of the time to ensure the independence of the Armenian Church. In 719 he visited Omar Khalif in Damascus and secured exemption of the Armenian Church from certain taxes, freedom to profess the Christian faith and the cessation of persecution in Armenia. In return he promised the obedience of the Armenians. He convened the Council of Dvin in 720, to establish rules for church services and the moral conduct of believers, and the Council of Manazkert in 726 to settle a dispute between the Armenian and Syrian churches over differing interpretations of the nature of Christ. The Council

Visitors to Ardvi are likely to have pointed out to them 'the snakes', a stratum of hard pink rock running more or less horizontally through softer pale rock where a spring issues from the cliff face in a gully near the monastery. Legend relates that one day when Odznetsi was praying two snakes (or dragons) appeared, terrifying his assistant. Odznetsi made the sign of the cross over the snakes (or dragons) and they immediately turned to stone, water gushing from them. There they remain to this day, petrified in the cliff face and with water still flowing from them. The water is considered an antidote to snake bites but it is suggested to follow the advice on page 76 rather than relying on the efficacy of the spring. *Odz* is the Armenian for snake. The connection with the name Odzun is obvious. It is also interesting that the shape of the unusual funerary monument beside Odzun Church harks back to the shape of *vishaps*, or dragon stones (see box, page 50).

agreed statements to ensure the unity of the churches and thus strengthen their Monophysite position against the Chalcedonic doctrine. His literary output was mainly on administrative, doctrinal and legal topics, together with philosophical subjects which earned him the honorific Imastaser (Philosopher). He was the first to collect and systematise the canon law of the Armenian Church. His monumental work *Canon Law of the Armenians* is still used. He was canonised in 1774. The cemetery, on an adjoining hillock, has a very fine collection of khachkars; graves here span the centuries from the 6th to the 19th.

**Alaverdi**  Back on the main road it is a short distance north to the copper-mining town of Alaverdi ('Allah gave' in Turkish). This industrial city clings to the side of the gorge and is the commercial centre of the Debed region. The conspicuous copper-smelting plant spews industrial-grade smoke into the air and is the town's main source of employment. While much of the town is down in the gorge there is also the district of Sanahin up on the plateau. Upper and lower districts are linked by road; local minibuses run the route regularly. A now defunct cable car opened in 1978 and had the steepest climb of any in the former Soviet Union. It has a drop of 200m and could carry a maximum of 15 people until it ceased to operate in 2015 when the owner (the director of the copper mine) claimed financial difficulties and closed it down. There are two road crossings of the river, at the south and north ends of the town, and a pedestrian-only medieval bridge (note the carved animals on top of the parapet), built in 1192, towards the north end of the town centre. From the east end of the southern road bridge the road to the Sanahin district and monastery goes off right and winds up to the plateau.

Most of the main facilities (including the train station) are in the centre of Alaverdi in the gorge, though several hotels and B&Bs operate in the Sanahin district, as well as in nearby Haghpat (page 291). A **tourist information centre** (3 Sayat Nova St; ✆ 0253 24858; m 095 508971; e toumanianlori@outlook.com; w toumanianlori.com; ⊕ 09.00–17.00 Mon–Sat) opened in 2015 to assist with visits not only to Alaverdi but also to all the sights of the Debed Gorge; the English- and French-speaking staff are very helpful. Minibuses depart from the main bus station on Tumanyan Street in the centre of town near the river, serving (unusually) many of the popular sites of interest in the vicinity, including Odzun, Haghpat, Akhtala and Ardvi. Minibuses also leave for Vanadzor (5 daily from 08.00; AMD800), the

Bagratashen border crossing (2 daily at 08.50 & 15.30; AMD500) and Stepanavan (10.00 daily; AMD800). The Yerevan–Tbilisi train (page 85) passes through in the early hours; the timing, however, is too antisocial to be of much use.

**Sedvu Monastery**   Visitors rarely reach this site on the dead-end road to the village of Kachachkut, former name Sedvi (giving the site its name). It is a trip made for the breathtaking views, not for the site itself, which in no way matches the splendours of the better-known monasteries. In Alaverdi take the road which goes off westwards under the railway bridge near the lower cable-car terminus. The road runs through the suburbs, turning to run southwards parallel to the river. Take the second right, beside a pharmacy. The road climbs up to the village of Akori then continues to climb to Kachachkut with ever more impressive views. The structures are hidden among trees some distance below the road. Go down through the cemetery by taking the track which goes off left 9km after leaving the main road in Alaverdi. The church of St Nshan and the ruins of the surrounding defensive wall are all that remains of the 13th- to 14th-century monastery. The very plain barrel-vaulted basilica church, built of dark grey stone, is somewhat sombre. With only a few small windows, it looks as if it was built as much for defence as for worship. More fortifications can be found a little further down the slope.

**Sanahin Monastery**   Added to UNESCO's World Heritage list in 1996, this famous monastery complex is just outside Alaverdi's upper district of the same name. To get here by road cross the river by the southern bridge in Alaverdi and continue up the hill past the Debed Hotel before bearing right to reach the monastery; local minibuses run from Alaverdi's main bus station on Tumanyan Street. Nowadays one of Lori's most frequently visited sights, it was established in 966 by Queen Khosrovanush, wife of King Ashot III Bagratuni, on the site of two existing churches, St Jacob which dates from the 9th century and the Mother of God which was built sometime between 928 and 944. Sanahin became a centre of considerable cultural influence during the 10th and 11th centuries with its monastic school and important library where copyists worked to produce illuminated manuscripts. Sanahin's role declined as Armenia suffered waves of invaders, although the local Argutyan family was exceptional in managing to retain its estates through to the 20th century.

The ensemble is very picturesque but does rather give the impression of having grown piecemeal. It is dominated by the **Church of the Holy Redeemer** with its conical dome; construction probably began in 966. This church, built of basalt, has its eastern façade decorated with arcature and the main window is similarly decorated. The gable of this façade has a sculptural relief depicting Smbat and Gurgen Bagratuni, two of the three sons of the founder, with a model of a church, the first appearance of such a scene in Armenia. Smbat became King Smbat II of the Bagratid dynasty, rulers of Ani, and Gurgen was the father of David Anhoghin who constructed Lori Berd. The Church of the Holy Redeemer is separated from the smaller **Mother of God Church** by a gallery covered by a barrel vault, the **Academy of Gregory Magistros**, which is believed to have been used for teaching. Possibly the students sat in the niches between the monumental pillars.

On the west side of the churches are large **gavits** constructed in 1181 and 1211 and somewhat different from each other in style. The gavit of the Church of the Holy Redeemer is the earlier. It has four tall free-standing internal pillars supporting arches. The bases and capitals of the columns are decorated with carvings and reliefs depicting the heads of animals, fruits and geometric patterns. The gavit of

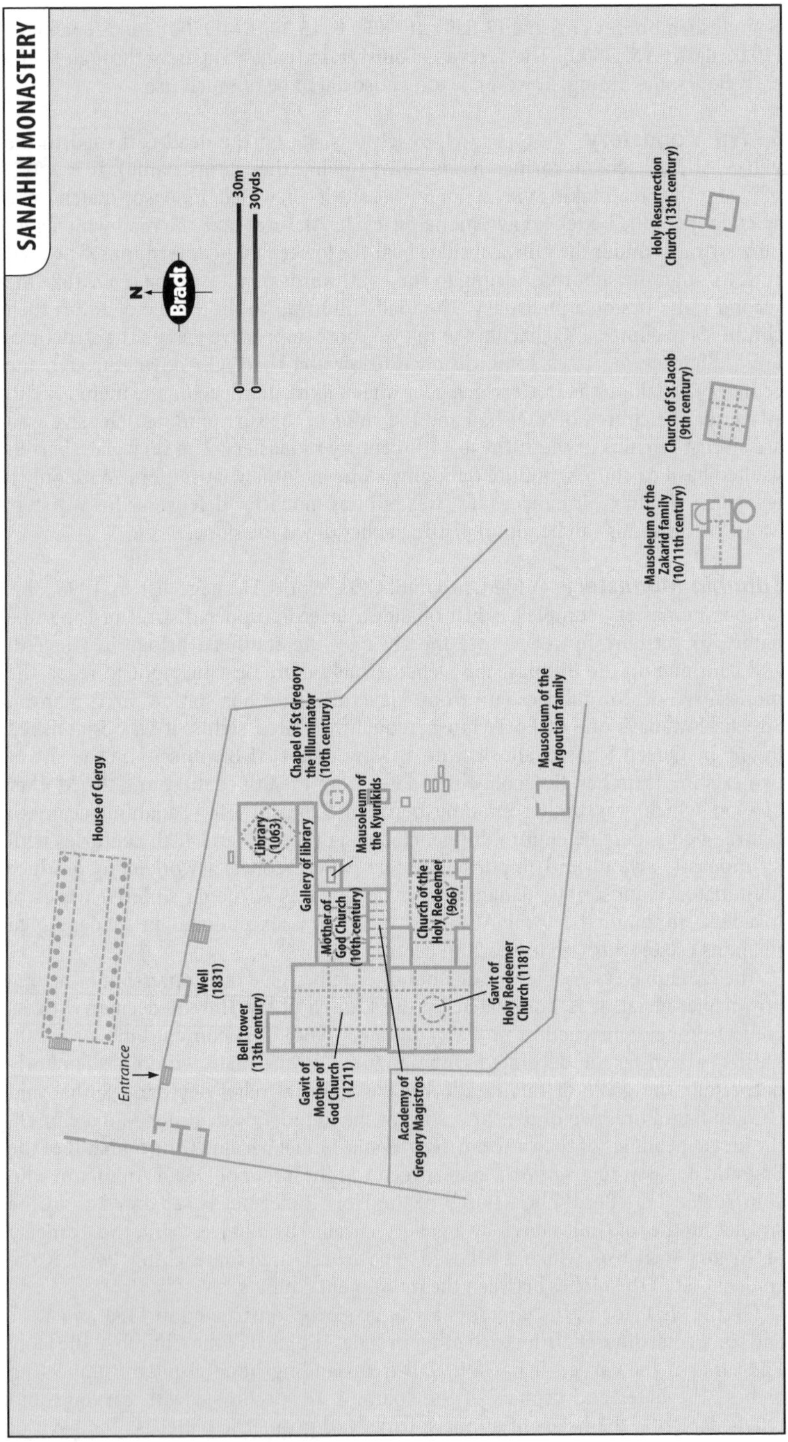

SANAHIN MONASTERY

N

Bradt

0 ———— 30m
0 ———— 30yds

House of Clergy

Entrance

Well (1831)

Bell tower (13th century)

Gavit of Mother of God Church (1211)

Academy of Gregory Magistros

Library (1063)

Gallery of library

Mausoleum of the Kyurikids

Chapel of St Gregory the Illuminator (10th century)

Mother of God Church (10th century)

Church of the Holy Redeemer (966)

Gavit of Holy Redeemer Church (1181)

Mausoleum of the Argoutian family

Mausoleum of the Zakarid family (10/11th century)

Church of St Jacob (9th century)

Holy Resurrection Church (13th century)

Sanahin's other claim to fame is as the birthplace of the brothers Anastas (1895–1978) and Artem Mikoyan (1905–70). A **museum** devoted to them is located in a former school down the hill from the monastery (✆ 0253 32574; m 091 909436; ⊕ 09.30–17.00 Tue–Sun; guiding inc but only in Armenian, AMD500). Anastas achieved the distinction of being the longest-serving member of the Soviet Politburo. He survived a series of political upheavals to remain a member from 1935 to 1966 and was involved in many important events. In 1939, he was responsible for the discussions with Germany on trade prior to the signing of the Nazi–Soviet pact; in 1955 he was part of the delegation which sought to heal the rift with Tito in Yugoslavia; in 1962 he dealt with Cuba during the missile crisis (he spoke Spanish); in 1964 he was instrumental in ousting Khrushchev. Artem Mikoyan, by contrast, played a leading role in the development of Soviet fighter aircraft. He was named head of a new design bureau in 1939. His bureau collaborated with that headed by Mikhail Gurevich and at first produced a number of relatively unsuccessful planes. Then the turbojet-powered MiG-15, which first flew in 1947, proved a world-beating design and was the forerunner of a series of light fighter aircraft which saw extensive deployment during the Cold War era. MiG is actually an acronym for Mikoyan and Gurevich.

In the museum itself, downstairs are everyday artefacts belonging to the family including furniture made by the illiterate father of the brothers. Upstairs is an exposition of their careers. In the forecourt is a MiG-21 fighter plane and a car belonging to Anastas.

---

the Mother of God Church is a three-nave hall with much lower arches than the earlier gavit and with less elaborate bases and capitals for the columns. Externally the western façade of this gavit has six arches, two to each gable. Abutting the gavit at its western end is the **belltower**, crowned by a small rotunda, which is also early 13th century and thought to be Armenia's earliest. The floors of the gavits are paved with gravestones and throughout the site there is a wealth of khachkars, not all of them religious: one commemorates the building of the bridge at Alaverdi in 1192 and another the construction of an inn in 1205. Some particularly fine ones stand in front of the gavits.

On the complex's north side is the **library** of 1063 which has an octagonal tent roof resting on diagonally arranged arches which spring from four short pillars, one in the centre of each wall and each differently decorated. At the eastern end of the library is the small domed round **Chapel of St Gregory the Illuminator** built in the late 10th century. It is a two-storey structure with a pointed roof. To the northeast of the main complex are two **mausoleums** which date from the 10th and 11th centuries and beyond them are the 9th-century **church of St Jacob** (the nearer one) and the early 13th-century **Holy Resurrection Church** which has two identical apses. By the boundary wall on the north side is the monastery's **spring**. It is covered by a structure which dates to 1831.

**Haghpat Monastery** Haghpat is contemporaneous with Sanahin and very similar in style. Both were added to UNESCO's World Heritage list in 1996, the first Armenian sites to be so listed. Pilgrims in the monasteries' heyday were inevitably driven to compare the two and from this comparison derive the present names: Haghpat means 'huge wall' because that was one of its striking features, whereas Sanahin means 'older than the other'. Although Haghpat can be seen from Sanahin, to reach it by road requires that you return to the bottom of the gorge, then head east along the main road for about 5km and turn right up the hill, from where the left fork leads to the monastery which can be seen high on the hillside. A better option if you have time is to walk between the two sites via the village of Akner on a very popular signposted hiking trail which also passes Kayan Fortress (see opposite); allow 3 hours to complete the 8km hike. Haghpat is much more attractively sited than Sanahin, and consequently more pleasant to visit, as the approach is not through an area of run-down Soviet-era buildings. It is, however, frequented by bus tours and surrounded by hotels and B&Bs to house their clients. The **main church** with its huge dome is dedicated to the Holy Cross and was built between 976 and 991 at the behest of Queen Khosrovanush, also the founder of Sanahin. From the exterior it appears rectangular but internally is cross-shaped and, as at Sanahin, there is a relief of Smbat and Gurgen holding a model of a church on the east façade. Frescoes were added to the church in the 13th century; some are still faintly visible in the apse. Unlike Sanahin the buildings, which were gradually added, do not lead directly off each other. A smaller church, dedicated to **St Gregory the Illuminator**, was added in 1005 at the southwest side of the site and a domed **Mother of God Church** was added on the northwest side in 1025. The St Gregory Church lost its dome during rebuilding in 1211. A **gavit** was built in 1185 to the west of the cathedral and the cathedral itself gained a magnificent porch in 1201.

The three-storey **belltower** was built in 1245, a much more substantial structure than at Sanahin. Its ground floor has the plan of a cross-dome church and serves as a chapel. The second storey by contrast is rectangular with the corners cut off, thus

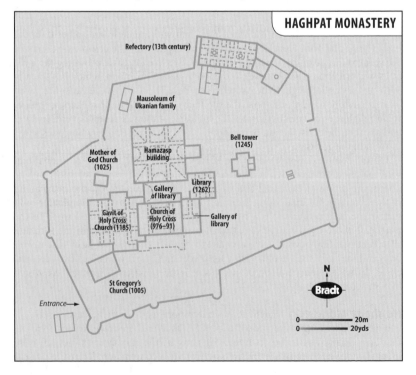

HAGHPAT MONASTERY

Refectory (13th century)

Mausoleum of Ukanian family

Bell tower (1245)

Mother of God Church (1025)

Hamazasp building

Library (1262)

Gallery of library

Gavit of Holy Cross Church (1185)

Church of Holy Cross (976–91)

Gallery of library

St Gregory's Church (1005)

Entrance→

N

Bradt

0 ———— 20m
0 ———— 20yds

turning into an octagonal shape. The transition between the two shapes is ingenious. The third storey, the belfry, is unusually seven sided and supported by seven columns. Another gavit, called the **Hamazasp building** after its donor, was built to the north of the cathedral in 1257 and is unusual for a gavit in being free-standing. The **library**, originally built with a wooden roof in the 10th century, was rebuilt with a stone roof in 1262. One of Armenia's most famous and beautiful khachkars, the **Holy Redeemer khachkar** of 1273, is in the passage leading to the library. This amazing work shows Christ crucified surrounded by saints and apostles with angels looking down and God the Father raising his hand in blessing. Haghpat's library became a storeroom after invaders had taken the manuscripts and the floor now has many storage jars sunk into it. The 13th-century **refectory** is an isolated building on the north side of the site. It is a long building whose tall roof is borne by intersecting arches supported by pairs of free-standing columns. The central section is crowned by octagonal domed vaults which admit light. This unusual structure adjoins the defensive wall of the monastery. Also notable to the west of the refectory is the **spring**. It is in a three-arched structure built in 1258. There are stone troughs along the back wall for watering cattle and a reservoir for general use.

***Kayan Berd (fortress)*** The ruins of this small fortress are probably most often seen while coming down the road from Haghpat Monastery. There are also good views of it from parts of Haghpat village. Standing on a peninsula-like promontory of the plateau between Sanahin and Haghpat, the fortress is not as inaccessible as it looks and can be reached by a pleasant, relatively easy 30-minute walk from the bottom, if not visited en route while hiking between the two monasteries (see opposite). Starting from the lay-by on the road to Haghpat at the junction for Tsaghkashat, follow the path which goes down to the river and across a renovated medieval bridge then uphill to the right. After the first uphill stretch the path is mostly level along the side of the hill until it reaches the final short climb to the top. Much of the route is through woodland so there is some shade. There are the remains of defensive walls with semicircular towers round two sides of the triangular site. The best-preserved building is the small black tuff Dsevank Mother of God Church built in 1233. Its

## THE 40 MARTYRS OF SEBASTE

Western visitors familiar with biblical narratives will have no difficulty in recognising what most of the frescoes depict at Akhtala (page 294), but they may be less familiar with the story of the 40 martyrs of Sebaste on the west wall of the south aisle. They were Roman soldiers martyred under Emperor Lucinius at Sebaste, Lesser Armenia, in AD320. Refusing to renounce their Christian faith, they were condemned to die by being exposed naked on a frozen lake with a north wind blowing. A warm bath nearby added to the temptation to renounce their faith. Only one succumbed and accounts vary as to what happened to him. Some say he expired immediately on entering the warm bath, others that he lived, repented and made amends for his apostasy by spending the rest of his life preaching the Gospel. The number of martyrs, however, remained at 40. A sentinel watching events was so impressed by a vision of the martyrs receiving their heavenly reward that he immediately became a Christian, stripped off his clothes and joined the 39 on the ice. The Feast of the 40 Martyrs of Sebaste is 9 March in the eastern churches, 10 March in the western.

## KHUCHAP AND KHORAKERT MONASTERIES

Although some maps still show Khuchap and Khorakert monasteries as being in Armenia, both are in fact in what is now a disputed border region. At the time of research it was **not possible to visit either of them independently** from Armenia. The authorities will detain any unauthorised person found in the disputed territory. Only through negotiations with the Armenian border guard unit headquartered in Pushkino village might it be possible to visit Khuchap from the Armenian side; if Khorakert can be visited it must be from the Georgian side. Descriptions of both are given here in any case, though they might not necessarily be fully up to date. The monasteries are only 5km apart.

**RECENT HISTORY** Khuchap and Khorakert monasteries have long been on the Armenia–Georgia border. In the early 2000s they were both indisputably in Armenia, although one had to cross slivers of Georgian territory to reach them. At that time this was no problem; the Armenian border guards simply phoned their Georgian counterparts for permission. Since then, the exact position of the border has become contested. Khorakert Monastery is now in Georgia-controlled territory and must be visited from Georgia. Khuchap technically remains in Armenia but is off limits because of the territorial dispute.

In 1918 Georgia and Armenia fought a short (17–31 December) war over disputed territory in the Lori, Javakheti and Borchalo districts which until 1917 had been part of the Tiflis Governate of the Russian Empire. A British-brokered ceasefire resulted in a neutral zone which was later divided between the Armenian SSR and the Georgian SSR, Lori going to Armenia, and Javakheti (which has an ethnic Armenian majority) and Borchalo to Georgia. With the collapse of the USSR, the border dispute between the two independent countries resurfaced.

The whole of northern Lori had numerous minor crossing points to Georgia but even locals are now not allowed to go to and fro. Armenians living in the village of Jiliza, only 1km from the border with Georgia, are not allowed to cross the local checkpoint to visit either Khorakert Monastery, some 4km away, or their relatives on the other side of the border. Instead they must now travel about 100km via Alaverdi and the main international border crossing at Bagratashen.

**KHUCHAP MONASTERY** Khuchap sits at the foot of Mount Lalvar and is a 7km walk from Jiliza. One can reach a closer point by 4x4 via the Wolf's Gate Pass (1,787m) north of Privolnoye, but the road is closed in winter and absolutely dreadful in summer. It takes about an hour to walk to Khuchap from the road. The beautiful

black, red and white dome was damaged by an earthquake in 1827. The church is perched right on the edge of the site; one corner had to be built on boulders.

***Akhtala Monastery*** (⊕ site always; church all day) Akhtala is further north towards the Georgian border and receives only a fraction of the visitors who go to Sanahin and Haghpat. It is built in a quite different style but its setting is equally dramatic, perched up on a cliff. Unfortunately the view from outside is marred by copper mining taking place on the opposite side of the valley, but the inside of the main church, featuring Armenia's finest frescoes, makes the visit to Akhtala worthwhile. There is also an excellent café and visitor centre just before the site's entrance (page 283). To reach it, take the M6 walk along the river, through orchards and forest, involves both wading across the river and the company of a border guard.

The monastery is delightfully situated, hidden away in its small wooded valley. It was abandoned in the 1940s when the last nuns left, but the main church (13th century) is intact. Red felsite was used for the outer walls and forms an unusual and pleasing contrast with the yellow felsite used for the window surrounds, large crosses on two of the gable ends, and to produce a banded effect on the tall tambour. Inside, the church is rectangular with a very high cupola and two supporting octagonal pillars. There are separate naves at the west end of the church and vestibules were added at the east end sometime after construction. Outside, the decoration is amazingly varied with door and window surrounds being carved with a whole range of geometric patterns, while carved figures of animals and projecting carved animal heads can be seen high up on the tambour. Every one of the 12 carved windows around the tambour has a different geometric pattern. On the west façade are the remains of a gallery-like addition with four arches. North of the main church are the remains of other monastic buildings, much plainer and built of grey andesite.

**KHORAKERT MONASTERY** Khorakert can now only be visited from Georgia (see opposite). Built in the late 12th and early 13th centuries, the really striking, unique, feature is that the tambour (which has ten sides – very rare in Armenia) is not a solid construction but comprises in the lower part 30 separate six-sided columns. The interior of the cupola is also most unusual: six intersecting arches form a six-pointed star in the centre of which is a hexagon which itself encloses another six-pointed star. The gavit of 1257 was also highly distinctive. It was roofed by another set of intersecting arches but unfortunately this collapsed in an earthquake in 1965. The whole ensemble gives the impression that it would not survive another. Outside the church on the south side is a stone frog which has been placed on a plinth. It looks as if the frog could originally have been mounted on a roof and there is certainly an unidentified animal on top of the cupola of the church. Traces of the main gateway, chapels and various other buildings also survive as does the well with its secret passage down to the river.

It may be possible to visit Khorakert from the Georgian side of the Bagratashen/Sadakhlo crossing. Take the Sadakhlo–Tsobi–Aghkyorpi road to Aghkyorpi; the monastery is a few kilometres outside the village. When it is dry the minor roads are drivable in an ordinary car to within about 100m of the monastery. This is a border zone and locals say that strictly speaking a pass is needed to visit the area – enquiries could perhaps be made at the border post at Sadakhlo.

main road east from Alaverdi for about 15km. The monastery is well signposted from the main road, from where it is a further 3km uphill through the village.

Akhtala is surrounded either by precipitous drops or by defensive walls. Entry is through the main gate in the defensive fortifications. Although this may be locked, entry can be achieved easily as there is an inconspicuous wicket gate within the main gate. Take very great care on the site as the long grass conceals drops into subterranean rooms of the original fortress whose roofs have collapsed. (The windows of some of these rooms can be seen in the defensive walls as one approaches the monastery.) The 10th-century fortifications, constructed of basalt, were built by the Kiurikian branch of the Bagratid dynasty: the Kiurikian kingdom was a vassal state of the king at Ani. The fortress is contemporary with that at Lori (page 280). Akhtala, like Lori, was a highly defensible site and one of the main strongholds of northern Armenia. The large round tower beside the entrance can be accessed with care. There are three partially remaining storeys, each divided into sections by arches which radiated from a central column to the circumferential wall. Within the fortress stands the monastery, and the remains of other buildings can be seen. The **main existing church**, dedicated to the Mother of God, was built between 1212 and 1250 at the behest of Prince Ivan Zakarian who belonged to the same dynasty that obtained control of Lori Berd and Kobayr Monastery. It was therefore built as a Georgian Orthodox church but is on the site of an earlier Armenian one. It is of the domed basilica type with four massive pillars, two of which are free-standing. The dome collapsed in the 18th century and the existing small pyramidal roof dates from 1978. There are plans to rebuild the tambour and dome. Built, like the fortress, of basalt, the monastery is quite different in appearance from those at Sanahin and Haghpat, reflecting the Georgian influence on its design. The interior frescoes are absolutely magnificent. Especially notable is the Virgin Mary enthroned in the apse. Her face has been defaced either by the elements or by artillery (accounts vary); a hole in the wall can be seen in the centre of the cross high up on the exterior of the east façade. Beneath the Virgin Mary is a depiction of the Last Supper with Christ giving the bread to St Peter on the left and the wine to St Paul on the right. Two ranks of saints stand below. Other scenes include the Last Judgement over the west door, the trial and Crucifixion of Jesus and the Resurrection. Figures of saints adorn the pillars which divide the building into three naves.

Large relief crosses on each façade, together with smaller more intricate crosses on the elaborate arcaded porch and the small chapel built on to the southwest corner of the church, also show Georgian influence. Remains of domestic buildings line the inside of the east wall between the entrance gate and the main church; it is here that care must be taken to avoid falling into the underground rooms (page 80). The small church in the west of the precinct is sometimes called the winter church – presumably it was easier to heat a smaller building.

## TAVUSH PROVINCE

Armenia's heavily forested northeastern province is bounded to the north by Georgia and to the east by Azerbaijan. Tavush's two largest towns, the provincial capital of **Ijevan** and the former spa town of **Dilijan**, are sited on the Aghstev River, whose valley broadens out as it flows northeast towards Azerbaijan, where it joins the Kura River to reach the Caspian Sea south of Baku. This valley comprises the most visited and easily accessible part of Tavush, with two of its major historical sites (**Goshavank** and **Haghartsin** monasteries), the lion's share of accommodation (in the town of Dilijan), and of course the 240km² **Dilijan National Park**, encompassing mature beech, oak and hornbeam forests, alpine wild-flower meadows and dramatic limestone cliffs, with enough to entertain hikers for several days, including a newly rebuilt (in 2017–18) and well-signposted trail network.

Elsewhere in Tavush, the road north towards **Noyemberyan** and the Georgian border is often used as an alternative route between Yerevan and Tbilisi and can sometimes be heavy with goods traffic, though the views out to the plains of Azerbaijan are impressive and several lesser-known historical sites (including **Makaravank**) are accessible from this route. The east of the province centred around **Berd** is understandably less visited, but it is here that some of the most scenic roads are to be found. The lush and forested **Getik Valley** – its river a tributary of the Aghstev – is an underrated gem and its gentle, winding road makes an excellent scenic route to Lake Sevan. The highland interior of the province bordering with Lori, though dramatic, is remote and inaccessible, home only to herders in the summer months and with no permanent settlements.

Many Tavush villages were once populated by ethnic Azeris living in Soviet Armenia and have been resettled by Armenians fleeing Azerbaijan. The village names have since been changed, though locals will often refer to regional landmarks by their old Turkish names. Azeri cemeteries are not an uncommon find. The formerly mixed ethnic population is also reflected in the regional accent, which has similarities with that of Karabagh and Syunik, with many Azeri words still in common use – indeed, some still remember how to speak the language. Some villages were abandoned altogether by both sides and their ruins can still be found; Aghkilisa/Chermakavan, meaning 'white church', is one of the more accessible of these, with hiking trails leading from both Gosh and Khachardzan.

The aftermath of the war is evident in other ways in Tavush. Some sites close to the border, notably Khoranashat Monastery, are inaccessible because of the risk from Azeri snipers, and the former road and rail routes from Yerevan to the rest

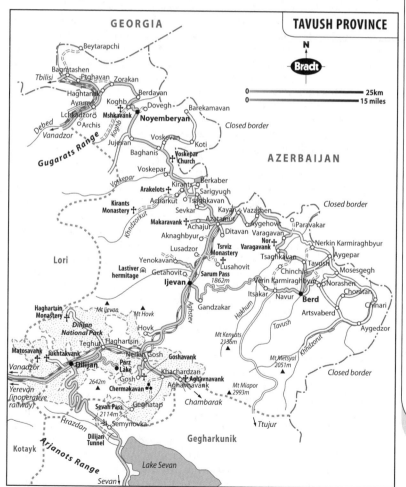

of the former Soviet Union are closed at the border with Azerbaijan. The M16/H26 road between Ijevan and Noyemberyan crosses *de jure* areas of Azerbaijan which, since 1994, have de facto been part of Armenia, with the result that maps of this area can look rather confusing (page 5).

The region is best explored from either Dilijan or Ijevan, the latter being more suitable for northern Tavush. Dilijan is nearer the more popular monastic sites and is convenient for those wishing to explore the National Park or travel south to Lake Sevan. There is plentiful accommodation in the region, particularly in Dilijan. See page 92 for general comments on accommodation.

**GETTING THERE AND AROUND**  Two main highways enter southern Tavush: one from Vanadzor from the west and one from Yerevan (via Sevan) from the south, these roads meeting in Dilijan. Travelling from Sevan became easier in 2003 as a new road tunnel was opened avoiding the **Sevan Pass** (2,114m), though those not in a hurry may prefer to enjoy the spectacular views from the much quieter (and still paved) old road via Semynovka. In the north of the province, a single road links up with the Debed Gorge road in northern Lori and the road from the Georgian border at Bagratashen.

Ijevan, Dilijan and Noyemberyan all have bus stations served by **minibuses** from Yerevan. To Dilijan there is an hourly service in both directions between 09.00–17.00, taking around 90 minutes and costing AMD1,000; getting to Ijevan takes just over 2 hours and costs AMD1,500. Tickets should be bought at the bus station before boarding; you do not pay the driver directly. These services depart from Yerevan's Northern Bus Station (*hyusisayin kayaran*) on the city outskirts on the M4 Tbilisyan Highway to Lake Sevan, which itself can be reached by bus route 259 from central Yerevan via Komitas Avenue. Since 2018, Dilijan also has daily minibuses to nearby villages including Teghut, Haghartsin, Khachardzan and Gosh. Ijevan has connections with most regional destinations, including Berd (14.00 daily from outside the main market; AMD1,000), Vanadzor (15.00 daily from the main bus stop outside the city hall; AMD500) and Dilijan (hourly 09.00–17.00 from outside the city hall on the same bus that continues to Yerevan; AMD500). Do check for the latest timings; village services are designed around the needs of people making shopping trips to Ijevan market, arriving in Ijevan in the morning and returning in the afternoon. As with everywhere else in Armenia, public transport to historical sites is non-existent, but **taxis** are a convenient and relatively cheap way of reaching them. A round trip from Dilijan to Haghartsin and Goshavank monasteries should cost about AMD10,000, including waiting time. Despite the railway line running alongside the main road from Margahovit to Dilijan, Ijevan and the Azerbaijan border, there are have been no passenger services for many years (though plans for a major upgrade of the Yerevan–Dilijan line are on the table and it seems only to be a matter of time). For general comments on transport see page 85.

**WHERE TO STAY**  Dilijan is the accommodation centre of Tavush, with the broadest range of options and an estimated 3,000 total bed spaces; see the map (page 302) and listings (page 301). Several of the surrounding National Park's more popular attractions have accommodation on-site or en route (see opposite). Ijevan also has several B&Bs and hotels, though nothing approaching the variety or quality of Dilijan. The main route to the Georgian border at Bagratashen via Noyemberyan now has several motels which have sprung up due to the (perhaps temporary) increase in goods traffic on this route in response to major roadworks on the route via Alaverdi. Elsewhere in the province, accommodation is sparse and scattered.

We have indicated where our listings are plotted on one of the maps in the book.

## Ijevan

Map, page 312

🏠 **Guest House Anahit** (5 rooms) 4 Tavrizyan St; m 077 012274/292979; e anahitalaverdyan@mail.ru. Anahit's quiet & very welcoming family homestay has a lovely shaded terrace & simple twin/trpl/family rooms with shared bathrooms. A favourite with backpackers. Excellent home-cooked lunches/dinners on request (AMD3,000–4,000). $

🏠 **Hotel Mosh** (10 rooms) 3 Yerevanian St; \0263 35611; e moshhotel@mail.ru. Central & near the main market, therefore possibly somewhat noisy. An acceptable basic budget hotel with dbl/trpl rooms, some en suite. Rooms without bathroom even cheaper. Cards accepted. B/fast AMD1,500 pp or bring your own. $

🏠 **Kamar B&B** (16 rooms) 2 Nalbandyan St; m 093 191200/767673; e khamzyan@gmail.com. Hosting guests since 2000 in 7 twin/dbl rooms on the 1st floor of the large family home, Gyulnara's B&B is now expanding with new deluxe rooms in a separate building. Kitchen for use of guests. $

🏠 **Ruzan Hotel** (8 rooms) 5/7 Yerevanian St; \0263 41110; m 077 670667, 093 632942. Opened in 2016, this modern, central riverside hotel has pleasant twin/trpl en-suite rooms on 3 floors. B/fast extra, served in ground-floor café (page 312). $

## Elsewhere in the province

🏠 **Apaga Resort** (22 rooms) 38 First St, Yenokavan village; \0263 60703; \060 650651, m 077 004413; e info@apaga.info; w apaga.info, yellextremepark.com. See page 313. Family-oriented nature resort 3km uphill from Yenokavan, mainly offering complete packages inc activities such as horseriding, trekking, zip lining, 4x4 tours, etc, of course dependent on weather. Popular with Russians, locals & the diaspora. Dbl/twin rooms can be booked without packages. Good restaurant & bar on-site. Buffet b/fast. Camping space also available. $$$

🏠 **Hotel Levon 2** (9 rooms) 29 Noyember St, Noyemberyan; m 091 201410 (Flora Antonian). This hotel, a former office block, provides much-needed accommodation in the north of Tavush. On the right as one enters Noyemberyan from the north. Also functions as a very pleasant restaurant. Own produce inc eggs & honey. Homemade jams. BBQ & picnics available. B/fast AMD2,000 pp.

Rooms without en suite AMD7,000, with en suite AMD10,000. $

🏠 **Mkhitar Gosh Hotel** (10 rooms) Gosh village; m 093 758595, 098 441019; e hotelgosh@rambler.ru. En-suite shower-rooms are small but smart. Superb views of the monastery from front bedrooms. Meals only during tourist season (Apr–Oct). $

🏠 **Parz Lake Rest Area** (6 huts) Parz Lake Rd; \0263 61011; m 093 331144; e parz-lich@ararathotel.am; w ararathotel.am. Closed in winter. 10km from main road. The activity centre (page 310) is mainly aimed at Armenian family day trips or w/end holidays but may also be of interest to hikers. Restaurant. Accommodation comprises 6 wooden huts (3 with 2 beds, 3 with 4 beds); AMD3,000 pp. Separate toilet/washing area. B/fast extra at adjoining restaurant. Camping allowed on an informal basis. $

🏠 **Utik Hotel** (14 rooms) 4 Hayk Nahapat St, Berd; m 093 373090. Twin/dbl rooms in a newly renovated (2018) hotel, the only one in Berd at the time of research. Price of room depends on facilities. Most rooms can fit a 3rd guest on a sofa bed. B/fast AMD500–1,000. $

🏠 **Zikatar Environmental Centre** (7 rooms (sgl, dbl & trpl), 3 cottages) 10km from Koghb village; \010 562318, 0266 52772; e zikatar_center@yahoo.com. Within the government-run Caucasus Regional Forestry Training Centre. Official accommodation for training groups but can provide rooms for visitors. No food or drink is available: visitors are expected to bring it with them. Centre's kitchen can be used. There is a service charge of approx AMD3,000 for using the dining room. May suit those who wish to hike in the area. Bicycles for hire AMD1,000/hr. $

🏠 **Lastiver** (5 huts) Khachaghbyur River, near Yenokavan; \0263 31465; m Vahagn 091 365437, 093 365437, Hovhannes 094 603010, 096 603010; f. Accommodation in rustic wooden huts from May to Nov (overnight stay AMD5,000 pp inc b/fast; FB AMD15,000 pp inc guiding to local caves). In winter there is accommodation for up to 8 people in a cave with bedding & a wood-burning stove provided (call in advance). The brothers will collect guests from Ijevan or Yenokavan. Camping space for tents also available. $

✕ **WHERE TO EAT AND DRINK** Dilijan boasts some of the better dining in Armenia outside of Yerevan and at generally lower prices. Ijevan is far less well endowed in this respect but still has a number of riverside cafés with canopied open-air tables on both sides of the river, as well as a few fast-food outlets opposite the main market. On the M4 and M16 main roads through the province there are plenty of basic eateries, with the exception of the section between Ijevan and Noyemberyan that passes through contested territory. Some of the hotels listed on pages 299 and 301 also function as restaurants, which we have noted in individual entries.

**OTHER PRACTICALITIES** Dilijan is the tourism hub of Tavush, and a new **tourist information centre** (15/2 Maxim Gorky; ☎ 094 040994; ◫; ⊕ Apr–Oct 09.00–20.00 daily; reduced hours in low season) opened in August 2018. The centre has maps of Dilijan and the surrounding National Park and can help with booking accommodation and tours, with mountain bikes and hiking, camping and snowshoeing equipment available for hire. Useful **maps** of the town produced by the Youth Co-operation Centre of Dilijan NGO can also be picked up at most hotels and cafés, including Café #2 (page 303). Dilijan Community Centre has developed a 'Yellow Line' self-guided and signposted **walking tour** around the town. At the time of research, the mapping organisation Cartisan (w cartisan.org) intended to publish a 1:25,000-scale **topographical map** of Dilijan National Park by the spring of 2019, including all established hiking trails in the area.

Ijevan has the biggest food and produce **market** in the province and is slightly better for shopping than Dilijan. Koghb village (page 318) offers good local information in the Culture Centre. For local information and guiding in and around Gandzakar contact Zarmayil (Zarmo for short) Mardanyan (m 094 469607; e zarmayilmardanyan@ ymail.com). The Ijevan-based Tourism Development Agency of Tavush NGO operates the relatively useful English-language website w visit-tavush.com.

**DILIJAN** Dilijan is known colloquially as 'Armenia's Switzerland'. The former spa town nestles in the depths of the Aghstev Valley, overlooked by forests and limestone crags, its suburbs reaching up into the surrounding woodlands and gorges. Though having suffered a decline after the Soviet collapse, Dilijan is currently undergoing a renaissance led by Russian-Armenian philanthropist Ruben Vardanyan through the charitable IDeA Foundation (w idea.am), with extensive redevelopment of the town centre in the planning stages. Other entrepreneurs have been catalysed to move here from Yerevan, with the result that today's Dilijan is becoming a hotbed of hip cafés, boutique homestays and innovative social enterprises, as well as keeping the Russian-influenced 19th-century architecture for which it was always known. Dilijan's good road link with Yerevan makes it suitable for day trips, though there is enough to see and do in the area to occupy four to five days or more.

The town's revival has spread to **Dilijan National Park**, with modern-day Armenia's first **purpose-built hiking trails** developed in 2017 by the Armenian branch of the Transcaucasian Trail (see box, page 114) in partnership with HIKEArmenia (page 111) and Caucasus Nature Fund. Several more trails were added in 2018 by IDeA Foundation and many existing trails renovated, giving nature lovers plentiful opportunities to explore the verdant old-growth forest and its historical sites via an extensive and clearly signposted **hiking trail network** incorporating over 200km of trails. The five well-known **monasteries** (pages 306–10) within the park's territory all fall within the trail network too. The park stretches over the forested slopes of the Pambak, Areguni, Miapor, Ijevan and Halab mountain ranges, all part of the Lesser Caucasus mountain chain. Unfortunately the park faces an ongoing battle with illegal logging, evidence of which can sometimes be seen (and heard) while out hiking.

**Where to stay**  *Map, page 302*

 **Best Western Plus Paradise Hotel**  (50 rooms) 156 Kamo St; **𝄞** 0268 24016; **m** 077 288247; **e** info@paradisehotel.am; **w** paradisehotel.am. A franchise hotel on the edge of town on the road south to Sevan, this former Soviet-era complex is renovated to a high international standard. Swimming pool, sauna, 'kids' club', indoor sports. Restaurant has both à la carte & buffet. Standard rooms have 1 dbl bed (no twins), more expensive rooms have twin dbls (for 2 people). Accepts cards. **$$$**

 **Hotel Dilijan Resort & Spa**  (70 rooms, 12 cottages) 66 Getapnya St; **𝄞** 010 207755, 0268 24303; **m** 055 047755; **e** info@hoteldilijan.am; **w** hoteldilijan.am. This one-time Soviet hotel has undergone further renovation to transform itself into one of high international standard. Cottages sleep 4–8. Sports facilities, swimming pool, children's play areas & spa treatments available. Disabled access. Restaurant. Reduced rates Nov–Apr excluding Christmas & New Year. Cards accepted. HB (b/fast & lunch). **$$$**

 **Ananov Guesthouse**  (12 rooms, 2 apts) Sharambeyan St; **𝄞** 060 501010; **e** dilijan@ tufenkian.am; **w** tufenkianheritage.com; see ad, page 126. Part of the Old Dilijan Complex, the most reasonably priced of the Tufenkian properties consists of a restored 19th-century town house with 2 floors, each forming an apt for 2–3 people with lounge & balcony, & dbl/twin rooms in adjoining historical buildings. Tufenkian's hallmark attention to detail is evident. With several privately operated workshops, handicraft outlets & a museum in the same complex & the public free to wander through, the feeling is of inhabiting a historic neighbourhood. B/fast served in Haykanoush Restaurant (page 303) within the complex. Reception open ⏰ 09.00–21.00. Cards accepted. **$$–$$$**

 **Art Guesthouse Dilijan**  (24 rooms) 12/1 Kalinini St (650m from the main road, follow signs via Ivanov St); **m** 093 486882; **e** art_ guesthouse@yahoo.com; **f**. Large guesthouse in a quiet neighbourhood uphill from the Vanadzor main road, opened in 2015. Owner Gevorg speaks some English. Lovely south-facing aspect & plentiful outdoor areas for relaxation. En-suite sgl/

dbl/twin/family rooms are light, clean & pleasantly furnished. 2 small kitchens for the use of guests. Parking a short distance away. Lunch & dinner available (AMD3,750 pp). Cards accepted. **$$**

 **Daravand Hotel**  (7 rooms, 1 cottage) 46 Abovyan St; **𝄞** 0268 27857; **m** 094 420965, 091 411766; **f**. Iranian-Armenian proprietor & former actor Razmik has acquired legendary status for providing the most enigmatic hospitality in town. The cosy hotel showcases his carpentry skills (the hotel itself is 'just a hobby'). Delicious home-cooked food, personal service & a convivial atmosphere. The quietly situated hotel is popular both with foreign visitors & w/end escapees from Yerevan, with 7 dbl/twin rooms with shared bathrooms & a private cottage housing up to 7 more guests. Regular bus service to the town centre. Dinner by arrangement & highly recommended. **$$**

 **Toon Armeni**  (8 rooms) 4 Kamarin St; **m** 098 787899; **f**. Beautiful renovated historical property with vast gardens, dbl/twin & family rooms & an excellent restaurant open to non-residents. Very family-friendly. Ground floor rooms open on to a veranda & are preferable to the smaller first-floor rooms. Cards accepted. **$$**

 **Eco House & Camp**  (1 trpl, 8 dorm beds) 10 Getapnya St; **m** 093 265576; **f**. Budget hostel accommodation run by a local NGO; the proceeds fund efforts to combat illegal logging in the National Park. Staff are highly knowledgeable on hiking & adventure tourism opportunities in the region. Close to UWC Dilijan College (page 304) & hikes to Jukhtakvank/Matosavank monasteries & further afield (page 306). **$**

 **Nina's B&B**  (5 rooms, 1 cottage) 18 Myasnikyan St; **m** 091 767734. An old favourite with backpackers. Well located 2mins' walk up the unsealed road behind Dilijan Local Lore Museum. Nina speaks a little English and her attentive approach makes this guesthouse-hostel a welcoming home for budget solo travellers, if a little sparse inside. Meals are lavish, communal & delicious. Small shared kitchen. Shared dorms (AMD7,000 pp) & dbl/twin rooms; a private cottage sleeps 8. B/fast extra, other meals on request. **$**

 **Where to eat and drink**  *Map, page 302*

**✗ Carahunge Café & More**  25 Kalinini St (2nd entrance on Getapnya St); **m** 043 220003;

**w** carahunge-cafe.com; ⏰ 10.00–23.00 daily. Opened in 2017 by the owners of the Stepanavan

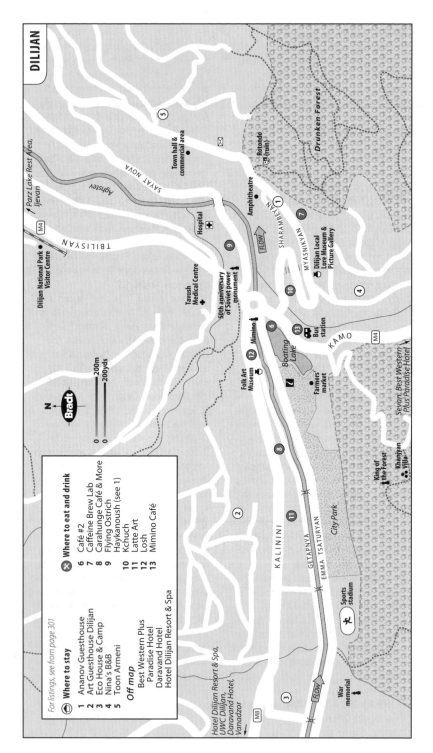

DILIJAN

For listings, see from page 301

**Where to stay**
1 Ananov Guesthouse
2 Art Guesthouse Dilijan
3 Eco House & Camp
4 Nina's B&B
5 Toon Armeni

Off map
Best Western Plus
Paradise Hotel
Daravand Hotel
Hotel Dilijan Resort & Spa

**Where to eat and drink**
6 Café #2
7 Caffeine Brew Lab
8 Carahunge Café & More
9 Flying Ostrich
Haykanoush (see 1)
10 Kchuch
11 Latte Art
12 Losh
13 Mimino Café

Hotel Dilijan Resort & Spa,
UWC Dilijan,
Daravand Hotel,
Vanadzor

Parz Lake Rest Area,
Ijevan

Dilijan National Park
Visitor Centre

Aghstev

SAYAT NOVA

Town hall &
commercial area

Amphitheatre

SHARAMBEYAN

Hospital

Tavush
Medical Centre

50th anniversary
of Soviet power
monument

Dilijan Local
Lore Museum &
Picture Gallery

MYASNIKYAN

Bus
station

KAMO

Sevan, Best Western
Plus Paradise Hotel

Mimino

Boating
Lake

Folk Art
Museum

Farmers
market

City Park

King of
the Forest

Khanjyan
Villa

KALININI

GETAPNYA

EMMA TSATURYAN

Sports
stadium

War
memorial

Drunken Forest

Rotondo
(ruin)

FLOW

FLOW

N

Bradt

0        200m
0        200yds

302

café of the same name (page 280), this is a café, restaurant, wine bar, bookstore & community hang-out in one, located in a renovated historical building. The Levantine-inspired menu is good & varied and the 'VIP' wine cellar truly impressive. One of Dilijan's few options for an evening drink in a bar/lounge setting.

**✗ Flying Ostrich** 6 Sayat Nova St; ✆ 060 655080; ⏰ 10.00–23.00 daily. Large, stylish restaurant set in extensive grounds on a quiet back street, opened by the company behind the famous Dolmama in Yerevan (page 142). Traditional Armenian fare inc *dolma* & *khorovats* cooked to a good standard, with a few more unusual dishes available too. The prices reflect the prestige of the brand; you can certainly eat as well for less elsewhere. Perhaps best for larger groups or special occasions.

**✗ Haykanoush Restaurant** Sharambeyan St; ✆ 060 501010; e dilijan@tufenkian.am; w tufenkianheritage.com; ⏰ 08.00–23.00 daily. Part of the Old Dilijan Complex (page 301) in the style of a late 19th- or early 20th-century Dilijan dining room. Wooden floors covered with handmade Tufenkian carpets. The menu, updated in 2017, has a good range of more traditional & revivalist Armenian dishes at reasonable prices, as well as a good selection of wines.

**✗ Kchuch** 37 Myasnikyan St; m 041 886010; ☐; ⏰ 10.00–22.00 daily. Opened in 2016, Kchuch has such a good reputation that diners are known to come from Yerevan just for dinner. Owner Varda served her apprenticeship in Chicago before setting up this fantastic fusion restaurant. Meticulously sourced local ingredients come together in clay dishes (*kchuches*) baked in wood-fired brick ovens, producing twists on old favourites (highlights: wild mushroom pizza, osso buco, lamb with plums & honey, *shakshuka*, grilled vegetable platter). Excellent homemade fruit vodkas & delicious pomegranate wine. Don't leave without trying the peach cobbler.

**✗ Losh/Tava** 1/2 Kalinini St; m 041 886018; ☐ LoshDilijan/TavaDilijan. Opened in 2018, this is a large, convivial 2-in-1 restaurant from the founder of the immensely popular Kchuch (see above). Losh (on the ground floor) is named after

the Armenian word for Arabic flatbread & serves a lighter, healthier menu, while Tava (on the 1st floor) is named after the flat iron skillet found across West & South Asia, making extensive use of the implement & specialising in meat & wine.

**✗ Mimino Café** 50 Maxim Gorky St; ✆ 0268 22440; ⏰ 11.00–23.00 daily. Cheap restaurant/ café next to the bus station in the town centre with an attached take-away snack bar. Georgian-style food is passable but service was poor at the time of research. Some outdoor seating. Plans for a full makeover in the face of stiff competition. Soups AMD700–1,000, Georgian main courses AMD900–1,600, individual *khachapuri* AMD800–1,000.

**☐ Café #2** 17/1 Maxim Gorky St; ✆ 060 700805; ☐ Cafenumber2; ⏰ 09.00–22.00 daily. Trendy & relaxed café by the lake, serving Italian-style coffee as well as local herbal teas & juices, light meals & snacks, & alcohol after 18.00. Built by the same foundation behind the UWC international school (page 304) to provide hospitality training & employment for local youth: it seems to be working. Perennially popular with international students & an obvious first stop for visitors disembarking at the bus station opposite.

**☐ Caffeine Brew Lab** 38 Myasnikyan St; m 091 073733; ☐; ⏰ 09.00–22.00 daily. Experimental & über-trendy coffee joint opposite the upper entrances of the Tufenkian complex on the road to Dilijan town hall. Opened in 2016 by two emigrés from Yerevan. The menu changes daily & the barista roasts coffee beans in front of you as you inspect the bewildering array of scientific apparatus involved in its preparation. If you're a coffee aficionado, of course, the results are worth waiting for. Fabulous baked goods also.

**☐ Latte Art** 2/14 Getapnya St (entrance near back of building); ✆ 098 900191; ☐; ⏰ 09.00–23.00 daily. Opened in 2017, serving a full range of well-made Italian-style coffees & teas, along with salads, pasta, pizza & other light bites at reasonable prices. Cocktail menu for evening visitors.

**What to see and do** The **boating lake** is the de facto town centre for visitors, with several cafés and restaurants nearby, as well as the town's bus station and much useful signage. At the northwest corner of the lake is the new and very modern-

The Northern Provinces    TAVUSH PROVINCE

5

looking **tourist information centre**; a few steps south is the newly opened **farmers' market**, both of which Dilijan sorely lacked until their openings in 2018. To the east of the roundabout is a striking Soviet-era **monument** erected to mark the 50th anniversary of Soviet power in the Caucasus; its (today ironic) design was intended to represent the eternal union of Armenia, Georgia and Azerbaijan under Soviet rule. The statue with its drinking water fountain on the west side of the roundabout depicts the three principal characters from the popular Soviet comedy film *Mimino* and is thus a popular photo opportunity for Armenian and Russian tourists. Directly north and across the road, a dilapidated double staircase leads to the overgrown grounds of one of Dilijan's several Soviet-era **sanatoria**, long privatised but still awaiting redevelopment.

As you head west, the first point of interest is the **Folk Museum** (1 Getapnya St; m 094 433292 (Anahit); ⊕ 11.00–17.00 Tue–Sat, 11.00–16.00 Sun; guided tour in Armenian AMD2,000; AMD1,000) in a late 19th-century house, originally the summer house of Mariam Tamanyan. It was latterly the home of the painter Hovhannes Sharambeyan (1926–86), whose *Early Spring* is in the National Gallery, Yerevan, and after whom Sharambeyan Street is named after he initiated its reconstruction. Items from the 19th century to the present day are on display and it is possible to buy locally made handicrafts. All along the main road through this western portion of Dilijan, and in the backstreets on the hillside above, can be found a plethora of guesthouse accommodation (page 301). Those who venture further north and uphill into the suburbs might come across a sprawling space-age campus: this is the fee-paying **Dilijan Central School** built by the Ayb Foundation (*ayb* is the name of the first letter of the Armenian alphabet) with funding from the Central Bank of Armenia (see below), presumably in part to provide top-end education to the children of the bank's well-paid executives. At the far western end of town, a second impressive-looking campus across the river is in fact **UWC Dilijan College** (7 Getapnya St; ✆ 060 750800; e welcome@uwcdilijan.org; w uwcdilijan.org), an international co-educational boarding school teaching the International Baccalaureate; its first students were admitted in September 2014, which incidentally helps explain the number of foreign-looking teenagers inhabiting Dilijan's cafés. On the northern side of the main road from the college is Abovyan Street: follow this road for 2.8km to reach the starting point for a looping hike to both Jukhtakvank and Matosavank monasteries (page 306), as well as a much longer (20km) route to Haghartsin Monastery. Dilijan's well-known **mineral water spring** is at the far end of this road; the water bottled here is a familiar sight throughout Armenia.

Northeast on the M4 main road towards Ijevan there is little of interest except perhaps the **Dilijan National Park Visitor Centre** (⊕ 09.00–17.00 Mon–Fri). Turn left under the railway bridge 850m after leaving the roundabout, then left at the T-junction. The centre houses a collection of plant specimens and stuffed animals and would be of more interest to a botanist or biologist than a general visitor or hiker; the new tourist information centre (see above) looks set to do a better job in this regard. A few hundred metres further east is the now defunct **railway station**. The circular edifice with the mirrored glass façade overlooking this stretch of road from the north is the Training and Research Centre of the **Central Bank of Armenia**, opened in 2013.

Southeast from the roundabout, a short walk up Myasnikyan Street to the first hairpin bend will bring you to the lower entrance of **Sharambeyan Street**, rebuilt in a traditional style in the late Soviet era and continued in the 2000s by the Tufenkian hotel chain to offer visitors a historical experience of 19th-century Dilijan. The reconstructed main street features the **Yesayan Museum** (⊕ ask at reception;

free tour in English) exhibiting artefacts of traditional Dilijan life, along with woodworking and ceramic workshops rented by local craftspeople, and a range of private souvenir shops selling (among other things) couture and jewellery.

Exiting the complex by one of the stairways to the upper part of Myasnikyan Street, cross the road and make a 180m walk west to the **Dilijan Local Lore Museum and Picture Gallery** (28 Myasnikyan St; ✆0268 24450; ⏺ 10.00–17.40 Tue–Sat, 10.00–16.00 Sun; AMD500), often incorrectly referred to as the Geological Museum. You'll recognise it from the bust of Lenin by the entrance stairs. The museum hosts an array of historical artefacts telling the story of Dilijan's history through the ages, as well as permanent artwork collections and temporary exhibitions.

Double back east past the Romanesque open-air amphitheatre of 2009 to your left and look for a narrow stairway to your right leading up into the forest. Following this signposted route will take you first past the derelict **Rotondo** open-air theatre of 1981, then on a quiet walk up through the **Drunken Forest** – a mature pine plantation whose trees have begun to fall at angles as if inebriated – with some excellent lookout points over the town. Signed trails continue to Parz Lake (13km; allow 3–4hrs) among other destinations and loops, the scenery ever more spectacular as the town becomes more distant, but you may also return directly to Dilijan through the southeastern suburb of Takhta; as the trail dips back into the residential area, following any of the streets downhill and in a northeasterly direction will eventually bring you back to the **commercial centre** of Dilijan. Several more guesthouses can be found on or nearby Myasnikyan Street on both sides of this municipal centre.

Southwest from the central roundabout are two of Dilijan's quirkier sites of interest. Follow the M4 main road past the bus station for 200m and take the first paved road on your left, leading uphill. Follow the switchbacks up until you reach a large gate across the road with a gatekeeper's kiosk to its right. Walk around the gate and continue until on your right, through the trees, you see the sadly ruined **Khanjian Villa**. Born in 1901 in Van in present-day Turkey, Aghasi Khanjian and his family fled to Russian Armenia in 1915. As a student he was an active Marxist, and by 1930 he was the First Secretary (ie: leader) of the Armenian Communist Party and a popular figure within Soviet Armenia. Unfortunately his popularity seems to have been his downfall: on a 1936 visit to Tbilisi at the request of Georgian party leader Lavrentia Beria, the most powerful politician in Transcaucasia, he was reported to have mysteriously committed suicide. Popular theory has it that he was in fact assassinated for being seen as a threat to Beria's monopoly. In any case he never got to enjoy this grand summer mansion, which was completed in the same year. Left to ruin after independence, this majestic building is now a shadow of its former self and continues to collapse through neglect. Warning signs indicate that exploring the building's interior might be best avoided, but its unique circular structure can at the time of research still be admired from a distance (though rumours suggest that the area may be redeveloped in the near future). A few steps to its north among the trees can be found **The King of The Woods**, a bizarre wood carving of a crowned head set in the crook of a large sycamore tree, whose 'arms' appear to embrace the valley below.

## AROUND DILIJAN AND DILIJAN NATIONAL PARK
The popularity of Goshavank, Haghartsin and Parz Lake is such that there are plentiful eating options at all three sites, as well as some accommodation (page 299). As noted on page 298, however, there is no public transport besides a minibus to Gosh. All of the sites described on pages 306–10 except Aghavnavank are connected by the long-distance **Transcaucasian Trail** hiking route through the region (see box, page 114).

**Jukhtakvank and Matosavank (monasteries)** Visits to these two small monasteries can easily be combined, as both are accessed via Abovyan Street at the far western end of Dilijan, and a pleasant walking route through the forest has been created between the two, creating a loop from the trail head. Turning right along the signposted dirt track will take you first to **Jukhtakvank** (*jukht* means 'pair' or 'couple': the site has two remaining churches). Drivers are advised to park by the river at the bottom of this dirt track, on which it is about 10 minutes' walk to the monastery. Compared with the architectural glories of Haghartsin and Goshavank this monastery is modest indeed with its two small churches. The nearer one, dedicated to St Gregory, has lost its dome, although it retains some very elaborate carving inside. The further church, probably the older one, is dedicated to the Mother of God and bears an inscription indicating that it was built in 1201. This peaceful site in the wooded valley makes for a very pleasant visit, and picnic facilities and a freshwater spring can be found nearby. Just below Jukhtakvank is the starting point for a long (20km) and challenging day's hike over the mountains to Haghartsin Monastery: head back downhill on the dirt road for 250m, and look on your left for the entrance to a narrow path leading up into the forest. Take plenty of water and protection from the elements.

The looping route through the forest to **Matosavank** (Monastery of St Matthew) is also clearly marked from just below Jukhtakvank, as well as from the trail head on the road (allow an hour for the complete loop). In springtime the woodland floor is carpeted with cowslips, violets and blue anemones. One is almost upon the small 13th-century monastery before seeing it, with its ruined roofs partially covered in vegetation, contrasting with the wealth of attractive khachkars inside. The barrel-vaulted gavit leads into a small barrel-vaulted chapel to the east and into a domed chamber on the south.

**Haghartsin Monastery** (⊕ site always; church all day) Haghartsin sits deep in a picturesque forested valley and has long been one of Armenia's most visited monasteries. On the approach to the monastery are some small chapels (a good photographic vantage point) and some particularly fine khachkars (the modern construction beyond was once planned to become the upper terminal of a cable car from the road below, but was abandoned before completion). Haghartsin is also the starting point for several good hikes, including a short walk to a nearby waterfall and two much longer routes, one back to Dilijan over the mountains and another to the village of Hovk in the direction of Ijevan. The latter route incorporates sections

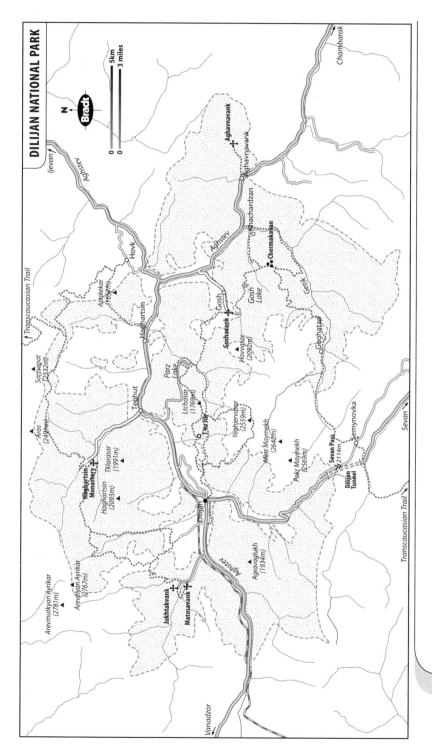

DILIJAN NATIONAL PARK

5km
3 miles

N

Ijevan

Aghstev

Transcaucasian Trail

Hovk

Aghstev

Aghavnavank

Aghavnavank

Khachardzan

Chermakajan

Apekekar
(1652m)

Gosh

Goshavank

Gosh
Lake

Getik

Hovkasar
(2092m)

Geghatagh

Sarkapat
(2532m)

Haghartsin

Teghut

Parz
Lake

Aros
(2490m)

Litchasar
(1769m)

Tzurtur

Yeghievdar
(2559m)

Tkorasar
(1991m)

Haghartsin Monastery

Mets Moymekh
(2642m)

Semynovka

Haghartsin
(2093m)

Pokr Moymekh
(2569m)

Sevan Pass
2114m

Sevan

Dilijan

Dilijan
Tunnel

Transcaucasian Trail

Arevmutkyan Ayrikar
(2781m)

Arevelyan Ayrikar
(2767m)

Aghstev

Agravaglukh
(1934m)

Jukhtakvank

Matosavank

Vanadzor

Chambarak

The Northern Provinces   TAVUSH PROVINCE

5

307

of ancient footpaths found in the surrounding forests and mountains which at one time probably linked Haghartsin with Aghchkaberd (page 314). There is no accommodation on-site, but camping is allowed behind the monastery on an informal basis; do ask permission first.

In 2010 the ecclesiastical authorities, having decided that Haghartsin would once more become a working monastery, undertook renovation of the site (although rebuilding might be a more accurate term). Over the centuries Haghartsin has seen many such changes but for those who prefer historic medieval buildings to look their age, the reconstruction of Haghartsin might be a disappointment. Externally, much of the site now looks as if it is newly built, although the interior of many of the churches is unchanged. The addition of a museum, extensive car parks, public toilets, a gift shop selling homemade honey and jam, a *gata* (page 101) bakery and a snack bar have imparted more of the feel of a mainstream tourist attraction than an ancient historical site. It is also popular among locals for pre-wedding photo shoots.

As at so many monasteries, the original small church was joined by other buildings over the centuries and is now rather dwarfed by its less ancient neighbours. The oldest part is the **St Gregory Church**, probably dating from the 10th century, and with an octagonal tambour. This church was damaged by Seljuk invaders and had to be reconstructed after the Georgian victories over them. This reconstruction was followed by a large increase in the monastery's size and an important school of church music became established here which developed a new system of notation for the Armenian liturgy. The original church acquired a **gavit** at a lower level reached by steps; it is unusual in that part of the pillar in the south wall to the east of the central arch rotated to provide a secret hiding place for when the monastery was under threat. **St Stephen's Church** was built in 1244, the large **refectory** (divided into two parts by arches and with stone benches along its sides) in 1248 and the bigger **Mother of God Church** with a high 16-sided tambour, and also with a **gavit**, was added in 1281. (Most histories give this date, but our source, a publication from the 1954 Etchmiadzin archives, states that an inscription was unearthed in the 1950s giving

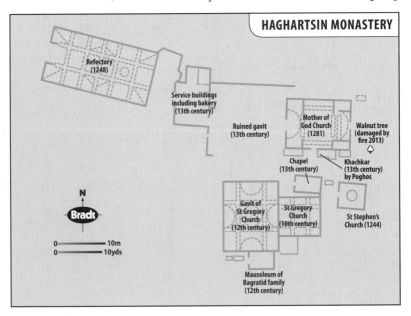

HAGHARTSIN MONASTERY

Refectory (1248)

Service buildings including bakery (13th century)

Ruined gavit (13th century)

Mother of God Church (1281)

Walnut tree (damaged by fire 2013)

Chapel (13th century)

Khachkar (13th century) by Poghos

Gavit of St Gregory Church (12th century)

St Gregory Church (10th century)

St Stephen's Church (1244)

N

Bradt

0 ——— 10m
0 ——— 10yds

Mausoleum of Bagratid family (12th century)

a date of 1071 for the church, and that the 1281 date in fact refers to a renovation.) A relief of the donors with a dove (symbolising the Holy Spirit) above them can be seen on the east façade, pointing to a model of the church. Finest of all the many **khachkars** in the monastery is the one carved by Poghos in the 13th century, which is outside the south door of the Mother of God Church. Among the other buildings which can be seen are the monastic **bakery** complete with oven. To the south of the gavit of St Gregory's are the reconstructed royal tombs of the Bagratid dynasty.

Upsetting for many was the destruction by lightning in 2013 of the old walnut tree at the southeast corner of the Mother of God Church. Contemporaneous with the 13th-century spate of building, it was estimated to be around 700 years old. Generations of Armenians enjoyed picnics in its shade and ate its nuts in autumn; only the scorched trunk remains.

## Gosh and Goshavank (monastery)

Gosh village has one small hotel (page 299), a couple of convenience stores, and several cafés in and around the square below the monastery, where a variety of refreshing herbal teas, made with local mountain herbs, can be enjoyed. The village can be reached on foot from Parz Lake (page 310) via a popular 8km hike on a well-signposted but hilly footpath (allow at least 2½hrs to enjoy the views). For keen hikers, the signposted trail from Dilijan to Parz Lake can be combined with that to Gosh for an excellent full day of walking. In the other direction, trails extend through fields and forest to Gosh Lake (4km) and onwards via the ruined village of Chermakavan to Khachardzan (16km).

**Goshavank** itself (⊕ site always, church all day; guided tour of the monastery AMD1,000 – ask at museum) was established in the late 12th century by the cleric Mkhitar Gosh (1130–1213) with the support of Prince Ivan Zakarian to replace the monastery of Getik, about 20km further east, where he had previously worked but which had been destroyed in an earthquake. Originally called Nor (New) Getik, it was renamed in honour of its founder immediately after his death. The earliest part of the complex, the **Mother of God Church**, dates from 1191; its **gavit** was completed in 1197 followed by the two **St Gregory chapels**, the free-standing one with its particularly fine carving in 1208 and the one attached to the gavit in 1237. The **library** and the adjacent school buildings were built in 1241 of large rough-hewn stones. In 1291 the **Holy Archangels Church** with belltower was added on top of the library, access to the church being via the external cantilevered steps. The belfry later collapsed and the building is now protected by a conical transparent dome. At its peak the library held 1,600 volumes until Mongol invaders set fire to it in 1375. It was at Nor Getik that Mkhitar Gosh first formally codified Armenian law (partly as a defence against the imposition of Islamic sharia law) and also wrote his fables which make moral points using birds as the protagonists. Another feature of the monastery is the particularly fine **khachkar,** by the door of the 1237 St Gregory chapel, which dates from 1291. Poghos, its sculptor, carved two identical khachkars for his parents' graves and the other is in the History Museum of Armenia in Yerevan. The delicate filigree of his carving led to his sobriquet 'Poghos the Embroiderer'. The two small rooms to the south of the gavit were used as studies by religious students. There is a walnut tree at the north of the site, of a similar age to the monastery.

Mkhitar Gosh spent the last years of his life as an ascetic in a retreat at some distance from Nor Getik. Although it was normal for founders to be buried at the monastery they had established, he requested that this should not be done and a mausoleum was built away from the site.

In the grounds of the monastery is a **small museum** (⊕ 09.00–17.00 Tue–Sun; AMD500). By far the most interesting items on show are the large pottery bell-

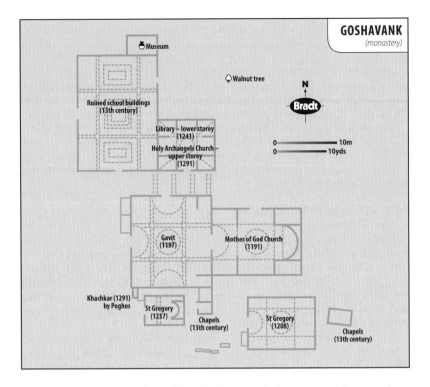

Museum

Walnut tree

N

Bradt

Ruined school buildings
(13th century)

Library – lower storey
(1241)

Holy Archangels Church –
upper storey
(1291)

0 ——————— 10m
0 ——————— 10yds

Gavit
(1197)

Mother of God Church
(1191)

Khachkar (1291)
by Poghos

St Gregory
(1237)

Chapels
(13th century)

St Gregory
(1208)

Chapels
(13th century)

shaped objects that were hung from the dome with the open end downwards to try to improve the acoustics by reflecting sound back down into the church. The solution to the problems of some more recent concert halls such as the Royal Albert Hall, London, was clearly anticipated at Goshavank!

## Aghavnavank (monastery)
This small 12th- or 13th-century church may not merit a special visit but the road journey here, especially the last stretch through the Getik Valley, is very enjoyable and can easily be combined with a visit to Goshavank. It is a lovely walk on a signposted trail through the woods beside the stream, taking about 30 minutes to the church. Situated on the wooded slopes of Mount Tsaghkot in the Miapor mountain range, the Mother of God Hermitage Church is of the cross-dome type with a relatively tall tambour. It abuts a rocky outcrop, suggesting that it may have been built on the site of a pagan spring shrine. In the vicinity are virgin yew *Taxus baccata* groves, some of the trees estimated to be 300–400 years old.

## Parz Lake
An outdoor recreational centre with accommodation and a restaurant has been established on the bank of this small lake in the hills northeast of Dilijan. It is aimed mainly at local family day trippers and weekend holidaymakers and can be very busy on summer weekends. It is also the trail head for several excellent hikes, one of which climbs through the forest to an alpine meadow before dropping down to Dilijan (14km; allow 3–4hrs) and another, very popular, route to Goshavank (8km; allow 2½hrs), from where onward transport should be available. There is also a short (1km), family-friendly loop trail around the lake, with signboards describing the species that may be seen in the area.

The bumpy and pot-holed 10km road to Parz Lake leaves the M3 main road about 7km beyond Dilijan and can be tackled (slowly) by regular cars. Activities at the resort itself include zip lines (AMD3,000/session) and boating (AMD2,000/½hr). Swimming is forbidden. There is a good restaurant on-site and some basic accommodation (page 299). The name, which means 'clear lake', dates back to before the natural site was 'improved' by developers who dredged the lake and thus destroyed the delicate ecosystem: today the water is a stagnant green.

**Hovk**  While not a destination in and of itself, the village of Hovk is the starting point for several good hikes, including a newly developed route to the nearby peak of Apakekar (3km); a significantly longer loop that consists of a historical forest trail below the limestone cliffs northwest of the village and a parallel route above the cliffs, with a dramatic stone staircase etched out of the rock face connecting the two; and a similarly long route through to Haghartsin Monastery (page 306). All routes are signposted from the village square. It is also possible to hike over the ridge to the north and connect to the Khachaghbyur Valley, Lastiver, Yenokavan and Ijevan (see below), though this would be a very long hike to complete in a single day.

**IJEVAN**  The name of Ijevan, meaning 'inn', recalls the scarcely imaginable days when silk route traders passed through this gateway to the Lesser Caucasus mountain range – indeed, the ruins of a bathhouse are preserved on the town's southern outskirts, and the town's (Persian) name until 1919 was Karavansara. Its strategic importance on the edge of the Kura basin was highlighted when, in 1920, an invading Red Army from Soviet Azerbaijan imposed Bolshevik rule first in Ijevan before conquering the rest of Armenia's First Republic (page 23). On the theme of regime change, it is perhaps fitting that Nikol Pashinyan, the leader of the 2018 Velvet Revolution (page 33), also hails from here.

Ijevan today is still a trading centre, dominated by its main market, with villagers coming from across Tavush to buy and sell produce, as well as housing the offices of the provincial government and church diocese. The town's appearance is enhanced by the extensive use of white felsite for building, the local architectural style seeming to reflect the low vaults and broad arches of the caravanserais of old. The region's dry white wines, made from grapes more usually associated with Georgia, were long among Armenia's best, though those of many modern wineries have now surpassed them. Although it is just 35km downstream from Dilijan, the climate and geography of Ijevan is noticeably more subtropical.

**Minibuses** from the bus stand on the main road at the west end of the town centre serve local destinations including Berd (timed for locals, so departing Berd at 09.10 and returning 14.00 daily; AMD1,000), Vanadzor (15.00 daily; AMD1,000) and Yerevan via Dilijan (hourly 09.00–17.00; AMD1,500; to Dilijan AMD500).

## ✖ Where to eat and drink  *Map, page 312*
The area around the market is replete with fast-food stands serving kebabs and *khorovats*; it is worth noting that Ijevan's **pork** is highly regarded and this is a good opportunity to try some. All along both sides of the river are numerous summertime cafés and a few year-round indoor options.

⌨ **Café Cascade**  Just up from Hotel Dok, off Ankakhutyan St, in the open area; ⏰ 10.30–midnight daily. A pleasant café with tasty food & friendly staff.

Sandwiches AMD350–750, soups AMD600–1,000, pizza AMD2,500, *khorovats* AMD1,500–2,200, tea AMD250, Armenian coffee AMD200.

🍴 **Café Ruzan** Ruzan Hotel (page 299);
⊕ 10.00–23.00 daily. On the ground floor of the
hotel. Clean & airy café with an English menu &
indoor/outdoor seating by the river serving the
usual barbecues & salads as well as pizza, *lahmajo*
& *khachapuri*. Hot/cold & alcoholic drinks. Outdoor
entertainment in summer evenings.

**What to see and do** The main street of Ijevan follows the west bank of the
Aghstev River, with the **market**, **post office**, **police station** and **bus station** lined up
next to each other. The east bank is a favourite place to stroll with plentiful summer

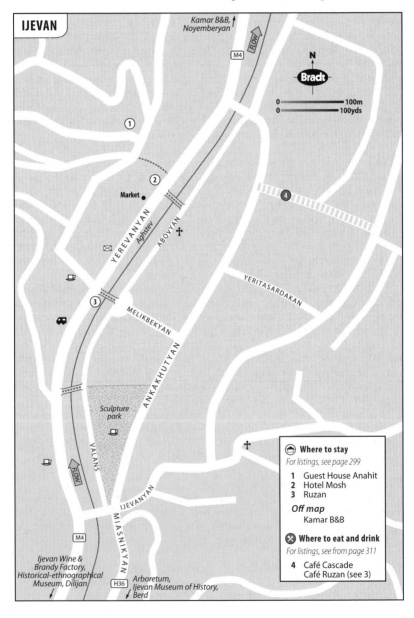

IJEVAN

Kamar B&B,
Noyemberyan

M4

FLOW

N

Bradt

0 ——————— 100m
0 ——————— 100yds

① 

②

Market

YEREVANYAN
Aghstev
ABOVYAN

YERITASARDAKAN

④

③

MELIKBEKYAN

ANKAKHUTYAN

Sculpture
park

VALANS

FLOW

IJEVANYAN

✝

MIASNIKYAN

M4

Ijevan Wine &
Brandy Factory,
Historical-ethnographical
Museum, Dilijan

H36

Arboretum,
Ijevan Museum of History,
Berd

🛏 **Where to stay**
*For listings, see page 299*

1 Guest House Anahit
2 Hotel Mosh
3 Ruzan

*Off map*
Kamar B&B

✖ **Where to eat and drink**
*For listings, see from page 311*

4 Café Cascade
Café Ruzan (see 3)

cafés and recently renovated gardens, fountains and walkways. Also on the east side are the **banks**, the **sculpture park** and various provincial government offices. A relaxing hour or two can be had wandering through the park and continuing southeast, past the statue of mounted Bagratid monarch Ashot Yerkat and a monument to the Great Patriotic War (World War II) to the **arboretum** (m 055 525688, 091 525688, 094 525688; ⊕ 09.00–22.00 daily). Established in 1962, the 14.5ha 'dendropark' houses some 640 species of trees and shrubs, some of which are labelled with their Latin names. A skeleton crew keeps the gardens tidy but the site as a whole remains sadly neglected.

Opposite the bridge over the river near the arboretum's entrance, on the M4 main road about 1km south of the town centre, is the **Ijevan Museum of History** (5 Yerevanyan St; m 098 002223; ⊕ 09.00–17.00 Mon–Fri). The wide-ranging collection includes geological and biological specimens, farming implements and domestic items. The elderly curator certainly knows his stuff and talks enthusiastically about each exhibit. For him one of the prized items is a radio given by Stalin to troops, together with a newspaper carrying Stalin's obituary.

Beyond the museum on the opposite side of the road is the **Ijevan Wine and Brandy Factory**, established in 1951, with a factory outlet selling regular and reserve grape wines and brandies, as well as fruit wines and compotes. English-language tours of the factory are possible (m 077 093993 (Elina); w ijevangroup.am; ⊕ 09.00–17.00 Mon–Sat, though groups can visit outside of these hours by appointment; AMD2,000–5,000 pp depending on whether tasting is included & of how many wines & brandies).

**AROUND IJEVAN** Two tourism enterprises have been developed near the village of Yenokavan just north of Ijevan in the spectacular canyon of the Khachaghbyur (Cross-spring) River. The first is Apaga (Future) Resort, a family holiday retreat popular with locals and Russians, with the Yell Extreme Park activity centre on-site. The second is Lastiver, a rustic campsite in an exceptionally beautiful spot by the tumbling waters of the Khachaghbyur River. To reach both, take the main road from Ijevan north for about 5km and, after crossing the Khachaghbyur, turn left for **Yenokavan** which lies about 8km further on. Apaga only allows parking for its residents, so if making for Lastiver either leave vehicles in Yenokavan or park on the rough ground outside the gates. There are about three marshrutkas a day from Ijevan to Yenokavan but you will still need to walk a further 3km uphill or arrange onward transport from the village. A taxi from Ijevan costs around AMD3,000.

**Apaga Resort** (page 299) offers packages which include full-board accommodation in attractive chalets. **Yell Extreme Park** runs the activity side of the business, offering hiking and horseriding day excursions from the centre (AMD30,000/day pp) and longer camping trips (AMD35,000/day pp). What it is best known for locally, however, is its growing network of **zip lines**. At the time of research there were five in operation, ranging from 135m to 750m in length (AMD11,000–15,000 pp). Under construction in 2018 was what was hoped to be the **world's longest zip line**, which will be an incredible 2.7km in length (though it seems the claim may have been pre-emptively foiled by an even longer project in Ras Al-Khaimah).

The **riverside campsite Lastiver** (page 299) is best approached via Apaga along a beautiful 3km hiking trail. The flowers in the forest here are among the most attractive in Armenia and the paths winding along the steep sides of the gorge offer fantastic views. The (signposted) final scramble down to the campsite, however, is steep and awkward. The camp with the waters cascading by has been developed by three brothers, Vahagn, Tatoul and Hovhannes Tananyan, because they have such fond memories of coming to this place in their childhood. Rock climbing, hiking and fishing are available (guiding AMD5,000 pp). Such is the popularity of the site with guided day tours that it can become very crowded at lunchtime during peak season; evenings tend to be quieter.

Not far from the campsite is **Lastiver hermitage** (or *anapat*). It comprises several rooms carved out of the rock on different levels, some of which are reached by ladder. In the caves there are carved faces and animals, strange enough that we wondered if they were modern but apparently they are very old, possibly Stone Age. Archaeological excavation has enlarged the cave opening, enabling the carvings to be seen by daylight, but a torch is useful too. There are also later Christian carvings.

From the trail above Lastiver it is possible to continue hiking up the valley, turning left at the fork and crossing a small footbridge over the Khachaghbyur before leaving the forest to reach the tiny hamlet of **Okon**. From here it is a two-day trek across the remote interior of Tavush and Lori to the village of Atan following the Vazgen Sargsyan Military Road, or alternatively a spectacular but very long day's walk to connect with the Dilijan National Park trail network (page 300) above Hovk village. Hikers have even been known to walk for 4–5 days to reach Alaverdi or Koghb on the network of remote tracks that criss-cross the mountains.

Elsewhere, approximately 10km southwest of Ijevan in the mountainous forests north of the main road is the ruined **Maiden's Fortress** (Aghchkaberd), though it would take a particularly determined hiker to track it down. For those interested it can be found on a knoll at the approximate decimal co-ordinates 40.8230, 45.0582.

**EASTERN TAVUSH** The former main rail and road routes to Azerbaijan follow the gradually broadening valley of the Aghstev. The first turn right after leaving Ijevan leads to the village of **Lusahovit** where the **Tsrviz or Moro-Dzor Monastery** is located. (The right turn is signposted for Khashtarak. In Khashtarak turn right 2km from the main road, almost a U-turn, and then continue straight ahead until Lusahovit is reached and you see the church below the village.) Established in the 5th century, the main **Mother of God Church** was rebuilt in the 12th and 13th centuries and has been restored fairly recently. It is a tiny four-apse church, one of only nine such early medieval churches in Armenia. Three of the four apses are seen externally, the fourth rectangular west wing concealing its internal apse. The four wings cluster closely round the relatively high tambour giving a somewhat curious appearance. The lower courses are of rough-hewn basalt, the upper of dressed stone. After 32km the main road now bears right at Kayan before reaching the border: even newer maps still show it going straight ahead into Azerbaijan. At the village of **Aygehovit** is a church called **Srvegh**, or (by locals) Srvis, high up on the hillside to the south. Its name, which means 'long pointed neck', is very apt. The ruined church, with its tall tambour and pointed dome, is very similar to Kirants Monastery (page 316) both in style and the use of bricks for construction. To reach it, turn right in Aygehovit on to an unpaved road which becomes a track going uphill through a field. Park here and walk the rest of the way, about 30 minutes up a steep rutted track, or park in the village, in which case it would take about an hour to walk. The entrance to the monastery is through a gate on the left where there is a welcome spring. The path to the church goes from the far end of the barbecue shelter.

After Aygehovit the main road winds up and over a pass with numerous hairpin bends as far as the village of **Varagavan**. Turn right on to the main street of the village (Nor Varagavank is signposted 4.5km) and continue through it. A good road to the monastery winds up through attractive forest where both green and black woodpeckers can be found. The **monastery of Nor Varagavank** is very important historically. Having been in a sadly ruined state for a long time, work to renovate the façades and stabilise the walls is under way. It was founded, as Anapat (Hermitage), by David Bagratuni, son of King Vasak I. The oldest part of the complex is the small Church of the Holy Cross built in 1198 at the southeast side. A two-storey burial vault was added at its north side in 1200. The monastery's importance, however, increased considerably in 1213 when it was chosen as the site for a relic, a piece of the True Cross brought to Armenia by Sts Hripsime and Gayane, which had been removed from the monastery of Varagavank, near Van in present-day Turkey, when that monastery was threatened by Mongol invaders. Hence the name Anapat was changed to Nor (New) Varagavank. (The relic, back by then at the original Varagavank, was destroyed along with the monastery during fighting in 1915.) The larger Mother of God Church was built between 1224 and 1237 by David Bagratuni's son King Vasak II. A massive gavit adjoins the west wall of this church and another, very ruined, gives entry to Holy Cross Church and its flanking chapels. There are unusual door portals, fine carving and interesting khachkars at this attractive site overlooking the forest. Continuing south the main road winds up and down the hills with views across the plains of Azerbaijan. From the village of **Tsaghkavan,** a rough dirt track leads to the picturesquely situated **Shkhmuradi Monastery.**

Although **Berd**, the main town of eastern Tavush, was important historically (its name means 'fortress') it now suffers from its remote position, former links to Azerbaijan having been cut. There is little to detain visitors, though accommodation is available (page 299). However, it is the gateway to two spectacular roads in Tavush.

The first is the H36 road east from **Ijevan to Berd via Gandzakar and Navur.** The road is shown on maps as dauntingly sinuous, which accurately reflects its topography, but it is a surprisingly good and well-maintained dirt road. It climbs up to the Sarum Pass (1,862m) through steep wooded hills then down through mixed woods of hawthorn, oak, ash, hazel, elm, beech, elderberry and wild rose, interspersed with grassland. In early summer the variety and colour of the wild flowers are overwhelming. From the village of Itsakar the road is good asphalt to Berd.

At the village of **Navur** is the junction with the **Berd to Ttujur** road, the second spectacular road mentioned on the opposite page. The road goes south with Mount Kenats (2,136m) to the west and Mount Metsyal (2,051m) to the east, finally descending from the Ttujur Pass (2,092m) to Ttujur village in Gegharkunik province northwest of Chambarak. This road also has a better surface than might be anticipated. Not long after leaving Navur there is a statue of General Andranik Ozanian, on horseback, carrying a child and holding his sword aloft – towards Azerbaijan. There are summer villages in the mountains where livestock is brought for summer grazing. It is a good place to see eagles.

Note that the 8th-century **Khoranashat Monastery**, to the east of Chinari village, is located just 500m from Azeri military positions and is **not safe to visit at the time of research**. It is also worth noting that the UK government advises against all travel within 5km of the Armenia–Azerbaijan border in Tavush province; this is particularly relevant to the northeast.

## Makaravank (monastery)  (⊕ site, always; church, daily) Makaravank, on the slopes of Mount Paytatar, is beautifully situated with fine views over the Aghstev Valley and into Azerbaijan. It is well restored and has probably Armenia's finest carvings. Road improvements have made this splendid monastery more accessible.

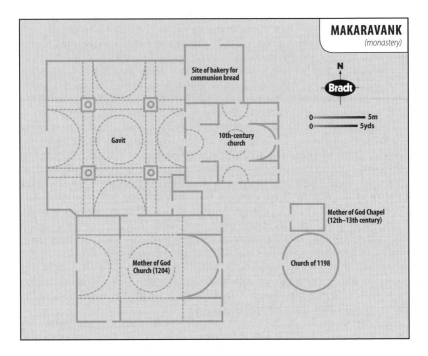

To reach Makaravank from Ijevan take the main road towards the Azeri border as far as the junction with the road to **Noyemberyan**. At this junction turn left on to a road heading for the village of **Achajur**. In the village centre a sign points right to Makaravank. It is then 6km to the monastery; for the last 3km the road deteriorates but is still drivable.

If the monastery gate happens to be locked, simply walk along the path to the right, past domestic monastic buildings, to gain access. The **oldest church**, whose dedicatee is unknown, was probably built in the 10th century. Inside it has beautifully carved window surrounds and an equally beautiful front to the altar dais with floral and linear designs. However, even this fine carving is wholly overshadowed by the amazing carving of the main **Mother of God Church** built in 1204 by Vardan, son of Prince Bazaz. The carving here is wonderful. In particular the front of this altar dais is covered with eight-pointed stars separated by octagons in each of which is a different elaborate design: a man in a boat, sphinxes, sirens, birds, floral arrangements and other unusual designs. Outside there is more fine carving; the south façade has a sundial above the main window and a bird below it, while the smaller round windows each have a different intricate design. The **gavit** was added by Prince Vache Vachutian early in the 13th century. Plain outside except for a bull and lion fighting to the left of the door and a winged sphinx with a crown on its head to the right, it is a riot of carving inside. Adjoining the north side of the original church is the site of a **bakery** for making communion loaves. East of the main church is the small **Mother of God Chapel**, which is very unusual, being round in its lower part and octagonal in its upper part. It is surmounted by a round tambour. It was built in 1198 and like other parts of the complex has richly carved decoration.

**NORTHEASTERN TAVUSH** To get to **Kirants Monastery** and other sites in the same side valley, turn off the main road for the village of Acharkut and continue for about

4km until the road ends at a barrier erected to stop illegal logging. It is possible to get the barrier opened but the track is so bad beyond here that walking is preferable, at least after the next kilometre or so. The walk through the forest with the Karahan River close by is extremely pleasant. At the barrier are information boards about the places and wildlife. Some of the sites are difficult to find; a local guide may be a good idea. It is 10km from Acharkut to Kirants Monastery along a difficult, rutted and often very muddy track; allow 2½–3 hours to Kirants alone.

**Arakelots Monastery** is the first site to be signposted, off right. The 13th-century fortified monastery occupies an extensive area on a rock outcrop. The main church, a small basilica with a tall round tambour and dome, has remains of frescoes in the apse, sadly defaced by graffiti. The church is entered through the gavit on its west side. The open dome of the gavit is a good example of the *hazarashen* method of construction where stones are added across angles to make an aperture of decreasing size (*hazar* is Armenian for 'thousand'). The north wall of the church together with the north and west walls of the gavit form part of the defensive wall around the site. Outside the south wall of the church stands a notable khachkar. To the south through the trees are the substantial ruins of domestic buildings. A short distance beyond Arakelots a bridge over the river on the left brings you to a picnic area and a **medieval bridge**. About 2km further, on the right, is an extensive picnic area with a spring. A short path leads from the far left of the clearing to a low cave with a collection of domestic and farming items.

**Deghdznut and Samson monasteries** are next to be signposted, off left, across the Zayghoshan Bridge which has a Persian inscription from the Hijra year 1207 (Gregorian 1792). Both are small ruined 12th- to 13th-century monasteries, requiring a further 3km hike up another badly rutted dirt road before descending the hillside to the left for 300m at a final signpost. Finally, **Kirants Monastery** is signposted uphill to the right of the main track. Beware of dense thickets of giant hogweed (page 81). The monastery is very unusual in that it is constructed of fired tuff bricks. The main church dates from the 13th century and has a tall octagonal tambour, a long window in each side, with an octagonal dome. The tambour is decorated with glazed tiles. The monastery was built as a Georgian Orthodox foundation and Georgian influence can be seen in the interior frescoes, most evident in the apse and tambour. Unfortunately these are covered in graffiti, some written in Russian and some in Armenian. On the west and south sides of the church are gallery-like halls with pointed entrance arches. To the west of the church is the barrel-vaulted refectory built of large boulders. This unusual, remote monastery is somehow a sad place: derelict, overgrown and defaced.

**NORTHERN TAVUSH** The main road via Noyemberyan is one of the most spectacular in the country due to its eastern outlook across the lowlands of Azerbaijan. However, an upshot of this is that it comes very close in some places to Azeri territory which since 1994 has been controlled by Armenia, and in one instance crosses it; a potential concern to anyone reviewing maps of the area. Though in practice visitors are unlikely to encounter issues (the road has been rerouted away from the line of contact, is a major haulage and transit route, and in any case is the only way to access the towns and villages of the region), the UK government was advising against all travel on this road at the time of research. Certainly it is inadvisable to stop between Kirants, Voskepar and Baghanis villages, from where Azeri positions are close enough to be seen with the naked eye; these villages continue to be the target of occasional potshots. The road passes through several ruined villages in some of which just one wall of each building has been left standing. A weird sight on a hillside right of the road is the completely restored 7th-century **Voskepar Church** surrounded by ruined and abandoned houses.

The town of **Noyemberyan** was damaged by Azeri shells in the early 1990s and by an earthquake in July 1997. It has a single hotel (page 299), a couple of cafés and other basic facilities, and makes for a natural stopping point when travelling between Ijevan and the Georgian border.

At the north end of **Koghb**, more or less opposite a big military base, is Koghb Culture Centre. On the second floor are two gems: an information centre and a museum. The staff of the **information centre** (✆0266 52599; ◷ 09.00–17.00 Mon–Fri) can help with bus times, accommodation information, etc, and can arrange a guide to local places such as Mshkavank (see below). They are also very happy to show visitors around the small but well-presented museum.

**Mshkavank (monastery)** lies about 6km southwest of Koghb. From the Culture Centre follow the blue signs to the Zikatar Environmental Centre. After about 3km a signposted track goes left to Mshkavank. The final 3km is a rocky track which needs a 4x4 to drive but makes a pleasant walk up through the wooded countryside. Tortoises have been spotted on this track. The 12th-century gavit almost overwhelms the smaller 5th- to 6th-century Mother of God basilica which is entered from the gavit. The gavit is on a stepped base and has remnants of decoration around the entrance. The roof is supported by two pairs of arches at right angles to each other and the open dome is constructed in a similar fashion. On the east façade of the church there is an unusual cross.

# 6

# Southern Provinces

Southern Armenia is characterised by its remoteness and its dramatic mountain scenery, with the main road zigzagging over some of the highest passes in the country as the territory narrows towards the Iranian border. Two of Armenia's best-known monasteries are here; **Noravank** in Vayots Dzor province, a day trip from Yerevan, and **Tatev** in Syunik, requiring an overnight stay. Petroglyphs, cave villages, Armenia's best-known megalithic site and one of the world's best-preserved caravanserais are among the other gems of the south. The farthest reaches of Syunik are famed for the figs, pomegranates and persimmons that thrive in the dry heat of the Arax Valley, and large parts of southern Syunik are state-protected conservation areas. The second main route from Yerevan to Nagorno Karabagh traverses both of the southern provinces, branching off at Goris towards Shushi and Stepanakert. Given all of that, it is perhaps surprising that southern Armenia – particularly south of Tatev – sees fewer tourists than any other part of the country.

## VAYOTS DZOR PROVINCE

Popular etymology translates Vayots Dzor as the 'gorge of woes', which some say derives from the catastrophic eruptions of the Vayots Sar volcano (page 336). The area today seems a much happier place, perhaps partly owing to a post-Soviet renaissance of **winemaking** in the region, fusing traditional grape varieties and techniques with modern technology to produce wines which are now internationally renowned. That this is happening in Vayots Dzor is no coincidence: recent excavations at the **Areni-1** cave complex (page 325) have uncovered the earliest known evidence of winemaking, dating back around 6,100 years. The lineage is also apparent in geographical names: the town of Areni is named after the endemic black grape used in most of the region's red wines, and the name 'Gnishik' – given to a river, a gorge and a village – is derived from *gini shek*, meaning 'red wine'. The appeal of wine to visitors has not been ignored: **wine tourism** is now one of the region's fastest-growing niches.

Vayots Dzor also lives up to the *dzor* (gorge) part of its name. The province is dominated by the deep valleys following the Yeghegis and Arpa rivers, which combine near the provincial capital of **Yeghegnadzor** before flowing west into Nakhichevan, together with innumerable side valleys that are home to clusters of remote villages interspersed with historical sites and unending dramatic landscapes. These all combine to offer plentiful hiking opportunities, either to reach points of interest or simply for the pleasure of walking in such stunning countryside (see page 111 for general comments on hiking). The narrowest and most spectacular parts of the gorges are on the M2 main road between Areni and Arpi, on the old

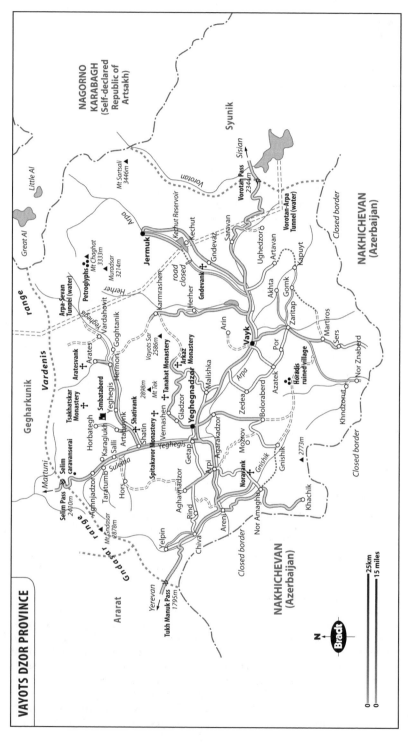

VAYOTS DZOR PROVINCE

NAGORNO
KARABAGH
(Self-declared
Republic of
Artsakh)

Little Al

Great Al

Vardenis range

Gegharkunik

Ararat

NAKHICHEVAN
(Azerbaijan)

Closed border

NAKHICHEVAN
(Azerbaijan)

Closed border

Syunik

Vorotan Pass
2344m

Vorotan-Arpa
Tunnel (water)

Vorotan

Sisian

Mt Sortsali
3446m

Arpa

Kechut Reservoir

Jermuk

Kechut

Gndevaz

Saravan

Ughedzor

Artavan

Akhta

Gomk

Kapuyt

Zaritap

Martiros

Sers

Nor Znaberd

Khndzorut

road
closed

Gnevank

Herher

Karmrrashen

Arin

Por

Vayk

Mozrov

Mt Choghat
3333m

Muradsar
3214m

Petroglyphs

Arpa-Sevan
Tunnel (water)

Vardahovit

Goghtanik

Hermon

Vayots Sar
2586m

Arkaz
Monastery

Tanahat Monastery

Yeghegnadzor

Malishka

Zedea

Boloraberd

Azatek

Horadis
ruined village

Khndzorut

2773m

Khachik

Gnishik

Gnishik

Mt Tek
2898m

Shatin

Shatinvank

Smbataberd

Yeghegis

Tsakhatskar
Monastery

Aratesvank

Arates

Horbategh

Karaglukh

Salli

Sulema

Hors

Artabuynk

Vernashen

Gladzor

Spitakavor Monastery

Getap

Arpi

Agarakadzor

Norayank

Gnishik

Aghavnadzor

Rind

Yelpin

Chiva

Areni

Nor Amaghu

Selim
caravanserai

Selim Pass
2410m

Mt Gndasar
2878m

Aghnjadzor

Tartumb

Maralik

Tukh Manuk Pass
1795m

Yerevan

Gnadar range

0        25km
0    15 miles

N

Bradt

road to Jermuk beyond Gndevank, and in the canyon between Noravank and Gnishik (the latter two only reachable on foot). There are many other gorges in the province, of course, the wooded ones being good places to see golden orioles in the breeding season, flocks of rose-coloured starlings, and the occasional view of a Levant sparrow-hawk.

Many day trippers come from Yerevan to see the monastery of **Noravank** (page 325), often in combination with Khor Virap in Ararat province. If you're staying nearby, this beautiful monastery is well worth an early morning trip up the canyon to beat the tour buses, as well as to enjoy its spectacular setting amid towering cliffs of red rock. A second major attraction, particularly for Russians and the diaspora, is **Jermuk**, Armenia's best-known medical spa resort since the Soviet era and the source of the namesake brand of bottled mineral water.

**GETTING THERE AND AROUND** Most visitors coming from Yerevan take the M2 main road and enter at the **Tukh Manuk Pass** (1,795m) from Ararat province. This route carries heavy goods traffic between Yerevan and Iran. A second road route enters from Gegharkunik province in the north via the **Selim Pass** (2,410m), and a third from Syunik province in the south via the **Vorotan Pass** (2,344m). These three routes converge at Yeghegnadzor and form the principal road structure of the province, with almost all other routes being one-way trips up side valleys. Conditions are generally poor on the M2 main route, with the current attitude to maintenance seemingly to do the minimum necessary while waiting for the new North–South Road to reach the area. Paved provincial roads are often in better condition.

**Minibuses** travel from Yerevan's Intertown Bus Station to Areni, Yeghegnadzor, Vayk and Jermuk (page 337). The 120km trip to Yeghegnadzor takes about 2 hours. From these centres minibuses head off to local villages but, as usual, to reach many of the historical sites a car or taxi is needed. A few can only be reached by hiking, mountain biking or with a 4x4. Minibus travel back to Yerevan is easily arranged, but onward travel from Yeghagnadzor south is more complicated as it will involve your host or hotel reserving you a seat on a minibus departing Yerevan (and you paying the same price as a journey from Yerevan to your final destination). Regular routes include Goris, Tatev and Stepanakert; others may be possible by negotiation. Minibuses from the towns of Syunik travelling to Yerevan will also make drop-offs in Vayk, Yeghegnadzor and Areni on negotiation with the driver. There are no train or air routes to or from Vayots Dzor.

**WHERE TO STAY** While accommodation in Vayots Dzor is relatively abundant and well distributed, the terrain and road layout makes **Yeghegnadzor** an obvious base for overnight visitors, especially since many popular sights can be reached from here as day trips. There is a growing number of family-run B&Bs in the town, thanks in part to the Yeghegnadzor B&B Network (\ 0281 24837; m 077 024837; e aterjanian@yahoo.com; w yeghegnadzorbandbnetwork.weebly.com). The network can host groups of up to 50, and Antoine and Sheila, the Canadian-Armenian founders, can arrange transfers, cultural experiences and regional tours, and are very accommodating of special requests. All the member B&Bs are highly rated and similarly priced and thus are not listed individually in this guidebook. The excellent **campsite** outside Yeghegnadzor is a popular place to meet other travellers (page 322).

Almost as central to the sights (or perhaps more convenient, depending on your interests) is **Areni**, which is also well served by family guesthouses. For those who wish to explore the further reaches of the province, accommodation can also be

6

found in the villages of Aghavnavank, Hors, Hermon, Gomk, Martiros, Artavan, Herher and Yeghegis; there are several B&Bs in Chiva. Homestays exist in most other villages and are best arranged by a travel agent (page 67).

**Jermuk** is something of a one-trick pony but has the largest number and range of hotels, including the most upscale in the province. **Vayk** has little to offer per se but its small collection of hotels may be useful, and many roadside restaurants on the M2 double as motels for people passing through.

## Yeghegnadzor

🏠 **Old Bridge Winery** (3 rooms) 16 Levonyan St; m 093 219756, 091 800240; e info@ oldbridgewinery.am; w oldbridgewinery. com. 2 dbls & 1 quad with shared bathroom in a small family guesthouse. Far more than just accommodation. English-speaking couple Armen & Ashken lay on an immersive (!) winemaking & tasting experience for their guests. Pricey for Yeghegnadzor but the experience is a cut above – there is even a (seasonal) outdoor pool. Reservations strongly suggested as their offer is understandably popular. **$$$**

🏠 **Gohar's Guesthouse** (7 rooms) 44 Spandaryan St; ☎0281 23324; m 094 332993; e sargisyan@hotmail.com. The longest-running of Yeghegnadzor's many B&Bs is still deservedly popular, combining the convenience of a small hotel with the experience of being part of an Armenian household. Gohar's excellent food is all either home-grown or produced locally by relatives. Coffee/tea always available & inc as part of the hospitality. Airport pick-up on request. Taxi-type transport can be arranged, inc 4x4, to sites in Vayots Dzor & Syunik. Light meals (AMD2,000 pp) can usually be provided without notice; a full dinner (AMD5,000 pp) needs a day's notice. **$$**

🏠 **Hotel Arpa** (14 rooms) 8/2 Narekatsi St; ☎0281 20601; e info@hotelarpa.am; w hotelarpa. am. In the centre of town, this hotel opened in 2010 & provides business standard (ie: somewhat impersonal) accommodation. Taxi stand nearby. No sign outside. Evening meal for hotel guests available with notice. Cards accepted. **$$**

⚔ **Crossway Camping** (2 bungalows, 2 dorms) 1/8 Yerevanyan Hwy at the M2/M10 junction west of Yeghegnadzor; m 093 001606; e armcamping@gmail.com; w armcamping.am. One of the few bona fide campsites in Armenia, with vehicle access & space for 25–30 tents. Well located for overlanders, cyclists, etc, & a good place to meet fellow travellers. Facilities inc hot showers, communal kitchen, laundry (AMD500/

load) & covered pavilions in an attractive orchard setting. Note: no RV hook-up. B/fast AMD2,500 pp & dinner on request (AMD4,000 pp). Equipment hire extra. Off-season discounts. There are 2 raised bungalows (AMD4,000 pp) & 7 dorm beds in 2 rooms (AMD6,000 pp) also available. **$**

## Jermuk
Map, page 338

🏠 **Armenia Wellness & Spa Hotel Jermuk** (60 rooms) 2 Myasnikyan St; ☎0287 21290; e contact@jermukarmenia.com; w jermukarmenia.com. Next door to the Mineral Water Gallery. Jermuk's priciest sanatorium has been splendidly refurbished to its former glory. Large & prominent bar serves non-residents. The hotel's medical complex offers a large range of investigations & therapies. Gym. Swimming pool. Price inc all meals & medical treatment, whether taken or not. Cards accepted. **$$$$**

🏠 **Hyatt Place Jermuk** (92 rooms) 7/5 Shahumyan St; ☎060 741234; e jermuk.place@ hyatt.com; w jermuk.place.hyatt.com. Built in 2015 to the usual Hyatt standard, in an unmissable location in front of the Mineral Water Gallery. Twin/ dbl/suite rooms available. Bright & airy lobby bar open to the public (& probably the only place in town to get a good Italian-style coffee). The Gallery Café overlooks the lake & is also open to non-residents. Private medical spa in basement with a variety of treatments inc mineral baths at extra cost. Gym. Swimming pool. Off-season special packages available. **$$$$**

🏠 **Jermuk Olympia** (52 rooms) 16 Shahumyan St; ☎0287 22366; m 094 444904; e info@jermukolympia.am; w jermukolympia.am. This fully renovated sanatorium looks light & airy with carefully thought-out décor. Wheelchair access to hotel, but not to the pleasant dining room overlooking the grounds. Indoor sports, bar, sauna, conference hall. Offers a range of medical investigations & spa therapies. FB & medical treatment inc. **$$$**

**Ani Hotel** (11 rooms) 26 Shahumyan St; 0287 21727; m 091 211727, 077 211727, 055 211727; e contact@jermukani.am; w jermukani. am. Small hotel with good quality, interestingly shaped rooms. No lift; 4 floors. A brisk 10min walk from the town. Cards accepted. FB. **$$**

**Anush Hotel** (16 rooms) 2 Vardanyan St; 0287 22441; m 094 444908/06; e info@ jermukanush.am; w jermukanush.am. A renovated Soviet building in the centre of town. Lots of steps up to front entrance. No lift; 4 floors. Cards accepted. **$$**

**Central Guesthouse** (12 rooms) 12 Myasnikyan St; 0287 21607; m 093 177770, 055 840444. Entered from Shahumyan Street. Town-centre building opened 2012. Rooms on floors 2, 3 & 4. Shops on 1st floor, b/fast room in basement. Lunch/dinner not available. **$$**

**Nairi Hotel** (21 rooms) 7/1 Myasnikyan St; 0287 22008; m 098 101070; e info@ jermuknairi.am; w jermuknairi.am. Set on the edge of the Arpa Gorge, with superb views. Very near town centre. Pleasant hotel with restaurant & bar. FB available. **$$**

**Verona Rest House** (20 rooms) 9/1 Shahumyan St; 0287 22050; m 091 402615, 093 402615; e info@jermukverona.am; w jermukverona.am. Within the Town Park at the side of one of the lakes. Do not be too put off by the huge derelict Sport Complex nearby; the hotel is pleasant & new in well-kept grounds with easy access to parks, the Mineral Water Gallery & the town centre. FB available. **$$**

**Cascade** (8 rooms) At the southern end of Shahumyan St; m 095 603007. Reception is the nearby portacabin. The luxe building is divided into a pair of 2-storey apts each with 2 twin bedrooms (AMD30,000/apt). The other house is divided into quarters giving 4 2-storey apts, each with 1 twin bedroom (AMD20,000/apt). Prices in low season are AMD10,000/apt cheaper. **$**

**Evmari** (pronounced Yevmari) (1 dbl, 5 suites with 2 dbl rooms, 1 suite with 3 dbl rooms) 3 Shahumyan St; 0287 21814; m 099 011814; e hayro@inbox.ru. In town centre. B/fast approx AMD1,000 pp. **$**

**Hotel Life** (4 rooms) 10/1 Shahumyan St; 0287 21256; m 055 811118, 093 721256; e info@ jermuklife.am. Budget self-catering hotel in the town centre. All rooms en suite with small lounge areas. Small shared kitchen. B/fast not inc. **$**

## Elsewhere in the province

**Hors Guesthouse** (3 rooms) 2km west of Hors village; m 091 195478. Intended to be rented as a whole property, this new self-catering ecolodge in the Gndasar mountain range near Hors village accommodates up to 10 people & may be of interest to groups wishing to explore the nearby peaks & lakes. Only accessible by 4x4 but the manager can arrange pick-up. Reservations via Airbnb or Booking.com. B/fast AMD3,500 pp. **$$$**

**Areni Wine Art** (8 rooms) 20 Second St, Areni; m 094 536329; . Converted family home at the top of the village with a spacious garden & covered eating area, catering for group lunches & hosting overnight guests since 2015 in light & airy en-suite twin/trpl/quad rooms. Young proprietor David speaks English & can arrange guided hiking, trekking & 4x4 tours. Homemade wine & honey for sale. Traditional *lavash*-baking classes on request. Dinner AMD3,000–4,000 pp. **$$**

**Hotel Arevi** (10 rooms) At the eastern end of Yeghegis village; m 093 306556; e hotelarevi@ gmail.com; w arevi.am/hotel; . New in 2018, this ultra-modern riverside B&B is built from recycled shipping containers & very convenient for the attractions of the Yeghegis Valley. En-suite dbl/twin rooms available, all with tea-/coffee-making facilities. Owned by Arevi Tour (page 67) who can also organise hikes & activities in the area. **$$**

**LucyTour Hotel Resort** (60 rooms) Hermon village; 0281 21080; m 098 779778/005829; e info@lucy-tour.com; w lucy-tour.com. On the Yeghegis Valley road. Prices very reasonable for what is included – indoor swimming pool, bicycles, gym, volleyball & basketball. Detailed information leaflet about the province, inc map, provided. Can arrange tours with 4x4 & guides. Accepts cards. Hotel accommodation in chalet-like buildings. Restaurant on-site. **$$**

**Arakelyan Family Homestay** (3 rooms) Herher village; m 093 995573. The Arakelyan family regularly host foreign visitors in their large family home in Herher, from where the beautiful surrounding valley can be explored. Family members can act as local guides. B/fast & other meals by arrangement. Most produce is locally grown or raised & delicious. Traditional group meals also catered for. **$**

**Horseback Tours Farm** (5 rooms) 11 Fifth St, Gomk village; m 094 996460, 077 016692;

**e** benson.armenia@gmail.com; **w** bensontour. am. Offers horseback riding in a fabulous location but also a standalone B&B/hostel in its own right, perched below a spectacular gorge with plenty of excellent hiking. Twin/dbl rooms in one building & dorm beds/bunks in a second newer unit. Shared bathrooms. Small kitchen & BBQ. Lunch/dinner on request & highly recommended. Camping space in garden. **$**

**Vayk Hotel & Restaurant** (10 rooms) 10a Jermuk Rd, Vayk; ☏ 0282 92809; **m** 093 021170; **e** vaykhotel@gmail.com. This hotel-cum-private information centre has nice rooms with photographs of the region taken by the owner. Very helpful staff. Information desk. Owner can arrange cultural/wine/camping tours & leads caving expeditions himself. Accepts cards. B/fast AMD2,000 pp. **$**

✕ **WHERE TO EAT AND DRINK** There are plenty of **restaurants** on the M2 main road serving standard Armenian fare, as well as more varied roadside 'food courts' in Vayk and just east of Yeghegnadzor. Most overnight visitors are likely to eat their morning and evening meals with their B&B hosts, almost all of whom can offer delicious home-cooked dinners on request. Standalone eating options in the towns and villages are somewhat thin on the ground for this reason, but there are restaurants at Noravank, Areni-1 cave and the Hin Areni Winery; traditional kitchens in Areni and Yeghegnadzor that can provide meals by advance arrangement; and fast-food places in the centres of Yeghegnadzor and Vayk. In Jermuk it is possible to eat in the restaurants of any of the large hotels, but note that the evening meal for full-board guests is usually served rather early. There are few other restaurants in Jermuk and those that do exist (page 338) are often busy for that reason.

**OTHER PRACTICALITIES** The towns in the province have basic facilities such as shops, post offices, banks, ATMs, cafés and taxis. Any special requirements should be brought from Yerevan. On the main road junction for Yeghegnadzor is the Arpa Protected Landscape **visitor information centre** (page 328; ⏱ 09.30–18.00 Mon–Fri), whose English-speaking staff can help with the planning of hikes and nature-watching excursions throughout the province, as well as arranging guides and accommodation. Vayk has a private **tourist information centre** within the Vayk Hotel (see above; information desk ⏱ 10.00–19.00 Mon–Fri, 10.00–16.00 Sat) and the proprietor can help with arranging almost anything locally. Antoine and Sheila of the Yeghegnadzor B&B Network (page 321) can also share a wealth of local knowledge with guests of their member B&Bs. Signposting to historic sites is generally good in Vayots Dzor, and some of the more popular hiking trails are now signposted and waymarked.

**ARENI** Though the vineyards themselves are in the surrounding hills, the village of Areni has become synonymous with Armenia's wine industry. The main part of the village straddles the Arpa River south of the M2 main road at the foot of dramatic ochre cliffs. An annual wine festival of growing fame is held on the first Saturday of October, part trade fair, part local celebration with wine tasting, dancing and a demonstration by young girls of treading grapes in the traditional barefoot manner. Areni takes its name from the indigenous black grape variety mainly used for making dry red table wines. Several establishments in the area advertise **wine tasting and tours**; try the Hin Areni Winery (⏱ 09.30–20.00 daily; **m** 041 234111; **w** hinareniwine.am; English guided tours & tasting AMD1,000 pp) for a showcase of a mixed traditional/modern approach; Zorah Wines (⏱ on request, usually via local tour operators; **w** zorahwines.com) in nearby Rind whose wines have won awards internationally; Momik Wines (⏱ by arrangement; **m** 095 480450; **f**) who operate the first of several planned 'wine cube' tasting rooms across the region; or one of the many family-run places to see how it's done the old-fashioned way. Should you wish to purchase the homemade variety, try one of the roadside stalls that sell large bottles, often labelled as Coca-Cola (most people who buy these are Iranian truck drivers taking home to alcohol-free Iran a beverage with considerably more body and flavour). The quality varies but it is normal practice to taste before buying. During the grape harvest you can also buy from the same stalls *matchar*, which is fresh grape juice having undergone two to three days' fermentation; in other words a fruity precursor to actual wine. Don't be tempted to keep it in storage: the yeast is still active and the bottle will explode.

On the southern bank of the Arpa is a **red cross-dome church**, built in 1321 and restored in 1997. The church's most remarkable feature is the tympanum of the west door, which is a wonderfully carved effigy of the Virgin Mary created by Momik, one of Armenia's greatest stone carvers and also a great illustrator of manuscripts. He worked in this region in the late 13th and early 14th centuries and his museum is now located at Noravank (see below). High on the west façade, the representation of a head gazing down is said to be that of a Mongolian, a reminder that at the time the church was constructed when Armenia was under Mongol rule and that persecution of non-Muslims was increasing. Inside the church in the pendentives below the tambour are more fine carvings, again by Momik, of the symbols of the four evangelists. The graveyard too has some exceptional carving. One tombstone shows a horse and also a person playing a *saz*, a musical instrument rather like a lute and the ancestor of the Greek *bouzouki*. Other tombstones appear to reinforce Areni's long winemaking history as they show a figure with a wine flask or wine glass.

## Areni-1 cave
(⊕ on demand, ask the security guard or at the restaurant next door; AMD1,000) Areni's long history of winemaking has been confirmed by excavations by a team of Armenian and Irish archaeologists during 2007–10 in a cave complex known as Areni-1. The Areni-1 winery is 6,100 years old, making it the world's oldest known winery and showing that grapes had already been domesticated by 4000BC. Items found included a wine press, fermentation vats, storage jars and cups as well as grape seeds and the remains of pressed grapes and other fruit. (It was in the same cave that the world's oldest shoe was found in 2008, now on display in Yerevan's History Museum of Armenia; page 176.) The site is carefully managed, as further excavations are still to take place; but it is possible (and worthwhile) to tour the caves. The route is well lit and interpretative panels help make sense of what you see.

## NORAVANK (MONASTERY)
(⊕ always, though snow may restrict access in winter) Just south of Areni, next to the Areni-1 cave, a paved road leads west from the main road across a bridge and enters the narrow gorge of the Gnishik River. The first, narrow part of the gorge is spectacular and popular among rock climbers, with several routes established for both sport and trad climbing. Beyond that, the road leads to one of Armenia's best-known tourist sights, Noravank (New Monastery), approximately 7.5km from the main road. En route is Vardges's Stone Bar (⊕ 10.00–dusk daily in high season; no electricity), a popular **café** set in a small cavern, serving light meals and drinks – look for the wrought-iron railings and khachkar-like stones fronting the cave. As the gorge opens out and the valley floor fills with fruit trees, Noravank can be seen high on the slopes below the cliff face to the left. Its construction in red stone set against the similarly coloured rock of the mountainside is particularly evocative in the early morning or late evening light. If at all possible avoid coming to Noravank in the middle of the day as the place is thronged with tour buses from Yerevan. It is also stiflingly hot in the valley in summer.

An alternative route to Noravank involves a short but spectacular **hike** and some excellent views from above. Follow the H40 paved road from Areni as far as

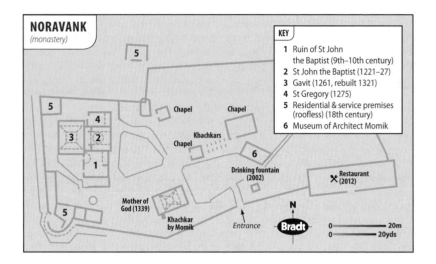

**NORAVANK** (monastery)

**KEY**

1 Ruin of St John
  the Baptist (9th–10th century)
2 St John the Baptist (1221–27)
3 Gavit (1261, rebuilt 1321)
4 St Gregory (1275)
5 Residential & service premises
  (roofless) (18th century)
6 Museum of Architect Momik

Chapel
Chapel
Khachkars
Chapel
Drinking fountain
(2002)
Restaurant
(2012)
Mother of
God (1339)
Khachkar
by Momik
Entrance
**Bradt**
N
0 — 20m
0 — 20yds

the ruined village of **Nor Amaghu** (ie: New Amaghu) on a plateau on the left of the road, then follow either of the two signposted trails through the ruins and down into the gorge – the easternmost option is the more dramatic, winding along a narrow historic footpath. At the bottom of the gorge, cross the road to find a bridge and a trail continuing up to the monastery. From the same starting point (Nor Amaghu) it is possible to hike along the canyon through Arpa Protected Landscape (page 328) by continuing 500m on the paved road towards Khachik and taking the dirt road at the sharp right-hand bend. Proceed past the barrier and follow the waymarks for 14km to reach Gnishik, allowing at least 3–4 hours. The route passes through the ruined settlement of Hin Amaghu (ie: Old Amaghu) and past a spectacular rock outcrop before descending into the canyon itself. There was one very steep and hazardous section at the time of update, involving a couple of hundred metres of nervous scrambling, though plans to rebuild the section are on the table. More details about hikes in the Noravank area can be found on information boards installed at the monastery as part of the WWF-sponsored Barev Trails project (w barevtrails.com).

As you approach the monastery itself, the striking two-storey building that you come to first is actually a mausoleum with another church on top of it, and is the newest part of the establishment. The larger complex of buildings beyond is older; the oldest part of all is the ruined 9th- or 10th-century **church of John the Baptist** at the southeast corner. The site was developed mainly in the 13th century by the Orbelian princes, a branch of the Mamikonian family which had settled in Georgia in the 9th century and members of which had held the position of commander-in-chief of the Georgian forces in the 10th and 11th centuries. The Georgian army, which included many Armenians, defeated the sultan in 1204 and many families from Georgia moved into Armenia including the Orbelians who settled in Syunik. The Orbelians built several churches to act as burial places for the family and the see of the bishopric of Syunik was moved here to Noravank. The **oldest surviving church** is the one in the centre of the further complex of buildings. Erected in 1221–27, it is also dedicated to **John the Baptist** and is of the cross-dome type with two-storey corner rooms. To judge from a fragment of the church model which has survived, it originally had an octagonal tambour with an umbrella cupola but this collapsed during an earthquake in 1840 and has been replaced by a circular tambour and conical cupola. The more modest **church of St Gregory** was added on the north side in 1275 as the burial place of the Orbelians. In the floor are gravestones including one dated 1300 for Elikum, son of Prince Tarsayich Orbelian, who is represented by a lion figure resting its head on one paw. There are two carved doves by the altar dais, which is flanked by khachkars, and the remains of frescoes can be seen, the red colour of which is apparently the highly prized red dye, *vordan karmir* (page 213), which was used in Armenia's illuminated manuscripts.

The original **gavit of the John the Baptist Church** was built on the west side in 1261 by Prince Smbat Orbelian but it was completely rebuilt in 1321 following earthquake damage. Both the gavit and the Mother of God Church are the work of Momik who was also responsible for the fine carvings at Areni (page 325) and the intricate khachkar in Yeghegnadzor Regional Museum (page 329). The two tympana (one above the other, separated by a window opening) of the doorway are in every way remarkable. The carved relief of the upper, pointed one shows God, with his almond-shaped eyes looking straight ahead while a dove is entangled in his beard. He is raising his right hand in blessing while holding a head in his left. Whose head must remain a matter of speculation: possibly that of John the Baptist to whom the church is dedicated and who was decapitated, or perhaps it is the head of the Son or perhaps that of Adam. Above the head is a dove symbolising the Holy Spirit. To the right there is the winged head of a child, the medieval symbol of a seraph, while to the left the scene of Crucifixion. The lower tympanum is semicircular and depicts Mary sitting with Jesus in her arms on a patterned rug. On the right is the Prophet Isaiah together with a banner that reads 'Holy Virgin Isaiah'. On the left is St John the Baptist with further words visible in the tracery. The whole is surrounded by an inscription which, according to a recent Armenian booklet describing Noravank, reads: 'Here is the blessed and awful name of my God from the beginnings to the verge of edges that is out of ends and ruptures.' Inside the gavit there is further carving but nothing to rival the tympana.

The two-storey **Mother of God Church** also has very fine carving. Built by Prince Burtel Orbelian, it was completed in 1339, proving to be Momik's last work. Considerable damage was caused by the 1840 earthquake, and the church lost its tambour and cupola which were not restored until 1997. The appearance of this church is very unusual: the lower storey is rectangular but the upper is of cross-dome form. The lower storey can be accessed by descending six steps at the west end and comprises the burial vault of the donor and his family. Over the doorway the tympanum depicts Mary with Jesus in her arms, but sitting on a throne this time, flanked by the archangels Gabriel and Michael. Inside the vault can be seen the figures of the evangelists. The church, in the upper storey, is accessed by narrow steps cantilevered up the outside face of the lower façade – only those who are happy on narrow ledges should climb them. The tympanum over the upper doorway depicts a half-length Christ flanked by the apostles Peter and Paul. From the ceiling of the corner room to the right of the altar the head of a lion looks down.

The reinstated conical cupola is, unusually, not supported by a tambour but by 12 columns. On three of the columns at the western end can just be seen (binoculars help) carved figures of Mary with Jesus and of two donors of the church, one of whom is holding a model of it. There are still some very fine khachkars here although the finest of all have been moved to Etchmiadzin. One good and very intricate one which remains was carved by Momik in 1308. To the right of the entrance gate is the **Museum of Architect Momik** ( ⊕ 10.00–19.30 daily; closed mid-Nov–early Apr, depending on the weather; guide available; AMD500) which depicts his work as a manuscript writer and illustrator. There is a 15-minute video presentation about Noravank generally and helpful casts of the important Noravank tympana enabling one to see the details close-up. Other displays show examples of 'vivifying flower teas'; the natural pigments used

6

in manuscripts; and the 54 ingredients (herbs, spices and oil) used in the preparation of *meron*, the Armenian Church's chrism (consecrated oil for anointing).

The **Noravank restaurant** (⊕ Mar–Oct 09.30–20.00 daily; m 093 368700) belongs to the church and has something of a refectory feel: a simply furnished large dining hall lined with the large clay pots found in the area. Prices are extremely reasonable. Groups are advised to book in advance. Its future is currently uncertain; Noravank is under consideration for inscription in the UNESCO World Heritage list but the presence of such commercial buildings goes against the strict criteria.

From where the road crosses the river below Noravank, a track leads to the small **Chapel of St Pokas** (cross the sluice gate and continue uphill – about a 5-minute walk), in which is a 4th-century khachkar, oval with a simple cross, and a sacred spring whose water is covered by a film of oil, supposedly oil from the saint's burial ground. According to Stepanos Orbelian writing in the late 13th century, surprising miracles formerly occurred here: all manner of pains, whose cure by men was impossible, such as leprosy and long-infected and gangrenous wounds, were cured when people came here, bathed in the water and were anointed with the oil. However, in cases where the diseases were incurable, the people died immediately upon drinking the water. A small bathing pool has been constructed just downhill from the chapel for those who wish to test these theories.

**AROUND ARENI AND NORAVANK** Travelling south from Areni on the H40 will bring you to **Khachik** (Little Cross), a remote village with some of Armenia's highest-altitude vineyards and perilously close to the militarised border with Nakhichevan. Unless you are here as part of a cultural tour organised by a local operator, one of the few reasons you might find yourself in Khachik is for its annual *gata* (page 101) **festival** on the second weekend of September.

About 4km east of the Noravank junction is a paved road north to **Aghavnadzor** and **Ulgyur** (13.5km). At Ulgyur, 5km northwest of Aghavnadzor, there are two fine *vishaps*. A 4x4 is needed to reach the site, but leaving your vehicle in Aghavnadzor and walking is also a good option. The rough track winds round the mountain, zigzagging higher and higher until you reach the Mother of God Chapel (11th–14th century). Beside the chapel stand two impressive *vishaps*, the taller being over 3m high. The dragon heads can be seen clearly. Both had crosses added in the 11th–12th centuries. The gravestones of several family members of Momik, the architect of Noravank, were found in the chapel cemetery.

**Arpa Protected Landscape**, is a conservation zone covering a triangular area roughly bounded by the Noravank Canyon, the Arpa River and the closed border with Nakhichevan. Its **visitor information centre** (1/8/1 Yerevanyan Hwy, Yeghegnadzor; m 095 959025, 096 331131; ⊕ 09.30–18.00 Mon–Fri; e gnishik.himnadram@gmail.com; f GNISHIK) is on the main road below Yeghegnadzor. The area was established with the help of the WWF in 2014, originally as Gnishik Protected Landscape, in order to maintain a continuous ecological corridor for critically endangered species. The centre's English- and French-speaking staff can advise and arrange tours not just to the protected area itself but throughout Vayots Dzor. The centre also displays a map of local **hiking trails** and natural/cultural monuments, and the staff can arrange a variety of services and experiences including guided hikes, horseback riding, 4x4 trips, spelunking (caving), birdwatching and wildlife-watching tours, and homestay accommodation. A small gift shop and café are also on-site.

**YEGHEGNADZOR** The centre of the provincial capital **Yeghegnadzor** (Valley of Reeds) lies to the north of the M2 main road, the junction marked by a statue symbolising

*Wisdom*. It is famous for its **goats' cheese**, which is made by sealing curds and herbs in a clay pot with wax and burying it underground to mature: the resulting cheese is excruciatingly strong, sharp and (some say) delicious. The town itself is well kept and has a relatively prosperous feel and, though there are no particular highlights for sightseers, those who are curious or who find themselves staying at one of the many B&Bs will find sufficient interest to occupy a few hours. One of the quirkier attractions is a perfectly preserved Soviet-era **knitwear factory** that employed 500 people until 1992, whose owner is happy to show visitors around; this is best arranged via your host or via the Yeghegnadzor B&B Network (page 321).

Through a striking horseshoe-shaped entrance, **Yeghegnadzor Regional Museum** (4 Shahumyan St; ☏ 0281 23392; **e** museum68@rambler.ru; ⏰ 09.00–17.00 Mon– Sat (if door is locked call the displayed number); Sun visits possible if booked in advance; AMD500) contains a treasure trove of interest. Pride of place goes to a broken 1330s khachkar by Momik, one of Armenia's greatest stone carvers. The two pieces were found separately and reunited in the museum. Other significant items include a stone altar with a Greek inscription from Areni, pottery from the second millennium BC, an Urartian bronze belt from the first millennium BC found in the town, and colourful glazed pottery from the 12th–13th centuries AD. A cradle displays an ingenious contraption to prevent bed-wetting by its (male) occupant and there are two stones said to be the female equivalent of phallic symbols. The storeroom has artefacts which can't be displayed for lack of space, including petrified sea urchins and starfish found in the vicinity showing that Yeghegnadzor, high as it now is (1,194m), was once below sea level.

**AROUND YEGHEGNADZOR** There are a number of interesting sights outside the town including the Museum of Gladzor University, the related Tanahat Monastery, and Spitakavor Monastery (page 330). Near the junction of the two main roads outside the town is the **13th-century Dadal Bridge over the Arpa**. The bridge can be reached by taking the track next to the auto mechanic's workshop about 100m east of the M2 main road's junction with the M10 Selim road. Follow the track through the fields and cross the new bridge over the river, then turn left for 0.5km on the road which goes along the hillside parallel to the river. The old bridge, which once upon a time stood on the Silk Road route between Julfa (in present-day Iran) and the Selim Caravanserai (page 335), consists of a single arch of 16m span. It is unlike other medieval Armenian bridges in being a lancet arch, an acutely pointed arch having two separate centres of equal radii. This gives it a pointed appearance with a high clearance over the river in the centre. The bridge is picturesquely situated away from any main road and makes an ideal place for a picnic.

## The Museum of Gladzor University (⏰ 09.00–17.30 Tue–Sun; the keyholder
lives next door & is happy to show visitors around at any time; she speaks Armenian & Russian; AMD500) From the centre of Yeghegnadzor a road leads northeast up the hill through residential areas. The **Museum of Gladzor University** is a few kilometres beyond the town in the village of Vernashen, on the left, housed in a former basilica church. This museum does not rank among Armenia's must-sees but a visit will help make sense of the mentions of Gladzor University at other sites (it moved from place to place according to the wishes of the principal of the day). The seven modern stones outside the entrance represent the seven subjects of medieval learning: the trivium or lower part comprised grammar, rhetoric and logic while the quadrivium or higher part comprised arithmetic, geometry, astronomy and music. The museum has photographs of the various monasteries to which the university moved, illustrations

of illuminated manuscripts produced at the university, and photographs of places where former students went to establish schools. In all, 350 *vardapets* graduated between 1282 when the university was established by Momik (page 327) and 1338 when it ceased to function. Throughout its working life the university was concerned with maintaining the independence of the Armenian Church and the rejection of papal authority.

**Spitakavor Monastery** The monastery of Spitakavor (essentially meaning 'white') can be reached from the Museum of Gladzor University (page 329) either by car or on foot. Driving definitely needs a 4x4, good weather and an experienced driver. Even then it is a difficult 8.4km journey. The walk of about 6km is very pleasant, if rather steep at times. The track to the monastery goes off left a few metres beyond the museum. The first short section is through the village, after which the stream is crossed. The vehicle track turns left but walkers should carry straight on while keeping the stream and a small dam on the right. The rocky path then ascends up the side of the ever-narrowing and dramatic gorge until it angles left and emerges into an alpine meadow as the gorge widens out. The next section of the path is through a summer village where farmers from the villages below come to pasture their stock during the warmer months. Beyond the summer village keep right and you will soon see Spitakavor high above you. In places the path has been washed away but it is fairly easy to follow the stream, which flows down the steep mountainside from the monastery. There is a very welcome spring at the top. Watch

## GAREGIN NZHDEH – THE SAVIOUR OF ARMENIA

Born Garegin Ter-Harutyunian in 1886, Garegin Nzhdeh was the son of a village priest in Nakhichevan. Later he led an Armenian band fighting alongside the Bulgarians in 1912 as Bulgaria battled for independence from the Ottoman Empire. During World War I he fought alongside the Russian troops against Turkey. By 1921, his guerrilla band was holding off both Bolshevik and Turkish forces in Syunik and Zangezur (southern Armenia) and he declared an independent Republic of Mountainous Armenia at Tatev Monastery in May 1921. This he used as a bargaining tool with Lenin to ensure that both Syunik and Zangezur were incorporated into Armenia, rather than into Azerbaijan as the Bolshevik government had at first agreed in its bid to achieve good relations with Turkey. After agreement with Lenin was reached, the tiny state capitulated in July 1921 and Nzhdeh went into exile via Persia. He later negotiated fruitlessly with Nazi Germany in a bid to recover the lost territories of Western Armenia and in 1945 he was arrested in Bulgaria by Soviet troops. He was executed in 1955 for 'anti-Soviet activities'. He is regarded as the person who saved southern Armenia for the nation and, in the light of more recent events, he may almost be regarded as the saviour of Armenia since it is doubtful whether Armenia could have survived the early 1990s without the lifeline to Iran which those territories provided. His remains were secretly brought to Armenia in 1983 and kept in the cellar of one of those who had returned his remains. In 1987 he was reburied at Spitakavor. In his will, Nzhdeh had said that he wished to be buried on Mount Khustup so in 2005 parts of his body were taken from Spitakavor and buried for a third time on the slopes of Mount Khustup, near his memorial in Kapan. It is said that only his heart now remains buried in his grave at Spitakavor.

out for interesting reptiles on the way, such as the nose-horned viper and Caucasian green lizard. Drivers will follow the main track left at the location mentioned on the opposite page. The track winds up round the hillside, giving magnificent views over the mountains and the valley in which Yeghegnadzor lies. It appears to go past the monastery but then doubles back to a small car park. Walkers can of course do a loop, walking up one way and down the other. It is also possible to combine this hike with the approach from Shativank (page 332).

The **church**, dedicated to the Mother of God, dates from 1321 and was built by Prince Prosh of the Proshian family on the site of a 5th-century basilica. The belltower was added in 1330. The gavit has seen some restoration. The church itself is a cross-dome construction with tall cylindrical tambour and conical cupola. High up in the apex of the dome are carvings of the symbols of the four evangelists; the ox is the easiest to see. There are interesting carvings outside. The tympanum is richly carved in a style similar to Areni and Noravank: stalactite decoration arches over a beautiful Madonna and Child and geometrical patterns surround the whole. On the east façade is a curious irregular and asymmetrical cross. The cross on the south façade is more regular but, rather like a tree of life, it seems to grow out of a pot and it has pentagonal stars within its arms. Outside the church the **modern grave** is that of Garegin Nzhdeh (see box, opposite).

The track to the monastery continues uphill. At the crest of the track a path goes off right to the remains of the small **fortress of Proshaberd**, also built by Prince Prosh, on top of a rocky hill. The walk up is easy apart from a scramble at the end. Allow about an hour to walk up, look round and return. A rectangle of walls survives with a tower at each corner. Otherwise not much remains but the views are excellent. One thing that does survive is a deep, dungeon-like pit. Be careful not to fall into it – it would be very difficult to climb out again.

## Tanahat Monastery

Tanahat Monastery, where Gladzor University was probably first established, is 5km beyond the museum on the same road. A monastery was first established here in 753 but the present buildings date from 1273–79. The lavishly laid out car parks and remains of other facilities were provided for celebrations in 1982 that marked the 700th anniversary of the university's founding. The **main church**, St Stephen's, is a cross-dome structure with a 12-sided tambour and umbrella cupola. Rather plain inside, it has much elaborate carving outside with a heavy preponderance of depictions of animals and birds. Above the sundial on the south façade, two doves drink from a common cup. The crest of the Orbelian family (a lion and a bull) is high on the tambour; that of the Proshians (an eagle holding a lamb in its talons) is on the side over the door. Another eagle has a smaller bird in its claws and around the top of the tambour can be seen a whole range of animal heads. To the north of St Stephen's Church is the small 14th-century **Church of the Holy Cross**. There are more animals here – the tympanum depicts a mounted horseman attacking a lion. The reason for so much animal carving is not known. The foundations of numerous other buildings can be clearly seen, indicating that the monastery was once large and important.

## NORTHERN VAYOTS DZOR AND THE YEGHEGIS VALLEY

About 15km east of Areni, the main road passes the confluence of the Yeghegis and Arpa rivers to meet a junction with the M10 road from the north of Vayots Dzor. A number of sights reside in this northern region – some walking is required to reach most of them. The road splits at the village of **Shatin**, from where the road eastwards along the Yeghegis Valley allows access to the monastery of Shativank; Tsakhatskar Monastery and the fortress of Smbataberd; Yeghegis village (Zorats Church and the Jewish cemetery); Arates Monastery; and a purpose-built observation point for Bezoar goats in Shatin village. **Hermon** village offers several accommodation options; from here it is possible (in summer) to continue south on a dirt road over a 2,234m pass and to rejoin the main road via Herher – a worthwhile loop for those with time and suitable transport.

## Shativank (monastery)

In Shatin, 0.5km after turning off the M10, turn right where there is a shop on your *left* (ignore an earlier right turn with a shop on the right) and then take the road which *bears* right (not the sharp right turn). About 150m after crossing the river fork right, then after another 500m go left up a hill to the cemetery. If you get lost ask for the cemetery (*gerezman*); the road to the monastery goes through the cemetery. In a 4x4, in good weather and with an experienced driver, it is just about possible to drive beyond here to the monastery of Shativank, but it is a pleasant 7km walk along the track with fine views down into the valley on each side from the crest of the ridge. Note there is an alternative path direct up the gorge (left beyond the bridge where the track to the cemetery forks right). It is shorter but much steeper, frequently muddy, and there are no views. From the village cemetery the track to the monastery goes up between the graves and then bears left. After a few kilometres it is possible to see Shativank in the distance and the track winds down to it. Hikers wanting a full day's walking may continue to Spitakavor Monastery (page 330) and be picked up on the H47 paved road to Yeghegnadzor at Vernashen.

Shativank was founded in 929 but was destroyed in the 14th century and then rebuilt. Like other Armenian churches in the late medieval period it was provided with massive fortified walls which are well preserved, and the substantial remains of three round defensive towers can also be seen on the south side. The **Zion Church** itself, rebuilt again in 1665, is a three-aisle basilica built of basalt and of limited interest apart from its evocative site. There is evidence of a gallery on the church's west side and remains of other monastic buildings.

## Tsakhatskar Monastery and Smbataberd (fortress)

The next two sights along the Yeghegis can be combined for a pleasant walk along signposted trails. Continuing east from Shatin village, take the left fork towards **Artabuynk**. About 1km beyond Artabuynk a track angles steeply down on the right-hand side, crossing an irrigation channel as it descends. At the bottom of the hill the track formerly crossed the Yeghegis by a bridge but this is questionably safe for vehicles, although it can be used by pedestrians. The river can be forded by 4x4s, but it is risky for others unless the river is exceptionally low. It is better to walk from here, especially as some of the track is in poor condition.

**Tsakhatskar Monastery** should be visited first as this gets the greater part of the climbing accomplished earlier in the day. A moderately fit person should allow 90 minutes to walk from the river up to Tsakhatskar, then 45 minutes from Tsakhatskar to Smbataberd, and 30 minutes back from Smbataberd to the river plus some time at each site and to admire the views. Follow the signposts up the main track from the far side of the ford or bridge. In about 500m there is a spring on the right where water bottles can be filled, although it may be dry towards the end of summer. There is another spring at Tsakhatskar itself. The monastery can be seen high up on the mountainside to the left long before reaching it, but in practice it is hard to detect, so similar is the colour of its basalt stone to the colour of the mountainside. The ruined monastery is reached after about 5km of continuous ascent and is astonishingly large for so isolated a place. According to a 13th-century historian, the monastery was built in the 5th century as the burial place for those who died in battles against the Persians (page 18) and rebuilt in the 10th and 11th centuries. There are two 11th-century churches, restored in 2010, and older ruined monastic buildings to the west.

The easternmost of the two churches, **Holy Cross**, dates from the 11th century and appears to have been a mausoleum. A square entrance area, above which is a second storey, leads through to a lower chapel. A large stone structure has been built across the original entrance for the full width of the building and on it stand large khachkars.

The more western of the two churches, **St John the Baptist**, was built in 1041. It is a cross-dome church with circular tambour and conical cupola. On the south façade there is a carving of an eagle clutching a lamb in its talons (symbol of the Proshians) and the doorway is elaborately decorated with geometric designs and inscriptions. The north wall has a carving of a lion tearing a bull (symbols of the Orbelians and Bagratunis); the west and east windows are surrounded by geometric carving. The front of the altar dais has a row of carved jugs. Outside there are many khachkars, including two very large ones near the entrance.

The main part of the **monastery** was at a distance from these churches on the west side. Extensive remains of buildings can be seen, most of them presumably the service buildings of the monastery, although including further churches dedicated to the Mother of God (10th century) and, at the southern end, to St John. The latter bears an inscription dated to 999. There are what appear to be the remains of cloisters and all of these buildings on the western side were once surrounded by a defensive wall, of which only the eastern part with its gateway survives. An inscription at the gateway records its restoration in 1221. The sheer scale of these remains, which stretch for over 200m, indicates clearly the former importance of this now forgotten place. From the site the view is over alpine meadows and apple trees down into the valley below; a mountain ridge stretches away to the south, on the furthest summit of which is the **fortress of Smbataberd**. The walk again provides magnificent views down into the valley on each side and is mostly downhill apart from the final slope up into the fortress. Stabilisation work has been carried out on the walls of the fortress and a paved path leads to one of the postern gates outside of which a small viewing platform has been built.

Smbataberd (fortress of Smbat, Prince of Syunik) was probably founded in the 5th century but considerably strengthened in the 10th and is one of Armenia's most impressive fortresses. Few can fail to be impressed by the gigantic ramparts built on the precipitous cliff face, especially those on the eastern side. Smbataberd is in a magnificent defensive position, crowning the southern end of the ridge and guarded by steep cliffs on three sides. Even on those sides, walls with frequent towers were built wherever the drop was less than precipitous and much of this survives. Inside the walls relatively little remains, although the outline of buildings can be discerned around the walls as well as the fortress's keep at the highest point of the site. According to local legend, Smbataberd fell to the Seljuk Turks when they employed a thirsty horse to sniff out the water supply: it came in an underground pipe from Tsakhatskar. This would indicate an 11th-century date. However, other reports suggest that the castle was defended until the 13th century, which would imply that it was eventually captured by the Mongols rather than the Seljuks.

Should you wish to walk to Smbataberd from **Yeghegis** village (the view of the fortress is actually better from this approach), the track begins at the western end of the village and is signposted.

**Yeghegis** The ruins of the ancient town of Yeghegis lie by the river of the same name. The town had two separate periods of prosperity: first, during the Syunik princedom (10th–11th century) at the end of which it was destroyed, possibly by an earthquake or volcano; and then under the Orbelians from the 13th century to the 15th. Present-day Yeghegis is the village to the northeast. It is a pleasant, unspoiled village with three churches and an old Jewish cemetery. The three-aisle basilica, the **Mother of God Church** with a grass-covered roof in the centre of the village, was built in 1708. Four massive pillars support the barrel-vaulted roof. The church is built into the hillside, a feature suggesting an earlier origin. Over the west door are carvings of two sirens. At the east end of the village the 13th-century **church of John the Baptist** is a small cross-dome church. However, the village's most notable church is the **Zorats (Army) Church** dedicated to St Stephen. It is highly unusual in that the congregation stood in the open air facing the altar. The roof was built to only cover the east end of the church and covers just the altar in the centre with a sacristy on each side. The name Zorats, and possibly the reason why it was an open-air structure, came from its use as the place where arms and horses were consecrated before battle. The church was constructed in 1303 by a grandson of Prince Tarsayich Orbelian, governor of the province of Syunik. Excavations have uncovered medieval foundations on the north side of the church and to the east are many tombstones and an extensive area with large boulders forming walls and pathways around a plateau overlooking the valley. In season the walnut tree planted below the church still yields excellent fruit.

The **Jewish cemetery** here was rediscovered in 1996 by the Bishop of Syunik. It is one of the oldest known in the world and has been excavated since 2000 by a team from the Jewish University of Jerusalem under Professor Michael Stone. It is reached by a footbridge over the Yeghegis River. So far more than 60 gravestones have been identified including those used for the foundations of the footbridge and others used in the foundations of a mill. At the cemetery, some of the stones are positioned on open graves while others are on sealed graves. A number of the stones have magnificent ornamentation. Some of the symbols on the Jewish gravestones – like a spiral wheel – were also in use on Armenian Christian stonecrafts around the same time. It is most interesting that the same decorative motifs were shared by Jews and Christians. While some of the inscriptions were worn down over the centuries, a lot of them are decipherable. One stone dated the 18th of Tishrei of AD1266 is of 'the virgin maiden, the affianced Esther, daughter of Michael. May her portion be with our matriarch Sarah.' The opposite side quotes 'Grace is a lie and beauty is vanity' (Proverbs 31:20) and continues with a statement that Esther was 'God-fearing'. Another gravestone contains an emotional statement from a father mourning his son's passing in which the father claims that the soul is eternal and cites passages from the book of Isaiah that relate to the resurrection of the dead.

Comparing the style of the Jewish stones with those in Christian cemeteries of the period, it seems likely that they were carved by the same craftsmen who served both communities. The evidence suggests that Jews were important members of the society at Yeghegis, probably engaged in flour milling, since the remains of three watermills have been uncovered in the Jewish district. On the evidence of the graves discovered, Jews probably arrived here in the 13th century during the period of Mongol rule, remained throughout the era of Turkmen control but left in the 15th, possibly around the time of Ottoman takeover.

Opposite the Jewish cemetery on the same side of the river as the road, there is a field where gravestones have been pushed over. This used to be an Azeri village before the war over Nagorno Karabagh.

**Aratesvank (monastery)**  Some 10km east of Yeghegis are the ruins of Arates Monastery. Few visitors reach it, apart from those with a particular penchant for monasteries. Beyond Yeghegis the road deteriorates but a 4x4 is not required. There are three small churches side by side – the 7th-century **St Sion Church** (probably the middle of the three), the 10th-century **Mother of God Church** and the 13th-century **St John the Baptist Church** – and a **gavit**, flagged with gravestones, built in 1265–70 by order of Prince Smbat Orbelian. Multiple small chapels lead off the churches. The village of Arates itself, having been an Azeri village, is deserted although the orchards are well tended. The steeply sided river gorge between Yeghegis and Hermon, the hills surrounding Arates and the wild flowers en route all make this an attractive extension to the visit of the Yeghegis Valley.

**Selim Caravanserai**  Also referred to as Orbelian's Caravanserai after the dynasty who built it, Selim Caravanserai is the best-preserved caravanserai in Armenia and one of the best preserved in the world; its remote site high on the Selim Pass (2,410m) prevented its being quarried for building materials. The caravanserai is situated just below the summit of the pass, with ample parking and a picnic area on-site, and affords wonderful views south along the valley, as well as access to the Gndasar and Vardenis mountain ranges to the west and east respectively.

Constructed of basalt and with a roof of flat tiles, the caravanserai is a long building with a single entrance at one end (having only one entrance made the building more readily defensible against thieves). To the left of the doorway of the entrance vestibule is a griffin while to the right there is a lion. Above it is an inscription in Persian, while inside the vestibule to the right there is one in Armenian, recording that the caravanserai was built in 1332 by Chesar Orbelian during the reign of Khan Abu Saeed II. The main hall of the caravanserai is divided into three naves by means of seven pairs of pillars. The two narrower side naves were used for the merchants and their wares while the animals were kept in the central one. Stone troughs were provided for feedstuffs for the animals and there is a basalt trough in one corner to supply them with water. Light and ventilation were provided by small openings in the roof but the interior is dark and a torch is useful. Looking at all these arrangements it is possible to capture an image of the life of the 14th-century merchants who passed this way, to an extent which can rarely be experienced anywhere in Europe. The restoration carried out in 1956–59 did nothing to mar the atmosphere and it is only to be hoped that the greatly increased numbers of visitors will leave it similarly unscathed.

**VAYK**  East of Yeghegnadzor, the M2 main road to Syunik passes through the large town of Vayk, which itself has little to distract the visitor but has all basic facilities, several supermarkets and food courts, a number of accommodation options and a private tourist information centre (page 324). It is also the closest major town to the sights of eastern and southern Vayots Dzor (page 339).

### EASTERN VAYOTS DZOR
**Herher Valley**  About 6.5km east of Vayk there is a junction signposted **Herher**. This road, which was undergoing reconstruction as far as Herher village at the time of research, follows the Herher river gorge and skirts the Herher Reservoir before reaching the village and its surrounding valley. Much of the east side of the valley constitutes the 61km$^2$ **Herher Open Woodland Sanctuary**, an official protected area since 1958. The village itself was resettled by Armenians from Persia in the early 19th century and now has a population of about 700. It is highly self-sufficient, with a

hydro-electric power source and a network of irrigation canals ensuring all the village gardens remain watered throughout the year, producing abundant fruit and vegetables to supplement the rich foraging opportunities for herbs, berries, mushrooms and wild vegetables. Hunting and logging in the sanctuary is strictly forbidden and remarkably well self-enforced. The result is a pristine yet almost unvisited pocket of countryside featuring oak and juniper forests, waterfalls, fortresses, volcanoes, river rapids and yet-to-be-investigated archaeological sites, as well as wildlife including bear, mouflon, Bezoar goat and eagle, not to mention several species of lizards and snakes (see page 76 for general comments on snakebites). All of this makes the valley certainly worth an overnight stay for those of an exploratory nature – note that there are no facilities in Herher besides a single shop of the open-on-demand variety. Walking routes are not yet marked but you should easily find someone to guide you. Local geology professor Samvel Arakelyan has published a small trilingual book listing seven suggested hiking routes together with background information; copies are available at his family's homestay, where they can also help you find a local guide (page 323).

South of the village, a tiny hermitage (1297) with a square western façade is visible on top of a small hill to the east. This is **Chikivank** (or St George), reachable in about 3km on foot from the village. Within the village itself there is the three-aisled, barrel-vaulted basilica of **St George** (locals call it St Karapet, meaning 'holy herald', ie: John the Baptist). The 19th-century restoration is probably of a much earlier church, given the evidence of stones with eye-holes and chambered graves in the surrounding cemetery. The east end of the church is built into the hillside, a feature of originally pagan sites. Here it is easy to see the deliberate use of turf on top of stone roof slabs. Old khachkars have been used as building material. There is a rather nice touch on the west façade where the gable end has been shaped around someone's head. Others were not so lucky; having been cut in half, their heads point in all directions.

Directly northeast of the village across the river, a prominent rock outcropping on a nearby spur conceals the remains of **Kapuyt Berd** (Blue Fortress). A large 14th-century stone inscription in classical Armenian can be found on the western approach, mentioning several people's names and that of a church – perhaps a list of donors. From the outcrop's summit, reinforcing walls can be easily identified, and the ruins of a village and its terraces on the hillside below are conspicuous.

North of the village are the twin churches of **St Sion** and **Mother of God** (villagers call the site Goshavank) perched on the edge of the gorge and surrounded with interesting khachkars. The monastery is first noted in the 8th century and was abandoned in 1604 at the time of the forced migration to Persia of thousands of Armenians, ordered by Shah Abbas during Persian–Ottoman clashes. **St Sion**, the older church, is built of rough-cut stone and, very unusually for a basilica church, has an apse at both eastern and western ends. **Mother of God Church** (1283) is built of smoother stone and has a double eastern apse, another uncommon feature.

Further upstream on an eastern tributary is a well-known **waterfall** with a very inviting plunge pool beneath it: bring bathing gear in summer. To the west, the domed peak dominating the skyline is the volcanic cone **Vayots Sar** (2,386m), or 'mountain of sorrows', in whose crater a small 8th-century chapel can be found, and whose last eruption supposedly gave the province its name. It is a relatively easy hike but longer than it may appear from Herher village; perhaps employ a local guide and 4x4 to take you to the base of the cone and walk from there.

Some 7km north of Herher is the even smaller and higher-altitude village of **Karmrashen**, whose inhabitants are mainly engaged in cattle herding and bee-keeping. The dirt road then continues northwest up the valley and over a 2,234m pass before descending to the **Yeghegis Valley** (page 331); a highly recommended scenic route if vehicle and season allow. As the crow flies it is not far from here to northern Syunik's Ughtasar petroglyphs (page 345), although it is much further by road. Petroglyphs are widely scattered over the mountains of this part of Armenia and there are some on the slopes of Muradsar which, being at a lower elevation, are accessible for a slightly longer period than those at Ughtasar (in mid-June the route had recently become snow-free). The **Muradsar petroglyphs** are at a height of 3,070m and are 26km from Herher village. An off-road vehicle is essential; LucyTour Resort Hotel (page 323) can arrange transportation and a guide. About 2km before the petroglyphs are reached the route passes a large 6,000-year-old cemetery.

### Gndevaz and Gndevank

On the main road slightly beyond the Herher junction the Arpa River bears north away from the M2 main road. There is a road each side of the river; the new road is up on the plateau on the east side of the river and allows tour bus access to Jermuk, while the old road follows the west bank of the river within the gorge itself and is far more spectacular. The closest vehicle access to the **monastery of Gndevank** is via this old road, about 11.5km from the junction with the main road, and is signposted as such. However, a little way beyond the Gndevank turn-off it is blocked to motor vehicles by several major landslides (though it is still possible to walk to Jermuk this way; see below).

Gndevank was founded in 936 by Princess Sophia of Syunik who claimed that 'Vayots Dzor was a ring without a jewel; but I built this monastery as the jewel for the ring'. The main church, dedicated to St Stephen, is of the cross-dome type with circular tambour and conical cupola. A gavit was added in 999. Unlike most gavits which are square, this is more like a barrel-vaulted tunnel leading to the church. Encircling fortified walls were added later, the southern and western stretches lined with other buildings used by the monks. The complex was restored between 1965 and 1969 following earthquake damage and underwent further restoration in 2013. There are some particularly fine gravestones here: one shows ibex being hunted alongside falconry while another depicts a boar hunt. There are picnic tables at the monastery and a spring.

It is possible to hike between Gndevank and the orchard-filled village of **Gndevaz** above, via two spectacular historical footpaths which can be combined into a loop. It takes about 45 minutes to descend; the walk up may take longer depending on your degree of fitness. The northernmost path is signposted; the southern alternative offers a short detour just below the village to an impressive cavern and (in spring and early summer) waterfall.

The blocked northern part of the **old road** to Jermuk, between the Gndevank turn-off and the southwest end of the Kechut Reservoir, is a real gem for walkers. It hugs the side of the narrow gorge underneath beetling cliffs with breathtaking views of the river and the ravine. Rockfalls continue and it would be unwise to walk this route at times of high avalanche or landslide risk; on the other hand the lack of motor traffic makes it prime wildlife-spotting territory. At the upstream end of the gorge, the road along the west side of the Kechut Reservoir provides access to Jermuk itself via a small cave shrine (look for the sign on the left of the road as the valley narrows close to the town). A good day's walking might involve a drop-off at Gndevaz followed by a hike down to Gndevank and the old road back up to Jermuk, or vice versa.

### Jermuk

Jermuk was a large and popular Soviet-era spa resort, and remains Armenia's primary medical tourism destination on account of the supposedly restorative properties of its **natural hot mineral** water **springs**. These are mainly favoured by Russians and the diaspora, as Western visitors may find it hard to get on board with the spirit of what was a very Soviet phenomenon – that of taking a holiday in a 'sanatorium', in which general recuperation was combined with a staggering variety of nature-based medical treatments. That aside, Jermuk's splendid setting among forested slopes, alpine meadows and distant peaks, together with its mild summer climate and well-kept parklands and boulevards, makes it worthy of a visit regardless. Some of the old sanatoria have been renovated and are combining this role with that of a modern hotel; several new hotels have also been built. The town is gradually losing its previously run-down air, although some derelict concrete buildings and wasteland remain, meaning that in the off-season Jermuk can still feel somewhat abandoned.

## ✗ **Where to eat and drink**   Map, below

✗ **Gndevank Restaurant**  24 Shahumyan St, next door to Jermuk Restaurant; ⏱ 09.00–midnight daily. A more limited menu than the Jermuk Restaurant but the food is satisfactory. Loud music in evenings.

✗ **Jermuk Restaurant**  22/2 Shahumyan St, near the Ani Hotel; ⏱ 08.00–midnight daily. The food is very good; their homemade wine rather 'young'. Can be very busy & noisy with loud music in evenings.

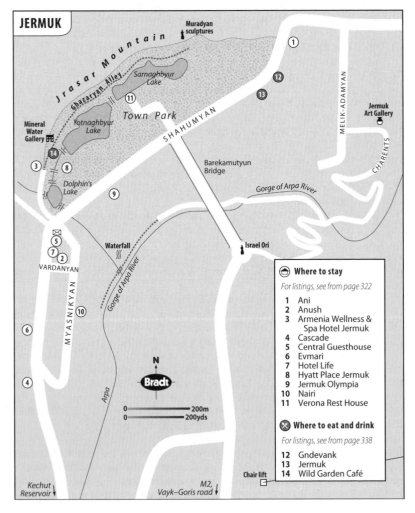

**JERMUK**

Muradyan sculptures

Jrasar Mountain

Ghazaryan Alley

Sarnaghbyur Lake

Yotnaghbyur Lake

**Town Park**

Mineral Water Gallery

SHAHUMYAN

MELIK-ADAMYAN

Jermuk Art Gallery

CHARENTS

Dolphin's Lake

Barekamutyun Bridge

Gorge of Arpa River

Waterfall

Gorge of Arpa River

Israel Ori

VARDANYAN

MYASNIKYAN

Arpa

**N**

**Bradt**

0 ——— 200m
0 ——— 200yds

Kechut Reservoir ↓

M2, Vayk–Goris road ↓

Chair lift

### 🏨 Where to stay
For listings, see from page 322

1  Ani
2  Anush
3  Armenia Wellness & Spa Hotel Jermuk
4  Cascade
5  Central Guesthouse
6  Evmari
7  Hotel Life
8  Hyatt Place Jermuk
9  Jermuk Olympia
10  Nairi
11  Verona Rest House

### ✗ Where to eat and drink
For listings, see from page 338

12  Gndevank
13  Jermuk
14  Wild Garden Café

🍴 **Wild Garden Café** Myasnikyan St, between the Hyatt Place & the Mineral Water Gallery; ⏰ 10.00–18.00 daily. Bright, modern & airy café serving light meals inc pizza, barbecue, etc & hot/cold drinks. Plentiful outdoor seating with good aspect over the lake. The music is quieter here.

**What to see and do** Shahumyan Street is the main road of the resort area. Along its western side is the **town park** with many statues and manmade lakes fed by springs and streams from the slopes of Mount Jrasar above. At the west end of the town park is the **Mineral Water Gallery**, a colonnaded building constructed in 1956 containing a row of urns, each of which has natural mineral water of a different temperature – from 30°C to 53°C (86°F to 127°F) – pouring into it, where visitors fill their mugs, jugs and vacuum flasks. From here the Ghazaryan Alley goes along the far side of the park lakes to the **Muradyan sculptures**, a series of ten busts of Armenian revolutionaries, some of which are beside the path while others nestle among the rocks and trees of the hillside. The **commercial centre** of Jermuk is centred on the southern part of Shahumyan Street. At the far end of the bridge over the Arpa Gorge is the **statue** of Israel Ori (1659–1711), Armenia's first diplomat, who from 1678 onwards travelled throughout Europe and Russia seeking protection for Armenia against the Persians and Turks, and who in 1709 headed the Armenian delegation to the Persian shah (king).

Down in the gorge is Jermuk's beautiful **cascade waterfall**, known locally as the Mermaid's Hair Falls, with water cascading some 70m over rocks. It is reached by a road which goes off just north of the Ani Hotel and zigzags down to a parking area in the gorge, from where the waterfall is a short walk. Jermuk would be a good centre for more serious hiking, especially in high summer, and indeed is one of the staging posts for forays into the Vardenis Range to the north, **Jermuk Hydrological State Sanctuary** to the east, and the Big Al and Little Al high-altitude lakes across the border in Nagorno Karabagh. However, there are no detailed maps beyond those mentioned on pages 65 and 112 and no marked trails; some of the more adventurous local operators and guides (page 67) do lead occasional expeditions.

The small **Jermuk Art Gallery** (1 Charents St; ☎0287 22132; ⏰ 10.30–17.30 Tue–Sun; guide in Armenian or Russian AMD1,500; AMD200) exhibits paintings from the last hundred years and includes evocative landscapes and portraits as well as abstract works. A two-seater **chair-lift** (⏰ 11.00–19.00 daily; return trip AMD1,500) at the new road's entry to the town carries passengers from an altitude of 2,100m to 2,500m. The ski area consists of a single 2.6km slope of medium difficulty; skis and accessories can be hired at the lower terminal. There are cafés (⏰ same hrs as ski lift) at both terminals. Talk of additional lifts and ski slopes continues to percolate but nothing has yet materialised.

**SOUTHERN VAYOTS DZOR** The southern side valleys of the Arpa River all play host to spectacular mountain landscapes, unusual historical sites and sparsely populated but welcoming villages in which tourism is barely seen. The ever-comprehensive Armeniapedia (w armeniapedia.org) mentions many of the more esoteric and remote sites; this section represents a selection of the most accessible.

Just east of Vayk on the M2, a good road leads to **Zaritap**, a centre of tobacco growing and the municipal seat of the surrounding villages. Keep right at the fork and continue with the river on the left to reach the new (ie: relocated due to unstable ground) village of **Martiros**. The village has a homestay and a couple of tiny shops; it is also on the route to the old village, first established in 1283 and containing a half-finished monastic complex. From here, signboards provide directions to the **Holy Mother of God** subterranean church some 2km southeast from the village, built by the Proshian family in 1286. It comprises a small entrance gavit, the main church and a small separate chapel. There is a little light inside from windows high up in the hillside but a torch is useful. Standing inside this extraordinary excavation, you find an interior similar to that seen in any normal Armenian church. It is possible to hike on a newly built and waymarked trail from here to the village of Gomk (or hike the same route from Gomk itself).

Opposite the junction for Martiros a dirt road leads across open fields to the ruins of **Horadis** village, in which stands the partly restored church of **St Nikoghos** – a 4x4 or a long walk is required to reach this remote site, in which only a couple of bee-keepers remain. The church is unusual for having a belfry above the entrance (the bell can be rung using the supplied rope!). The village is said to have been abandoned in Soviet times when central planners decided it was too remote to qualify for utilities and infrastructure. South of these sites are the border villages of Khndzorut, Nor Aznaberd and Bardzruni; their exposure and proximity to Azeri military positions (as little as a few hundred metres in some cases) excludes them from being recommended at this time.

Back in Zaritap, forking left at the junction mentioned on page 339 (and perhaps asking locals for directions) leads to a broken asphalt road to **Gomk**, whose resident families are Armenians from Azerbaijan displaced during the Karabagh war. This picturesque village has a highly recommended B&B (page 323) with an attached horse farm, and is a good staging post for hiking and horseback riding in the nearby gorges. Particularly spectacular is the canyon directly east of the tiny hamlet of **Kapuyt**, from where waymarked **hiking trails** lead to (among other places) a magnificent natural rock arch and a collection of 10th- to 15th-century inscriptions and khachkars carved directly into a rock face. Good rock climbing is also reported in the valley. Energetic hikers can climb an ancient trail up the impossible-looking south side of the gorge to the clifftop before looping around to the north side, and either back down to Gomk via the abandoned former Azeri village of **Akhta**, or onwards to Artavan in the valley to the north via a beautiful trail through oak forests. The whole area is noted as a habitat for bears, though you will be lucky to see anything other than their scat – more likely you will bump into a herd of roaming cattle grazing the steep slopes.

**Artavan** is reachable by road from a junction further east along the M2 main road. The village sits beneath a splendid oak forest with a 17th-century bridge spanning the river; a single homestay makes it possible to explore the region's landscapes in more depth. Several forest trails lead to as-yet-undocumented archaeological sites including an ancient village and forge, as well as to a permanent ice cave which stays frozen all year round (a local guide may be necessary; ask at the homestay). On the slopes and meadows to the east can be found a nicely situated **cascade waterfall** and a reed-filled **mountain lake** whose appearance from above is said to resemble a map of the world. On the ridge north of the lake are the spectacularly located remains of **Andranik's Fortress**, and the watershed in general is dotted with the ruins of ancient settlements. Dirt roads to haymaking fields make these sites easily accessible; the area in general lends itself well to a day or two of exploration. Trails to these and other sites were being waymarked at the time of research, and the route of the Transcaucasian Trail (see box, page 114) was planned to link Martiros, Gomk and Artavan into a continuous hiking route; see page 111 for general comments on hiking.

# SYUNIK PROVINCE

Armenia's southernmost province is dominated by vertiginous mountain ranges and the second-largest forested region in the country. Syunik, also known as Zangezur, has two well-known historical sites (**Tatev** and **Karahunj**) and one (**Ughtasar**) which, although much less well known, ranks as one of the most interesting in the country. Syunik's long western border with Nakhichevan is closed and heavily militarised. The even longer eastern border with the self-declared Republic of Artsakh (Nagorno Karabagh) has one main road crossing between Goris and Shushi/Stepanakert. The far south along the Iranian border is the warmest part of Armenia and a centre for growing certain fruit to which this climate is better suited; there is a single border crossing with Iran at Agarak. Two main roads connect Kapan and Meghri, one via the mining town of Kajaran in the west and a newer, quieter road through Shikahogh State Reserve (page 366) in the east. The routing of this new road caused

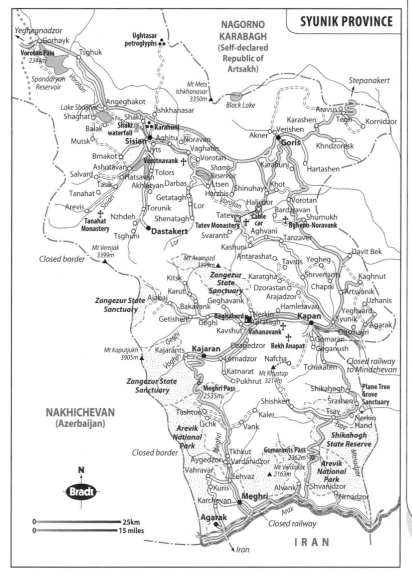

controversy because of fears about the impact on wildlife and also because it could open the area to illegal logging; it was completed in 2006 regardless. Both roads traverse spectacular scenery and if possible it is highly recommended to travel both as a loop. There are several other protected areas including Arevik National Park and Khustup State Sanctuary: visitors who make the effort to explore these regions will find they have the stunning landscapes practically to themselves.

**GETTING THERE AND AROUND** Most visitors enter Syunik along the main road from Vayots Dzor via the **Vorotan Pass** (2,344m), which is marked by two austere concrete belltowers on each side of the road: the symbolic Gates of Syunik. The road then descends past the Spandaryan and Shaghat reservoirs running parallel to the Vorotan River which lies some distance to the south. Pot-holes can be a significant problem on this stretch of road. **Minibuses** run daily from Yerevan to Sisian, Goris, Kapan, Meghri and Agarak (page 87). Limited regional services also operate between the main towns and the surrounding villages. A few sites can only be reached by walking or with a 4x4. A high-speed **cable car** to Tatev Monastery has cut travelling time somewhat as the road journey can terminate at Halidzor. Still, allow the best part of a day if travelling from Yerevan. Daily **domestic flights** between Kapan and Yerevan were supposed to commence in 2018 but were still not operational at the time of research. It is also possible to enter Syunik from **Iran** via the sole border crossing at Agarak, where the same procedures are followed as at all other border crossings (page 69). The crossing can become very busy during Iranian public holidays.

**WHERE TO STAY** Sisian, Goris and Kapan all have accommodation and can act as bases from which to visit their respective parts of the province. Goris is the most popular and has the best variety of overnight options. The sights of the far south can be covered in a day trip from Kapan; there is also good accommodation in Meghri. Those travelling to or from Iran may prefer the convenience of Agarak itself, which has a handful of budget and mid-range options. Tatev village has numerous homestay-style B&Bs and a camping area from which the region can be explored in depth; Halidzor (at the far end of the cable car) has a couple of more upscale places. Motel-style accommodation can be found at various locations on the main road, though being on a major trucking route these establishments are not necessarily the most reputable. As well as the accommodation listed below, **homestays** in other villages can be arranged through tour operators in Yerevan (page 67) and the tourist information offices in Tatev, Goris and Sisian. Where listings are plotted on a map, this is indicated below. See page 92 for general comments on accommodation.

## Sisian
Map, page 348

**MJA Resort** (10 rooms) 9km from Sisian between Ashotavan & Hatsavan villages; m 041 374100; e info@resortmja.am; w www.resortmja. am. Upscale & very well-appointed new property in the countryside outside of Sisian with a wide range of services, as well as sgl/dbl/trpl/suite rooms & apts. Favoured by visiting diplomats & families looking for a quiet retreat. On-site bar & restaurant. Swimming pool, laundry & room service available. **$$$**

**Basen Hotel** (23 rooms) 2 Ara Manukyan St; 02832 4662; m 093 434727; e contact@

basenhotel.am; w basenhotel.am. Owner Hasmik speaks excellent English, is a font of knowledge on the local area & hiking opportunities, & can arrange tours of all types. The hotel comprises 3 separate, fully renovated buildings, each with several dbl/trpl rooms. Restaurant in separate building with outdoor terrace serving excellent food, & a small souvenir shop selling local handmade ceramics & artwork. Traditional *tonir* bakery on-site with demonstrations on request. **$$**

**Lalaner Hotel** (16 rooms) 29 Sisakan St; 02832 6600; m 091 481606; e info@lalahotel.am; w lalahotel.am. This hotel on the main square was being extended at the time of update. Sauna (AMD10,000/hr). Restaurant. Online reservations possible via **w** armhotels.am. **$$**

🏠 **Zorats Qarer B&B** (6 rooms) 29b Nelson Stepanyan St; **☎** 02830 4242; **m** 093 988809; **e** suren@tourism-sisian.com; **w** tourism-sisian. com; **f**. Family-run B&B in the north of the town. Owner Dr Suren's wife speaks English. Can arrange local tours. Home-cooked meals on request. **$$**

🏠 **Dina Hotel** (31 rooms) 35 Sisakan St; **☎** 02830 3333; **m** 093 334392; **e** sisiano@mail. ru; **w** dinahotel.am. Long-established budget option with a somewhat sparse feel, but clean & renovated, & the staff are cheerful & friendly. There is information about local sites of interest & staff can arrange transport & guides. The small restaurant can provide meals with advance notice. Sgl rooms without bathroom AMD3,000 pp, b/fast AMD2,000 pp. En-suite dbl rooms AMD12,000–14,000. **$**

## Goris
Map, page 355

🏠 **Hotel Christy** (20 rooms) 9 Mashtots St; **m** 055 019006, 077 000047; **e** christyhotel@ gmail.com. A welcoming, warm hotel with good hot showers & sgl/dbl/trpl/family rooms. Very close to town centre. Rooms & dining room non-smoking. Meals available with 2hrs notice. **$$**

🏠 **Hotel Mina** (40 rooms) 169 Mashtots St; **☎** 0284 30119; **m** 099 030119; **e** hotelminagoris@ gmail.com; **w** hotel-mina.am. A little further from the centre than most other hotels, on the main road to Stepanakert. This smart, business-oriented hotel has sgl/dbl/trpl/suite rooms & a swimming pool, gym & restaurant. Cards accepted. **$$**

🏠 **Hotel Mira** (6 rooms) 24/3 Ankakhutyan St; **☎** 0284 24880/1; **m** 093 595947, 096 595947; **e** mira.hotel@mail.ru. A family-run guesthouse with a personal touch in a renovated house on 3 floors. Own fruit from garden. Shared kitchen, lunch/dinner by arrangement. **$$**

🏠 **Hotel Mirhav** (31 rooms) 100 Mashtots St; **☎** 0284 24612/32; **m** 098/099 284402; **e** hotelmirhav@yahoo.com. The best-known boutique hotel in Goris, tastefully decorated in natural materials. The restaurant serves excellent meals (the apricot pilaf is wonderful); 1–2hrs' notice is required. Some of the smaller rooms are quite cramped. The hotel stocks a good range of postcards & maps. Cards accepted. Discounts for groups & children. **$$**

🏠 **Hotel Goris** (20 rooms) 53 Khorenatsi St; **☎** 0284 30003. The approach to this Soviet building is not encouraging, but once inside you will find a renovated hotel with a bar & restaurant. Reviews were mixed at the time of research, however. Lunch/dinner by arrangement. **$–$$**

🏠 **Eden Hostel & Guesthouse** (5 rooms) 4 Orbelyanner St; **m** 043 615999; **e** edenhouse2016@ gmail.com; **w** edenhostel.am. New in 2016, this quiet & cosy family-run hostel has 18 beds spread over 2 dorms, 1 trpl & 2 twin. Shared kitchen & bathroom, nicely decorated communal area. The property has an extensive orchard/garden for summer use. Laundry AMD1,000/load. **$**

🏠 **Hostel Goris** (3 rooms) 55 Khorenatsi St; **☎** 0284 21886; **m** 093 425220; **e** jirmar28@ freenet.am. The 3 rooms (2 dbl, 1 trpl) share 1 bathroom. A favourite backpacker joint. The host, Jirayr Martirosyan, is an artist & member of the Armenian Painters' Union. His gallery is in a rock cave & visitors are welcome. Guided tours of Goris can be arranged (AMD15,000 inc lunch). Members of the family speak English, Russian & Turkish. Meals for non-residents can be arranged with a day's notice. B/fast AMD1,500 pp. **$**

🏠 **Hotel Vivas** (6 rooms) 65 Syunik St; **☎** 0284 24812; **m** 093 746892; **e** info@vivas.am; **w** vivas.am. One of the oldest B&Bs in Goris with a cheerful, helpful proprietor. Only 2 of the rooms en suite; others share a bathroom. Restaurant, order in advance. Accepts cards. **$**

## Kapan
Map, page 359

🏠 **Fenix Complex** (21 rooms) 8/1 Aram Manukyan St; **m** 093 666669/449944. Kapan's newest mid-range hotel opened in 2016 & is a 20min walk from the city centre along the south side of the Voghji River. Sgl/twin/dbl/trpl en-suite rooms all have lounges, minibars & AC. Use of large gym & 25m indoor swimming pool inc. Billiard hall (AMD2,000/ hr) & massage parlour (AMD5,000 for a 45min full body massage). Pleasant terrace restaurant overlooks the Voghji with live music every evening & is open to non-residents. Cards accepted. **$$–$$$**

🏠 **Hotel Darist** (32 rooms) 1a Aram Manukyan St; **☎** 0285 62662; **e** hotel_darist@ yahoo.com. Decent mid-range option in central Kapan. Reception on 4th floor (room 404), rooms on 3rd & 4th floors, restaurant on 2nd floor. There is a lift. The restaurant serves good food & is open to non-residents although the occasional live music is too loud for some tastes. Booklet (AMD1,000) about Kapan & map (AMD500) of the town available. **$$**

🏠 **Hotel Lernagorts** (33 rooms) 2 Demirchyan Sq; 📞 0285 28039; e lernagorts@mail.ru; w lernagortshotel.am. A budget Soviet-era hotel renovated to a good standard. Price depends on room size, facilities & occupancy; sgl/dbl/twin/trpl en-suite rooms available. Basic b/fast AMD1,000. Some English spoken. Has a pleasant new outdoor café/restaurant (📞 0285 28473) in front & to the left of the main entrance. Lifts. **$**

🏕 **ARK Armenia Campsite** 1.2km up Azatamartikneri St in Baghaburj district; m 093 812683, 098 887894; e arkarmenia@gmail.com; w arkarmenia.com. Kapan's only campsite, with wooden sleeping cabins for rent, tent space & a small outdoor kitchen, all set in a verdant permaculture garden on the outskirts above town. Facilities are very rustic & will mainly appeal to the adventurous. Accommodation can also be 'paid for' by volunteering for the NGO that runs the place (see opposite). Call in advance, as the site is locked when vacant. **$**

## Meghri

Map, page 364

🏠 **Arevik Guesthouse** (4 rooms) 20 Mejnumynan St, Pokr Tagh; m 077 305124 (Armine, the owner). Delightful restoration of a 17th- or 18th-century house, with a monastic feel, in the old district of Meghri. To find it, follow the signs for the church at the top of Pokr Tagh, climbing through the maze of streets, alleys & stairs. Shortly before reaching the church, look for the faded placard on wooden dbl doors. Vehicles have to be left some distance below, beside a white garage door with green lettering. Rooms (1 twin, 1 dbl, 1 trpl, 1 quad with en suite) around an attractive courtyard. Dining room downstairs. Quiet, no TV/radio. Wonderful meals by advance arrangement. The drawback is that the entrance is padlocked shut at night on the outside, meaning that guests are locked in. The only other way out is via balconies in 2 of the bedrooms, to the garden

of the house below & it is a long way down. If you do decide to stay here, & unless the arrangements have changed, make sure you have the keyholder's mobile number (but note she lives some distance away in the town). **$**

🏠 **Haer B&B** (5 rooms) 14 Qarakert; m 093 545414. B&B sign outside. Established in 2003, this family-run homestay/B&B is a little way north of Mets Tagh centre but has long been welcoming guests in Meghri in renovated twin/trpl rooms with shared bathroom. Some English spoken. B/fast AMD2,000, dinner AMD4,000. **$**

🏠 **Hotel Edem** (8 rooms) 31 Zoravar Andranik St; m 077 242526. Dbl, trpl & quad rooms. One of several basic hotels on the main road south opposite the turn-off into the town. Restaurant. **$**

🏠 **Rosa's B&B** (3 rooms) 300m uphill from the main road junction on the H50 provincial road; m 077 154501. A second homestay option in Meghri, this one in Pokr Tagh. Twin/trpl rooms in a family home with a large garden, relaxing shaded terrace & communal dining room. Note no sign visible from the street. **$**

## Elsewhere in the province

🏠 **Hostel Samuel** (3 rooms) Agarak; m 094 842422. Opened in 2017 to cater for budget travellers crossing the border; as such it is not in the town but rather a 10min walk from the border checkpoint itself. To reach it, proceed 400m west beyond the turn-off for the checkpoint, then turn right on to a dirt road for 150m to reach the gate of the property. There are 9 dorm beds in 3 basic but clean & modern trpl rooms, each of which has a bathroom. The owners have converted a shipping container into a dining room. Meals extra & on request. (Samuel is the name of the family's horse!) **$**

🏠 **Hotel Kajaran** (48 rooms) 3 Abovyan St; m 098 575810, 077 180577; e kajaran.hotel@ mail.ru. If desperate to stay in Kajaran, try the renovated Soviet hotel owned by the Zangezur Copper Molybdenum Combine. B/fast AMD1,500–2,000 pp. Restaurant, but order in advance. There is a 2nd building with cheaper rooms (AMD5,000/ bed). Cards accepted. **$**

✕ **WHERE TO EAT AND DRINK** The main towns and tourist destinations have standalone eating places. All homestays can provide evening meals by arrangement. Many of the hotels listed can also provide a full meal with notice; where they have walk-in restaurants this is mentioned in the reviews above. There are summer cafés in Sisian (page 347), Goris (page 356), Old Khndzoresk (page 357), Tatev village near the cable-car terminal (page 351), and Kapan (page 360). Eating places exist on the M2 main road as far as Kapan and Kajaran, but the roads south to Meghri and Agarak are poorly provided for, particularly the new road through Shikahogh. See individual destination sections for additional listings.

**OTHER PRACTICALITIES**  Sisian, Goris and Kapan are the larger towns and have most facilities but bring any special requirements with you. There are tourist information offices next to Goris and in Tatev Monastery; one was under development in central **Sisian** at the time of research and was planned to open by the end of 2018. **Goris Tourist Information Office** (3 Ankakhutyan St; ⏰ 09.30–18.00 Mon–Fri; ☏ 0284 22690; m 077 277765; e touristeoffice_goris@yahoo.fr) is staffed by volunteers, so opening hours can vary. English and French are spoken. They have some information leaflets and basic maps of Goris, can help to arrange homestays, and offer a 2-hour tour of Goris. Ara Atasunts of **Goris Tours** (m 094 002322; e goristours@gmail. com; w goris.tours) is one of the best local guides in town and speaks excellent English. **Sisian's tourist information centre** (38/1 Sisakan St; m 093 262533; ⓕ SisianDevelopmentInitiativesNGO; ⏰ 10.00–17.00 Mon–Fri) opened in October 2018 and is run by a local NGO, whose very knowledgeable director also manages Basen Hotel (page 342). **Tatev Information Centre and Café** (page 350) is opposite the cable-car terminal car park just above the monastery. The privately run centre can arrange homestays, guides for hikes, and pretty much anything else you might wish for. In Kapan there is no information centre but a local social enterprise **ARK Armenia** (4/4 Charents St; m 093 812683, 098 887894; e arkarmenia@gmail.com; w arkarmenia. com) expressly offers language support and information to tourists in the region, particularly regarding hiking and ecotourism. Also in Kapan is the administrative headquarters of **Zangezur Biosphere Complex** (page 366), whose tourism division is the first port of call if you wish to visit protected areas in the far south.

As with Vayots Dzor, walkers and hikers should take precautions regarding the possible presence of snakes (page 76).

**UGHTASAR**  Visitors wishing to see the immensely worthwhile and fascinating **petroglyphs** at Ughtasar will need to arrange a local guide and probably transport via a travel agent or one of the Sisian or Goris hotels. The 17km track climbs 1,400m from the nearest settlement, requiring a very capable 4x4 and some walking at the far end. The petroglyphs, all above 3,300m elevation, are accessible only from July to September because of snow and it can be bitterly cold even in summer. To anyone who has seen supposed rock carvings in museums the petroglyphs here are an absolute revelation with numerous designs scattered on boulders over a large area. The 1.5km × 1km caldera is beautiful in itself with the eroded rim of the volcano towering above wide areas of natural grassland and seasonal pools. Most of the petroglyphs are on boulders around the permanent glacial lake within the caldera. It is also the haunt of bears and wolves, as is attested by the droppings and footprints.

Petroglyphs, called 'goat letters' in Armenian, are found in several parts of Armenia. They are scattered over tens of square kilometres at sites in the mountains of Syunik, but these at Ughtasar are among the more accessible and many thousands of petroglyphs have been recorded here. Some of the carvings depict animals, mostly the wild animals of the region but also domestic ones. Wild goats are especially common. There are carvings of hunting scenes and ones showing the impedimenta of hunting. Birds are rarely depicted, while snakes and leopards feature more frequently. People also feature in scenes depicting dancers, either two dancers together or communal dancing. Some rocks have just a single design but others have a whole collection of carvings, as many

Although carved on rock the petroglyphs are fragile, many of them eroding in the harsh climate. They have also suffered damage from visitors walking on the carved surfaces (and from graffiti). Please help to prevent further damage to this wonderful rock art and the delicate balance of the site's rich natural environment.

**NEVER**
- Stand or walk on the carved surfaces
- Touch the panels unnecessarily
- Use any substance to enhance the carvings
- Use anything (including water) to 'clean' the rock surface; never try to remove graffiti
- Remove lichen from rock art panels
- Remove turf from buried or partially buried panels
- Scratch anything on or close to the carved panels
- Make fires close to rock carvings or light candles on the rocks

**ALWAYS**
- Take all litter away with you
- Take all food away; it is dangerous if the bears and other wild animals which frequent the site associate visitors with food
- Leave the carved rocks and other archaeological features as you find them
- Pass on this advice to others visiting the site

as 50 in extreme cases. The presence of hunting scenes and cattle has led to speculation that the people who carved the rocks lived partly by hunting and partly by animal husbandry, presumably pasturing their animals here in summer. They must have been at least semi-nomadic since it would not be possible to survive here in winter. The age of the carvings is difficult to ascertain but the majority of carvings at Ughtasar and elsewhere in Armenia probably date from the 5th to the 2nd millennium BC. A team of British and Armenian archaeologists is systematically surveying the petroglyphs at Ughtasar. Details of their work and results, including photographs, can be found at w ughtasarrockartproject.org. Members of the team have provided advice (see box, above) on caring for rock art.

**KARAHUNJ** (Note that Karahunj is off the M2 main road, just west of the more easterly turn-off for Sisian; it is not near the village of Karahunj to the south of Goris.) Much better known than the petroglyphs is another, slightly more recent site. Karahunj (also known as Zorats Karer) is sometimes called Armenia's Stonehenge, although the appellation is misleading since the two look very different. The whole site occupies about 7ha of plateau at the edge of a small ravine in the hills above the Vorotan River. The area is covered with numerous stone circles, cists and mounds as well as the best-known arrangement of standing stones which comprises 204 rough-hewn stones. These are arranged in an elaborate layout and the most quoted theory is that they formed an ancient astronomical observatory dating from sometime prior to 2000BC. The stones are basalt and the largest, 3m tall, weighs 10 tonnes. Of the stones, 76 have apertures near the top. The configuration is of 39 stones laid in an oval formation with its main axis running east–west for a distance of 43m. Within this oval are some contemporary graves. Bisecting the oval is an arc comprising a further 20 stones. Three arms of stones lie off this central shape running to the north, south and southeast. The north and south arms are much longer than the southeast arm and bend west towards their tips. Stones with apertures occur only in the arms but not all stones in the arms have apertures.

There has been much theorising on how the monument was used. It certainly seems clear that the apertures must be significant, but they are too large (at least 5cm diameter) to look through a single one in a precise direction and they don't seem to be lined up with each other for looking through pairs of apertures, which would have facilitated more precise observation. Conceivably the stones could have been used for observing the moon, but observation of stars seems difficult to imagine. In 2000 a team of archaeologists from the University of Munich in conjunction with the Armenian Academy of Sciences examined the site. Their opinion was that it is mainly a necropolis from the Middle Bronze Age to the Iron Age, citing the tombs found in the area. Later, they suggest, possibly in the Hellenistic/Roman period (c300BC–AD300), the site was used as a refuge with a wall of rocks and soil, the large vertical stones (today the only remaining elements) reinforcing the structure.

Some sizeable lizards (40cm in length) of rather prehistoric appearance clamber about on the stones. They are Caucasian agama (*Laudakia caucasia*), a species, despite its name, with a range from northeast Turkey to Pakistan.

**SISIAN** Sisian is the northernmost city in Syunik, known for its cool climate and bisected by the Vorotan River which broadens in this area. While the city hasn't seen as much development as others in the province, it was in Soviet times an important hub with its own airport and much industry. Today it is a rather low-key place with relatively few visitors, though the surrounding countryside is replete with interesting sights and quiet back roads and is by all accounts excellent walking, fishing, hunting and even ski-touring country.

**Sisakan Street** and parallel **Israelyan Street**, on the north side of the river, have most of the facilities including the **tourist information centre** (38/1 Sisakan St; m 093 262533; ⓕ SisianDevelopmentInitiativesNGO; ⏰ 10.00–17.00 Mon–Fri), as well as several cafés and all of the accommodation (avoid the so-called 'bar' opposite Dina Hotel, however, unless you are looking for additional services from the waitresses). Across the main bridge, the south side of town, known as **Getap** (Riverbank), has a couple of eateries and the best supermarket in town (Sisian City), as well as a functioning Soviet-era children's funfair hidden in overgrown parkland just to the east of the bridge.

## ✖ Where to eat and drink  Map, page 348

✖ **Jrahars (Mermaid) Restaurant**  39 Israelyan St; ☎02832 5386; m 094 866808; ⏰ 09.30–22.00 daily. Slightly hard to find – go down the steps opposite Rico supermarket at the northeast corner of the bridge over the river. This basic restaurant with private dining rooms serves a limited 2-page Armenian menu of barbecues, mains, soups, salads & side dishes.

🍴 **Flamenco Café-Pizzeria**  1/1 Vorotan St; m 093 550518; ⏰ 11.00–23.00 daily. Clean & modern new 1st-floor café serving a wide variety of mains, eg: pizza, pasta, burgers and Georgian-style *khachapuri*. Good Italian-style coffee. Outdoor seating on terrace. Serves cocktails in the evenings.

**What to see and do**  If you have a good imagination it is possible to imagine the 'pearl of Armenia' at its peak while strolling along once-majestic riverside promenades, the pedestrian footbridges at each end of town allowing a long walking

6

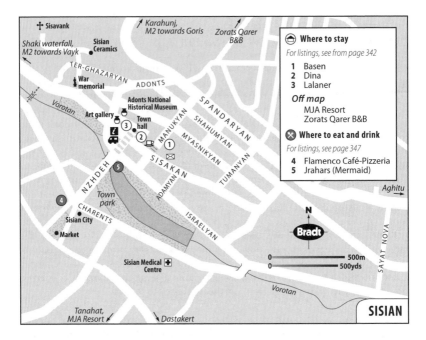

Map labels:
Sisavank
Karahunj, M2 towards Goris
Zorats Qarer B&B
Shaki waterfall, M2 towards Vayk
Sisian Ceramics
TER-GHAZARYAN
War memorial
ADONTS
Adonts National Historical Museum
Vorotan
Art gallery
Town hall
SPANDARYAN
MANUKYAN
SHAHUMYAN
MYASNIKYAN
TUMANYAN
Aghitu
SISAKAN
ADAMIAN
NZHDEH
Town park
CHARENTS
ISRAELYAN
Sisian City
Market
SAYAT NOVA
N
Bradt
0 — 500m
0 — 500yds
Sisian Medical Centre
Vorotan
Tanahat, MJA Resort
Dastakert
SISIAN

Where to stay
For listings, see from page 342
1 Basen
2 Dina
3 Lalaner
Off map
MJA Resort
Zorats Qarer B&B
Where to eat and drink
For listings, see page 347
4 Flamenco Café-Pizzeria
5 Jrahars (Mermaid)

loop. Should you happen to be in Sisian at the end of July, you may be lucky enough to happen upon the city's annual **raspberry festival**.

Some material excavated from Karahunj is in the **Adonts National Historical Museum** (1 Adonts St; ☎ 02832 3331; ⊕ 10.00–17.00 Tue–Sun; guided tour in English AMD2,000; photographic fee AMD1,000; adult AMD400) in the centre of Sisian. In the small park outside is a good collection of gravestones in the form of sheep, as well as stones bearing petroglyphs which were (perhaps ill-advisedly) relocated from Ughtasar (page 345) and have now been defaced; booklets about the stones and about other items in the museum are on sale inside. On the opposite side of the park is the **art gallery** (m 094 236361; ⊕ 10.30–17.45 Tue–Sun; guided tour in English AMD1,000; adult AMD500) with exhibitions on rotation in the main gallery, as well as a room dedicated to local Sisian artists and a first-floor exhibition of Aghtamar cathedral in present-day Turkey.

In the hilly northwest of the town can be found the workshop of **Sisian Ceramics** (42 Grigor Lusavorich St; m 093 615661; visits by appointment) in which pottery demonstrations and classes can be arranged and handmade ceramics purchased. Nearby **Sisavank** is a fine early church dedicated to St John. Similar in style to the church of St Hripsime at Etchmiadzin, this was built of basalt by Prince Kohazat and Bishop Hovsep I between 670 and 689. Like St Hripsime it has three-quarter-circle ante-rooms leading into the corner rooms. It is notable for its regular geometrical composition; all four apses are of equal size, as are the ante-rooms; the volume under the dome is an exact square in plan; there are two deep triangular niches on all façades. Of cross-dome style, it has a conical cupola supported by a tambour, which is octagonal internally but 12-sided externally, decorated with 12 graceful arcatures with twin half-colonnettes: a window is positioned directly over each of the four apses. The interior of the church is decorated by a sort of frieze depicting vine leaves and grapes which runs around most of it, presumably a reference to Jesus being the true vine since this is not a district traditionally associated with winemaking. The altar table with a carved eagle on its front is new (2001) and was carved by the son of the present caretaker. The font, to the left of the *bema*, is also new (2008) and was carved by the caretaker's grandson. The church has a small collection of old books, the oldest dating from 1686, and also some miniatures by Eduard Ghazaryan carved on items such as rice grains, which can be viewed through a microscope.

## AROUND SISIAN

**North of Sisian** A few kilometres northwest of Sisian is the **Shaki Waterfall** (⏰ 11.00–18.00 daily; the flow is shared with the hydro-electric station so the sluice is on a timer) on a tributary of the Vorotan River. While not large by global standards it is still impressive. It can be reached via Sisian's western connecting road with the M2 main highway: the junction is just south of the village of Shaki itself. After about 2km you come to the hydro-electric station. There is no signage but do not be deterred; pass through the station's grounds and continue to a parking area. From here, the path to the waterfall follows the stream for a couple of hundred metres to the waterfall. Those with a head for heights can scramble up beside it, cross the top via stepping stones, and return on the opposite bank.

From the same point, it is possible to walk beside the river along the beautiful gorge to the Shaghat Reservoir and the village of **Angeghakot**, a sprawling settlement perched on the valley side with excellent views into the Vorotan Valley and several unique sites of its own. The **Shaghat** area is known to archaeologists as the site of several Bronze Age settlements, as well as for 5th-century fortifications of what was then the Kingdom of Syunik.

**Southeast of Sisian** To the southeast there are several seldom-visited points of interest set in dramatic and deepening valleys. Stay on the north side of the river and follow Sisakan Street out of Sisian towards the village of **Vorotan**. If asking for directions (the road out of Sisian is confusing at times) note that locals may still refer to Vorotan by its old name, Urut. After about 5km the first village is **Aghitu** where there is an unusual 6th- or 7th-century **funerary monument** to an unknown individual, unlike anything else in the country apart from the monument at Odzun Church in Lori province. The scenic road continues to the **monastery of Vorotnavank**. The oldest church, dedicated to **St Stephen**, was built in 1000 by Queen Shahandukht. It is barrel-vaulted and has a much lower gavit on the west side. (Beware the extremely deep hole at the west end of the gavit.) In 1007 the queen's son, Sevada, built a second church, dedicated to **St John the Baptist**. There are remains of frescoes on the north wall and in the apse. It is a cross-dome construction and lies to the southeast of the first church. Both churches have arcaded galleries, but of different styles and presumably of different dates. A further smaller church, various service buildings and a fortified wall complete the complex. There was severe damage here in the 1931 earthquake but it has mostly been repaired. There is a plethora of gravestones which have rich figure carving, some of which have at some point been incorporated into the buildings.

A little further on are the scant remains of the **fortress of Vorotnaberd** on top of a steep hill to the left. This was a key site in Armenian history from AD450 when it was a stronghold of rebels under Vardan Mamikonian. It then changed hands many times: to the Seljuk Turks in 1104, recaptured by the Armenians in 1219, taken by the Mongols in 1386 who returned it to the Orbelians, conquered again by the Turks in 1407 then recovered by David Bek (page 20) in 1724. It is a short but difficult climb to the top. There is not much to see of its momentous past apart from low remains spread over two hills – and the view. If you don't cross the river but detour through the village of **Vorotan**, turn right through some derelict Soviet buildings rather than left into the village to find a **hot spring** which is piped into a pool. Were it not for the derelict buildings and litter it would be an idyllic place to soak outdoors amid the mountains. The road through the village then crosses the **Melik Tangi bridge** of 1855, directly below Vorotnaberd, before rejoining the main route through the valley past Shamb Reservoir. The road terminates at the tiny village of **Ltsen**, from where a challenging 15km dirt track leads through the woods and over the hills to Tatev (see below). In the vicinity of Ltsen is a small **hermitage** of 1347 known simply as Anapat, whose modest structure has become curiously embraced by a singular juniper tree estimated to be up to 600 years old.

## Southwest of Sisian

Heading southwest, a road passes north of the Tolors Reservoir via Ashotavan and Hatsavan to follow the Sisian River. The journey along the valley is extremely beautiful and worth experiencing for its own sake. Just after a road branches off right for Tanahat village, the remains of **Tanahat Monastery** can be seen on an outcrop on the valley side across the river. Unlike its namesake, Tanahat Monastery in Vayots Dzor, this monastery is very ruinous, but reaching it involves a pleasant walk with many flowers in early summer and myriads of butterflies in midsummer. There is a footbridge across the river some way past the monastery. It has partly collapsed but it is still possible to cross. A footpath leads across the hill to the monastery. At times it may be possible to wade across or ford the river in a vehicle just after the road branches off to Tanahat village, but this is impossible when the river is in spate. The pink 5th-century single-nave church has remnants of carved tulip-like decoration – highly appropriate since wild white tulips are one of the earliest flowers to appear here after the snow has melted. Some of the graves in the cemetery look very like the chambered tombs of northwest Europe, the burial vault being covered by up to three large slabs. One 11th-century khachkar found here re-used a stone with an earlier cuneiform inscription; it is now in the museum at Erebuni.

## TATEV

Syunik's best-known historical site, Tatev Monastery, is dramatically situated on the cliffs above a deep section of the Vorotan Gorge. The farming village of **Tatev** itself has precious little else to offer, but several good hikes begin here and the abundance of **homestay** accommodation makes it a good base for exploring the area. There is a **camping** area just uphill from the monastery on the left; ask at the information centre (see below). A couple of cafés and restaurants can be found by the road leading down to the monastery, as well as lines of stalls selling trinkets to tourists, all overlooked by an unfortunate forest of high-voltage electricity pylons. If you plan to do more than simply visit the monastery, be sure to check in at the **visitor information centre and café** (m 093 880230; e tatevinfocenter@gmail.com; w tatevinfo.com; ⊕ Apr–Oct 09.00–21.00 daily) opposite the cable-car parking area. The exuberant co-founder Anna Arshakyan is not always here herself, but if she is she will happily share with you her wealth of knowledge in fluent English, Italian, Russian or Armenian over a hot drink and a freshly baked pastry. The centre can also make arrangements for accommodation, guided tours and hikes, and homestays in other villages in the region. It sells local handicrafts and hosts an excellent library of books and travel literature.

Tatev is 29km from the M2 main road via the H45 side road. The road is asphalt as far as Satan's Bridge (page 353) at the bottom of the gorge, then a good dirt road climbs to the village (4x4 not required). An alternative route, suitable only for walkers, mountain bikers and very capable 4x4 drivers, begins in the village of **Ltsen** to the northwest and follows an abandoned dirt road some 15km through the mountains to Tatev. Walkers can enhance the spectacular descent into the village by following the track near the clifftops via **Mount Kkvasar**, rather than the waymarked route. Another mountainous dirt road connects Tatev with **Kapan** via Khotanan, Tandzaver and Aghvani, but this can become extremely muddy after rain to the point of being impassable, even by 4x4.

The typical route to Tatev has been expedited by the **Wings of Tatev cable car** (⏰ Tue–Sun: Jan–Apr & Oct–Dec 10.00–18.00; May & Sep 10.00–19.00; Jun–Aug 09.00–20.00; departures at approx 15min intervals; last departure from Tatev approx 30mins before closing; one-way ticket AMD3,500, return ticket AMD5,000; under-7s free; bicycles charged as an extra passenger; advance tickets online via **w** tatever.am), whose Halidzor terminal has ample parking for the many coach tour groups that make use of it, as well as a good (if overpriced) restaurant. Each of the two cabins carries 25 passengers for the spectacular 12-minute ride high above the valley of the Vorotan River to a terminal next to the monastery, including an audio narration of the journey in Armenian, Russian and English. Profits from the Guinness World Record-holding cable car – the world's longest reversible single-track cableway at 5,752m – help fund the ongoing Tatev Revival programme (**w** idea.am/tatev-revival-project). Otherwise, there is a twice-weekly minibus from Tatev to Goris and back for locals (Mon & Fri only; Tatev to Goris 09.00; Goris to Tatev 15.00; the 30km journey takes 1½hrs; AMD700), while a taxi from Goris, including an hour's waiting time, costs about AMD10,000. Finally, it is worth mentioning that many Yerevan-based tour operators run overnight trips to Tatev; some even manage to fit the whole visit into a single day.

**Tatev Monastery** The fortified clifftop monastery of Tatev dates to the 9th century. Its greatest importance was in the 14th and 15th centuries under Hovnan Vorotnetsi (1315–88) and Grigor Tatevatsi (1346–1411). The date of the now vanished first church at the monastery is unknown, but in 844 Bishop Davit persuaded the Princes of Syunik to grant lands which would support the founding of a monastery worthy to house the relics which the church in Syunik possessed. His successor, Bishop Ter-Hovhannes, built the **main church**, dedicated to Sts Paul and Peter between 895 and 906. (Incidentally, legend has it that the architect couldn't get down when he finished the cupola, and cried out: '*Togh astvats indz ta-tev*', which means 'May God give me wings' – and so the monastery got its name.) It is somewhat intermediate in style between the earlier domed basilica churches and the later cross-dome churches. The umbrella cupola is supported by an unusually tall decorated circular tambour. On the east façade, above the triangular niches, long snakes are looking at two heads while on the north façade, above a window, two shorter snakes are looking at a person: Armenians supposedly regarded snakes as protectors of their homes. On the north façade are also representations of the founders of the church – Prince Ashot, his wife Shushan, Grigor Supan (the ruler of Gegharkunik), and Prince Dzagik. In 930, the walls of the church were decorated with frescoes but these have almost totally vanished except for some scant remnants in the apse, and the interior is now rather plain. Grigor Tatevatsi is buried inside the small chapel on the south side of the main church. His tomb is the highly decorated structure which abuts the church.

Outside the church on the south side is a monument erected in 904 called the *gavazan* (meaning a priest's or clergyman's pastoral staff). It is an octagonal pillar built of small stones with an elaborate cornice and a small khachkar on top. The pillar formerly detected earth tremors by rocking on the horizontal course of masonry on which it is constructed. It is currently undergoing investigation with a view to restoration.

The modest **St Gregory Church** adjoins the main church also on the south side. Dating from 1295, it replaced an earlier 9th-century building. To the west of the St Gregory Church there was a vaulted gallery with arched openings on the southern

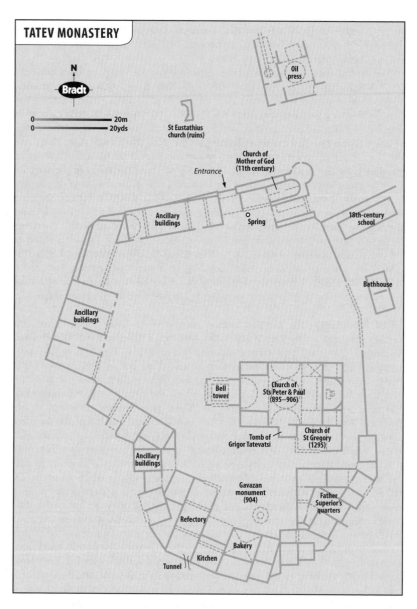

**TATEV MONASTERY**

N

Bradt

0 ————— 20m
0 ————— 20yds

St Eustathius
church (ruins)

Oil
press

Church of
Mother of God
(11th century)

*Entrance*

Ancillary
buildings

Spring

18th-century
school

Bathhouse

Ancillary
buildings

Bell
tower

Church of
Sts Peter & Paul
(895–906)

Tomb of
Grigor Tatevatsi

Church of
St Gregory
(1295)

Ancillary
buildings

Gavazan
monument
(904)

Father
Superior's
quarters

Refectory

Bakery

Tunnel   Kitchen

side. To the west of Paul and Peter Church the **belltower** was built in the 17th century on the site of a gavit which had been destroyed in an earlier earthquake. Above and to the left upon entering the complex is the unusual 11th-century **Mother of God Church**. It is a small cross-dome church with an octagonal tambour and umbrella cupola. The chambers of the clergy, the refectory with a kitchen and storerooms, and the dwelling and service premises form a rectangle around these structures within the fortified, one of which allows the intrepid visitor to emerge on to the hillside below the walls via a concealed (and very claustrophobic) tunnel. These chambers date from the 17th and 18th centuries.

Tatev Monastery has seen successive waves of restoration since an **earthquake** in 1931 destroyed much of the complex. The work has not always been sensitive, and the site was yet again surrounded by metal fencing and construction equipment at the time of research, but the results do give an excellent idea of how the monastery must have looked when it was a thriving centre of learning and science and up to a thousand people lived here. Most recently, a 2017 reconstruction of the monastery's 18th-century **water fountain** has been installed in its original location inside the reopened main entrance, whose floor also contains a glazed inset display of the ceramic plumbing system that supplied the water. Outside the walls can be seen the ruins of various other 18th-century buildings; the **oil press** has been restored to working order as a 'living museum' and gift shop. Wild red tulips (*Tulipa julia*) grow behind the monastery in late spring; unfortunately, they often end up as cut flowers.

**AROUND TATEV** Several spectacular hikes of varying difficulty and length begin from Tatev village. Deep in the gorge is the impressive monastic complex of **Tatev Grand Hermitage** (or Mets Anapat), which can only be reached on foot. A steep path descends through woodland and the ruins of terraced gardens. It begins from the signpost at the second switchback of the road down into the gorge; follow the waymarks and allow about 1½ hours to reach the hermitage. It can also be reached from a closer starting point opposite Satan's Bridge (see below), where an information board and map have been installed and a new trail and bridge constructed as part of the Barev Trails project (w barevtrails.com). From the hermitage, another trail can be followed to the village of Tandzatap and then back to Tatev, forming a very appealing half-day loop.

The hermitage is surprisingly large. Built in the 17th and 18th centuries, it was both an educational and spiritual centre, accommodating 500 monks. The central **Mother of God Church**, dating from 1663, is a three-aisle barrel-vaulted basilica with a small central belfry. It has a gallery at its west end and a gavit was added on the north side in 1743. The rectangular site is surrounded by high defensive walls, built in the middle of the 18th century, with the main gateway to the northwest. An extensive range of domestic buildings lines the wall, including monks' cells, a kitchen with a large fireplace in the southeast corner, an adjacent dining room and possibly inn accommodation, with water troughs, for travellers. At the time of research, it was populated by a single bearded hermit growing tomatoes in the courtyard.

**Satan's Bridge**, officially listed among Armenia's protected natural monuments and sometimes rendered as 'Devil's Bridge', consists of a natural rock bridge above the Vorotan River as it gushes through a series of caves and fissures. On the same site are several natural mineral springs of varying temperatures; one has had a small bathing pool built around it with a changing cubicle nearby. From just beyond this point, visitors with a head for heights can clamber (at their own risk) down a rickety ladder into the depths of the canyon; indeed, it is rather difficult to appreciate this marvellous creation of nature without doing so, particularly as the site is otherwise dominated by the road, the parking area, bright green guardrails and a deplorable amount of litter.

Another good hike, though much longer, begins from the top of the village and traverses the hillsides north, passing below Mount Petroskhatch (an alternative route leads to the peak) before winding down into the gorge and back up the northern side to the village of **Old Harzhis**. It is signposted from the visitor information centre and waymarked throughout; allow 5–6 hours and consider arranging return transport, or double back to the bottom of the gorge and climb up to Halidzor to take the cable car back. Backpackers and hikers with sufficient time can follow a dirt road **walking route to Kapan**. The journey is best tackled in two or three days; Tatev visitor information centre (page 350) or ARK Armenia in Kapan (page 345) can arrange accommodation in Aghvani and Arachadzor, and camping opportunities are easy and plentiful. Three years in the planning, **Tatev National Park** is due to be inaugurated in late 2018, aiming to conserve the forests, mountains and communities around the village, with new hiking trails proposed to the nearby villages of Svarants, Bardzravan and Tandzatap in one direction, and to Goris in another.

Further afield, an excellent view of Tatev Monastery and the gorge can be had from **Harsnadzor** (Bride's Canyon), a lookout point just south of Halidzor. The path to the viewpoint starts from the lay-by at the top of the climb from Halidzor. The watchtower is variously said to mark the signalling point from which the monastery could be warned of approaching enemies, or alternatively the spot from which a young lady threw herself into the gorge rather than submit to an unwelcome marriage with a local Muslim ruler – perhaps both are true. The ruined village of **Old Halidzor** can be seen on the hillsides below. It is possible to walk a loop between this and some of the other old villages on the side of the Vorotan Gorge, including those of **Old Shinuhayr** and **Old Khot**. The old villages were abandoned in the 1970s when the inhabitants moved to flatter land higher up with better access to the main road. The tracks down may be just about drivable (but not recommended) with a 4x4 but are more suitable for the donkeys and horses used by locals, and for walking. The villagers still use the old gardens for growing food and collecting firewood. Allow about 5½ hours for this loop, including plenty of stops to look at the ruined villages and to admire the scenery. It would be as well to try to arrange transport from the far end. Otherwise it is a 5km walk back along the main road to one's starting point if transport has been left there.

The track down from the present village of Shinuhayr winds down giving good views into the valley of the Vorotan River with its striking rock formations. A track then goes off left and zigzags down to **Old Shinuhayr** through orchards, at one point becoming either the bed of a stream or an irrigation channel through which it is difficult to find a dry route. Old Shinuhayr has two ruined churches. The first one reached is the 17th-century church of St Stephen, a large three-aisled, barrel-vaulted basilica. The second, a little further towards the river, can be seen from high up but is more difficult to find once in the village when the vegetation is high. It seems to have been a monastic complex with a surrounding wall, a church (17th-century Mother of God) with a small entrance hall and, on a lower level, the barrel-vaulted 17th-century Hermitage of the Virgins. Elsewhere within the walls are domestic buildings.

Returning to the main path down from the main road, the track continues along the hillside. Where the track starts an impressive zigzag course down to the river (and up the other side to Bardzravan), a narrow path continues more or less level along the hillside and eventually reaches Old Halidzor. Both the Shinuhayr and the Halidzor thirds of the path are reasonably obvious but the middle third disappears into the vegetation. It is a case of continuing on a more or less level course until the path becomes clear again. **Old Halidzor** was a large village and the streets and houses, although ruined, can be traced. Some of the buildings have unusual curved façades and there is a large cemetery. The church, seen as one approaches the village, has been restored. Nearby is a welcome spring, piped into a series of water troughs.

# GORIS

**GORIS** Goris is situated at the southern base of a high mountain range near the headwaters of the Goris River. It is the most architecturally and geologically distinctive town in southern Armenia, with its chessboard-like layout of two-storey grey stone buildings with wooden doors and balconies (apparently influenced by a German architect who lived here in the 19th century) overlooked from the east by the conical rock formations and caves of Old Goris (page 356). The climate is characterised by a relatively high possibility of rain and fog throughout the year. Culturally, Goris residents appear somewhat close to their Nagorno Karabagh neighbours to the east and those to the south, whose dialects all contain a higher proportion of Turkish/Azeri and Persian borrowings. *Jhingalov hats*, the herb-stuffed bread of Karabagh (see box, page 379), is ubiquitous in Goris, as are other dishes of a shared heritage. The town is noted for its traditional *lavash* and its desperately strong homemade fruit vodka (*oghi*).

Accommodation is scattered throughout (page 343), catering for all budgets, and the town is thus a popular base for exploring the northern part of Syunik.

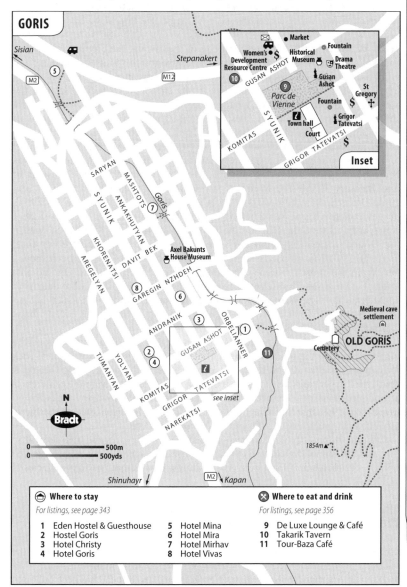

**GORIS**

**Inset**

**N**

**Bradt**

0 ———— 500m
0 ———— 500yds

Shinuhayr ↓        M2 ↘ Kapan

| 🛏 Where to stay | | 🍴 Where to eat and drink | |
|---|---|---|---|
| *For listings, see page 343* | | *For listings, see page 356* | |
| 1 Eden Hostel & Guesthouse | 5 Hotel Mina | 9 De Luxe Lounge & Café | |
| 2 Hostel Goris | 6 Hotel Mira | 10 Takarik Tavern | |
| 3 Hotel Christy | 7 Hotel Mirhav | 11 Tour-Baza Café | |
| 4 Hotel Goris | 8 Hotel Vivas | | |

## Where to eat and drink   *Map, page 355*

**✗ Takarik Tavern**   25/1 Syunik St; ☎ 0284 20515; 📱 091 051575; ⏰ 09.30–23.00 daily. Small, traditionally decorated Caucasian tavern with a wood-fired oven baking several local specialities inc *pide* & *jhingalov hats*. The food is excellent & very good value. Private dining rooms available.

**⬛ De Luxe Lounge & Café**   In the Parc de Vienne, Komitas St; ☎ 0284 24400; 📱 091 224477, 095 406630; ⏰ 11.00–23.30 daily. Popular mainly with aspirational locals who can afford the relatively high prices, this spacious, modern lounge-café features an extensive international menu (albeit Armenian interpretations). Outdoor seating in summer. Good for a morning coffee or an evening beer.

**⬛ Tour-Baza Café**   1 Grigor Tatevatsi St; ☎ 0284 30078; ⏰ 09.00–midnight daily. Popular outdoor café with a lovely view over Old Goris (depending on where you sit), serving regular Armenian barbecues & drinks. No English spoken. It can get rather busy.

**What to see and do**   The southern end of the town at the bottom of Mashtots and Ankakhutyan streets is the commercial centre and this is also where taxis and minibuses to local villages wait. The stand for long-distance buses is on the east–west highway in the north of the town. At the end of Ankakhutyan Street is the arched entrance to the **Parc de Vienne**, a favourite place for strolling which has a children's funfair and summer cafés. Next to this is the renovated **city square** with its fountains, benches, old-fashioned street lamps and cobbled walkways.

On the south façade of the **St Gregory Church** can be seen the trajectory of an artillery shell, which narrowly missed the building while the town was being bombarded during the conflict with Azerbaijan. The **house museum of Axel Bakunts** (41 Mesrop Mashtots St; ☎ 0284 22966; ⏰ 10.00–17.00 Tue–Sun; guide (French, Russian) AMD1,000; AMD300), a writer who died in Stalin's purges, contains his personal belongings in a typical Goris villa with a well-kept courtyard and veranda. Outside the **Historical Museum** (28 Komitas St, within the Drama Theatre, museum entrance round to the left of theatre entrance; ⏰ 10.00–17.00 Mon–Fri) are some sheep gravestones which have been moved here from the church. The displays are mostly of domestic items. One notable artefact is a five-sided stone with a face carved on each side, thought to date from 4,000 years ago. The **Women's Development Resource Centre** (7/14 Ankakhutyan St; ☎ 0284 30054; ⏰ 09.00–18.00 Mon–Sat) is a good place to buy locally made handicrafts and embroidery.

**Old Goris** is the name generally given to the region east of the river beyond the inhabited area of the town, with its manmade caves and distinctive conical rock formations scattered all over the west-facing hillsides of the Goris Valley. The area is relatively compact and easy to explore on foot if you are suitably fit; the cemetery is a good place to start, with several trails and tracks leading among the rocks and up to the ridge. Note that the area of most archaeological significance (ie: the formerly inhabited manmade caves) is fenced off for conservation.

Cultural events include the **sheep-shearing festival** in June, the *oghi* **festival** in July, and the annual **Days of Goris** parade (whose exact date has not yet been settled upon) in celebration of local hero Axel Bakunts, in which some streets are closed and locals lay out homemade food.

### AROUND GORIS

**Verishen**   The village of Verishen lies north of the main east–west highway, 2km northwest of Goris. It has two interesting churches and some cave dwellings still in use for storage or for housing livestock. On the hillside above the northern end of the village, with good views over the village to Goris and the surrounding hills, is the 17th- to 18th-century **church of Noraknunk** (New Baptism). Its west end has been built into a rocky outcrop, up the centre of which steps have been carved. If the church is open, you can see the bare rock at the west end inside the church. The easiest way to find the church is to go through the village until an area of cave dwellings can be seen to the right of the road, from where an obvious path leads uphill to the church. Within the village is the 5th-century **St Hripsime Church**, rebuilt in 1621. It can be spotted across gardens from the old town hall on the main street. It is a tall, relatively narrow barrel-vaulted basilica with thick walls built of rough stone. The eastern apse projects and looks as if it has been added later, a feature said to indicate conversion from a pagan temple. Certainly, the massive stones of the base of an earlier rectangular building are visible at the southeast corner. The west door has a pointed arch over the khachkar lintel. Much of the interest is in the stones of the graveyard around the church. Some are carved with figures of people, animals and implements, and there are stones with the same sorts of eye hole as those at Karahunj. A carved capital has a tulip-like image, like those at Tanahat Monastery.

**Old Khndzoresk** To reach the **cave village** of Old Khndzoresk, take the Stepanakert road from Goris for about 6km until the road to the present-day village goes off right, underneath a metal gateway which bears the legend 'Welcome to Khndzoresk' in Russian and Armenian. There are two ways into the cave village. The first leads to a viewing platform on the west side of the gorge from where one can walk down to the village. The second goes through the present village to reach the eastern road down into the gorge. To go to the viewpoint, turn first right from the Khndzoresk road on to a dirt road. It goes through fields and ends at the viewing platform where, in the summer, there is a small café. The platform gives a good overall view of the cave village. To walk down to the gorge, go through the gate at the far end of the paved area and follow a fairly steep path down to a suspension bridge across the gorge (5–10mins down, 15mins back uphill). One can then either cross the suspension bridge to the far side of the gorge or take the path to the left of the bridge which ultimately leads right to Sparapet's grave (see below) or left to St Hripsime Church. For the alternative approach continue on the asphalt road to the present village. At the far end of the village, turn right down the hill (following the better asphalt road) to Old Khndzoresk. Eventually the road becomes a dirt road and it is best to continue on foot. Most visitors give themselves half an hour here but half a day is needed to do justice to the place. The old village comprised cave dwellings hewn into the soft rock amid the spectacular limestone karst rock formations. The caves ceased to be used for housing people in the 19th century though some are still used even today for storage and for livestock (and some were temporarily reoccupied during the Karabagh war while Goris was being shelled). As the villagers left the caves they built surface buildings nearby, but the village was devastated by the 1931 earthquake and a decision was made to relocate to the higher position of the modern village.

The caves are spread out over a surprisingly large area indicating that a sizeable population lived here. Some of them are very simple and some quite elaborate with windows and niches cut into the hillsides. The two churches both date from the 17th century and survived better than most of the other surface buildings. The upper one, St Thaddeus, is a single-nave church with a carved portal with remnants of red paint decoration. The lower one, St Hripsime, was in the centre of the village and dates from 1663. It is a three-aisled church, also with a carved portal. Across the stream at the bottom of the gorge and slightly further south is the 17th-century hermitage where Mkhitar Sparapet is buried along with his wife and followers. He succeeded David Bek as leader of the rebellion against Ottoman rule. In 1730 he was murdered by the villagers of Khndzoresk because of Turkish threats that they would be attacked if they harboured him. Apparently, the Turkish *pasha* (governor) in Tabriz to whom they presented his head had the murderers themselves beheaded for what he regarded as their treachery.

**SOUTHERN SYUNIK** South from Goris the road follows the narrow gorge of the Goris River through spectacular countryside, with the rock pinnacles continuing along the east side. After leaving the gorge the road descends a long series of hairpin bends to meet the Vorotan River, which is eventually bridged close to a hydro-electric station. In Soviet days, the road south of this point followed the boundary between Armenia and Azerbaijan and was actually on the Azerbaijan side of the border at times. Since 1994, however, the de facto border is further east, though landmines remain a risk in places – best not to venture off the beaten path (page 78). At the top of the next big climb after crossing the Vorotan, the right turn signposted to **Bardzravan** leads after 3km to a track which goes off right to the remains of the **monastery of Bgheno-Noravank** in thick forest. The only surviving part is a small, reconstructed basalt church of 1062 which incorporates several stones carved with human figures, and geometric carvings including swastika designs around the doorway and on the pillars.

On cliffs above **Artsvanik** village, about 10km north of Kapan, is the 6th-century **monastery of Yeritsavank**. To reach it, take the main road junction for Kaghnut and turn left after 6.8km on to a rough track where the asphalt road bears right through about 90°. Where the rough track forks take the left fork for the monastery; the right leads to a large picnic area. The monastery is hidden among trees and does not present the startling appearance it once did according to ancient chronicles. The St Stephen Church, although ruined, is the best-preserved building. There is a chapel to the south and between them evidence of a walled monastic precinct. **St Stephen** is a tall basilica with a pointed vaulted roof. The long north and south walls have three arches which were originally open. Nowadays it is difficult to know how the west and east ends of the church appeared; presumably there would have been an eastern apse. At one time a separate wall surrounded the whole church but this no longer exists. One theory is that the church was originally open to the outside on three sides, which might explain why it was described as being so astonishing. The surrounding wall may have been built later as a defensive wall, a known feature of Armenian churches (page 49). An alternative theory is that the church was never open to the elements but that the body of the nave, with its arches supporting the upper reaches of the walls and the roof, were built as one and that the external wall of the church was built as a shell – a device used to limit earthquake damage to the main hall.

**Kapan** Kapan is the capital of Syunik and the largest and most populous city in the province. The approach from the north hints as to its former industrial status: ruined Soviet-era factories adorn the valley floor, the remains of the previous airport and rail links to Azerbaijan are still visible, and high-rise workers' flats dominate the suburbs. Today the old industries have mostly vanished and Kapan's main economic function is to support regional mining operations; the increasing number of Iranian visitors are hinted at by the Persian-language signage in public places and at hotels. The city is bisected by the eastward-flowing Voghji River and the northward-flowing Vachagan River, which converge in the centre of Kapan at one of the main road bridges across the Voghji. Central Kapan is quite compact and most of what there is to see can be covered in a walk of a couple of hours. Most

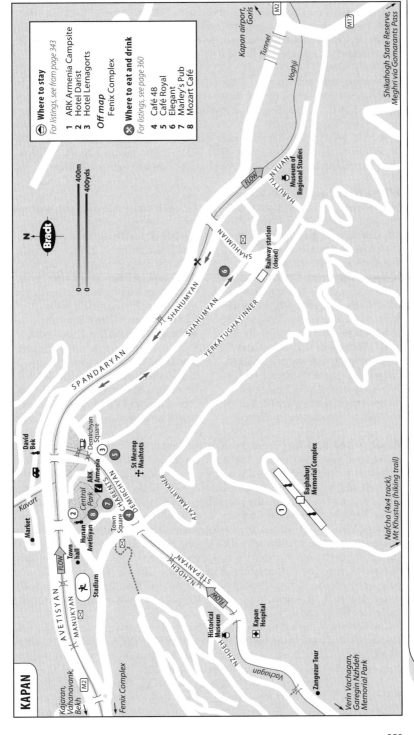

# KAPAN

**Where to stay**
For listings, see from page 343

1 ARK Armenia Campsite
2 Hotel Darist
3 Hotel Lernagorts

*Off map*
Fenix Complex

**Where to eat and drink**
For listings, see page 360

4 Café 48
5 Café Royal
6 Elegant
7 Marley's Pub
8 Mozart Café

facilities are within a short distance of each other in the centre of the town on the south bank of the river; the grocery market area is on the north bank, and many other shops can be found on Shahumyan Street. The statue of a horseman by the main bridge in the centre is of David Bek (page 20).

A daily **minibus from Yerevan** (AMD3,500) departs at 07.30 from the Intertown Bus Station (see box, page 87), taking 6–7 hours and stopping en route for refreshments. The return service departs from outside Café Royal on Demirchyan Square at 09.00. Depending on demand, a daily minibus to **Meghri** (and then Agarak) via Kajaran departs from the M2 main road junction with Myasnikyan St at 15.00 (AMD2,000–3,000), taking 2 hours. A minibus to **Goris** (AMD1,500) departs from the same location at 09.00 (AMD1,500), taking 3 hours. Schedules change regularly, so do check with your hotel or host before making plans.

## ✕ Where to eat and drink  Map, page 359

✕ **Café Royal** 2 Demirchyan Sq (next to Hotel Lernagorts); m 098 624006; ⊕ 10.00–22.00 daily. Convenient, central & cheap eatery with a basic Armenian menu of soups, salads & main courses, with a snack bar next door.

✕ **Elegant Restaurant** 32/1 Shahumyan St; ✆0285 21505; ⊕ 11.00–23.00 daily. A busy place with loud music in the evenings but it serves good Armenian food, hence its long-standing popularity.

✕ **Mozart Café** Southern cnr of Central Park; m 098 213060; ⛶; ⊕ 11.00–midnight daily. This standalone 2-storey restaurant serves good food from an extensive menu of Armenian & European dishes & may possess the only Italian espresso machine in town. Spacious open-air 1st floor with comfortable armchair seating. Also serves flavoured hookah (*nargile/shisha*) pipes. Additional charge for live music in evenings (AMD500 pp).

⌂ **Café 48** Straddling the Vachagan River next to the main square; m 096 489648; ⊕ 24hrs daily. Easy to miss as there are no signs & the curtains are always drawn, this terrace café on the river is in fact one of the nicer & more convenient spots in town for a drink. Varied menu & comfortable seating.

⌂ **Marley's Pub** 1 Charents St; m 098 898088; ⛶ Marleys.Pub.Cafe; ⊕ noon–late daily. Somewhat hard to find, down an alley off Charents Street behind the main square, this (unusual for small-town Armenia) Western-style bar has found favour with Kapan's progressives, as well as Yerevantsis, expats & travellers. Expect live music, ongoing special events & – of course – drinking.

**What to see and do** Demirchyan Street, which becomes Stepanyan Street, follows the east bank of the Vachagan River. The **church**, built in 2002 and dedicated to Mesrop Mashtots, is a large cross-dome church with a balcony at the west end for the choir. A short distance beyond the church Azatamartikner Street goes off left, opposite the post office, and winds up the hill for about 1km to the **Baghaburj Memorial Complex.** The memorial commemorates the Great Patriotic War (World War II), the 1915 genocide, the 1988 massacres in Sumgait and Baku, and the soldiers who died during the Karabagh war. It is a typical grandiose Soviet construction; the two female figures of the 1940–45 memorial, one young and one old, are remarkable for the sadness they so vividly and poignantly portray. Continuing up this road you will eventually reach the badly rutted 4x4 track to **Nafcha**, from where ascents of Mount Khustup are usually made (see box, page 362).

The **Garegin Nzhdeh Memorial Park** is 2km from the town centre up the same road on the east bank of the Vachagan. The memorial of the 'Saviour of Armenia' is set against the magnificent backdrop of Mount Khustup, where Nzhdeh's remains were eventually buried, as he wished (see box, page 330).

The **Historical Museum** (24/41 Garegin Nzhdeh St; ✆0285 028591; ⊕ 10.00–18.00 Tue–Sat) has been partially renovated. One room is devoted to the Karabagh war. It displays photographs of the town during the war, a reminder that the border is not far away. The museum is not directly on Nzhdeh Street but is in the block behind the first row of buildings. The **Museum of Regional Studies** (3/1 Harutyunyan St; m 098 258018; ⊕ 09.00–18.00 Mon–Fri; AMD1,000), to the east of the town centre, has ethnographically themed displays of local artefacts.

Behind Hotel Darist, west of the main square, is **Central Park**, with a children's funfair from May to October. The **statue** on the western edge of the park is a memorial to Hunan Avetisyan, a local boy who died in the Great Patriotic War (World War II), having sacrificed himself so his comrades could advance. The austere fortified edifice on the southeast edge is not a renovated castle but a newly built children's entertainment complex.

**Around Kapan** In the forest south of Bekh village at the west end of Kapan is **Bekh Anapat**, a little-known hermitage with a small chapel nearby. The 10th- to 11th-century hermitage was only recently uncovered and has undergone some restoration. The very pleasant woodland site is only accessible by foot or horseback: from the top of **Bekh** village, cross the river on the dirt road where the trail bends sharply right, then follow the signs 3.5km up through the forest. Allow an hour to reach the hermitage. It is possible to continue walking beyond the hermitage and return to Kapan via **Verin Vachegan** village by bearing downhill at the point where the trail leaves the forest.

Further along the main road to Kajaran, 1km after the leaving Kapan sign, a signposted road goes off left to the fortress of Halidzor (3.3km, not to be confused with Halidzor near Tatev) and the monastery of Vahanavank (2.2km). Shortly after crossing the river the road forks; left on a dirt road for the fortress, right on asphalt for the monastery. The road to **Halidzor Fortress** needs a 4x4 and dry weather: it is extremely muddy when wet. It forks several times; keep taking the upper fork. Built as a convent in the 17th century, it was used by David Bek as his headquarters. In 1725 Bek and 300 followers withstood a seven-day siege by an invading army of 70,000 Ottoman Turks. He led a charge downhill which so terrified the invaders that they fled. Bek died in the fortress in 1728 and is thought to be buried there. The heavily restored site has little atmosphere but does give an idea of the warren of rooms in the complex. To the right of the *bema* of St Minas Church is a large hole, perhaps the entrance to the secret 500m tunnel to the river which allowed the defenders to withstand the siege.

The **monastery of Vahanavank** was founded in 911 by Vahan, son of Prince Gagik of Kapan, who sought to become a monk in order to rid himself of the demons which possessed him. He built the main church, St Gregory the Illuminator, and is buried there. In the 11th century Queen Shahandukht of Syunik built the two-storey Mother of God Church to act as a burial site for her and her relatives.

**ECOTOURISM IN KAPAN**

Several of the sites around Kapan can be connected together into longer walks, thanks in large part to the work of the local social enterprise **ARK Armenia** (page 345; w arkarmenia.com), which has mapped and waymarked several local trails and published trail guides on its website. It hopes by doing so to help diversify the region's economy away from mining and heavy industry. Staying at one of its rustic properties supports its ongoing work to develop ecotourism in Kapan; backpackers are also encouraged to volunteer via the Workaway or WWOOF networks (page 124).

Southern Provinces  SYUNIK PROVINCE

South Syunik's most famous peak, Mount Khustup (3,206m), dominates Kapan's southern skyline on a clear day and is a favourite among hikers and mountaineers. The non-technical climb can be attempted via a variety of routes, depending on time, conditions and availability of 4x4 transport, but in any case should only be attempted in good weather, July to September being the most reliable and snow-free period.

The **simplest route** from Kapan makes use of an 11km dirt road from the Baghaburj district of Kapan to Nafcha, a cluster of summer houses often used as a 'base camp'. Here the flat ground and a spring make for good camping, or you can rent a small cottage (arranged through ARK Armenia; page 345). From Nafcha, a steep 5km track wraps around the mountain's eastern flanks, climbing over 1,000m to a shoulder just south of the peak, from where it is a few minutes' easy scramble to the summit itself. On a good day it seems one can see across the entire Caucasus region from the top. This route can be managed in one very long day of hiking, or more easily by taking a 4x4 as far as Nafcha.

**Alternative routes** exist. Nafcha can also be reached via Verin Vachegan by following a dirt route out of the village as it traverses the northern slopes below the peak; a guide is recommended as this route is less well known. From Verin Vachegan it is possible to climb a very scenic old footpath up to the ridge before following it to Khustup; this is by far the most scenic route but a very long and challenging one, probably necessitating an overnight camp. The closest 4x4 access to the peak is in fact via Shishkert village, some 50km distant from Kapan along the M17 road to Shikahogh. From Shishkert, a very challenging dirt road ascends the southern slopes of the mountain to the same shoulder reachable on foot from Nafcha; this drive should only be attempted by a very experienced driver in a 4x4 with very good clearance. A summer campsite has been established 1km from Shishkert village by Zangezur Tour and makes a good base camp for the climb (page 367).

The monastery has undergone considerable restoration. Both St Gregory and its western gavit are entered through an arcaded gallery which runs along the south side of both buildings. Part of the gallery has been left unrestored so that the large arches for which the monastery is famous can still be seen. St Gregory is a cross-dome church with two free-standing pillars separating the main space from the two very narrow side aisles. The tall tambour is decorated with arcatures with twin half-colonnettes, similar to those at Sisavank.

After the turn to Vahanavank, above the river at the tightest point in the gorge, there is a **statue of a bear** with a ring and key in its mouth – the arms of Syunik. Some 3km west of the village of Hamletavan on top of a hill is the **fortress of Baghaberd.** It is difficult to see the main part of the fortress when heading south (although much easier heading north) but a small fortification (and a square concrete construction) adjacent to the road on the right is conspicuous. A waymarked path leads up from the main road; some parts are steep and difficult because of the loose scree. Baghaberd was briefly capital of the Syunik kingdom in the 12th century before it was sacked by the Seljuks in 1170. It was reoccupied by David Bek (page 20) in the 18th century and has significant remains of the boundary wall but little else. The main gateway is near the northern end of the wall which defended the only side of the triangular hilltop lacking precipitous cliffs.

Continuing south on the old main road, the route follows the valley upstream through wooded mountains as far as the molybdenum-mining town of **Kajaran**, which was relocated here in the 1960s after earthquake damage on its former site further up the hill. Extensive mining operations and the proximity to the Nakhichevan border preclude serious expeditions into the Zangezur Mountains above the town, including Armenia's second highest peak, Kaputjukh (3,906m). The main road makes a U-turn over the river, then climbs south over the **Meghri Pass** (2,535m) before descending to the Iranian border.

**Meghri** The principal town in the far south, Meghri is enclosed by the natural defences of the surrounding mountains, its green irrigated gardens starkly contrasting with the arid slopes. It's a world apart from the rest of the province: at an average of 610m above sea level it is one of the lowest-lying areas of Armenia, becoming savagely hot in high summer. For this reason the area is famous for its figs, pomegranates and persimmons – indeed, the name Meghri means 'like honey' and supposedly refers to the sweetness of its fruit. The oldest surviving residential areas were built in the 18th–19th centuries from rough-hewn stone, lending the buildings a unique architectural appearance; wooden beams were incorporated into the walls for reinforcement that have since survived several earthquakes, and wooden balconies protrude from the upper storeys. On the steeper slopes the houses were literally built on top of each other, the roofs of one level forming the gardens of those above. Walking around the narrow, cobbled alleys with their canopies of vines reinforces the impression of an ancient cultural crossroads.

A daily **minibus from Yerevan** (AMD5,000) departs from the bus stand behind the main railway station and Sasuntsi Davit metro station at 07.30 and takes 8–9 hours to reach Meghri town square. The return service leaves the town square at 07.30 and costs the same. Depending on demand, a minibus to and from **Kapan** (AMD2,000–3,000) departs at 07.30, returning at 15.00, also to and from the town square. All these services start and terminate in **Agarak**, another 30 minutes distant.

### ✕ *Where to eat and drink* Map, page 364

✕ **Phalanga** 20 Adelyan St; ☎091 304334, 093 304334; ◷ 11.00–00.30 daily. On the main highway just north of the bridge over the river into the town, at the bottom of the Cascade. Newly built in a classical Greek style (the name refers to the 'phalanx' military formation) with indoor/outdoor seating & a broad menu of salads, mains, desserts & drinks. The pick of the many roadside joints on the main road through Meghri.

⌨ **Family Café** 1 Hraparak; ◷ 10.00–20.00 daily. A 1st-floor café above the VivaCell shop on the north side of the main square in Mets Tagh. Enter via the ground-floor doorway on the right of the shop. This new, relaxed central café serves mainly hot & cold drinks with freshly baked snacks from the bakery in the same building.

**What to see and do** The town is divided into two districts by the Meghri River and the M2 main road which runs alongside it. East of the river is **Mets Tagh** (Big Quarter) with the central triangular 'square' housing most facilities; the Cultural Centre and Town Hall face each other on opposite sides, with the old Soviet cinema adjacent (now a greengrocer's). The grandiose **Culture Centre** houses a children's art gallery and a local museum; opening times are somewhat flexible.

Downhill from the square by the police station is the top of **Meghri Cascade**, a series of flights of stairs reminiscent of Yerevan's Cascade and a shortcut between the town centre and the main road. Overlooking Mets Tagh from a horseshoe-shaped ridge are the remains of six watchtowers. These **fortifications** were originally built

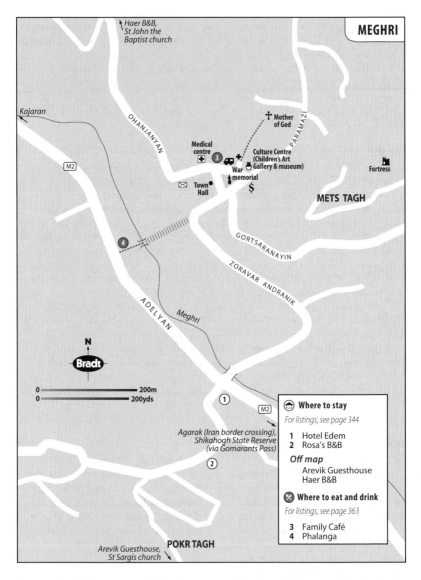

Haer B&B,
St John the
Baptist church

Kajaran

OHANJANYAN

Medical
centre

PARAMAZI

Mother
of God

3

Culture Centre
(Children's Art
Gallery & museum)

War
memorial

Town
Hall

Fortress

METS TAGH

GORTSARANAYIN

4

ZORAVAR ANDRANIK

ADELYAN

Meghri

N

Bradt

0                200m
0                200yds

1

M2

Agarak (Iran border crossing),
Shikahogh State Reserve
(via Gomarants Pass)

2

Arevik Guesthouse,
St Sargis church

POKR TAGH

**Where to stay**

For listings, see page 344

1   Hotel Edem
2   Rosa's B&B

**Off map**
     Arevik Guesthouse
     Haer B&B

**Where to eat and drink**

For listings, see page 363

3   Family Café
4   Phalanga

in the 10th–11th century and rebuilt in the 18th by David Bek (page 20), the first in Armenia to be modified for artillery. The two towers closest to the town have been rebuilt and are relatively easy to reach on foot: take the road uphill to the right of the Cultural Centre as far as the children's playground, then look for a narrow stairway between two old houses on the right. Locals say that all six towers may be connected by a suitably sure-footed hiker, though it would be wise to take a guide; see page 111 for general comments on hiking.

The **Mother of God Church** in the centre of the town (take the small street to the left of the Cultural Centre) was built in the 15th century and rebuilt in the 17th. It had the distinction of housing the first piano in Armenia, brought from Berlin to form part of the dowry of the daughter of a local family. The piano currently sits on a veranda of the house of the local priest. The pale-coloured stonework of the church contrasts with the very tall 12-sided pink tambour and cupola. The plain exterior also contrasts with the flamboyant interior, which is covered with 19th-century murals. Those on the arches and cupola are mainly abstract or floral in design but the walls and pillars depict saints or Bible stories. In the *Baptism of Jesus* He is shown standing on a snake, and Hell looks suitably chaotic in the *Last Judgement*. The church was used as a store in the Soviet era and the murals were apparently painted over, so it is pleasing to see how well they have survived.

There are two other churches in Meghri. **St John the Baptist Church** is reached by taking the street which leads north from the town square, parallel to the north–south highway. The church is tucked away behind a storage barn, built deliberately to obscure the church in Stalin's era. It has a domed basilica with three aisles and there are the remains of frescoes on the columns. The arches are all slightly pointed in a style reminiscent of Persian architecture, as is the brickwork above the main door. Like the houses, wooden beams were incorporated into the structure for reinforcement, though the church was badly damaged in the 1960s by an earthquake. It was undergoing extensive renovation at the time of research.

**Pokr Tagh** (Little Quarter) to the west of the river has **St Sargis Church** perched on top of a hill overlooking the town. It is best reached on foot through the tangle of steep alleys and stairways between houses that form perhaps the best-preserved historical district; two enormous plane trees (*Platanus orientalis*) shade a water fountain and seating area at a halfway resting point. The church is at the highest point. It was restored in the 1990s and at the time of research was undergoing further restoration under the patronage of the US Ambassador, the resplendent frescoes inside being sensitively renovated and drainage improved. The Persian-style brickwork of the cupola is said to have deterred invading Muslim forces from sacking the building. Attached to the outside of the church is the morgue, in which the bodies of the dead were washed before being taken into the church. Such a building is unusual in Armenia, the ablution normally being performed at home.

**Around Meghri** South from Meghri the road continues another 12km to the Iranian border checkpoint near **Agarak**. The town is dominated by the copper-molybdenum mine to the north and is really only of interest to travellers for the border crossing. A relaxation of visa rules for locals has resulted in increased cross-border traffic; a dedicated trading centre selling imported Iranian goods was yet to open at the time of research.

The **new road to Kapan** instead follows the border eastwards before turning north at the village of Andadzor. It is worth driving the stretch between Andadzor and Agarak to see the magnificent landscape along the River Arax, which forms the actual border. There is an alarmed and patrolled fence on the Armenian side of the river, photography is forbidden and one is advised not to stop, although driving moderately slowly seems to be tolerated. An abandoned railway follows the border – only tunnels and retaining walls are still intact – which once connected Nakhichevan with Azerbaijan proper.

There is a **scenic side trip** along the Arax River after the main road has turned north at Andadzor, where a stretch of rail track has been lifted and converted into 9.5km of good dirt road. After a junction for Nrnadzor village, a deteriorating but drivable asphalt road continues east and climbs for 6.5km to reach the former border post with Azerbaijan. Given the situation regarding landmines (page 78 and 370) it would not be wise to venture beyond this point, nor to stray from the road on the way up, but the views to the Arax River flowing between the mountains of Armenia and Iran are superb. (**Note**: There is an old parallel dirt road which might make a good hiking route – do not attempt it in a vehicle as it becomes dangerously narrow.) **Nrnadzor** itself, whose name means 'valley of pomegranates', contains extensive ruins and is one of the access points for Arevik National Park (see opposite).

Shortly after the main road to Kapan turns north is **Shvanidzor** village where there is a 17th-century aqueduct which is still in use for irrigation. To reach it, take the Shvanidzor turn-off from the main road and then the first left turn, just before entering the village itself. There is a church in the village where, in Stalinist times, a cultural civic centre was built on to the west end thus blocking the main entrance and, as with St John the Baptist in Meghri, disguising the fact that it was a church. Embedded high up on the inside walls of the church are ceramic pots. They were used to improve the acoustics of the church by filling them with variable amounts of ash until the required result was obtained. Shvanidzor, founded in the 13th century, has moved several times as necessitated by lack of water and poor soil fertility. Evidence of one previous location can be seen on the road north. Water continues to be a problem and work has recently started to re-establish an ancient system of supply based on *kakhrezes*, a series of wells connected by underground channels. The *kakhrez* system is found in areas of historic Persian influence and also in India and China. Shvanidzor has five *kakhrezes*, four dating from the 12th to 14th centuries and one built in 2005.

From Shvanidzor the road climbs to the **Gomarants Pass** (2,362m) then passes through Shikahogh State Reserve (see below). This road is more remote and scenic than the older road through Kajaran, partly because of the absence of human habitation for much of the way and the lack of traffic.

## Zangezur Biosphere Complex
In 2013, several of the protected areas of southern Syunik were brought together as a single unit, Zangezur Biosphere Complex, whose offices are in Kapan (42/27 Stepanyan St; ✆ 0285 20064; m 077 733000; e info@zangezurkh.am; w zangezurkh.am). Its tourism operation, **Zangezur Tour**, has English- and French-speaking staff who organise guided tours in the protected areas. A total of 13 day-long itineraries have been developed, covering a range of activities and interests. It can also arrange 4x4 transport, horseback tours and equipment hire.

To enter **Shikahogh State Reserve**, which has the highest level of protection, it is necessary to buy a **permit** (AMD5,000 pp/day) and to be accompanied by a ranger (AMD10,000/day) which can be arranged via the office in Kapan (see above) – unless you simply wish to travel the paved main road through the area, in which case the rule does not apply. The second-largest forest reserve in Armenia consists of densely tree-clad mountains of mainly Georgian oak, Caucasian oak and Caucasian hornbeam, spanning both sides of the Tsav and Shikahogh rivers and covering 100km$^2$, as well as incorporating the ruins of many historical settlements, fortresses, bridges and churches. Of particular note is **Mtnadzor** (Dark Canyon), evangelised by local writer Axel Bakunts in a book of the same name, where the north–south orientation of the canyon sides and the thick virgin forest create a perpetual twilight. A number of threatened species on the international Red List (w iucnredlist.org) are found in the reserve; mammals on the list include Syrian brown bear, Bezoar ibex, Armenian mouflon and, rarest of all, Persian leopard (also known as the Caucasian leopard). Wild boar have been spotted, hares are quite abundant, and the rivers have some large freshwater crabs. Unfortunately, its eastern border with Nagorno Karabagh still suffers from the problem of uncleared landmines.

Near the village of **Nerkin Hand** is a relict grove of oriental plane trees along the Tsav River. The **Plane Tree Grove Sanctuary** is signposted at the junction for Nerkin

Hand. Keep going down towards the river and turn right just before the large school building. There is a place to park and a small bridge over the river from where you can walk among the tall plane trees, of which more than a thousand extend for 10km along the riverbanks. Cuttings from the oriental plane take root readily in moist conditions: new trees have been planted simply by sticking a length of wood in the ground, the same method by which, it is speculated, the plane trees first took root here when merchants on the silk route stuck their staffs in the ground and then forgot them.

About 1km upriver from Shishkert village on the approach to **Mount Khustup** (see box, page 362) is a seasonal summer **campsite** (⊕ approximately Jun–Sep; AMD5,000 pp inc tent, mattress & sleeping bag), operated by the protected area authorities with communal barbecue facilities and staff on-site. From here it is possible to arrange 4x4 transport to a point close to the summit if you do not wish to tackle the whole climb on foot. The protected area visitor centre in Shikahogh village offers basic **accommodation** in a region otherwise devoid of overnight options; this can be booked online or via the office in Kapan.

**Arevik National Park** and **Zangezur State Sanctuary** are extraordinarily rich in natural beauty and do not require permits to enter but are among the least-developed protected areas in Armenia; the only touristic infrastructure at the time of research was a summer campsite near the village of Lichk, stays at which could be arranged through Zangezur Tour (see opposite). Note that the western border of these areas with Nakhichevan is strictly off-limits; do not consider climbing any of the border peaks (including Kaputjugh, at 3,906m Armenia's second-highest mountain) unless you wish to become target practice for Azeri snipers.

**ARMENIA ONLINE**

For additional online content, articles, photos and more on Armenia, why not visit **w** bradtguides.com/armenia?

6

# 7

# Nagorno Karabagh

Although it is known by the name Artsakh to its inhabitants and to many Armenians, the more widely known name Nagorno Karabagh dates from the Khanate of Karabagh's formal entry to the Russian Empire in 1813, *nagorno* being Russian for 'mountainous' and *karabagh* Turkish for 'black garden'. Today Nagorno Karabagh is very predominantly inhabited by ethnic Armenians – according to a census of 2015 they make up 99.7% of the population. The language in the streets of its towns is Armenian – albeit a strikingly different dialect thereof – and the currency in use is Armenian. However, it is not part of Armenia: it has its own president and a government with its own foreign ministry, its own flag, its own stamps and its own national anthem. Despite all this, its existence as a sovereign state is unrecognised by any UN member state (including Armenia) and no foreign government can provide consular services there; *de jure* it is internationally considered part of Azerbaijan, yet in reality it can only be entered from Armenia. Why go? One answer is that it has some magnificent scenery – it isn't called Nagorno for nothing. Even within the pre-1994 boundaries the land rose to 2,725m at Mount Kirs; the incorporation of territory that formerly separated Nagorno Karabagh from Armenia means that the highest point is now the 3,584m summit of Mount Tsghuk, which falls on the border with Armenia in Syunik province. It also has some very fine monasteries, and some thought-provoking damaged buildings and streets from which the ethnic Azeri population has fled. There are differences from Armenia. Inevitably, the military presence is more conspicuous. Additionally, Christian repression was greater here in Soviet days and all 220 churches which existed in Nagorno Karabagh during the Tsarist era had closed by the 1930s. Since 1989 there has been a steady reopening programme. A more mundane difference

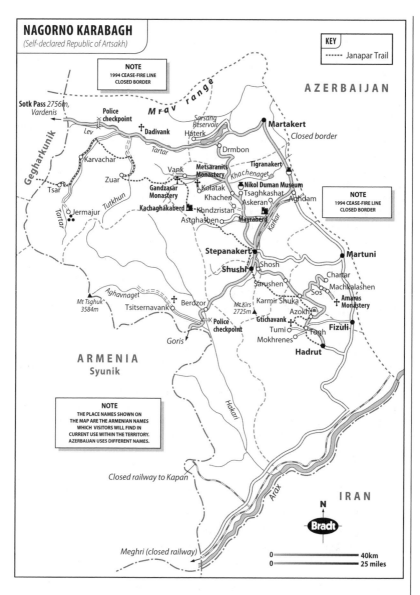

## NAGORNO KARABAGH
*(Self-declared Republic of Artsakh)*

NOTE
1994 CEASE-FIRE LINE
CLOSED BORDER

A Z E R B A I J A N

M r a v   r a n g e

Sotk Pass 2756m,
Vardenis

Gegharkunik

Police
checkpoint

Lev
✝ Dadivank
Háterk

Sarsang
Reservoir

Martakert

*Closed border*

Karvachar

Tartar

Drmbon

Tsar

Zuar

Tutkhun

Vank
✝ Metsaranits
Monastery

Gandzasar
Monastery

Kolatak
Khachen
Kachaghákaberd    Khndzristan

Khachenaget

Tigranakert

Nikol Duman Museum
Tsaghkashat
Askeran
Aghdam

NOTE
1994 CEASE-FIRE LINE
CLOSED BORDER

Jermajur

Tartar

Astghashen

Mayraberd

Kartar

Stepanakert

Martuni

Shushi    Shosh

Chartar
Machkalashen

Aghavnaget

Mt Tsghuk
3584m

Tsitsernavank ✝ Berdzor

Mt Kirs
2725m

Sarushen

Karmir Shuka    Sos

Amaras
Monastery

Azokh

Police
checkpoint

Gtichavank
Tumi
Mokhrenes

Togh    Fizuli

Goris

Hadrut

A R M E N I A
Syunik

NOTE
THE PLACE NAMES SHOWN ON
THE MAP ARE THE ARMENIAN NAMES
WHICH VISITORS WILL FIND IN
CURRENT USE WITHIN THE TERRITORY.
AZERBAIJAN USES DIFFERENT NAMES.

Hakari

*Closed railway to Kapan*

Arax

I R A N

N

Bradt

*Meghri (closed railway)*

0 ——— 40km
0 ——— 25 miles

from Armenia is that the groups of men in the street are often playing cards rather than backgammon, which is the norm in Armenia.

Nagorno Karabagh has some interesting sights although they do tend to be rather spread out. Certain of the best sights are inaccessible because of their proximity to the ceasefire line and the risk from snipers. The 270km Janapar Trail (page 381) allows many of the accessible sites to be visited as part of a long-distance village-to-village hike across the region; hiking elsewhere would be superb but should not be attempted beyond recognised trails without a local guide because of the continued existence of minefields (see box, page 370 and page 78). Many of these have been cleared but local knowledge is vital before leaving obviously used routes. Some visitors consider the abandoned Azeri villages with their ruined houses to be of interest, perhaps as a tangible reminder of the tragedy of war. Burnt-out military hardware can still be seen in places. The territory is under martial law: problems can arise with roads being closed for military manoeuvres.

## HISTORY *(See also page 25)*

Nagorno Karabagh was under Persian rule in 1805 when, along with other areas in eastern Transcaucasia, it was annexed to the 'everlasting rule' of the **Russian Empire**. The Gulistan Treaty of 1813 signed by Russia and Persia ratified this. The collapse of the Russian Empire in 1917 resulted in a changed arrangement of states in the Caucasus. The newly formed Republic of Armenia and the equally new Azerbaijan Democratic Republic both sought control over Nagorno Karabagh between 1918 and 1920. From the outset the Azerbaijan Democratic Republic made territorial demands for large areas of historic Armenia, even though the Tsarist census of the whole Karabagh region showed in 1917 a population which was 72% Armenian. (These figures are disputed by the Azeris who consider the Russian Imperial Census of 1897, showing an Armenian population of about 40%, to be more reliable.) Taking advantage of the confused state of affairs resulting from World War I, the collapse of the Russian Empire and continuing persecution of Armenians by Turks, Turkish forces along with Azeri military units destroyed hundreds of ethnically Armenian villages. (It was a feature of the whole region that most villages were dominated by one ethnic group: some Armenian, some Azeri, and elsewhere some Georgian and some Turkish.) Only in Nagorno Karabagh did the Armenian population succeed in repelling the attacks. In July 1918, the **First Armenian Assembly of Nagorno Karabagh** declared the region to be self-governing and created the Karabagh National Council. In August 1919, this National Council entered into a provisional treaty arrangement with the Azerbaijan government to try to halt the military conflict. This, however, did not prevent Azerbaijan's violation of the treaty, culminating on 28 March 1920 with the massacre of Armenians, accompanied by burning and plundering, in Shusha (Shushi), the then capital. As a result the Karabagh Assembly nullified the treaty and declared union with Armenia.

The First League of Nations had its inaugural meeting in late 1920. Applications for membership were considered by the fifth committee, chaired by Chile, which

## SAFETY – ADVICE ON AVOIDING MINES

The following list of points for travellers is provided by the HALO Trust (see box, page 375) which carries out mine clearance in Nagorno Karabagh:

- Mines and unexploded ordnance (UXO), including cluster munitions, litter the region and can be found in both remote areas and close to towns and villages
- Always speak to the local people before entering an area
- Keep to well-used tracks and paths
- If a track does not look used then avoid it
- Be aware that although a track may be used it could pass through a minefield or area contaminated with UXO
- Do not touch anything which looks like a mine or ordnance
- If you don't know what something is then don't touch it

recommended that Azerbaijan should not be admitted (mainly because of its Bolshevik government) while consideration of Armenia's admission should be postponed (because it was occupied). However, the League of Nations, before final resolution of the issue, recognised Nagorno Karabagh as a disputed territory since it had not in practice been ruled by any outside power since the Russian collapse in 1917. That only changed when Bolshevik forces occupied Nagorno Karabagh in 1920. Immediately following the establishment of the Soviet regime in Armenia, the Azerbaijan Revolutionary Committee on 30 November 1920 formally recognised Nagorno Karabagh, as well as Zangezur (southern Armenia) and Nakhichevan, to be parts of Armenia and in June 1921, Armenia itself declared Nagorno Karabagh to be part of Armenia.

Meanwhile the **Bolshevik** leaders in Russia were having visions of an imminent international communist revolution and believed that the new Turkish government under Atatürk was a believer in their cause. This resulted in a change of attitude regarding Turkey's ethnically close relations with Azerbaijan and the question of the disputed territories including Nagorno Karabagh. Stalin, Commissar of Nationalities in the Council of People's Commissars in Moscow, therefore persuaded the Caucasian Bureau of the Russian Communist Party to adopt on 5 July 1921 a policy of annexing Nagorno Karabagh to Azerbaijan rather than Armenia. This was despite the fact that both Armenia and Azerbaijan were still independent, albeit communist controlled, countries: the Soviet Union into which they would be incorporated along with Russia was not formed until December 1922 and it was no business of the Russian Communist Party to decide on the wishes of the Karabagh population. This Russian decision was put into effect but with the proviso that Nagorno Karabagh would be granted the status of an autonomous region.

On 7 July 1923, the Soviet Azerbaijan Revolutionary Committee resolved to dismember Nagorno Karabagh and to create – on only part of its territory amounting to 4,400km$^2$ – the promised **autonomous region**. A large part of the remainder, comprising the present-day districts of Lachin and Kelbajar, became the Kurdistan Autonomous Soviet Socialist Republic. Thus Armenia and Nagorno Karabagh were now separated by the territory of Kurdistan. In 1929, Kurdistan was abolished and the territory fully incorporated into Azerbaijan, so that from 1929 onwards, Armenia was separated from Nagorno Karabagh by Azerbaijan proper.

In 1935, there were protests in the region against Nagorno Karabagh remaining within Azerbaijan and these became an almost annual feature after 1960 following the Khrushchev thaw. Gorbachev's policy of openness, established after he came to power in 1985, merely served to bring matters further into the open.

The year 1988 became a turning point in the history of Nagorno Karabagh. Mass demonstrations started here on 11 February 1988 demanding union with Armenia. On 20 February in an extraordinary session of the Nagorno Karabagh Autonomous Republic Council, the People's Deputies voted to secede from Azerbaijan and join Armenia and appealed to the Supreme Soviet of the USSR to recognise this decision. This was matched by massive demonstrations in Yerevan, accompanied by a petition signed by 75,000 Armenians, demanding the annexation of Nagorno Karabagh. A pogrom on 28 February at **Sumgait**, Azerbaijan, which was directed against ethnic Armenians, resulted in around 30 deaths (or some estimates claim up to 120) of Armenians at the hands of their Azeri neighbours. This unprecedented killing shocked the Soviet Union and the Soviet authorities arrested 400 rioters. Some 84 perpetrators were tried and sentenced in Moscow. (The incident which purportedly led directly to the Sumgait massacre was the killing five days earlier of two Azeri young men by youths reported by the press to be Armenians, in a skirmish between the two ethnic groups in the Aghdam region of Karabagh.) Thereafter ethnic tensions continued to rise and during the fighting over Nagorno Karabagh there were civilian deaths on both sides. (Perhaps the incident which gained most international notice and condemnation was the deaths of 161–613 (numbers are disputed) Azeri civilians, fired on by Armenian forces in February 1992, as they tried to leave Khojaly, near Aghdam, as it was about to be occupied by Armenian forces. Khojaly was used as a military base by the Azeris to shell Stepanakert, or Khankendi as it is known by the Azeris.) The Sumgait massacre was followed by even bigger mass protests in Armenia itself when almost a million people were estimated to have participated. The inaction by Moscow produced massive unrest with an estimated 200,000 Azeris fleeing Armenia and 260,000 Armenians fleeing Azerbaijan. In July the Nagorno Karabagh Supreme Soviet, Nagorno Karabagh's supreme governing body, took the decision to secede from Azerbaijan and adopted measures to become part of Armenia.

The members of the **Karabagh Committee**, a group of nationalist intellectuals leading the fight for union with Armenia, were arrested in December 1988 and held in Moscow without trial, while on 12 January 1989 direct rule of Nagorno Karabagh from Moscow was imposed. International protests eventually led to the Karabagh Committee members being freed on 31 May. Showing how little control of events Moscow had by now (the Soviet Empire in central and eastern Europe was fast disintegrating at the time) Azerbaijan started partially blockading Armenia in September. With a breathtaking disregard for the likely consequences, Moscow abandoned direct rule of Nagorno Karabagh on 28 November and handed control to Azerbaijan.

Armenia's response was swift and on 1 December the Armenian Supreme Soviet voted for unification with Nagorno Karabagh. The vote was declared illegal by the Supreme Soviet of the USSR to which Yerevan's response was to pass a new law giving it the right of veto over laws passed in Moscow. The year 1990 was to be a year of conflict between Armenians and central Soviet forces with massive protests over the Karabagh issue and often brutal police and military repression: six Armenians were killed in Yerevan by Soviet troops in a confrontation on 24 May. Eventually, after two changes of leadership, the appointment of Levon Ter-Petrosyan (one of the members of the Karabagh Committee) as Chairman of the Supreme Soviet of Armenia on 4 August led to Armenia declaring independence within the USSR on 23 August.

The next year was to see momentous change. The failed coup against Gorbachev on 19 August 1991 led to the inevitable break-up of the Soviet Union at the end of the year. More immediately, Azerbaijan's response on 27 August was to annul Nagorno Karabagh's status as an Autonomous Region which then led, on 2 September, to the declaration of the independent **Republic of Nagorno Karabagh** – the goal had changed and union with Armenia had ceased to be the objective. A plebiscite in Nagorno Karabagh on 10 December resulted in an overwhelming vote for independence. Azerbaijan began a blockade of the territory (which it completely encircled) and launched military attacks using the equipment of the USSR 4th Army stationed in Azerbaijan. Meanwhile newly emergent Russia saw Armenia as a key ally – notably because of its long border with Turkey, a member of NATO. Accordingly, Russia signed a treaty of friendship and co-operation with Armenia on 29 December, two days before the demise of the USSR. This was to be followed, much more crucially for Nagorno Karabagh, by a collective security pact signed by Russia and Armenia along with Kazakhstan, Kyrgyzstan, Tajikistan and Uzbekistan on 15 May 1992.

Azeri military attacks made initial territorial gains but by 8 May 1992 they had been driven back from Martakert and Shushi while on 18 May the Armenian army was able to force a corridor through the Azeri lines at Lachin and break the blockade of Nagorno Karabagh. This, however, was to be followed by a renewed Azeri offensive which resulted in considerable further Azeri gains so that by the end of July they had taken the whole of the Shahumyan region, a great portion of the Martakert region, and portions of Martuni, Askeran and Hadrut controlling about 60% of the entire territory. These Azeri victories had several effects: there were demonstrations against Ter-Petrosyan, by now the Armenian president, and he survived an assassination attempt on 17 August; the US Congress adopted a resolution condemning the actions of Azerbaijan and prohibited US government economic assistance; and Ter-Petrosyan on 9 August invoked the less than three-month-old security pact asking for Russian help.

Russian support arrived in the form of supplies and equipment. By March 1993 the Armenian army was able once more to go on the offensive and it not only recouped its losses over the next few months but also gained almost all of Nagorno Karabagh, together with the former Kurdistan and a considerable swathe of Azeri territory bordering Iran. Finally, on 5 May 1994, a **ceasefire** – brokered by Russia, Kyrgyzstan and the CIS Interparliamentary Council – was signed which took effect on 12 May. By this time Azerbaijan had lost control of a substantial area of its territory, though it continued to control small portions of what had previously been the Nagorno Karabakh Autonomous Oblast. By contrast the self-declared

## NAGORNO KARABAGH OR ARTSAKH?

On 20 February 2017 a public **referendum** was held in Nagorno Karabagh on a variety of constitutional reforms. One of the proposed amendments would result in the official **name** of the self-declared republic being changed from the Nagorno-Karabakh Republic to the Republic of Artsakh, reflecting the name for the region traditionally used by many Armenians, including its current inhabitants. The referendum passed with 90.1% in favour and a turnout of 76.5%, according to the republic's own Central Electoral Commission, and was of course immediately dismissed as illegitimate by Baku.

This poses a particularly challenging situation for guidebook authors whose goal is to present practical information with no political bias. In spite of the referendum, the region remains commonly known as Nagorno Karabagh or simply Karabagh (or some similar transliteration thereof), and many Armenians have always referred to and will continue to refer to it as such. What is now the self-declared Republic of Artsakh has begun to implement the name change within its official institutions, but at the time of research many (including both the embassy in Yerevan and the Ministry of Foreign Affairs website) continue to bear the former name and to express the interchangeability of the two in any case. While it is likely that the name Artsakh will gradually come to predominate in the region itself, it seems equally likely that the non-partisan international community will continue to use Nagorno Karabagh on the grounds that it was the name in use when the dispute over the territory began.

In this guide we have chosen to continue using the common name **Nagorno Karabagh** to refer to the region generally; the **Nagorno-Karabakh Republic** in the past context of the self-declared republic between 1994 and 2017, and the **Republic of Artsakh** in the present context of the self-declared republic which has now formally adopted that name.

Nagorno-Karabakh Republic would eventually incorporate into its administrative districts even the occupied areas of Azerbaijan which were not in the former autonomous region, considerably increasing its size in the process, establishing a long border with Armenia itself, and creating an additional dispute: while Armenia argued that this 'buffer zone' was critical to the safeguarding of Nagorno Karabagh, Azerbaijan would not accept such a huge loss of former sovereign territory along with the expulsion of its Azeri populace.

The job of finding a solution to the conflict was placed in the hands of the **Minsk Group** of the Organization for Security and Co-operation in Europe (OSCE) which was set up in 1992. It was discussed that Nagorno Karabagh might be handed over in exchange for southern Armenia (Zangezur, ie: Syunik) but that was unacceptable to Armenia since it would lose its important direct link to Iran. Armenia wanted a resolution of the problem which it believed would help economic growth but Armenians felt that they could not desert their kith and kin. Nagorno Karabagh also continued to be a key factor in the frozen diplomatic relations between Turkey and Armenia. The ceasefire mostly held but, with no peacekeeping force in place, instances of breach were frequent. Usually this was limited to exchanges of sniper fire, but more serious skirmishes began to occur as time went on: in November 2014 an Armenian military helicopter was shot down in an area of no man's land near Aghdam, and in April 2016 what became known as the Four-Day War resulted in the first movement of the ceasefire line since 1994 (in Azerbaijan's favour) and the deaths of several hundred military personnel and also some civilians (on both sides). Many international commentators criticised the action as setting a dangerous precedent for the continued escalation of violence, and this and other incidents have brought the question of resolving the conflict back to prominence. It has been noted that Armenia's newest prime minister Nikol Pashinyan is the first leader in more than 20 years who is not a member of the 'Karabagh clan'; while the previous ruling elite portrayed first-hand participation in the conflict as favourable, others argued that new voices were needed to break the stalemate. Meanwhile, the Minsk Group negotiations continue, as does life in Nagorno Karabagh, with no war and no peace either.

## GOVERNMENT

Although still part of Azerbaijan under international law, the self-declared Republic of Artsakh is a de facto independent state with the necessary organs of government. The president, who is eligible to stand for not more than two five-year terms, and the 33 members of the chamber of deputies are directly elected by the population of around 151,000. A set of constitutional reforms in 2017 included the renaming of the self-declared republic from the Nagorno-Karabakh Republic to the Republic of Artsakh (see box, page 373). Nagorno Karabagh has its own police, court system, education system and so on. The national flag of Nagorno Karabagh is basically the Armenian one but with a white five-toothed stepped arrow pattern on the right-hand side. Though the Nagorno Karabagh dram (NKD) was officially created in 2005, the notes and coins produced are no longer legal tender; the currency in circulation continues to be the Armenian dram (AMD).

The government has given assistance to the estimated 40,000 people who have settled in Nagorno Karabagh since 1991 (mostly ethnic Armenian refugees fleeing Azerbaijan) in the form of allocating housing, providing livestock, and charging half the Armenian price for electricity. There are also incentives in place for couples to have larger families.

**Landmines** were used extensively (by both sides) during the war in Nagorno Karabagh, as were large amounts of cluster munitions and other explosive ordnance. Between the ceasefire in 1994 and August 2017, 370 people were killed or maimed by landmines and **unexploded ordnance** (UXO). The presence of minefields leaves farmers unable to cultivate vast swathes of fertile agricultural land and also inhibits development and infrastructure projects. Towns and villages alike are affected.

The HALO Trust (page 122), the largest humanitarian mine-clearance organisation in the world, has been active in Nagorno Karabagh since 2000 and provides the only large-scale mine-clearance capacity in the region, employing more than a hundred staff. All known minefields have been surveyed and signposted, and by July 2018 90% of known minefields were cleared, with the help of crowdfunding campaigns that saw all donations doubled by a private US-based donor. Most of this land has been returned to cultivation. At current funding levels HALO believes that Nagorno Karabagh could be mine-free by 2020.

## RED TAPE

Non-Armenian passport holders require **visas**. Information and an application form (for use in Stepanakert) can be found at w nkr.am. Visas can be obtained from the Nagorno-Karabakh Republic Permanent Representation to the Republic of Armenia in Yerevan in the suburb of Arabkir to the north of the centre (17a Nairi Zaryan St; ☎010 249705; e yerevancons@mfa.nkr.am; ⊕ 09.00–13.00 & 14.00–17.00 Mon–Fri). It is advised that visa applications are made in the morning, especially if same-day visa service is requested. A 21-day tourist visa costs AMD3,000 if collected the following day. Same-day service costs AMD6,000. If there is any possibility of travelling in future to Azerbaijan then it is essential to obtain the visa on a separate piece of paper; requesting this is quite normal. A Nagorno Karabagh visa entered in a passport means that entry to Azerbaijan will be refused. It is also possible to obtain a visa from the Ministry of Foreign Affairs (28 Azatamartikner St; ☎047 941418) after arrival in Stepanakert, provided you show identification documents at the border. In either case you will be asked to list the towns and sites of interest you wish to visit on a separate form; for the Janapar Trail (page 381) this should include every overnight stop on your intended route. You should carry this form with you when you travel; it has to be handed in at the border post when you leave and it may be requested by the police or military at any time, particularly if you travel to areas not usually visited by tourists. Note that visiting Aghdam is not officially permitted.

## GETTING THERE AND AWAY

At present Nagorno Karabagh can only be entered from Armenia. There are two good asphalt roads that can be combined to form a loop. The newer of the two goes from **Vardenis** via the **Sotk Pass** (2,367m). After the pass the road follows the beautiful valley of the Lev, at times with toweringly high cliffs on each side until its confluence with the Tartar where the road meets another coming along the Tartar Valley from Karvachar. It then follows the Tartar until Nagorno Karabagh's pre-1994 territory is entered just past the monastery of Dadivank. The road is extremely scenic all the way along the valley to Sarsang Reservoir (page 391). Since its opening in 2017 this has been the principal route for travellers between Yerevan and Stepanakert, as it shortens the journey time by at least an hour; allow 5–6 hours if driving via this route.

The second road goes from **Goris** and crosses the so-called Lachin Corridor through what was, from 1929 to 1994, part of Azerbaijan proper. After an impressive climb the road descends to the valley of the Aghavnaget where there is a new chapel up on the left dedicated to soldiers who died in battle in Karabagh. The checkpoint is immediately after the river crossing. The road continues and enters Nagorno Karabagh's pre-1994 boundaries just before the town of Berdzor (previously Lachin). This is the last sizeable place before Shushi 43km further on. Although over 50% of its houses were damaged in the war many, but not all, have been rebuilt. The houses not destroyed were largely occupied by refugees who chose to settle here. The road then climbs up and after the summit runs through sparsely populated country to bypass Shushi and descend rapidly into Stepanakert. Allow about 6–7 hours to drive from Yerevan via this route.

There are several **minibuses** daily from Yerevan to Stepanakert, the capital, which leave hourly (07.00–10.00) from Yerevan's Central Bus Station, taking around 6 hours for a fare of AMD5,000. **Car** drivers must stop at one of the two **checkpoints** on entering and leaving so as to register the vehicle. Visitors are asked for their passports and visas at the checkpoint. If you do not have a visa you will be instructed to obtain one in Stepanakert (page 385).

There are **other roads** into Nagorno Karabagh from Armenia. Most of those marked on maps are minor mountain tracks which are likely to be in dire condition. The only such track likely to be of interest to visitors is that used by the section of the Janapar Trail (page 381) between Vardenis and the village of Tsar. See also the warning about landmines in the box on page 370.

**Stepanakert Airport** lies some 20km north of Stepanakert. Flights stopped in 1990 during the Karabagh war. Repair and upgrading started in 2009 and after several postponements it was announced that the airport would start to operate flights to and from Yerevan in the summer of 2012. Certainly in August of that year it looked as if opening was imminent, with a new building, state-of-the-art security and passenger handling and all staff training having been completed, but flights did not resume: citing international aviation laws, Azerbaijan threatened to shoot down any unauthorised flights in its *de jure* air space, and the Turkish government threatened to close its air space to Armenia if the opening went ahead. The airport, it seems, has become part of the bigger problem of the resolution of the Karabagh conflict under the auspices of the OSCE Minsk Group (page 374). In the meantime the only international civilian flight yet to have landed at the airport was a single paramotor pilot from Yerevan as part of the 2017 Artsakh Airfest (in all other respects a domestic light aviation event).

## IMPORTANT NOTES

- Nagorno Karabagh can only be entered from Armenia.
- A visa for the self-declared Republic of Artsakh is required.
- Azerbaijan cannot be entered from Nagorno Karabagh.
- The visa is not valid in Azerbaijan and entry to Azerbaijan will be denied to anyone with a visa in their passport.
- The Republic of Artsakh is not recognised internationally and no consular services of any kind are available.

# GETTING AROUND

Most places of interest to tourists can be visited as day trips from Stepanakert. The two most popular, Dadivank and Gandzasar, can be visited on the same day if travelling by car. The **north–south highway** has made travelling in Karabagh much easier than it was, as has the **Vardenis–Martakert highway**, both built with funds from the charitable Hayastan All-Armenian Fund (page 122). In spite of their names they are both single carriageways, albeit good quality paved ones, and have catalysed a number of roadside cafés and filling stations to be built in what were previously very poorly served regions in such regards. As in Armenia it is possible to travel between most towns and villages by **minibus** (marshrutka). The best way to find out current departure times is by asking at either the tourist office in Shushi or Stepanakert (page 380) or at your hotel or homestay. The well-organised bus station in Stepanakert has detailed information on departures to places within Karabagh and to Armenia. **Taxis** are plentiful and cheap and are a reasonable and convenient alternative to the marshrutkas. **Car hire** can be arranged through Gala Tour based in Park Hotel (page 378) in Stepanakert; a cross-border supplement may be due on cars hired in Yerevan (page 91).

##  WHERE TO STAY

The website of the Artsakh Tourism Development Agency (**w** artsakh.travel) lists accommodation options in Karabagh. There are several modern hotels in Stepanakert and a couple in nearby Shushi. Several B&Bs now operate in both cities; Shushi in particular was seeing a rapid increase in guesthouse openings at the time of research. While hosts in Armenia tend to prefer Booking.com for online reservations, those in Nagorno Karabagh seem to favour Airbnb (**w** airbnb.com), where apartments and hotel rooms can be found as well as plentiful homestay accommodation in Stepanakert and Shushi. Elsewhere, **homestays** are also widespread; every village on the Janapar Trail (page 381) has at least one such option, all of which are listed on the trail's website. They can most easily be booked via a Yerevan travel agent before leaving or through the tourist information offices in Shushi or Stepanakert (page 380). Most hotels offer lower rates in low season, approximately November to April. Note that hotel accommodation may be difficult to obtain 1–3 September as the government reserves it all for Independence Day celebrations on 2 September; at this time hostels and homestays are likely a better bet.

### STEPANAKERT
Map, page 383

 **Vallex Garden Hotel** (57 rooms) 35 Stepanyan St; \047 973393/7; **e** info@vallexgarden.com; **w** vallexgarden.com. A grandiose complex occupying a large portion of the centre of town. The architect seems to have had imperial Rome in mind; the interior décor is more tasteful. Restaurant serves an imaginative & above avg menu. Fitness club, large indoor swimming pool & sauna, pleasant terrace bar. Cards accepted. **$$$$**

 **Armenia Hotel** (55 rooms) Veratsnund Sq, 4 February 20th St; \047 949400; **e** info@armeniahotel.am; **w** armeniahotel.am. A prominent hotel of international standard next door to the National Assembly (parliament) building. Restaurant & bar with outdoor patio on the square. Gym. Finnish sauna & plunge pool. Cards accepted. **$$$**

 **Hotel Europe** (32 rooms) 26 Azatamartikner St; \047 975752/975782; **m** 097 258033; **e** info@hoteleurope.am; **w** hoteleurope.am. A modern building with a curved façade next to the Ministry of Foreign Affairs. Swimming pool. Formal restaurant in basement; café on roof (extra AMD2,000 for comfortable sofas). Cards accepted. **$$$**

🏠 **National Artsakh Hotel** (10 rooms) 9a/1 Nelson Stepanyan St; 📞047 970770; m 097 330770; w nationalnkr.am. Tasteful & modern upscale hotel, opened in 2014, with deluxe twin/dbl rooms, all en suite. Good restaurant on ground floor. Cards accepted. **$$$**

🏠 **Park Hotel** (28 rooms) 10 Vazgen Sargsyan St; 📞047 971971; e info@parkhotelartsakh.com; w parkhotelartsakh.com. This attractive boutique hotel in a fully refurbished 19th-century building is decorated & furnished in traditional style. Helpful staff. Restaurant, bar & summer café inc outdoor seating. Price varies with size of room & view. Somewhat basic b/fast. **$$$**

🏠 **Hotel Heghnar** (28 rooms) 39 Abovyan St; m 097 266666; e heghnarhotel@yahoo.com; w heghnarhotel.com. A fully renovated hotel with sgl/dbl/trpl/quad rooms tastefully decorated in natural materials, with healthy plants gracing lobby & landings. Attractive original modern paintings, many for sale, adorn the walls. Lunch/dinner can be provided with notice. Own fruit trees; guests are welcome to sample the fruit. Summer café in garden. **$$**

🏠 **Yerevan Hotel** (16 rooms) 62 Tumanyan St; 📞047 977888, 060 277888; e yerevanhotel@gmail.com, info@yerevanhotel.travel. Occupies part of a converted wine factory, so there is lots of space. Reception on 2nd floor. Meals except b/fast have to be ordered 2 days in advance. Accepts cards. **$$**

🏠 **Hotel Tirun** (9 rooms) 107 Tumanyan St; 📞047 955996/945996; m 097 223366. A small, friendly basic hotel. Has family rooms. B/fast AMD3,000 pp. **$**

🏠 **Raffo & Karine's Hostel** (4 rooms, 12 dorm beds) 6 Nalbandyan St; m 097 335288; e carinerooms7@gmail.com. Popular budget option in a rustic suburban house where Karine has hosted guests since 1997. Private dbl/trpl/quad rooms upstairs, dorm beds (AMD3,000 pp) downstairs. Shared bathroom for all but the quad room which also has a living area. Shared kitchen, BBQ & outdoor terraces. B/fast AMD1,500. **$**

## SHUSHI
Map, page 386

🏠 **Avan Shushi Plaza Hotel** (30 rooms) 29 Ghazanchetsots St; 📞047 731599/733377; e avanplaza@hotmail.com; w avanshushiplaza.com. A very well-renovated Soviet-era hotel in the centre of town. The tallest building in Shushi; 10 floors with a lift. Gym. Cards accepted. **$$**

🏠 **Shushi Grand Hotel** (45 rooms) 2B Manukyan St; 📞047 733337/38/40; m 097 264446; e info@shushigrandhotel.com. This was a sanatorium in Soviet days but is now purely a hotel. Very well renovated & very good value with large, pleasant rooms; 3 floors, no lift. Set in 2½ha of parkland near the green church. Restaurant & bar open to non-residents & serving Armenian & Middle Eastern cuisine. Accepts cards. **$$**

🏠 **Avetyans B&B** (3 rooms) 3 Karaglugh St; 📞041 019018. One of several new family-run homestays in Shushi, offering quad & family rooms in a renovated historical house. Kitchen & pleasant terrace. Homemade b/fast. Undergoing refurbishment at the time of research. **$**

🏠 **Shushi Hotel** (12 rooms) 3 Amiryan St; 📞047 731357; m 097 251599; e shushihotel@yahoo.com; w shushi-hotel.com. In the centre of the town, close to the cathedral. Rooms warm & comfortable; 4 floors, no lift. Can also organise guided tours. **$**

## ELSEWHERE IN KARABAGH

🏠 **Sea Stone Hotel** (14 rooms) Vank village, Martakert region; 📞010 500168 (Yerevan number); m 097 286285/235072. This hotel is 3km outside Vank (the village below Gandzasar) & is run by the same people as the Eclectica. It is a more luxurious hotel, with comfortable rooms, but is just as ostentatious. Restaurant, café. Can arrange tours of Karabagh. **$–$$**

🏠 **Ani Paradise Hotel** (8 rooms) Khndzristan village, Askeran region; m 097 282000. This small, pleasant hotel in a country house 18km from Stepanakert has sgl/dbl/trpl/quad rooms & a swimming pool & can arrange horseriding, fishing & hiking. Lunch/dinner can be provided with notice. Priced per room, rather than pp. **$**

🏠 **Hotel Eclectica** (18 rooms) Vank village, Martakert region; 📞010 500168 (Yerevan number); m 097 286285. Situated just below Gandzasar Monastery in Vank village. Rooms basic. The 6 rooms on the ground floor (1 dbl, 2 twin, 1 trpl, 1 quad, 1 room for 5) share 2 bathrooms, as do the 13 rooms upstairs (9 dbl, 4 sgl). This hotel lives up to its name: the extraordinary entrance hall is decorated as an undersea world with perspex cases, containing models depicting Armenian life, set into the floor. The restaurant ceiling is held

Food and drink in Nagorno Karabagh is similar to that in Armenia (page 96), but one local speciality is herb bread, *jhingalov hats*. This is a classic flatbread into which are incorporated anywhere between seven and 15 seasonal wild herbs and vegetables. The dough is rolled out into a flat sheet, a generous pile of chopped greens is placed on top, the sides of the dough are folded over and the whole is rolled out again. It is then cooked on a griddle brushed with oil. It's absolutely delicious when fresh, though beware of some inferior imitations. You can watch it being made at the market in Stepanakert and buy it fresh and warm straight off the hotplate. *Jhingalov hats* makes excellent picnic food.

up by half a dozen Atlas-like figures & Corinthian columns, between which is a frieze embellished with casts of Armenian coins. The pictures on the wall are reproductions of works by Van Gogh. Outside, an open-air stage has tiered green & yellow plastic seats. Restaurant, bar, café. No rooms en suite. **$**

**Samvel Arakelyan's Hostel** (3 rooms) Hadrut; m 097 204205. Useful if starting the Janapar Trail (page 381) from Hadrut. Samvel hosts tourists (& sometimes military personnel) in trpl rooms with a shared bathroom in this comfortable, renovated B&B. He can also arrange hiking tours locally & has his own vehicle. **$**

## WHERE TO EAT AND DRINK

Stepanakert is considerably better served by standalone restaurants and cafés than Shushi, which until recently had no eating options worth mentioning beyond its few hotels; this does seem to be changing as the town rebuilds, and in both towns a pleasing number of cafés and restaurants are non-smoking. Some hotels have restaurants and/or cafés where non-residents can eat. See maps and listings on pages 377 and 383.

Opening hours and prices are similar to those in Armenia (page 142). Most villages have a well-stocked shop where food can be purchased, and petrol stations sometimes have a small shop or fast-food outlet attached. When spending a day away from the main towns in lesser-visited places, a picnic is possibly the best option, though the roads to the main sights are now relatively well served by roadside eateries. Those walking the Janapar Trail (page 381) will experience village life more intimately by eating at homestays, though provisions suitable for camp cookery can be found in most villages, as can local produce such as cheese and honey. Several good supermarkets and grocery stores exist in Stepanakert, and the market on Sasuntsi Davit Street is a good place to buy provisions.

## SHOPPING

Most **shops** are to be found in Stepanakert on or near Vazgen Sargsyan Street (formerly, and sometimes still, called Yerevanyan Avenue) or Azatamartikner Street. Maps can be bought at Kanzler, a **stationery shop** (26 Vazgen Sargsyan St); English-language books are rare.

The **market** on Sasuntsi Davit Street (page 384) sells household items and clothes as well as food, while for souvenirs, **Nereni Arts and Crafts** (10 Grigor Lusavorich St; ☎047 984711; m 097 217711; e nereni_nk@yahoo.com; ⨍ nereni.artsakh) is the best option, with a good range of handmade local crafts. For handmade **carpets** try the Shushi Carpet Museum (page 387).

# OTHER PRACTICALITIES

At present Stepanakert has far more facilities than Shushi (though historical Shushi is arguably the more attractive of the two towns), with most **banks**, a **post office**, **internet cafés**, **currency exchanges**, etc on or near Vazgen Sargsyan Street or Azatamartikner Street. All banks offer currency exchange, and **ATMs** accept international cards as in Armenia (page 83). **Telephone** and **internet** services are provided by Karabakh Telecom (14 Nelson Stepanyan St; ✆047 979702; e info@karabakhtelecom.com; w karabakhtelecom.com). **Emergency phone numbers** are the same as in Armenia: fire ✆101, police ✆102, ambulance ✆103, general emergencies ✆911. Anyone wishing to use a **mobile phone** in Nagorno Karabagh should note that Armenian SIM cards will work on (affordable) roaming tariffs if activated *before* you arrive; see the website of your provider for details. If you're staying longer it may be cheaper or more practical to buy a Karabakh Telecom SIM card, particularly if you plan to use a lot of data. Options available include prepaid and post-paid cards with tariffs dependent on whether domestic, Armenian or international access is desired. Information on cards and tariffs is available from Karabakh Telecom's website. **Postage** rates are similar to Armenia's, and all major towns have post offices. There is a philatelic corner in the main post office on Hakobyan Street in Stepanakert.

There are **tourist information offices** in Shushi (3 Garegin Nzhdeh St; ✆047 733296; ⏲ 10.00–18.00 daily) and Stepanakert (opposite the Armenia Hotel on Veratsnund (Renaissance) Sq, February 20th St; ✆097 399175; ⏲ 09.00–19.00 daily). Both have English-speaking staff who can help with accommodation bookings, transport enquiries, local tours and the like. The offices are run by the rebranded **Artsakh Tourism Development Agency** (2 Knunyantsner St, Stepanakert; ✆047 949172; m 097 399175; e info@artsakh.travel; w artsakh.travel), whose website has some useful background information (amid much flowery language) including details of the regions of Nagorno Karabagh, accommodation, transport, museums, local tour operators and cuisine. It also publishes a guidebook, *Discovered Paradise*, which contains similar information, and a series of free booklets which contain background information and good photographs but few practical details. Titles include *Karabakh*, *Stepanakert*, *Gandzasar*, *Tigranakert*, *Carpets* and *Nikol Duman* and can be obtained from the tourist information offices in Shushi and Stepanakert.

Another good internet source is w armeniapedia.org, which has information on Nagorno Karabagh; a counterpart to the excellent book *Rediscovering Armenia*, entitled *Rediscovering Artsakh*, was being prepared for (digital) publication at the time of research and promises to cover exhaustively the great many minor historical sites of Nagorno Karabagh not included in this guide. Finally, even if you do not

---

## TELEPHONE CODES IN NAGORNO KARABAGH

Landline phone numbers comprise the code for Nagorno Karabagh (047), followed by an area code which indicates the town (Stepanakert 9, Shushi 7, Askeran 6, Martakert 4, Hadrut 5, Martuni 8) followed by the five-digit local number. The area code is usually given as part of the number. Karabakh Telecom mobile numbers (see above) start with 097. If calling from abroad, remove the initial 0 and add the international country code +374, as for Armenia. If calling from Armenia, no country code is required; Nagorno Karabagh numbers can be treated as local.

plan to walk it you will find a great deal of useful information on the **Janapar Trail** website (**w** janapartrail.org) about the sites and villages along the way.

There is a useful, if old (2001), **printed map** of Nagorno Karabagh, with street plans of Stepanakert and Shushi and notes on sites of interest. Although you can see it on display at the Shushi tourism information office, it is their only copy: you might find it at the stationery shop Kanzler (page 379). Both tourist offices can supply a free folding street map of Stepanakert, though it was last updated in 2011. A small folding map (you may need a magnifying glass or magnifying compass) can be bought at Nereni Crafts (page 379). The Collage maps of Armenia (page 65) also cover Nagorno Karabagh.

In terms of **digital mapping**, be aware that Google Maps does not at the time of research show the line of contact; also, administrative labels include both Armenian and Azeri names in the script of each language but not in English (presumably because transliterating one but not the other would imply a political position). Open-source mapping such as OpenStreetMap tends to follow a policy of representing the de facto situation, is currently more detailed in remoter regions, and *does* show the ceasefire line; similar advice applies as for Armenia (page 112) regarding its accuracy and that of the Soviet-era mapping.

**THE JANAPAR TRAIL** Conceived in 2007, the Janapar Trail is now a well-developed, waymarked, **long-distance hiking route** that was originally designed to connect a variety of cultural and natural heritage sites across Nagorno Karabagh. The 270km route can be completed in 15 days and homestays are available at each suggested stopping point, eliminating the need to carry camping equipment (although many backpackers do choose to camp at least some of the time). The more popular **southern section** of the route – for which six days are recommended – begins in Hadrut and proceeds via Togh village, Azokh Cave, Karmir Shuka with its 2,000-year-old plane tree, Zontik (Umbrella) Waterfall and the Hunot Canyon to reach Shushi. (The section to the waterfall is also a popular and highly recommended day hike to/from Shushi; page 388.) The more challenging and less travelled **northern section** of the route in Nagorno Karabagh continues to Stepanakert, Patara and Kolatak; the natural limestone fortress of Kachaghakaberd; Gandzasar Monastery (page 390); Zuar with its hot springs; the desolated clifftop city of Karvachar (page 392); and ultimately Tsar village (page 392), from where the final gruelling 34km section crosses the ridge dividing Armenia and the self-declared Republic of Artsakh and ends in Vardenis. From Vardenis a 'virtual' – insofar as there are no trail markers – extension continues to Dilijan National Park, where it is possible to join the Transcaucasian Trail (see box, page 114) or continue to Yerevan. Interested hikers can download the GPS route from the Janapar Trail website.

The trail is marked both with **blue and white painted blazes** on trees and rocks, as well as with occasional trail markers emblazoned with the trail's **blue and yellow footprint logo**. In 2017 the government's head of tourism proclaimed the trail a 'national treasure', and in 2018 a crowdfunding campaign raised funds to perform much-needed maintenance on several sections of the trail and reinstall all of its blazes and markers. As a result, the route is now much easier to follow and the previously unmarked northern section comprehensively marked as well. In addition, several improvements were made to the route, homestay listings were expanded, and a new bridge was built near Zontik Waterfall.

The project's **website** (**w** janapartrail.org) contains a wealth of information for the interested hiker, including downloadable GPS files, supported navigation apps for smartphones, printable maps and step-by-step descriptions of the route, as well as the contact details and addresses of families who have agreed to host hikers on the trail and who have been assisted in preparing their homes to accommodate the weary and hungry. The trail's developers have consulted closely with the HALO Trust to ensure as far as possible that the trail can be considered as safe as anywhere else in the region, but walkers are advised to remain vigilant regarding mines and unexploded ordinance (see box, page 370) in what is a post-conflict zone and to stay on the marked route at all times.

## WHAT TO SEE AND DO

The most popular historic sites for visitors in Nagorno Karabagh are the monasteries of **Gandzasar** (page 390) and **Dadivank** (page 391). The excavated site and museum of **Tigranakert** (page 388) are well worth a visit. The architecturally distinctive town of **Shushi** (page 385) still provides thought-provoking evidence of the conflict over Karabagh, evidence which has now largely disappeared from Stepanakert and which is rapidly disappearing from Shushi, too. Entrance to museums in Nagorno Karabagh is generally free or very cheap. A contribution, and perhaps a tip to the guide, is always welcome. Historic sites which are in ruins are always open. Where there is a church which is now active it will be open every day (at least 09.00–18.00 and often longer). The rest of a monastery site is usually accessible at all times.

Several annual **festivals** have begun to establish themselves in Nagorno Karabagh, including the Artsakh Wine Festival held each autumn in Togh village (page 394) to celebrate the end of the grape harvest. Event listings can be found at w artsakh. travel/events.

**STEPANAKERT** Formerly Khankendi, the capital of Nagorno Karabagh (population 55,200 as of the 2015 census) was renamed Stepanakert in 1923 in honour of the Armenian Bolshevik Stepan Shahumyan (1878–1918) after whom Stepanavan is also named. His statue stands in Shahumyan Square at the northern end of Vazgen Sargsyan Street, one of the main shopping streets. Newly independent Azerbaijan renamed it back to Khankendi in 1992, but Stepanakert remains the name in use within Nagorno Karabagh today. The town suffered considerable damage in the war but this has now been repaired and the bustling town centre has the feel and appearance of a capital city, albeit a small one.

### ✘ Where to eat and drink  Map, opposite

✘ **Pandok Karas**  18 Azatamartikner St; m 097 148000; ⏰ 11.00–23.00 daily. A reliable traditional tavern-style restaurant on the main drag through Stepanakert, serving the usual salads, soups & grills as well as some regional specialities inc *jhingalov hats* (see box, page 379) & *korkot*, a variant of *harissa* (page 100) made with pork instead of poultry. Also serves draught Alaverdi unfiltered beer. Non-smoking.

✘ **Tashir Pizza**  20 Azatamartikner St; ☎047 971117; ⏰ 10.00–midnight. A branch of the popular Armenian fast-food chain. A wide variety of pizzas can be bought by the slice or whole. Also serves pasta, salads, soups, etc.

✘ **Ureni Restaurant**  66 Tumanyan St; ☎047 944544; ⏰ noon–midnight. Once the poshest restaurant in Stepanakert apart from those in hotels. Still popular with locals. Armenian & Russian cuisine.

🍽 **Renaissance Tea House & Restaurant** 28/53 Knunyantsner St; ☎047 108180; m 097 108108; 🇫; ⏰ 11.00–midnight daily. Delightful non-smoking café, new in 2016, serving a large range of international & local herbal teas (also sold loose), Armenian/Italian coffees, chocolates & pastries, as well as an extensive European lunch/dinner menu. Indoor & outdoor seating. Deliberately no Wi-Fi to encourage socialising. Take-away coffee available.

Askeran,
Tatik yev Papik

TIGRAN METS STREET

Victory
Square

South–north
highway

0 ———— 500m
0 ———— 500yds

ALEK MANOOGYAN ST

ABOVYAN STREET

SAROYAN STREET

MKHITAR GOSH ST

DAVIT BEK STREET

AZATAMARTIKNER STREET

KAMO STREET

TUMANYAN STREET

Ministry of
Foreign Affairs

PARUYR SEVAK STREET

TERTERYAN ST

SASUNTSI DAVIT ST

Stepanakert
Republican Stadium

DANIELYAN ST

Lovers'
Alley

Market

South–north
highway

KHACHATRYAN ST

National Assembly
building

Stepan Shahumian
Monument

Artsakh Museum
of History

Stepanakert
Art Gallery

VERATSNUND SQ

HISTORICAL
QUARTERS

GAREGIN
NZHDEH ST

Fallen Freedom Fighters' Memorial Museum

Museum of
Missing Soldiers

STEPANYAN ST

HAKOBYAN ST

Vahram Papazyan
State Drama Theatre

KNUNYANTSNER ST

LUSAVORICH ST

Nereni Arts
& Crafts

NELSON ST

VAZGEN SARGSYAN STREET

VARDAN MAMIKONYAN ST

Republic
Hospital

BAGHRAMYAN STREET

Memorial Complex
of Stepanakert

Cemetery

MARTUNI ST

GENERAL ANDRANIK ST

MKRTCHYAN ST

Holy Mother of
God Cathedral
(under construction)

Children's
Hospital

VAGHARSHYAN ST

**NOTE**
THE PLACE NAMES SHOWN ON
THE MAP ARE THE ARMENIAN NAMES
WHICH VISITORS WILL FIND IN
CURRENT USE WITHIN THE TOWN.
AZERBAIJAN USES DIFFERENT NAMES.

**Where to stay**

*For listings, see from page 377*

| 1 | Armenia | 7 | Raffo & Karine's Hostel |
| 2 | Hotel Europe | 8 | Vallex Garden |
| 3 | Hotel Heghnar | 9 | Yerevan |
| 4 | Hotel Tirun | | |
| 5 | National Artsakh | | |
| 6 | Park | | |

**Where to eat and drink**

*For listings, see from page 382*

| 10 | Bardak Pub |
| 11 | Pandok Karas |
| 12 | Renaissance Tea House & Restaurant |
| 13 | The Roots |
| 14 | Tashir Pizza |
| 15 | Ureni |

7

🍴 **The Roots** 16/38 Vazgen Sargsyan St; m 097 315004; w the-roots-stepanakert. business.site; ⏰ Mon–Sat noon–23.00, Sun 14.00–23.00. Spacious & welcoming community-oriented café serving good European cuisine inc burgers, fresh pasta & wood-fired pizza (from 19.00). Aims to act as a much-needed cultural space for local youth to meet, exchange ideas, display artwork & hold events.

🍺 **Bardak Pub** 2/1 Tevosyan St; m 097 333004; 🅕; ⏰ 20.00–01.00 daily. Stepanakert's (& perhaps Nagorno Karabagh's) first real pub opened in 2017 southeast of the town centre & has quickly become a favourite place for young locals & foreigners to meet & mingle, where relaxed evenings turn to late-night dancing sessions. Proprietor Azat is very knowledgeable about hiking & climbing in the region, and runs the Free Step Trekking Club (🅕).

**What to see and do** The National Assembly (parliament) building on Veratsnund (Renaissance) Square is topped by a transparent cupola reminiscent of Armenian church architecture. The square itself is a popular place for locals to gather and stroll on hot summer evenings, with several outdoor cafés and terraces in the vicinity. It also hosts an outdoor stage during public holidays and festivals. From Veratsnund Square, steps go down to **Lovers' Alley** which continues to undergo renovation and landscaping. At the bottom is a sculpture of two hands with a wedding ring; beyond this is the renovated Stepanakert Republican Stadium, originally opened in 1956 as the Josef Stalin Stadium, now an all-seater **stadium** seating 12,000 and since 2012 home to the Artsakh national football team, whose first international fixture was against Abkhazia (another unrecognised de facto state in the Caucasus region). Until recently Stepanakert had no churches; to address this issue the construction of a new **cathedral**, dedicated to the Mother of God, was launched in 2006 just south of the historical quarter, but dwindling funds seem to have stalled the project. The smaller and less ambitious **church of St Jacob** in the northeast of the city was opened in 2007 and remains the only working church at the time of research. In the **market** (⏰ 07.00–18.00 daily) it is possible to see the herb bread *jhingalov hats* being made (see box, page 379); this is a good place to buy food for picnics and self-catering.

The **Artsakh Museum of History** (4 Sasuntsi Davit St; 📞047 941042; e tangaran@ktsurf.net; ⏰ 09.00–17.00 Mon–Fri, 09.00–16.00 Sat, lunch break 13.00–14.00; Russian, English & French spoken) is just up the hill from the market. It gives an interesting portrayal of Nagorno Karabagh from prehistoric times to the present day. The Soviet era is not totally ducked as sometimes happens but, World War II apart, the focus is on the positive side (industrialisation) rather than the negative (the purges). The two sides in the days of the First Armenian Republic, the Bolsheviks and the Dashnaks, are given complementary displays opposite each other. The final room covers the Karabagh war. Two museums related to the Karabagh war are close to each other on a small square between Nzhdeh and Hakobyan streets: the **Fallen Freedom Fighters' Memorial Museum** (25 Vazgen Sargsyan St; 📞047 950738; w kniga.am; ⏰ 09.00–18.00 Mon–Sat) is devoted to soldiers who died during the war and whose graves are known. The **Museum of Missing Soldiers** remembers those who are missing, presumed dead (although their relatives still hope that they are alive as prisoners of war and that one day some will return). Both museums have collections of anything at all connected with those remembered (personal belongings, letters, flags, uniforms, medals, etc) as well as walls densely covered with portraits. What makes a visit even more poignant is that the volunteers who staff the museums, and show you round, are relatives of the dead or missing soldiers. One comment in the visitors' book reads 'To come to Karabagh and not visit these museums means not to have visited Karabagh.'

| | |
|---|---|
| 1 January | New Year |
| 6 January | Christmas |
| 8 March | International Women's Day |
| March/April | Good Friday |
| March/April | Easter Monday |
| 7 April | Motherhood and Beauty Day |
| 24 April | Armenian Genocide Remembrance Day |
| 1 May | Workers' Solidarity Day |
| 9 May | Victory and Armed Forces Day |
| 28 May | First Republic Day |
| 2 September | Independence Day |
| 10 December | Constitution Day |
| 31 December | New Year's Eve |

The **Vahram Papazyan State Drama Theatre** (18 Hakobyan St), founded in 1932, is an elegant theatre but in need of significant funds for restoration. Nonetheless, there is still much beautiful plasterwork. The season is usually May to October; it does not function during the winter because of the problem of heating it. The programme is advertised at the theatre and in the town. Tickets cost AMD500. The theatre seats 425; the crossed-off seats on the seating plan do not indicate those which are already booked, but rather those which are unusable at present. If you happen to call in when the manager is there he will probably be delighted to show you round and perhaps offer you a taste of his own mulberry vodka.

The delightful **Stepanakert Art Gallery** (Vardan Mamikonyan St, just before its junction with Sasuntsi Davit St; ⊕ 09.00–18.00 daily; English spoken) opened in late 2013 and is well worth a visit. The ground floor houses temporary exhibitions of a varying nature, while the upstairs display of sculpture is permanent with labels in Armenian, English and Russian. The **Memorial Complex of Stepanakert**, in the southeast of the town, was built in memory of the 22,000 inhabitants of Nagorno Karabagh (of all ethnicities) who died during the Great Patriotic War (World War II). A separate part of the complex holds the graves of Armenian soldiers killed during the Karabagh war.

Last but not least, on a small hill on the north side of Stepanakert is a **statue** reproduced in a thousand Karabagh souvenirs. Created by the sculptor Sargis Baghdasaryan in Soviet times, it is officially called *We Are Our Mountains*, though it is usually referred to as **Tatik yev Papik** (sometimes 'Mamik yev Papik', Granny and Grandad). Portraying an elderly couple in national costume, the statue is intended to symbolise the unity of the Karabagh people with their mountains. While it is a couple of kilometres from the city centre, a good pavement leads all the way there and refreshments are on sale at the foot of the hill.

**SHUSHI** The important historical centre of regional culture and the former capital of the Karabagh khanate, known to its present Armenian residents as Shushi and to Azeris as Shusha, is visible from Stepanakert on its dominating hilltop position to the south, set on a precipice overlooking the impressive gorge of the Karkar. It is notable for its distinctive 18th- to 19th-century architecture. Unlike Stepanakert the scars of conflict are still very evident in Shushi, with many ruined buildings, but the reconstruction efforts of recent years are also obvious. Prior to 1988 the town was one of the few in the region to have a mixed and relatively well-integrated Armenian and Azeri population. Now the Azeri population has fled while the Armenians remain. Some of the blocks of flats are still burnt-out shells while others have been fully rebuilt, and more and more of the older houses and buildings are being restored in their original historical style, lending the town an increasingly cultured feel and making for pleasant urban walking. Something of the complexity of emotions surrounding Shushi is perhaps captured in the language used today to refer to the battle of 8–9 May 1992 in which the town fell to Armenian forces, with Armenia celebrating the town's 'liberation' and Azerbaijan lamenting its 'occupation'.

## ✖ Where to eat and drink  *Map, below*

There are a couple of snack bars and cafés dotted about the town, and with the increase in rebuilding and guesthouse accommodation the number seems likely to grow. The Shushi Grand Hotel (page 378) has a good restaurant which is open to non-residents and serves Armenian and Middle Eastern cuisine.

✖ **Old Shushi** 3 Garegin Nzhdeh St; ☏097 212268; ⊕ 10.00–23.00 daily. On the 1st floor above the tourist information centre, opened in 2018 & serving traditional regional dishes in a small but pleasantly decorated dining room.

**What to see and do**  Shushi has a **tourist information centre** (page 380) with helpful English-speaking staff and one of the town's few **restaurants** (see above). The town has several points of interest. Part of the medieval town wall remains

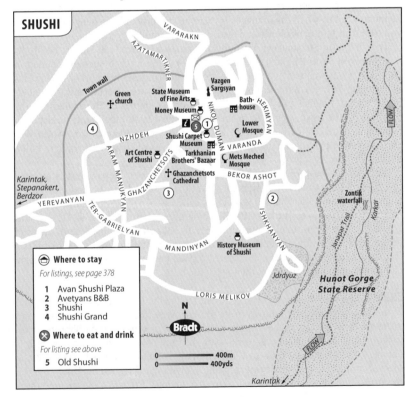

**SHUSHI**

VARARAKN
AZATAMARTIKNER

Town wall
Green church
NZHDEH
ARAM MANUKYAN
TER-GABRIELYAN

State Museum of Fine Arts
Money Museum
Shushi Carpet Museum
Art Centre of Shushi
GHAZANCHETSOTS
Tarkhanian Brothers' Bazaar
Ghazanchetsots Cathedral

Vazgen Sargsyan
NIKOL DUMAN
Bath-house
Lower Mosque
VARANDA
Mets Meched Mosque
HEKIMYAN
BEKOR ASHOT

*Karintak, Stepanakert, Berdzor*
← YEREVANYAN

MANDINYAN
LORIS MELIKOV

History Museum of Shushi
ISHKHANYAN

Jdrdyuz

Zontik waterfall
Janapar Trail
Karkar
FLOW

**Hunot Gorge State Reserve**

N

**Bradt**

Where to stay
*For listings, see page 378*
1  Avan Shushi Plaza
2  Avetyans B&B
3  Shushi
4  Shushi Grand

Where to eat and drink
*For listing see above*
5  Old Shushi

0 ———— 400m
0 ———— 400yds

FLOW

*Karintak* ↙

and two 19th-century churches have been restored; both of them, with their very pale stone, are striking in appearance. The massive, almost white **Ghazanchetsots Cathedral** ('Ghazan' refers to some very large vessels which were gifted to the church) was built between 1868 and 1887 and has been fully restored. Like all Karabagh churches it was closed during the Soviet period and saw service variously as a granary, a garage and a munitions store. Oddly enough the belltower, decorated with figures of angels playing musical instruments which stands beside it, was built earlier, in 1858. All but one of the angels decorating the belltower were destroyed in the war, the remaining one being christened the 'guardian angel of Artsakh'. After renovation the church and belltower, with new angels, were reconsecrated in 1998. The other church, the so-called **green church** (*kanach zham*), in the northwestern part of the town, has a silver metallic cupola and was completed in 1847.

Elsewhere in the town **mosques** survive: religious buildings were not destroyed after the war. In 2005 the government of the self-declared Republic of Nagorno-Karabakh took the most interesting one, the **Mets Meched** or **Upper Govhar Agha Mosque** of 1883, under its protection and invited the religious authorities in Tehran to send specialists to restore it. In Soviet days it served as the town's historical museum. It is possible to climb one of the minarets for an excellent view over the town. Across the square from the mosque the **Tarkhanyan brothers' bazaar** has been rebuilt to its original design, with the hope it will function again as a market. Down the road opposite the bazaar is an overgrown second mosque, the **Lower Govhar Agha Mosque**, of 1875. A hammam or **bathhouse** (east of the main square) has also been restored.

On one side of the main square, at the junction of Ghazanchetsots and Garegin Nzhdeh streets, the 18th-century caravanserai has been magnificently converted to become the **State Museum of Fine Arts** (24 Ghazanchetsots St; ⌕047 731410; ⏰ 09.00–18.00 Tue–Sun; AMD250) which opened in 2013. A visit is highly recommended. All the works of art displayed have been gifted to the gallery either by the artist or by collectors. The splendid collection is well displayed and is labelled in Armenian, Russian and English (but unfortunately without dates for the artists or the works). A catalogue with excellent reproductions of the paintings is available for AMD5,000. Next door is the small, well-presented **Museum of Money** (⌕047 731960; ⏰ 10.00–13.00 & 14.00–16.00 Tue–Sun; entrance free), opened in 2018, with collections of medieval coins found during excavations at Erebuni (page 172) as well as more modern coins, banknotes and bonds issued and used in Armenia and Nagorno Karabagh from the Tsarist era to the present day. Exhibits are well labelled in English, Russian and Armenian.

On the square, the **statue** of the seated man, usually surrounded by flowers, is Vazgen Sargsyan. Sargsyan, the main commander of Armenian forces during the Karabagh war, was Defence Minister of Armenia (1995–99) and Prime Minister of Armenia from June 1999 until his assassination in October the same year (page 28). Opposite the cathedral, in a former printing house, is the **Art Centre of Shushi** (Ghazanchetsots St; ⏰ 10.00–18.00 daily) which has an exhibition of carpets on the ground floor and temporary exhibitions on the upper floor. The **History Museum of Shushi** (17 Mesrop Mashtots St; ⌕047 731948; ⏰ 09.00–17.00 Mon–Sat) displays the history of Shushi in a mid-19th-century house. There are the usual domestic and archaeological items together with interesting information about printing, education and music. Labels are in English. The private **Shushi Carpet Museum** (31 Ghazanchetsots St; e artsakhgorg@mail.ru; ⏰ 10.00–19.00 Tue–Sun; donations towards the upkeep/renovation of the building welcomed) is well worth a visit, even for those who do not have a special interest in carpets. Two rooms contain antique carpets from various regions of Armenia and Karabagh, all the personal collection of the owner. A full explanation from the excellent guide could well occupy a couple of hours but she realises that not everyone has that much time and is able to tailor her information as appropriate. The attached showroom has both new and antique carpets for sale. New carpets cost from US$400 per square metre. For those who wish and are able to buy, the showroom can manage all the red tape involved in export and delivery.

On the southeast edge of town there is a recreational parklike area, **Jdrdyuz**, from where one can look down into the impressive gorge of the Karkar River. It is possible to explore the gorge either by following the footpath down from Ishkhanyan Street on the eastern edge of town north of the hospital (ask locally for *zontiki arahet*) or from **Karintak** village which lies at the foot of the cliffs below Shushi. Karintak suffered badly during the war but is recovering, its cobbled streets presenting a picture of village life. The path between Shushi and Karintak is one of the most spectacular parts of the Janapar Trail (page 381) and follows the Karkar River through the Hunot Gorge State Reserve, past the iconic moss-covered **Zontik (Umbrella) Waterfall** and through the ruins of Hunot village (so deep in the gorge that no road could be built to it and which was abandoned in Soviet times) where the remains of several medieval watermills can be seen. If you only have time for one hike in Nagorno Karabagh, it is strongly suggested to make it this one.

## NORTHEASTERN NAGORNO KARABAGH
Some 15km north of Stepanakert just before the town of **Askeran** the main road passes right through the fortress known variously as **Mayraberd** (Mother Fortress) or Zoraberd (Powerful Fortress). It was reinforced in 1788–89 by the Persians because of the increasing Russian threat and most of what can be seen today dates from then. The fortress is on both sides of the Karkar River. What survives is a triangle of walls breached by the road on the northern side plus a smaller fortification together with several towers and a length of wall with the remains of a walkway on top on the southern side.

Beyond Askeran the road continues another 5km to the ghost town of **Aghdam**. Aghdam was a sizeable town, formerly inhabited by Azeris, but it was destroyed by the Karabagh army after they captured it to prevent it falling back into Azeri hands and is now an uninhabited ruin. Many visitors choose to visit in spite of (or perhaps because of) the desolation, although official permission to visit will not be given.

Beyond Aghdam, on the Martakert road, is the **excavated site and State Archaeological Museum of Tigranakert** (**w** tigranakert.am; ⊕ 09.00–19.00 daily; English-speaking guide sometimes available; AMD250). (The website's English pages were not active at the time of writing but photographs of this fascinating and impressive historical site can be viewed on the Armenian and Russian pages.) A medieval fortress sits at the foot of the dramatic site of the ancient city of Tigranakert, founded by Tigran the Great (ruled c95–55BC). Behind the medieval castle a wave-like escarpment on the southeastern slope of Mount Vankasar (879m) rises from the plain. The triangular fortified city, with the citadel at its apex, occupies the lower third of the slope above the castle. The site covers some 50ha and excavations, started in 2005, are continuing. Already two of the main walls of the city have been uncovered. Built of local white limestone, without mortar, the stone blocks were dovetailed together by means of triangular joints. Also notable are the steps carved into the rock on the edge of the escarpment. The many finds, dating from the 5th century BC to the 17th century AD, are now displayed in the museum which opened in the medieval fortress in June 2010. Information is in Armenian, English and Russian. Note that, although the museum entrance is signed straight ahead of the entrance gate, to follow the exhibition chronologically either go in via the door to the left or make your way there once inside.

South of the castle the foundations of a 5th- to 7th-century basilica have been excavated. Beyond the fortified site a small renovated cross-dome church stands on the peak of Mount Vankasar. The church holds nothing of interest but it makes a good endpoint for a walk which gives a bird's-eye view of Tigranakert and views across the Azerbaijan plain. It takes about an hour of moderately steep walking to reach the church, the first part made easier by the ancient steps carved into the rock. It is worth starting early in the day before it becomes too hot. Even if not wishing to reach the church, walking to the top of the excavated site is worth it for the overall impression of this important location.

Driving north to the town of **Martakert** there is much evidence of the war and the departed Azeri population: ruined houses, a well-preserved Islamic burial chamber, a toppled Azeri cemetery and a ruined Soviet memorial. Martakert centre appears prosperous and has all the facilities expected of a town.

**NORTHWESTERN NAGORNO KARABAGH** Some 22km north of Stepanakert, in the village of **Tsaghkashat** (Ghshlagh), is the **house museum of Nikol Duman** (m 097 236327 (Mariam); ⊕ 10.00–14.00 & 15.00–18.00 Mon–Fri; AMD250). The lower floor of the restored 19th-century house is dedicated to the life and work of the Armenian national liberation movement figure Nikol Duman (1867–1914), born Nikoghayos Ter-Hovhannisyan, and includes collections of military and domestic items. The upper floor shows a typical living room of the era. Other ethnographical displays are nearby. Within the complex is a souvenir shop selling local handicrafts and produce. Snacks are available and traditional meals can be organised. There is overnight accommodation for up to 13 guests in the village (AMD4,000 pp with breakfast or AMD3,000 pp without) which can be booked through the museum.

Clearly visible on a mountaintop to the west is the prominent limestone outcrop of **Kachaghakaberd** (Magpie's Fortress), which can be reached on foot from either Patara or Kolatak. Both ways are marked as part of the Janapar Trail (page 381); allow a full day for the return trip. The natural fortress, which dates back to the 8th century and is referred to in some historical sources as Khachen (see also page 390), was said to be impregnable and served as an important refuge during successive waves of Arab invasion, with additional manmade fortifications added (and still visible). According to one legend, its popular name derives from a particular event during which the invading force began to retreat after an unsuccessful siege of many months. As they began to do so they noticed a large flock of magpies atop the fortress. Investigating soldiers disturbed the birds, who took flight en masse; at the same time they discovered that the besieged locals had chosen to starve to death rather than give themselves up, and the image of the magpies remained in memory.

North of Kolatak, on an upgraded dirt road which is passable by car, is the ruined **Metsaranits Monastery**, which is thought to have been constructed around the same time as the fortress, though its exact foundation date remains unknown. Like Dadivank it has a complex layout with buildings on two levels, most of which date from the 8th–18th centuries. The oldest inscription, on a khachkar pedestal later built into a wall, refers to 851, while others relate to a rebuilding in 1212. Repairs were probably carried out in the 15th and 16th centuries. Another inscription records the construction of domestic buildings in 1725.

On the upper level there are two churches, a gavit and an arcaded entrance gallery which leads into the other three buildings. On the lower level are other monastic and domestic buildings. The whole complex is surrounded by a largely intact, high wall with a tunnel-like western entrance. The oldest building is probably the easternmost church, the smaller of the two churches. Its style, with a high bema underneath which are small cells, suggests a 12th-century rebuilding on an older construction. The arcaded gallery adjoins the west wall of this church and in turn it has the second, larger, church to its north. This larger church has a gavit on its west side. All four buildings (churches, gallery and gavit) are barrel-vaulted and are paved with massive slabs and gravestones. The north walls of the gavit and the larger church form part of the monastery's external wall.

It is known from manuscripts that Metsaranits Monastery was the centre of a diocese and, in the 13th century, the residence of the Katholikos; bishops and katholikoi were buried here. It was an important educational and manuscript centre in the Principality of Khachen (1261–1750), the most important of the region's medieval Armenian principalities and which was situated on part of present-day Nagorno Karabagh. Being nearer to Stepanakert and on the way to Gandzasar, and with good road access, one imagines that if restored it could one day rival Dadivank.

## Gandzasar Monastery
Gandzasar (Treasure Mountain) is once more a working monastery and seminary. Open to the public, it is accessible via a good road on a hilltop outside **Vank** (Monastery) village, Martakert district, with ample parking for the many tour groups that visit the site. Dedicated to John the Baptist, the monastery's name derives from the presence of silver deposits in the area and it has been fully restored since 1991. It is particularly notable for its exquisite carved detail. Surrounded by walls, it is a cross-dome church with its 16-sided tambour topped by an umbrella cupola. Owing to its inaccessibility, Nagorno Karabagh partly avoided the large-scale Seljuk invasion in the 11th and 12th centuries, as well as the Mongolian invasions in the 13th century. Consequently some of the finest church architecture of the period is found here. The monastery was founded in 1216, the church being built between 1232 and 1238, while the gavit was added in 1261. The founders were Hasan-Jalal Dawla, ruler of Khachen, together with his wife Mamkan and son Atabek. The monastery served as the burial place of the Khachen rulers, and until the 19th century as the seat of the Katholikos of Aghvank.

The tambour of the **church** is an outstanding work of art, decorated with numerous sculptured images between the triple columns separating each side. On the western side two bearded figures with long moustaches are sitting in an oriental posture with their feet tucked under them. On the south side are kneeling figures facing each other with arms outstretched and haloes round their heads while angels spread their wings over them in blessing. One side shows the Virgin and Child, there are two bulls' heads and an eagle with spreading wings. The gavit obscures another sculptural composition – a crucifix under the gable of the west façade with seraphs hovering over Jesus and Mary, and John the Baptist kneeling in prayer with outstretched hands. The north façade shows a bird in the western sky and the south façade has galloping horses. The west and east façades have large relief crosses. The **gavit** has an immense west portal which shows two birds as well as much varied abstract design. Over the north door are two lions, emblems of the Hasan-Jalalian family. The six-pointed star in front of the right-hand creature is associated with Armenian royalty. The gavit is surmounted by a belfry supported by six columns. The interiors of both church and gavit have yet more carving including the finely carved front of the altar dais, the pattern of each triangle or square being different.

Compared with the tranquil traditional appearance of the monastery, Vank village is certainly a contrast. Someone has painted all the gas pipes yellow and green to match the tiered plastic seats of the outdoor theatre attached to one of the hotels, part of which is in the form of a ship and one of whose walls has been (perhaps tastelessly) decorated with old Azeri numberplates. There are a couple of other places nearby serving snacks and refreshments.

**Dadivank (monastery)** Dadivank, one of the largest medieval Armenian monastery complexes in the region, is on the northern route to Armenia from Nagorno Karabagh. The road to Dadivank bears right after the junction with the Gandzasar road just after the Khachenaget bridge and continues north through the hills until eventually Sarsang Reservoir can be seen with the village of **Drmbon** in the foreground and the Mrav range forming a backdrop. Drmbon is an important mining area and the signposted road to Dadivank goes off left beside the large white and green building of the Base Metals Mining Company. Initially mining activities are evident along the Sarsang Reservoir but eventually these are left behind and then the rest of the journey is extremely beautiful along the gorge of the fast-flowing Tartar River as far as the monastery. Since the road was upgraded in 2017 a number of roadside eateries have appeared, as well as several filling stations, and it is no longer quite the expedition it used to be: there is even a small snack bar above Dadivank itself. It is possible to drive right up to the monastery, whose access road was paved at the same time as the main road through the region.

Dadivank is traditionally believed to be on the site of the grave of St Thaddeus who was martyred in the 1st century for preaching Christianity, 'Dadi' being a phonetic transposition of his name. Although there was probably a church here by the 4th century, the oldest surviving remains date from the 9th century. The church was pillaged in 1145–46 by the Persians but reconstruction started in the 1170s. The monastery went into decline in the 18th century and the monastery estates were only half occupied when the Khan of Shushi invited the Kurds to move on to them from Yerevan. The late 18th century saw further Persian military action, and plague and famine in 1798 saw the final abandonment of the site. There has been much restoration, which was ongoing at the time of research.

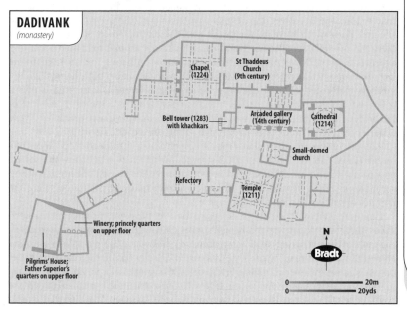

**DADIVANK**
*(monastery)*

Chapel (1224)

St Thaddeus Church (9th century)

Bell tower (1283) with khachkars

Arcaded gallery (14th century)

Cathedral (1214)

Small-domed church

Refectory

Temple (1211)

Winery; princely quarters on upper floor

Pilgrims' House; Father Superior's quarters on upper floor

N

Bradt

0 — 20m
0 — 20yds

7

The layout is exceedingly complex and there are buildings on two levels. The 9th-century **church of St Thaddeus**, built over his grave, is at the north side of the complex. Less than ideal restoration work following excavations has resulted in some loss of atmosphere from this ancient church. To its west lies a **chapel** resembling a gavit, said to be the burial vault of a princely dynasty, built in 1224. There are further contemporary buildings to the west. Southeast of St Thaddeus is the main **cathedral** which dates from 1214. The 16-sided tambour has graceful arcatures and the cupola is conical. On both the south and east façades are two figures holding a model of the church. In front of it is a 14th-century **arcaded gallery** which extends as far as the **belltower** of 1283. New steps at the belltower enable the two intricately carved khachkars to be fully appreciated. To the south there is a **small-domed church** with circular tambour and a tiled dome; its date is uncertain. The restoration of this church is also somewhat insensitive but the remains of frescoes can still be seen high on the north wall. On the lower level are the **kitchen**, **refectory** and **wine press**, as well as various accommodation quarters. The building with four round pillars on square bases is, according to an inscription of 1211, the **temple**. There is a spring at Dadivank, picnic tables, and a small shop above the site.

**Karvachar and around**  From the main road between Dadivank and Karvachar a road goes off south, signposted *tak jur*, ie: hot water. **Zuar** is reached after 17km and at least an hour of driving on a very poor road. The hot spring for which the village is known is a few hundred metres beyond the settlement. Very hot water bubbles up then flows into a pool where the temperature is bearable and several people can bathe, before it flows into the river. The springs are popular with locals and you are not necessarily assured an undisturbed soak; biting flies are also an annoyance. A couple of picnic shelters are nearby and a two-bedroom bungalow is available for overnight stays (ask at the village); the village has a small shop at its southern end where provisions can be bought.

The main road forks 10km beyond Dadivank, just beyond the last filling station in the region, which also has a decent restaurant attached. The right, northernmost, road follows the Lev River, then enters Armenia via the Sotk Pass (page 375). The left fork goes south through the gorge past the clifftop town of Karvachar and thence to the isolated village of Tsar, starting as a poor asphalt road then becoming a dirt road. In the Soviet period the road continued south for a further 12km to the Jermuk-esque health resort of **İstisu** (in Armenian Jermajur; both names literally mean 'warm water'). The bridge over the river beyond the Tsar turn-off is now a collapsed heap of broken concrete, but it is possible to ford the river just east of the bridge (in low water and in a 4x4 with good ground clearance driven by a very experienced driver) and continue through to the ruins of the resort.

The city of **Karvachar** (Kelbajar) itself is spectacularly situated atop sheer cliffs on the plateau above. It was mostly destroyed during the war but a few houses are now occupied and some infrastructure rebuilt, including at least one homestay and a couple of shops. In such a key strategic location many of the residents are the families of soldiers stationed in the region.

Continuing on the worsening road beside the river takes you through a steep-sided valley, the lower slopes wooded beneath sheer cliffs with basalt columns and caves. A couple of the **hot springs** feed into manmade pools where it is possible to soak and enjoy the warm mineral water. One is situated directly beside the road; the better option is across the river via a small bridge below the ruins of a large concrete building.

**Tsar** village (2,040m above sea level) is on a triangular plateau above the confluence of the Tartar River and its tributary, the Tsaraget. The cliffs that mostly surround the small plateau formed a natural defensive structure, which was supplemented by about 250m of fortifications on the remaining open side. (The short but narrow rocky track which zigzags up the side of the cliff to Tsar should only be driven in a 4x4 in good weather.) Tsar is mentioned in historical records from the medieval period onwards and once had four churches, two monasteries and cemeteries with numerous khachkars. With the changes in ruling powers (page 20) most Armenian Christians had left the Karvachar area by the mid 18th century. For over a century, villages such as Tsar were occupied only by nomadic herdsmen and only during the summer months. With the establishment of the USSR the area was incorporated first into Azerbaijan, then in 1923–29 into Kurdistan, then again into Azerbaijan. Only since the Karabakh war, when the region became part of the self-declared Republic of Nagorno Karabagh, have Armenian Christians again been the majority inhabitants. This chequered history has seen the destruction of much of Tsar's Christian heritage; only two small single-aisle barrel-vaulted churches remain among the ruined Azeri houses, St Gregory and St Sargis (both from 1274). Stone from destroyed buildings was re-used as building material and many fragments of churches, monasteries and khachkars have been discovered in secular buildings of the region, such as the Azerbaijani school in Tsar, built in the 1950s. In 2013 14 families, some 65 persons, lived in Tsar, many having relocated from Armenia proper. A very poor dirt road crosses the mountains via haymaking fields to Vardenis some 34km distant. This is the final, very challenging section of the Janapar Trail (page 381) for hikers who may at this point have been walking for two weeks or more.

Shortly after the Karvachar turn-off the **northern route to Armenia** via the **Sotk Pass** (2,367m) enters an incredibly narrow gorge where the overhanging cliffs tower high above the road beside the Lev River. The road then enters a broad valley where it crosses the river. The **border post** is at Nor Kharkhaput, some distance from the actual border, before the serious climb to the pass begins. If travelling by private means, you must be proactive in stopping for your papers to be checked here as there is no physical barrier stopping you from passing straight through. A snack bar sells coffee and refreshments. The road zigzags up the mountain, exchanging the rocky, sparsely tree-clad slopes of Karabagh for the more rounded grass-covered slopes of the hills towards Lake Sevan. Before reaching the actual pass the enormous spoil heaps of the Sotk gold mines come into view, shattering any illusions of remoteness. Descending through the gold mine on the Armenian side presents a desolate vista. The road descends to Sotk village and thence to Vardenis (page 237).

**SOUTHERN NAGORNO KARABAGH** A secondary road branches off the main Shushi–Stepanakert road just south of Stepanakert to **Shosh** where there are many plantations of mulberry trees, as silk was made here in Soviet days. There is a possibility that the industry might be revived but meanwhile the mulberries are used for producing mulberry vodka. The ruined 12th- to 13th-century **Pirumashen Church**, a single-aisle basilica, is passed on the right before the village of **Sarushen**. Restoration has started but seems to have stalled. The road winds down after Sarushen; at the bottom of the hill a 2,000-year-old oriental plane tree known as **Tnjri** is signposted left. This is a popular picnic site with locals and also acts as a shrine – witness the handkerchiefs tied to the tree. A fairly good 2.5km dirt road leads to the tree. The hollow tree has a circumference of 27m (several people can stand inside it at once) and a height of 54m. The canopy arises either from boughs growing from the rim of the trunk or from new growth at its base.

The main road continues to the large village of **Karmir Shuka** (Red Market). From Karmir Shuka it is possible to turn off the main road and travel eastwards along a good asphalt road to the **monastery of Amaras**, near the village of Matchkalashen. Amaras was founded by St Gregory the Illuminator in the early 4th century and Mesrop Mashtots is said to have taught here. It has been destroyed (by the Mongols in the 13th century, during Tamerlane's invasion in 1387 and again in the 16th century) and rebuilt several times. During the first half of the 19th century Russian troops used it as a frontier fortress. The Armenian Church reclaimed it in 1848. The monastery was abandoned during the Soviet period but is once again a functioning church. The complex comprises a 17th-century fortified wall within which is the church of St Gregory built in 1858 and restored in 1996. Beneath the east end of the church is the tomb of a grandson of St Gregory the Illuminator, also St Gregory (322–48). One of the rooms which line the south side of the fortified wall has a marriage fireplace, the sides of the fireplace being in the form of two heads facing each other. Should you need fuel for the car, or other purchases, make for **Chartar**, off the Amaras road. This sizeable town, which has a filling station and most other facilities, also has a gem in the form of the **Sevak Ghuvakyan Theatre**, within the cultural palace. The round, pink tuff building is modelled on Yerevan's opera house and has a delightful frieze of foliage, fruits and animals above its arcades as well as a lovely auditorium with comfortable seats. Local and Yerevan companies give a summer season with tickets costing AMD500–1,000.

South from Karmir Shuka and near Azokh village is **Azokh Cave**, reached by a scramble up the hillside. The eight linked caves have a total length of 600m and an area of 8,000m$^2$ with the largest chamber being 3,000m$^2$. The caves are just as famous for their stalactites and stalagmites as for the prehistoric finds which have been made there. These include the million- to 1.5-million-year-old remains of Palaeolithic and Mesolithic man together with more than 2,000 bones from 45 species of animal, some of them now extinct.

About 3km south of Azokh is **Togh** village through which the **monastery of Gtichavank** is reached. The monastery is signposted off the main road and at one further junction but not thereafter. It is possible to drive right up to the monastery, but the last 3km is extremely difficult and requires dry weather and a 4x4. Better to walk up the hillside with its wonderful views over the hilly countryside of southern Karabagh. The approach to the monastery is one of the finest imaginable but the monastery itself is an incredibly sad place. Where so many lived and worked to the glory of God vandals have spray-painted with graffiti every square centimetre inside, even climbing up to the most inaccessible parts of the cupola to cause as much desecration as possible. The graffiti comprise mostly people's names, written in Russian letters and often dated. The monastery was the seat of the archbishopric as early as the 5th century. The inscription records that the existing main cross-dome church was built between 1241 and 1248 by the brothers Sargis and Vrtanes, bishops at Amaras.

The church is entered through a barrel-vaulted gavit whose main hall is set asymmetrically to the church portal, perhaps to accommodate the large khachkar which stands to the right of the church entrance. The cross is supported by angels and above the cross, within the moulded frame, is the central figure of Jesus with six figures on each side representing the 12 disciples. The front of the church's bema is decorated with a geometrical design and a frieze of pomegranates. A very ruinous building lies to the north of the main church. Some restoration of the exterior of the church and gavit has been undertaken. If work continues and includes removal of the graffiti the monastery may some day match its attractive setting.

The main road continues south through yet more impressive mountain scenery to the town of **Hadrut**, the southernmost town in the pre-war autonomous region of Nagorno Karabagh and today the administrative centre of the de facto Hadrut province. The town is the starting point for the northbound Janapar Trail (page 381) and has basic facilities including a filling station, two banks, a police station and a hospital, as well as a basic eatery and several homestays. In terms of monuments there is a restored church and a war memorial with a statue of a resigned, kneeling woman.

South of Hadrut, the area beyond the Soviet-era borders of the Nagorno-Karabakh Autonomous Oblast and under the control of the Armenian military since 1994 remains all but uninhabited with dilapidated roads and no functioning infrastructure. Permission to visit will not easily be obtained, and travellers are likely to be stopped and questioned. In addition, a relatively high concentration of known minefields still exists.

**Tsitsernavank (monastery)** This monastery is very close to the Armenian border. The signposted turn-off north is immediately west of the Lachin border post. Keeping the Aghavnaget River on your left, continue for 15km on a dirt road (4x4 necessary in bad weather) until the monastery can be seen on an outcrop between the Aghavnaget and its tributary the Khovnavar. At the fork take the lower track which crosses a bridge. It is better to park at the bottom of the steep final slope up to the monastery and walk the last few metres. The narrow, tall three-aisle **basilica** was built in the 4th century but renovated in the 5th and again in the 7th. Unusually, there are three arches above the apse. There is some decoration on the square pillars and on the front of the bema. Near the bema some of the 13th-century floor stones have been exposed to view. Outside, one of the gravestones in particular shows very fine figure carving. The 16th-century refectory is now a small **museum** which the priest will open and show you if he is around. Items on display include clay communion vessels dating from the 5th or 6th century, carpets and khachkars. One early khachkar originally bore two carved doves but one has been defaced, possibly by order of a cleric who believed that Christ had one nature, not two (page 40). Both the church and the later fortified wall have been restored. The name Tsitsernavank derives either from the Armenian for 'swallow' (the bird) or from the word for the tip of the little finger; St Peter's was reputed to have been brought to the monastery.

Nagorno Karabagh    WHAT TO SEE AND DO

**UPDATES WEBSITE**

You can post your comments and recommendations, and read feedback and updates from other readers online at **w** bradtupdates.com/armenia.

7

# Appendix 1

## LANGUAGE

Armenian is an Indo-European language but a significant number of words have been borrowed from the country's various occupiers, mostly Persian and Turkish. There are differences in grammar, vocabulary and pronunciation between Eastern Armenian, the dialect spoken in Armenia and certain diaspora communities in Russia, Georgia and Iran; and Western Armenian, as formerly spoken in Anatolia and still spoken by much of the remainder of the diaspora, although the two are mutually intelligible. Many discrepancies in transliteration can be traced to the differing pronunciations of particular letters of the same Armenian alphabet. An older form of the language called Grabar is still used by the Church. Armenians in the present-day republic tend to incorporate much Russian vocabulary into their spoken language, while diaspora communities tend to do likewise with words from the primary language of their place of residence.

### SOME OF THE GRAMMATICAL RULES OF EASTERN ARMENIAN

- There is no gender and the same word is used for he, she and it. There are, however, separate masculine and feminine nouns where there is a clear difference, eg: man/woman; ram/ewe; male saint/female saint.
- The definite article (ie: 'the') appears as a suffix to the noun (as in a few other Indo-European languages such as Swedish and Norwegian). There is no indefinite article: a noun without the definite article suffix is assumed to be indefinite. (This is different in Western Armenian where the indefinite article appears as a separate word after the noun.) If the following word starts with a vowel, then the definite article suffix is spoken as if it were the first syllable of the following word rather than the last syllable of the noun of which it is a suffix.
- The stress is on the last syllable of a word but the definite article suffix is not regarded as a syllable for this purpose and is never stressed.
- There is no interrogative form. Questions are indicated only by tone of voice in speech, and in writing by a special mark (ˊ) over the stressed vowel of the word about which the question is being asked. For example, in the question 'You have an apple?' the question mark in Armenian would be placed either over the word 'you' or over the stressed vowel of 'apple' depending on precisely what the questioner wanted to know.
- Nouns decline (as in Latin, Russian and German). There are seven cases.
- Pronouns also decline. Infinitives can act as nouns and then they similarly decline.
- Adjectives are placed before the noun; they do not change to agree with the noun.
- Most prepositions follow the noun rather than precede it (and are therefore sometimes called postpositions) and they govern the case which the noun takes.
- There are two main conjugations of verbs plus irregular verbs.
- Some Armenian words are never heard spoken in Armenia, the Russian equivalent being used instead.
- The second person singular is used when addressing close family members, close friends and also God in prayer.

# THE ARMENIAN ALPHABET: PRONUNCIATION

(**Note:** while Armenian is largely a phonetic language, letters may sometimes be pronounced slightly differently in spoken Eastern Armenian in accordance with their position in the word.)

| | | | | | |
|---|---|---|---|---|---|
| Ա | ա | As the a in **f**ather (never as in apple) | Յ | յ | As the y in **y**ear |
| Բ | բ | As the b in **b**ook | Ն | ն | As the n in **n**ought |
| Գ | գ | As the g in **g**o | Շ | շ | As the sh in **sh**oe |
| Դ | դ | As the d in **d**og | Ո | ո | As the vo in **vo**lume at the beginning of a word; like the o in n**o**d within a word |
| Ե | ե | As the ye in **ye**s at the beginning of a word; like the e in p**e**n within a word | | | |
| Զ | զ | As the z in **z**oo | Չ | չ | As the ch in **ch**ildren |
| Է | է | As the e in **e**lf | Պ | պ | As the p in **p**iece |
| Ը | ը | As the u in b**u**t | Ջ | ջ | As the j in **j**uice |
| Թ | թ | As the t in **t**oday | Ռ | ռ | As the rolled Scottish **r** |
| Ժ | ժ | As the s in trea**s**ure (generally transliterated jh/zh) | Ս | ս | As the s in **s**oft |
| | | | Վ | վ | As the v in **v**oice |
| Ի | ի | As the ea in m**ea**t | Տ | տ | As the clipped t in bu**t** |
| Լ | լ | As the l in **l**ip | Ր | ր | As an English **r** |
| Խ | խ | As the ch in Scottish lo**ch** | Ց | ց | As the ts in lo**ts** |
| Ծ | ծ | As the tz in Ri**tz** | ՈՒ | ու | As the oo in f**oo**l |
| Կ | կ | As the clipped ck in tri**ck**y | Փ | փ | As the p in **p**ink |
| Հ | հ | As the h in **h**ealthy | Ք | ք | As the k in **k**ey |
| Ձ | ձ | As the ds in li**ds** | Օ | օ | As the o in st**o**ne |
| Ղ | ղ | As a French **r** (generally transliterated gh) | Ֆ | ֆ | As the f in **f**ool |
| Ճ | ճ | As the j in **j**ob | և | | (Lower case only) Pronounced *yev* at the beginning of a word but otherwise *ev*; it also has the meaning *and*. |
| Մ | մ | As the m in **m**oon | | | |

**NOTES ON TRANSLITERATION** As mentioned, extensive use is made of certain Russian words in preference to the Armenian. In this appendix Russian words have been given as transliterations direct from Russian into English although in some cases the transliteration into Armenian is also given, depending on how useful we thought it was likely to be. For simplicity, the Cyrillic alphabet, in which Russian is written, has not been used.

For the definite article ը when suffixed to a noun, as demonstrated in many phrases in this section, we have transliterated the letter as u (as distinct from oo). In this context it is pronounced as an unstressed *-uh*. The sound is known in linguistics as 'schwa' and has no direct equivalent in the Latin alphabet.

## One hybrid expression you must not fail to understand If you ask an Armenian if he or she can do something for you, the usual answer is *Problem chka*. This is a Russo-Armenian hybrid expression which means 'NO problem'. It does NOT mean that there is any difficulty!

## WORDS AND PHRASES
### Essentials

| | | |
|---|---|---|
| Good morning | Բարի լույս | *Bari luys* |
| Good afternoon/day | Բարի օր | *Bari or* (Not much used in spoken Armenian) |
| Good evening | Բարի երեկո | *Bari yereko* |

| Goodnight | Բարի գիշեր | Bari gisher |
| Hello (formal) | Բարև | Barev |
| Hello (informal) | Բարև ձեզ | Barev dzez |
| Goodbye | Ցտեսություն | Tstesootyoon |
| My name is ... | Իմ անունը ... է | Eem anoonu ... e |
| What is your name? (formal) | Ի՞նչ է ձեր անունը | Inch e dser anoonu? |
| What is your name? (informal) | Ի՞նչ է անունդ | Inch e anoonut? |
| Where are you from? | Որտեղի՞ց եք | Vordegheets ek? |
|  Australia | Ավստրալիա | Avstralia |
|  Britain | Բրիտանիա | Breetania |
|  Canada | Կանադա | Canada |
|  Ireland | Իռլանդիա | Eerlandia |
|  New Zealand | Նոր Զելանդիա | Nor Zelandia |
|  USA | Ամերիկա | America |
| I am from ... | Expressed by saying Ես (pronounced *yes*) followed by the name of the country in the ablative case, followed by եմ (pronounced *em*). The ablative case is formed from the nominative case listed above by adding the suffix յից (pronounced *yeets*) if the name of the country ends in a vowel; or the suffix ից (pronounced *eets*) if the name of the country ends in a consonant. For example: | |
| I am from Scotland | Ես Շոտլանդիայից եմ | Yes Shotlandiayeets em |
| How are you? | Ինչպե՞ս եք | Inchpes ek? |
| I'm fine | Լավ եմ | Lav em |
| Please | Խնդրում եմ | Khntroom em |
| Thank you | Շնորհակալություն | Shnorhakalootyoon |
|  | (most people use the French *Merci* for the sake of brevity) | |
| Excuse me/Sorry | Ներողություն | Neroghootyoon |
| Pleased to meet you | Շատ ուրախ եմ | Shat oorakh em |
| Yes | Այո | Ayo |
| No | Ոչ | Votch |
|  | (Armenians often say *ha* and *che* instead) | |
| I don't understand | Ես չեմ հասկանում | Yes chem haskanoom |
| Please speak more slowly | Խնդրում եմ ավելի դանդաղ խոսեք | Khntroom em avelee dandagh khosek |
| Do you understand? | հասկանու՞մ եք | Haskanoom ek? |

## Questions

| How? | Ինչպե՞ս | Inchpes? |
| What? | Ի՞նչ | Inch? |
|  | (This is frequently used when you don't understand, haven't heard, or are surprised.) | |
| Where is ...? | Որտե՞ղ է ... | Vordegh e ...? |
| What is it? | Ի՞նչ է սա | Inch e sa? |
| Which? | Ո՞ր | Vor? |
|  | (Used when, for example, you've been shown several rooms in a hotel, to ascertain which of them you would prefer.) | |
| When? | Ե՞րբ | Yerp? |
| Why? | Ինչու՞ | Inchoo? |
| Who? | Ո՞վ | Ov? |
| How much does it cost? | Ի՞նչ արժե | Inch arzhe? |

# Numbers

| | | | | | | | |
|---|---|---|---|---|---|---|---|
| 1 | *mek* | 11 | *tasnmek* | 21 | *ksan mek* | | |
| 2 | *yerkoo* | 12 | *tasnerkoo* | 30 | *yeresoon* | | |
| 3 | *yerek* | 13 | *tasnerek* | 40 | *karasoon* | | |
| 4 | *chors* | 14 | *tasnchors* | 50 | *hisoon* | | |
| 5 | *hing* | 15 | *tasnhing* | 60 | *vatsoon* | | |
| 6 | *vets* | 16 | *tasnvets* | 70 | *yotanasoon* | | |
| 7 | *yot* | 17 | *tasnyot* | 80 | *ootsoon* | | |
| 8 | *oot* | 18 | *tasnoot* | 90 | *innusoon* | | |
| 9 | *innu* | 19 | *tasninnu* | 100 | *haryoor* | | |
| 10 | *tas* | 20 | *ksan* | 1,000 | *hazar* | | |

# Time

| | | |
|---|---|---|
| What time is it? | ժամը քանի՞սն է | *Zhamu kaneesn e?* |
| It's … [AM]/[PM] | (The expressions AM and PM are not used in Armenian. Say instead '… hours in the morning/in the afternoon/in the evening/in the night.') | |

| | | |
|---|---|---|
| in the morning | առավոտյան | *aravotyan* |
| in the afternoon | ցերեկվա | *tserekva* |
| in the evening | երեկոյան | *yerekoyan* |
| in the night | գիշերվա | *gisherva* |

(Thus, 'It is 7.00AM' becomes 'առավոտյան ժամը յոթն է' – pronounced '*aravotyan zhamu yot ne*', literally meaning 'in the morning the hour seven is'. The suffix *n* on the word seven is the definite article, which is the letter *n* for all hours except two o'clock for which it is *sn*.)

| | | |
|---|---|---|
| today | Այսոր | *Ays-or* |
| this morning | Այս առավոտ | *Ays aravot* |
| this afternoon | Այս ցերեկ | *Ays tserek* |
| this evening | Այս երեկո | *Ays yereko* |
| this night/tonight | Այս գիշեր | *Ays gisher* |
| tomorrow | Վաղը | *Vaghu* |
| yesterday | Երեկ | *Yerek* |

| | | |
|---|---|---|
| Monday | Երկուշաբթի | *Yerkooshaptee* |
| Tuesday | Երեքշաբթի | *Yerekshaptee* |
| Wednesday | Չորեքշաբթի | *Chorekshaptee* |
| Thursday | Հինգշաբթի | *Hinkshaptee* |
| Friday | Ուրբաթ | *Oorpat* |
| Saturday | Շաբաթ | *Shapat* |
| Sunday | Կիրակի | *Kiraki* |

(The names of months do not require initial capital letters in Armenian.)

| | | |
|---|---|---|
| January | հունվար | *hoonvar* |
| February | փետրվար | *petrvar* |
| March | մարտ | *mart* |
| April | ապրիլ | *apreel* |
| May | մայիս | *mayees* |
| June | հունիս | *hoonees* |
| July | հուլիս | *hoolees* |
| August | օգոստոս | *ogostos* |

| September | սեպտեմբեր | *september* |
| October | հոկտեմբեր | *hoktember* |
| November | նոյեմբեր | *noyember* |
| December | դեկտեմբեր | *dektember* |

## Getting around

| I'd like … | Ես ուզում եմ … | *Yes oozoom em …* |
| … a one-way ticket | … տոմս մեկ ուղղությամբ | *… toms mek ooghghootyamp* |

(Return tickets are not issued for journeys within Armenia. Also trains and buses within Armenia are one class only. There are various categories of ticket on the overnight train to Tbilisi, Georgia; page 85.)

| I want to go to … | Ես ուզում եմ մեկնել … | *Yes oozoom em meknel …* |
| How much is it? | Ի՞նչ արժե | *Inch arzhe?* |

(In the following three sentences insert the word for bus, minibus, train or plane – given below – but with the suffix ը (pronounced like an unstressed *u*) to indicate the definite article.)

| What time does the … depart? | Ժամը քանիսի՞ն է … մեկնում | *Zhamu kaneeseen e … meknoom?* |
| The … has been delayed | … ուշանում է | *… ooshanoom e* |
| The … has been cancelled | … չի մեկնելու | *… chee mekneloo* |
| bus | Ավտոբուս | *Avtoboos* |
| train | Գնացք | *Gnatsk* |
| plane | Օդանավ | *Otanav* |
| minibus | (Use the Russian word pronounced *marshrootka*.) | |
| boat | Նավակ | *Navak* |
| platform | (Use the Russian word pronounced *platform*.) | |
| ticket office | Դրամարկղ | *Dramakurr* (Also used for the box office at a theatre.) |
| timetable | Չվացուցակ | *Chvatsootsak* |
| bus station | Ավտոկայան | *Avtokayan* |
| railway station | Կայարան | *Kayaran* |
| airport | Օդանավակայան | *Otanavakayan* |
| car | (Ավտո)մեքենա | *(Avto)mekena* |
| 4x4 | (Although 4x4 drive vehicles are common and useful in Armenia, there is no proper word for them. Use the words *Neeva* or *Vilis* which are the commonest Russian makes; or the word *Jeep* which is the commonest international make.) | |
| taxi | Տաքսի | *Taksee* |
| motorbike | Մոտոցիկլ | *Mototseekl* |
| moped | Մոպեդ | *Moped* |
| bicycle | Հեծանիվ | *Hetsaneev* |
| arrival/departure | Ժամանում/Մեկնում | *Zhamanoom/Meknoom* |
| here/there | Այստեղ/Այնտեղ | *Ays-degh/Ayn-degh* |
| Is this the road to …? | Սա … տանո՞ր ճանապարհին է | *Sa … tanorr janaparn e?* |
| Where can I buy petrol? | Որտե՞ղ կարող եմ գնել բենզին | *Vordegh karogh em gnel benzeen?* |
| … litres, please | … լիտր, խնդրում եմ | *… leetr, khntroom em* |
| … drams worth, please | … դրամի, խնդրում եմ | *… dramee, khntroom em* |
| diesel | (Use the international word *diesel*.) | |

| petrol | Բենզին | *Benzeen* |
| My car has broken down | Մեքենաս տրշացել է | *Mekenas pchatsel e* |
| danger | Վտանգ | *Vtang* |
| Go straight ahead | Ուղիղ գնաց եք | *Oogheegh gnats ek* |
| left | Ձախ | *Tsakh* |
| right | Աջ | *Aach* |
| traffic lights | (Use the Russian word pronounced *svetafor*.) | |
| north | Հյուսիս | *Hyoosis* |
| south | Հարավ | *Haraf* |
| east | Արևելք | *Arevelk* |
| west | Արևմուտք | *Arevmootk* |
| behind | Փետրե | *Hetev* |
| in front of | Առջև | *Archev* |
| near | Մոտ | *Mot* |
| opposite | Դիմաց | *Deemats* |

## Street signs

| entry | Մուտք | *Mootk* |
| no entry | Մուտքը արգելված է | *Mootku argelvats e* |
| exit | Ելք | *Yelk* |
| no parking | Կանգառն արգելված է | *Kangarn argelvats e* |
| open | Բաց է | *Bats e* |
| closed | Փակ է | *Pak e* |
| toilets | Զուգարան | *Zookaran* |
| information | տեղեկություն | *Teghekootyoon* |

## Accommodation

| hotel | Հյուրանոց | *Hyooranots* |
| | ('Hotel' is also understood.) | |
| guesthouse | Փհյուրատուն | *Hyooratoon* |
| Where is there a | Որտե՞ղ կա էժան/լավ | *Vordegh ka* |
| cheap/good hotel? | հյուրանոց | *ezhan/lav hyooranots* |
| Could you please | Խնդրում եմ հասցեն գրեք | *Khndroom em hastsen grek* |
| write the address? | | |
| Is there a vacant room? | Ազատ սենյակ կ՞ա | *Azat senyak ka?* |
| I'd like … | Ես ուզում եմ … | *Yes oozoom em …* |
| … a single room | … մեկդեղանոց սենյակ | *… mekdeghanots senyak* |
| … a double toom | … երկդեղանոց սենյակ | *… yerkdeghanots senyak* |
| … a room with two beds | … սենյակ երկու մահՃակալով | *… senyak yerkoo mahjakalov* |
| … a room with a toilet | … սենյակ զուգարանով | *… senyak zookaranov* |
| and shower | և լողարանով | *yev logharanov* |
| How much is it per night? | Գիշերը ի՞նչ արժե | *Geesheru inch arzhe?* |
| How much is it per person? | Անձը ի՞նչ արժե | *Andsu inch arzhe?* |
| Where is the toilet? | Զուգարանը որտե՞ղ է | *Zookaranu vordegh e?* |
| Is there water? | Ջուր կ՞ա | *Joor ka?* |
| Is there hot water? | Տաք ջուր կ՞ա | *Tak joor ka?* |
| Is breakfast included in | ՆախաՃաշը մտնու՞մ | *Nakhajashu mtnoom* |
| the price? | է գնի մեջ? | *e gnee metch?* |
| I am leaving today | Ես մեկնում եմ այսոր | *Yes meknoom em ays-or* |

# Eating and drinking

| restaurant | Ռեստորան | *Restoran* |
|---|---|---|
| breakfast | Նախաճաշ | *Nakhajash* |
| lunch | Ճաշ | *Jash* |
| dinner | Ընթրիք | *Untreek* |

(On entering a restaurant one is usually asked: Քանի° հոգի եք (pronounced *Kanee hokee ek*?). It means 'How many of you are there?')

| Is there a table for … people? | … հոգու համար սեղան կա° | *… hokoo hamar seghan ka?* |
| Are there any vegetarian dishes? | Բուսական ուտեստներ կա°ն | *Boosakan ootestner kan?* |
| Please bring me … | Խնդրում եմ … բերեք | *Khntroom em … berek* |
| … a fork/knife/spoon | … պատարաքաղ/դանակ/գդալ | *… patarakagh/danak/gtal* |
| The bill, please | Հաշիվը բերեք, խնդրում եմ | *Hasheevu berek, khntroom em* |
| soup | Ապուր | *Apoor* |
| bread | Հաց | *Hats* |
| butter | Կարագ | *Karag* |
| *lavash* (Armenian flatbread) | Լավաշ | *Lavash* |
| cheese | Պանիր | *Paneer* |
| honey | Մեղր | *Meghr* |
| oil | Չիթ | *Dset* |
| vinegar | Քացախ | *Katsakh* |
| pepper | Բիբար/պղպեղ | *Beebar/pghpegh* |
| salt | Աղ | *Agh* |
| sugar | Շաքարավազ | *Shakaravaz* |
| apple | Խնձոր | *Khndzor* |
| banana | (The correct word is Ադամատուզ – pronounced *adamatooz*, but the word generally used is Բանան – pronounced *banan*.) | |
| grapes | Խաղող | *Khaghogh* |
| orange | Նարինջ | *Nareenj* |
| peach | Դեղձ | *Deghdz* |
| pear | Տանձ | *Tandz* |
| watermelon | Ձմերուկ | *Dzmerook* |
| apricot | Ծիրան | *Tseeran* |
| sweet cherries | Կեռաս | *Keras* |
| strawberries | Ելակ | *Yelak* |
| plum | Սալոր | *Salor* |
| carrot | Գազար | *Gazar* |
| garlic | Սխտոր | *Skhtor* |
| onion | Սոխ | *Sokh* |
| sweet pepper | Բիբար | *Beebar* |
| potato | Կարտոֆիլ | *Kartofeel* |
| rice | Բրինձ | *Brindz* |
| tomato | Լոլիկ | *Loleek* |
| cucumber | Վարունգ | *Varoong* |
| salad | Սալաթ | *Salat* |
| salmon | Սաղմոն | *Saghmon* |
| tuna | Թյունոս | *Tyoonos* |
| whitefish | Սիգ | *Sig* |
| smoked whitefish | Ծխացրած սիգ | *Tskhatsrats sig* |
| beef | Տավարի միս | *Tavaree mees* |

| lamb | Ոչխարի միս | *Vochkharee mees* |
| pork | Խոզի միս | *Khozee mees* |
| goat | Այծի միս | *Aytsee mees* |
| chicken | Հավ | *Hav* |
| barbecued | Խորոված | *Khorovats* |
| sausage | Նրբերշիկ | *Nrpersheek* |
| ice cream | Պաղպաղակ | *Paghpaghak* |
| chocolate | Շոկոլադ | *Shokolad* |
| tea | Թեյ | *Tay* |
| coffee | Սուրճ | *Soorj* |
| juice | Հյութ | *Hyoot* |
| milk | Կաթ | *Kat* |
| water | Ջուր | *Joor* |
| mineral water | Հանքային ջուր | *Hankayeen joor* |
| wine | Գինի | *Ginee* |
| beer | Գարեջուր | *Garejoor* |
| brandy | Կոնյակ | *Konyak* |

## Shopping

| I'd like to buy … | Ես ուզում եմ գնել … | *Yes oozoom em gnel …* |
| How much is it? | Ի՞նչ արժե | *Inch arzhe?* |
| It's too expensive | Չափազանց թանկ է | *Chapazants tang e* |
| I'll take it | Ես սա կվերցնեմ | *Yes sa k'vertsnem* |
| Do you accept credit cards? | Կրեդիտ քարտ ընդունու՞մ եք | *Kredeet kart untoonoom ek?* |
| A little more | Մի քիչ ավել | *Mee keech avel* |
| A little less | Ավելի քիչ | *Avelee keech* |

## Communications

| Where is … ? | Որտե՞ղ է … | *Vordegh e … ?* |

(If any of the following nouns were used after *Vordegh e …?*, it would indicate the indefinite article: for example, 'where is there a church?'; 'where is there a museum?', etc. If the definite article is required, then add the unstressed suffix ը – pronounced -*uh* – when the noun ends with a consonant or the suffix ն – pronounced *n* – when the noun ends with a vowel. This results in the meanings: 'where is the church?'; 'where is the museum?', etc.)

| church | Եկեղեցի | *Yekeghetsee* |
| monastery | Վանք | *Vank* |
| castle/fortress | Բերդ, Ամրոց | *Berd, Amrots* |
| museum | Թանգարան | *Tangaran* |
| post office | Փոստ | *Post* |
| bank | Բանկ | *Bank* |
| market | Շուկա | *Shooka* |
| embassy | Դեսպանատուն | *Despanatoon* |
| exchange office | (Use the English word *change*.) | |

## Emergency

| Help! | Օգնություն | *Oknootyoon!* |
| Call a doctor! | Բժիշկ կանչեցեք | *Bzheeshk kanchetsek!* |
| There's been a road accident | Ավտովթար է տեղի ունեցել | *Avtovtar e deghee oonetsel* |

| | | |
|---|---|---|
| There's been an accident (non-road) | Դժբախտ պատահար է | Dzhbakht patahar e |
| I'm lost | Ես մոլորվել եմ | Yes molorvel em |
| Go away! | Հեռու գնա | Heroo gna! |
| police | Ոստիկանություն | Vosteekarnootyoon (or the English 'police') |
| fire service | Հրշեջ ծառայություն | Hrshetch tsarayootyoon |
| ambulance | Շտապ օգնություն | Shtap oknootyoon |
| thief | Կողոպուտ | Koghopoot |

## Health

| | | |
|---|---|---|
| hospital | Հիվանդանոց | Heevandanots |
| I am ill | Ես հիվանդ եմ | Yes heevand em |
| diarrhoea | Լուծ | Loots |
| nausea | Սրտխառնոց | Srtkharnots |
| doctor | Բժիշկ | Bzheeshk |
| prescription | Դեղատոմս | Deghatoms |
| pharmacy | Դեղատուն | Deghatoon |
| paracetamol | Պարացետամոլ | Paratsetamol |
| antibiotic | Հակաբիոտիկ | Hakabeeoteek |
| antiseptic | Հականեխիչ | Hakanekheech |
| tampon | Վիրախտոց | Veerakhtsoots |
| condom | Պահպանակ | Pahpanak |
| sunblock | Հակաարևահարման բույ | Haka-arevaharman ksook |
| I have ... | Ես ... ունեմ | Yes ... oonem |
| ... asthma | ... աստմա ... | ... astma |
| ... epilepsy | ... էպիլեպսիա ... | ... epilepsia |
| ... diabetes | ... շաքարախտ ... | ... shakarakht |
| I'm allergic to ... | Ես ալերգիկ եմ ... | Yes alergeek em ... |
| ... penicillin | ... պենիցիլինի | ... peneetseeleenee |
| ... bee stings | ... մեղվի խայթոցի | ... meghvee khaytotsee |
| ... all kinds of nuts | ... բոլոր տեսակի ընկույզների | ... bolor tesakee unkooyzneree |

## Other

| | | |
|---|---|---|
| my/ours/yours | իմ/մեր/ձեր | eem/mer/dzer |
| and | և (or) ու | yev (or) oo |
| some | մի քիչ | mee keech |
| this/that | այս/այն | ays/ayn (as in ice and nine) |
| expensive/cheap | թանկ/էժան | tang/ezhan |
| beautiful/ugly | գեղեցիկ/տգեղ | geghetseek/tgerr |
| old/new | հին/նոր | heen/nor |
| good/bad | լավ/վատ | lav/vat |
| early/late | շուտ/ուշ | shoot/oosh |
| hot/cold | տաք/սառը | tak/saaru |
| difficult/easy | դժվար/հեշտ | dzhvar/hesht |
| boring/interesting | ձանձրալի/հետաքրքիր | dzandzralee/hetakr'keer |

## PLACE NAMES

| | | | |
|---|---|---|---|
| ԵՐԵՎԱՆ | YEREVAN | ԷՋՄԻԱԾԻՆ | ETCHMIADZIN |
| ԳՅՈՒՄՐԻ | GYUMRI | ԵՂԵԳՆԱՁՈՐ | YEGHEGNADZOR |
| ՎԱՆԱՁՈՐ | VANADZOR | ՋԵՐՄՈՒԿ | JERMUK |
| ՍՏԵՓԱՆԱՎԱՆ | STEPANAVAN | ՍԻՍԻԱՆ | SISIAN |
| ԱԼԱՎԵՐԴԻ | ALAVERDI | ԳՈՐԻՍ | GORIS |
| ԴԻԼԻՋԱՆ | DILIJAN | ԿԱՊԱՆ | KAPAN |
| ԻՋԵՎԱՆ | IJEVAN | ՄԵՂՐԻ | MEGHRI |
| ՍԵՎԱՆ | SEVAN | ՍՏԵՓԱՆԱԿԵՐՏ | STEPANAKERT |
| ԾԱՂԿԱՁՈՐ | TSAGHKADZOR | | |

## FOLLOW BRADT

For the latest news, special offers and competitions, subscribe to the Bradt newsletter via the website **w** bradtguides.com and follow Bradt on:

🅕 BradtTravelGuides
🐦 @BradtGuides
📷 @bradtguides
𝓟 bradtguides
▶ bradtguides

# Appendix 2

## FURTHER INFORMATION

Thanks largely to the diaspora, the range of contemporary literature about Armenia is vast. There are also numerous out-of-print titles, many from Soviet days. It is clear that nobody could read more than a small fraction of the total. The following represents no more than some of the books which the authors have found interesting or useful.

NHBS (**W** nhbs.com) is a good source for books on natural history. Out-of-print titles can often be found through Amazon or via AbeBooks (**W** abebooks.co.uk). Armeniapedia (**W** armeniapedia.org) has extensive categorised listings of books about Armenia and the Armenian people.

Since Armenia's independence, members of the diaspora have published plentiful English-language web content covering practical concerns for the visitor, though local institutions and organisations in Armenia are catching up as the country's visitor base diversifies beyond its traditional market of Russians and the Armenian-speaking diaspora.

### HISTORY

*Archaeological Heritage of Armenia* Edited by Hakob Simonyan; Hushardzan Publishers, Yerevan 2013. A well-illustrated, bilingual (Armenian and English) introduction to the archaeology of Armenia. Also covers churches and monasteries from the 4th century to the 14th century.

*Armenian Churches – Holy See of Echmiadzin* Calouste Gulbenkian Foundation, 1970. Largely a book of black-and-white photographs with limited text, it is interesting to compare some of the 1960s photographs with the same churches today and see the extent of reconstruction. Also covers a few churches in present-day Turkey.

Galichian, Rouben *Countries South of the Caucasus in Medieval Maps* Printinfo Art Books, Yerevan & Gomidas Institute, London, 2007. Commentaries on a collection of fascinatingly impressionistic Christian and Islamic maps with their representations of Armenia at various points in medieval history. The full-colour book is rather expensive but PDF copies can be freely downloaded from the author's website (**W** roubengalichian.com).

Hasratian, Murad *Early Christian Architecture of Armenia* Inkombook, Moscow, 2000. Covers churches intact and ruined, large and small, well known and desperately obscure. Does not include churches from the later medieval period so some of the most famous are excluded. Detailed information explaining well the variety of forms found in Armenian churches. The absence of an index diminishes the usefulness of what is otherwise a well-produced book.

Hovannisian, Richard G *The Republic of Armenia* (4 volumes) University of California Press, 1996. An exhaustive and scholarly but readable account of Armenia's First Republic in the crucial years from 1918 to 1921.

Karapetyan, Samvel *Armenian Cultural Monuments in the Region of Karabakh* Gitutian Publishing House of NAS RAA, Yerevan, 2001. An interesting up-to-date account of what is to be found there. It includes territories occupied since 1994 but regrettably does not include all districts so that Nagorno Karabagh's best known sight – Gandzasar Monastery – is omitted.

Kevorkian, Raymond *The Armenian Genocide* IBTauris, 2011. This weighty tome describes itself as 'a complete history' of the genocide. It traces the roots of the genocide, the impact on the Armenian community and the development of the Turkish state. The section comprising a region-by-region detailed documentation of deportations, massacres and resistance is an encyclopedic work of reference.

Khalpakhchian, O *Architectural Ensembles of Armenia* Iskusstvo, Moscow, 1980. This thorough survey would have been more useful if only it had been better translated. It desperately needed review by a native English speaker. Standing with it in hand at the place being described it is, however, usually possible to work out what the author probably means. Covers only 19 sites but quite thorough.

Masih, Joseph and Krikorian, Robert *Armenia: At the Crossroads* Routledge, 1999. Although the English is occasionally curious the book does give a feel for Armenia's crossroads position – historically, geographically, politically and economically.

Nassibian, Akaby *Britain and the Armenian Question 1915–1923* Croom Helm, 1984. A good account of the British government's failure to help the Armenian people. Despite the title it includes the background to the events from the 1870s onwards.

Nersessian, Vrej *Treasures from the Ark* The British Library, 2001. The catalogue of the wonderful exhibition of Armenian art held in London that year. It is the best illustrated book of Armenian art treasures available.

Piotrovsky, Boris *Urartu* Nagel, 1969. Translated from the Russian by James Hogarth. Written by the director of Leningrad's Hermitage Museum and director of excavations at the Urartian site of Karmir Blur near Yerevan for over 20 years, this book brings to life the dry, both literally and metaphorically, remains of the kingdom of Urartu. Photographs of unearthed treasures, many of which are on display in the History Museum of Armenia, Yerevan.

*A Question of Genocide* Edited by Ronald Grigor Suny, Fatma Müge Göçek and Norman M Naimark; Oxford University Press 2011. Subtitled *Armenians and Turks at the End of the Ottoman Empire*, the book brings together essays by historians from both sides of the Armenian–Turkish divide, and from none, to examine in a non-nationalistic and non-partisan way the causes of the Armenian genocide in particular and communal violence in general.

Redgate, Anne E *The Armenians* Blackwell, 1998. A strongly recommended history of the Armenian people although rather sketchy on the period after 1100.

Rost, Yuri *Armenian Tragedy* Weidenfeld and Nicolson, 1990. A journalist's eyewitness accounts of the early stages of the conflict between Armenia and Azerbaijan and the devastating earthquake of 1988.

Thompson, Andy *Trucks of the Soviet Union: The Definitive History* Behemoth Publishing Ltd, 2017. Illuminating hardback detailing the histories of many of Soviet-era vans, trucks and 4x4s that can still be found in widespread use across Armenia. The author has also written a volume on cars from the same era.

de Waal, Thomas *Black Garden: Armenia and Azerbaijan Through Peace and War* A non-partisan history of the events that led to the Karabagh war of 1991–94, the war itself and much of the time since, told through the author's first-hand experiences, scholarly research and interviews with protagonists on both sides of the conflict, and illuminating much of its complexity and tragedy.

## NATURAL HISTORY

Adamian, Martin S and Klem Jr, Daniel *A Field Guide to the Birds of Armenia* American University of Armenia, 1997. An invaluable, well-illustrated field guide.

Asatryan, Anna *Remarkable Trees of Armenia* Published by the author, 2012. A slight, idiosyncratic volume written by a local academic, listing (with photographs) some two dozen noteworthy tree specimens in the country and recounting the lore surrounding them. Unavailable outside Armenia.

Baytaş, Ahmet *A Field Guide to the Butterflies of Turkey* Ntv, 2007. Although it doesn't specifically cover the area of Armenia it would be generally useful and certainly more portable than Tuzov's *Guide to the Butterflies of Russia and Adjacent Territories* (see below).

Gabrielian, Eleonora and Fragman-Sapir, Ori *Flowers of the Transcaucasus and Adjacent Areas* Gantner Verlag, 2008. Available from NHBS. Expensive.

Greenhalgh, Malcolm *A Pocket Guide to the Freshwater Fish of Britain and Europe* Mitchell Beazley, 2001. Does not include all Armenian species but quite useful.

Holubec, Vojtech and Krivka, Pavel *The Caucasus and its Flowers* LOXIA, 2006. Available from NHBS. Expensive.

MacDonald, David *Collins Field Guide to the Mammals of Britain and Europe* HarperCollins, 2005. Omits a few species such as leopard, but useful.

Pils, Gerhard *Flowers of Turkey* published by the author, 2006. The most useful field guide for the average botanical traveller, but expensive. No text but lots of photographs, arranged by plant families. Available from NHBS.

Shetekauri, Shamil and Jacoby, Martin *Mountain Flowers and Trees of Caucasia* Martin Jacoby, 2009. Available from NHBS. Paperback and the cheapest of the botanical guides.

Szczerbak, N N *Guide to the Reptiles of the Eastern Palearctic* Krieger, 2003. One sees lots of reptiles in Armenia and this guide is useful although it does not always make it clear how to distinguish between related species.

Tuzov, V K (ed) *Guide to the Butterflies of Russia and Adjacent Territories* (2 volumes) Pensoft, Sofia, 2000. A thorough guide illustrated with photographs of specimens and covering the whole of the former USSR but unfortunately not very portable.

## GENERAL

Petrosian, Irina and Underwood, David *Armenian Food: Fact, Fiction and Folklore* Yerkir Publishing, 2006. This is not a cookery book! Written by an Armenian wife and American husband, it's a fascinating and revealing insight into Armenia as seen through the country's food. Entertainingly written and very informative. Highly recommended.

Solomon, Susan *Culture Smart! Armenia* Kuperard 2010. A guide to the customs and culture of Armenia. Helpful tips on social etiquette, dos and don'ts.

## TRAVEL

Bachmann, Carine and Tufenkian, Jeffrey *Adventure Armenia – Hiking and Rock Climbing* Kanach, 2004. Describes 20 walks and five climbs in English and Armenian editions. The first attempt to publish practical information in guidebook form about the country's potential though it only scratches the surface. Sadly out of print and very hard to find (though copies have recently been seen in the gift shop of the Tufenkian hotel at Dzoraget).

Hepworth, Revd George H *Through Armenia on Horseback* Isbister, 1898. In one of the best accounts of life among the Armenians of Anatolia shortly before the genocide, the evidently unbiased author gives an account of their hardships and oppression.

Kiesling, Brady and Kojian, Raffi *Rediscovering Armenia* Tigran Mets, 2001. A travelogue-gazetteer which lists most of Armenia's historical sites together with scrupulously researched background information. Not really a guidebook itself but it was often very useful to the authors of this one in indicating what exists. Full text available online at **w** armeniapedia.org. An accompanying volume *Rediscovering Artsakh* was being prepared at the time of research.

Marsden, Philip *The Crossing Place* Collins, 2015 (2nd edition). Recounts a fascinating journey made by the author in search of Armenian communities across Europe and the Middle East, culminating in a visit to the newly independent republic itself amid Soviet collapse and the outbreak of war.

Nansen, Fridtjof *Armenia and the Near East* George Allen & Unwin, 1928. The great Polar explorer was appointed League of Nations Commissioner for Refugees and in that capacity visited Soviet Armenia in its early days accompanied by Vidkun Quisling (later to become Norway's prime minister during the Nazi occupation and consequently executed for treason in 1945) who acted as his secretary. He was favourably impressed by the plans to use the water from Lake Sevan to irrigate the Ararat Valley.

PP (ie: Peter Pears) *Armenian Holiday August 1965* Privately published, 1965. The English tenor's account of his visit with Britten, Rostropovich and Galina Vishnevskaya. The Russian soprano, Rostropovich's wife, also gives an account in her autobiography *Galina – A Russian Story* (Hodder & Stoughton, 1985).

Shaginyan, Marietta *Journey through Soviet Armenia* Foreign Languages Publishing House, Moscow, 1954. A wonderful period piece of Stalin-era writing – the Russian original was published in 1952 before his death. Unfortunately out of print but eminently worth seeking a copy for anyone with a taste for the bizarre.

*Yerevan: A Guide* Progress Publishers, Moscow, 1982. Another English-language publication from Moscow, aimed at foreign visitors to Soviet Yerevan and containing a healthy dose of communist propaganda. It is perhaps interesting to compare the modern-day city with that described here. Very hard to find, but the text has been reproduced in full at **w** armeniapedia. org/wiki/Soviet_Guide_to_Yerevan.

Youredjian, Raffi *Tour de Armenia* Published by the author, 2014. A humorous, personal account of a 1,000km bicycle journey around Armenia with plenty of cultural and historical information interspersed throughout.

## Bradt guides to nearby destinations

For a full list of Bradt's European and Middle Eastern guides, see **w** bradtguides.com.
Darke, Diana *Eastern Turkey* Bradt Travel Guides, 2014.
Burford, Tim *Georgia* Bradt Travel Guides, 2018.
Oleynik, Maria and Smith, Hilary, *Iran* Bradt Travel Guides, 2017.

## LITERATURE

*Armenian Poetry Old and New* Wayne State University Press, 1979. A bilingual anthology compiled and translated by Aram Tolegian. The English translations make available to non-Armenian-speakers a selection from a wide range of poets, including some mentioned in the literature section of this guidebook. For those who have a little knowledge of the language the bilingual nature of the book allows a rare glimpse into Armenian poetry.

*Folktales of Armenia* Translated into English by Leon Surmelian. Nahapet Publishing House, Yerevan. A charming collection of Armenian fairy tales revealing that the Armenian equivalent of 'Once upon a time …' translates literally as 'There was and there was not …'.

Pushkin, Alexander *A Journey to Arzrum* (ie: Erzurum) 1835, English translation by Birgitta Ingemanson published by Ardis, 1974. An excellent translation with extremely useful notes explaining matters unlikely to be familiar to modern Western readers.

Saroyan, William *The Human Comedy* 1943 and *Boys and Girls Together* 1963. Two works suggested as an introduction to the Armenian-American author.

**LANGUAGE** A variety of teaching material is now offered on the internet although much is for Western rather than Eastern Armenian. Try **w** armeniapedia.org or search via Google for Eastern Armenian courses.

Avetisyan, Anahit *Eastern Armenian: Comprehensive Self-Study Language Course* Published by the author, Yerevan, 2017 (3rd edition). The most accessible Eastern Armenian course we have found. Everything is provided in three forms: Armenian, Armenian transliteration and English translation. It also introduces the learner to cursive handwritten Armenian. It does tend to teach a formal form of the spoken language rather than the colloquial Armenian heard on the streets. Very expensive to buy outside Armenia.

Eurotalk *Learn Armenian* CD-ROM and download (W eurotalk.com) Introduces the reader to basic Eastern Armenian words and phrases in what it describes as a fun way. It has the advantage that one can hear as well as see the language and it provides an element of feedback.

Grigorian, Kh *English–Armenian/Armenian–English Dictionary* Ankyunacar Publishing, Yerevan, 2005. Compiled for English-speakers. The best small dictionary we have found. Apparently unavailable outside Armenia.

Muradyan, Lusine *Learning Armenian Headstart* Edit Print, Yerevan, 2011. A manual for English-speaking, absolute beginners. Based on conversational skills with the introduction of basic grammar. Extensive vocabularies. Includes a copy book section to learn cursive writing. The separate grammar section is in tabular form without explanations in English. CD included. Paper edition apparently unavailable outside Armenia. Kindle version available from Amazon (author listed as Lusine Mouradyan).

## RELIGION

Ghazarian, Jacob G *The Mediterranean Legacy in Early Celtic Christianity* Bennet & Bloom, 2006. Visitors to Armenia may well be struck by the similarities between the decoration on Armenian khachkars and illuminated manuscripts and that on the Celtic crosses and illuminated manuscripts of Ireland and Scotland. This book explores possible reasons for those similarities.

Ormanian, Archbishop Maghakia *The Church of Armenia* Ankyunacar Publishing, Yerevan, 2011. Translated by G Marcar Gregory. First published, in French, in 1910, the present English translation includes annotations reflecting changes in the century since it was written. An informative small book about the history, doctrine, clergy, hierarchy and liturgy of the Armenian Church. Clarifies some matters for those unfamiliar with the Armenian Church.

*Speaking with God from the Depths of the Heart.* The prayers of St Grigor Narekatsi (c950–1010) translated by Thomas J Samuelian. VEM Press, Yerevan, 2002. The prayers, or lamentations, of St Gregory of Narek have been compared to the psalms of David and occupy a unique place within the Armenian Church and Armenian literature. Gregory sought an intuitive communication with God; his prayers pile image upon image, metaphor upon metaphor.

**USEFUL WEBSITES** Some of the websites listed below are multilingual and may default to the Armenian language. All have language selection options; look for a small link reading 'Eng' or 'English', or an Armenian flag icon (three horizontal stripes in red, blue and orange) which when clicked should reveal the other available languages.

W **ace.aua.am/ecotourism** The American University of Armenia's ecotourism portal, with listings of relevant national and international organisations and websites, as well as details of the annual ecotourism conference.

W **armenia.travel** Official website of Armenia's State Tourism Committee, relaunched in 2018 and containing plenty of useful introductory information, as well as a festival and events calendar.

W **armenianchurch.org** The website of the Mother See of Etchmiadzin. Comprehensive information about the Armenian Apostolic Church.

W **armenianheritage.org** Website of the seemingly now inactive Armenian Monuments Awareness Project. Not the easiest of websites on which to find what one wants but has some useful information, eg: a guide to Noratus field of khachkars which is worth downloading to take with you when visiting the site.

w **armeniapedia.org** Still the best internet source for all things Armenian, including several categories of information not permitted by Wikipedia (recipes, language learning resources, etc), though some topical information eg: government is out of date. Also covers Nagorno Karabagh.

w **armhotels.am** Online information and booking for hotels in Armenia and Nagorno Karabagh.

w **artsakh.travel** Official tourism website of the self-declared Republic of Artsakh (Nagorno Karabagh).

w **azatutyun.am** Website of the independent Radio Free Europe/Radio Liberty branch in Armenia. Good for keeping up to date with Armenian news in English.

w **cyclingarmenia.com** Unofficial, volunteer-run website offering route suggestions and practical advice for cyclists of all types coming to Armenia.

w **gallery.am** Website of the National Gallery of Armenia with information on the collections.

w **gov.uk/foreign-travel-advice/armenia** UK government website offering official advice for travellers to Armenia.

w **haypost.am** Website of the Armenian Post Office. Has some useful practical information plus information on philately.

w **hikearmenia.com** Launched in 2018, this website and app aims to be a much-needed 'one-stop shop' for those interested in Armenia's hiking opportunities.

w **hotels.am** Another locally operated website offering hotel listings and online booking services.

w **mfa.am** The official website of the Armenian Foreign Ministry. Gives information on visa requirements and other official government announcements.

w **nayiri.com** Online Armenian–English and Armenian–French dictionary with the ability to cross-reference results between various digitised sources.

w **nkr.am** The website of the Nagorno Karabagh Foreign Ministry. Has information on visas, including a downloadable visa application form for use in Stepanakert but not if applying in Yerevan (page 375). Also information on geography, flora, climate, etc.

w **repatarmenia.org** Mainly created to support diaspora Armenians moving temporarily or permanently to Armenia, this organisation has collected reams of practical information on life in the country that is just as relevant to the non-Armenian visitor or expat.

w **spyur.am** Armenia's Yellow Pages is by far the most comprehensive, accurate and up-to-date source of contact information and street addresses.

w **tacentral.com** Useful practical information, although some of the country is not covered and the site can be a bit out of date at times. Interesting articles on topics such as Armenian carpets, flowers, language and archaeology. Useful guides to the History Museum of Armenia (a little out of date after recent redevelopment) and to Metsamor Museum.

w **uk.mfa.am** The website of the Armenian embassy in London. Has much useful information about Armenia. Details of visa requirements and a link to the application process for an e-visa, if required.

w **usa.mfa.am** The website of the Armenian embassy in Washington. Essentially the same information as on the UK site.

w **zvartnots.aero** Useful information about Zvartnots International Airport, including live departures. Also information about Shirak International Airport near Gyumri.

# Index

## INDEX OF ADVERTISERS